Banking on Slavery

American Beginnings, 1500–1900

A SERIES EDITED BY HANNAH FARBER, EDWARD GRAY, STEPHEN MIHM, AND MARK PETERSON

Also in the series:

A Great and Rising Nation: Naval Exploration and Global Empire in the Early US Republic
Michael A. Verney

Trading Freedom: How Trade with China Defined Early America
Dael A. Norwood

Wives Not Slaves: Patriarchy and Modernity in the Age of Revolutions
Kirsten Sword

Accidental Pluralism: America and the Religious Politics of English Expansion, 1497–1662
Evan Haefeli

The Province of Affliction: Illness and the Making of Early New England
Ben Mutschler

Puritan Spirits in the Abolitionist Imagination
Kenyon Gradert

Trading Spaces: The Colonial Marketplace and the Foundations of American Capitalism
Emma Hart

Urban Dreams, Rural Commonwealth: The Rise of Plantation Society in the Chesapeake
Paul Musselwhite

Building a Revolutionary State: The Legal Transformation of New York, 1776–1783
Howard Pashman

Sovereign of the Market: The Money Question in Early America
Jeffrey Sklansky

National Duties: Custom Houses and the Making of the American State
Gautham Rao

Liberty Power: Antislavery Third Parties and the Transformation of American Politics
Corey M. Brooks

A complete list of series titles is available on the University of Chicago Press website.

Banking on Slavery

Financing Southern Expansion in the Antebellum United States

SHARON ANN MURPHY

The University of Chicago Press
Chicago and London

The University of Chicago Press, Chicago 60637
The University of Chicago Press, Ltd., London

Published 2023
Printed in the United States of America

32 31 30 29 28 27 26 25 24 23 1 2 3 4 5

ISBN-13: 978-0-226-82459-8 (cloth)
ISBN-13: 978-0-226-82513-7 (paper)
ISBN-13: 978-0-226-82460-4 (e-book)
DOI: https://doi.org/10.7208/chicago/9780226824604.001.0001

Library of Congress Cataloging-in-Publication Data

Names: Murphy, Sharon Ann, 1974– author.
Title: Banking on slavery : financing Southern expansion in the antebellum United States / Sharon Ann Murphy.
Other titles: Financing Southern expansion in the antebellum United States | American beginnings, 1500–1900.
Description: Chicago : The University of Chicago Press, 2023. | Series: American beginnings, 1500–1900 | Includes bibliographical references and index.
Identifiers: LCCN 2022026308 | ISBN 9780226824598 (cloth) | ISBN 9780226825137 (paperback) | ISBN 9780226824604 (ebook)
Subjects: LCSH: Banks and banking—Southern States—History—19th century. | Banks and banking—United States—History—19th century. | Slavery—Economic aspects—United States. | Slavery—United States—History—19th century.
Classification: LCC HG2472 .M867 2023 | DDC 332.10975—dc23/eng/20220708
LC record available at https://lccn.loc.gov/2022026308

♾ This paper meets the requirements of ANSI/NISO Z39.48-1992 (Permanence of Paper).

For my children, Amalia Rose and Cono Joseph,
whose hugs and kisses were essential to writing this book

Contents

Illustrations

Figures

Tables

Maps

INTRODUCTION

Banking in the Nation's Largest Slave Market

New Orleans in the 1830s was a rapidly growing metropolis that rivaled New York as the nation's most important commercial port. Critically located at the mouth of the Mississippi River, the value of her exports "matched or exceeded" that of New York's from 1834 to 1844.[1] On any given day, newcomers to the thriving city included: slave traders from the upper South bringing untold numbers of enslaved bodies for sale in the city's numerous exchanges; wealthy planters coming to town to meet with their cotton or sugar factors, purchase additional enslaved laborers, or buy supplies for their plantations; free blacks and single (or widowed) women seeking independence and employment in the urban center; out-of-state merchants selling commodities they brought from home and purchasing goods for transport back North and East; foreign businessmen pursuing investment opportunities and trading partners in the bustling port; a cross section of Louisiana citizens who had business with the state legislature or court system; indigenous peoples with goods to trade and business to conduct; newly arrived migrants who dreamed of building their own cotton or sugar estates; and tourists from across the country and around the globe. The streets bustled with merchants and traders of all stripes who rubbed elbows with women, enslaved individuals, free blacks, rural farmers, and tourists, all speaking a mélange of French, English, Creole, and Spanish.

Many wealthy tourists—like the Swedish reformer Fredrika Bremer, the British writer Charles Weld, and the American architect Frederick Law Olmsted—considered New Orleans to be a must-see destination on their American tour. Intent on getting the most out of the experience, a typical tourist might purchase a guidebook like *Norman's New Orleans and Environs* (1845), supplementing it with a street map of the city like L. Hirt's 1841 *Plan of New Orleans* (figure I.1), which included etchings of the most important buildings to explore—churches,

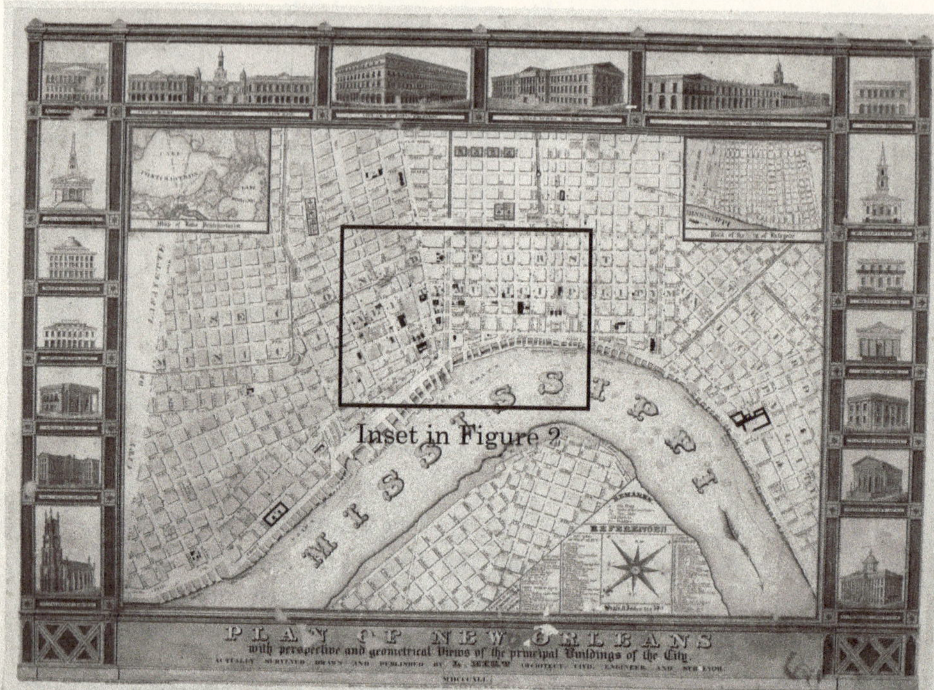

FIGURE I.1. Hirt, "Plan of New Orleans with Perspective and Geometrical Views of the Principal Buildings of the City," 1841. Lithograph, 22¼ × 30¼ in. http://hnoc.minisisinc.com/thnoc/catalog/1/2814. Courtesy of the Historic New Orleans Collection, Williams Research Center, New Orleans, LA. The L. Kemper and Leila Moore Williams Founders Collection.

banks, exchanges, theaters, a cotton press, a sugar refinery, the courthouse, and the city hall.[2]

Upon arrival by Mississippi riverboat, Bremer noted that "the harbor which we entered was beautiful and inviting in its crescent form, but the roadstead was bad, and the quay of wood, and ill built."[3] Disembarking near St. Louis Street in the heart of the French Quarter, our anonymous visitor would need to walk a distance of less than three blocks from this gritty harbor to the recently built St. Louis Hotel and Exchange (also known as the City Exchange)—the "most respectable" hotel in the city (the third building pictured along the top of figure I.1, and location M in figure I.2).[4] The impressive structure had been built in 1838 and financed through the New Orleans Improvement and Banking Company (location N), which was one of several joint banking-improvement companies in the city.[5] According to Norman's guide, the "combination of [the hotel's] brilliant and business-like appearance, is not an inappropriate representative of their national character."[6] Spanning

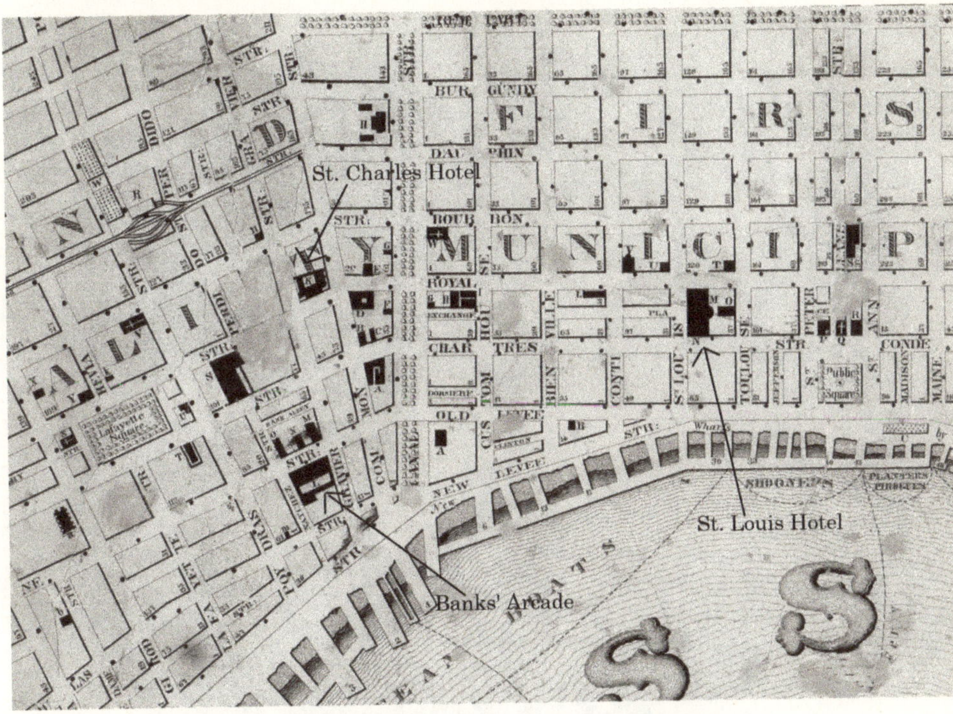

FIGURE I.2. Inset of figure I.1, highlighting the main slave-trading and financial districts.

the entire block of St. Louis Street, with entrances on both Royal and Chartres Streets, the building was "intended . . . to combine the convenience of a city exchange, hotel, bank, large ball rooms, and private stores."[7] Among the properties bought up and replaced by the hotel was Hewlett's Exchange (formerly Maspero's Exchange and Coffeehouse), a prominent location of the city's slave auctions during the first decades of the century.[8] When a massive fire destroyed the new hotel in February of 1840, it was quickly rebuilt in all its splendor by May 1841, with financial help from the adjacent Citizens' Bank.[9]

Without even leaving the hotel, on most days our visitor could experience the city's renowned public slave auctions, which occurred between noon and three in "one of the most beautiful rotundas in America" (figure I.3).[10] As one architectural historian describes it, "auctions of every conceivable form of property, including enslaved human beings, were conducted beneath the 88-foot-high dome surrounded by towering Tuscan columns, like a scene out of ancient times."[11] Bremer tried to attend an auction here at the "splendid rotunda, the magnificent dome of which is worthy to resound with songs of freedom," but she arrived too late on that particular day.[12] To support this trade in enslaved lives, "dozens of salesrooms . . . were located in the streets

FIGURE I.3. William Henry Brooke, engraver. "Sale of Estates, Pictures and Slaves in the Rotunda, New Orleans." Engraving with watercolor, $3^{13}/_{16} \times 5^{1}/_{16}$ in. In James Silk Buckingham, *The Slave States of America*, vol. 1 (London: Fisher and Son, 1842). http://hnoc.minisisinc.com/thnoc/catalog/1/34408. Courtesy of the Historic New Orleans Collection, Williams Research Center, New Orleans, LA.

surrounding" the hotel, although pens to house the enslaved men and women themselves had been banned from the French Quarter in 1829, forcing these depots to arise a few blocks away in the second and third municipalities.[13]

But our visitor did not come to New Orleans to remain inside. If she were to exit the hotel from the rear of the building toward Toulouse Street, she would pass through a "yard held in common with the Citizens' Bank" which was "devoted to public use every day from 9 o'clock A. M. to 3 o'clock P.M."[14] The Citizens' Bank (location O, and the second-to-last building on the right panel of figure I.1), which abutted the rear of the hotel, was the nation's largest financial institution after the Second Bank of the United States, having been incorporated in 1833 as a plantation bank with a massive capital of $12 million.[15] Turning right toward Royal Street, our visitor would quickly realize that she was in not only the city's slave-trading district, but also its financial heart. The late 1830s marked the height of commercial banking in the South, and nowhere were southern banks more concentrated than in New Orleans. In 1838 the city contained seventeen state-chartered banking institutions—traditional commercial banks, joint banking-improvement companies, and the newly developed plantation banks—with a total capitalization of $55 million between them.[16] This was the nation's most sophisticated financial infrastructure outside New York City.[17]

Across the street from the St. Louis Hotel on the corner of Toulouse and Royal was the Consolidated Association of Planters of Louisiana (location T), the nation's first plantation bank, incorporated in 1827. A specialized type of property bank, the very foundation of the capital for these plantation banks were the mortgaged land and enslaved lives at the center of Louisiana's economy. Walking left down Royal toward Canal, within two blocks our visitor would admire three more major bank buildings, starting with the Louisiana State Bank (location V), one of the last buildings designed by renowned architect Benjamin Henry Latrobe—best known for the United States Capitol building—before his death from yellow fever in 1820. This was "a handsome building based on a plain cubic symmetrical exterior with a large domed banking room and dignified by an elegant treatment of windows."[18] Across Conti Street on the corner of Royal was the branch building of the Second Bank of the United States. Originally the home of the Planters' Bank of Louisiana (chartered in 1811), the Second Bank purchased it upon the closure of the Planters' Bank in 1820. When Congress declined the recharter of the Second Bank in 1836, the newly chartered New Orleans Gas Light and Banking Company purchased the lot, buildings, and furniture for $50,000.[19]

Located directly across the street was the Bank of Louisiana (location L, and the fifth building on the right panel of figure I.1)—"a fine Ionic building at the south-west corner of Royal and Conti streets, surrounded by a handsome court." Built in 1826 and 1827, "the whole edifice is well arranged, the banking room in particular, is admired for its good architectual [*sic*] effect . . . with a fine gallery above."[20] Continuing down Royal toward the edge of the French Quarter, our visitor would pass the Union Bank (location I, and the fifth building down on the left panel of figure I.1) and the Bank of Orleans (location G), both near the Merchants' Exchange (location H, and the third building on the left panel of figure I.1). With a capitalization of $7 million when it was chartered in 1832 as a plantation bank, the Union Bank was the nation's third-largest bank in the 1830s.[21]

Having walked only about one-third of a mile down Royal Street, our visitor would already have reached Canal Street and the end of the French Quarter. Crossing the broad avenue, she would find both the Mechanics' and

Traders' Bank (location F) and the New Orleans & Carrollton Railroad and Banking Company (location G) facing Canal Street. On the side street between these two banks was the beautiful yet "squeezed" new building that the Gas Bank had finished in 1839 (location E), opposite the City Bank's "building of the Ionic order" whose "banking room is admired for its elegant simplicity" (location D).[22] Passing these institutions would bring our visitor to the St. Charles Hotel & Exchange (location K, and the bottom building on the right panel of figure I.1), which had been built by architects James Gallier Sr. and Charles Dakin from 1835 to 1838. The St. Charles had been financed by another improvement bank—the Exchange and Banking Company—which was housed a block away (location B), next door to the City Bank (location C).[23] Of the St. Charles Hotel, Norman's guide noted that "this magnificent establishment . . . for size and architectural beauty, stands unrivalled."[24] Bremer initially stayed at this "magnificent building resembling the Pantheon at Rome, shining out white with its splendid columns, not of marble, but of stucco," before she moved to a more private—and economical—room in the boardinghouse of a respectable widow overlooking Lafayette Square.[25] The St. Charles Hotel spanned the full length of St. Charles Street between Gravier and Common Streets, amid the slave depots. Our visitor could also experience slave auctions here, which "were regularly held in the octagonal bar" located in the center of the building.[26]

Just outside the St. Charles was the complex of slave depots which served as holding pens for enslaved individuals awaiting auction in both the French and American Quarters. The depots roughly encompassed the three square blocks from Common to Poydras Streets, between Baronne and Camp Streets.[27] Walking just two blocks from the hotel down Gravier Street toward the river, our visitor would see a third collection of improvement banks between Gravier and Natchez Streets: the New Orleans Canal and Banking Company (location M), the Atchafalaya Railroad and Banking Company (location N), and the Commercial Bank (location O), which built the city's waterworks. Directly across the street from these banks, spanning the entire block, was Banks' Arcade (location L), a three-story, glass-covered building that was "a great resort for merchants and others."[28] Although many sales of enslaved people also took place in smaller locations (such as the house where Bremer finally witnessed an auction, which she found "repulsive") or even directly out of the slave pens, it was the St. Louis Exchange, the St. Charles Exchange, and Banks' Arcade that accounted for most of the city's slave auctions.[29] If our visitor were to wander two blocks farther down Camp Street, she would find Lafayette Square, which Bremer described as "a market-place planted with young trees still green, and with a grass-plot in the centre."[30]

Overlooking the square was the Merchants' Bank (location T, and the third building down on the right panel of figure I.1), the final major financial institution of the city. As our visitor returned to the St. Louis Hotel, this entire walking tour—not including stopping for lunch, exploring the slave pens, or wandering into shops down side streets—would have encompassed about a mile and a half.

The New Orleans slave auction, with its public spectacle in the heart of the city, was the physical embodiment of the South's full embrace and celebration of slavery as the engine behind its antebellum economic prosperity. It was an essential part of the massive movement of people—both enslaved and free—into the fertile lands from Georgia to the Mississippi River valley in the aftermath of the War of 1812 (figure I.4). Numerous scholars have documented important aspects of this story: the retreat of European claims to the heart of the continent; the expulsion of indigenous peoples from the land; the massive forced migration of hundreds of thousands of enslaved men, women, and children from the upper South; the inhumanity of the slave market; the economics of the plantation system; the violence of its labor practices; and the financing and consumption of slave-produced commodities.[31] Yet it was expensive to move people great distances, to improve the land, and to create the critical infrastructure necessary to survive and thrive on the frontier. How did southerners finance this rapid settlement of the Southwest? Our visitor's walking tour amid the bank buildings and slave auctions of New Orleans in the early 1840s, representing the pinnacle of commercial banking in the frontier South, also marked the height of the involvement of commercial banking with the financialization of slavery.

Despite the rich and ever-growing literature on the history of slavery, the question of how slaveholders financed the settlement of the frontier South remains an understudied topic. The conquest of the Deep South with the growth of large-scale cotton and sugar plantations paralleled the separate maturation of a commercial-banking industry in the United States during the first half of the nineteenth century, yet scholars have only recently begun examining the intersections of these two concurrent developments. Calvin Schermerhorn and Edward Baptist discuss the short-lived plantation banks of the 1830s.[32] Joshua Rothman details the experiences with banks of one Mississippi slaveholder during the Panic of 1837, while Rothman and Jeff Forret examine some of the financial practices of slave traders.[33] Others, such as Richard Kilbourne Jr. and Bonnie Martin, interrogate the use of enslaved people more generally in credit transactions.[34] Both J. Carlyle Sitterson's groundbreaking 1953 book on the sugar industry and Harold Woodson's 1968 investigation of cotton financing focus mainly on the factorage system.[35] Historians who deal

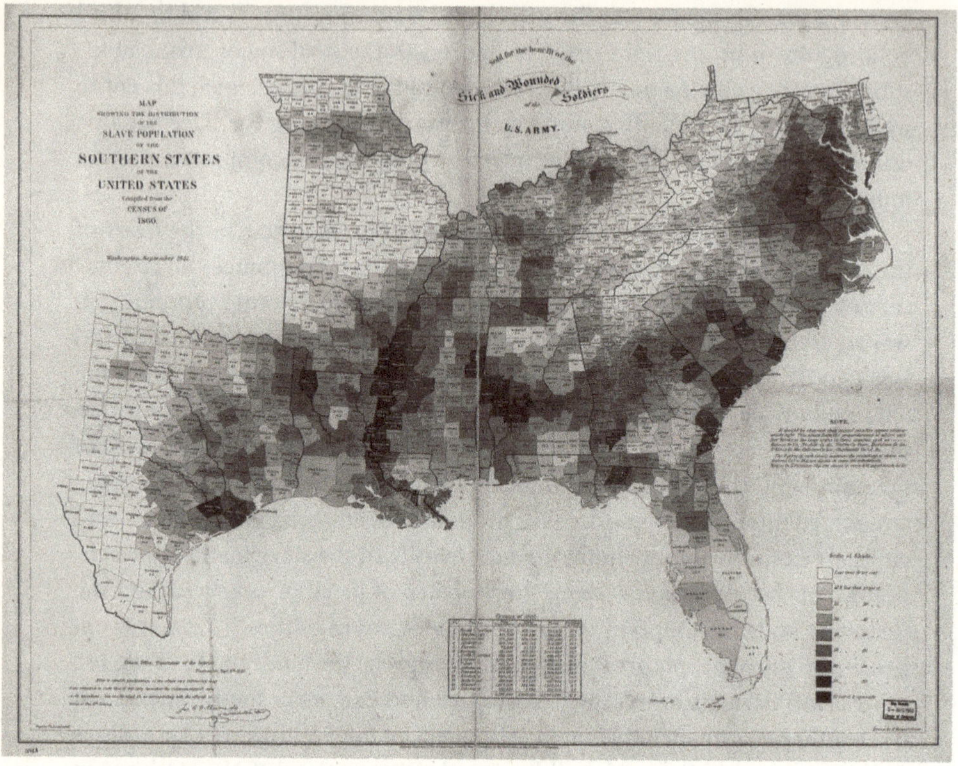

FIGURE I.4. E. Hergesheimer, "Map Showing the Distribution of the Slave Population of the Southern States of the United States. Compiled from the Census of 1860" (Washington, DC: Henry S. Graham, 1861). https://www.loc.gov/item/99447026/. Courtesy of the Library of Congress Geography and Map Division, Washington, DC.

extensively with southern banking, such as Larry Schweikart and Howard Bodenhorn, make only limited references to slavery.[36] With the exception of Kilbourne's work on the Natchez branch of the Second Bank of the United States and a recent article on Nicholas Biddle by Stephen Campbell, historians of the national banks—and especially of the first Bank of the United States—make almost no mention of slavery.[37] Many scholars seem simply to assume that enslaved individuals functioned as financial assets without any understanding of how these contracts worked, how they changed over time, or how they impacted the slave system as a whole. And yet, the ability and willingness of banks to alter traditional banking operations to meet the unique needs of a frontier economy was critical to the success and expansion of the slave economy by mid-century.

As Stephen Mihm emphasizes in his 2016 essay "Follow the Money: The Return of Finance in the Early American Republic," capitalism is more than just the interaction between "production and wage labor on the one hand, and commodities and consumption on the other." Central to these relationships is a sophisticated financial system that serves as "the connective tissue of capitalism, the invisible infrastructure that underwrites enterprise and fuels the speculative, creative, and at times, destructive, aspects of capitalism." In order to fully understand the depth and breadth of the slave system in the United States, we need to unmask the relationship between slavery and the "institutions, practices, and people that collectively constitute a tangled web of money, investment, credit, and debt."[38] Southerners adapted increasingly sophisticated financial tools and institutions to fit the slave system in order to facilitate investment, market exchange, and profit maximization; and they were aided and abetted by that same financial system. And yet, these adaptations were often inadequate, forcing bankers and legislatures to change the banks to fit the needs of the slaveholders more fully. A full assessment of the willingness, and sometimes eagerness, of bankers to push the boundaries of accepted banking practices and break altogether with banking norms in order to engage with slavery provides a more accurate picture of the true depth to which the slave system had penetrated the country's economic institutions. More importantly, it sheds light on *how* these financial relationships worked across the South throughout the nineteenth century.

As the commercial-banking industry rapidly developed during the nineteenth century, its engagement with slaveholders and the system of slavery throughout the South evolved as well, resulting in the increased financialization of human property—particularly on the southern frontier. Enslaved people had always generated wealth for slave owners through their physical labor, their reproduction, and their appreciation in market value. Yet one of the most salient features of a modern financial system is the willingness and ability of participants to *leverage* assets—borrowing against the market value of an asset in anticipation of repaying the debt either from future profits or the appreciation in value of the asset itself. As legal historian Katharina Pistor details, a central part of this process was the use of "contract law, property rights, collateral law, trust, corporate, and bankruptcy law" to redefine an asset—in this case, enslaved people—legally into capital.[39] Financialization transformed enslaved lives from physical bodies into abstract capital assets that could be used as collateral in sophisticated loan contracts or exchanged for shares of corporate stock.

This financialization occurred in a series of overlapping waves that was driven by the financial demands of the slaveholders pouring into the frontier

South, by the boom-and-bust cycle of the nineteenth-century economy, and by the related state-level experimentation with the legal structure and function of commercial banks. Part I examines the origins of commercial banking in the South. As a valuable financial asset, human property had always been vulnerable to seizure and sale at the hands of creditors like banks as part of foreclosure proceedings whenever a debtor failed to repay a loan. By the first decade of the nineteenth century, banks were additionally accepting enslaved individuals as mortgage collateral for the securitization of existing short-term loans upon their renewal. This was especially the case for banks operating in the growing states of Kentucky, Tennessee, Mississippi, and Louisiana.

The largely positive experiences of both debtors and banks with these mortgage contracts during and after the Panic of 1819 convinced bankers that enslaved lives were not only acceptable, but were superior to other assets. Thus, during the 1820s and 1830s, bankers operating on the frontier were increasingly willing to initiate new long-term loans secured by enslaved individuals, and even to finance the initial purchase of plantations and enslaved lives secured by this same property (part II). These long-term loans, many of which were for extremely large amounts, were unique among banks of the period and thus forced both bankers and legislatures to rethink traditional banking practices within the context of a dynamic slave system. This shift to long-term lending secured by enslaved lives was most evident in the booming cotton and sugar regions of the southwestern frontier from Georgia to Louisiana. Bankers initially innovated their lending practices to meet the growing demands of slaveholders without (technically) breaking the legal conditions of their incorporation, while others operated in open violation of their charters. Rather than awkwardly fitting slavery into traditional banking practices, by the 1830s several state legislatures responded by restructuring commercial banks to fit the needs of the slave system more efficiently. The apex of this financialization of slavery was the development of plantation banks in which the capital stock for the bank itself was obtained through mortgages on plantations and enslaved lives. This banking infrastructure was critical to the development of the frontier South during the 1820s and 1830s.

The Panics of 1837 and 1839, and the resulting recession, highlighted the shortcomings of relying so heavily on human property in credit relationships (part III). Frontier banks had become so dependent on slavery that they faced two equally bad choices: foreclose on slaveholding customers and sell their plantations and enslaved workers at a severe loss, or renegotiate more-lenient terms with debtors in the hopes of a quick economic recovery. Both the liquidity of enslaved individuals and their shifting legal status as either movable or immovable property, which banks initially viewed as the major advantage of using enslaved people as collateral during the economic boom, turned out to be a huge disadvantage during a downtown. In addition to declining in value like land could, enslaved people could be physically moved out of state, die or run away, be claimed as the separate property of wives, or be sold to innocent (or not-so-innocent) third parties, making it difficult for creditors to recover on these debts. Even in the case of successful foreclosures, banks often found themselves saddled with owning and managing plantations with their enslaved workforce—property they were either unable or unwilling to sell at the going market rates. Thus banks more often opted for leniency over foreclosure, providing much-needed stability to a slave system in crisis. Yet this choice also more directly threatened the fiscal soundness of the banks by undercutting their immediate liquidity. In effect, many frontier banks sacrificed themselves at the altar of the slave system. Slavery would survive, but at the expense of the banks.

The panics not only decimated the banking industry, but also caused bankers, debtors, and legislatures alike to reconsider the wisdom of continuing this interwoven relationship between banks and slavery (chapter 9). Although banks had played a critical role in the expansion of the slave economy during the 1820s and 1830s and had successfully helped to navigate indebted slaveholders through the panics, they had been merely a means to achieve this financial end. Even as the slave economy triumphed and cotton became king during the 1840s and 1850s, frontier legislatures rejected the continued dominance of banks in the financialization of slavery, and only the most capital-intensive sugar planters remained dependent on state-chartered commercial banks. With many southern states now rejecting banks altogether, private bankers, out-of-state-bankers, and merchants attempted to fill this void, but most lacked the economic resources available to incorporated institutions for financing large-scale endeavors. The most successful of these newcomers would develop into some of the nation's investment banks—but that is a story for another book. By the late 1850s, a few southern states re-embraced traditional commercial banking through the free-banking model developed in New York, but these new banks were less accommodating to the financial needs of slaveholders and the slave system. Banks on the southern frontier fulfilled a specific need during a crucial moment in the expansion of the slave system, and then retreated to the background.

The three groups of protagonists in this story are southern banks, the slaveholders who were their customers, and the enslaved people used as collateral. Credit relationships do not necessarily require financial intermediaries like banks, and many—if not most—credit transactions in the early republic happened outside of formal institutions, appearing as entries in merchant ledger books or agreements between neighbors.[40] Although American slaveholders had always financialized their human property by various means, an increasingly sophisticated economy required the emergence of intermediaries to accommodate more complicated and capital-intensive needs. The institutionalization of this practice within commercial banks was a critical intensification and formalization of slave finance. As Sean Patrick Adams has so cogently argued, institutions represent "a formal set of rules within a prescribed boundary of authority" which are "visible remnants of political and economic tussles, cultural assumptions, and both formal and informal power arrangements." While informal relationships certainly matter, the policies and practices a community chooses to institutionalize—even as they are "remade countless times over the course of their existence"—represent and reflect the collective choices of a given society.[41] To fully understand slavery we must examine the *formal* institutions—including financial institutions—that protected, promoted, and transformed the system.

The most important financial institutions of the early nineteenth century were commercial banks. These banks facilitated the exchange of funds between borrowers and available creditors by centralizing the process of lending. Commercial banks specialized in judging the riskiness of potential debtors and spreading these risks across many creditors. Additionally, banks were better equipped than individuals to enforce payment through the often time-consuming, costly, and confusing legal system. Thus before we can understand the financialization of slavery, we need to examine the structure and function of southern commercial banks; this is as much a story about southern banking as it is about slavery.

But the issues at the center of this inquiry still all reside at the immediate intersection of banking and slavery. I am *not* concerned with questions about the profitability of southern banks, their impact on general economic development at the state and local levels, or their role within the national and international macro economy. I also largely ignore northern and European banks, whose relationship with slavery was usually more indirect, through the financing of the cotton trade or through investment in southern bonds. Although these questions and relationships are not irrelevant to the system of slavery, they are not dependent upon it either. Bank financing of the international cotton trade, for example, could have occurred in a counterfactual universe without slavery. This study instead focuses exclusively on those ways that southern commercial banks directly, knowingly, and explicitly interacted with the slave system. Similarly, this study largely ignores the financialization of slavery that occurred outside of formal state or federally chartered institutions—especially through merchants and private bankers who operated without the official sanction and oversight of the state (and who would eventually develop into investment banking houses). These choices are made as much for ideological reasons (government-sanctioned institutions matter) as for practical reasons. I could not hope to take a long view of the financialization of slavery across the frontier antebellum South with any precision or detail if I included all the direct and indirect interactions with slavery by all possible financial firms.

But institutions don't just exist on paper; they only matter because of their interactions with real people. Institutions—both financial institutions and the slave system—evolved through the reciprocal relationships between the people who ran the institutions and their clientele. The slaveholders at the heart of this study were often also the legislators, directors, and stockholders who incorporated, ran, and invested in the banks. They had to navigate complicated loyalties as bankers running solvent financial institutions that still met the credit needs of their family, friends, neighbors, and themselves during the dramatic booms and busts of the antebellum period. The evolving financial demands of planters, particularly in the growing regions of the southern frontier, propelled the development of innovative banking institutions to address their unique credit needs. It likewise drove them largely to abandon bank finance in the 1840s and 1850s.

Yet in the end, the main reason this study matters is because of the enslaved individuals themselves. While we often focus on slavery as a labor system, the financialization of enslaved people took dehumanization to a new level. In moving beyond the physical and psychological violence of the plantation, the financialization of slavery turned human beings into abstract financial assets that both expanded the local money supply and circulated globally as bonded debt. On the one hand, using enslaved lives as loan collateral was often an alternative to selling those same people to raise needed funds. Thus mortgaging human property frequently prevented family breakups and the destruction of enslaved communities. Debtors wishing to sell a particular enslaved person also needed to petition the bank for a legal release of the person from the mortgage contract, which added a layer of bureaucracy and expense to the selling process. On the other hand, the expansion of southern banking to embrace large-denomination mortgages secured by enslaved individuals greatly facilitated the indebtedness of planters. They built their substantial cotton and sugar plantations with enslaved lives imported from other parts of the country, stimulating and supporting the growth of the domestic slave trade. And when these indebted planters did fail, especially during economic downturns, it had catastrophic consequences for the enslaved lives who were seized and sold as part of the foreclosure proceedings.

Despite their centrality to the system of slave finance, it is the voices and experiences of the enslaved themselves that are most absent from this study. At its core, slavery is a system of dominance, but dominance for an economic end. At every turn, this book unintentionally reproduces the violence and commodification of the slave system by focusing on people as financial assets. Recent scholars of slavery have done an amazing job of unearthing enslaved voices and telling their stories. But the entire purpose of financialization is to erase stories. Finance is all about abstraction. By turning assets—even human assets—into dollar equivalencies, they become fungible, interchangeable, without identity. While I have tried to maintain the humanity of the individuals, they are everywhere property, collateral, assets. In telling a financial story, I employ the language of finance. People are foreclosed, settled, liquidated. Understanding the economics behind *how* the system of slavery accomplished a massive migration of people to the frontier South, creating the foundations of the modern American economy by mid-century, is essential to our understanding of the slave system. Yet beyond enslaved people being under the constant threat of sale due to the indebtedness of their owners, this study reveals little about the individual experiences of the enslaved themselves. These silences remain deafening.[42]

PART I

Financing Southwestern Expansion through the 1810s

At the turn of the nineteenth century, the United States was growing, and Americans were on the move. The southern seaboard states of Delaware, Maryland, Virginia, and North and South Carolina grew in population from approximately 1.7 million people in 1790 to 2.6 million in 1820 (a moderate growth rate of about 20 percent each decade) through a combination of natural increase, immigration, and the continued Atlantic slave trade (legal through 1809).[1] Many more Americans pushed west. In historian Ira Berlin's summation, "During the last decades of the eighteenth century, [the slave regime] breached the easternmost Blue Ridge range, inundated the Shenandoah Valley, and spilled across the Cumberland Plateau into Kentucky and Tennessee. At the same time, slave-owning planters enlarged their base at the mouth of the Mississippi River. The purchase of Louisiana from a beleaguered France . . . created . . . an empire for slavery" (maps PI.1 and PI.2).[2]

Georgia's population doubled between 1790 and 1800, before doubling again by 1820. Kentucky and Tennessee's populations both tripled during the 1790s; the latter then grew fourfold by 1820 while the former almost tripled again. The new states of Mississippi, Alabama, and Louisiana—which had few non-indigenous inhabitants in 1800—ballooned to 75,000, 128,000, and 153,000 people, respectively. As historian Dan Dupre writes, "Thousands traveled the wagon roads through mountain passes in the years just before and after the War of 1812, leaving familiar communities in Virginia, the Carolinas, Georgia, and Tennessee to carve out new homes on the frontier."[3] With a total non-indigenous population of fewer than two hundred thousand in 1790, these six frontier states claimed almost 1.7 million inhabitants by 1820; about one-third of them were enslaved men, women, and children.[4] "Before they reached their adulthood, most slaveholders had been conditioned to accept migration as the prerequisite to success," historian James Oakes concludes. "What united small slaveholders with the sons of planters was the goal of purchasing land and slaves and moving west in pursuit of that goal. By the nineteenth century, westward migration had become so much a part of upward mobility in the South that it took on a lure almost independent of the profitable potential of the actual move."[5]

Simultaneous with this first wave of westward migration, state legislatures as well as the federal government began chartering commercial banks to provide much-needed financial support and liquidity for the young nation. Primarily designed to address the monetary needs of eastern merchants and commercial traders, these early financial institutions were of limited worth to the agricultural interests of the frontier, which required larger loans with longer payment terms and the ability to offer property as collateral. On the southern frontier, where farmers believed the ownership of enslaved labor

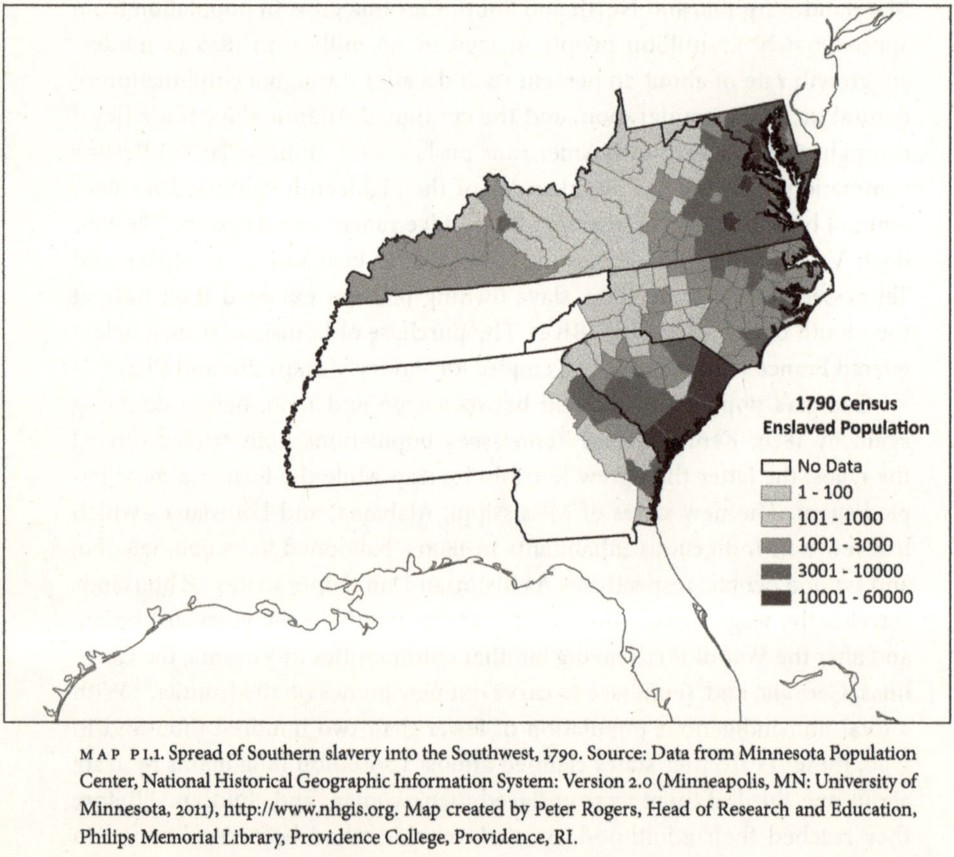

MAP P1.1. Spread of Southern slavery into the Southwest, 1790. Source: Data from Minnesota Population Center, National Historical Geographic Information System: Version 2.0 (Minneapolis, MN: University of Minnesota, 2011), http://www.nhgis.org. Map created by Peter Rogers, Head of Research and Education, Philips Memorial Library, Providence College, Providence, RI.

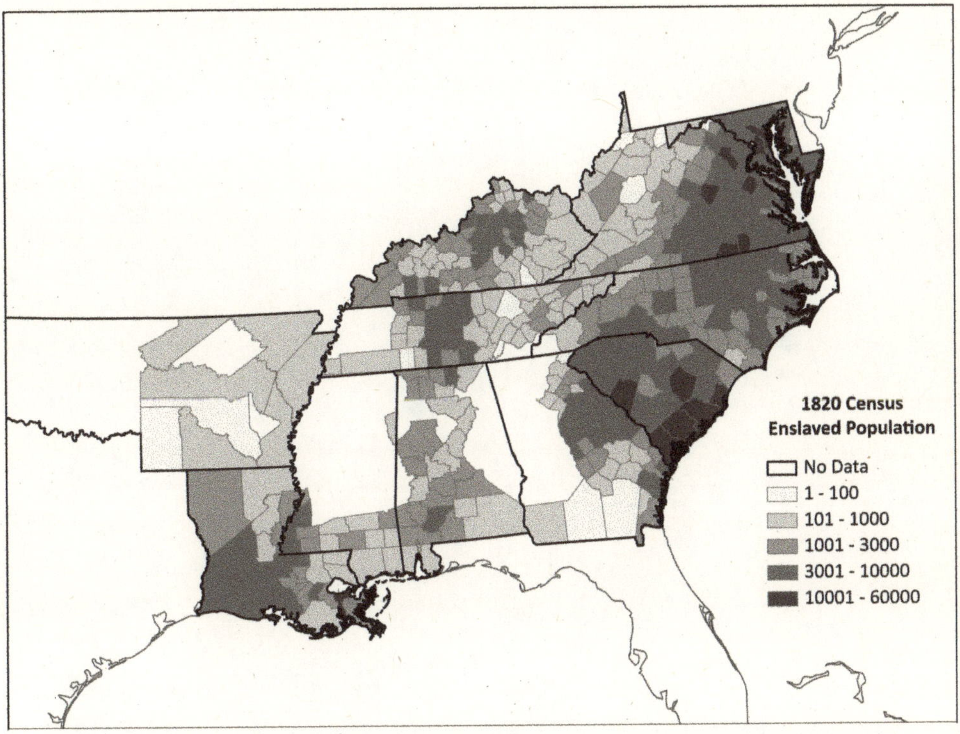

MAP PI.2. Spread of Southern slavery into the Southwest, 1820. Source: Data from Minnesota Population Center, National Historical Geographic Information System: Version 2.0 (Minneapolis, MN: University of Minnesota, 2011), http://www.nhgis.org. Map created by Peter Rogers, Head of Research and Education, Philips Memorial Library, Providence College, Providence, RI.

to be essential to their success, and where much of the region's wealth was invested and stored in these same enslaved bodies, this discrepancy between banking practices and local demands initially hampered growth. Chapter 1 details the economic and legal limits of banking in the southern context, and early attempts to navigate around these limitations. During the post–War of 1812 boom and the ensuing Panic of 1819 (chapter 2), frontier bankers became increasingly comfortable with actively treating enslaved people as financial assets, even as traditional banking norms continued to constrain their support of westward expansion. Ultimately, these lessons from the nation's first boom and bust would transform southern banking during the next, much-larger push into the Southwest during the 1820s and 1830s, when frontier banks would become an essential part of this burgeoning "empire of slavery" (part II).

1

The Limits of Early Bank Financing of Slavery

Prior to the American Revolution, George Galphin had used his position as a major merchant and Indian trader to make a name for himself as an "intermediary for Creek and European peoples."[1] He additionally owned over two hundred enslaved individuals across his Silver Bluff plantation in South Carolina and Old Town plantation in Georgia.[2] Yet upon his death in 1780, his substantial estate became mired in the disputed claims of both his personal creditors and the creditors of his firm: Galphin, Holmes & Co.[3] In 1796, the estate sold a large portion of Galphin's property to three Charleston businessmen, who agreed to honor Galphin's remaining debts to a London firm. The London firm accepted their promissory notes for future payment, secured by a combination of Galphin's landed estate, "together with mills, stock, tools, &c," as well as a group of twenty-five enslaved individuals, another group of forty-eight people, a house and lot in Charleston owned by one of the businessmen, and the endorsement of Wade Hampton—one of the wealthiest planters in the state.[4]

In April 1802, with the debt still unpaid, a representative of the London firm physically transferred the forty-eight enslaved people to Charleston for the purpose of selling them. One of the businessmen appealed to the newly opened State Bank of South Carolina for help, obtaining a loan to pay off the London debt in return for the bank's mortgage on the enslaved lives as well as the other property. Following standard banking practice, this loan was probably a sixty-day renewable promissory note payable by the Charleston businessmen to the London firm and further endorsed by Hampton. Hampton's position as a founding director of the State Bank likely helped convince his colleagues to accept these lending terms.[5] Thus, rather than dispersing the forty-eight enslaved individuals at auction, Galphin's Charleston creditors kept possession of them.[6]

When this mortgage loan remained unpaid a year later, Hampton became "uneasy at the great delay of payment, and the insolvency of two of the parties, [and] did warn the bank, that unless they used all due care and proper diligence to collect their debt, he should exert himself to get released from his securityship." His fellow bank directors took this warning to heart and immediately employed an agent to enforce the mortgage and sell the enslaved people. Galphin's creditors quickly obtained an injunction to stop this sale, claiming that the bank should liquidate other "primary" assets from the original mortgage first, such as the land or houses. The court, however, disagreed. The bank, it ruled, had assented to the 1802 loan in exchange for the mortgage on the human property, and "it would be extraordinary and unjust, that the multiplication of securities, which was intended as an inducement to the loan by the Bank, should be converted into a source of delay in the recovery of the debt. . . . It appears obvious that the [slave] mortgages were taken as an additional security, and it was intended that the Bank should be at liberty to resort to any of the securities, to enforce payment."[7] In other words, it was the bank's right to seize and sell any of the collateral used to secure the loan, and the enslaved lives were the easiest to transform into cash.

Court cases often deal with novel issues that break from the norm, but they can also reveal what was uncontroversial and widely accepted at the time. This loan was not typical for early banking institutions. The State Bank had been chartered with the primary purpose of "receiv[ing] money on deposit" and "discount[ing] bills of exchange . . . and notes with two or more good names thereon," as long as "said bills and notes have not more than sixty days to run."[8] In order to comply with these charter terms, the directors likely wrote the loan as a standard sixty-day renewable promissory note. Yet the long-term nature of this loan, which had originated before 1796, certainly violated the spirit of the charter and would have made most early bankers extremely uncomfortable. Indeed, even Hampton acceded to that point when the loan remained unpaid after another year.

Yet although early banks typically did not loan in this manner, mortgage contracts had existed long before the rise of banking institutions, and they were commonly secured by all types of real and personal property—from land and buildings to livestock and tools to enslaved men, women, and children.[9] No one in this case disputed the variety or types of collateral involved. On the other hand, the case revealed a growing awareness of the advantages of enslaved people as collateral over other types of property of equivalent market value. In a rapidly growing economy centered on slavery, the enslaved individuals themselves were often the most liquid assets available. Not only could creditors sell human property quickly at auction, they could also seize only the number of people necessary to repay the debt, tearing apart enslaved families and communities in the process. Landed property, on the other hand, was both less liquid and more difficult to apportion without losing market value. The State Bank thus preferred the ease of selling enslaved lives over the hassle of dealing in land. Yet while slaveholders sought greater flexibility to tap into the wealth stored in their human property, bankers needed to balance these demands against the requirements of their government charters and the accepted norms and practices of the financial community. The limited ability of early banks to meet the rapidly growing financial needs of slaveholders is thus where we begin this story.

Enslaved Collateral and the Law

Historically, most credit transactions have occurred without the intermediation of financial institutions such as banks. Debtors borrowed from family members, friends, business partners, or local merchants, with deals formally recorded in ledger books or sealed with a mere handshake.[10] Since enslaved individuals constituted a significant proportion of southern wealth even in the colonial period, mortgages involving enslaved lives were common.[11] Yet the legal designation of human property mattered greatly for these contracts.[12] Throughout the history of slavery in North America, colonies and then states struggled with how to define enslaved people. Whereas legal (de jure) definitions had significant weight, the treatment of enslaved lives in day-to-day (de facto) interactions sometimes contradicted the law. For example, bondspeople were almost universally defined as property. As George Stroud summarized in his *Sketch of the Laws Relating to Slavery* in 1827, "the cardinal principle of slavery—that the slave is not to be ranked among *sentient beings*, but among things—is an article of property—a chattel personal,—obtains as undoubted law in all of these states."[13] Yet some nineteenth-century *life* insurers routinely underwrote enslaved people as lives, where they would never underwrite valuable horses or livestock (which were also, arguably, living property).[14] In legal historian Katharina Pistor's words, "property rights . . . are negotiated case by case by matching actual practices to legal concepts. . . . the fashioning of property rights in law is a complex process that is pregnant with value judgments and power."[15] This question of personhood versus property would later form the core of many of the debates over abolition.[16]

Even if most southern whites agreed that enslaved bodies were legally property, the precise type of property was more debatable. Were they "real" or "personal" property? "Movable" or "immovable" property? The answers to these questions were less obvious than they might first appear, and shifted from location to location and across time. As one major historian of southern law summarizes, "Some judges analogized slaves to land and adopted rules reflecting that correspondence. For one reason or another rules of real property law were applied to slaves in some instances in over one-third of the jurisdictions that made up the slave South."[17] While this designation as realty or personalty was irrelevant to the day-to-day life experiences of the enslaved people themselves, legal definitions mattered greatly for the financialization of slavery since the laws surrounding realty differed from the laws surrounding personalty, especially in two instances: questions of inheritance and the property rights of wives and widows.

In English law, the real property of a person who died intestate (without a will) passed directly to his heirs, while personal property could be used by the executors of the estate to pay off any unsecured debts—meaning debts not backed by specific property as collateral—and then divided equally among the heirs.[18] Even without debts, if land descended to the eldest son (under the law of primogeniture) but human property was divided among the other heirs, "the plantation might sit idle, potentially forever, while [the eldest son] gathered enough funds either to purchase his father's slaves from his siblings or to purchase new slaves. Thus, inherited land was of little value if slaves were personal property."[19] A 1668 law in Barbados tried to solve this issue by classifying enslaved individuals as realty, tying them to the land and thus keeping them out of the hands of the executors. The Virginia legislature modeled its 1705 law on this Barbadian statute. "The primary objective was to assure that those who received the land of a slaveowner would also receive the slaves necessary to work the land." Continuing this logic, when enslaved lives were not directly connected to a plantation, their legal status remained as personal property.[20]

With the Debt Recovery Act of 1732, British creditors pushed back against this classification of the enslaved as realty, since it made it more difficult for them to foreclose on the property of delinquent debtors in the colonies.[21] Creditors also worried that debtors would "purchase slaves for the specific purpose of shielding wealth from the claims of creditors."[22] For the purposes of debt collection, the 1732 act required that both land and human property be treated as personalty. "The Act abolished the legal distinctions between real property, chattel property, and slaves in relation to the claims of creditors. Under the Act, land and slaves could be seized and sold to satisfy any type of debt, including many widely used forms of unsecured debt."[23] However, sheriffs typically had to sell off non-enslaved personal property first, then enslaved individuals, before seizing and selling landed property in the recovery of debts.[24]

An example of this designation problem appeared in the 1732 and 1736 court cases of *Jones v. Langhorn*. Sometime before 1705, Mary Rice inherited land and several enslaved individuals from her mother Mary Godwin for "use . . . during her natural Life," before becoming the property of any "heirs lawfully begotten of her body." The daughter first married a man named Myres, with whom she had four children, and the couple entered into a mortgage with another man named Jones, using this human property inherited from Godwin as collateral. Jones assumed that Myres—as the husband—was the legal owner of the enslaved people which Rice brought into the marriage. When Myres died, Mary Rice remarried to John Langhorn and had four more children. In 1732 and again in 1736, Jones sued Langhorn (the second husband) for the enslaved lives previously mortgaged to him by Myres (the first husband).[25]

Despite the 1705 law designating enslaved individuals as realty, both attorneys agreed that these individuals should be treated as personal property, since that was their status when Mary Rice first inherited them before 1705. Jones's attorney argued that when Myres married Rice, he acquired only managerial control of her realty "but as to chattels personal, marriage is an absolute gift of all such in possession, whether the husband survive or not." Therefore, the enslaved people were his to mortgage, and should pass to *his* heirs upon death, after all creditors were satisfied—ignoring the terms of Godwin's will. Langhorn's attorney conceded that the human property should be treated as personalty, but instead focused on the terms of the will which only granted Rice a life estate in the property, with the remainder descending to *her* heirs. Myres, as the first husband, only gained the use rather than the outright ownership of the personal property during his life. Langhorn's attorney then concluded that "it would be a hard case upon women, especially widows marrying second husbands" if marriage canceled the terms of a valid will, and "that it would be inconvenient too since the slaves might be taken in execution for the [first] husband's debts or sold by him to the prejudice" of her heirs. In both cases, the court decided in favor of Langhorn and, by extension, Mary Rice and her children.[26]

It is unclear whether Rice and Myres entered into the mortgage with Jones in exchange for a new loan (i.e., with Jones offering a loan of money directly in return for a mortgage on the enslaved lives), or as a means of securing an existing loan (i.e., with Myres already owing Jones a sum of money, and using the mortgage to secure the loan and delay immediate payment). However, numerous eighteenth-century court cases reveal that debtors from throughout the southern states mortgaged enslaved people both to secure existing debts and to obtain new loans.[27] They even purchased plantations and slaves on mortgage, using the same purchased property as collateral. For example, in April 1794, W. B. Mitchell and his brother John purchased a South Carolina plantation with its 137 enslaved laborers from a man named Neufville. Under the terms of the purchase, the Mitchells promised to pay 9400£ for the land in six annual installments, and 8905£ for the enslaved individuals in five annual installments. Neufville agreed to maintain a mortgage on this entire property as well as on another plantation with one hundred enslaved laborers owned by John, until the purchase price was fully paid.[28] There is also limited evidence that northern enslavers during the colonial period secured loans using their human property as collateral. For example, in 1840, the abolitionist newspaper the *Liberator* alleged that the "first mortgage ever given and put upon record in the Commonwealth of Pennsylvania" occurred on December 7, 1685, when Joseph Brown mortgaged his "negro man Jack" to Patrick Robinson for fourteen pounds, which he was to repay "by the delivery of 25,000 good, sound, merchantable bricks."[29] Nor were these contracts an American innovation. Archaeologists excavating the ancient city of Pompeii have found wax tablets from the first century AD detailing loan contracts secured with enslaved individuals.[30]

As the states attempted to create viable governing regimes during and after the American Revolution, most concluded that "the Debt Recovery Act subjected landowners to an undesirable level of financial risk" in that the failure to pay one's debts could result in the loss of one's landed property.[31] Each state thus needed to consider what balance to strike between creditors and debtors. Virginia's law of 1792 redefined enslaved individuals as personalty in most instances, while Kentucky's law of 1798 defined them as realty for the purposes of inheritance, but as personalty in cases of debt. By 1852, Kentucky reclassified human property as personalty in all cases. However, the new statute directed that creditors first claim non-enslaved personal property before seizing and selling enslaved lives.[32] The laws of Louisiana, which derived from its Spanish and French ancestry rather than the British tradition, classified property as *movable* or *immovable* (which were similar but not equivalent to the British terms *personalty* and *realty*). While the French *code noir* had initially defined enslaved lives as movable property, the law of 1770 reclassified them as "immovables for the purposes of sale and mortgage."[33] With its entrance into the United States, Louisiana's 1806 *code noir* declared that "Slaves shall always be reputed and considered real estates, shall be, as such, subject to be mortgaged, according to the rules prescribed by law, and they shall be seized and sold as real estate."[34] As commercial banks emerged in the South and began accepting enslaved individuals as collateral, these conflicting and confusing legal definitions remained problematic.

The Emergence of Commercial Banks

The first American commercial bank to open its doors was the Bank of North America in 1782. Initially chartered by the Continental Congress to aid in the financing of the Revolution, it transitioned to a Pennsylvania bank after the war.[35] During the early years of the republic, Secretary of the Treasury Alexander Hamilton famously convinced President George Washington to support the chartering of a national bank, over the protests of Thomas Jefferson and James Madison. Although Hamilton had described the Bank of the United States as a public institution, it was really a hybrid entity, part public and part for-profit. Only $2 million of its $10 million capital stock was owned by the government, and the government had no say in the election of board members, yet it provided loans to the government (as well as to private citizens), assisted in the collection of federal taxes, and served as a depository for all federal government funds—particularly import duties and western land sales—which gave it considerable financial power.[36] At its creation, this bank was more than three times larger than the combined capital of all the state-chartered banks. In terms of capital resources, it remained the largest business institution in the country throughout its twenty-year history.

Headquartered in Philadelphia, the directors of the Bank of the United States eventually opened eight branches (known as offices of discount and deposit) in major cities throughout the country. Six of the eight were located in the states of the slaveholding South: Baltimore, Maryland (1792); Charleston, South Carolina (1792); Norfolk, Virginia (1800); Washington, DC (1802); Savannah, Georgia (1802); and New Orleans, Louisiana (1805).[37] These southern branches helped tie the South and plantation slavery directly to the nation's financial system. And whereas state-chartered institutions could only operate as single (unit) banks or with branches within a state, the bank's nationwide branching further established its financial dominance.

The individual states also began actively chartering banks to supplement the services of the first Bank of the United States, although these state-chartered banks were often located in the same commercial centers as the national branches. Through early 1815, the southern states (including Washington, DC) chartered approximately fifty-nine banks (including the six aforementioned Bank of the United States branches), many of which opened (or were permitted to open) additional branches within their respective states (table 1.1). The five southern banks chartered during the 1790s were all located in the mid-Atlantic region (Delaware, Maryland, and the District of Columbia), and this same region accounted for almost two-thirds of all charters through 1815. The Bank of South Carolina officially opened its doors in Charleston in 1792, but failed to receive a charter from the legislature. It operated as an unincorporated (private) bank until the state finally relented in 1801. The legislature simultaneously decided to charter the State Bank of South Carolina (1802), also in Charleston, which was partially state-owned and controlled. Both banks focused on the commercial needs of the port city.[38] After the first Bank of the United States' charter expired in 1811, the state incorporated three more banking institutions, including the state-owned Bank of the State of South Carolina.[39]

In 1804, the Commonwealth of Virginia incorporated the Bank of Virginia, which was directly modeled on the Bank of the United States; Virginia owned one-fifth of the bank's shares and appointed one-fifth of its directors. Headquartered in Richmond, the bank also opened offices of discount and deposit in Norfolk, Fredericksburg, and Petersburg. Following the closing of the first Bank of the United States, the commonwealth chartered the Farmer's Bank, which was also headquartered in Richmond with the same three branches, plus Lynchburg in the west and Winchester in the northwest. New Orleans received its first bank—the Louisiana Bank—in 1804, which was the first southern bank chartered outside the original colonies. The state opened its second and third banks after the closure of the national bank branch in 1811, when it chartered the Planters' Bank and the Bank of Orleans, both of which were also in New Orleans. Additionally in 1804, the state of North Carolina incorporated the Bank of Newbern (with a branch in Fayetteville) and the Bank of Cape Fear in Wilmington. The partially state-owned Bank of the State of North Carolina opened in Raleigh in 1810, with six other state branches. The partially state-owned Bank of Kentucky opened in 1807 with the right to open future branches. The Nashville Bank appeared in 1808, followed by the state-owned Bank of the State of Tennessee in 1811. In anticipation of the closure of the Savannah branch of the first Bank, Georgia chartered its first two banks in 1810: the Bank of Augusta and the Planters' Bank in Savannah.[40] Similarly, the territory of Mississippi chartered the Bank of the Mississippi in 1809, which first opened its doors in Natchez in 1811.[41]

Like the numerous northern banks being formed at this same time, almost all these commercial banks were chartered on conservative banking principles that were primarily designed to meet the needs of businesspeople actively engaged in trade. They provided small, short-term loans backed by business paper, and a circulating medium—banknotes—to supplement the sparse supplies of gold and silver in the economy. In answer to the question "What are the objects of a Bank," the incorporators of the Louisiana Bank in 1804 helpfully responded to potential stockholders: "The loaning of money on lawful interest; and the substituting [of] their own promissory notes, as a

TABLE 1.1 Southern bank charters through 1820[a]

Region	*Bank charters through 1811*	*New charters 1812–15*	*New charters 1816–20*	*Closures through 1820*	*Total banks end of 1820*	*Percentage of banks closed through 1820*	*Growth rate of banking 1811–20*
Mid-Atlantic (MD, DE, DC)	19	15	11	(11)	34	24%	79%
Old South (VA, NC, SC)	10	2	6	(3)	15	17%	50%
Upper frontier (KY, TN, MO, AR)	3	1	8[b]	(6)	6	50%	100%
Lower frontier (GA, AL, MS, LA, FL)	8	1	9	(5)	13	28%	63%
Totals	40	19	34	(25)	68	27%	70%

[a] Includes branches of the First and Second Bank of the United States. Does not include individual branches of state banks.

[b] Kentucky passed one act chartering forty-six small independent banks in 1819, many of which never opened and none of which survived the panic. I only count these as one bank in the chart, to avoid an unrepresentative skew in the numbers.

Source: Warren E. Weber, Census of Early State Banks in the United States (2005), https://www.minneapolisfed.org/people/warren-e-weber; Warren E. Weber, "Early State Banks in the United States: How Many Were There and When Did They Exist," *Journal of Economic History* 66, no. 2 (June 2006): 433–55.

circulating medium in lieu of gold and silver."[42] Banks were a more efficient way to match the available funds of creditors with the needs of debtors. Additionally, they spread the risks of lending across many individuals and specialized in judging the riskiness of these loans.[43]

The most common type of lending engaged in by commercial banks was discounting, which was a specific type of short-term loan for businesspeople engaged in trade. A merchant would obtain goods from a seller by issuing a promissory note known as commercial paper, promising to pay the full amount at a specified future date after he had sold the goods in question. The seller could then add his name to the note—making it double-name paper—and take this note to a bank to be discounted; the bank would loan him the face value of the note less a discount reflecting the interest rate.[44] In promoting the creation of the Bank of Virginia, an editorialist in 1804 explained, "In this country [banks'] chief employment consists in discounting the promissory notes of merchants; and their chief profit arises from circulating" their own banknotes. The editorialist then continued to explain the process of discounting. "When a merchant in good credit, gives his promissory note payable in sixty days at farthest, and negociable at the bank, if it has an approved endorser, the Directors will, on application, advance the money to the holder of the note, first deducting the legal interest for the time it has to run. The money thus advanced is not specie, but bank bills, that is, its own promissory notes payable to the bearer, which have the same currency in gold and silver."[45]

When these discounted notes became due, usually after sixty to ninety days, the loan recipient could repay his or her debt or request a renewal of the loan for an additional discount. As long as the bank did not need the funds and remained confident in the debtor's eventual ability to repay, it was usually willing to renew the loan; this renewed obligation was often called an accommodation loan. As Howard Bodenhorn's extensive study of antebellum banks concludes, banks traditionally "preferred to loan at short term," even if repeated renewals might turn a ninety-day loan into a 180-day or 270-day loan. On the other hand, although "long-term noncommercial loans were sometimes made, they were rare."[46] As one Maryland bank proponent explained in 1805, "But it is a fact well known, that these accommodations, although nominally limitted [*sic*] to sixty days, yet are in reality seldom discontinued, where the security is undoubted, and the borrowers are industrious and thriving; but on the contrary, are renewed as long as customers may require, unless the bank is obliged to curtail its discounts, in which case timely notice is usually given."[47] In the parlance of the time, these institutions were even commonly referred to as "office[s] of discount and deposit," directly specifying their main functions.[48]

In this earliest period, sixty days was the most common limit on bank loans throughout the United States.[49] According to the bylaws of the first Bank of the United States, "Discounts shall be made at a rate not exceeding 6 per cent per annum on notes or bills of exchange that have not more than sixty days to run, and with at least two responsible names."[50] Both the Charleston (1792) and Savannah (1802) branches of the first Bank of the United States advertised their lending terms upon opening for business: "Discounts shall be made on Bills, Notes, or Acceptances, payable in Dollars, upon personal security only, with, at least two responsible names (one of which must be a resident in Savannah) for any term not exceeding Sixty days."[51] As the 1802 charter for the State Bank of South Carolina similarly delineated: "They shall receive money on deposit, . . . discount bills of exchange accepted and payable in the city of Charleston, and notes with two or more good names thereon . . . at a rate of interest not exceeding one per cent. discount for sixty days. *Provided* the said bills and notes have not more than sixty days to run."[52] The Louisiana Bank definitively stated in 1804 that loans were "payable every 60 or 90 days, according to their custom,"[53] while a Virginia promoter of banks explained that same year: "In the course of two months, at farthest, all the money due to the banks is collected, barring insolvencies."[54] The Union Bank of South Carolina was one of the few that was more lenient, allowing discounts of up to ninety days in its 1810 charter.[55]

These discount loans reflected a common belief among early bankers in the real-bills doctrine. Proponents of sound banking asserted that the safest types of loans were on short-term commercial paper because they were backed by "real" commodities: goods in transit, items awaiting sale, a harvest about to be shipped, and so forth. Yet although backed by "real" goods, these discounted loans were still unsecured loans, since the debtor offered no specific property in return for the loan. The requirement that the loan be endorsed by two people (usually the initial recipient of the note and a second party) was meant to provide adequate security, since any endorsers could also be sued for payment. And although, in theory, these notes were meant to represent transactions in progress, they were often just short-term promissory notes, known as accommodation paper. As banking historian Naomi Lamoreaux explains, accommodation loans were "notes that were not connected with any specific commercial transaction and that were routinely renewed upon maturity," which were "used to support a wide variety of investment activities" in the early nineteenth century.[56] Even business paper that initially reflected goods in transit effectively became accommodation paper upon renewal, having been divorced from its original purpose.[57]

Regardless of whether the note reflected an actual business transaction or was merely a loan, the short-term nature of the arrangement was its key feature; this feature is also what made these loans of little use to the agricultural sector. If the bank needed the funds or was not confident in the long-term soundness of the debtor, the bank could demand immediate repayment when the loan term was up. If the debtor failed to repay the loan, the bank could sue the debtor and/or any endorsers of the note in question. The court would issue an order of *fieri facias* (or *fi. fa.*, for short), which allowed the sheriff to seize and sell the property of the debtor (or any of the endorsers) in payment of the delinquent obligation.[58] And it was through these *fi. fa.* judgments that early banks first engaged directly with human property.

Seizing Enslaved Individuals

In October 1804, the Sheriff of Charleston advertised property for sale "By virtue of sundry writs of *fieri facias* to me directed." Included in the forthcoming sale was half of Timicaw or Dewee's Island in Christ Church Parish, as well as "Sundry NEGROES and a large CANOE," all of which was the property of a local slaveholder. This property had been seized to satisfy "the separate suits" of six different creditors, including the Charleston branch of the Bank of the United States. The purchaser of the enslaved individuals was required to pay 10 percent immediately, with the remainder in cash or specie at some unspecified point in the near future.[59] While all this property sold in the November sale, by December the sheriff was again advertising the enslaved individuals, who had "to be re-sold on account and risk of the former purchaser, who has not complied with the terms of sale."[60] This second sale was successful, with the exception of one enslaved individual. Although no details are available on this person, the sheriff continued to advertise "one NEGRO To be re-sold . . . as the property of John Lewis Poyas, at the separate suits of" his various creditors, including the branch bank, in February and March of 1805.[61]

Alternatively, in lieu of initiating foreclosure proceedings, the bank in this case could have demanded that the debtor supply additional security—i.e., particular identifiable assets as collateral—in order to renew the loan in the form of a mortgage on his or her property. This would have turned an unsecured loan into a secured loan. Most early bank charters contained language specifically permitting the mortgaging of property for this purpose. Although none of these early charters explicitly mentioned human property, they often permitted both real and personal property as security. The charter of the first Bank of the United States stated that the institution could "hold real and personal estate . . . such as shall have been bona fide mortgaged to it by way of security, or conveyed to it in satisfaction of debts previously contracted, in the usual course of its dealings, or purchased at sales upon judgments which shall have been obtained for such debts."[62] Most other early banks included the same language in their charters, including the first six New York banks (chartered between 1791 and 1805), three of the South Carolina banks (1801, 1802, 1810), both Virginia banks (1804, 1812), the three North Carolina banks (1804, 1804, 1810), the Bank of Kentucky (1806), both Georgia banks (1810, 1810), and the Bank of the State of Tennessee (1811).[63] Although the Louisiana Bank (1804) was vaguer in its charter terms, the description of functions that it released to potential investors explained: "For these loans they are paid an interest, and they receive in return as security for the re-payment of the sum lent, the notes of the borrowers, sufficiently endorsed, mortgages on real estates, or precious and valuable effects."[64]

Due to the limited extant documents from these earliest commercial banks, the most ample evidence of banks securing loans with enslaved individuals comes from the closure papers of the first Bank of the United States. When Congress voted not to renew the federal charter for the institution in

1811, the bank quietly closed its doors and settled its accounts. Philadelphia banker Stephen Girard purchased the bank's remaining assets, including any outstanding debts owed to the bank at its eight branches. In Charleston, Savannah, and New Orleans, the surviving records include loans collateralized with enslaved people.[65] For example, the prominent South Carolina couple James and Elizabeth Hamilton had received a loan of $2,700 from the Charleston office in November 1799, which they secured by a mortgage on their "Negroes & Plantation on [the river] Santée"; in 1811 they still owed the office $2,530.09 in principal and accrued interest, but the 103 enslaved individuals whom they listed in the 1810 census remained adequate collateral.[66] In July 1804, Henry Laurens Jr.—eldest son of one of the most important South Carolina statesmen of the eighteenth century—mortgaged his Mepkin plantation and human property on the Cooper River in return for a loan of $94,408 (about $2.1 million in 2021). Given both the odd dollar amount of this loan and the limits of acceptable banking practices, the mortgage was most likely to secure numerous accumulated (and repeatedly renewed) existing debts with the bank. Yet this debt was still striking for its size, which also challenged traditional banking norms even in the case of wealthy debtors. Laurens paid down much of the loan over the next several years, and the value of his 250 enslaved lives recorded in the 1810 census dwarfed the $18,881.88 he still owed when the bank closed its doors.[67]

As in the case of the Hamiltons and Henry Laurens, creditors like the Bank of the United States were often willing to renew a debt repeatedly as long as the underlying assets remained sound, the debtor paid the annual interest and a portion of the principal regularly, and the bank had no other pressing need for the funds. However, when the debt became questionable or the debtor died, the bank willingly foreclosed on any outstanding loans; it seized both real estate and personal property (whether or not this property had initially been secured as part of the loan collateral), and sold these assets for the benefit of the shareholders. Among the property often advertised for sale were enslaved people acquired for the bank in lawsuits. For example, after the death of one Savannah shopkeeper, the Bank of the United States seized his slave Scipio, selling him as part of a sheriff's sale at the Savannah courthouse on the first Tuesday of August, 1809.[68]

The foreclosure and sale of large estates was often much more involved. When the young John Habersham died unexpectedly in 1806, he was heavily indebted to the Savannah branch of the Bank of the United States.[69] Heir to one of the most prominent families in post-Revolutionary Savannah, John had inherited the Dean Forest plantation outside the city after the deaths of his parents John (1799) and Ann Sarah (1802).[70] His uncle Joseph Habersham, elder brother of his father, had become the first (and only) Savannah branch bank president when it opened its doors in 1802, and became administrator of his nephew's estate upon John's death.[71] In both April and May 1810, the entire Dean Forest plantation—including one thousand acres of land and several buildings, but only twelve enslaved individuals—was auctioned on behalf of the first Bank. The newspaper advertisements described the estate as an active rice plantation, with about 120 acres suitable for cotton or corn cultivation.[72] Lacking the federal census records for Georgia, it is impossible to know how many enslaved people had once resided on the plantation, yet it certainly was substantially more than the twelve included in the sale.[73] In all likelihood, the family chose to liquidate the land to pay off the debts while dispersing most of the enslaved lives to the surrounding family plantations of Silk Hope and Beverly.[74] The twelve remaining enslaved individuals were either of the estimated value to satisfy the remaining debt, and/or the least desirable of the slaves.

Dean Forest with its twelve enslaved individuals presumably found a buyer in that May 1, 1810, auction. It was no longer advertised for sale after that date; there was no entry for John Habersham in the record of branch debts at the bank's closing; and the bank did not include this plantation as part of its final real estate holdings.[75] Two years later, however, the Dean Forest plantation—still "levied on as the property of John Habersham, dec[eased]"—was again listed for sale in favor of the bank.[76] Perhaps the original transaction (likely also a credit sale) had fallen through and the bank reclaimed the property once the buyer defaulted. One of the largest bank debtors during this period was branch president (and John's uncle and estate administrator) Joseph Habersham, who owed $26,310 in February 1811; perhaps he had been the purchaser.[77] Regardless of the circumstances, the land alone was now advertised for sale at auction in April, May, and June 1812.[78] The thirteen enslaved people (probably the original twelve along with the child of Belinda), were not again advertised until May, separate from the second sale of the plantation. Of these thirteen, at least ten were female and at least two were children. Only two were clearly male, although their ages are unknown.[79] This severe gender imbalance implies that these enslaved people were selected for sale because they were less valuable to the Habersham family on the neighboring plantations. It also implies that the sale broke up several enslaved families at Dean Forest.

While the Dean Forest sale involved the liquidation of an estate, the bank also foreclosed on the property of delinquent living debtors. Lewis Johnston of Savannah discounted several notes with the national branch of that city, endorsed by Samuel Howard and James Johnston Jr. The latter two men had both been elected members of the bank's board of directors in 1803; James

Johnston remained a director in 1810.[80] By January 1810, Lewis Johnston owed the branch $12,514.40 including accrued interest, "the payment of which note is secured by a bond & mortgage by Lewis Johnston & Wife on Twenty three Negroes to said Cashier." Additionally, Howard and James Johnston put up "the residue of Fifty one Negroes after certain payments made as expressed in such conveyance to the Cashier."[81] Six months later, the bank began trying to sell this property to pay off the debt, starting with the "old coffee-house wharf."[82] Not finding a suitable buyer, the bank purchased the wharf property itself, valuing it on its books at $4,000.[83] But the bank waited another year to foreclose on any more of Johnston's property, deciding instead "to indulge him" until the bank's liquidation forced the sale. Howard, as an aggrieved endorser, later complained that "in the mean time," Johnston's property "depreciated much."[84]

During the summer of 1811, bank president David Lenox finally advertised Nanny, Elsey, Jimmy and Dora for sale at the courthouse in Savannah. That same day, another sale took place about sixty miles to the south "at the Market-house in Darien" of Johnston's plantation in McIntosh county, consisting of 498 acres and nineteen enslaved lives.[85] The Darien sheriff also auctioned off separately another "Twenty-seven NEGROES, now in the possession of Mr. Lewis Johnston, conveyed to the late Bank of the United States by James Johnston and Samuel Howard—terms of sale, cash."[86] The records do not indicate who purchased these three lots of enslaved people, or if they were further separated, but Howard later claimed that "much of it was bought by the Bank."[87] In addition to being an endorser on Johnston's notes, Samuel Howard was also separately indebted to the bank for approximately $34,770.71, which also remained outstanding as the War of 1812 broke out.[88]

Another major debtor of the Savannah branch was George Millen. Sometime after the Revolution, Millen settled on a plantation just three miles south of Savannah, Georgia, on the Little Ogeechee River, which he called Lottery Hall.[89] When the Savannah branch of the Bank of the United States opened its doors in 1802, Millen became a regular customer. He was certainly well acquainted with the branch president, Joseph Habersham. Since at least the early 1790s, both had been active members of the city's Union Society, an organization of elite Savannah citizens dedicated to providing education and relief to the city's poor.[90] By the end of the first decade of the century, Millen had amassed about $9,000 in debts to the bank.[91] Again, this debt was most likely an accumulation of smaller, short-term promissory notes that he had discounted and continued to renew with the bank. In order to secure this debt, Millen granted the bank a mortgage on his plantation and enslaved property.[92]

By 1810, the bank management made the decision to foreclose on Millen, rather than allow any more renewals of the debt. He was probably delinquent even in making his interest payments to the bank, since he was also listed as a defaulter on the city tax returns of 1809.[93] The branch successfully sued Millen, receiving a court order allowing it to sell his plantation and human property.[94] Yet the economy was already depressed from the effects of the 1807 Embargo Act and 1809 Non-Intercourse Act, both of which severely constrained trade with Britain.[95] The branch worried that the land, in particular, would sell for well below what its market value would be in better times. While the bank assessed the property at $2,700 on its account books, it noted that "the sum of three thousand dollars has been offered for the property, in better times it would bring Five thousand dollars." As it awaited improved market conditions for a sale, the board allowed Millen to remain on the land; presumably he continued to maintain the premises until either the bank could execute a final sale at better terms, or he could scrape together enough funds to pay off his debt and repurchase the land.[96]

But whereas the bank was willing to hold onto the landed property, it quickly began trying to sell off Millen's enslaved people in separate lots. In late March 1810, the *Savannah Republican* commenced advertising for sale (by name) fifteen individuals enslaved by Millen, to be sold at the Savannah courthouse in May on behalf of the bank. When they did not sell in the May auction, they were re-advertised for a June sale.[97] Almost a year later, the Bank of the United States was again advertising for sale thirteen of the same named slaves, along with five more belonging to Millen; only Sancho and Jenny were not relisted from the original sale.[98] Since there were no intervening advertisements, the most likely scenario is that the bank had sold these individuals in 1810 on credit terms (perhaps Millen himself had purchased them at auction), but when the new buyer failed to fulfill his end of the contract, the bank reseized them to sell again—adding on five more enslaved lives to the group. These eighteen enslaved people were presumably resold in April 1811 (either together or in smaller groups), since the bank stopped listing them and instead began advertising for sale twenty different enslaved individuals belonging to Millen—including Sancho, Jenny, and (possibly) Anthony from the original sale.[99] This second group of enslaved people proved much more difficult to sell. The same twenty were relisted by name regularly in ads for the monthly courthouse auction from May 1811 through March 1812.[100] Then, from April until June 1812, the bank tried to sell off "Pussy and her infant child" separate from the larger group, but to no avail.[101] By the summer of 1812, Pussy and her child were again being listed alongside six of the twenty enslaved people from Millen's second group, the other twelve presumably having (finally) been sold.[102]

In the meantime, Congress had allowed the charter of the bank to expire in 1811 without renewal, and all unpaid debts went into foreclosure. These latter suits were often executed in the name of David Lenox, president of the entire bank, to whom had been "made a general assignment of all its effects . . . in trust, for the purpose of closing its concerns."[103] In April 1811, the bank advertised for sale "the following NEGROES: Tom, Billy, Cato, Harry, Hamer and Lucy, *among the men are three Coopers*," all the property of Benjamin Maurice, who was indebted to the bank for $6,300.[104] While the enslaved individuals sold quickly, Cato—one of the coopers—was back up for sale from March 1812 through January 1813, "his purchaser at a former sale not having complied with the conditions thereof."[105] Despite this caveat, one has to wonder if there was not some other reason it took almost a year to find another buyer for this skilled enslaved man. Perhaps he was unhealthy, or rebellious, or prone to running away.

As war with Britain broke out in the summer of 1812, the now-defunct bank could no longer hang onto foreclosed property while it awaited improved economic conditions. It needed to be actively liquidating all of its assets, including the entirety of its real estate holdings such as George Millen's Lottery Hall. From May through July 1812, the bank started advertising an additional thirty-two unnamed individuals enslaved by Millen, along with Lucy, Binah, Jonathan, Jack and Little Isaac—five people never previously named in any of the Millen slave sales—and "2 Horses, 2 Mules, a stock of Cattle and Sheep (about 80 head); Riding Chair and Harness, Household and Kitchen Furniture, one Gold Watch and sundry Farming Utensils—taken in execution, as the property of George Millen, at the suit of the Bank of the United States."[106] It appears that the thirty-two enslaved lives were being offered as part of the larger plantation sale, while the other five could be split off in a separate sale.

In all, the Bank of the United States advertised seventy-four distinct enslaved individuals of George Millen for auction between April 1810 and August 1812, splitting the slaves into various groups as needed. On the one hand, the bank sought to maximize the proceeds from these sales by creating desirable groupings for different purchasers. On the other hand, it needed to make sure that all the enslaved people sold, regardless of age or condition; the bank had no desire to be left in possession of any enslaved people. Thus it had to create groupings in which young children, the elderly, the recalcitrant, and those with physical or mental impairments would sell alongside more desirable people—prime laborers, childbearing women, skilled artisans, trusted cooks and house servants. Family or community preservation was likely a secondary consideration—if it was factored in at all—although selling very young children with their mothers often made the most economic sense.

Millen's first group of fifteen (later eighteen) sold quickly on two successive occasions—perhaps this group contained the most desirable enslaved lives whose selling price would be highest when sold separately from the plantation. Yet the second group of twenty proved more difficult to sell, being repeatedly auctioned every month for almost an entire year. While it is impossible to know why, this group possibly contained too many weak, old, young, or rebellious individuals. Or perhaps the bank set a minimum sale price that the auctioneer had difficulty attaining. We only know their names: "Yarro, Sally, Polly, little Yarro, Judy & child, Phoebe, Pussy, Rose, Juno, Anthony, Affeba, Ben, Pleasant, Sarah, Charles, Polladore, May, Sancho and Jenny." They were a mix of male and female, a mix of generations (Judy and child; little Yarro as presumably a descendant of Yarro), with at least a few having direct family ties. The last to be sold were "Pussy and her child Pleasant, Sarah, Nelly, May, Affiba, and Poladore"—mostly females, perhaps the oldest and/or youngest of the lot. Either way, this group of twenty was not only broken apart from the other eighteen, thirty-two, and five Millen slaves sold for the bank, but they were further divided into smaller groups as some were sold off. All of these enslaved individuals presumably remained at Lottery Hall until sold, being brought the three miles to town every month for the auction. The final five people—Lucy, Binah, Jonathan, Jack and Little Isaac—were possibly never sold, remaining in Millen's possession. In the 1820 census, Millen's household included four enslaved males, one enslaved female, and one free woman of color, which roughly matches the few demographic details we have on these final five enslaved individuals.[107]

As the bank continued to wind up its affairs during the war years, one potential buyer of its foreclosed human property was sea-island cotton planter Pierce Butler. In 1813 he instructed his agent in Savannah to find out more about the remaining enslaved individuals from the bank's cashier: "The Bank informs me that it has a number of Negroes belonging to the Bank of the United States in the care of judge or doctor James, which he lets Planters have for maintaining them without cloathing [*sic*] them." Thus the enslaved people owned by the bank were loaned out to local planters for a pittance, until they could be sold. Butler hoped to negotiate a private sale with the bank "for a value on them" rather than bidding in a public auction. He also wished to find out more about the remaining bank debtors, hoping to "agree on a price" for their human property, which would "peremptorily stop the sale and get the present owner a discharge from the Bank." Given the fact that "their Negroes must be sold" and "the times are trying and critical," he "would not go to 300 dollars average" on the price. This $300 maximum was approximately the average reduced market price for enslaved people in Georgia during the war years.[108]

While slaveholders like Butler saw the depressed conditions of the ongoing war as an opportunity to buy enslaved labor cheap, the declining value of slaves concurrently hampered the ability of the bank's debtors to pay off their loans with their existing assets. By the fall of 1813, the bank's trustees were negotiating compromised terms with the remaining debtors. Jacob Read, a former senator from South Carolina, wrote to George Simpson, the bank's cashier in Philadelphia, hoping to take the bank up on its offer to "treat with the parties for some composition" in paying off their debts. As Read explained: "Non importation laws Embargoes & other Causes over which I had no control have lately borne very hard indeed, on the Southern States and now the War & the prospect of a continuance of it seems likely to rein in all." The problem, explained Read, was a lack of liquidity. "The embarrassments which have occurred have always acted with a double force on us, for while they increased the Prices of imported commodities, and of all the articles necessary for our Plantations and Negroes, they took from us . . . the power to dispose of a dollar's worth of our Crops & the produce of our Estates."[109]

William Stephens, former chief justice of the Georgia Supreme Court and then federal justice of the US District Court for Georgia, similarly begged for leniency with the Philadelphia office on both his own debt and that of the estate of F. Levett, for which he was executor. "I own about 100 Negroes old and young, Sea Island Cotton Lands, a vast body of Interior Lands, and some Houses, and Lots in Savannah," he wrote, while Levett's estate "possesses upwards of 200 negroes, valuable rice, and cotton lands, worth equal, in better times, thirty thousand pounds." Yet while all of this property should have been adequate to meet the debts, "there is no sales for rice, or cotton, or negroes." Bank president David Lenox read the letter at the board meeting and personally replied, but his response has not survived.[110]

Samuel Howard, who had repeatedly dealt with the bank before the war as an endorser of Lewis Johnston's debts, also hoped to negotiate a favorable settlement with the bank for his own outstanding obligations. As he later explained to the bank's cashier in Philadelphia, he "had previous to the War met great losses" which "left me totally without the means of paying my debts." He blamed this situation on "the whole of my property being swallowed up by claims of the United States for duties, or pledges to the bank of the US which holds a mortgage on all my property which remains unsold except my claim to two thirds of a wharf property, which was not mortgaged, but was bought in by the bank at the sales above referred to for duties."[111] The bank assessed the value of this property on its books in 1814 at $14,000.[112] By the winter of 1814–15, Howard had been "granted authority" from the General Assembly of Georgia "for the exclusive rights to navigation with boats propelled by steam on all streams under the jurisdiction of the state for a period of twenty years."[113] He thus wrote the bank in March 1815 to obtain a final settlement in order to free himself from the debts. Howard believed he "could obtain the assistance of a friend to advance $14000 to be secured by" the wharf property, and proposed "to pay that sum to the bank & to withdraw all opposition to foreclosing the mortgage on my remaining property, so that the bank may immediately make the most of that property." In return, "the Bank would of course expect to cancel all claims under its judgments against me, or my late firms and to return me any notes which may not have been put in suit against me."[114] Whether the bank ultimately agreed to this particular settlement or reached some other deal, Howard did manage to free himself from his creditors. He teamed up with his brother Charles, and by January 1816 they launched the first successful steamboat on the Savannah River between Savannah and Augusta.[115]

The bank continued to sell enslaved lives seized from debtors after the war. For example, from January to March 1815 the Charleston sheriff advertised for sale a plantation in St. John's Parish, two lots of land in the city, and "a gang of 47 negroes. All which to be sold as the property of Theodore Gaillard, jun. at the two several suits of David Lenox [of the Bank of the United States] and the Union Bank."[116] In August, the sheriff of Savannah auctioned off twenty enslaved men, women, and children of another slaveholder "to satisfy an execution in favor of the Bank of the United States."[117] And the following October, a marshal's sale was held in Alexandria, Virginia, on "Three *Negro Men* and one *Negro Woman* and two *Boys*—Also a large and general assortment of *Household Furniture* of a superior quality, the property of Ferdinand Marsteller; to satisfy two executions in favor of David Lenox [of the Bank of the United States] and others."[118]

Despite the minimal extant records from the first Bank of the United States, it is clear that its southern branches willingly accepted enslaved individuals as collateral to secure existing debts, possibly granted new loans secured by enslaved individuals, and were active in foreclosing on this property whether the cause was an estate sale, a delinquent debtor, or the liquidation of the bank's assets after its charter expired. While the records are not detailed enough to assess the exact proportion of debts that were collateralized with enslaved lives, we can estimate what percentage of outstanding debts at the Savannah branch (for which the documents are most complete) were owed by people who had at least *partially* secured their loan with slaves. For example, Bryan Morel owed the bank $5,941.16, which was secured by a mortgage on his Ossabaw Island, Georgia, sea-island cotton plantation and ten enslaved individuals. His brother Peter Morel owed the bank $4,236.75, secured by a mortgage on his neighboring plantation and twenty-three enslaved lives, while a third brother, John Morel Jr., secured his $17,651.25 loan with forty-five enslaved people (and no land). With the exception of John, the precise valuation of land versus enslaved property for the purposes of the collateral is unknown.[119] Often, the bank just vaguely listed "a plantation and sundry Negroes" in its records, such as for Solomon Prevost's $7,840 loan with the New Orleans branch.[120]

With this substantial caveat that we cannot know what percentage of each debt was secured with human property, the debtors who included at least some enslaved individuals as part of their collateral were responsible for between 35 percent and 45 percent of all outstanding debts larger than $5,000 to the Savannah branch of the Bank of the United States between February 28, 1811 and October 31, 1812. If we include debtors with an endorser who put up human property as collateral for the endorsement, that percentage increases to between 57 percent and 62 percent of all outstanding large debts.[121] Large debts made up approximately two-thirds of the value of all debts to the Savannah branch. If we assume that *no* debts under $5,000 were collateralized with enslaved lives (an unlikely proposition), then slaves accounted for at least 24 percent to 30 percent of all outstanding debts, and at least 38 percent to 41 percent when the collateralized human property of endorsers is included.

Merchants vs. Planters

Even during this earliest period of commercial banks, farmers throughout the United States often complained that the traditional banking practice of short-term discounts on commercial paper catered to the needs of urban merchants and ignored the credit needs of the agricultural community; in this complaint they were absolutely correct. As banking historian Howard Bodenhorn notes, "Although political and economic tensions between urban merchants and rural farmers played out everywhere, they were especially pronounced in the southern and western United States."[122] Farmers needed both longer credit terms of at least six to twelve months (which I will refer to as intermediate-term loans) and the ability to use their property as the primary security for these loans. But many merchants and bankers worried that "agricultural lending froze a bank's assets and made the money supply prone to rapid overexpansion."[123] Even though sixty-day loans were repeatedly renewed, they could theoretically be called for payment at the end of any period, giving the bank more flexibility in its lending.

The first slaveholding region to innovate in terms of banking was the mid-Atlantic, when Maryland incorporated its Farmers' Bank in 1805. As its charter indicated, the purpose of the institution was "to promote the agricultural and manufacturing interest" by making "loans on more extended principles than have heretofore been adopted by similar institutions in this state." Based in Annapolis with a branch in Easton, the bank loaned up to $1,000 for up to six months upon "reasonable personal or landed security as the directors of the bank and branch bank respectively may require," thus providing the option of much-needed intermediate-term loans for at least some of its clientele.[124]

In the weeks and months before the passage of its charter, the new bank's supporters blanketed the newspapers with a defense of these two unique features: intermediate-term loans secured directly by property. The most prominent of these defenses noted that "land banks" formed under similar principles had operated successfully for decades in England and Scotland, and were now appearing in places like Boston and New York, giving northern farmers a competitive advantage against Maryland's agriculturalists.[125] Despite this assertion, I can find no evidence for such banks in the Northeast prior to this Maryland incorporation in 1805.[126] For example, none of the charters for the seven banks incorporated in New York through 1805 contain language to this effect.[127] The most likely candidate, the Farmers' Bank of the City of Troy, New York (1801), specifically advertised that "discounts are limited to 56 days, with three days of grace" and gave no indication that it was willing to lend money exclusively secured by mortgaged property.[128]

A more likely comparison would have been with the colonial loan offices that operated in most North American colonies at various points during the eighteenth century. While not actually banks, these government institutions lent landholders state-issued paper money up to half the value of their property, which borrowers paid back over the course of several years with interest. These institutions were largely successful at providing a circulating medium of exchange and stimulating the economies of Pennsylvania, New Jersey, New York, and Maryland, where legislatures limited the amount of money issued, were careful about the acceptance of collateral, and devised a clear taxation plan for retiring the money from circulation. On the other hand, as one historian of the system concludes, "excessive currency inflation and low land values . . . combined to produce ruinous depreciation in New England"; and a similar assessment could be made about loan offices in the Carolinas.[129] But supporters of Maryland's 1805 Farmers' Bank gave no evidence that they were modeling this new banking experiment on colonial antecedents.

Challenging the principles of the real-bills doctrine directly, one proponent of the Farmers' Bank asserted that "notes issued on landed security have this solid advantage, that the security can never be diminished nor removed, it must remain for ever unimpaired." In contrast, this author continued, "notes issued on the paper of merchants, depend for their solidity on the life, skill, integrity and good fortune, not only of the merchants themselves, who are known and trusted, but also on the life, health, skill, integrity and good fortune, of their numerous and unknown correspondents, and upon the safety of perishable commodities, exposed to the casualties of an uncertain element." In short, real estate was more reliable and permanent as an asset than goods in transit of a merchant "who depends upon the safe return of a ship and cargo employed in foreign commerce."[130] Although this idea would soon be directly challenged by the bubble in land prices in the 1810s and again in the 1830s, and the severe depreciation of the Panics of 1819, 1837, and 1839, for the moment this argument for the permanence of the value of landed assets seemed sound.

This same author also defended lending on renewal terms of six months rather than two, since few merchants ever paid their obligations in sixty or even one hundred and twenty days. "It cannot be supposed, that a bank established for the accommodation of the landed interest, would subject its safe customers to more inconvenient conditions than are imposed on merchants in mercantile banks."[131] Two years later, Delaware chartered a bank on this same model, lending up to $2,000 for six months on "reasonable personal or landed security" to aid any "farmer, mechanic, or manufacturer of this state."[132] Similar provisos were sometimes included in the charters of future banks incorporated in these two states, including the 1812 charter of the Commercial Bank of Delaware.[133]

This idea of securing intermediate-term loans with property remained limited to the mid-Atlantic. Although Georgia, South Carolina, Louisiana, and Virginia all chartered so-called "planters" or "farmers" banks between 1810 and 1812, the lending practices of these banks stayed focused on discounting short-term notes.[134] The preamble to the charter for the Planters' Bank of New Orleans justified its existence by stating that "the establishment of an additional Bank in New-Orleans will greatly tend to the extension of Commerce and the encouragement of Agriculture," yet it was still primarily "a Bank of Discount, Deposite and Exchange."[135] Similarly, the legislature of South Carolina "deemed beneficial to the citizens of this state" the establishment of "a bank under the name of the Planters and Mechanics Bank" located in Charleston. Although it was "authorized to establish branches in different parts of this state," these branches were "for the purposes of discount and deposit only."[136] These banks attempted to cater to the needs of the agricultural sectors of their states either by locating offices outside the commercial centers and/or by reserving a certain portion of loanable funds for rural residents. Yet rural residents continued to clamor for better access to credit, beyond short-term discounts.

The planters of South Carolina finally succeeded when that state incorporated the Bank of the State of South Carolina in 1812. Headquartered in Charleston with a branch in the capital city of Columbia, its stated purpose was "to establish a bank on the funds of the state, for the purpose of discounting paper, and making loans for longer periods than has heretofore been customary, and on security different from what has hitherto been required." Entirely state-owned, the capital came from all the assets owned by the state, including stock in other banks or corporations, "loan office bonds . . . and all bonds and notes due the state." Additionally, it served as the depository for "all the unexpended money in the treasuries of this state, and all the taxes to be hereafter collected."[137] Whereas discounted loans were still limited to sixty days, the bank was uniquely permitted to lend up to $2,000 for up to one year upon mortgaged real or personal property. These loans were renewable annually, upon the debtor paying a discount (interest in advance) and one-tenth to one-quarter of the principal. In effect, these were long-term loans of four to ten years in duration.[138]

Although the charter referenced both real and personal property, most of the explanatory clauses focused on landed property. For example, applicants needed to "submit their titles to the lands intended to be mortgaged," the bank "appoint[ed] five commissioners in each election district, to value and appraise the lands which may be offered in mortgaged," and "every valuation of land" needed to be certified by the commissioners. But at one of the first meetings of the board of directors in May 1813, it passed a resolution to ensure that loans secured by personal property—most likely human property—would be similarly scrutinized. "[E]very person applying for a loan upon a mortgage of personal property, shall be required to produce his titles to the said property" or "prove his titles by the affidavit of one or more respectable persons." Additionally, he needed to produce certificates from various state and local officials of any claims against the property in terms of other mortgages, trust deeds, legal suits, taxes due, or other encumbrances.[139] Yet as the nation entered the postwar boom with the conclusion of the War of 1812, the Bank of the State of South Carolina and the handful of mid-Atlantic banks willing to lend on intermediate terms secured by property remained as outliers.

*

On January 31, 1809, North Carolina bank agent John Steele submitted the weekly return of the Salisbury Office of Discount to the main office of the Bank of Cape Fear. Among the renewals was a bond for $1,440 of George Fisher. Steele worried that this note "exceeds the amount limitted" for individual loans of $1,000, and otherwise "transcended our instructions"; he thus sought "the opinion of the Bank on the subject." Steele explained that "the excess was owing in part to his renewing of bonds . . . and to a loan of $600 . . . which he [Fisher] was extremely solicitous to obtain for the purpose of enabling him to effect an advantageous purchase of Negroes at the time." Although we do not have the Bank of Cape Fear's response, it was likely appalled at the unconventional underwriting of a direct loan for the purchase of an enslaved man, which violated traditional bank lending practices and possibly even its state charter. Yet for Steele, the bank's agent in the field, this request seemed like a perfectly logical use of loanable funds. Steele's main concern was rather the potential violation of the $1,000 loan limit. He hoped that because the loan renewals were extended on different days, "what we have done will be approved." If not, "we may avoid the like in future."[140] Steele was trying to navigate carefully between the specific needs and available assets of southern customers, without fully recognizing the constraints on banks from both their charter restrictions and the accepted practices of the banking industry.

During the 1810s, most banks in both the North and the South remained committed to short-term discount loans on commercial business paper. These loans were often renewable, and an individual could potentially accumulate significate debts across multiple loans. Whereas southern banks initially only seized enslaved people as part of *fieri facias* foreclosure proceedings against debtors, banks increasingly permitted debtors to secure these renewable short-term loans with mortgages on specific land and human property. And there was growing pressure from southern planters—particularly on the frontier—for banking services that could accommodate longer-term loans, for larger dollar amounts, directly secured by land and human property. The logical final step—which Steele quickly grasped despite its remaining a radical idea for bankers—would be providing direct loans for the initial purchase of plantations and enslaved laborers, using this same property as collateral for the mortgage. As the nation entered a postwar boom, bankers and legislatures in the Southwest increasingly sought ways to address these competing demands and constraints.

2

Adapting Slave Financing to the Needs of the Frontier South during the Nation's First Boom and Bust

During the height of the post–War of 1812 boom, brothers-in-law and business partners Armistead Morehead and Robert Latham of south-central Kentucky habitually discounted their short-term business paper with the Russellville branch of the Bank of Kentucky. While the partners occasionally repaid these notes, they more often renewed them repeatedly with the bank to maintain greater liquidity for their business operations.[1] By October 1817, the pair owed the Bank of Kentucky $15,914 (about $320,000 in 2021) on more than a dozen notes worth $250 to $3,000 each. Feeling uneasy with this substantial debt, the bank requested that they provide additional security. As a result, the partners mortgaged to the bank twenty enslaved individuals, the house and lot in Russellville where Morehead resided, Morehead's distillery (where one of Latham's brothers lived), and several outlying tracts of land. The cashier of the parent bank in Frankfort advised his counterpart at the Russellville branch to give the pair "reasonable time" in repayment, as long as they had "unquestionable security" for the protested bills.[2]

The following spring, the partners additionally discounted a $1,000 note signed by another brother of Latham's, a $2,600 note from a business transaction, and several notes of the firm of Robert Latham & Co. worth $3,800. They reaffirmed with the bank their mortgage on the real estate and on nineteen of the same enslaved individuals (the twentieth presumably having died). Sixteen of the slaves—nine males and seven females—belonged to Morehead, and three males belonged to Latham; their ages are unknown. On December 30, 1818, Morehead discounted another $4,720 note from one of Latham's brothers, adding this sum to the debt covered by the mortgage. Each of these mortgage instruments stipulated that the bank "might proceed to sell the mortgaged property, in case of default in payment of the calls which should be made by the bank." Treating this mortgage as a line of credit, the pair periodically repaid earlier debts while adding new ones onto the same mortgage.[3] While this arrangement technically did not violate the bank's charter, repeatedly renewing such a large debt did challenge traditional conservative banking principles. It also placed the bank in the difficult position of having to seize and sell land and human property if the pair defaulted. And in the event of an economic downturn—such as the unprecedented Panic of 1819—the collateral might prove insufficient to cover the balance due.

Like the Bank of Kentucky, many southern banks—particularly those operating on the frontier—began pushing the boundaries of both their charter limitations and accepted banking practices in order to take advantage of the financial opportunities presented by the booming postwar economy. Human property had always been susceptible to seizure and sale under *fieri facias* proceedings when unsecured debts went unpaid. Yet banks now were increasingly willing to secure existing commercial debts in a mortgage contract with enslaved lives as the collateral. As was the case with Morehead and Latham, this practice often resulted in banks permitting debtors to discount and continuously renew numerous business notes, amassing thousands of dollars in debt. Banks also began creatively interpreting the discounting privileges written into their charters, initiating mortgage loans *directly* secured by land or human property, with the courts supporting these interpretations. As a logical extension of this policy, some banks began lending money for the initial purchase of human property, accepting those same lives as collateral for the loan. In pushing these boundaries, banks had to navigate several new challenges, especially as the Panic of 1819 forced many debts into foreclosure. While banks needed to decide which property of a delinquent debtor (or his endorser) to seize and sell, the proffered collateral sometimes proved to be insufficient—due to either declining market values or fraud on the part of the debtor. Banks thus had to balance selling property at a loss, taking possession of land and people until market conditions improved, or renegotiating mortgage terms; all these options threatened a bank's immediate liquidity and its continued existence.

Creative Discounting from Boom to Bust

In the aftermath of the War of 1812, the economy began to boom; trade was reestablished with Europe, while fledgling American industries—given a boost during the years of embargo—started to take off. Exports of agricultural goods in particular surged in response to rising European demand for American cotton, tobacco, and grain. As the economy grew, commercial banks in this period

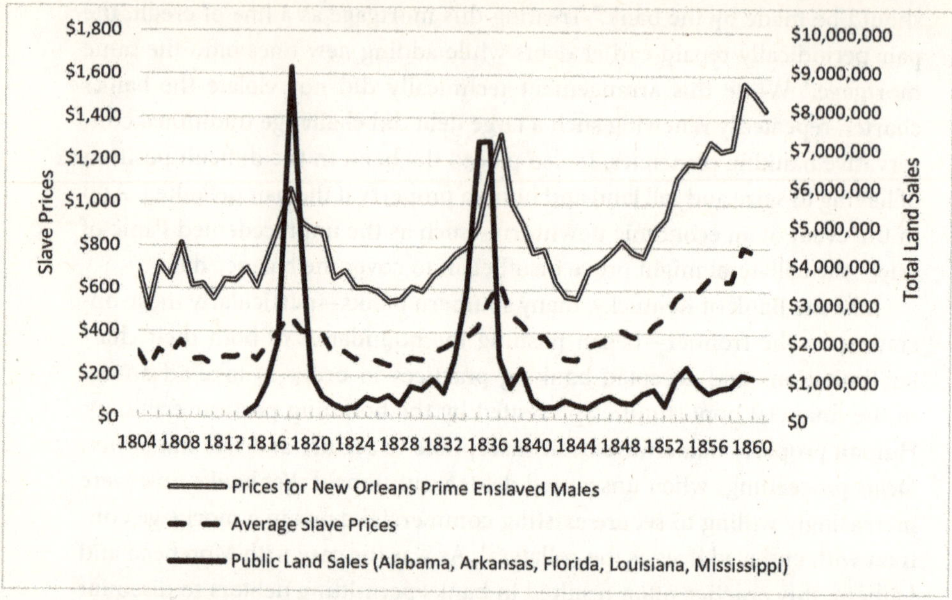

FIGURE 2.1. Public land sales and slave prices, 1804–1861. Source: Richard Sutch, "Appendix: The Value of the Slave Population, 1805–1860," in Roger Ransom and Richard Sutch, "Capitalists without Capital: The Burden of Slavery and the Impact of Emancipation," *Agricultural History* 62, no. 3 (SUMMER 1988): table A.1, 150–51; and Douglass C. North, *The Economic Growth of the United States, 1790–1860* (New York: W. W. Norton, 1966); table A–X, 257.

extended credit generously and expanded the money supply rapidly by issuing increasing quantities of banknotes. With export prices on the rise, farmers borrowed heavily both to improve their existing acreage and to bring new lands into production. Land speculators contributed to this rapid expansion of the economy, buying up western lands—again on credit—in anticipation that continued rising land prices would quickly cover this debt. Federal law only required a purchaser of federal lands to pay one-quarter of the price within forty days. The second quarter was due within two years, and the remaining half within four years. This policy encouraged both farmers and speculators to acquire land far in excess of their immediate ability to pay. Additionally, the seemingly insatiable demand for cotton from British and New England textile factories not only drove up land prices and sales in the states of the Deep South but also increased the demand for enslaved people to work these lands. The average price of enslaved men and women increased by 40 percent during this period (figure 2.1).[4]

State legislatures chartered numerous banks in response to the boom. Yet, with the notable exception of a handful of Maryland and Delaware banks and the Bank of the State of South Carolina (1812), all of which extended loans directly secured by property, the charters of these new southern banks remained conservative—even on the frontier. In 1815 the newly chartered Bank of the State of Georgia, headquartered in Savannah, promised to open branches in Milledgeville, Augusta, and anywhere else "they shall think fit within this state," specifically "for the purpose of discount and deposit only."[5] The 1818 charter of the Bank of Darien in Georgia allowed discounts for ninety days, while the Northwestern Bank of Virginia (Wheeling, 1817), the Bank of the Valley in Virginia (Winchester, 1817), and the Louisiana State Bank (1818) all permitted discounts up to 120 days.[6]

The focus of these banks, at least as defined by their legislatures, remained with discounting short-term business paper. Yet riding high on the postwar boom, many banks defied these legislative limits and pushed the boundaries of their charters well beyond short-term discounts, repeatedly renewing loans (as was the case with Morehead and Latham's debts to the Bank of Kentucky) and even underwriting loans directly using property as collateral.[7] In order to meet the technical restrictions of the charter, the bank still required the borrower to issue a formal promissory note endorsed by at least one other party. But there were no goods in transit or commodities about to be sold as the primary means of payment. Rather, land and human property itself was now the main source of security.

An extreme example of this practice was the case of William Fleckner. In March 1818, Fleckner purchased a plantation and slaves in Louisiana from John Nelder for $90,000 (about $1.9 million in 2021). He issued Nelder several promissory notes for the property, binding himself to pay $15,000 in four months (i.e., by September 1818), $25,000 in twelve months (i.e., by March 1, 1819), $20,000 on March 1, 1820, and the final payment of $30,000 on March 1, 1824, with "[t]he Bargained property mortgaged [to Nelder] to secure pay[men]t of all the notes." The latter notes were divided into smaller promissory notes of $10,000 each.[8] In order to get immediate access to this money, Nelder endorsed and then discounted these notes; at least one of the notes due in March of 1820 was discounted by the Planters' Bank of Louisiana. The bank gave Nelder $10,000 in banknotes minus an up-front discount fee (likely 8 percent, or $800). The $10,000 principal was directly secured by Fleckner's plantation and enslaved laborers, although—should this property prove insufficient—the bank could pursue other assets of either Fleckner or Nelder (as the note's endorser).[9]

The Planters' Bank had been incorporated in 1811 with a capital stock of $600,000. By 1817 the president and certain directors wanted greater freedom to discount notes than their charter allowed. In August 1817, a meeting of the board of directors resolved that "the president and cashier were authorised to discount notes which had more than sixty days to run." When some of the board balked that this resolution went too far, it passed a revised resolution in September only authorizing the president to discount notes "by consulting three or four directors, the majority of whom (including the president) should agree to the discount."[10] With this power in hand, which violated both the charter provision requiring the approval of at least four directors on all discounts and the bylaw limiting discounts to under sixty days, the president and three directors went on a discounting spree, largely for their own benefit. Court documents estimated that of the $1.8 million in bank discounts issued between September 1817 and October 1819, more than $1 million exceeded the sixty-day limit, and approximately $1.2 million benefited these four individuals alone.[11] Among the few discounts not for their own benefit was Fleckner's $10,000 note. While the fraud on the part of the Planters' Bank president and directors certainly was exceptional, this practice of turning short-term discounted loans into long-term mortgages was increasingly commonplace during the late 1810s, and—as we shall see—would be endorsed by the courts.

In addition to new state-chartered institutions, the federal government also incorporated a massive new bank during the boom. The financial challenges of waging the War of 1812 without the support of a national bank had caused many people's opinions to shift.[12] Only five years after the contentious battle over the recharter of the first Bank of the United States ended the life of that institution, a new twenty-year charter for the Second Bank of the United States easily passed Congress in April 1816. The final legislation bore many resemblances to its recently deceased predecessor. The federal government again owned 20 percent of its stock, although it was now capitalized at $35 million—three and a half times the size of the first bank. The bank still served as a depository for government funds, assisted in the collection of taxes, and was expected but not required to issue loans to the government as needed.[13]

Like the first Bank of the United States, the Second Bank's main office was in Philadelphia—still America's financial capital—and it had the power to establish branches in other locations throughout the country. It quickly opened eighteen offices of discount and deposit in 1817, including eleven in the slaveholding South. In addition to the six southern cities where the first bank branches had been located (Washington, DC; Baltimore, Maryland; Norfolk, Virginia; Charleston, South Carolina; Savannah, Georgia; and New Orleans, Louisiana), it also opened offices in Louisville and Lexington, Kentucky; Richmond, Virginia; Fayetteville, North Carolina; and Augusta, Georgia.[14] Once again, these southern branches tied the region and its slave-dependent economy tightly to the national financial system. Also like the first bank, the Second Bank's charter limited its lending to loans backed by short-term commercial paper.[15] Under its official "Rules and Regulations for the Government of the Offices of Discount and Deposit" passed in 1817, the bank's board of directors specifically stated that "no bill or note shall be discounted the unexpired term of which exceeds sixty days."[16]

Yet despite these rules, William Jones—who was president of the Second Bank during these boom years—allowed the individual branches relative freedom in terms of banknote issuance and lending policies. As one early history of the national bank contends: "Although by its fundamental regulations the bank apparently had the power to supervise and restrict the branches in their operations, it did not effectively exercise this right during its early management."[17] The same historians continue by noting that under Jones, "when the branches were encouraged to discount heavily, large loans were made on security which in the last analysis was real estate."[18] In the South, where many (if not most) of the presidents, directors, and cashiers of these branches were themselves slaveholders, these offices willingly engaged in loan contracts involving enslaved people.

On October 5, 1818, Baltimore residents Philemon C. Wederstrandt, Henry Didier Jr. (in trust for Rebecca Smith), and Henry Thompson entered into a seven-year partnership to purchase from Samuel B. Davis a fully operational sugar plantation in St. Bernard Parish, Louisiana, named Magnolia Grove. Sugar production was on the rise in Louisiana, and these Baltimoreans wanted to get in on this emerging, lucrative market.[19] Included in the purchase price of $140,000 (about $3 million in 2021) were the land, buildings, improvements, stock, crop, utensils, and forty-three enslaved workers. Paying $30,000 down in cash, the partners promised to remit to Davis the remainder in five equal installments of $22,000 on each first of May from 1819 to 1823. Davis retained a mortgage on the property until these payments were completed.[20]

The year after the agreement was signed, Rebecca Smith's husband Dennis A. Smith—one of the directors of the Second Bank of the United States—successfully applied for a loan of $24,000 with the local Baltimore bank branch, offering his wife's one-third interest in Magnolia Grove as collateral.[21] Although the property was still under mortgage to Davis, Dennis argued that the plantation had already increased in value to $180,000 due to the addition of forty more enslaved workers and the expected success of the sugar crop. Dennis intended to use this loan as the down payment for the purchase of another Louisiana sugar plantation.[22] Unlike the discounting and purchase of the Fleckner note that same year, this agreement to lend directly on the landed and enslaved collateral of Magnolia Grove lacked even the pretense of a traditional discounting contract. In acquiescing to this mortgage, the

Second Bank—through its Baltimore branch—both defied prevailing banking principles (as well as its federal charter) and openly embraced the financialization of slavery.

Unfortunately for all involved, the postwar boom was much more fragile than anyone at the time realized, and 1819 was an inauspicious year to be borrowing money in anticipation of future agricultural profits. As is often the case with economic downturns, there was no one cause for the Panic of 1819. Rather, several events of both global and domestic origin placed increasing pressure on the financial system, chipping away at weak points in the foundation until the whole system finally gave way. Growth in global specie supplies had begun to slow as political problems erupted in the major gold- and silver-mining regions of Latin America, disrupting mining production. Additional downward pressure on prices emerged as American cotton farmers began to face increased competition from East Indian cotton producers. Demand for American foodstuffs likewise declined as European farms, hurt by years of war and bad harvests, returned to full production. By the winter of 1818–1819, commodity prices had begun a steep downward slide. The western land boom, driven by soaring global agricultural prices, collapsed; prices for land, slaves, and goods plummeted by as much as 50 to 75 percent off their post–War of 1812 peak values (see figure 2.1).[23]

Simultaneously, as the fall of 1818 approached, the directors of the Second Bank—led by bank president William Jones—realized that the institution was in grave danger of becoming insolvent. In addition to overissuing banknotes, $4.5 million of the bonds that the United States had sold to pay France for the Louisiana Purchase in 1803 were due for redemption in the fall of 1818 and spring of 1819. Most of the remaining bondholders were foreigners, which would require the export of specie abroad. The Second Bank, as the depository of government funds, held this specie in its vaults as part of its reserves. This bond payment would wipe out most of the specie reserves the bank used to support its loans and banknotes. President Jones decided that the bank had to adopt a policy of monetary contraction—severely reducing banknotes in circulation, declining loan renewals, and calling in loan payments from both individuals and other financial institutions—in order to keep from suspending specie payments, which would have violated its charter and undermined confidence in the fledgling institution. President Jones resigned in January 1819, but his successor, Langdon Cheves, believed that it was necessary to continue this contractionary policy in order to save the Second Bank.[24]

This sudden decision to contract the money supply, combined with the contractionary impact of changes in global supply and demand for specie and commodities, had a domino effect throughout the banking system. With specie reserves running dangerously low, many state banks began to call in their own loans, contracting the money supply even more. Banks now told debtors, who had come to expect their short-term loans to be regularly renewed, that they needed to pay off their balances. But many could not. Farmers who had made long-term investments in improving their land, speculators who had purchased western lands on the expectation of rising prices, enslavers who had invested in a larger labor force, and merchants who were dependent on future cotton sales all found themselves unable to pay off their debts. Many began to default on their loans.[25] Fleckner's discounted note with the Planters' Bank, Morehead and Latham's business debts to the Bank of Kentucky, and the Second Bank's mortgage on Smith's Louisiana sugar plantation all remained unpaid during the panic.

The fraudulent actions during the period of 1817 to 1819 of the Planters' Bank's president and directors—in which they lent large sums of the bank's capital on long repayment terms—placed the bank in peril as the panic descended on New Orleans in the spring and summer of 1819. By September 1819, the bank was itself heavily indebted to the New Orleans branch of the Bank of the United States, which had begun to call in payment on its various loans. In order to reduce this "substantial debt," the Planters' Bank endorsed and discounted with the Second Bank several of the promissory notes it owned, including one of the $10,000 notes originally issued by William Fleckner, which was still secured by his plantation and human property and due for payment on March 1, 1820.[26] If Fleckner defaulted, the Second Bank could seize this property and/or sue the note's endorsers (Nelder and now the Planters' Bank) for payment. But the questionable practices of the bank's officers had left it on the verge of ruin. The cashier—who was privy to and complicit in many of these transactions—absconded in October.[27] The bank's losses were further compounded when "in winding up its concerns, which soon became necessary, the corporation lost a sum of one hundred and twenty thousand dollars, by the purchase and resale of a sugar plantation and slaves, which it was induced to take, in order to secure a doubtful debt."[28] Although the court documents do not indicate how this sugar plantation became the property of the bank, it was possibly that of Joseph Tricou and sons, upon whom the bank foreclosed in the spring of 1821.[29] Like Fleckner, Tricou had probably offered this property as security on his accrued debts with the bank.

Meanwhile, Fleckner failed to pay the $10,000 note when it came due in March 1820, and the Bank of the United States sued to foreclose on his collateral. As part of his defense, Fleckner denied that the Second Bank, as purchaser of the note, had any claim on his land or human property. In fact, his attorneys argued that the bank's charter provisions prohibited it from "trading" in any "note . . . given for the purchase of real property." Fleckner's defense was referring to charter rule 9, which limited bank lending to loans backed by short-term commercial paper such as "bills of exchange, gold or silver bullion, or in the sale of goods, goods really and truly pledged for money lent . . . or of goods which shall be the produce of its lands." The bank, led by President Langdon Cheves, countered that rule 7 of the charter allowed it to secure existing loans—which were traditionally short-term discounts on renewal—through mortgages on real estate.[30] Therefore, it could discount notes backed by "any thing whatever in payment or as security for debts *bona fide* due."[31]

When a Louisiana jury ruled against the bank in 1820, it appealed the case all the way to the US Supreme Court. Justice Joseph Story's 1823 opinion hinged on two points: first, reconciling the two seemingly conflicting clauses (rules 7 and 9) that appeared in some form in almost every bank charter; and second, understanding the definition of a "discount." If the bank's charter only permitted it to discount short-term commercial paper (as rule 9 implied and as most banks had always acted in practice), then it "would defeat the powers given in other parts" of the charter, such as the specific ability to secure debts with property in rule 7. Thus "the true interpretation" of rule 9 was that it prohibited the bank "from doing the ordinary business of a trader or merchant, in buying and selling goods, &c., for profit" and that "there are no words" in the charter "restricting the discounts to any particular kind of paper."[32]

"But," Justice Story continued, "in what manner is the bank to loan? What is it to discount?" Since "it is notorious, that banking operations are always carried on in our country by discounting notes," which was exactly what the bank did when it discounted Fleckner's note for the Planters' Bank, it would make the charter "a mere mockery" if the courts "depart[ed] from this settled construction" of that word and placed limitations on a practice with an accepted meaning. As long as the bank made "a deduction or drawback . . . upon its advances or loans of money, upon negotiable paper, or other evidences of debt, payable at a future day," it was legitimately discounting within the privileges granted by the charter. The initial security attached to that debt—in this case, Fleckner's plantation and enslaved workers—thus remained liable for seizure by each person or institution who purchased the note by discount. In Story's interpretation, "Nothing can be clearer."[33] By providing such an expansive definition of discounting, Story opened the door for traditional banks to engage in all kinds of lending practices, so long as the loan took on the formal structure of a discount.

At this point, the historical record on Fleckner's plantation and enslaved people falls silent. There is no record of a seizure or sale. Within a few months of the ruling, Fleckner died, but the property was not listed as part of his estate probate in July 1823. Perhaps Nelder or another creditor had seized the property prior to the conclusion of the case. Regardless, Fleckner's failed challenge to the bank's operations demonstrated the extent to which some banks during the postwar boom years were actively pushing the boundaries both of their written charters and of traditional banking practices. Yet rather than breaking new legal ground, Story's 1823 ruling effectively rubber stamped the existing discounting practices of many southern banks—particularly those operating on the burgeoning frontier during the 1820s.

Foreclosing on Endorsers

One of the critical features of the discount loan was the requirement of one or more endorsers, who pledged to repay the loan in the event that the principal debtor failed to do so. Endorsers were often family members or business partners with intimate knowledge of the debtor's finances, who had confidence in the debtor's ability to repay, and/or felt obligated to support the debtor due to their kinship or business connections. And the reciprocal nature of endorsements often meant that the principal debtor for one note was the endorser on another, and vice versa. As one later lawsuit involving endorsers noted, it was quite common for the same people to be "in the habit of constantly endorsing for each other, to very large amounts."[34] With unsecured loans, the creditor could then use *fieri facias* proceedings to seize and sell any property of either the debtor or one of the endorsers.

Debtors and (especially) their endorsers, could try to evade the *fieri facias* claims of creditors by transferring property ownership before the bank had an opportunity to sue and stake its claim. Such conveyances were illegal if explicitly done to outwit creditors, and it was relatively easy to prove fraud when the *primary debtor* gifted or sold property at a considerable loss to family and friends, leaving few assets for courts to seize. *Endorsers* on unsecured loans, on the other hand, were unrestricted in the use and alienation of their property until formerly sued, making it much easier for them to disperse their property before seizure—unless a creditor could explicitly demonstrate fraudulent intent. In 1819, George Norton discounted with the Lexington, Kentucky, branch of the Bank of the United States a $4,700 note which was payable in sixty days.[35] Although Norton listed fourteen enslaved individuals in the 1820 federal census, he was so heavily indebted to a number of different people—including another $3,000 note and $2,000 note, both due to the Bank of the United States—that the bank did not believe it could get the money from Norton.[36] The institution thus decided to sue instead all the endorsers of his notes for payment, including Abraham Venable who owned two large tracts of land and thirteen enslaved people.[37] Between the lawsuit's initiation in November 1821, and the Kentucky circuit court's ruling in the Bank's favor in May 1822, Venable deeded a portion of the land and all the enslaved individuals to his brother-in-law.[38] The bank alleged that the deed had been made fraudulently, with the sole intent of placing these assets out of the hands of his creditors. As Justice Story would later summarize in his 1829 US Supreme Court opinion: "Here then is the case of a person upon the eve of a decree being rendered against him for a large sum of money, which it is admitted would go far to his ruin, making conveyances of his whole property real and personal to his brother-in-law, for an asserted consideration equal to its full value."[39]

Part of the evidence against Venable was the fact that his brother-in-law did not have the means to purchase this property either for cash or on credit. Instead, the land and enslaved lives were deeded to him partially in exchange for administering the estate as guardian on behalf of Venable's stepchildren. The land and enslaved individuals, however, were "to remain in possession of the former tenant," i.e., Venable. The brother-in-law borrowed the remainder of the purchase price from a third party, which he paid to Venable. The next morning, Mrs. Venable took the money paid by the brother-in-law (and borrowed from the third party) and loaned it back to the same brother-in-law, who used it to repay his loan from the third party. This third party even testified that he had required no collateral of the brother-in-law, since he expected to (and did) receive the loaned money back almost immediately. Justice Story thus continued that "the borrowing of the money was merely to exhibit before witnesses a formal payment, and that there was no real bona fides in this part of the transaction."[40] The court ruled in favor of the Bank, which subsequently sold several of Venable's enslaved people to pay the debt he had endorsed.[41]

This type of fraudulent conveyance was particularly problematic for unsecured loans. By securing a loan with a formal mortgage, specific property was set aside for payment in the case of default. A debtor could secure a loan by mortgaging property directly to the creditor (as Morehead and Latham had done with the Bank of Kentucky), or the debtor could mortgage property to their endorser which would protect the endorser in case of the primary debtor's default. Under either option, both creditors and endorsers received an extra level of protection. Endorsers expected creditors to seize first the mortgaged property, while creditors held the priority of claim to the property over other *unsecured* creditors and thus possessed a more direct legal path to recovery of their loans. Yet the precise rights of debtors, creditors, and endorsers were still unclear, which forced the courts to weigh in on these relationships. And these mortgage contracts could still be the subject of fraud.

By the spring of 1819, Morehead and Latham were deeply indebted to the Bank of Kentucky for $15,914 on more than a dozen notes, and were scrambling to save their business. The intricate chain of debtor-creditor relations often meant that the liquidity of any given debtor depended on the timely payment of debts by others along the chain, and no one seemed to be able to pay off their obligations during the panic. Morehead appealed to the bank for permission to release the house, the lot in Russellville, and the distillery from the mortgage lien, desiring to sell these properties for cash. The bank acquiesced, believing that the nineteen enslaved individuals also listed on the mortgage constituted sufficient security for the remainder of their debt.[42] Yet as asset and commodity prices plummeted and credit markets froze, Morehead and Latham found it increasingly difficult to repay their mounting debts, especially as their own debtors became delinquent.

One of these outstanding debts was a bill of exchange that the pair had drawn up with Morehead's nephew, Turner Morehead, in Baltimore. Presumably, Turner had received $4,500 worth of goods from the Kentucky partners, which he planned to sell at a profit within ninety days before repaying the partners. He gave Latham and Morehead the bill of exchange (a type of long-distance promissory note) to pay for the goods. The pair sought to discount the bill to acquire immediate access to the funds, but it appears that the Russellville branch bank was unwilling to advance them any more money. They probably sought credit instead from a bank thirty miles away in Clarksville, Tennessee, where both they (and their debt history) were less known, and they solicited local Clarksville merchant Samuel Vance to endorse the bill; he promised to pay the balance should the partners become delinquent.[43] Perhaps Vance had a history of trading with Latham and Morehead, but—being uncertain of their liquidity—he wisely required further security in exchange for his endorsement. The partners offered him a mortgage on the same nineteen slaves, which "he might proceed to sell . . . to raise the money" if they failed to pay. It is unlikely that Vance realized that these enslaved people were also subject to prior mortgages with the Bank of Kentucky.[44]

At this point, Morehead and Latham's precarious house of debt finally came crashing down. The partners failed to repay their obligations either to the Bank of Kentucky (which still totaled $7,784, with interest and costs of protest) or make good on the $4,500 Baltimore bill of exchange. Latham fled the state (apparently without his three slaves), relocating to New Orleans where he died bankrupt the following year at the age of thirty-five. Although Latham and Morehead were the "primary endorsers" on the note, Vance's position as "secondary endorser" made him equally liable to any creditors, especially with Latham absconding. In mortgage deeds recorded with the county courts, the Bank of Kentucky typically included a statement "that the said Bank may resort to them as endorsers for the whole or any portion of the said debt, for which they are or shall be respectively bound as endorsers for the said" debtor.[45] As the president of the main bank explained to its Louisville branch in 1820, "There is no point of law I am told more clearly settled than this . . . the Bank has an equal claim on all the endorsers." The only rights that a secondary endorser retained was that "he might certainly recover the am[oun]t from any prior endorser," meaning that the endorser could also file a claim against the debtor.[46] Vance, realizing that—as an endorser—he was now responsible for the $4,500 due on the Baltimore bill, needed to act quickly to limit his own financial exposure. He took possession of the nineteen enslaved individuals and immediately sold one for $350.

Simultaneously, the Bank of Kentucky appointed trustees to sell the enslaved people, but was outraged to learn that Vance had preempted it. Citing its earlier mortgage claims, the bank obtained a court order to stop Vance from selling any more individuals. He was required to deliver them back to the bank trustees, who promptly sold eleven enslaved people for $4,146.[47] Vance now countersued, which halted the bank's sale of the remaining seven individuals. In Vance's estimation, the bank's mortgage was no longer valid since the original notes upon which it had been based had been repaid and replaced with newer obligations. His attorneys argued that the bank needed to record new mortgages covering the new debts, rather than treating the original mortgage as if it were a line of credit. Additionally, they contended that even if the mortgage remained valid, "that the [landed] real estate mortgaged to the bank, is sufficient to satisfy the debts due to them, and that they should be compelled to resort to it in the first instance, and leave the slaves to satisfy his demand, being the only fund to which he can have recourse for that purpose." The bank's attorneys disagreed. It no longer had any claim on the distillery, or the house and lot in Russellville, which Morehead had sold with its permission. Although three outlying tracts of land also remained part of the mortgage, the bank deemed them "in remote places and . . . of little value." Thus "they insist upon their right, as first mortgagees, to have their debts satisfied out of the slaves."[48]

By the time the Kentucky Court of Appeals made its final ruling on the dispute in October 1823, Vance had also just died at the age of thirty-nine. The justices determined that the bank's mortgage gave it the first lien on the enslaved individuals over the claims of Vance, even when the bank permitted the partners to repay and add new debts continuously to the same mortgage.

Additionally, the bank had the right to settle its claims against Morehead and Latham by seizing and selling any of the property included in the original mortgage, in any order. If the sale of the enslaved lives alone fulfilled the debt, then "any surplus should go towards satisfying Vance's demand." Once the bank's debt was settled, it should "assign to Vance's representatives, the mortgages upon the real estate . . . to subject the lands aforesaid to sale, in satisfaction of his demand." The hassle of selling the undesirable lands would fall upon Vance's administrators, while the bank benefited from the easier task of selling the enslaved individuals.[49] We know nothing about the ultimate fates of these twenty individuals. Sold in (at least) three separate lots, they may have been purchased by the same buyer, or their family groups might have been further broken apart. No advertisements, receipts, or other records exist of their sales.

Whereas the point of adding endorsers to a debt contract was to increase the likelihood of the creditor recovering the money, it also created a complicated set of relationships. Banks needed to decide which property it was in their best interest to pursue, while endorsers often disputed the extent or order of their liability. Endorsers, like Vance, commonly argued that a creditor could not claim their property without first exhausting all other options. This claim was particularly put forward when notes had been repeatedly discounted and included the names of numerous endorsers. In September 1817, Ashton Garrett mortgaged his house, his interest in the firm of Trimble and Garrett, and "sundry slaves"—likely the six people he would list in the 1820 census—to his endorsers, who then discounted the note with the Bank of the United States branch in Lexington, Kentucky.[50] David Trimble, one of the original endorsers on the note, withdrew as an endorser upon its first renewal. He also secretly held a prior lien from 1816 on the mortgaged house, but reasoned that this lien did not matter since "the negroes mortgaged were worth the sum due on the note." When the bank foreclosed on the property for nonpayment, it sold a portion of Garrett's enslaved lives for $1,300, leaving a balance of $500 to $600. Charles, one of the enslaved men on the mortgage, had run away. Another had been sold, but the bank could not prove whether or not this enslaved individual "was one of the mortgaged negroes." With several other endorsers being insolvent, the bank in February 1823 sued William Mosely for the remaining $565.68 due. Mosely, in turn, sued Garrett and the other endorsers for withholding the house that had originally been included as collateral. The court sided with Mosely, ruling that Trimble could not accept the house as mortgage collateral for a note he was endorsing, while simultaneously holding a prior lien on the same property. The house and lot were thus liable for the remainder of the debt, and Mosely was "not bound to pursue the negro, Charles."[51] With no further records, Charles presumably succeeded in his escape.

Even when no potential fraud was involved, the process of foreclosing on endorsers was rarely straightforward. For example, in August 1818 the firm of Throckmorton & Girault was indebted to the Bank of the State of Mississippi for $6,000 on several notes, endorsed by Francis S. Girault and Henry Nelson. Nelson was also indebted to the bank for another $15,000 through his firm Hall, Nelson & Co. By December 1818, Nelson convinced the bank to combine these debts into a sixty-day note, adding the endorsements of Charles B. Green and another man. Both men were prominent citizens of Natchez, Mississippi, but Green was heavily indebted himself with the firm of Hall, Nelson & Co., who served as his commission agents in New Orleans. Yet as a director of the Mississippi bank, Green's endorsement carried considerable weight, despite his own indebtedness.[52] This complicated web of debts and endorsements was quite common among the commercial businessmen in a given locale. Even as other New Orleans firms began to fail in the winter of 1818–1819, the bank was unaware that the finances of Hall, Nelson & Co. were also questionable, "nor did they feel any uneasiness except what might naturally arise from the circumstance of so large a sum in Bills with their indorsement returning under protest for non payment." In fact, at the time "the said Firm was in creditable repute and had many substantial & excellent friends at Natchez and in the vicinity." Thus the bank agreed to renew the note in February, and repeatedly throughout 1819.[53]

By December of 1819, Green was increasingly concerned that the firm would not pay, and that he—as a tertiary endorser—would be liable. He offered to sell some town property he owned "at a great sacrifice to reduce" the debt, as well as his bank stock which was "richly worth its nominal am[oun]t." But he specifically stated that he wished to protect his plantation and enslaved laborers from seizure. By March, his financial situation had worsened. A bad harvest combined with "the reduced price of cotton have curtailed, very much, my means of meeting the requisitions of the Board." Not only did he still need to pay his "merchants, Physicians, Overseer, Smiths &c. &c." from this meager harvest, but his own debtors were now failing. Edward Broughton and others "to whom I sold my Lake plantation" known as Waterloo for $16,100 on credit terms "and from whom an instalment is now due, inform me, that they cannot pay any part of that instalment out of the crop of 1819." These delinquent owners were simultaneously trying to sell the fully operational Waterloo plantation, including all of its enslaved laborers and livestock, in order to get out from the mortgage, but they were unsuccessful and the plantation reverted back to Green.[54] Even worse, Green's own attempts to sell some other property had failed: "I have on several occasions offered property at a reduced price solely for that purpose" of meeting these bank obligations "but have not met with purchasers. I would now sell any property I have (plantation and negro [still] excepted) to make a payment to the Bank. It is scarcely necessary to add, a sale at present cannot be effected."[55]

The bank, however, was also feeling increasingly uneasy about these debts. "[T]he Board cannot yield the indulgence required, without receiving from you, such further security as you can readily offer and they deem satisfactory."[56] It was also uninterested in receiving Green's bank stock in payment. "That money was wanted and not Stock is very certain. That Stock was at the time considerably under par in the market."[57] The bank wanted a mortgage on *all* of his property, the plantation and enslaved laborers included. At this point, Green began to argue that he was not actually an endorser on the notes due to the bank, but that "the notes of Hall Nelson & Co indorsed by myself were given as collateral security only" on different bills. The bank disagreed with this interpretation, and continued to demand more security.[58]

Also in March of 1820, Francis S. Girault, another endorser on the notes, proposed a formal mortgage to the bank of both his and Green's property, in return for extending their terms of payment over four years. Girault and his wife Jane Kempe mortgaged several tracts of land in the parish of Concordia, Louisiana, which he had purchased with his late father-in-law Colonel James Kempe and others, including its twelve enslaved laborers, "a new mill & gin," house, "negro cabbins," farming utensils, and livestock. He also mortgaged another tract of land in Jefferson County, Mississippi, a town lot in Natchez, and four enslaved men—all property that he owned along with his wife's siblings as the heirs of her late father, and which was under a prior mortgage to Green. He then added another three slaves and a smaller property in Natchez that he owned separately. As part of the same mortgage, Green included the Waterloo plantation (which he had previously sold under mortgage to Broughton for $16,100 but now valued at only $12,000), and his "House and Lot in Natchez in the Public Square which now rents for 50$ per month." Altogether, Girault estimated this combined property to be worth (after deducting prior liens) $34,230.[59] Under the terms of the mortgage, Girault and Green would together repay the bank in four equal payments of $5,250, due annually on April 1, from 1821 to 1824.[60] Green argued that the property offered in the mortgage was "amply sufficient" and that "he has not any more to offer."[61]

At the same time, Girault's wife Jane was separately appealing to the bank for leniency on her own debts. Mrs. Girault owed $1,739 on two notes to the Bank of the State of Mississippi, partial payment of which was due in May 1820. Mrs. Girault had tried to pay her debts, but "the only means I had left was to take a negro out of the field." Failing to sell him during the downturn since "there are no purchasers," she feared that "the boy will have to be sacrific'd for I have no money . . . If I am compelled to pursue that plan, it will be plainly seen that my all will be sacrific'd; & besides the complete loss of my crop, which is now flourishing." She begged the bank to "extend their liberality to save me from ruin, which will be the case if I am not relieved," and concluded her letter with a postscript: "If no other arrangement can be made, I will voluntarily & with pleasure mortgage my property for the payment of all my Bank accom[modatio]ns payable annually."[62] It is unclear how much property she owned separately from her husband, nor how the bank responded to this particular request.[63]

When Green and Francis Girault's first payment on the new mortgage fell due in 1821, they were still unable to pay. At this point, Green accused the bank of taking "ungenerous & fraudulent advantage" of him, charges which the bank found to be "most scandalous and unfounded." In its 1822 lawsuit to recover the debts, the bank argued that "in every part of their conduct towards him [the bank has] acted with the most liberal and patient forbearance. . . . [I]nstead of using that power [of foreclosure] which [Green] acknowledges would have crushed him, [the bank has] uniformly manifested a disposition to indulge and to favor and protect [him] from ruin."[64] The fault for Green's situation lay not with the bank, but was "because of an unfortunate responsibility which you incurred and which this Bank had no more agency in creating than the Bank of England."[65]

As the legal proceedings continued, in December 1823 Green again offered to give the bank his Lake Concordia plantation of Waterloo, *not* including "the stock, farming utensils and personal estate thereon," as well as his town property in Natchez.[66] Although Green was "sensible, that a monied institution does not need property of this description," he argued that this would be better than trying to squeeze payment out of him through the delay of law suits and executions which would only result in a sheriff's sale "at a great sacrifice." The bank faced few options, given that "I [Green] have not, nor can I command cash."[67] The bank thus agreed to his terms, releasing him from all of his obligations in exchange for the plantation.[68] Despite this acrimonious dispute and Green's failure to pay, by 1826 Green would again become indebted to the bank by a new mortgage on his land and enslaved laborers.[69]

The bank now owned the Waterloo plantation and its enslaved workforce. Edward Broughton had originally purchased the property from Green under mortgage for $16,100 in the 1810s, only to be foreclosed by Green during the panic. With prices still depreciating, Broughton now offered to buy it back from the bank "provided I could obtain it at a reasonable price and upon accommodating terms." However, he would not be able to take possession of it for a full year, "by which time, I expect such an addition to my force, as would enable me to cultivate it with ease."[70] When the bank and Broughton could not agree on terms, the bank instead advertised it for sale in June of 1824.[71] James A. Girault (Francis's brother) expressed an interest but balked at the bank's terms: $10,000 payable in five annual payments. Girault concluded that "the place is too small & Confined to authorise such a price," and counteroffered for only $8,000—less than half Broughton's original purchase price and a fraction of the $21,000 debt (not including accrued interest) for which the bank had taken possession.[72] It is unclear if the bank agreed to this much-reduced price, but James Girault remained indebted to the bank at least through 1831 when "to satisfy all my debts" to the bank he had to "dispos[e] of my plantation & negroes."[73] As for Francis Girault's share of the original $21,000 debt, it appears to have remained unpaid well into the 1820s.

Once banks were willing to take the large step of securing existing loans with land and human property, it was just a small step further to justify granting loans for the initial purchase of such property—with the same property being offered as the loan collateral. For example, the cashier of the Bank of Orleans William McF. Saul solicited a loan from the Bank of the State of Mississippi (in which he was also a stockholder), specifically for the purpose of purchasing a plantation and enslaved laborers near Baton Rouge.[74] By January 1819, he had already purchased twenty enslaved individuals with the proceeds from $8,000 in discounted notes, people whom he was able to obtain "very cheap" due to "the extreme pressure of the times." He estimated that he could resell them at auction at "a profit of from 9 to 10000$," although "it is not however my intention to sell them again." Rather, he was "now negotiating for a plantation" and he hoped the bank would discount another note for "a further loan of 4 or 5000$." He believed that in "3 or 4 years" he could "see my way clear" to paying off these notes from the profits of the plantation.[75] The following November, he sought to renew the original $8,000 note. But Saul was now also feeling the pressure of the times and was concerned that the bank would not agree to the renewal. He explained that since he had "some heavy payments to make for negroes & as it is impossible for me to sell the Stocks of this City without great sacrifice I wish you to sell my [stock of the] B[an]k of S[tate]. of M[ississippi]. if you can get it within two or three per cent of par," using the proceeds to "pay off my note, should it be required."[76] The bank had willingly financed his long-term investment in a plantation and enslaved laborers, and now had to decide how long it was willing and able to wait for Saul to meet his obligations. The historical record is silent as to whether the bank accepted the stock in payment of the debt, foreclosed on the property, or reached some other agreement with Saul. But regardless of the outcome, the bank was pushing the boundaries of its charter privileges in underwriting these various long-term loans secured by enslaved individuals.

The Advantages of Secured Mortgages

As the Girault and Green dispute with the Bank of Mississippi demonstrates, converting a short-term unsecured loan into a longer-term secured loan held both advantages and disadvantages for both parties. A secured loan defined the specific assets that the bank could seize and sell, creating a lien on this property that legally prevented debtors from selling, altering, or otherwise destroying the value of the property. It also gave a creditor priority of claim to this property over other, unsecured creditors. For the debtor, it bought them time to raise funds for the payment of their original debt, hopefully saving most of their property from the auction block. With rapidly appreciating prices for land and enslaved lives after the War of 1812, bank loans secured by property became particularly attractive. Yet the characteristics of slave collateral which made it most desirable for banks—especially the high demand for enslaved individuals on the frontier, and thus the ease with which they could be sold to recoup delinquent debts—also made it a highly risky form of collateral. Unlike land, enslaved lives were both portable and perishable. They could lose value through age, illness, or death, or be physically moved beyond the claims of creditors.

When banks secured loans with specific property—either when renewing existing debts or, as was becoming increasingly common, when they directly issued loans secured by land or human property—the mortgagor was legally required to register this deed with the local county where the contract took place. Deeds of trust, in which property was secured for the separate use of a wife or other dependent, likewise had to be registered. In this way, a creditor performing due diligence before issuing a loan could investigate whether there were any prior claims on the property in question. It also established the priority of claim to the specific property; deeds filed first took precedence over later filings. The local recording of deeds involving immovable land was generally unproblematic, but enslaved lives—although often legally classified as immovable—were much more challenging for creditors to track. Judges repeatedly ruled that as long as the original deed of trust had been filed properly in the county of the original transaction, it satisfied the legal requirements in subsequent jurisdictions. This placed an even greater burden and expense on creditors since deeds involving enslaved lives could conceivably have been filed in thousands of different counties around the country.[77] Failing to register, on the other hand, often left these mortgages unenforceable in court. In September 1821, Joseph Towles of Kentucky mortgaged some enslaved property to Andrew Barnett and others, "to indemnify them against some liabilities, as his sureties to the Commonwealth's Bank." But seeing as "this deed was not proved or acknowledged, and deposited in the property office for record, within sixty days, as is required by the statute of 1820," the court determined that the mortgage was "legally invalid against 'any creditor.'"[78]

In August 1820, Randolph Ross of White County, Tennessee, was deeply in debt. He owed William Galt of Richmond, Virginia, $3,457 from a debt incurred in July 1816 and originally due in July 1817. Then, on August 12, 1820, he took out a loan for $15,000 with the Bank of Virginia, payable in three installments of $5,000 each on January 20, 1822 to 1824. To secure these loans, he mortgaged several tracts of land in Tennessee, the stock of two stores in Tennessee and another in Virginia, and fifteen enslaved individuals then in the possession of two different Virginia relatives. If he failed to repay William Galt before January 1, 1822, or missed any installment payments to the Bank of Virginia, this property could be seized and sold. Eleven months after Ross made this mortgage agreement, one of his relatives moved from Virginia to Sparta, Tennessee, with nine of the enslaved individuals listed in the contract.[79]

Ross was simultaneously taking out loans in Tennessee. In June 1820, two months *before* the mortgage to Galt and the Bank of Virginia, but four years *after* he was already indebted to Galt, Ross obtained a loan from the Winchester branch of the Nashville Bank for $750, with Anthony Dibrell as his endorser. In August 1821 (just a few months before his debt payments to Galt and the Bank of Virginia were due, but immediately after his relative had moved to Tennessee), he sold to this same relative several tracts of land and ten enslaved individuals, all of which had previously been mortgaged for his various debts in Virginia and Tennessee. The relative agreed to pay $20,000 for this property, which he promised to deliver in annual installments of $2,000 each. Acknowledging Ross's continued debts, the relative promised to direct these annual payments toward his various creditors—who continued to renew for him at his "urgent and repeated solicitations" for "indulgence." By January 1828, the Bank of the State of Tennessee (which had taken over the debts of the Nashville Bank when it closed in the early 1820s) renewed his note (now $785) for six more months, but indicated that this would be the final renewal.[80] At the end of this period, the Bank of the State of Tennessee sued the estate of Ross's relative (who had recently died) for payment of $832.10 (the debt plus past interest and costs). The ten enslaved individuals were sold on February 12, 1830, to satisfy the bank's claim, purchased by Anthony Dibrell for the bargain-basement price of $1,000 (just $100 apiece, on average)—enough to satisfy the Tennessee bank debt but little more. Given that average slave prices in 1830 were around $273 each, Dibrell's purchase likely reflected only a fraction of the slaves' true market value. Galt, as the original creditor, cried foul and sued Dibrell.[81]

In defending his claim, Dibrell brought up several issues that highlight some of the weaknesses of using enslaved lives as collateral. First, he challenged Galt's claim on the specific enslaved individuals he had purchased. In describing the collateral "not by name, but by number and place of residence," the mortgage of Galt and the bank was too vague. Indeed, most mortgage contracts listed, at a minimum, the name and approximate age of any enslaved person, while others included color, occupation, or other identifying characteristics. The court struck down this challenge, since the number of slaves listed with Ross's relatives were identical to what they possessed and what Dibrell had purchased. But the court admitted that "it would have been different had only a portion of them been sold, as it would then have been impossible without further description to identify them."[82]

The court next examined the question of registration of the 1820 mortgage deed that Ross had contracted with Galt and the Bank of Virginia, placing his human property in trust with his relatives. Most states wrote their registration laws with immovable land in mind, an approach that failed to take into account the ability of a slaveholder to move enslaved lives to another jurisdiction. The potential mobility of human property raised two important issues. First, did an indebted slaveholder need to re-register a mortgage or deed of trust when he moved? Registrations, which required the use of a notary public, cost money. Additionally, in the case of a mortgage contract, the registration primarily protected the creditor (and forewarned any future creditors) of the property lien. There was thus little incentive for a debtor to pay to re-register a debt obligation when he or she moved.

Second, while a future creditor could easily check for prior liens on land in the county where it existed, how could the creditor ensure that enslaved lives did not have prior liens from another jurisdiction? Most courts ruled that the initial registration complied with the requirements of the law, and that no subsequent registration was required. Thus, as one historian of debt has noted, "land is an ideal form of collateral because it cannot be moved or hidden from creditors."[83] The court ruled that Ross could have complied with the law by registering the deed in either jurisdiction. In August 1822, he finally registered the deed in Tennessee, acknowledging in one document both the debt to Dibrell and the sale of his enslaved property to his relative "subject to the trust in favor of Galt and the Bank of Virginia."[84] The court ruled that this placed Galt, the Bank of Virginia, and Dibrell on an equal footing as claimants, and that the underpriced sale of the slaves to Dibrell was unfair to the other creditors.[85] While resolving the specific dispute at hand, the ruling left unresolved the problem of the physical mobility of people. As long as courts continued to treat enslaved bodies as if they were the equivalent of immovable realty, the possibility of both future disputes between creditors and deliberate fraud by debtors would remain a pressing issue.

The Hazards of Deflation

Whereas slave mobility was one risk of accepting that specific form of collateral, rapidly declining asset prices during the Panic of 1819 revealed other risks inherent in securing loans with any property. The editor of the *Frankfort Argus* reported from the Kentucky state capital on April 16, 1819, that "never, within the recollection of our oldest citizens, has the aspect of times, as it respects property and money, been so alarming. . . . We have but little money in circulation, and that little is daily diminishing by the universal calls of the banks. Neither lands, negroes, or any other article, can be sold for half their value in cash."[86] If a bank foreclosed on delinquent debtors and sold depreciated property immediately at a loss, it might only recoup a fraction of the debt. Yet if it waited for asset prices or the debtor to recover in order to receive full payment, it risked the failure of the bank itself. Thus banks across the South had to balance their own needs for liquidity against the hassle of litigation and potential loss from foreclosure.

Alpha Kingsley, the proprietor of a large tavern called the Nashville Inn, was indebted to the Nashville branch of the Bank of the State of Tennessee for $5,000, due on August 17, 1819. Believing that Kingsley would be more likely to repay the full debt if he were allowed to continue what had once been a profitable business, the bank extended this debt until September 1820, secured by "certain negroes, several articles of household furniture, two horses, four cows and calves, and other personal property." Although he continued to pay regular discounts on the note, business during the downturn remained depressed and Kingsley did not earn enough to pay off the loan. He "urg[ed] the officers of the bank to renew his note," which it agreed to do for another five months, at which point it decided that Kingsley was not likely to repay and that it was better to sell the property, even at a loss. On February 21, 1821, the bank advertised that the mortgaged property, included the enslaved individuals—would be sold at auction the following month. The sheriff's sale was again delayed, but finally took place on April 2, 1821, and the bank received the proceeds of $2,495.82 ½—roughly half the nominal amount of the original debt.[87]

Banks during the panic found themselves in a difficult position. They needed liquidity to pay noteholders and depositors. Yet the enforcement of debt payments often led to property sales at severely reduced prices. Foreclosures also could lead to the ruin of the debtor, who was frequently a prominent citizen, friend, neighbor, relative, and/or possibly even a member of the bank's board of directors. The bank's only alternative when facing such severe losses was to suspend specie payments, which was a violation of its terms of incorporation and could result in the legislature revoking its charter. Yet failed banks—with their lost deposits, worthless banknotes, and dead stock shares—would only worsen the state of the local economy. Thus state legislatures soon realized that turning a blind eye to most bank suspensions during the panic was ultimately in the best interests of the community. As early as February 1819, the Maryland legislature debated a string of resolutions which would "grant indulgences to the debtors of banks" and to allow a bank to "suspend its operation until the first day of January 1820."[88] In state legislatures throughout the nation, politicians debated the pros and cons of allowing a bank to suspend without punishment, versus enforcing the letter of its charter obligations to pay specie on demand. As planter Sterling Ruffin wrote in September 1819 to his son Thomas—a prominent North Carolina judge and future chief justice of the state Supreme Court: "The pressure for money here continues to increase & the end cannot be conjectur'd by any. Should the Banks alter their present accommodating system, and again call upon their debtors for the usual installments before the last crop of tobacco is dispos'd of, ruin in many instances, will immediately succeed independence."[89] Lending policies and charter provisions which made sense under normal economic circumstances needed to be reconsidered in times of panic.

The most vocal response to the crisis came from Kentucky, where citizens met throughout the state during the spring of 1819 to debate the situation. The legislature in 1818 had just passed one of the most aggressive banking bills in the country, which created forty-six small "independent banks" scattered throughout the state to supplement the services of the partially state-owned Bank of Kentucky and its branches, as well as the two branches of the Bank of the United States in Louisville and Lexington.[90] Since most of these independent banks were still in the process of organizing, the majority of the debates centered on the actions of the Bank of Kentucky and the branches of the Bank of the United States. In the capitol of Frankfort, attendees at a public meeting were concerned that "the present scarcity of money, the pressure by the Banks upon those indebted to them, the pressure by creditors for their debts by suits and executions, the difficulty of raising very moderate sums of money even by enormous sacrifices of property . . . [and] the general embarrassment which seems to encircle the commercial world, which is recoiling on the agricultural and mechanical classes" was leading to "forced sales" of "the most valuable property" at "depreciated prices and ruinous sacrifices." Recognizing that this was "a time of such *general* calamity and dearth of money," the meeting attendees sought "*even-handed public justice*" for creditors and debtors. Since "banks are the great money holders as well as great creditors, they can also be great and efficient instruments in alleviating the present distress." The meeting thus called on all banks "immediately to suspend their payments of specie, suspend their calls, and make moderate issues of paper upon good security"—thus expanding rather than contracting the money supply—and for the legislature to use its "wisdom and intelligence" to validate this suspension.[91] Meetings the following month in the counties of Bourbon, Harrison, and Mason echoed these calls for a state-sanctioned bank suspension. On the other hand, the citizens of Jefferson (Louisville), Washington, Greene, Wayne, and Mercer counties disagreed. Whereas the latter citizens also hoped that the banks would "extend as much indulgence, and exercise as much forbearance as possible, towards all honest debtors," they still believed that the banks should remain bound by the strict terms of their charters to pay specie on demand.[92]

By the summer of 1819, the Bank of Kentucky decided that a suspension of specie payments was its only viable option for dealing with the continued depression; the state took no action against the bank for this decision. In suspending, the bank alleviated its pressing liquidity crisis, which enabled it to deal with debtors more leniently in the hopes of recouping a higher proportion of the money owed in the future. Rather than demanding immediate payment of short-term loans from insolvent debtors, the bank could seek additional security for the loan, extending the payment terms in the hopes that the economy would recover quickly. In February 1820, the Kentucky legislature additionally passed a law allowing debtors to postpone repayment of their debts for one to two years, if they added a suitable endorsement to the debt. Throughout the country, other banks made a similar calculation to suspend specie payments to avoid bankruptcy. While these decisions were always controversial—especially among the most vocal critics of banks—most legislatures permitted these charter transgressions.[93] In the frontier South, this leniency led to more debts being secured with land and enslaved lives.

During the summer and fall of 1819, numerous debtors from Franklin County (where the capital city of Frankfort was located) renegotiated their notes with the Bank of Kentucky using enslaved individuals as collateral.

On July 1, Catesby Gill mortgaged "one negro aged about nineteen named Harvey" to secure his note of $315.[94] On September 1, Lewis Castleman Jr. mortgaged three enslaved men, an enslaved woman, and her young son (five of his six slaves), along with his one-third portion of "the new Steam boat Providence, now lying in the Ohio River, at or near Louisville" to secure one note of $2,000 due in sixty days and another of $3,000 due in seven months.[95] In October, Eliza P. Hickman offered the bank "two negroes Eda & Javiard" to secure her $400 note, due in sixty days.[96] John R. Campbell mortgaged a seventeen-year-old named Bob and a twelve-year-old named Frank to guarantee his $600 debt.[97] On his note of $486, William Littell offered "one negro girl slave named Charlotte aged about ten years, one negro girl Slave named Molly aged about eight years[,] one negro girl slave name Mary aged about six years, one negro boy slave named James Anderson aged about six months."[98] Littell mortgaged these four children, but not the two young women and one young man, all aged fourteen to twenty-six, whom he also owned.[99]

While these mortgages offered temporary relief for many debtors, they provided few liquid funds for the bank and often resulted in prolonged legal battles over the property. When John R. Campbell was still unable to pay his bank debt by the summer of 1821, he tried to evade his creditors by selling his enslaved collateral—Bob and Frank—out of their reach. By August, the bank board of directors learned that he had already sold Bob "to Hillary Offutt," a well-known slave trader, "and [Bob] has been transported by the said Offutt to Louisville for the purpose . . . of carrying him to New Orleans."[100] The bank resolved to intervene in order to claim Bob while he was still in the state, "and also to take the measures which may be necessary to prevent another negro Frank also conveyed in a similar measure for the same purpose from being withdrawn from the control of the court."[101] A year later, on October 8, 1822, the bank auctioned off Bob and Frank "before the door of the Mansion house in the town of Frankfort."[102]

In 1823, debtor William Littell still owed the bank $636.91 on his original note plus interest. Charlotte, Molly, Mary, and James Anderson remained mortgaged to the bank, and Littell now added two enslaved women named Sophia and Maria, and the children Nelly and George Riley (who had been born since the original mortgage), as well as two carriage horses and a tract of land.[103] But his one prime-aged enslaved man remained outside the mortgage.[104] Eliza Hickman was also still delinquent on her $400 note. In 1824, she proposed renewing and combining this debt with that of Littell (to whom she was now married), adding her enslaved couple to his mortgage; the bank assented to this proposal.[105] John Smith had mortgaged three hundred acres of land to the Bank of Kentucky in September 1819, securing his debt of $3,320 on two notes. When the bank "instituted suits" to foreclose on this property in 1824, Smith pleaded that he was "desirous and anxious to obtain a farther indulgence and forbearance upon said debts." The bank agreed, receiving an additional mortgage on two enslaved families totaling eleven people. Smith did not repay this debt until 1828, when the bank finally released him from his mortgage.[106]

Following the lead of the Bank of Kentucky, the Lexington and Louisville branches of the Second Bank also discounted notes and renewed discounts on the security of land and human property. James B. and Thomas January had discounted several notes totaling $3,500 with the Lexington branch of the Second Bank in 1820. Instead of foreclosing on the loan when the brothers failed to repay it by the following year, the bank agreed to accept several tracts of land in Fayette County as well as "Anthony aged about forty one Years, Chloe aged about thirty one Years, Seechey about forty one Years, Mary about thirteen Years, Melinda about eight Years, Jesse about seven Years, Bartlet about six Years, Matilda about four Years and Bety about two Years . . . with the increase of the females" as collateral.[107] These individuals comprised nine of the nineteen enslaved people James and Thomas listed themselves as owning in the 1820 census, and focused on the youngest and oldest individuals. They offered six of the nine lives under the age of fourteen, and three of the seven individuals over the age of twenty-six (two of whom were in their forties), but none of the three prime enslaved lives aged fourteen to twenty-five.[108]

State representative Thomas Fletcher of Bath County offered the Lexington branch twenty-seven of his thirty-nine enslaved people as collateral in order "more effectively to secure" five notes totaling $9,850 which had been discounted between 1819 and 1821. Divided roughly evenly between thirteen males and fourteen females, ten of the males and five of the females were children aged fourteen or younger. Of the remaining twelve, five of the females were thirty or older, and two males were each forty and sixty.[109] Only one of the enslaved individuals included as collateral was a prime-aged male of twenty, despite Fletcher listing several prime-aged slaves on the 1820 census.[110] Twenty-one of the twenty-seven were listed in family groups. Five of these groups consisted of a mother with one to six children, while a sixth group included a husband and wife, their two daughters and a grandchild.[111] Whether or not these families would be sold together if the property foreclosed is impossible to predict, but at least they would all go up on the auction block together. Taken as a whole, this policy of accepting enslaved lives as collateral in exchange for extending loan terms greatly expanded the experience of banks with this type of collateral.

Toxic Assets

As banks quickly discovered, one of the major dangers of foreclosure was that the land or enslaved lives would fail to sell at an acceptable price and the bank itself would actually end up taking ownership of the property, as when the Bank of the State of Mississippi acquired Charles Green's Waterloo plantation and enslaved laborers on Lake Concordia. Several frontier banks suddenly found themselves owning plantations with their enslaved men, women, and children, forcing them to manage land and people until they could sell the property for an adequate return. These toxic assets weighed on a bank's balance sheet and, in combination with rising debt defaults, threatened the existence of the bank itself. As the 1910 history of the Second Bank of the United States explains, "As a result of this ill-advised policy there was a considerable volume of suspended debt in the South and West and a large amount of real estate was thrown back upon the bank. . . . If the security was insufficient, the mortgage was foreclosed and the property sold, usually to be purchased by the bank and then improved."[112] As the president of the Bank of Kentucky explained to his Glasgow branch bank president in 1822, "The cumbrous and inconvertible nature of real estate, cause the acquirement thereof to be incompatible with the operations of monied corporations; and nothing but an inability to secure or realize debt in any other way, justifies the taking it in payment." In theory, the Bank of Kentucky would do anything in its power to avoid foreclosing upon and seizing property in the payment of debts. "Such is the principle upon which we have attempted to act here, and no man[']s property has been received in any instance, where it was believed, that there existed a prospect of making the money from other means."[113] Yet, by the very act of accepting land and enslaved individuals as loan collateral, these banks were also accepting the potential burden of property ownership.

Despite the president's repeated warnings against the Bank of Kentucky acquiring property, the failure of debtors to pay their mortgages forced that bank to take possession of and then resell enslaved people on several occasions. At a board of directors' meeting in May 1823, the president himself informed the board that "he ha[d] purchased on account of the Bank a negro woman for the sum of three hundred & ten dollars." The board resolved to "recognise the s[ai]d purchase as made on their behalf & that the president be instructed to make sale of the said negro woman for money as early as he may deem it expedient."[114] There is no record of when the bank resold this woman, nor where she resided and worked in the meantime.

Similarly, the bank foreclosed on the property of Richard Taylor, the proprietor of the Mansion House hotel in Frankfort. In November 1819, Taylor had secured his $4,500 bank debt with eleven enslaved lives "and also all the beds and bedsteads of which he . . . is now the owner and possessed."[115] Taylor had separately mortgaged the building to the Lexington branch of the Bank of the United States. Although the Bank of Kentucky received a court judgment in the summer of 1822, it took more than a year for a bank representative to take possession of Taylor's "furniture and negroes." The property was put up for sale on August 18, 1823, with the bank purchasing the property itself. In all likelihood, the bids for the property were too low to satisfy Taylor's debts, and the bank gambled that it could get a better price for the property at a later time.[116] The Bank of United States also seized the building, advertising it for rent in December 1823. "This is one of the largest establishments in the state of Kentucky, and is in every respect, fitted for comfortable accommodations on the most extensive scale, having numerous chambers, extensive dining and other rooms, (in all, more than seventy:) a Stable and Sheds, sufficient to contain 75 to 100 horses, and all other requisite buildings for such an establishment."[117]

The Bank of Kentucky held onto the hotel furnishings and enslaved workers for almost three years before selling them in March 1826 for $6,200. The new buyers paid the bank $1,800 in cash, with the remainder spread over eight payments (plus interest) between April 1826 and September 1829. These payments were secured by a mortgage on the property, including "sixteen high post cherry bedsteads[,] eighty four common hight [*sic*] bedsteads[,] one hundred feather beds[,] one hundred pair of sheets[,] one hundred Blankets[,] and one hundred counterpanes" as well as twelve enslaved workers: "Anderson a Blacksmith[,] Bill a hostler[,] Dick a Cook[,] George and Richardson waiters the latter indicating some irregularities of mind[,] Harry a farm servant[,] Judy Sail and her child Henry [or Harry,] Harriet and Patience house and domestic servants."[118] On July 20, 1830, the buyers completed their payments to the bank, and the bank issued to them a deed of sale on the property.[119] It thus took more than a decade for the bank to receive full payment on a debt which had started out as several short-term, sixty-day discount loans.

Whereas most of the mortgages with the Kentucky banks secured loans of under $5,000 (about $120,000 in 2021), mortgages in Mississippi and Louisiana were already ballooning to four or five times this amount. The Baltimore branch of the Second Bank, for example, had lent Dennis Smith $24,000, secured by his wife's one-third share of the Magnolia Grove sugar plantation in Louisiana. Yet with sugar prices in rapid decline, the owners quickly found themselves delinquent on all their debts. Reaching a top price of 13 cents per pound in 1815, sugar in New Orleans had settled in to just under 10 cents per pound from 1816 to 1819, before sharply dropping off to 6 cents per pound during the early 1820s.[120] Smith reported to the Baltimore branch in March 1820 that "the unexampled reduction in the value" of sugar was putting the Magnolia Grove plantation in danger of foreclosure, and that he needed an additional loan of $5,000 to meet his wife's portion of the mortgage payment due to Davis—who possessed the first mortgage on the property.[121] When the branch balked at this further investment, Mrs. Smith's Magnolia Grove partners pleaded with the bank on her husband's behalf. Henry Thompson warned that the "decision was probably made without knowing how important this loan would be towards your [the bank's] security," while Philemon Wederstrandt informed it that Davis "has arriv'd with the express design of seizing upon the estate & slaves if payment is not punctually made."[122] The bank relented, extending to Dennis another $5,000 loan secured by his wife's portion of the plantation and enslaved laborers and further endorsed by his brother.[123] Yet Smith was not only overextended in Louisiana. He was also implicated in an embezzlement scandal that engulfed the Baltimore branch bank's cashier, James W. M'Culloh.[124] By April 1822, with Smith embroiled in lawsuits and still unable to pay his bank loans, the Baltimore branch took full ownership of Mrs. Smith's one-third portion of the estate.[125]

That same fall of 1822, Helen Wederstrandt wrote to the New Orleans branch cashier, pleading that the bank assist her husband Philemon, who ran Magnolia Grove on behalf of the partners (which now included the bank). In addition to his continued difficulties meeting his portion of the mortgage payments to Davis due to "the depreciated price of sugar since the purchase," she ironically asserted that this white enslaver suffered from "the labor and fatiguing duties of the Estate . . . in a climate hostile to health and responsibility." She requested that the bank "grant Mr Wederstrandt a loan equivalent to that which he will be deprived of by the injury his credit has sustained" both for Wederstrandt's sake as well as "to hold [the bank's] interest in the Estate."[126] In April and May 1823, the Second Bank extended two loans to Wederstrandt totaling about $20,000, which enabled him to pay the final mortgage installment to Davis. Four years later, with Wederstrandt still unable to pay his bank debts, the bank finally foreclosed on the property, taking full possession of the plantation and its enslaved workers, and endeavoring to operate the same—at least in the short term—for its own profit.[127] While this outright ownership of a plantation and its enslaved workforce may not have been the norm in the immediate aftermath of the Panic of 1819, it was a logical outgrowth of the lending decisions made by southern banks during the panic, as well as a foreshadowing of the direction frontier banking was going to take during the 1820s and 1830s.

❋

Despite the massive disruption of the first national panic, the banking system of the South emerged largely intact. Approximately fifty banks chartered before the panic survived past the early 1820s, but more than half of these remained concentrated in Maryland, Delaware, and the District of Columbia. In addition to the southern branches of the Second Bank of the United States, the states of Virginia (1804), Kentucky (1806), North Carolina (1810), Tennessee (1811), Mississippi (1811), South Carolina (1812), Georgia (1815), and Louisiana (1818) each had at least one large bank that was partially or wholly owned by the state, with branches spread throughout the state. The remaining dozen or so banks scattered throughout the South were small entities, capitalized at $500,000 or less. With only a few exceptions, the business model of all these banks—including the Second Bank and the large state-owned banks, as well as those in the frontier South—was the discounting of short-term commercial paper, which could be regularly renewed and secured with mortgages on land or human property. Outside the Maryland region, the only southern bank *permitted* to extend loans directly secured by land and enslaved individuals remained the Bank of the State of South Carolina. Yet a few banks—especially those operating on the frontier—actively pushed against these boundaries, allowing businessmen to accumulate increasingly large debts from discounting business notes, which were repeatedly renewed using land and enslaved individuals as collateral. In a few cases, such as the Baltimore branch bank's financing of Magnolia Grove in Louisiana, banks blatantly defied these charter limits by directly securing large loans with enslaved lives.

All this changed during the 1820s and 1830s. While most existing banks continued discounting on conservative banking principles as their primary function, frontier institutions found new and inventive ways to push against the boundaries. Yet the financing needs of the people pouring into western Georgia, Alabama, Mississippi, and Louisiana greatly surpassed what these conservative banks could offer—even with their most creative interpretations of the discounting function. Frontier southerners were intensifying their demands for new institutions to help them finance and expand their operations by leveraging their land and human wealth in loan contracts. By the eve of the next panic, legislatures in the most rapidly developing southern states were openly experimenting with entirely new forms of banking institutions in an attempt to harness the full economic potential of slavery. The enslaved had always generated wealth for owners through their physical labor, their reproduction, and their appreciation in market value. The experiences of bankers and their clientele during the Panic of 1819 now highlighted the potential to leverage enslaved lives in credit relationships as well, opening the way for the transformation of enslaved individuals into fully abstract financial assets.

PART II

Financing an Empire of Slavery in the 1820s and 1830s

In the aftermath of the War of 1812, the rich and abundant lands from Georgia to the Mississippi River opened for settlement. The indigenous peoples of the Southwest had been severely weakened by the war. In the following years, Andrew Jackson negotiated several treaties with the Creek, Chickasaws, and Choctaws in which these tribes exchanged millions upon millions of acres of extremely fertile land for inferior lands further west. Although the government would not fully expel these tribes from the region until the 1830s, under the inhumane policies of Jackson's presidential administration, their military defeat and the signing of these treaties opened up the land for settlement starting in the 1820s.[1] Historian Adam Rothman notes: "Potential settler interest in those ceded lands soared as Andrew Jackson's soldiers returned home with tales of abundant and productive land." Additionally, the end of the Napoleonic Wars solidified the United States as the dominant power on the eastern half of the continent, as most of the European powers retreated from the area and relinquished their claims to parts of the United States frontier.[2] Ballooning European demand for cotton and the continued protective tariff on sugar further encouraged internal migrants to take advantage of the government's already generous policies toward federal land sales.[3]

Population growth in the southern seaboard states stagnated during the 1820s and 1830s, only increasing from 2.6 million to 3 million people over twenty years. The frontier states of the interior (Kentucky, Tennessee, Missouri, and Arkansas) approximately doubled from 1.1 million to 2.1 million people, but enslaved individuals constituted less than one-quarter of the population in these states. In contrast, the growing concentration of large plantations along the most fertile lands from the western border of Georgia, across Alabama into eastern Mississippi (the cotton black belt) and then down the alluvial lowlands along the Mississippi River to New Orleans captured the greatest number of migrants. The population of these states tripled from under seven hundred thousand people to about 2.1 million, with enslaved men, women, and children accounting for close to half (maps PII.1 and PII.2).[4] The cotton and sugar revolutions drove this surging population. Whereas the South produced fewer than three hundred thousand bales of cotton in 1815, the annual harvest more than doubled within five years. By mid-century, the region produced more than four million bales per year.[5] Louisiana experienced a similar tenfold increase in sugar production, from fewer than fifty thousand hogsheads produced annually during the early 1820s, to five hundred thousand hogsheads by mid-century.[6] And critically, these twin agricultural revolutions were built on the backs of the enslaved population. As historian Walter Johnson argues, "The extension of slavery

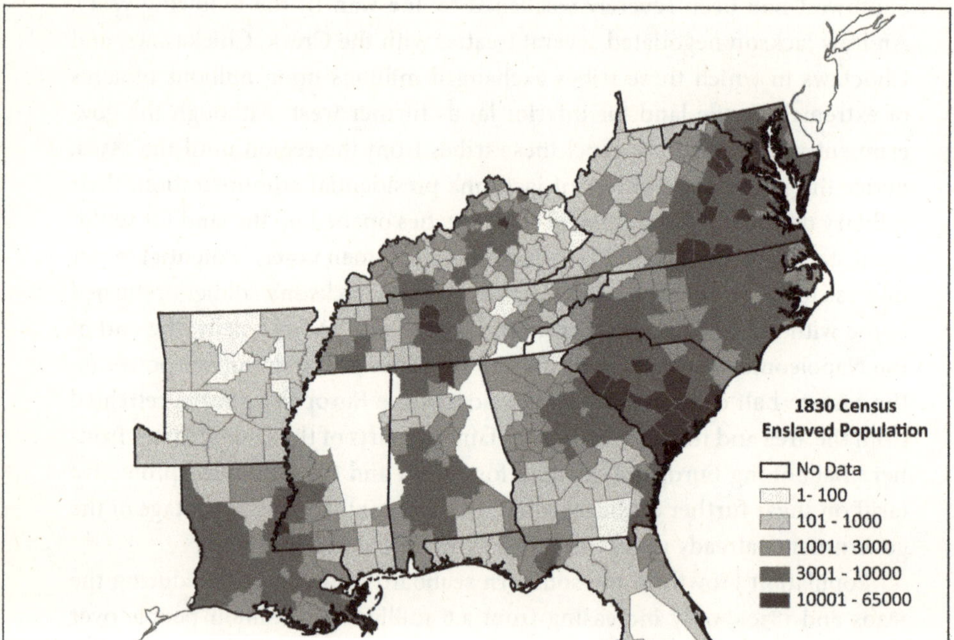

MAP PII.1. Spread of Southern slavery into the Southwest, 1830. Source: Data from Minnesota Population Center, National Historical Geographic Information System: Version 2.0 (Minneapolis, MN: University of Minnesota, 2011), http://www.nhgis.org. Map created by Peter Rogers, Head of Research and Education, Philips Memorial Library, Providence College, Providence, RI.

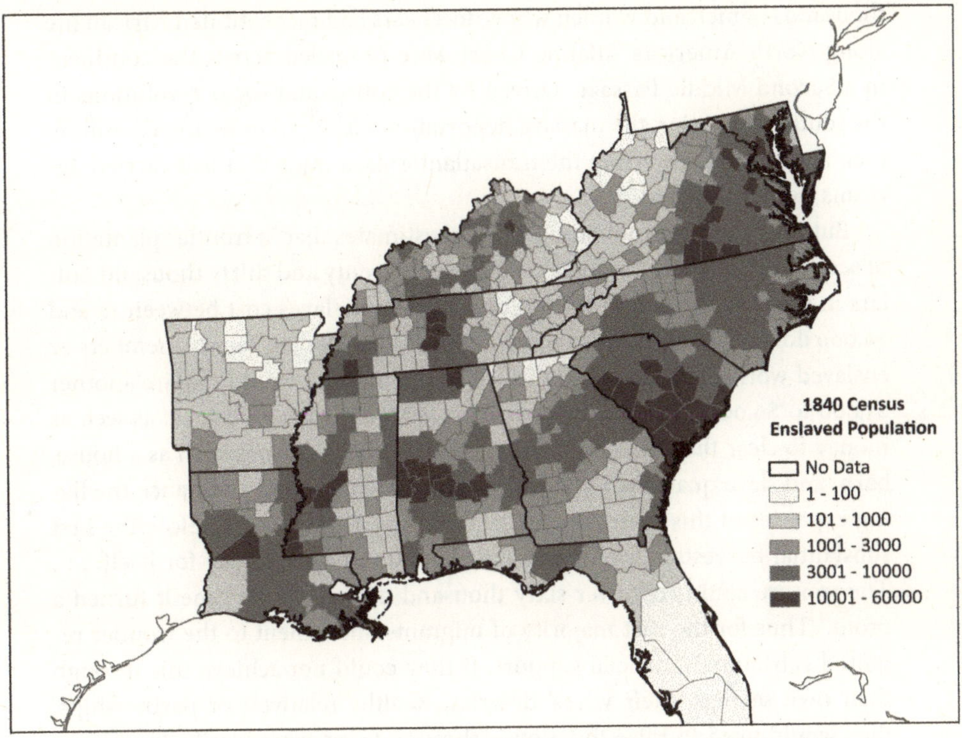

MAP PII.2. Spread of Southern slavery into the Southwest, 1840. Source: Data from Minnesota Population Center, National Historical Geographic Information System: Version 2.0 (Minneapolis, MN: University of Minnesota, 2011), http://www.nhgis.org. Map created by Peter Rogers, Head of Research and Education, Philips Memorial Library, Providence College, Providence, RI.

into the Mississippi Valley gave an institution that was in decline at the end of the eighteenth-century new life in the nineteenth."[7]

This migration was propelled in large part by young southern men "who faced the diminishing economic opportunities" of the Eastern Seaboard states, and who were attracted both by the fertile southwestern lands opened up for settlement after the War of 1812 and the burgeoning international market for cotton. Historian Joan Cashin has documented how rich planters' sons who were both concerned about the soil exhaustion of the Old South and unwilling to wait decades to inherit these landed estates "believed that the best way to ensure their independence was to leave for the Southwest." While men of all ages and economic backgrounds headed west, "most . . . were in their twenties, and most wanted to be planters."[8] And in addition to their wives and children, they brought their human property with them. In historian Ira Berlin's memorable summation: "During that half century [from 1810 to 1861], thousands of men and women whose forebears had reconstituted African life along North America's Atlantic Coast were propelled across the continent in a Second Middle Passage. Driven by the cotton and sugar revolutions in the southern interior, the massive deportation displaced more than a million men and women, dwarfing the transatlantic slave trade that had carried Africans to the mainland."[9]

But migration was not cheap. Cashin estimates that "a frontier plantation of several hundred fertile acres cost between twenty and thirty thousand dollars in the mid-1830s, and a workforce of twenty slaves cost between 18 and 20,000 dollars." In addition to transportation costs for any family members or enslaved workers brought from the East, the migrant would require another $5,000 to $6,000 to outfit the plantation with tools and livestock, as well as money to clear the land and build any necessary structures such as a house, barn, and slave quarters. Finally, the migrant would need to finance the living expenses of this entire operation "for two or three years before the first substantial harvests came in and the plantation began to pay for itself. . . . The venture could cost over sixty thousand dollars by the time it turned a profit." Thus for the vast majority of migrants, movement to the frontier required substantial financial support. If they could not achieve this through their own savings, their wives' dowries, wealthy relatives, or partnerships, they would need to raise the money through loans from family, friends, or financial institutions.[10]

As frontier southerners scrambled to obtain prime land and labor amid rapidly rising prices, they demanded banking services that reflected their need for long-term loans secured by their land and human wealth. Chapter 3 examines how banks of the old South (including coastal Georgia) and the early frontier (especially Kentucky and Tennessee) were drawn into financing slavery's expansion as their existing customers moved West and South. Although these banks were incorporated with conservative charters that restricted them to short-term discount loans, some still sought innovative ways to include land and human property in their loan portfolios, either by exploiting the silences and technical loopholes in their charters, or by openly defying their incorporation provisions. By contrast, in the most rapidly expanding parts of the frontier South, legislatures began explicitly permitting traditional commercial banks to extend large, long-term loans secured by the rapidly appreciating value of the region's land and enslaved lives (chapter 4). During the 1830s boom, a few frontier legislatures even began experimenting with radically new banking structures that completely reimagined how slaveholders could capitalize on their land and human property (chapter 5).

3

Old South Banks and Frontier Finance

Throughout the Nicholas Biddle Papers at the Library of Congress, which record his correspondence as president of the Second Bank of the United States from 1823 to 1836 and the subsequent United States Bank of Pennsylvania from 1836 to 1839, Biddle explicitly mentioned slavery in only one exchange, from 1831. That spring, Roswell L. Colt, a prominent director of the bank branch in Baltimore, inquired about a loan to John Spear Smith. Smith was the son of the powerful, pro-bank US senator from Maryland, Samuel Smith, who chaired the Committee on Finance from 1823 to 1833.[1] The younger Smith jointly owned a sugar plantation and about a hundred enslaved individuals in St. James Parish, Louisiana, with his aunt Esther (Hetty) Smith Carr (youngest sister of Samuel and the widow of Thomas Jefferson's nephew Peter Carr).[2] The pair sought to use this property as collateral for a $50,000 loan (about $1.5 million in 2021) from the Philadelphia office of the bank.[3] In consultation with the bank committee, Biddle responded that they were "desirous of serving" Smith "for his own as well as his father's sake" and were "well disposed to make the loan." Having Senate allies for the bank, especially on the Committee on Finance, was always critical. However, openly listing enslaved lives as part of the collateral gave the committee pause. In Biddle's words:

> There is one part of the subject which jars with our habits and opinions here as you may well understand. It is the voluntary acceptance of a mortgage by which the Bank might be under the necessity of selling off to strangers the negroes on the estate. In Louisiana and in Maryland these operations are necessary and excite no feelings. Here [in Philadelphia] the case is different, and, as you know, matters of feeling do not yield to considerations which seem very strong to those who look at the question in a merely pecuniary point of view.[4]

Four days later, Biddle again wrote to Colt, suggesting that they "avoid the Slave question" in this case by using Smith's "country and town house" in Maryland as extra collateral, but this arrangement did not meet with Smith's approval.[5] Indeed, it is curious that Smith solicited this loan from the main bank office in Philadelphia rather than from the branches in either Baltimore or New Orleans, both of which regularly accepted enslaved lives as collateral. Perhaps he was trying to exploit his father's position and relationship with Biddle for his own financial benefit.

Discussions continued for two more weeks, until Biddle and Smith finally agreed to a plan that satisfied the latter without exposing the Philadelphia office to unnecessary scrutiny.[6] Through their legal proxies in New Orleans, Smith and Carr received a $50,000 loan from the Philadelphia office, offering six promissory notes payable over six years at the Baltimore branch and endorsed by Baltimore commission merchants Harrison & Sterett. As collateral for the loan, Smith and Carr offered the bank "a certain plantation, together with all the buildings and improvements thereon (*but without the slaves attached to the same*)" [emphasis added].[7] This explicit caveat in the contract was striking for its novelty. Mortgages defined in often excruciating detail what property *was* included but rarely, if ever, mentioned exceptions; debtors commonly offered land alone as collateral without feeling the need to mention excluded items such as enslaved people, livestock, or household goods. Biddle wanted this exception to appear prominently in the document, providing plausible deniability to the Philadelphia office.

That same day, Smith and Carr's proxy signed a second, separate mortgage binding them to Harrison & Sterett. In return for the Baltimore firm's essential endorsement on the aforesaid $50,000 bank loan, Smith and Carr mortgaged to it "about one hundred slaves to secure them against all the risks they have incurred by endorsing the said six notes; which slaves belong to them and are at present on their plantation situated in the said Parish of St. James." The mortgage included a list describing each enslaved individual by name, age, color, and role on the sugar plantation.[8] The enslaved bodies were effectively securing the $50,000 bank loan, with the third-party endorsement serving to hide this collateral from the "opinions" and "feelings" of Biddle's more skeptical Philadelphia board members. As Biddle warned Colt in sketching out this plan, "it will be well to confine the subject to the parties interested as we might otherwise be burdened with applications from all quarters which we would be obliged to decline."[9] Given the timing of this exchange mere months before the bank applied for an early recharter in January 1832, Biddle was likely trying to downplay the bank's direct relationship with slavery in order to shore up northern support for the institution, while still placating important southern senators like Samuel Smith.

While novel in its details, this arrangement reflected the many ways that banks of the seaboard South navigated the constraints both of their charters and of accepted banking practices so as to meet the growing demands of southerners on the frontier. Banks regularly manipulated the standard practice of endorsing loans to bypass charter restrictions. Others entered into formal or informal relationships with more-permissive frontier banks. Although some northerners likewise migrated South and became slaveholders during this period, I have found few examples of northern banks (beyond the federally chartered Second Bank of the United States) being similarly drawn into slave finance. This interstate financing of the expansion of slavery was complicated by differing state laws with regard to the rights of creditors and debtors, which became especially contentious in cases involving women and children. Yet ultimately, this willingness of some traditional banks to accommodate the expansion of slavery still fell far short of the needs of frontier slaveholders.

Exploiting Loopholes

As the country emerged from the Panic of 1819, states tentatively began expanding their banking systems. In addition to the about three dozen existing southern banks (outside of Maryland, Delaware, and Washington, DC) from the pre-panic era, southern legislatures incorporated a handful of banks from 1820 to 1825, and then exploded with over one hundred bank charters from 1826 to 1838. By the mid-1830s, the economy had entered another speculative boom similar to that of the late 1810s (see figure 2.1 in chapter 2). Both international and domestic demand for cotton again skyrocketed, driving up prices for land and enslaved workers. Additionally, growing British investment in transportation stocks and bonds, the British opium trade with China, silver inflows from Mexico, and a French legal payment to the United States over shipping losses during the Napoleonic wars all expanded the American money supply and contributed to the economic bubble.[10] At the same time, as part of President Andrew Jackson's war against the Second Bank of the United States, the treasury secretary began moving government deposits out of the national bank and into the vaults of "politically friendly" banks throughout the country. By 1836, these "pet banks" (as Jackson's opponents dubbed them) numbered around ninety, and used their increased funds to justify even more loans and banknotes.[11]

The number of state-chartered banks in the South approximately doubled during these boom years, but the majority of that institutional growth was concentrated on the frontier (table 3.1). For the five states of the lower frontier, the number of banks grew by more than 400 percent. Yet despite this speculative environment, roughly half the new southern banks remained exclusively committed to discounting only on short-term business paper, and still only encountered enslaved individuals through *fieri facias* foreclosure suits, or when they requested additional security upon note renewals. Even when the discounted notes resulted in large outstanding debts, these institutions were still operating within the confines of traditional banking practices. But on the frontier, agricultural interests were pressuring legislatures to allow banks greater leniency in their lending policies, which would cautiously begin to open up more opportunities for the direct finance of slavery.

In 1820, Kentucky replaced the failing Bank of Kentucky with the Bank of the Commonwealth of Kentucky. Fully state-owned with a capitalization of $2 million, the new institution was charged with opening twelve branches throughout the commonwealth.[12] The legislature also extended the charter of the Bank of Kentucky until 1829, to allow for an organized liquidation of its assets and liabilities.[13] That same fall, Kentucky's southern neighbor incorporated the fully state-owned Bank of the State of Tennessee, with agencies or branches in every county of the state. Capitalized with $1 million, the legislature explained that it was "deemed expedient and beneficial both to the state and the citizens thereof, to establish a bank on the funds of the state for the purpose of relieving the distresses of the community and improving the revenue of the state."[14]

Both chartered at the height of the depression after the Panic of 1819, one of the main purposes of these two new large state banks was debt relief, especially for rural debtors, which they largely achieved by relaxing the restrictions on lending.[15] In terms of discounting, these banks remained conservative. The Bank of the State of Tennessee, for example, still only allowed discounts renewable every sixty days.[16] Instead of expanding discounting (which would be of little benefit to rural debtors), these banks modeled themselves on the Bank of the State of South Carolina in extending loans backed by real or personal estate. Both the Bank of the State of Tennessee and the Bank of the Commonwealth of Kentucky permitted twelve-month loans for up to half the value of the mortgaged property. These loans were renewable for up to ten years, with the requirement that the debtor pay interest and one-tenth of the principal each year. The Kentucky bank placed a limit of $1,000 on these property loans (about $24,000 in 2021).[17] As had been the case with the 1812 charter of the Bank of the State of South Carolina, the legislature seemed

TABLE 3.1 Southern bank charters, 1820–1838[a]

Region	Total banks end of 1820	New charters 1821–25	New charters 1826–38	Closures 1821–38	Total banks end of 1838	Percentage of banks closed 1821–38	Growth rate of banking 1821–38
Mid-Atlantic (MD, DE, DC)	34	1	15	(14)	36	28%	6%
Old South (VA, NC, SC)	15	2	11	(8)	20	29%	33%
Upper frontier (KY, TN, MO, AR)	6	1	12	(9)	10	47%	67%
Lower frontier (GA, AL, MS, LA, FL)	13	2	70	(19)	66	22%	408%
Totals	68	6	108	(50)	132	27%	94%

[a] Includes branches of the Second Bank of the United States. Does not include individual branches of state banks.

Source: Weber, *Census of Early State Banks.*

to assume that property loans would be based on land alone. The bank was directed to appoint commissioners "to value and appraise the lands which may be offered in mortgage to the bank" and at least three commissioners to approve "every valuation of land." This charter made no specific mention of valuation for human property.[18] Yet whereas the legislature did not seem to anticipate the use of enslaved individuals as collateral, debtors immediately began demanding such lending conditions, forcing bank directors to adapt.

The older Bank of Kentucky quickly found itself caught between the desires of customers for property loans and its reluctance to risk having to seize property in foreclosure proceedings. In April 1822, the president of the Shelbyville branch of the Bank of Kentucky requested permission from the main bank to extend a real estate loan to "a respectable and widowed female struggling to sustain a young and helpless family." President Harvie, however, was unmoved, and reminded his branch president that "it must be obvious to all who think on the subject that the acquisition of real estate is militant to all the sound principles of Banking policy and should be resorted to for the securement and indemnification of debts of the most equivocal and hazardous character only." Although the bank secured existing loans on discounted paper with property, it drew the line at direct loans. "Such is the principle upon which this Board have hitherto acted, having invariably rejected all propositions for the reception of real estate in payment of debts which were held to be unquestionably safe and responsible." Even in a case "strongly prompted by the dictates of sympathy," he concluded that "a deviation from the rule" would be "highly replete with mischief to the Institution." The president backed this decision by referring to the bank's charter, which "only authorises the reception in extinguishment of debts of such estate alone as is pledged to the Corporation for the securement of the debts" already existing through discounts. "[W]e have therefore no power even if the will existed of" engaging in such loans backed by property, and could only treat the widow with "every indulgence and forbearance . . . which the interests of the Institution will authorise."[19]

Despite the apparent hard line taken by President Harvie, the Bank of Kentucky regularly issued loans backed by land and human property by making these loans *appear to be* discounted promissory notes. In doing so, it adopted a structure similar to the much-later 1831 loan of Smith and Carr with the Second Bank, in which the enslaved individuals were mortgaged to the note endorser rather than directly to the bank. If a bank was permitted to discount *any* promissory notes that crossed its desk—as the Bank of the United States was just then arguing in the 1820 and 1823 *Fleckner* cases down in Louisiana—then the bank only needed to perform a little legal smoke and mirrors to put itself in compliance with its charter privileges. In a typical discounting scenario any agreements between the initial debtor and his or her endorsers were separate from the agreement between the debtor and the bank as creditor. Going back to the 1819 example of Latham and Morehead, the partners discounted their $4,500 bill of exchange, endorsed by Samuel Vance, with a bank in Tennessee. As far as the bank was concerned, Latham, Morehead, Vance, and the originator of the bill (Morehead's nephew) could all be held equally liable for payment. This discounting contract was entirely separate from the mortgage agreement reached between Vance and the partners, in which Vance could seize their human property if Morehead and Latham failed to pay the bank and he were called upon as an endorser. Family, friends, and business partners often endorsed notes without requiring any additional security; Vance was actually being more proactive than most, even if doing so still failed to protect him fully.[20]

This two-step process for obtaining loans secured by enslaved individuals through an endorser was inefficient and cumbersome. The Bank of Kentucky thus developed a streamlined process that adhered to the letter if not the spirit of the bank's charter. Most of the property loans issued by that bank from (at least) 1819 through 1822 or 1823 collapsed these separate agreements into one contract, thereby mimicking the traditional discounting process for what was really a loan secured by property. The debtor (designated as the "first party") would find someone (the "second party") to endorse his promissory note in exchange for a mortgage on his property. That note would then be discounted by several of the bank clerks—usually Harrison Blanton, John Wilkinson, and Samuel J. M. Major (the "third party")—as representatives of the bank. The debtor would then receive the desired loan from the bank. The bank could say that it had discounted a valid promissory note with two endorsers (the first and second parties). The endorser (the second party) was protected from most of the risk due to the mortgage on the property of the first party, which property the bank representations (the third party) could seize in the event of a foreclosure. Indeed, what made this process so unique from a normal discounted note was that the second endorser was not actually assuming much, if any, risk. He was merely serving as a name to satisfy the form of a proper discount.

One typical example of this "dummy discount" was in January 1821, when Daniel Weisiger, a director of the bank, sought a $2,000 loan secured with his human property; the agreement gave no indication of Weisiger's purpose for this loan. The bank held "the Note of said Weisiger, indorsed by said Dudley dated on this day and payable sixty days after date," although Weisiger could renew it as desired. Jeph Dudley, as the endorser, "consent[ed] to the security hearinafter [*sic*] mentioned," which consisted of ten enslaved individuals owned by Weisiger. The bank, for its part, agreed "to resort to the means of payment hereby intended to be secured"—i.e., the enslaved people of Weisiger—"before they [Dudley] are called upon to respond as endorsers." Thus, although the enslaved people were being mortgaged to the endorser, the bank would bypass this endorser and seize the people directly in case of default. Even more, it was explicitly with the bank's representatives (and not the endorser) that Weisiger "doth covenant and agree" that he had full ownership of the enslaved and "hath lawful right to sell and convey" them if and when they should be claimed by the bank in payment for the loan. Indeed, the remaining pages of the contract ignored altogether the existence of the endorser and even, to some extent, the bank's third-party representatives (Blanton, Wilkinson, and Major) as intermediaries to the loan. "[T]he said party of the first part . . . doth covenant and agree to and with the President Directors and Company of the Bank of Kentucky that he will well and truly pay and satisfy them in the said debt . . . and that upon default in that behalf that it shall and may be lawful for the said Trustees [Blanton, Wilkinson, and Major] . . . to sell . . . such part or parts of the property as will be sufficient."[21] Rather than being an extra level of security for the bank, the endorser in this case was merely a means of disguising the true nature of the contract—a new loan secured directly by property. This example was not an exception but was typical of the Bank of Kentucky's loans during the post-panic period.[22]

One of the biggest advantages for a bank of mortgaging property through an endorser was that the endorser was then responsible for seizing and selling the property. For example, when William Hatton failed to pay his bank debt in 1824, his endorser advertised "A likely negro Boy, aged about 5 or 6 years" in the *Kentucky Gazette*. "[S]aid sale is made to secure myself as security for said Hatton in a note executed to the Bank of the Commonwealth of Lexington."[23] On the other hand, eliminating the endorser—as the Bank of Kentucky was now doing—could instead saddle the bank with the property. A July 1822 mortgage between Henry and John Perkins ("of the first part") and Blanton, Wilkinson, and Major ("of the third part") ignored the pretext of an intermediary endorser altogether. The Perkins family mortgaged ten-year-old Peter and nine-year-old Hannah directly to the bank representatives in exchange for a $200 bank loan, payable or renewable in sixty days. By April 1823, when the Perkinses were unable to pay and the bank was unwilling to continue renewing, the enslaved children were deeded to bank representative Harrison Blanton.[24] More than two years passed before Peter (now thirteen) and Hannah (now twelve) were sold "to the highest bidder, at the Court-house door in Lexington" in July 1825 "to satisfy and pay" the Perkins family's debt to the bank.[25]

By late 1822, these "dummy discounts" by the Bank of Kentucky were becoming less common, particularly as the new Bank of the Commonwealth of Kentucky began operations in October 1822 with explicit permission to extend property loans of up to $1,000—eliminating the necessity of the ruse. Around this time, State Representative Thomas Fletcher of Bath County owed the Bank of Kentucky just under $4,000. In September 1822, the bank allowed him to secure this loan by agreeing to mortgage his land and human property. In a highly unusual move for the older Bank of Kentucky, the institution structured the loan as a long-term property mortgage, payable in three annual payments of $1,314.83 each on September 25, from 1822 to 1824.[26] Presumably Fletcher paid off this mortgage before he listed these exact same enslaved individuals in his mortgage agreement of August 5, 1824, with the Lexington branch of the Bank of the United States.[27] Yet this long-term mortgage to Fletcher was an outlier in the Bank of Kentucky's books. For the remainder of the 1820s and 1830s, the bank openly lent only small sums of money (usually under $1,000) secured by land or human property, renewable every sixty days.

Like President Harvie of the Bank of Kentucky, Nicholas Biddle of the Second Bank of the United States was wary of writing mortgages secured by property. As the bank president explained in 1825 to one inquirer: "The Bank does not lend . . . on landed security for a term of years. It would occupy more time than would be agreeable to either of us, to explain why this particular species of loan is of all others the most inconsistent with the very nature and purposes of a Bank."[28] On several other occasions throughout the 1820s and 1830s, he reminded the local branch presidents that "the Bank . . . does not habitually lend on mortgage,"[29] and insisted "Our great object is business men and business paper."[30] Of course, the fact that both Harvie and Biddle repeatedly had to remind their branches *not* to engage in loans on property belies the fact that this was exactly what many of the branches were doing. The administrators of several of the Second Bank branches viewed property loans as a profitable use of its capital stock, particular as the economy again heated up during the late 1820s and 1830s. One early historian of the bank asserts that in the West and Southwest "money was advanced to grow the crops, and the loan paid out of the proceeds when they came to market. The bills of exchange by which these loans were made were frequently six months' paper."[31] Although Biddle repeatedly "counseled the western and southern branches to adopt more conservative methods, the advice was not heeded. Indeed, the branch officers defended their operations as wise and necessary."[32]

As had been the case before the panic, the two Kentucky branches of the Second Bank of the United States actively accepted enslaved lives as collateral from their debtors. In February 1822, John Lowry discounted several notes totaling $7,000 with the Lexington branch of the Bank of the United States, with the payment due in sixty days. In order to further secure these notes, Lowry and his wife, Flora, offered as collateral a tract of land in downtown Lexington as well as seven enslaved adult men, a group that was a subset of the nineteen males and one female the Lowrys listed in the 1820 census but that included two of their three eldest individuals.[33] If Lowry failed to pay off the loan within sixty days, he "would warrant the title of the said slaves to the President Directors & Company of the Bank of the United States and their successors forever, free from the claim or claims of all and every person or persons whatever."[34] In 1824, Dr. Richard Pindell (brother-in-law of Henry Clay) offered the Lexington branch four enslaved individuals and "also two Poneys" to secure his unpaid $1,790 debt from 1821.[35] Neither loan contract indicated the reason for the loans.

The Louisville, Kentucky, branch of the Second Bank also accepted enslaved lives as collateral to secure debts. In 1824, Harrison Blanton of Franklin

County offered Isaac and his wife Judy as collateral for a $500 note to this branch, agreeing that if he, Blanton, failed to pay or receive a renewal of the note within sixty days, the bank "may proceed by their agent or attorney to take the said negroes in possession and after having advertised the same two weeks in some public paper proceed to the sale of both or either of them in such a manner as they may direct, either for cash in hand or on a credit."[36] John Smith offered eleven of the forty enslaved people he had listed in the 1820 census to secure a $2,500 loan from the same branch in 1825, including two families each consisting of a mother and two children under the age of five.[37] (These named individuals were different from the eleven he had simultaneously mortgaged to the Bank of Kentucky for a separate debt.)[38] When Smith failed to pay back the loan, he appealed to the bank for leniency. While he was "unable to pay the same without great sacrifice," he hoped the bank would "grant him further time upon condition that he shall execute to them a new note for the said debt." The bank branch agreed to these new terms, and the eleven enslaved lives remained as collateral on the loan.[39] In each of these cases, the future of these enslaved individuals—and the possibility that they would be placed on the auction block—depended on their owner's fiscal responsibility in paying off these debts, and the aggressiveness of the banks in pursuing these debtors.

Appeasing Planters

In Georgia, most of the banking capital through the 1820s remained focused on the older commercial strongholds of Savannah and Augusta. While mainly discounting short-term commercial paper, these banks regularly foreclosed on enslaved individuals through *fieri facias* proceedings. For example, the Savannah sheriff's sale for the first Tuesday in March 1825 included "six negroes . . . levied on under a fi. fa. on foreclosure from Jon Hunter to the Planters' Bank" as well as "5 negroes . . . levied on as the property of James Bilbo, to satisfy an execution in favor of the President, Directors and Company of the Bank of the U. States," and "A negro man named Soloman, levied on as the property of John Womack, to satisfy executions in favor of the Bank of the State of Georgia." The April sale on the steps of the Savannah courthouse included "seven negroes . . . levied on under a fi fa on a foreclosure of a mortgage as the property of Joseph Carruthers to satisfy the Bank of the State of Georgia" and "18 negroes . . . levied on under a fi fa. on a foreclosure of a mortgage as the property of Wm. C. Wayne, to satisfy the Bank of the State of Georgia."[40] These banks also occasionally underwrote mortgages directly secured by enslaved individuals. The Planters' Bank of Georgia, for example, discounted a $7,000 note of Jeremiah and William H. Cuyler in March 1828. Both residents of Savannah, Jeremiah was a US district court judge for the District of Georgia, and his son William was a local physician and member of the bank's board of directors.[41] Secured by a mortgage on their land and thirty enslaved people, the note was payable or renewable in sixty-one days.[42]

The Savannah branch of the Second Bank of the United States also regularly advertised for sale enslaved property it had seized by court order, such as George, the property of Dimas Ponce, and five enslaved women belonging to John Gribbin: "a negro girl named Charlotte," as well as Jane and her daughters Martha, Mary, and Eliza.[43] In February 1826, the bank advertised for sale twenty enslaved individuals of Peter T. Merchant. After eight sold at the March auction at the Savannah courthouse, the bank continued listing the remaining twelve for sale through the July auction, when they presumably sold.[44] And in 1828, the bank seized sixteen "very young and prime negroes averaging about eighteen years of age," as the property of M. H. McAllister, who was the endorser for another delinquent debtor.[45]

In September and October 1824, the Savannah branch advertised for sale eight enslaved lives belonging to Eleazar Early: Sally and her three children, and Delia (or Delila) and her three children.[46] Early held a contract with the postmaster for the mail routes between Savannah and Augusta, Georgia. In 1822 and 1823, he had made significant investments in a steamboat on the Savannah River and stagecoach lines to fulfill the four-year contract. Unfortunately for Early, disagreements with both the postmaster general and his connecting mail carriers had rendered the service unprofitable. By December 1823, he owed the General Post Office $5,500 in postal fees, which he promised to deposit with the Savannah branch and then transfer to the District of Columbia branch of the Second Bank. Yet problems and disputes continued into 1824, likely leading to the Savannah branch's decision to foreclose on his debts and sell these enslaved families.[47] Sally's family sold first, yet evidently the sale was unsuccessful. All eight were again listed for auction on the first Tuesday of December, with "Sally and her three children, sold on account of the former purchaser."[48] By late December, only Delia and her offspring remained for sale, disappearing from the record (presumably sold separately from Sally's family) after the January 1825 sheriff's sale.[49]

Yet these banks and branches along the South Carolina border failed to address the needs of the planters migrating into the indigenous lands of central and western Georgia. Continued demands for longer credit terms finally led to the incorporation in 1828 of the Central Bank of Georgia, with its headquarters in the capital city of Milledgeville. In the preamble to the charter, the legislature explained: "It is deemed expedient and beneficial both to the State and its citizens, to establish a bank on the funds of the State, for the purpose of discounting paper, and making loans upon terms more advantageous than has been heretofore customary." Fully owned by the state, the capital funds consisted of "the money in the treasury of this State, not otherwise appropriated," all shares of stock in other banks owned by the state, "all bonds, notes, specialties, judgments due the State; and all moneys arising from the sales of fractions and town lots . . . and all other debts and moneys at any time due the State." In short, it was created as the fiscal agent of Georgia. In return, its charter authorized it to discount notes up to $2,500, requiring "two or more good securities" and any "additional security . . . when, in their opinion, the interest of said bank shall require it." These loans were designed to be treated as long-term by the bank, with borrowers permitted to renew every six months for up to five years, paying back one-fifth of the principal plus interest annually "unless the exigencies of the bank shall require it."[50] Although a few other states had operated banks on a similar model for several years, Georgians still viewed the long-term loans suspiciously. The legislative debate on the bank focused "particularly, as to the time at which money should be lent. A great variety of opinion prevailed on this point. It was finally settled at six months."[51] In 1836, the legislature revised this provision, allowing renewals on an annual basis.[52]

From the beginning, the Central Bank was not without its detractors. One editorialist predicted failure if security was based on "mortgages upon the worn-out lands of the Landlord."[53] Another editorial, published in the *Niles' Weekly Register*, entitled "Banks a Curse to Farmers," went viral, being reprinted up and down the Eastern Seaboard, from Georgia to Massachusetts. Focusing on the "long periods" of the Central Bank's loans, the author predicted that it would "probably bankrupt from one third to one half of the *planters* who shall deal liberally with it, in the space of ten years." Instead of risking his assets by endorsing bank loans for five years, the writer advised the planter to use instead "his *real* capital in the purchase of lands and slaves, at reduced rates, if so he shall wish to employ it." Those in need of loans "should avoid banks as they would *scorpions*—unless under particular circumstances and with a decided understanding and resolution, that all engagements made with them *shall* be cancelled at maturity—without any extension of what is called *accommodation*." Indeed, the long-term nature of these loans was what scared the writer most. "All projects of this kind . . . by whatever name *protracted payments* have been allowed for the *relief* of farmers, have had one uniform effect, to destroy them in the end."[54] As the bank began opening agencies for discounting in the spring, the critiques continued.[55] A writer in the Savannah *Daily Georgian* had "misgivings" that "the distribution of money easily obtained, will bring back the reign of prodigality and speculation" among "those borrowers composed of the landed interest." In particular, the lending practices of the Central Bank would "give a fictitious value to property."[56]

Despite these continued attacks, the Central Bank underwrote mortgages on the land and human property of Georgia's planters until after the Panic of 1837. But its role as a fiscal agent of the state put it in a unique relationship with the system of slavery. In 1829, the state appropriated $50,000 (approximately $1.4 million in 2021) "for the purchase of such a number of able bodied negroes . . . as will, in addition to the number now owned by the State, amount to the number of one hundred and ninety" to aid in the "improvement of roads and rivers of this State."[57] By October 1830, the state owned 207 "public hands."[58] Yet just four years later, in 1834, the state decided that this experiment as a slaveholder was not working out—the enslaved workers were deemed "unsatisfactory as labor" and expensive to maintain—and the legislature directed the Central Bank to sell the enslaved individuals.[59] "Together with all the Horses, Mules, Carts, Tools, and Implements belonging to the State of Georgia," the superintendent of roads advertised 187 enslaved laborers who would be sold at the courthouses of eight different counties in March. Buyers could finance their purchases by discounting their notes at the bank "on such terms as are usual in discounting on loans: *Provided* the sum shall not exceed twenty five hundred dollars," which was the lending limit under the bank's charter.[60] Those individuals not sold in March were sold in April.[61] By July, only four enslaved laborers remained for sale, being those "who were absent from their respective companies on the day of sale." The superintendent listed four more runaways who would also be sold should they "be apprehended before the day of sale." Finally, since "the former purchaser" of Phillip "refused to comply with the terms of sale," Phillip was resold.[62]

In the end, the state received $118,148.37 from the sale of 198 enslaved individuals (about $597 each), "all of which sum has been deposited in the Central Bank in notes discounted and cash" except for $4,477.95 which "remains unsettled on account of . . . a difficulty which arose on account of the unsound health of one of the negroes." This total did not include "eight runaways to be disposd [*sic*] of when apprehended," although most of their value would be consumed by "the expenses of their apprehension, jail fees, physician's bill and other incidental charges."[63] A year later, the governor was pleased to announce that all eight runaways had been recovered and sold, netting the state an additional $2,930.71, which had "been paid over to the Central Bank."[64]

In contrast to the Central Bank, other older Savannah-based banks, such as the Planters' Bank (chartered 1810) and the Bank of the State of Georgia (chartered 1815), continued to concentrate on discounting, often using endorsers as intermediaries for loans secured by enslaved lives. For example, in June 1837 Ann Box of Savannah mortgaged two enslaved men named Hammond (aged twenty-one) and Tom (aged nineteen) to Thomas Box to secure her promissory note of $300 due in sixty-one days. Thomas Box immediately discounted that deed of mortgage with the Bank of the State of Georgia, who assumed both Ann Box's debt and the claim on her human property.[65] The following month, Robert Pooler mortgaged to the firm of Gaudry & Branch "two certain Sloops or Vessels. . . . Also two certain negro men slaves the one named Harry about thirty two years of age and the other named July about forty five years of age" to secure his $1,345.10 note due in ninety-one days. The mortgage specifically stated that Gaudry & Branch "intended to have the said promissory note negotiated at the Bank of the State of Georgia." A second document of the same date transferred the debt from Gaudry & Branch to the bank, granting it "full power to foreclose and collect all sums mentioned and expressed arising or accruing from in, to or out of the within deed."[66] Three days later, Gurdon Miller of Savannah mortgaged fifteen-year-old Harry to Henrietta Miller to secure his debt of $210. Henrietta immediately transferred to the Bank of the State of Georgia "the within deed of Mortgage, and all every right and title to the negro Boy named therein, together with the original debt for which the said Mortgage was given."[67] The Planters' Bank of the State of Georgia followed a similar practice, although its discounts were often for much-larger amounts. For example, in December 1837, George Glen mortgaged fifteen enslaved individuals to the firm of Bayard & Hunter to secure his $5,000 note, payable in sixty-one days. Bayard & Hunter sold both the note and the right to foreclose on the mortgaged people to the Planters' Bank.[68]

These Georgia banks were also often willing to discount directly with their debtors. In October 1837, one slaveholder mortgaged to the Planters' Bank of the State of Georgia a piece of land in Savannah and eleven enslaved individuals "together with the future increase and issue of the said female slaves" to secure his debt of $13,500.[69] In February 1838, another slaveholder mortgaged eleven enslaved individuals to the same bank, securing a $3,500 promissory note due in sixty-one days. The bank granted this mortgage not just on this particular note, but also on "all other notes which may be hereafter discounted at and by the aforesaid Bank in renewal thereof."[70] A third slaveholder mortgaged an enslaved family of four to the Bank of the State of Georgia in May 1838 to secure a note of $1,400, due in sixty days, with a similar stipulation on renewals. This debtor renewed the note repeatedly, until it was finally "Cancelled and Satisfied" on January 14, 1840.[71] A female slaveholder likewise repeatedly renewed her $2,300 note with the Bank of the

State of Georgia, which she had secured with land in the city of Savannah, and eighteen enslaved individuals. Originally due sixty days after June 28, 1838, the bank finally "Cancelled" the debt upon full repayment on November 19, 1840.[72]

With its established coastal communities and its newly opened indigenous lands, Georgia's experience with banking straddled that of the old and frontier South. A number of small, older, traditional banks met the needs of the commercial community, while cotton planters in the western part of the state demanded more access to capital, which was only partially met by the Central Bank. Yet the eastern banking influence remained a powerful force in the state's legislature. While the legislatures of other frontier states would respond to these demands with a combination of plantation banks and joint banking-improvement companies during the 1830s, Georgia exclusively turned to the joint banking-improvement company model (chapter 4).

Financing Movement

Just as for any other merchant, access to credit was critical for the numerous slave traders who transported hundreds of thousands of surplus enslaved individuals from the states of the old South to the booming cotton and sugar plantations of the frontier. As Allen Gunn of Yanceyville, North Carolina, complained in 1835 to his slave-trading partner Joseph Totten, who was then traveling in Alabama: "[E]very man that can get credit in the Bank and his situation will let him leave home is a negro trader."[73] Yet as far as southern bankers were concerned, slave traders were little different from any other interstate merchant. Traders discounted their own sixty-day promissory notes at a Virginia or North Carolina bank and purchased enslaved individuals with the proceeds. They then transported the people to Mississippi or Louisiana, selling them at a profit—sometimes for cash but often receiving another promissory note as payment, which they discounted at a local bank. With the balance, they repaid their original promissory note and began the cycle anew.[74] As Isaac Franklin of the slave-trading firm Franklin & Armfield advised his Richmond, Virginia, associate Rice Ballard (of the firm of R. C. Ballard & Co.) in January 1832, "should you stand in need of funds you may borrow from your Banks at 60 or ninety [days] with full confidence that the money will be remitted to meet it."[75] And in June, when Franklin reported that his partner John Armfield was "considerably in debt and the banks have all stop[p]ed discounting in" Natchez, he instructed Ballard that he and Joseph Alsop (another trading associate) "must sustain [Armfield] through the Fredericksburg and Richmond Bank for from sixty to ninety"—again not needing to indicate that he meant days. "[I]n that time I have no doubt I will be able to forward you funds to meet any engagement you may make[;] you must sustain his credit for that time."[76]

Yet in an economy without a uniform currency, this interstate trade in remitting money was not quite so straightforward. Banknotes declined in value based both on the reputation of the issuing bank and the distance the banknote traveled from that bank. Mississippi banknotes would be worth far less once they arrived back in Virginia.[77] On one occasion in 1834, an associate of Rice Ballard who was then in charge of preparing "40 odd Negroes suitable for shipping" complained that he had tried to cash a check of Ballard's from the Bank of Virginia but "they did not want Virginia funds."[78] One alternative to this interstate movement of funds was for a merchant to obtain a bill of exchange from one bank, payable at another bank with which the bank had a correspondent relationship. For example, several southern banks solicited agreements with the private Girard Bank in Philadelphia during the 1830s. The Girard arranged with the Bank of Louisiana in June 1834 to accept foreign exchange in each other's name for up to $250,000.[79] At the same time, the bank was willing to discount notes arriving in Philadelphia of the Planters' Bank in Natchez for up to $50,000.[80] The Girard Bank reached other correspondent agreements during the 1830s with the Northern Bank of Kentucky, the Mechanics' and Traders' Bank of New Orleans, the Commercial Railroad Bank of Vicksburg, the Union Bank of Mississippi, the Grand Gulf Banking and Railroad Company of Mississippi, and the New Orleans Gas Light and Banking Company.[81]

Once these agreements were in place, banks and their customers could more easily move funds between locations. In April 1832, the Planters' Bank of Mississippi issued a bill of exchange for $7,000 payable "at sight" at the Phenix Bank in New York, to the order of R. C. Ballard & Co. Two months later, Ballard received another bill of exchange from the Planters' Bank, payable at the Phenix Bank for $10,000. Presumably, Ballard or one of his associates had discounted $7,000 and then $10,000 in promissory notes with the Planters' Bank—the proceeds of slave sales in Mississippi. Ballard or a representative of his firm could then present each bill at the Phenix Bank to receive New York banknotes. When payments due to the Planters' Bank arrived in New York—perhaps from the sale of cotton in England—these funds would be deposited at the Phenix Bank to the credit of the Planters' Bank, canceling its debt from the bill of exchange. R. C. Ballard & Co. similarly received bills of exchange from the Union Bank of Louisiana payable at the Merchants' Bank in New York for $15,000 in December 1832, for $10,000 in April 1833, for $5,000 in November 1833, and for $15,000 in December 1833.[82] Although the issuing bank would typically charge a fee to customers like R. C. Ballard & Co. for this service, it was more economical for the firm than making transactions in less desirable banknotes.

Whereas the reputation and location of these New York and Philadelphia banks made their funds highly valuable in trade, the most sought-after banknotes were those of the Bank of the United States, which circulated at par throughout the United States during the bank's existence. In May 1832, the Bank of Orleans issued R. C. Ballard & Co. a bill of exchange for $6,000 payable at the "Philadelphia Bank"—the main office of the Second Bank of the United States. Even better, it obtained a bill of exchange directly from the New Orleans branch of the Second Bank, payable at the Philadelphia office, for $5,000 in February 1832.[83] Whenever possible, banks tried to establish these correspondent relationships directly with the Second Bank, in order to increase the desirability of their own services. Stephen Duncan, president of the Bank of the State of Mississippi, traveled to Philadelphia in 1826 with a charge from the bank board to "affect any operation with the U.S. Bank here, 'greatly to the advantage' of our institution." Although the bank had a relationship with the Louisville branch bank, Duncan believed that "the enlargement of our credit" with the main bank would be beneficial, especially among "the negro traders & large dealers" who "w[oul]d always prefer checks" drawn on Philadelphia banks over Louisville ones.[84]

In many ways, the short-term renewable notes of traditional banks fit the needs of the slave traders quite well, but slaveholders moving to the frontier often required much-longer credit terms for the expansion of their labor force. As Isaac Franklin reported to Rice Ballard from Natchez, Mississippi in the summer of 1832, "nothing has kept the prices up this season but [that] the Branch US Bk[,] the Planters Bank [of Mississippi] and the old State Bank [of Mississippi] in the early part of the Season loaned out at twelve months."[85] The banks of the old South, in contrast, were less willing to bend their lending restrictions to fit these needs, yet the movement of their existing customers to the frontier often unwittingly pulled them into longer-term contracts secured by enslaved lives.

In July 1833, former bank cashier Marcus Cicero Stephens of North Carolina begged his onetime boss—Bank of Newbern president William Gaston—to deal leniently with his son Godfrey, who was past due on several notes to the bank, notes for which the father and Robert Primrose (a director of the New Bern branch of the State Bank) were endorsers. Godfrey had migrated to Florida and was now "in possession of a considerable property in land, stock and negroes." The son was planning to return to North Carolina "prepared to satisfy his friends here, by which I understood him to mean, furnished with means to discharge his bank debt past due since 1 April last, concerning which I had repeatedly and urgently written," but he had fallen ill on the trip and was delayed. The father was particularly concerned that the bank would no longer be willing to grant his son "a long indulgence" since its charter was expiring, and it might be "under the necessity of closing its business very soon." Regardless, the father thought that "his [son's] past conduct gave him no right to expect" an indulgence.[86]

While Stephen's long-term plan was to have Godfrey "transfer the debt to the Bank in Tallahassee, where he could attend to it with less trouble and expence [*sic*]," that would not solve the immediate issue. "I wish if possible that the Board will forbear taking ultimate and decisive steps in this matter until I can go to Florida and bring things to a close in some way or other." While he hoped to "save my son without disposing of his capital," he was prepared "to sell the negroes and bring or remit the money for the liquidation of the debt." Stephens believed that this would be a better outcome than "if the Bank of Newbern tired, as they may indeed, . . . with waiting," and consequently "order[ed] judgment to be taken, and execution to follow" on the father's North Carolina property, which would leave the family "destitute and houseless."[87]

Upon arrival in Florida, Stephens found that his son Godfrey's "affairs were in a very deranged situation, yet they were far from being irretrievable." He owed money "in the shape of notes and judgments," but also was the creditor on several "open accounts." Although the father tried "to negotiate a loan from the Bank of Tallahassee," he "found it impossible, not because of the insufficiency of the security offered but because the situation of the bank, real or pretended, forbid the accomodation [*sic*]." First chartered in 1828, the Bank of Florida at Tallahassee had largely ceased operations by this point in March of 1834. The Central Bank of Florida at Tallahassee had been chartered in 1832 to absorb the old bank, but it did not go into active operation until 1835.[88] Godfrey was only "enabled . . . to escape the loss of a Sh[eri]ffs sale" through the timely intervention of some wealthy friends. "That debt and several others have been discharged, his negroes and Cotton have been saved, the latter he has shipped to New York and ordered insurance, and what I esteem best of all, Godfrey has awakened from his lethargy and now sets about big business like a man ought." The father, as well, was converted to the potential of Florida as a country "that gives the strongest appearances of reward to the industrious and prudent planter. Every one of them who attends to his business is getting rich." If the Bank of Newbern was willing to lend Stephens $1,500 repayable in three years, it "would enable me to set in with means that afford a reasonable prospect of success." For security, he offered his existing property in Newbern, along with the land and enslaved lives he planned to acquire in

Florida.[89] While is unclear if the bank granted this new loan, this pressure on existing commercial banks to address the credit needs of citizens moving to the frontier only became more persistent during the boom years of the 1830s.

In May 1837, Thomas Green of Richmond, Virginia, was deeply in debt, owing the Bank of Virginia $17,400 and the Farmers Bank of Virginia $91,350 (over $4 million total in 2021). In order to "convince . . . the Directors of the Virginia Bank of my desire to place the debt I owe on the safest footing and to guard against the possibility of loss," he sent each bank several promissory notes, secured with a mortgage on his entire Red River plantation in Louisiana and its enslaved workers. Green believed that this land and human property "may reasonably be estimated at $80,000." He was simultaneously in the process of trying to sell this plantation, presumably to pay off these debts more quickly. His local manager had "<u>in three instances</u> made contracts of sale at $75,000 within the last 90 days, but neither was consummated as the <u>security</u> was not satisfactory." The third potential buyer had gone to Vicksburg, Mississippi, "to endeavor to get the security." In closing, Green promised: "I mean to exert myself, to the utmost, to pay the debts due, just as speedily as if I had not made this transfer" of promissory notes, "which is made, purely to satisfy all concerned of my desire to do what is proper."[90] Having allowed Green to accumulate such large debts, the Bank of Virginia was likely unable to refuse Green's offer of this plantation and its enslaved workforce as collateral, even if accepting it defied the institution's established banking practices. For the commercial banks of the upper South, short-term discounting of business paper remained their main form of lending; they were only reluctant participants in the speculative frenzy on the frontier, and their participation still remained limited.

Jurisdictional Disputes and the Vexing Problem of Heirs and Women

As banks crossed borders and dealt with collateral in other states, they often had to grapple with differences in property law. In southern courtrooms throughout the 1820s and 1830s, creditors and debtors battled over the priority of claims on mortgaged property, the legal requirements for recording mortgages and trust deeds on property classified as immovable (which could actually be physically relocated), and questions of fraudulent property conveyances. Most states required the registration of property sales, trust deeds, and mortgage liens at the county or city courts within a certain period of time, in order to establish legal ownership and protect future buyers or creditors from competing claims.[91] The question of whether enslaved people were legally classified as personalty or realty was especially relevant in the case of inheritance, married women's property, and the dower rights of widows; thus, these jurisdictional fights became particularly fraught when one of the parties involved was the wife (or minor children) of the debtor.

Under English common law, a woman's personal property merged completely with that of her husband, while he only retained managerial control of her realty. This meant that he needed her consent to sell or mortgage the real property she brought into the marriage, especially since doing so would impact her dower rights should she be widowed.[92] Upon his death, a widow was entitled to a life estate (for use during the remainder of her lifetime) in one-third of the real estate of her deceased husband (one-half if they were childless), which was protected from the claims of her husband's creditors. She also typically inherited outright one-third of the personal estate that remained after all debts had been paid (one-half if they were childless). Upon her death, the realty descended to the husband's heirs, while personalty descended to her heirs.[93] If she remarried, her new husband gained only managerial control of this dower realty during her lifetime, but absolute control of her personalty.[94]

Although there were variations in interpretation of this common law throughout the colonies, by the eighteenth century all colonies except Maryland and Virginia only recognized dower in realty. The classification of human property as realty or personalty could thus have an enormous effect on the widow's dower.[95] In South Carolina, where enslaved lives were defined as personalty, a widow inherited no bondspeople as part of her dower.[96] Even in Virginia and Maryland, where dower in personal property remained, the distinction was significant. Virginia, for example, defined enslaved individuals as personalty except in the case of dower, when they were defined as realty—which protected the human property from the claims of creditors but limited it to a life estate for the widow. Maryland, on the other hand, declared enslaved lives to be personalty—giving the widow an absolute right to one-third of the enslaved, but only after the settlement of her husband's debts.[97] Only in Louisiana, which had never operated under British common law, were women better protected (chapter 4).[98]

In property disputes between banks and their debtors, courts almost always sided with the bank when the debtor had behaved in a clearly fraudulent manner—for example, if a debtor secretly sold or conveyed his slaves to another person to evade the claims of a creditor, as Abraham Venable had done in 1821 in attempting to outwit the Lexington, Kentucky, branch of the Bank of the United States (chapter 2).[99] Yet during foreclosure proceedings, wives (especially widows) often claimed ignorance of their husband's financial dealings with banks, and sought to prevent the seizure of their enslaved people regardless of their husbands' fraudulent behavior. Even in substantiated cases of fraud, if the wife could portray herself as an unwilling victim of the husband's misdeeds, court rulings became much more unpredictable. A bank often had to prove not only that the husband had acted fraudulently, but that the wife had knowingly participated in the fraud and was not an innocent victim. Or, it had to prove that the (usually now-deceased) husband had *not* acted in bad faith, and that the wife's assertion of a prior claim on the enslaved individuals was instead truly fraudulent. The courts' moral concern for the impact of these loan contracts on financial dependents ignored altogether both the contractual rights of the banks *and* the ultimate fate of the human collateral at the center of these disputes.

In 1808, Ann Cross had received in trust four enslaved people as a gift from her mother for her personal use during her lifetime, a life estate that would descend to Cross's children upon her death (similar to the case in chapter 1 of Mary Rice from a century earlier). During the nineteenth century, trusts were a common legal mechanism used by the wealthy to shield their assets from creditors. The trust deed legalizing this transaction was recorded eighteen months later in Louisa County, Virginia, where Cross resided with her husband Oliver, although Virginia law required such deeds to be filed within eight months in order to be valid.[100] The mother-in-law allegedly purchased three more bondspeople from her son-in-law Oliver in the early 1830s, and then willed these enslaved individuals to her daughter upon her death in 1834, with the same stipulations. Ann Cross added these three individuals to the same trust deed. Yet there was no concrete evidence that a valid sale between mother and son-in-law had ever taken place; the Crosses could produce no bill of sale and their neighbors never saw any change of ownership of the enslaved people in question.[101]

In 1835, the Crosses relocated first to Tennessee and then (in 1836) to Mississippi with these seven enslaved individuals. At that point, Oliver solicited a loan from the newly chartered Northern Bank of Mississippi (1837), offering Ann's human property as collateral but representing them as his own. Ann was present for the appraisal of the property, and thus was later unable to deny her knowledge of the loan. Yet when Oliver died in 1838, Ann still protested the claims of her husband's creditors, contending that the enslaved individuals were her own property and thus out of their reach. Despite her clear knowledge of the loan, her lawyers asserted that she had been under no obligation to reveal to the bank the true status of the property as protected by a trust deed. Citing another recent Supreme Court case involving slave collateral in Virginia and DC, the defense argued that it was not "the duty of

Mrs. Cross to give notice of her title to the various persons from whom her husband may have obtained credit," since "such a duty imposed on a wife would conflict with the quiet and harmony of the nuptial relation, and would, in effect, be requiring the wife to publish to the community, that her husband was designing to defraud them."[102]

Despite all the evidence of Ann's complicity in the fraud—including the likelihood that Oliver had illegally gifted three slaves to his wife through his mother-in-law to evade creditors as well as Ann's presence at the loan appraisal—the Mississippi High Court of Errors and Appeals still viewed this *feme covert* as the innocent victim of her husband's misdeeds. In the words of Judge Alexander Clayton: "The law has thrown certain guards around a married woman to protect her from the influence of her husband. . . . Without undertaking to say that the conduct of a married woman may not be so fraudulent as to destroy her rights in some cases, we do not believe that this is a case of that kind." This court had effectively set an extremely high bar of proof for creditors to attain if they wanted to recover property claimed by widows.[103]

But whereas the courts were very sympathetic to wives and widows—even with proof of fraud—there was little concern for the enslaved individuals themselves, who were at the heart of these disputes. An example of this was the case of "a colored woman" named Milly—whose experiences were a preview of the famous Dred Scott case a few decades later.[104] In October 1826, David Shipman of Shelby County, Kentucky, was indebted to the Bank of the Commonwealth for $800, and to four other creditors for $1,067 more. To secure these debts, Shipman mortgaged all his property to his nephew Stephen Smith (as his endorser): twenty-six acres of land on Guess's Creek (likely Guist Creek), his grist- and sawmills, livestock, farm utensils, beds, household furnishings, one clock, and thirty-year-old Moses, twenty-five or twenty-six-year-old Milly, eighteen-month-old David, sixteen-year-old Harry, twelve or thirteen-year-old Bill, twenty-seven-year-old Sarah, and fifteen-year-old Eliza.[105] Law professor Lea VanderVelde, whose 2014 book documents this case in detail, identifies Moses as Milly's husband.[106] They named their son "David Shipman" after their owner, who had promised to free them.[107]

Overwhelmed by his debts and the prospect of losing everything, Shipman decided that it was better to pack up his property and leave the state: "Soon after the execution of said mortgage, said Shipman being greatly embarrassed, took the said Milly with several other of his slaves, and secretly ran away with them to Indiana . . . [and] executed a deed of emancipation to said slaves," which was dated less than two weeks after the mortgage contract itself.[108] Shipman set himself up on a farm in Tazewell County, Illinois, near a Quaker settlement where—according to Milly—they "resided in the same place exercising their freedom without the control of any person." But by January 1827, Smith had tracked them down and "seized them and claimed them as his property." The emancipated family appealed the action to the Illinois Circuit Court, which ruled in their favor and "discharged the petitioners from his custody." The family returned to live with Shipman "free and unmolested." Yet Smith came back on May 4, and "they were again seized by said Smith assisted by others and violently taken away in nighttime, and carried by compulsion to the City of St. Louis." Moses, who escaped from the abductors, returned to alert their Quaker allies of what had happened, and the Quaker community sent help to St. Louis. Five days later, Milly filed a petition with the St. Louis Circuit Court asking "that they and each of them may be permitted to sue as paupers to establish their freedom." Her petition to sue was granted.[109]

In the ensuing court cases, Milly was suing for her freedom based both on the deed of emancipation and her residence in free states. But in order to ascertain Milly's freedom, the courts first needed to determine how the mortgage lien affected her status as property. Although Shipman retained the "right of possession" as her owner, did the mortgage lien prevent him from selling or otherwise altering the collateral property's value without the consent of the creditor? In the first case, the Supreme Court of Missouri decided that "Smith had only a lien on her to secure the payment of debts; which lien Shipman might, at any time, have defeated, by paying those debts" to the bank, and thus Shipman, the debtor, retained full ownership rights by the laws of Missouri. But since the mortgage had been executed in Kentucky, the court remained sufficiently uncertain as to send the case back to the circuit court for reconsideration. Even if Shipman still owned Milly, did Smith's property lien prevent him from emancipating her?[110]

When the case made its way back to the Missouri state Supreme Court, the justices thought it was important to point out that, by the "statues of Kentucky . . . for the purposes of descent, slaves are real property, and that for the purposes of contract and execution they are personalty." They then sharply criticized Shipman as being "a man largely indebted, hiding his property, and in fact destroying it, to prevent his creditors from reaping any benefit there from, and in this case, Shipman has been base enough to emancipate the slave to injure and ruin his security. We feel disposed to view him in a light but little below that of a felon." Yet the court could not find his fraudulent intentions to be illegal. Unless and until Smith actually foreclosed on the mortgage, the enslaved woman was not legally his. In fact, the court ruled that—up until the creditor foreclosed—the property was Shipman's to do with as he wished, despite the lien. Ignoring Shipman's deed of emancipation, the court instead ruled that "by the act of residence in Illinois," Milly was now free.[111]

But by "general rule" of the court of chancery, mortgage creditors in Kentucky had twenty years to claim any collateral used to secure a debt; "after twenty years, the equity is stale, and the presumption is strong, that the mortgaged debt is satisfied."[112] Thus Milly's "free" status came with an asterisk. Her freedom was granted under the condition of being sub modo—that is, she was only free until Smith's "lien is enforced by some mode known to the law." He could not kidnap her, as he had tried to do, but if the bank tried to seize Smith's property as an endorser on Shipman's debt, Smith could legally foreclose on Shipman and claim Milly as property. "[I]f Smith should delay this for twenty years after his right to do so has arisen, then the presumption would arise that he had no demand, and her right to her freedom would be unconditional."[113] Milly's grant of freedom was thus extremely tenuous during this intermediate twenty-year period.

This problem of selling, removing, or otherwise altering assets used as collateral was not unique to human property, but the results were unique. In other cases in which property was sold to an innocent third party out of the reach of creditors, the courts ruled that this buyer could not be held liable—unless he had knowingly acquired property upon which there was a valid prior lien. The debtor could not just seize property that a third party had purchased "in good faith."[114] However, the courts treated Milly differently. Although she had also obtained legal "ownership" of her "property" in herself as an innocent third party, the lien on her remained.

Narrating the Experiences of Enslaved Individuals as Collateral

Whereas enslaved people certainly knew of the risks of sale and family separation that might occur with the death of an owner, it is less clear how aware they were of their use as collateral and the heightened risk of sale and separation that might come with foreclosure. Court cases and petitions where we hear enslaved voices—like that of Milly—were relatively rare. An alternative source, although still often mediated through white abolitionists, were the many slave narratives written by individuals after escaping to the North. Debt, bankruptcy, and the sale of enslaved men and women were common themes throughout these narratives. As Moses Grandy of North Carolina concluded in his 1843 narrative: "The proprietors, though they live in luxury, generally die in debt. . . . Many of them are great gamblers. At the death of a proprietor, it commonly happens that his coloured people are sold towards paying his debts. So it must and will be with the masters, while slavery continues."[115]

Grandy's account is filled with references to debts and mortgages. During the first decade of the nineteenth century, he recalled witnessing the arrest of one enslaved man. "I asked what he had been doing, and was told that he had done nothing amiss, but that his master had failed, and he was sold towards paying the debts."[116] Grandy's own father "was often sold through the failure of his successive owners," while his sister Tamar was auctioned in Norfolk after her master went bankrupt. The purchaser "treated her exceedingly well . . . but it was not long before she was claimed by a person, to whom Culpepper had mortgaged her before he sold her to Johnson."[117] Later, Grandy purchased himself from his master, but the master didn't honor the sale and instead mortgaged him to another slaveholder.[118]

In a few cases, mortgage contracts were central to the storyline and the person's ultimate escape to freedom. For example, after the death of Lunsford Lane's master in 1829, the Bank of New Bern (where his master had been the cashier) foreclosed on the North Carolina estate through a *fieri facias* suit in order to redeem $40,000 in unpaid bank debts. The widow was forced to sell "some of her slaves, and hired out others." Despite it being a violation of the law, Lane convinced her to allow him to hire out his own time, repaying her $100–$120 annually, but keeping the remainder for himself.[119] In this way, Lane was able to purchase his freedom by 1834 or 1835.[120]

Oftentimes, debt and bankruptcy resulted in the sale of enslaved people to the frontier South. Josephine Brown, the daughter of escaped slave and abolitionist writer William Wells Brown, later recounted his childhood. Born in 1815 in Lexington, Kentucky, Brown and his enslaved family were relocated to St. Louis by his owner (who was also his father) around 1828. As was the case with many frontier slaveholders, "speculation and mismanagement had so far reduced the Doctor's finances, that he found himself compelled to sell some of his slaves to repair his affairs, and Elizabeth, William's mother, was among the first that were sold." Although William remained with his father, "William had three brothers, who, together with his mother, were taken to the St. Louis negro market, and sold to the highest bidder." While a local "gentleman" purchased his mother, his brothers passed into the hands of a slave trader and were then sold to a planter "on the Yazoo River" in Mississippi, never to be heard from again. Writing in the mid-1850s, Josephine surmised that "If still living, they are lingering out a miserable existence on a cotton, sugar, or rice plantation, in a part of the country where the life of the slave has no parallel in deeds of atrocity. Nothing can be worse than slavery in Louisiana and Mississippi, on the banks of the noblest river in the world."[121]

Williams Wells Brown drew on this personal experience when writing what experts consider to be "the first African American novel" in 1853. In

Clotel; or, The President's Daughter, Brown indicted the system by focusing on the ruinous effects of slavery on marriage—which he called "the first and most important institution of human existence—the foundation of all civilisation and culture—the root of church and state"—for both slaveholders and their human property. As had been the case with Brown's own mother, the fictional enslaved woman Currer was the mistress of a rich slaveholder (who, in this case, happened to be none other than Thomas Jefferson) and together they produced two daughters: Clotel and Althesa. Yet Jefferson was not Currer's owner; she hired out her service and "kept house" for him, paying her wages to her owner. As the story unfolds, the fate of this woman and her daughters is intricately tied to the fate of the white men who control their lives, and particularly to the indebtedness of these men.[122]

The novel opens with the death of Currer's owner, and the sale of his "entire stock" of "thirty-eight negroes." Although Brown did not expound upon the details of the fictional owner's finances, mid-nineteenth-century readers would recognize that this sale was likely necessary to satisfy the owner's outstanding debts upon his death. Currer, sixteen-year-old Clotel, and fourteen-year-old Althesa all are placed on an auction block in Richmond, Virginia, where "farmers who make a business of raising slaves for the market . . . [and] slave-traders and speculators were also numerously represented." The same slave trader purchases both Currer and her daughter Althesa, and he immediately takes all forty recently purchased lives and marches them to the southern frontier. He sells Currer in Natchez, where she will later tragically die of yellow fever just before being emancipated by her new owner's daughter.[123]

The trader continues with Althesa to New Orleans, where the beautiful young girl is spared the worst atrocities of the auction when "a teller in one of the banks, who had just been married, and wanted a maid-servant for his wife" spied her in passing. "Pleased with the young slave's appearance," he "purchased her, and in his dwelling the quadroon found a much better home than often falls to the lot of a slave sold in the New Orleans market." Clotel, on the other hand, has attracted the love and admiration of the son of a local Richmond planter. Her white savior arrives at the auction "with a blank bank check in his pocket, awaiting with impatience to enter the list as a bidder for the beautiful slave," whom he successfully purchases and then lives with as his wife (until later in the novel, when his political ambitions clash with this illegal romance).[124]

Like Clotel, Althesa likewise attracts the attention of a young white Vermont physician living with her new owner. The doctor purchases and (believes) he marries Althesa, assuming that she is now free, and they have two daughters together. Yet when both Althesa and her husband die in 1831 during a yellow-fever outbreak, it becomes clear that he "had been dealing extensively in lands and stocks; and though apparently in good circumstances was, in reality, deeply involved in debt." The law did not recognize their marriage, and thus "his wife was, in fact, nothing more than his slave . . . and . . . his two daughters, Ellen and Jane, were his slaves." When his brother arrives from Vermont to settle his affairs, he is entirely unaware of the enslaved status of his deceased sister-in-law, and never includes the girls on "an inventory of the property" which was "placed in the hands of the creditors." Nonetheless, as they are all leaving the city, the girls are seized and their uncle arrested "upon the charge of attempting to conceal the property of his deceased brother." The uncle, "overwhelmed with horror at the idea of his nieces being claimed as slaves . . . even offered to mortgage his little farm in Vermont for the amount which young slave women of their ages would fetch." Yet despite his clever effort to use a mortgage as a means of their emancipation rather than their further enslavement, "the creditors pleaded that [the girls] were 'an extra article' "—likely a reference to their potential value as sexual objects—"and would sell for more than common slaves; and must, therefore, be sold at auction."[125] Brown interweaves bank checks, bank tellers, mortgages, and debts throughout the novel, not needing to explain their functions or justify their role in the plot development for his readers.

These same financial themes recur throughout the nonfiction slave narratives of the period. In the *Biography of Rev. Jermain Wesley Loguen*, the author is the son of Jane (renamed Cherry), who was kidnapped from Ohio as a child and sold into slavery in Tennessee, and David Logue, one of her masters. Logue had promised Cherry that he would free their son Jarm, but the slaveholder was soon overwhelmed by debts. "His real estate was considerably encumbered, and such was the pressure of his creditors that he foresaw he must sell his slaves, as well as his plantation, to escape hopeless bankruptcy." In order to save this estate, Logue reneged on his promise to Cherry. He "overcame his justice and instincts, and compelled a determination to convert his slaves, and even his own flesh and blood, into money to pay his debts."[126] Logue sold his entire enslaved community to a slave trader, but convinced the trader to sell Cherry and her children to his brother, Manasseth. This brother turned out to be a brutal master, and Jarm was relieved when he and his mother, along with some other enslaved individuals, were "mortgaged . . . to a neighboring planter, as a matter of personal economy, or as a means of raising money" sometime during the 1820s.[127] Yet unlike most traditional mortgage contracts, the creditor took physical possession of Jarm, Cherry, and the other collateralized people until the debt was resolved. His original cruel master later repaid his debt and, much to Jarm's dismay, redeemed these enslaved individuals.[128] Around 1834, Jarm successfully escaped to Canada on the Underground Railroad.[129]

Lewis Clarke of Kentucky was similarly aware of his master's monetary problems. In his biography, he comments on the "habits" of his master, which "did not produce great thrift in their worldly condition, and myself and other slaves were mortgaged from time to time to make up the deficiency between their income and expenses."[130] By the mid-1830s, Clarke was "put up upon the auction block for sale," but the sale failed because "there were two or three old mortgages which were not settled."[131] In this way, the mortgage created a legal obstacle that prevented his quick sale. On the other hand, Clarke also commented on the experiences of an enslaved woman named Susan, who "was taken by Mrs. Banton on mortgage" and thus separated from her husband.[132]

Perhaps the most well-known slave narrative involving a mortgage contract is *Twelve Years a Slave*. In 1841, Solomon Northup was kidnapped into slavery and sold by slave traders to William Ford. Soon afterward, Ford was forced to sell eighteen enslaved individuals to repay a debt to John Tibeats. Whereas he sold seventeen of these people outright to a local planter, he transferred Northup directly to Tibeats, retaining a mortgage on him for $400 since "the price agreed to be given for me [was] more than the debt." As Northup then foreshadows, "I am indebted for my life, as will hereafter be seen, to that mortgage."[133] After an altercation with Tibeats, the slaveholder was about to hang Northup when the sympathetic overseer intervened, reminding Tibeats of his mortgage with Ford. "If you hang him, he loses his debt. Until that is canceled you have no right to take his life."[134] Once again, the mortgage contract inadvertently helped an enslaved person by diminishing and dispersing some of the master's dominion over his human property.

While neither Loguen, Clarke, nor Northup specifically referenced bank mortgages, several other narratives did. For example, around the year 1840, William Craft of Georgia was working as an apprentice to a cabinetmaker. "But before our time expired, my old master wanted money; so he sold my brother, and then mortgaged my sister, a dear girl about fourteen years of age, and myself, then about sixteen, to one of the banks, to get money to speculate in cotton." Craft, however, only became cognizant of their use as collateral later, when the debt went unpaid. "This we know nothing of at the moment; but time rolled on, the money became due, my master was unable to meet his payments; so the bank had us placed upon the auction stand and sold to the highest bidder." While Craft, himself, "was knocked down to the cashier of the bank to which we were mortgaged," his sister was sold to a distant planter who eventually brought her to Mississippi.[135]

But in most cases, the narrative discusses mortgages without a specific reference to the creditor. After her escape to Canada, Mrs. Christopher Hamilton remarked that "the people who raised me failed; they borrowed money and mortgaged me."[136] Robert Nelson, another successful refugee, recalled that in 1845 "my master got involved and I was mortgaged. The mortgage was out and closed—the sheriff got after me, and I ran to Canada. I was to have been taken to a cotton farm in Louisiana."[137] William Walker, who was enslaved on a cotton plantation in Louisiana during the 1840s, discovered that the overseer had plunged the owner deep into debt. "During the week prior to the sale it was found out that there was an indebtedness upon almost every thing on the kingdom. All of the stock and more than two-thirds of the slaves were covered with mortgages, and the most of them were due, and his creditors came in swarms." The owner was forced to sell for a loss, since "the damage to the plantation wrought by the cyclone and the many mortgages and bills of credit made it impossible . . . to realize from the sale more than enough to satisfy his creditors."[138] As Annie Burton recounted in her memories of being enslaved around the Civil War, "At New Year's, if there was any debt or mortgage on the plantation, the extra slaves were taken to Clayton [Alabama] and sold at the court house. In this way families were separated."[139]

As these slave narratives attest, it was not only creditors who seized and sold enslaved bodies. The debtors themselves often had to resort to property sales to redeem their debts. The nature of the short-term discount loan—what made it most attractive to banks—was that it was in a constant state of liquidation. Every sixty to ninety days, debtors either had to repay the loan in full, pay an additional discount for the renewal, and/or secure the debt with collateral. In many cases, the ability of the debtor to offer a given enslaved individual as loan collateral may have prevented the necessity of selling that person and helped to stabilize communities—at least temporarily. But the incessant pressure to pay off debts left enslaved property particularly vulnerable to sudden sales.

❋

Charles Willson of Milton, North Carolina, owed several small debts in early 1825, including a short-term note with the State Bank of North Carolina. Knowing that he was in need of funds, in February he "sent out to georgia a negro to sell for the purpose of raising the instalment and paying one or two other small debts." Unfortunately, the representative he sent to perform the sale was delayed in South Carolina and would not be back with the funds for at least another month. Although it was Willson's "wish to renew the note immediately on his arrival," this delay made him delinquent with the bank. With no other recourse, he "confessed judg[men]t in favour of Debt due the State Bank of North Carolina for the am[oun]t of what I owe that execution." Yet he still hoped that his representative would return with the proceeds of the slave sale before the sheriff was able to complete the seizure of his property. He pleaded with Superior Court Judge Thomas Ruffin to "instruct the Clerk not to ishue [*sic*] the execution" for at least two more weeks. "If . . . my property is sold I shall be ruined thereby, and my endorsers property taken also." Willson believed that this request was reasonable since the creditor was a bank and not an individual. "If the debt was due to an individual and that individual was compeled [*sic*] to have the money at all events I should then feel willing to meet whatever might be my fate." But the bank was not facing such a precarious destiny and could afford to be a little more lenient, especially since "the debt is a very solid one and the Bank apprehends no doubt and her object is interest and gain by the loans she makes."[140] While the bank might not have liked this rationale, it was true that institutional creditors—with their investments spread across numerous risks—usually had much-greater ability to deal indulgently with individual debtors than a small creditor could.

Yet the conservative banks incorporated in the first decades of the century could never meet the rapidly growing credit demands of the frontier South—even if they had wanted to do so. During the 1820s and 1830s, the legislatures of this burgeoning region instead looked to charter their own state banks to inject liquidity into the booming economy. But to finance the needs of large-scale sugar and cotton planters, these banks had to adopt a lending model that was more amenable to securing loans with the vast wealth embodied in enslaved lives. While frontier legislatures would initially try to do this through incremental changes to existing charters (chapter 4), they would eventually experiment with an entirely novel banking model that inverted this relationship and instead based banking policy on the needs of the slave system (chapter 5).

4
Pushing Financial Boundaries with Traditional Banks

On February 24, 1820, the widow Le Breton (most likely Marie Vincent Le Breton, widow of François Joseph Le Breton D'Orgenois, marshal for the district of New Orleans and briefly mayor of the city) sold off many of her enslaved people at Maspero's Coffeehouse in New Orleans, with the help of her relative Charles Derbigny. Already a prominent lawyer (and future senator), Derbigny was the son of Louisiana Supreme Court justice and future governor Pierre Derbigny. Le Breton and Derbigny advertised "a gang of Forty Negroes, almost all of them creoles and honest fellows. There are amongst them, brick moulders, coopers, carpenters, cartmen, ploughers, shoemakers, seamstresses, ironers and cooks." The pair offered to finance the purchase on one and two years' credit.[1] Auctioned off to (at least) eleven different buyers, this sale shattered the community on Le Breton's plantation.[2]

The following month, Le Breton and Derbigny discounted with the Louisiana State Bank a $10,000 note, payable in four months and backed by the thirteen separate promissory notes obtained from this purchase "portant hypothèque sur les esclaves, en payement desquels ils nous ont été donnés" ["bearing mortgage on the slaves, in payment of which they were given."][3] Under its original 1818 charter, the Louisiana State Bank had vaguely been permitted to negotiate mortgages secured by real or personal property and to discount "on banking principles," implying short-term discounts of business paper. Yet just one year later, a charter amendment specified that it would "be permitted to discount paper having more than one hundred and eighty days to run," or six months.[4] One of the most important functions of banks was an expansion of the money supply through the issuance of loans, which promoted necessary economic development by facilitating exchange.[5] In the rapidly growing economy of the Southwest, where a large percentage of the region's wealth was tied up in land and human property, the ability to tap into these assets was essential for the region's economic success. Presumably, Le Breton and Derbigny would use their $10,000 bank loan to make other purchases of land or commodities, ensuring that the money continued to circulate in the economy, rather than stagnating in unpaid promissory notes.

In the aftermath of the Panic of 1819, the response of legislatures in Alabama, Mississippi, and Louisiana initially looked similar to that of legislatures in Kentucky, Tennessee, and Georgia. States chartered new banks and extended the privileges of existing banks to allow for lending of limited sums on longer terms secured directly by land and human property. In direct contrast to the banking system of the Northeast, many banks throughout the South were either fully or partially owned by the state, with the capital usually based on state revenues from land sales and other public funds.[6] Despite this contrast in organizational structure, northern and southern legislatures still chartered banks that adhered to the same traditional banking assumptions that lending should be based on short-term commercial paper and that long-term lending secured by property should be the exception rather than the rule. Yet what appeared similar on paper became something very different in practice.

In responding to the demands of slaveholders like Le Breton and Derbigny for greater access to loans directly secured by enslaved individuals, many frontier banks openly and actively embraced large-scale lending secured by the rapidly appreciating values of land and human property, often in open defiance of their charter provisions. And rather than reining in these banks, legislatures slowly adapted charter regulations to reflect the reality on the ground. These banks enabled the development of the expansive cotton and sugar plantations from Georgia to Louisiana that would form the core of the South's economy by mid-century. Frontier state legislatures likewise experimented with joint banking-improvement companies to finance internal-improvement projects to meet the infrastructure desires of the growing region. Yet the traditional banking model still fell short of meeting the financial needs of a rapidly developing slave economy. In Louisiana, in particular, the capital-intensive requirements of the developing sugar industry magnified the demand for large, long-term loans secured by enslaved individuals, ultimately forcing the legislature to reimagine completely how banks could best support an economy based on slavery (chapter 5).

Financing the Long-Term Demands of Louisiana Planters

With its thriving commercial port at the mouth of the Mississippi River, New Orleans had the most developed banking infrastructure of the frontier

South, yet it was still initially focused on the commercial interests of the city's traders and failed to address the acute credit needs of Louisiana's planters—particularly on capital-intensive sugar plantations. Although the Bank of Orleans and the new Louisiana State Bank were able to survive the Panic of 1819, the Louisiana Bank and the Planters' Bank both closed their doors in its aftermath, leading to competing demands from both New Orleans businessmen and rural planters for greater access to capital. For the planters, large long-term loans secured by their plantations and enslaved workers were essential for their survival and growth.

In 1824, the legislature chartered the Bank of Louisiana to meet the demands of both constituents. The state owned half its $4 million capital, which it financed through the sale of state bonds in the northern and European markets.[7] While the bank was permitted to discount notes for up to four months, it was *required* to lend at least half of its capital in long-term mortgages of up to $5,000 (about $143,000 in 2021), payable in five years. "Two millions of the capital stock of the said bank, shall be appropriated to the sole purpose of being loaned upon notes or bonds, secured by mortgages on immovable property," lending in sums of up to half the value of that property.[8] Headquartered in New Orleans, the bank opened three branches in the cotton-producing parishes of West Feliciana, St. Landry, and Rapides, one in East Baton Rouge—a mixed cotton-and-sugar parish—and only one in the sugar parish of Ascension (map 4.1).[9] For these branches, the Louisiana legislature required that "two thirds at least of the capital of such offices of discount and deposit shall be appropriated by them, for the purpose of loaning or discounting upon mortgages" for twelve months, which could be renewed for up to five years with the annual payment of interest and one-fifth of the principal.[10]

Recognizing that enslaved property was legally classified as immovable in Louisiana and thus could be used as part of the mortgage security, the 1824 "Rules and Regulations for Conducting the Business of the Bank of Louisiana" stipulated that "when the property proposed to be mortgaged, consists in a rural estate, the proposals must contain a statement of the number of acres of land actually cleared and cultivated; of the whole number of negroes, and of the number employed to work in the field."[11] The following year, the legislature revised the charter of the older Louisiana State Bank, allowing it to issue long-term renewals of discounted loans worth more than $500, with the debtor paying in four equal installments annually "on giving likewise approved mortgage, security or endorser, or other security, at the choice of the debtor." Loans of $300 to $500 could be paid in two years, while smaller loans could be renewed for a year, with similar security.[12]

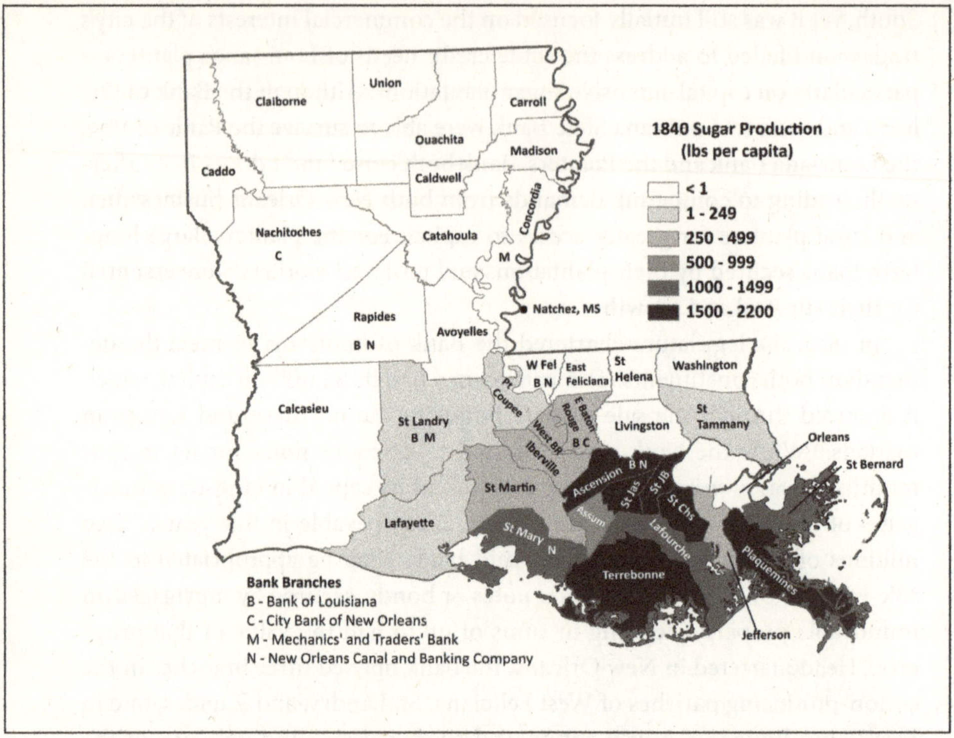

MAP 4.1. Louisiana sugar-producing parishes (1840) and commercial bank branches. Source: *Compendium of the Enumeration of the Inhabitants and Statistics of the United States, Sixth Census* (Washington, DC: Thomas Allen, 1841), 240; *An Act to Incorporate the Subscribers to the Bank of Louisiana* (New Orleans: Benjamin Levy, 1838): 22–23; "An Act to Incorporate the City Bank of New-Orleans," *Acts Passed at the First Session of the Tenth Legislature of the State of Louisiana* (New Orleans: John Gibson, 1831): 30; "An Act to Incorporate the Subscribers to the New-Orleans Canal and Banking Company," *Acts Passed at the First Session of the Tenth Legislature* (New Orleans: John Gibson, 1831): 56–58; George D. Green, *Finance and Economic Development in the Old South: Louisiana Banking 1804–1861* (Stanford, CA: Stanford University Press, 1972): 15. Map created by Peter Rogers, Head of Research and Education, Philips Memorial Library, Providence College, Providence, RI.

The Bank of Louisiana charter was also the first to reflect explicitly the unique property rights of married women in that state, and to address the potential problem of debtors hiding assets as part of the separate property of their wives. Unlike most other states, which derived their marital laws from the British precedent, Louisiana's civil laws reflected its past as both a Spanish and French colony. A woman maintained separate ownership of both her dowry—"that which she brings to the husband to assist him in bearing the expenses of the marriage"—as well as her paraphernal property, which was any additional property she might own or attain by gift or inheritance.[13]

Husbands possessed only managerial control over this property, and could neither reduce its value nor sell any immovable property—which included human property—without the consent of the wife. All additional property accruing during the course of the marriage was communal; the wife inherited one-half of this property outright upon her husband's death.[14]

This rather clear delineation of married women's property rights made it much easier for Louisiana banks to regulate mortgage contracts. The 1824 Bank of Louisiana charter stated outright that a wife could bind her property as part of the mortgage agreement.[15] The bank's rules and regulations then further stipulated that "no loan on mortgage security shall be made to any man having a wife living, unless the bond of mortgage be executed by the wife, jointly with her husband; she binding herself *in solido* with him, for the re-payment thereof."[16] In practice, this stipulation meant that every mortgage contract in Louisiana included a signed affidavit from the wife verifying her willingness to use her own property as collateral. For example, when Manuel Garcia mortgaged his St. John the Baptist sugar plantation and fifty-six enslaved lives to the Bank of Louisiana in 1834, his wife Aimée Masicot had to meet with the notary "out of the hearing of her said husband." The notary then read out loud her specific property rights under Louisiana law, citing each relevant article of the civil code. When finished, she had to "declar[e] herself to be fully informed of the rights which the law accorded or accords her upon the Estate of her husband . . . & that of her own free will and accord she formally renounces by these presents, in favour of" the bank all of her rights in the mortgaged property.[17] Other Louisiana banks followed this same policy, making wives' challenges to the mortgage claims of creditors much rarer than in other states. As one Louisiana judge explained in 1846:

> The establishment of banks necessarily threw upon them the business of lending money, and we can say, without danger of exaggeration, that nine-tenths of the whole debt due by the landed interest in this State, was due to the banks; so that, as far as the general policy of the State can be inferred from legislation and its necessary result, it was in favor of removing the disabilities of married women to bind themselves for the debts of their husbands, rather than of restraining them from making such contracts.[18]

In this judge's estimation, the credit needs of the state mandated the passage of laws allowing for married women to mortgage their property.

The shift to long-term property lending had a substantial effect on the credit options of planters in Louisiana. Large mortgages directly secured by land and human property became the norm for institutions like the Bank of Louisiana. According to the charter, branch loans and discounts were limited to $5,000 (about $138,000 in 2021) per individual, "without the express authorization of the board of directors of the mother bank."[19] In practice, however, the bank regularly approved loans of four to five times this amount. For example, one slaveholder in March 1830 received a $20,000 loan secured by a mortgage on his St. Charles sugar plantation and forty-nine enslaved workers, which he would not pay off until eight years later.[20] The following year, the bank lent the same amount to another pair of planters on their plantation and fifty-eight enslaved lives in Lafourche Parish. The partners remained indebted to the bank until 1838, when they sold the plantation to other slaveholders who assumed payment on the mortgage.[21] In April 1831, another pair of slaveholders mortgaged their sugar plantation in Jefferson Parish with 149 enslaved workers in exchange for a $25,000 loan. They faithfully paid it off over the next five years, fulfilling the terms by February of 1836.[22]

Although property loans at the bank were supposed to be limited to five years, they extended beyond that limit in two of the three examples above. The Bank of Louisiana regularly permitted longer terms, as long as the debtor continued to make at least partial annual payments, and the bank deemed the debtor still to be a sound risk. One cotton planter in West Feliciana mortgaged his plantation and eighty-three enslaved individuals to the bank in January 1826 in return for a loan of $28,260.80. The planter must have consistently paid enough of the principal and interest of this loan that the bank permitted it to extend for over twelve years. Finally, on August 3, 1838, the bank "received the full amount of the said Loan" and it released him from the mortgage.[23] In 1827, another slaveholder mortgaged a New Orleans city lot with its buildings and nine enslaved people for a $10,000 loan. When the owner died in 1834, a portion of this loan remain unpaid, but his estate settled with the Bank of Louisiana on April 23, 1838.[24] It is likely that this debtor's son paid the remaining balance by taking out his own mortgage. Just one day after the settlement (on April 24), the son received a relatively small $2,000 loan from the same bank, secured by his own plantation in the parish of Iberville and "sixty one Slaves now on and attached to the aforesaid plantation." Full payment on this modest loan was due in one year.[25]

On March 3, 1828, Philip Hicky and his wife Anna Mather mortgaged their sugar plantation, located four miles south of Baton Rouge, and fifty enslaved workers to the Bank of Louisiana in exchange for a loan of $15,000. Later that same month, Bennet H. Barrow of West Feliciana Parish took out a loan with the bank for an identical amount, secured by a mortgage on his cotton plantation on the Little Bayou Sara and sixty-seven enslaved individuals. Both Hicky and Barrow struggled to repay their loans, and remained indebted to the bank eight years later in 1836. But the bank still considered both of them to be good credit risks. For Barrow, who had paid back $9,000 of the principal, the bank extended the loan on the remaining $6,000 secured only by his land. The enslaved individuals were released from the mortgage, which protected this property from being seized in case the bank had to foreclose (unless the land still under mortgage proved to be insufficient). It also freed Barrow to sell these enslaved individuals without special permission from the bank, or to take out a new loan secured by his enslaved property. For Hicky, who had paid just $7,000, the bank extended the mortgage on the remaining $8,000 secured only by the enslaved property. If Hicky failed to maintain regular payments, the bank would seize and sell as many of these individuals as necessary to satisfy the debt.[26] In 1838, Hicky used his now unencumbered plantation and twenty-seven different enslaved laborers to purchase a hundred shares of stock (worth $10,000) in the Citizens' Bank of Louisiana, a new type of property bank discussed in chapter 5.[27] Barrow, for his part, paid off his remaining debt to the Bank of Louisiana by 1845, reapplying to the same bank for a new mortgage of $20,000 secured by this same cotton plantation and, now, 140 enslaved people.[28]

Louisiana merchants and planters both lobbied the legislature for even more banks; the legislature responded by chartering the City Bank of New Orleans in 1831 with a capital of $2 million and branches in Baton Rouge and the cotton parish of Natchitoches. Complaining that the existing New Orleans banks had "been converted into political engines" for the benefit of the merchants of the city, a competing group of businessmen successfully chartered the Mechanics' and Traders' Bank of New Orleans in 1833 as "a republican institution, got up to rescue the honest mechanic from the grasp of the opposition, and grant him facilities which he can enjoy without the sacrifice of his elective franchise."[29] Also capitalized at $2 million, this bank opened two branches in the cotton parishes of Concordia and St. Landry (see map 4.1).[30] The third new commercial bank chartered on the traditional model was the Merchants' Bank of New Orleans in 1836, with a capital of $1 million. The Merchant's Bank permitted up to eight years for the payment of mortgages and specifically listed "land and slaves" as suitable collateral on these loans. One-third of the bank's capital was designated for "planters of this State living out of the city of New-Orleans."[31] This latter bank would become the linchpin of Biddle's "national" banking system in the late 1830s (chapter 5).

The City Bank was to grant mortgages "on the terms and conditions contained in the charter of the Bank of Louisiana," the state's principal commercial bank, which capped mortgage loans at $5,000 and required the property assessment to be twice the value of the loan.[32] Also like the Bank of Louisiana, the charter of the City Bank of New Orleans stipulated that "at least one half the capital" (but "not more than two-thirds") would be "loaned on mortgage for the term of five years," with the debtor paying the interest and one-fifth of the principal each year.[33] Descriptions of banking functions throughout the period continued to highlight discounting as the main function of banks, and as the principal means of extending loans to the community. As Justice Martin of the Louisiana Supreme Court explained in an 1832 ruling: "Discount, in banking operations . . . is by far, the most important and the most common of the operations of a bank, and that through which (with a very few exceptions indeed) loans are exclusively obtained from any of these institutions."[34] And yet, by the time of this ruling, Louisiana banks had already shifted a substantial portion of their portfolios away from discounting and into long-term loans secured by land and enslaved lives. The reality of banking was diverging from the rhetoric of banking, at least on the southern frontier.

Upon opening its doors in 1832, the City Bank board of directors at the Baton Rouge branch immediately went to work issuing loans secured by land and human property. When the bank received an application, it assigned two directors to assess the value of the property being offered as security. On May 1, 1832, three slaveholders applied for $4,500 "to be secured by mortgage on their sugar plantation and slaves."[35] The property in East Baton Rouge on the Bayou Fountain included 120 arpents of land that were cleared and under cultivation, "all the Buildings & improvements thereon . . . and Ten Slaves."[36] The bank's assessment committee "rate the plantation & buildings $4000. The Slaves 5000. Total $9000," and the board voted to grant the $4,500 loan—exactly half the value of the property.[37]

That same day, another planter's application "for a loan of Five Thousand Five hundred Dollars to be secured by mortgage on his Plantation and slaves was read and referred to a committee."[38] A week later, the assessors also reported positively that this property offered sufficient collateral for the loan. They valued the plantation at $1,500, and the eighteen enslaved individuals at $5,400, for a total valuation of $6,900. The board voted to accept this application "on condition that the application . . . would cause all mortgages now existing on his property to be erased before the execution of the act of mortgage in favor of the Bank."[39] He received his desired loan of $5,000 on June 18, although his property assessed well below the $10,000 required.[40] In order to further protect the bank from multiple claims on a property, on May 15 it passed a resolution requiring all debtors "to produce a certificate from the Recorder of mortgage dated one day after" the mortgage approval, "certifying that since said inscription, no other mortgage had been recorded on the same property mortgaged to the Bank."[41]

In the case of Mrs. Mary Collingsworth, who had applied for a loan in late April, the assessment committee was "of opinion that no loan ought to be made on a property so much incumbered with mortgages."[42] While it is unclear what property she had originally offered as collateral, a week later she reapplied for a $4,000 loan secured by a plantation on Ward's Creek outside of Baton Rouge, "together with all the buildings & improvements thereon, and also on ten slaves." She added the names of two endorsers to improve her security.[43] Yet the bank committee still "reported unfavorably" since she had "not furnished satisfactory evidence of her title to the property offered to be mortgaged." Her application was again rejected.[44]

The board assessors were also unimpressed with the collateral of another slaveholder from St. Helena, who sought a loan of $5,000 secured by a cotton plantation and thirty enslaved lives.[45] They reported on May 15 that "the validity of the titles" to the property was questionable, and the board rejected his application.[46] He reapplied two weeks later, offering the same property: "1440 acres of Land . . . 250 of which are cleared and under cultivation, with all the buildings and improvements thereon, viz. a large dwelling house, cotton gin & press, also Thirty Slaves." Apparently he did a better job than Mrs. Collingsworth proving his title to this property in the second application. The assessors valued the property at $16,645, and the board approved his $5,000 loan on June 23.[47]

In all, the City Bank branch in Baton Rouge lent $31,000 on property mortgages during just its first month of operation (or about one-seventh of the capital allotted to that branch). Of these loans, $27,500 (or 89 percent) was secured by a combination of land and human property; only $3,500 was secured exclusively by land.[48] By the end of June 1832, the bank branch had lent $50,350 (one-quarter of its capital), three-quarters of which ($37,500) was partially secured by enslaved individuals.[49] In contrast, as of July 1832 the bank branch had only discounted short-term notes worth $8,558.33.[50] Although the balance sheets for this branch do not continue, the limited evidence indicates strong demand for property loans, and that enslaved lives were a critical component in securing these mortgages. And unlike the Bank of Louisiana, the Baton Rouge branch of the City Bank was resolute in sticking to the $5,000 loan limit in its charter. None of these early mortgages were granted for more than $5,000. When one slaveholder applied for a larger amount, the cashier informed him of the rule "which gives him the privilege to mortgage his land and slaves for Five thousand Dollars only."[51]

At the City Bank branch in Natchitoches (which also had a capital allotment of $200,000), the board was much more willing to lend for larger amounts, in direct violation of the charter. For example, by 1833 Absalom Barney Gill and his wife Ann of Alexandria owed the Natchitoches branch of the City Bank $15,000: $5,000 on discounted notes and another $10,000 for a mortgage on their cotton plantation and enslaved labor.[52] In April 1838, the Natchitoches branch again exceeded the limit, lending another planter $11,000 secured by his plantation on the Red River and thirty enslaved lives.[53] And one year later, a merchant mortgaged to the bank his entire property including a dwelling house, sawmill, warehouse, several tracts of land, and six enslaved workers, all of which he valued at $40,340 (about $1.2 million in 2021). The merchant stated that his "intention" in taking out this mortgage was "of giving a new course to his commercial transactions" by providing "all the necessary sureties and guaranties to those who may desire to become connected with him according to the new mode of transactions which he intends to follow." It appears that he wanted this mortgage to act as a line of credit for him to draw on as needed for his mercantile business. "The Said valuation may be changed from time to time, as circumstances may require and the amount increased by mortgaging other property."[54]

With a total capitalization of $10.5 million, Louisiana's five commercial banks (not including the New Orleans branch of the Second Bank) pushed the boundaries of traditional banking practices to extend large, long-term loans secured by land and enslaved laborers. Yet these adaptations were not enough, especially for the capital-intensive needs of the burgeoning sugar economy. Thus, at the same time that the legislature was expanding the types of permissible loans for traditional banks, it was also experimenting with new types of banks that were better adapted to the needs of its plantation economy (chapter 5).

Expanding into the Frontier of Alabama and Mississippi

In 1818, Alabama chartered its first two banks: the Tombeckbe Bank (in St. Stephens, just north of Mobile) and the Bank of Mobile, although the latter did not begin operations until 1820. Each had a capitalization of $500,000, 40 percent of which was owned by the state.[55] In 1820, the legislature chartered a much-larger institution with multiple branches to address the needs of citizens throughout the state. Capitalized at $2 million, the state initially owned half of the Bank of the State of Alabama. But before it opened its doors in 1825, the legislature decided to take full ownership of the institution, because it was "deemed highly important to provide for the safe and profitable investment of such public funds, as may now, or hereafter be in the possession of the state, and to secure to the community, the benefits as far as may be, of an extended and undepreciating currency."[56] In trying to strike a balance between the conflicting demands of planters for longer-term loans and more-conservative banking principles, the bank charter still emphasized its discounting functions, and no individual could be indebted to the bank as either a drafter or endorser for more than $5,000 in total.[57]

Upon opening branches in several cities, the state tried to further define this balance. At the Montgomery (1832) and Huntsville (1835) branches, total indebtedness was capped at $2,000. The legislation opening the Mobile (1832) and Huntsville (1835) branches quoted permissible interest rates for loans up to twelve months. In 1834, the legislature likewise amended the charter guidelines on the Bank of Mobile to permit loans up to twelve months. These intermediate-term loans could presumably be renewed as they came due, as long as the endorsements were still sound, but the total amount of indebtedness was sharply limited. Moreover, neither the charter of the Bank of the State nor that of the Bank of Mobile made any mention of securing loans through mortgages on property. In fact, the Bank of the State was forbidden from dealing in real estate "unless it be to secure a debt due said bank" through foreclosure on an overdue obligation. Still adhering to older banking practices, it could secure existing loans with property, but it could not initiate new loans in which property was the sole source of collateral.[58]

Despite the strict limitations implemented by the Alabama legislature, customers of the bank accrued significant loans secured by their enslaved laborers, which the bank turned into long-term loans through repeated renewals. Since the evidence documenting these practices mainly appears in the records from the bank's closure after the Panic of 1837, they will be thoroughly discussed in part III. Somewhat ironically, the legislature dramatically loosened the bank's charter restrictions during this panic—encouraging it for the first time to engage in the types of slave-secured mortgages that it was already practicing unofficially—in a desperate attempt to save the failing institution. Yet among banking institutions in the rapidly growing frontier states, Alabama's banks remained the most conservative in both their legislative mandate and actual function.

While the capital demands of cotton planters in Mississippi were likewise severely restrained by the legislature, slaveholders were much more effective in pushing for both amendments and new bank charters to meet their financial needs. Mississippi's first constitution upon attaining statehood in 1817 required that all banks be at least one-fourth owned by the state.[59] An 1818 amendment to the 1809 territorial charter of the Bank of the Mississippi thus renamed it the Bank of the State of Mississippi, expanded its capital from $500,000 to $3 million, and gave the new state a one-quarter stake in the institution. The amendment likewise guaranteed the bank a monopoly on banking services in the state until 1840.[60] Another amendment in 1822 allowed the bank to discount notes for up to 180 days (six months), "subject to one renewal, if the maker of the note desire it, and the endorsers continue to be satisfactory to the president and directors of said bank."[61] Yet this moderate amendment—combined with the conservative practices of its board—still severely limited the bank's long-term loans.

Even under these moderate lending terms, the Bank of the State of Mississippi often found itself in the position of buying and selling the land and human property in its possession. In 1821, for example, one slaveholder sent the bank "a valuable Negro, a black Smith by trade" named Moses, instructing the bank to sell the enslaved man "on account of his bad temper" and then to "apply the proceeds to the C[redi]t of my note." Originally purchased for $1,400, Moses was "now in jail, for beating his wife, & I fear to take him home lest he should kill her." But "with a master that could manage him," this slaveholder believed Moses "would be a most valuable man as he is a very good work man at the trade he has been brought up to." While he hoped that Moses "would bring 12 to 1500$" if the bank sold him in New Orleans, the slaveholder was willing to take "the best price he will bring." He also "expect[ed] to pay . . . commission on the proceeds" to the bank for its service.[62] It is unclear if the bank agreed to serve as the sales agent in this instance.

By the mid-1820s, Mississippi planters were increasingly complaining that the bank's lending policies were not meeting their needs. Some planters began lobbying for a branch of the Bank of the United States to open in the state, while others wanted the legislature to break the banking monopoly and open new banks with long-term lending privileges.[63] In response to these challenges, the Bank of the State began expanding its loan portfolio. For example, in settling the estate of Mrs. Jane White in 1826, the bank sold both her Mount Hope plantation and Botany Hills plantation on a mortgage payable over three years. "The personal estate consisting of Negroes, Horses, Mules, Cattle, Sheep, Hogs, and plantation utensils, will be sold on a credit" as well: sixty days for amounts less than $100 and twelve months for purchases over $100, implying that the enslaved workforce could not only be sold separately from the livestock and farm implements, but might also be broken into smaller lots.[64] That same year, another slaveholder solicited a loan of $6000, "payable one half next march & the balance the year after." In addition to the endorsement of his neighbor, he offered the bank "a Mortgage on his real estate & 30 slaves."[65]

By accepting mortgages collateralized with land or enslaved individuals, the bank risked having to take possession of that property through foreclosure proceedings; it would then have to own and manage the property until it could be sold for an acceptable price. In September 1819, Francis S. Girault's father-in-law, James Kempe, suddenly passed away during a yellow-fever outbreak in Natchez, Mississippi. Kempe left behind three married daughters (including Francis's wife Jane) and three minor sons, his wife having predeceased him in 1818. Kempe's extensive landed and human property holdings included the Rifle Point cotton plantation just across the river in Concordia, Louisiana (which he jointly owned with Francis), a neighboring plantation in Mississippi called Marengo, and another property forty miles south on the western shore of the Mississippi. With his death, the ownership of all of this property was thrown into chaos.[66] At this same time, Girault was already deeply indebted to the Bank of the State of Mississippi as the endorser for numerous notes (discussed in chapter 2).

Kempe's estate remained wrapped up in the probate court of Louisiana until 1826–1827, when the state finally began advertising the property for sale with the proceeds to be distributed evenly among the six heirs.[67] Francis, who owned half the Rifle Point plantation and had presumably been running the whole operation since Kempe's death, purchased the other half (of which his wife already owned one-sixth) for $8,500 in May 1827. This sum put the total value of the property at about $20,400. Lacking cash, he financed the purchase by issuing three notes equaling $8,500, payable to his wife's siblings. These notes were secured by the endorsement of his brother James Girault and a mortgage on the entire Rifle Point plantation, including all nineteen enslaved workers on the property.[68] The notes likely represented equal payments on the debt over the next three years.

Meanwhile, the Bank of the State of Mississippi was demanding payment on Girault's other outstanding debts. He quickly realized that he needed to deed the entire Rifle Point plantation to the bank to avoid wider foreclosure proceedings. In order to free the property from the mortgage lien of the Kempe heirs, Francis convinced his wife to mortgage to her siblings her one-sixth share in another of Kempe's properties—the Marengo plantation—to secure the $8,500 obligation. "He then got the husbands of the other two daughters, and the curator and tutor of the three minor sons and heirs of Kempe [who was also one of the brothers-in-law], to execute a release of the mortgage on the Rifle Point Plantation and the slaves sold at the probate sale, without the consent of a family meeting, or before payment of the mortgaged debt." Thus released from the mortgage on the property, in the fall of 1827 Francis conveyed the whole Rifle Point plantation to the bank, which valued it at $19,000 toward his debts.[69] The suddenness of this transfer was apparent from its timing in the middle of the cotton harvest. When the bank took possession there was "at this time about 90,0000 [*sic*] weight of cotton picked, and from 60 to 70,000 weight yet to pick."[70]

Having no desire to own or operate a plantation, the bank advertised the entire operation for immediate sale, including "500 acres, on which there is a good Gin, Mill and Press, overseer's house, negro cabins, &c. &c. About 140 acres cleared and now in cultivation, together with 21 slaves, 12 horses and mules, 3 yoke of oxen, a stock of cattle and hogs, farming utensils, and every thing else appertaining to the place." Hoping for a quick sale, the bank promised that "The *price* will be moderate if possession is delivered *immediately*," and it would even throw in all the cotton already picked. Additionally, the bank would finance the purchase with a mortgage payable in five annual installments—although there was nothing in its charter permitting such a long-term mortgage contract.[71] Unfortunately for the bank, there were no immediate takers. The bank was thus forced to run the plantation until a suitable buyer could be found. Extant receipts from the summer and fall of 1828 record the bank's purchases of various meat products for the plantation, including bacon, ham, chidlings, and two barrels of pulled pork.[72] Finally, in September 1828, it was able to sell the entire plantation to Dr. Thomas Hunt for an unknown amount.[73] Presumably, he would pay the bank in five annual installments from 1829 to 1833.

Despite Girault's attempt to appease his debtors, the bank and several other creditors still sued in the state of Mississippi, successfully receiving a court order to foreclose on another of Girault's plantations. On May 1, 1828, the sheriff of Adams County, Mississippi, auctioned off "the plantation where the defendant now resides," which consisted of 250 acres of land about 2.5 miles from Natchez, including the dwelling house which—the ad noted—was "handsomely finished." Also included in the sale were seven enslaved individuals, listed by name, as well as all the livestock, farm implements, buildings, and "also, a large and elegant assortment of household and kitchen furniture, (except such as is exempt by law)."[74] At this point, his wife Jane must have realized that not only her family's home but her entire inheritance was being consumed by the debts of her husband. In February 1829 she "went before the parish judge and protested against the act of mortgage, executed by herself and husband on the Marengo plantation" from two years prior "and disavowed the whole proceeding."[75] Her siblings, who would be left with nothing if Jane's disavowal succeeded, sued for the original collateral—the Rifle Point plantation and its enslaved laborers—who were now in the possession of Thomas Hunt. Even Jane decided to cast her lot with her siblings over her husband, filing for a legal "separation of bed and board" from Francis sometime around 1832; she would remarry two years later.[76] In April 1832, the district court ruled that the Kempe heirs had not legally signed over their rights and still held a valid mortgage on the Rifle Point plantation. Hunt and Francis Girault were ordered to pay $22,000 to settle the dispute with the siblings, which they both appealed.[77]

Francis appears to have been completely bankrupt by this point, so the only recourse of the heirs was to go after Hunt. But if the heirs foreclosed on Rifle Point, Hunt would cease payments on his mortgage to the bank, and might even sue the bank for all the purchase money he had already paid. Therefore, the bank hired prominent attorney (and future associate justice of the Louisiana Supreme Court) Abner Nash Ogden to defend Girault and Hunt at the Supreme Court of Louisiana. The bank agreed to pay Ogden $200 for arguing the case, and another $200 if he either "should succeed in the Supreme Court in obtaining a final judgment in favour of the Defendants" or if the case were remanded back to the district court, where he would "attend to it" as well.[78]

Despite this robust defense counsel, the court ruled in October 1832 that the heirs had "a right to pursue their claim to recover the original debt against the purchaser at the probate sale," meaning Thomas Hunt, "and to require the mortgaged property to be seized . . . and sold to satisfy their judgment, unless he prefers to pay the amount for which it was mortgaged, or voluntarily surrender it to be sold." The court gave Hunt just ten days "to satisfy said judgement."[79] But before Hunt could sue the bank to recover his past payments, the bank quickly accused him of being delinquent on his debt and foreclosed on his mortgage for the plantation, forcing him to "surrender it to the Bank because of [his] embarrassment."[80] By an act of the legislature of March 7, 1834, the State of Louisiana then granted to the Bank of the State of Mississippi permission to own this out-of-state plantation with its twenty-one enslaved lives, pending final sale.[81] The bank resold the plantation later in 1834 to Lemuel P. Gustine for a greater sum than it had received from Hunt, satisfying the claims of the Kempe heirs and making a further profit in the deal.[82]

Thomas Hunt was incensed by this outcome, especially since he was the most innocent of all the parties to the entire transaction. In a letter spewing vitriol—even the rushed handwriting seemed to drip with anger—Hunt lashed out at the bank and its president Stephen Duncan. "The Bank st. Missi. has forced me as far as it could & since I ask it no favors, because of its inability to hurt me any more, what I have to say on the subject of the Rifle Point plantation shall be said in a Court of Justice where I hope I will have full credence for my statements." Hunt recognized the cleverness of the bank in turning his missed mortgage payment into a timely foreclosure proceeding on a property rapidly rising in value. "You & the Bank in the Plenitude of your Power & wisdom as to foresight (about my Embarrassments) have decreed that I am broke & must be sacrifised [*sic*] to Bank interest." He concluded that the bank had been shortsighted in its decision. "If you had let me keep the Rifle Point plantation I would have paid you more than you have been paid, & now have been comparatively rich. But no! I must be sacrificed."[83]

In a second letter of the same date—still written in anger but with a slightly calmer hand—Hunt reiterated "The Bank forced me to a closure of the debt due by me for the Rifle Point plantation. I would have paid more for it by this time than has been paid without any difficulties & consider I have lost several thousand dollars thereby."[84] Finally, a third letter arrived the next day—signed in Hunt's name but, based on the handwriting and spelling, clearly written by someone else who believed in the power of honey over vinegar in the art of persuasion. Offering "an apology for some harsh expressions contained in my letter of yesterday," the writer explained that it was "the manner of the Rifle Point plantation slipping through my hands" that "provoked" him in "the idea of how much better off I might have been since the rise of property [values], had I retained it." This representative—perhaps his wife, an attorney, or just an interested friend—pled with the bank to "receive this apology as satisfactory" and consider returning to Hunt what "a sense of justice tells me it is due"—presumably the payments he had made on the plantation mortgage.[85] But this satisfaction never came, and Thomas Hunt died less than three months later at the age of thirty-six. By then, the new owner, Lemuel Gustine, had already been dead a full year (passing at the age of thirty-nine), and Rifle Point and its enslaved occupants passed to his older brother, Dr. Samuel Gustine—who happened to be the brother-in-law of the Bank of the State's president, Stephen Duncan, as well as a banker in his own right.[86]

The elder Gustine grew the plantation over the next decade. By the time of his death in 1845 at the age of sixty-one, the plantation consisted of "2000 acres of land—700 in cultivation, ditched and under excellent fence . . . the finest Cypress, Ash and Cotton wood timber . . . a most comfortable dwelling house," numerous outbuildings, gins, presses, and livestock, and 175 "of the finest acclimated negroes" including "two excellent blacksmiths; two engineers, capable of running a steam saw mill; three good carpenters, able to frame and make sash; two shoemakers; one excellent brick layer and plasterer; one good painter and plasterer and one good body servant and barber." The estate sale promised that these enslaved people "will be sold in families," although there was no way to guarantee that outcome.[87] Presumably he had paid off the original mortgage, since the estate sale mentioned no outstanding debts on the property.

Even as the Bank of the State of Mississippi expanded its lending practices in response to the demands of local planters, the calls for more banking facilities in Mississippi continued. On February 10, 1830, the legislature chartered the Planters' Bank of the State of Mississippi, with the stated purpose to "give impulse and vigour to agricultural labour, activity to commercial enterprise, and increased value to our lands."[88] The state provided two-thirds of the bank's three-million-dollar capital fund; it funded half of this by removing one million dollars in state funds from the Bank of the State, essentially hobbling that institution.[89] The state financed the other half of its investment through the sale of one million dollars in long-term bonds, much as Louisiana had financed the Bank of Louisiana.[90] Yet this was not a plantation bank (discussed in chapter 5), despite its misclassification as such by some scholars.[91] The state-backed bonds of plantation banks were ultimately secured by mortgages on the land and human property of stockholders. In the case of the Planters' Bank, the state itself was the stockholder and the bonds were backed solely by the taxing ability of the state. In his January 1835 message to the state, Governor Hiram Runnels critiqued the limited lending capacity of the new Planters' Bank as "a mockery of banking principles" and instead "recommend[ed] the establishment of a bank on the principle of the Union or Citizens' Bank of Louisiana, the stock of which to be taken by planters on the mortgage of their lands"—i.e., a plantation bank.[92] But, in the words of one Mississippi banking historian, "The legislature had no legal power to incorporate a planters type bank."[93] Mississippi would not charter its first plantation bank until 1837, when it incorporated the Union Bank of Mississippi.[94]

Rather than being a plantation bank, the Planters' Bank was modeled more on the Bank of Louisiana, both in its capitalization and its lending practices. Its charter specifically granted the "power to make loans to citizens of this state in the nature of discounts on real property, secured by mortgage" for up to $4,000 for one year, and renewable for up to four years "upon the payment of one fourth of the principal due and the regular and prompt payment of the interest."[95] That same day, the legislature also amended the charter for the Bank of the State to allow it "to discount paper for twelve months," although this brief amendment made no mention of either dollar limits or renewals.[96] Several months later, the legislature also approved the opening of a branch of the Second Bank of the United States at Natchez.[97]

Proponents of the Planters' Bank defended its embrace of twelve-month property mortgages. One editorialist, who directly addressed his letter to the president of the Bank of the State of Mississippi, endorsed the structure of the new Planters' Bank as "preferable to renewals every sixty days, or to our accommodation loans," which unnecessarily forced planters into the habit of "retaining for contingencies several hundred dollars in the coffers . . . money so kept is of no use either to the owner or the public."[98] Another commentator asserted that the new bank's charter "has been drawn with great care and talent, and its provisions adapted to the peculiar situation and interests of this State." Unlike other banks that relied for their "stability on the uncertain and often delusive support of extensive mercantile establishments," the Planters' Bank was "based on the rich staple commodity of the country." Reflecting rapidly appreciating prices for land and enslaved lives of the time, this editorialist averred that "it is further impossible that there ever can be a total failure of a Bank based on the planting interest of this State. . . . Such a thing as the failure of a planter, is hardly known amongst us; and it is hardly possible, even, with the most gross mismanagement, to sink the profits, much less the whole capital, of an institution so carefully guarded, and so firmly supported as the Planters' Bank." If this bank were to fail, it would mean that the state had already descended "into the most abject poverty and disgrace."[99] This commentator, who had clearly forgotten about the Panic of 1819, never anticipated that an even more intense economic depression would occur by the end of the decade.

While the Planters' Bank was still in the process of organizing, the Bank of the State began lending under its amended charter, even directly financing mortgages for the purchase of enslaved individuals. One slaveholder, for example, "made an investment in negro property" in November 1831 that "not only exhausted my means, but the Balance due must be paid in a very few days." Lacking immediate funds although he had "very considerable sums of money owing me," he sought a loan from the bank to pay off this purchase of enslaved lives. He was willing to "cheerfully submit to any terms you might think reasonable and just."[100] The following month, another slaveholder found himself similarly indebted. He had purchased "some ten or fifteen negroes" from his father-in-law's estate in South Carolina, but was short "four or five hundred dollars" to finish paying the sale's agent due to "the storm which verry [*sic*] nearly destroyed his present crop." This bank loan would prevent the agent from reclaiming the enslaved property.[101] Two days later, a third slaveholder sought to discount a note for $525, payable in twelve months, to finance the "negroe" he had "this morning purchased."[102]

Yet even as it attempted to satisfy the financial needs of slaveholders with more-lenient banking practices, the Bank of the State simultaneously challenged the very existence of its new competition—both by undermining sales of Mississippi bonds intended to capitalize the Planters' Bank, and by citing the monopoly privileges granted in the Bank of the State's 1818 recharter as a bar to the new bank's existence. Cashier Gabriel Tichenor, for example, wrote to the cashier of the Mechanics' Bank of New York in June 1831 that "Mississippi Bonds for the New York money market are now on the way there." He warned his New York counterpart that "these bonds as you probably know, form the basis of a new Bank which has been lately got up by persons of no experience or sober calculation, in violation of the chartered rights of our Institution." Tichenor likewise implied that the bank might never even open its doors. His letter stated that the old bank had consulted with prominent Philadelphia lawyer Horace Binney, who was of the opinion "that the Bank Charter is not only unconstitutional but its operations can be suppressed by an injunction." In the meantime, he encouraged the Mechanics' Bank cashier "to lay this information before any persons interested in it, at least among your friends suppressing the source whence you have gained the facts," in order to undermine bond sales.[103]

Tichenor was being a bit deceptive, since the bank had not yet heard back from Binney with his legal assessment. During the months of June and July, bank president Stephen Duncan separately laid out his argument as to the unconstitutionality of the Planters' Bank charter, soliciting Binney's opinion as how best to "stay the proceedings" of the new institution.[104] In addition to violating the Bank of the State's monopoly privileges, Duncan believed it also violated the "unequal taxation" prohibition in the United States Constitution. While the Bank of the State had been paying state taxes on its stock and dividends since 1820, "the charter of the 'Planters Bank' exempts that Institution from all taxation." Not only was this "personal tax on our stock . . . oppressive," but—echoing the language of Chief Justice John Marshall in his 1819 *McCulloch v. Maryland* ruling—Duncan asserted that "If the Legislature presses the right to tax one State Institution and exempt the other, they have also the power to destroy the 'Bank State Missi' by onerous taxation."[105]

Duncan awaited Binney's quick reply, but if Binney's "health will not admit of the necessary application to enable you to accomplish this" assessment of the situation, "I must beg the favour of you to hand the papers over to Daniel Webster Esqr of Boston" for his expert legal opinion.[106] And "if you should not find it convenient to secure the services of Mr Webster I presume the opinion of Chancellor [James] Kent [of New York] would next be proposed."[107] By September, Duncan was separately pressing his case with Senator Webster. He had sent him a "memorial" containing "a correct history of the origin of this Institution, which may be important in determining its rights." If he could obtain Webster's legal assessment, "It is the intention of our Directory to publish your opinion . . . in Pamphlet form for distribution throughout the State." The bank would pay his legal fee "through the Office of the United States Bank in your city."[108]

Yet by November 1831, even as rival banking proponents continued to argue in the press, the board of directors of the Bank of the State had given up any hope of being able to compete with both the new state institution and the new branch of the Second Bank of the United States.[109] Duncan negotiated a deal with Planters' Bank president Samuel Gustine—his brother-in-law and soon-to-be owner of the Rifle Point plantation—in which they agreed to transfer the majority of the business of the old bank to the new one.[110] In response to concerns "that the present capital of the Planters Bank will be considered too limited for the wants of the community . . . especially if our discounts are reduced," which "would be most injurious to the planting interest," the Bank of the State would continue renewing its existing discounts until 1837. Although this agreement benefited the new bank more than the old, Duncan believed it was unavoidable. Without this compromise, "[b]oth (Institutions if continued) would have to conduct their business more with an eye to safety than to profit, and the Branch Bank [of the United States] would reap all the benefits of our caution."[111] On November 17, the stockholders of the Bank of the State "unanimously determined to close the affairs of the Bank" in accordance with this agreement.[112]

As the two banks awaited legislative approval of the controversial deal, Daniel Webster finally sent his legal assessment of the situation. He unequivocally determined that the new Planters' Bank charter was in violation of the agreement made by the legislature with the Bank of the State, and thus "repugnant to the Constitution of the United States."[113] The editors of the *Natchez Gazette* ran his extended analysis in full on the front page, and then editorialized that the legislature now had no option but to sanction the proposed agreement between the two banks. "Should the Legislature, as has been intimated and feared, interfere, and attempt, by imposing restrictions, and chaffering down their proposals, place a barrier in the way of a conciliatory and final arrangement, between the two Banks, they will assume to themselves the responsibility of having plunged their constituents and even their discendants [*sic*], into the prospect of an awful state of confusion, if not, ultimate, irretrievable ruin." If the deal was not ratified, the elder bank would certainly use Webster's analysis to sue the new bank, putting the legislature in the position of "defending a law suit, doubtful in its result" which—"among other evils"—would "implicate the character of our state abroad—and prejudice the character of the [Planters'] bank, should it even survive the shock."[114] The legislature heeded this warning and soon authorized the deal. But Duncan was not done with banking. By March 1833, he had obtained a state charter for the new Agricultural Bank of Mississippi, which was capitalized at $500,000 without any state ownership.[115]

As per its agreement with the Planters' Bank, the Bank of the State continued renewing existing loans. In February 1832, one slaveholder was having a hard time paying off his discounted notes to the bank. He "understood that the Bank would extend the time to those indebted to them for a term of 5 years by paying interest. . . . [I]f this be a fact I would like this indulgence woul[d] be extended me." By thus renegotiating the terms of his debt, he would also be able to "make a purchase of 2 or 3 negro fellows that would enable me to carry on my farm to a much greater advantage."[116] The following month, another slaveholder inquired about "a rumour which is going the round here, that the several banks at Natchez refuse to discount for a longer period than 60 days." In all likelihood, this "rumour" referred to the newly opened Natchez branch of the Bank of the United States, which did indeed still limit discounts to sixty days (at least officially). These terms would not work for this planter; he did "not wish to effect a loan, for a shorter term than 12 months." But if the bank was willing to lend him $3,000 on those terms, he would be able to go to Virginia to purchase "a few negroes for my own use." He wanted to make it perfectly clear to the bank, however, that his purpose was not to speculate in enslaved lives, emphasizing "the negroes being for my own use & not for sale."[117]

The Planters' Bank finally opened its doors for business in 1833. By the language of its 1830 charter, the legislature seemed to have envisioned long-term mortgages mainly on land. Section 23, for example, discussed "mortgages on immovable property" and forbade it on "lands not in a state of improvement." Section 24 allowed for the appointment of local commissioners "to value and appraise the lands which shall be offered in mortgage" and called for the certification of "every valuation of lands" by at least three of these commissioners.[118] In contrast, it made no mention of the appraisal or valuation of enslaved individuals. Yet the bank quickly began approving large loans secured by both land and human property. In order to get around the $4,000 limitation on mortgages, the bank structured these loans as discounts through a third-party endorser—as several banks did in other southern states.

For example, in February 1835, John Tucker sought a $65,000 loan (about $2 million in 2021) from the Planters' Bank. He issued ten promissory notes of $6,500 each to James J. Chewning and William H. Washington, payable over the next five years, and secured the notes with a mortgage on three tracts of land and a group of fifty-two enslaved individuals. Tucker separately mortgaged another group of twenty-three people to secure two more notes totaling $13,000, issued to Benjamin F. Michie and John M. Chilton. If Tucker failed to pay any note as it became due at the bank "with all interest and costs," then the holder of the note in question could "take into possession so much of the said property as may be sufficient to pay the said note or notes so due and unpaid" and then "proceed to sell for cash the said property" in order to repay the bank. In addition to evading the mortgage limit, this structure helped the bank avoid having to take responsibility for seizing and selling the property in case of default. Chewning, Washington, Michie, and Chilton were effectively serving as endorsers on the notes, with a property mortgage to protect their interests.[119] The Planters' Bank executed a similar large loan with another slaveholder in 1835 for $70,000 (about $2.2 million in 2021).[120] On the other hand, the bank dealt directly with smaller debtors, such as when a husband and wife mortgaged their land, thirteen enslaved laborers, livestock, and farming utensils to the bank in October 1840 in return for a twelve-month loan of $2,700.[121]

This legislative expansion of banking practices in Mississippi, both through the incorporation of the Planters' Bank and the opening of the Second Bank branch at Natchez, still fell short of the needs of the state's economy. Yet once the Bank of the State's monopoly on banking had been broken, the Mississippi legislatures of the 1830s—like those of neighboring Louisiana—began considering more-innovative ways to meet the capital needs of the state's enslavers, such as through the incorporation of joint banking-improvement companies. Although these improvement banks were not exclusive to the South, the integration of these banks into the system of slavery did give them unique qualities.

Improvement Banks

Throughout the country, state legislatures of the 1830s began experimenting with bank incorporations as a magic bullet to provide funds for educational institutions and major internal-improvement projects without the necessity of raising taxes. As economic historians Richard Sylla, John Legler, and John Joseph Wallis argue, banks were an important mechanism of public finance for many states.[122] The chartering of corporations with ancillary banking privileges dates back (at least) to 1799 with the incorporation of the Manhattan Company to supply fresh water to New York City. Aaron Burr shrewdly inserted a clause in the charter of the company that allowed it to invest any extraneous capital not needed in the waterworks for "any other monied transactions or operations not inconsistent with the constitution and laws of this state or of the United States."[123] He then proceeded to apply $500,000 of the company's $2 million capital to the creation of a bank. In banking historian Howard Bodenhorn's assessment, "when public opinion opposed additional bank charters, surreptitious methods were resorted to so that legislators could charter banks and then claim to have been duped." The legislature repeated this scheme with the New York Manufacturing Company in 1812, the Aqueduct Association in 1818, the Delaware and Hudson Canal Company in 1824, and the New York Chemical Dock Company in 1825. Bodenhorn continues: "It was likely that legislators resorted to cloaking a bank in a nonbank charter when the demand for banking services increased, but chartering a single-purpose financial institution would have alienated an important or vocal constituency." With the exception of the Canal Company, each of these firms would eventually drop their initial improvement charge and become full-fledged banks.[124]

While these companies may have fulfilled their stated purposes—the Manhattan Company did construct and operate a waterworks until the 1840s—the main intent behind each was the creation of a bank.[125] In other parts of the country, this relationship was inverted. Legislatures in the South and the West, in particular, had often viewed banks as a means of financing public goods without having to resort to unpopular taxation—a form of what economic historian John Joseph Wallis terms "taxless finance."[126] In Virginia, both the 1812 charter of the Farmer's Bank and the 1814 recharter of the Bank of Virginia set aside shares of stock for the benefit of the state, to be paid for by a tax on shareholders.[127] Then, in 1816, the Virginia legislature passed a new law requiring all newly incorporated banks to pay a bonus premium and provide a portion of their stock to be invested in the state's internal-improvement fund. In this way, the state anticipated being able to raise $1,125,000 over ten years, and through "this novel though productive system of finance" accomplish many "public improvement[s]" with "a very inconsiderable part, if any, [being] derived from the pockets of the people, by the imposition of taxes."[128] The following year, the act incorporating the Northwestern Bank in Wheeling and the Bank of the Valley in Winchester designated that stockholders would pay an additional 15 percent for state-owned shares "for the benefit of the fund for internal improvement."[129]

The state of Kentucky, which owned half the stock in the Bank of Kentucky (incorporated 1806), expected to be able to fund desired projects ranging from internal improvements to education based on accumulated dividends, and to do so "without materially increasing the public burdens" [i.e., taxes]. In Governor Slaughter's 1817 address to the Kentucky legislature, for example, he urged it to allot a portion of the dividend along with "a tax on banks and such corporations, as from their nature are proper subjects of taxation . . . for the purpose of establishing an extensive and convenient system of education."[130] The following year, the Kentucky Senate likewise passed a bill "almost unanimously, appropriating $40,000 annually, out of the dividends arising on the State's Bank stock, for clearing out the obstructions on" four of Kentucky's major river arteries.[131] In South Carolina that same year, the state-owned Bank of the State issued $80,000 in state bonds to build a railroad between the cities of Charleston and Hamburg. Secured by the bank's capital, the state intended to pay off the bonds through the profits of the bank.[132] Even the 1830 charter for the Planters' Bank of the State of Mississippi was intended "by a creation of revenue, [to] relieve the citizens of this state from an oppressive burden of taxes, and enable them to realize the blessings of a correct system of internal improvements."[133] Bank incorporations could thus serve as a potential (magic) solution to the funding needs of various states.

This idea of skimming profits from banks for public projects—either through taxation, bonus provisions in bank charters, or state ownership of bank stock—was wholly different from chartering joint banking-improvement companies whose *main purpose* was to finance the construction and operation of a public utility through the profits from banking services. This latter model was initially developed in the mid-1820s by a handful of northern companies such as the Columbia Bank (& Bridge Company) in Pennsylvania (1824), the Delaware & Hudson Canal Company in New York (1824), and the Morris Canal & Banking Company in New Jersey (1826). But it never caught on extensively in the North or West. In contrast, these joint companies became widespread in the frontier southern states of Louisiana, Georgia, and Mississippi during the 1830s, where they financed canals, railroads, waterworks, and other public improvements. Half of all the banks chartered in these three states between 1830 and 1837 (approximately twenty-six out of fifty-one charters) were joint companies. Along with the plantation banks discussed in chapter 5, these banks encouraged the financialization of enslaved lives, both through their lenient lending policies and through their purchasing and hiring of enslaved labor for the construction of the improvement projects themselves.

Louisiana was the first southern state to embrace the joint banking-improvement company idea when it chartered the New Orleans Canal and Banking Company in 1831 with $4 million of capital. In total, the state incorporated sixteen banks between 1827 and 1837: four traditional commercial banks, three plantation banks, and nine improvement companies (one of which—the Clinton & Port Hudson Railroad—was also structured as a plantation bank, and a second—the Atchafalaya Railroad—that adopted some plantation bank features). These improvement banks included a canal, four railroads, a waterworks (the Commercial Bank [1833]), a gasworks (the New Orleans Gas Light & Banking Company [1835]), a hotel (the Exchange & Banking Company [1835]), and a complex of hotels, steam packets, and an exchange (the New Orleans Improvement & Banking Company [1836]).[134] The idea behind these hybrid corporations was that they could use the profits from banking to fund construction projects.

The charters of these improvement banks continued the aggressive lending policies first granted to the Bank of Louisiana (1824) and the City Bank of New Orleans (1831), while also including specific references to human property. While most of these improvement banks still placed a four-month limit on discounts (the exception being the Gas Light Company, which allowed six months), almost all were much more generous with loans secured by property. The Canal Bank, Clinton & Port Hudson Railroad, and Pontchartrain Railroad all permitted long-term loans payable over eight years in equal annual installments, while the Improvement Company lent at twelve months without specifying renewal terms. The Canal Bank, Gas Light Company, New Orleans & Carrollton Railroad, and Pontchartrain Railroad all required lending to be split two-thirds on property mortgages and one-third on discounts; the Clinton & Port Hudson Railroad split these fifty-fifty.[135]

Two-thirds of these improvement banks also included explicit discussions of enslaved lives. The Commercial Bank, Gas Light Company, Exchange Bank, and Improvement Bank all adopted nearly identical language: "The said company shall have power to discount notes or bills, and may loan money on stocks or other rights and credits, and on lands and slaves secured by mortgage, and may buy and sell bills of exchange, gold and gold coins, and silver bullion, and generally to transact any banking business."[136] Reflecting its incorporation as a plantation bank, the Clinton & Port Hudson Railroad adopted identical language to the Union Bank of Louisiana in stipulating that "mortgages may be taken on lands and slaves" and that "when the mortgage shall be on land and slaves, the value of the land shall be equal to two thirds at least of the stock for which the mortgage shall be given."[137] Both the Clinton & Port Hudson and the Pontchartrain Railroads also referenced "loans secured by mortgages on immoveable property or slaves" when discussing foreclosure proceedings.[138]

In November 1835, just months after receiving its charter, the New Orleans Gas Light & Banking Company purchased the assets of the New Orleans branch of the Second Bank of the United States, to go into effect on January 1, 1836, when the federal bank's charter officially expired. The *Niles' Weekly Register* observed that this addition would give the Gas Light Company "great advantages and ability to serve the commercial community."[139] The Gas Bank also began simultaneously underwriting mortgages with human property as collateral, and purchasing enslaved individuals for the use of the company. For example, in March of 1836 it lent $30,000 to a husband and wife on their mixed sugar-and-cotton plantation and fifty-two enslaved laborers in Assumption Parish.[140] Three months later, it purchased William from one slaveholder for $1,000; Tom from a second seller for $1,125; Jack from a third slaveholder for $1,100; Isaiah from a fourth vendor for an unknown amount; and Jim Davis, Armstead, George, and James Scott from a fifth supplier for $4,375, presumably all for employment in building the gasworks.[141] These sellers might have been offering individuals from their own workforce, or they might have been operating as slave brokers as part of the domestic trade. The bill of sale for Jack described him as a "Mulatto boy . . . aged about eighteen years, a creole of the country, house servant, accustomed to carry bucks, and to take care of horses, and fully guaranteed against the redhibitory vices, maladies & defects prescribed by law, with the exception that he has sometimes absented himself but has never left the city nor been absent more than twenty four hours."[142] On the other hand, when the bank purchased Billy for $950 from another slaveholder in March of 1838, he was guaranteed "with the exception of the vice of running away against which is not guaranteed."[143]

In November 1838, Catherine Wilkinson and her son Robert mortgaged their sugar plantation and thirty-four enslaved workers in Plaquemines Parish to the Gas Light Company in exchange for a $40,000 loan (about $1.1 million in 2021).[144] That same month, the bank purchased Messer for $900 and Peter for $1,050, but sold Jim Davis and Isaiah (purchased in June 1836) for $2,000—due to their history of running away.[145] By the summer of 1840, the Gas Light Company had decided to divest itself of its banking business and focus on operating the gasworks. Purchases of slaves for this purpose increased throughout the next few years. In almost all cases, the company acquired a single enslaved man in his early twenties from a local resident in New Orleans.[146] One exception was "Alexander or Ellick," whom the company purchased for $1,000 in 1838 from a resident of Virginia, through an agent from Tennessee.[147]

Other improvement banks similarly engaged with both large-scale property mortgages and the buying and selling of enslaved individuals. For example, in February 1836, one slaveholder sold the Commercial Bank four enslaved men for $4,800. The seller had purchased twenty-six-year-old Alexander "in Virginia whence he was imported about three years ago," twenty-five-year-old George from S. M. Woolfolk (a relative of and New Orleans agent for the notorious slave trader Austin Woolfolk), twenty-eight-year-old Tonny from another vendor in April 1834, and thirty-two-year-old Jacob from the firm of François Dugué & Co in August 1834.[148] The following day, this same slaveholder also sold the bank forty-eight-year-old Randel for $700, whom he described as "a good Black Smith & Engineer." For Randel, who had been in the seller's possession since April 1834, he stipulated "that should the said Slave turn out badly, that is to say be affected with or by any of the Vices or maladies prescribed by Law" within the next six months, that he would "immediately take back said Slave, and pay back to the said Bank in Cash" the purchase price. After that point, the condition of the enslaved man would be "at the entire risk of said Bank in every respect."[149] Presumably the bank intended to employ these enslaved laborers on the waterworks. In purchasing enslaved lives a decade later, the Commercial Bank board minutes specifically noted that they were "for the use of the Engines & yard."[150]

In April 1837, Louisiana planters Francis P. Corbin, Robert B. Corbin, and Edward Rawle decided to liquidate their Jefferson Parish sugar plantation, selling 102 enslaved individuals at an auction in New Orleans.[151] Among the buyers was the New Orleans Canal & Banking Company. The Canal Bank purchased twenty-one-year-old field hand and coachman Reed for $1,175; thirty-one-year-old Stephen who was "good at any kind of work on a plantation" for $1,125; twenty-three-year-old Watt and thirty-year-old Coleman—each of whom was described as a "good field hand & worker" for $1,175 each; twenty-seven-year-old "good worker" Amos for $1,150; and the family of twenty-two-year-old Ann Carter (also a good field hand), her four-year-old son Jack, and her nine-month-old son Cyrus, all for $1,250. Although described as field hands, the Canal Bank most likely intended to employ these enslaved workers in the construction and operation of the canal. The bank financed this purchase, promising to pay the $7,050 total in two installments of $3,525 each at the Bank of Louisiana, due in eight and twelve months with no right to renew, and "secured by mortgage on said slaves and to bear interest at the rate of ten per cent per annum."[152]

Like the other improvement banks, the Canal Bank embraced both its banking and improvement functions. In November 1838, it purchased Billy Christian from another slaveholder for $1,100, also for work on the canal project.[153] That same month, the bank issued a mortgage to the wealthy commission merchant and planter Glendy Burke of New Orleans and his wife Czarina Eliza Rogers on their Jon plantation in the parish of Madison, with its forty-four enslaved laborers, to secure an existing debt of $43,098.78 (about $1.2 million in 2021). The couple was to repay the debt in four equal installments, payable in six, twelve, eighteen, and twenty-four months.[154] By 1843, Burke would assume the presidency of that joint banking institution.[155]

While Louisiana was certainly the most creative in incorporating a variety of improvement banks, the idea also caught on in Georgia, Mississippi, and South Carolina. Georgia's first joint-banking ventures were technically not improvement companies but rather insurance companies. The charters of the

Marine & Fire Insurance Company (1812) and the Georgia Mutual Insurance Company (1822) were amended in 1825 and 1827 (respectively) to grant these firms banking privileges, renaming them the Marine & Fire Insurance Bank and the Augusta Insurance & Banking Company. In 1831, the legislature chartered the new Insurance Bank of Georgia with the justification that "the good of this State would be promoted by keeping within it, the large sums of money which are now annually sent to the North, to pay insurance on Southern property."[156] It is unclear if any of these firms underwrote slave-insurance policies.[157]

Unlike the later Ohio Life & Trust Company (1835) which was a bank disguised as an insurance firm, these all operated openly as both banks and underwriters. All three were small concerns, capitalized at only $300,000 to $500,000 each, with traditional commercial-banking privileges. Yet their limited funds did not stop them from engaging in property mortgages by the end of the 1830s. For example, in February 1838, one slaveholder mortgaged his land in Baldwin and ten enslaved individuals to the Marine & Fire Insurance Bank in return for a $3,500 loan, payable in twelve months. He renewed the loan over the next six years, finally finishing his payments in February 1844.[158] These small banks also occasionally paired with larger institutions to underwrite more substantial loans. In June 1838, a Georgia planter owed almost $20,000 to the Merchants' Bank of New York. To secure this debt, he mortgaged his land in Harris County, Georgia, farming utensils, mules, and enslaved workforce to the Merchants' Bank, depositing three promissory notes with the local Insurance Bank of Columbus, Georgia. He promised to repay the Insurance Bank annually over the next three years, and the latter bank would remit the funds to the Merchants' Bank.[159] While it is unclear why the two banks entered into this agreement, and even whether the Merchants' Bank was aware of the use of human collateral in this contract (which was filed with the local Muscogee County, Georgia, county clerk), it was highly unusual for a northern state-chartered bank to secure a southern mortgage using enslaved lives as collateral.

Georgia likewise chartered three railroad banks: the Georgia (1835), Central (1836), and Monroe (1836) Rail Road & Banking Companies. Charged with building various spans of track, these concerns hoped to attract stockholders by including banking privileges, as well as to raise additional building funds through profits from the banking business. As one legislator remarked during the various debates, the railroad "could not be built unless banking privileges were granted—no one would take the stock." Another legislator who "was as much opposed to increasing the number of banks as any one" reluctantly agreed: "deny banking privileges to this company and the rail road cannot be built."[160] A vocal opponent of the Central Rail Road & Banking

Company charter blamed this problem on the shortsightedness of the state, who relied on private investors to construct necessary improvements rather than contributing state funds. "What could the company have done, without the privilege of banking, for the purpose of raising the necessary funds to carry on and complete the work? The directors were well aware that they could not obtain from the legislature any assistance." This correspondent believed that "the state is rich enough to afford the means" of building railroads, if only the legislature "acted on enlarged views, and founded their plans on the future prosperity of the State."[161] Instead, it turned to the improvement-banking model—even as numerous other railroad companies were chartered in Georgia without banking privileges.[162]

Not surprisingly, these railroads were built primarily with enslaved labor, which required the railroad banks to either hire or purchase enslaved individuals on behalf of the company. The minute books of the Georgia Rail Road regularly discussed the need "to procure hands to go on the Road to work at such rates as will be reasonable," either by "purchasing Hands" or employing an agent "to hire hands."[163] In October 1836, it "authorised" the "purchase" of "twelve young negroes," and again in February 1837 appointed "agents to purchase . . . Sixty negro men suitable for labor on the Rail Road."[164] Just two months later, the company advertised for a runaway enslaved laborer named Philip, who was supposedly trying to return to his native Virginia.[165] In November 1837, it hired fifty-five more enslaved men for construction.[166] A year later, the board authorized the president "to sell any negroes belonging to the company that may be, from any cause unfit for the service for which they were purchased."[167] The Central Rail Road & Banking Company likewise employed enslaved labor, such as when it purchased several enslaved individuals from a local slaveholder in February 1839 for $2,000.[168] As the chief engineer of that company observed in his official report of May 1839, "That negro labour is perfectly adapted to the construction of works of internal improvement is now a well established fact."[169]

In addition to building track, these railroads also functioned as banks lending money secured by property. In the spring of 1836, one slaveholder applied to the Georgia Rail Road for a $25,000 loan, "to be paid 1837 and to be renewed annually." The board agreed to this loan, provided that the applicant mortgage his property as security. The following month it also granted another planter a loan secured by a property mortgage, although the terms were not specified in the minute book.[170]

As in Louisiana, Mississippi's improvement banks reflected that state's more aggressive approach toward underwriting mortgages with enslaved lives. The state incorporated three railroad banks in December 1833, eight more in

February 1836, and another four (plus the Vicksburg Water Works & Banking Company) in April and May 1837. Mirroring the permissive lending policies of the Planters' Bank (1830), at least thirteen of these sixteen improvement banks allowed discounts of twelve or more months. Only the West Feliciana Railroad was limited to four months, and the waterworks to six months. And all but these latter two companies designated that at least one-third to one-half of all loans be made on "long loans" of at least twelve months, secured by land and human property.[171] The five traditional commercial banks incorporated during May 1837 contained identical broad discounting-and-lending provisions.[172]

Chartered just a few months after the Mississippi Union became the state's first plantation bank, the Benton & Manchester Railroad (1837) was also capitalized on the plantation-bank model. In purchasing stock shares, its charter permitted its $1 million capital stock "to be paid in money, or to be secured by the pledge and mortgage of real estate, in this state," equivalent in value to at least double the stock purchased.[173] Similarly, the charter of the Mississippi & Alabama Railroad (1836) was amended in 1838 to allow the company to "dispose of their entire stock, and secure the payment thereof by mortgage on real estate, including slaves at half the estimated value thereof, upon which mortgages the said company may issue bonds."[174] Thus, as the Panic of 1837 began to descend upon the South, the banks of both Louisiana and Mississippi were committing themselves to long-term loans secured by the ballooning values of land and enslaved lives.[175]

❋

Throughout the 1820s, southern banks creatively adapted traditional banking practices to meet the growing credit needs of slaveholders, particularly those expanding into the frontier areas of Mississippi, Alabama, and Louisiana. These frontier institutions pushed the logic of traditional banking within the system of slavery to its limits. Yet this embrace of enslaved lives as collateral necessarily involved an imperfect adaptation of existing bank forms, and was always in tension with accepted banking practices. In order to fully harness the wealth potential embodied in the system of slavery, southerners needed to break free of these normative constraints. Rather than trying to fit the system of slavery into the traditional commercial-banking apparatus, southerners began reimagining the relationship between banking and slavery, resulting in the creation of plantation banks which drew their very capital from the land and human property of the region. These plantation banks marked the pinnacle of the financialization of slavery in the United States.

5
Reimagining Banking for a Slave Economy

Among the first subscribers in the newly chartered Citizens' Bank of Louisiana in 1833 were brothers Francis P. Corbin, Robert B. Corbin, and their business partner Edward Rawle.[1] The three men jointly owned a sugar plantation in the Cannes-Brûlées region of Jefferson Parish, Louisiana, about fifteen miles outside New Orleans, which Rawle managed on their behalf.[2] Francis was a businessman who split his time between Philadelphia and Paris, while Robert remained at "The Reeds"—the Corbin family plantation in Caroline County, Virginia, where he bred "fine horses." He would also represent that part of the state in the House of Delegates from 1838 to 1841.[3] But while his love of horses (and his fear of cholera) kept him in Virginia, Robert believed that the real money was in sugar. In contrast to cotton, which (in his estimation) "may be said to have attained its acme of success and must now decline from the excess of production and competition both foreign and domestic," he believed that sugar had "a good prospect of a gradual and steady advance" due to "the decline of Foreign competition" as "the probable result of the scheme of emancipation in the British West Indian Colonies"—a reference to the 1833 passage of the British Abolition Act. He also surmised that this projected success of sugar, while partially dependent on crop yields, would be based "mainly upon the abundance of Bank capital" which the massive new bank—capitalized at $12 million—could provide.[4]

The partners had purchased the sugar plantation and enslaved workers in December 1827; by 1831 they still owed the seller $28,000 for the property.[5] That year, they obtained a loan of $25,000 from the Bank of Louisiana (presumably to repay this outstanding debt), secured by a mortgage on the land and the 110 enslaved people then attached to it.[6] They likewise began accumulating debts with the New Orleans firm of A. & J. Dennistoun & Co., which amounted to $23,580 by 1833. They mortgaged the same property to secure this obligation.[7] But Robert was increasingly worried that they would need to sell the Louisiana plantation to meet all of these mounting debts, especially during the credit contraction of 1834 (caused by the ongoing Bank War between President Andrew Jackson and Second Bank president Nicholas Biddle).[8] He tried "to borrow $20,000 upon a mortgage" of The Reeds in Virginia, but he "could not obtain a dollar" from the traditional commercial banks in Richmond. Additionally, "the Banks refuse to grant accommodation loans"—renewals of short-term notes—and "the Capitalists or money lenders in this part of the country hold good Bonds but no money." Once again, he placed all his hope in the new bank. "If the Citizens Bank go into operation . . . I imagine sugar plantations will be more in demand, than they have been for several years past."[9] In that case, they could either sell their Louisiana estate for a tidy profit—Robert believed "$150,000 [about $5 million in 2021] would be a fair price for the Plantation as it stands"—or they could ride his predictions of an upward trend in the sugar market, paying off their debts with the inevitable profits.[10]

Whereas Robert was quite bullish on sugar, Rawle repeatedly expressed "his resolution to withdraw" from his one-fifth stake in the partnership, which might force them all to sell. But Robert had a plan. "If I can't sell for a fair price and [instead] the whole am[oun]t for which Rawle subscribed be obtained from the Citizens Bank, it may be expedient to renew the act of copartnership between members, pay off the debts due from the concern and release the property from incumbrance and apply the surplus to the payment of our debts in this question."[11] But this plan depended on timely financing from the new bank. Several months later, in June 1835, the partners finally acted upon their initial stock subscription, acquiring 1,054 shares of Citizens' Bank stock valued at $105,400; their outstanding debts to the Bank of Louisiana and A. & J. Dennistoun would have prevented the purchase of additional shares. As was the model of this new plantation bank, their stock "purchase" was secured not with money but with a mortgage on their sugar plantation and its now ninety-six enslaved workers.[12] Once the bank went into full operation, the partners would then be allowed to borrow up to $52,700—half the value of their stock—secured with the same property.[13]

Unfortunately, the bank did not start active lending to stockholders until the spring and summer of 1836, and the partners were in need of funds much sooner. By January 1836, their debt to A. & J. Dennistoun & Co. had grown to over $50,000, and Robert's bullishness was subsiding. He now "evinced an Earnest desire to sell the Property for any thing like a tolerable price."

Whereas in October 1834 he believed $150,000 to be the "fair" price, fifteen months later he "had resolved to take $110,000, if I could get it and return hither and pay off my most pressing debts."[14] In May 1836—just as the Citizens' Bank was on the verge of starting to lend—they transferred all their shares to other slaveholders and received a release of the bank's mortgage lien on their property.[15] The following year, they obtained legal releases from both the Bank of Louisiana and A. & J. Dennistoun & Co. "in order to facilitate the execution of the deeds of Sale of all the slaves belonging in common."[16]

On April 29, 1837, all 102 enslaved individuals were brought to New Orleans for a public auction.[17] Among the purchasers was the New Orleans Canal & Banking Company, who acquired five enslaved men, an enslaved woman, and her two young children.[18] This sale, which netted the partners $76,025, was "a very good one" in their estimation, especially "[w]hen we consider that a fifth of the number were very young children and that some men old and some diseased." Although the auctioneer tried to maximize the sale by selling most of the enslaved as individuals, "[s]ome sacrifice to humanity was made by putting them in families, which caused a loss" while "[i]n a few instances, the husband and wife were sold to different masters."[19] Yet this "humane" assessment is largely contradicted by the sales record itself, in which the 102 people were scattered across fifty different purchasers. Only seventeen of the transactions were for groups of two to five people; the remaining enslaved lives were all auctioned to separate slaveholders.[20] Additionally, many of these "humane" multiperson sales were probably designed for the practical purpose of making sure that there were no aged, infirm, or infant enslaved lives left unsold.

During this brief four-year period, these plantation owners had business relationships with a traditional bank in Virginia, a more planter-friendly bank in Louisiana, a joint banking-improvement company, and a new plantation bank. The partners' experiences reflected not only the many financial options open to slaveholders by the 1830s, but also the rapidly changing banking environment in the frontier South. The capital-intensive nature of sugar planting, in particular, required large, long-term loans that fell outside the scope of even the most permissive frontier banks. Rather than trying to fit the system of slavery into the traditional commercial-banking apparatus, the state of Louisiana pioneered a completely new banking model—the plantation bank—as a property bank explicitly drawing on the land and human capital of the region, in an effort to meet the unique financial needs of slaveholders on the frontier. This experiment with plantation banks would then expand into Mississippi, Arkansas, and Florida, before the Panic of 1837 wiped out most of these institutions.

A New Type of Property Bank

The one major constituency largely ignored in the expansion of Louisiana's commercial banks during the 1820s were the planters, and especially the sugar planters. Although the Bank of Louisiana, City Bank, and Canal Bank all had branches throughout the state, the majority of their banking capital and lending services centered either on the short-term commercial paper of New Orleans merchants or the needs of cotton planters (see map 4.1). And while the cotton and sugar planters controlled vast wealth in the form of land and human property, this wealth was not liquid, making it difficult to charter a new planters' bank on a traditional bank model. During the 1820s, a series of poor sugar crops, combined with a reduction of the tariff on imported sugar, hit the region hard. The average price dropped from a high of 15¢ per pound in 1815 to under 6¢ during the 1820s and most of the 1830s.[21] Whereas cotton could be profitably produced on plantations of all sizes with only minimal economies of scale accruing to larger producers, sugar was a capital-intensive crop that experienced substantial economies of scale.[22] Successful sugar planters appear to have required a minimum of at least $100,000 in assets (about $2.5–$3 million in 2021) for the requisite land, buildings, equipment, and enslaved labor, especially as "the thirties and forties brought revolutionary changes in sugar manufacturing." The required "new equipment increased the capitalization of plantations, as did also the trend toward higher land and slave values."[23] The capital-intensive nature of sugar production left the planters with an unmet need for access to banking services, especially long-term loans secured by this valuable property. The result of this growing demand was the formation of the Consolidated Association of the Planters of Louisiana (CAPL), chartered in 1827 with $2 million in capital, as a property bank focused mainly on plantations and their enslaved workers.[24]

Traditionally, commercial-bank charters required a specific amount of paid-in capital from their shareholders in order to begin operations. In contrast, the charters of plantation banks modeled on the CAPL required no paid-in capital to begin operations; the reserves of the bank were based solely on borrowed money. Investors mortgaged their plantations and enslaved laborers in return for bank shares, and the entirety of the bank's capital stock was based on these mortgages. But this practice still left the bank with no specie reserves for the issuance of banknotes or loans. Initially, the CAPL tried to sell bonds to raise the requisite specie; annual principal and interest payments by future mortgage debtors would pay the interest on these bonds.[25] But investors were wary of investing in mortgaged-backed bonds without any further security.

The bank appealed to the state for help. By an act passed in 1828, the State of Louisiana agreed to issue Louisiana state bonds, giving the bonds to the bank in exchange for collateral—the long-term mortgages on those plantations and enslaved lives. The bank sold these state bonds to investors in the Northeast or overseas, who paid the bank in gold and silver. The bond purchasers had more confidence in the securities since they were guaranteed by the state—and ultimately the taxpayers. This specie then enabled the bank to begin issuing banknotes and extending loans on a fractional-reserve basis. This financial setup was actually quite similar to the capitalization of the Bank of Louisiana in 1824, in which the state contributed $2 million of the total $4 million by selling state bonds. Yet unlike this semipublic institution, CAPL had shareholders who were all private citizens; the state would not gain directly from any profits. But Louisiana would indirectly benefit from a successful institution, and the state remained confident in the CAPL's ability to pay the interest and principal on bonds backed by the valuable land and enslaved workers of the region's booming cotton-and-sugar economy.[26]

The move to provide state backing was not without significant opposition, particularly from the cotton regions of the state, as well as from some commercial residents of New Orleans. One legislator in the Louisiana House of Representatives from that port city publicly expressed his reasons for voting against the bill, including that the legislature had no right to bind the state on behalf of a "certain class or description of citizens, to enable them to borrow money for their exclusive use and benefit, without any corresponding advantage to the public, or adequate security against loss," and that it would "destroy the public credit" of the state and "embarrass it in its necessary pecuniary operations." His supporters in the House felt so strongly that they insisted this protest be inserted in the official Journal of the Assembly. The protest was signed by thirteen members of the House of Representatives, including four from New Orleans and seven from the main cotton-producing parishes of Concordia, Rapides, Nachitoches, West Feliciana, East Baton Rouge, Catahuala, and Ouachita; the first five of these seven parishes also contained branches of competing banks. Ten other legislators tried to block this protest from being included in the official record—presumably indicating their strong support for state underwriting of the Consolidated Association bonds. These included two representatives from New Orleans, as well as representatives from the major sugar-producing parishes of St. Bernard, Plaquemines, and St. John the Baptist—none of which possessed a bank branch.[27]

Although the state's first plantation bank was successful, the limited capitalization of the CAPL still left planters—especially sugar planters—without adequate access to funding. In addition to possessing Louisiana bank branches, the largest cotton parishes (especially Concordia) were much closer in proximity to Natchez, Mississippi, giving them additional access to banking capital there. The Second Bank of the United States had just opened a branch at Natchez in 1831, and the bank would prove willing to provide planters with mortgages secured by enslaved individuals, as would the Planter's Bank of Mississippi (chartered in 1830; opened in 1833).

In response to this continued financing need, the state chartered a second plantation bank in 1832—the Union Bank of Louisiana. Located in New Orleans with eight additional branches, its capital of $7 million dwarfed the combined capital of all previous Louisiana banks. In order to "facilitate" the sale of the bank's bonds, which were payable in twelve, fifteen, eighteen, and twenty years, "the faith of the state" was "pledged for the security of the capital and interests" as part of its initial charter.[28] The Union Bank charter was the first to reference enslaved lives explicitly in its text. To secure their stock shares, subscribers had to mortgage "cultivated lands and slaves, . . . lots with houses, or other edifices yielding a revenue," that had a value "at least equal to the amount of their respective stock." No more than one-third of the value of the property could be enslaved, and "no mortgage on slaves alone shall be received."[29] The charter also stipulated that the bank would loan only one-third of the capital for short-term "promissory notes or bills of exchange," and the remaining two-thirds on twelve-month mortgages, which could be renewed annually for up to eight years upon the payment of accumulated interest and one-eighth of the principal.[30]

Although the reach of the Union Bank was more widespread than that of the CAPL, its branches still favored cotton growers. Four branches were in the cotton parishes of Natchitoches, Avoyelles, East Feliciana, and Lafayette; two were in the sugar parishes of Lafourche and St. Tammany; and two were in the mixed parishes of Iberville and St. Martin (map 5.1). In designating these eight sites, the charter also listed the parishes that these locations were intended to serve. Ignored in this list were two important cotton-growing parishes (the latter of which bordered Natchez, Mississippi) as well as the main sugar-growing parishes of the state: St. James, St. John the Baptist, St. Charles, St. Bernard, Jefferson, and Plaquemines. While planters in the first three of these sugar parishes might easily have accessed the branch in Lafourche, it is telling that the charter did not expressly state this fact.[31]

Interest in the Union Bank was immediate and overwhelming, with citizens of the city of New Orleans requesting mortgages in exchange for $12 million in stock, and residents of the remainder of the state subscribing for another $25 million in stock.[32] According to the charter, the directors would need to reduce the subscriptions back down to $8 million if oversubscribed

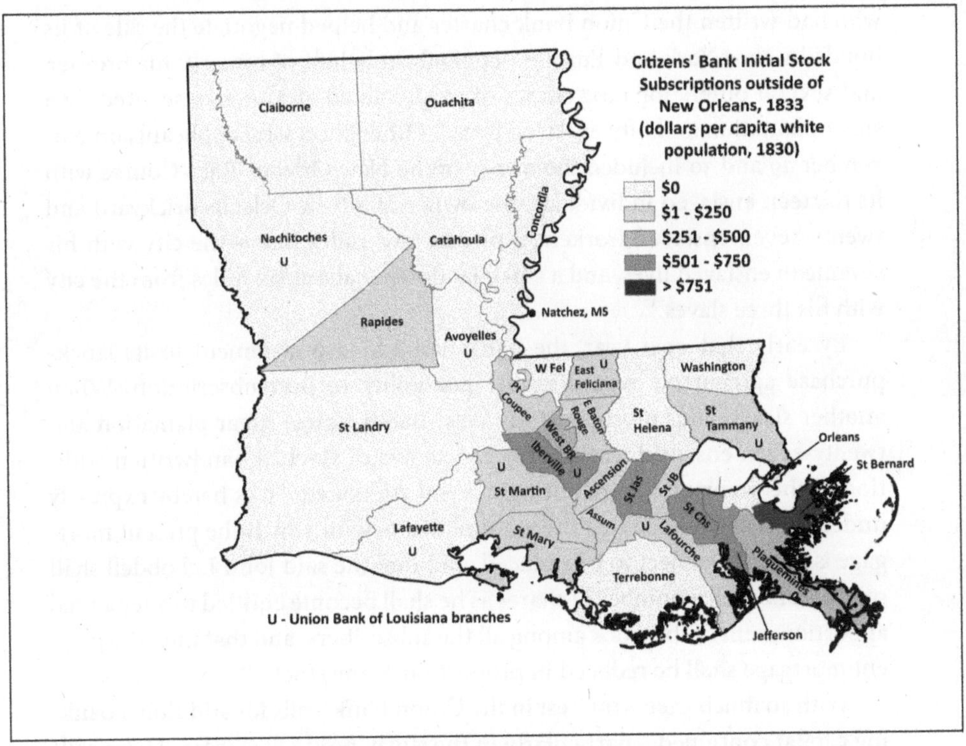

MAP 5.1. Union Bank branches (1832) and Citizens' Bank initial stock subscribers outside New Orleans (1833). Source: "Inventaire de titres et autres objets" [Inventory of securities and other objects], July 25, 1833, *Citizens' Bank*, reel 13; *Act to Incorporate the Subscribers of the Union Bank of Louisiana* (New York: Clayton & Van Norden, 1832): 15–16. Map created by Peter Rogers, Head of Research and Education, Philips Memorial Library, Providence College, Providence, RI.

by "deduct[ing] the amount of such excess from, first, the stock for which sufficient security shall not be offered, and then from the largest subscriptions, in such manner that no subscription shall be reduced in amount while any one remains larger."[33] Without a full listing of subscribers, it is impossible to know which sectors of the state this bank primarily served. However, while the location of its branches remained outside the main sugar regions, subscribers mortgaged both cotton and sugar plantations for their stock.[34]

Early subscribers included James Harvey Shepherd and John Fitz Miller, who jointly applied to the bank in November 1832 for 636 shares of stock. In granting a mortgage on their "steam saw mill establishment below this city," including its mill, forge, and thirty-six enslaved workers, the directors "deemed [the property] sufficient, and at least for the moment equal to the amount of the said six hundred and thirty six Shares of the said Stock," worth $63,600.[35] Later that month, New Orleans merchant Edmond Jean Forstall—

who had written the Union Bank charter and helped negotiate the sale of its bonds in New York and Europe—applied on behalf of himself, his brother, and several others for 1,012 shares of stock valued at $101,200, secured by a sugar plantation and fifty enslaved lives.[36] Other successful applicants on November 29 and 30 included the owner of the New Orleans Race Course with its thirteen enslaved individuals, the owner of a New Orleans brickyard and twenty-seven enslaved workers, a planter two miles below the city with his seventeen enslaved lives, and a small landowner about six miles from the city with his three slaves.[37]

By early that next year, the bank had added a statement to its stock-purchase agreements regarding the possibility of oversubscription. When another slaveholder mortgaged his West Baton Rouge sugar plantation and twenty-seven enslaved workers for 240 shares of stock, a handwritten addition to the preprinted purchase agreement stipulated: "It is hereby expressly understood and agreed that the amount of stock for which the present mortgage is given is subject to be reduced, and that the said John L. Lobdell shall only obtain such a number of shares as he shall become entitled to after a final apportionment of the stock among all the subscribers, and that then the present mortgage shall be reduced in proportion of the stock."[38]

With so much excess interest in the Union Bank, calls for additional banking capital continued—particularly in the sugar-producing areas. These calls culminated with the incorporation of the Citizens' Bank of Louisiana on April 1, 1833. Capitalized at $12 million, this massive third plantation bank permitted the mortgaging of human property up to one-third of the total value of the stock. And like the Union Bank, stock subscriptions quickly poured in, particularly from the sugar-growing areas of the state. According to the act of incorporation, the Citizens' Bank was permitted to sell subscriptions for $14.4 million of stock divided between the city and parish of New Orleans ($8.4 million) and the remaining parishes of the state ($6 million). It designated three prominent citizens in each parish to receive share subscriptions, a policy that was in stark contrast to the Union charter, which limited subscription locations to the eight cities designated as branches.[39]

Despite this more extensive outreach, the primary interest in this bank came from the sugar planters of the state (map 5.1). Subscriptions were concentrated in the parishes of St. Bernard, St. James, St. Charles, Jefferson, Iberville, Plaquemines, West Baton Rouge, St. John the Baptist, and Assumption. By 1833, planters from these nine parishes had subscribed a total of $7.4 million to the bank, accounting for 88 percent of the non–New Orleans subscriptions. On a per capita basis (white population in 1830), residents of these parishes contributed on average between $1,177 each in St. Bernard to $170 each in Assumption. Based on production recorded in the 1840 census, these locations were some of the top sugar-producing parishes of the state (see map 4.1). The other major sugar-producing parishes of Terrebonne, Ascension, Lafourche, and Saint Mary contributed very little to this initial subscription, yet they already contained three bank branches between them (the Union Bank branch at Thibodeauxville in Lafourche, and branches of the New Orleans Canal & Banking Company at Donaldsonville in Ascension and at Franklin in St. Mary). On the other hand, the major cotton-producing parishes demonstrated little interest in the new bank; thus, the Citizens' Bank would mainly support the sugar growers of Louisiana.[40]

One of the original incorporators of the Citizens' Bank of Louisiana was Jean-Bernard Xavier Philippe de Marigny de Mandeville, more commonly known as Bernard Marigny. A member of one of the most important and respected old aristocratic families of French Louisiana, Marigny owned several large plantations by the 1830s, including a sugarcane plantation and brickyard on the north shore of Lake Pontchartrain in the parish of St. Tammany, and another south of New Orleans in the parish of Plaquemines. In 1833, Marigny and his wife Anne Mathilde Morales mortgaged their Plaquemines sugar plantation—including the house, sugar mill, hospital, kitchens, slave cabins, a warehouse, barn, stable, carts, plowing equipment, animals, and seventy enslaved men, women, and children—in return for 490 shares of stock in the bank (figure 5.1).[41] At $100 per share, Marigny's stake in the bank (from this one mortgage) was worth $49,000. By 1834, he would mortgage more property including his sugar plantation and enslaved workers in St. Tammany, bringing his total stock subscription to 2,530 shares, which had a nominal value of $253,000 (about $7.3 million in 2021).[42]

Citizens' Bank stock was also popular with other elite sugar planters of the state. In July 1834, the descendants and heirs of Victorin Roman gathered to discuss the future of his two sugar plantations in the parish of St. James, the first with eighty-seven enslaved individuals and the second with eighty-three. The family, consisting of Victorin's widow and numerous adult and minor children, agreed "that it would be highly advantageous" to mortgage the property in exchange for Citizens' Bank stock, "which cannot fail to be profitable hereafter."[43] The family eventually subscribed for 1,165 shares.[44] The following month, Lucien Labranche and his wife Mathilde Fortier mortgaged their sugar plantation and 130 slaves in Jefferson Parish in exchange for 1,190 shares of Citizens' Bank stock worth $191,000.[45]

Whether written in French (as was the case with the Marigny, Roman, and Fortier contracts) or English, these contracts contained the same conditions. For example, in January 1835, another slaveholder, St. Julien Tournillon,

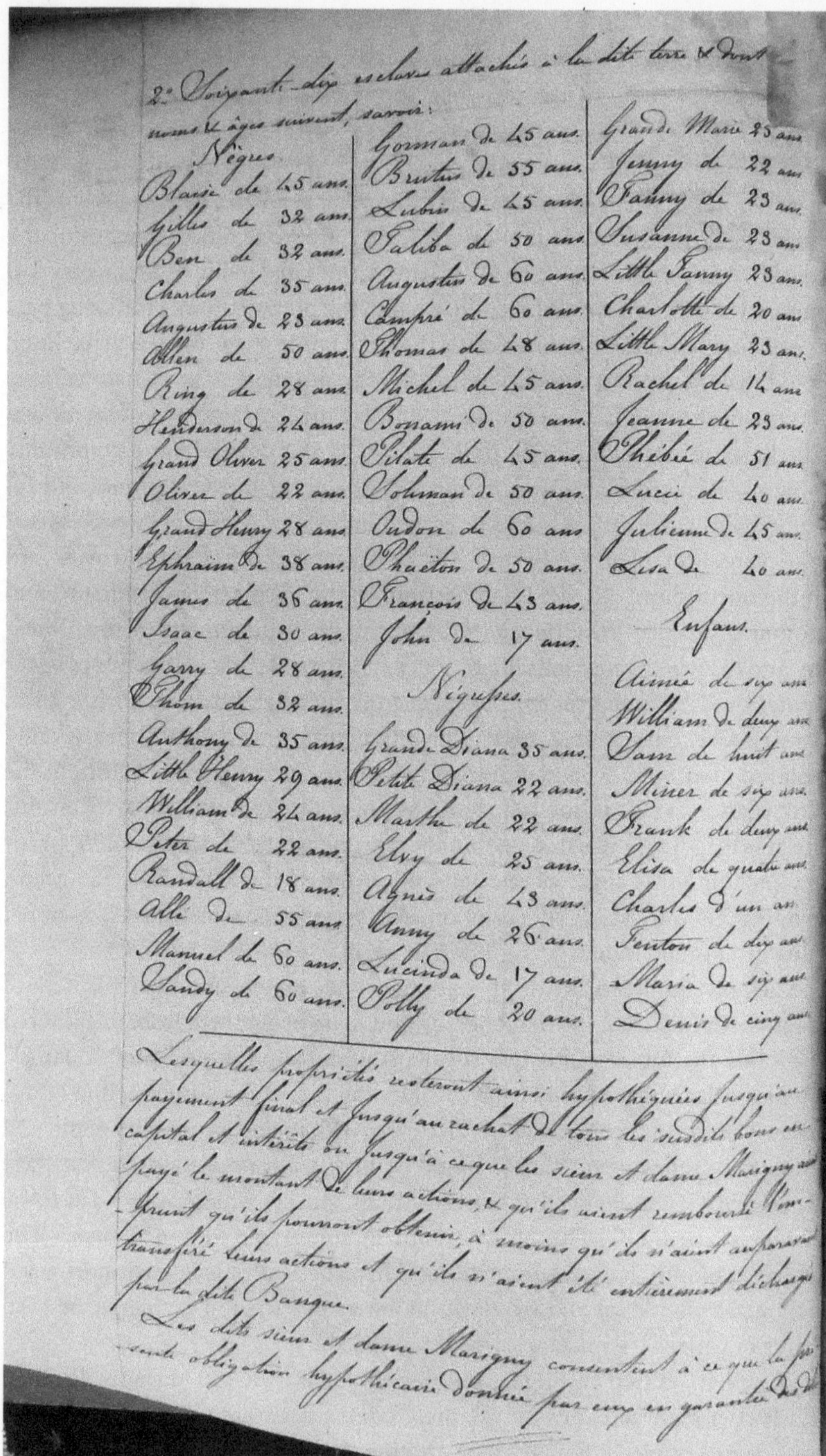

2° Soixante-dix esclaves attachés à la dite terre & dont [les] noms & âges suivent, savoir:

Nègres

Blaise de 45 ans.
Gilles de 32 ans.
Ben de 32 ans.
Charles de 35 ans.
Augustin de 23 ans.
Allen de 50 ans.
King de 28 ans.
Henderson de 24 ans.
Grand Oliver 25 ans.
Oliver de 22 ans.
Grand Henry 28 ans.
Ephraim de 38 ans.
James de 36 ans.
Isaac de 30 ans.
Garry de 28 ans.
Thom de 32 ans.
Anthony de 35 ans.
Little Henry 29 ans.
William de 24 ans.
Peter de 22 ans.
Randall de 18 ans.
Alle de 55 ans.
Manuel de 60 ans.
Sandy de 60 ans.

Gorman de 45 ans.
Brutus de 55 ans.
Lubin de 45 ans.
Taliba de 50 ans.
Augustin de 60 ans.
Campré de 60 ans.
Thomas de 48 ans.
Michel de 45 ans.
Bonami de 50 ans.
Pilate de 45 ans.
Soliman de 50 ans.
Oudon de 60 ans.
Phaëton de 50 ans.
François de 43 ans.
John de 17 ans.

Négresses.

Grande Diana 35 ans.
Petite Diana 22 ans.
Marthe de 22 ans.
Elvy de 25 ans.
Agnès de 43 ans.
Anny de 26 ans.
Lucinda de 17 ans.
Polly de 20 ans.

Grande Marie 23 ans
Jenny de 22 ans
Fanny de 23 ans.
Susanne de 23 ans
Little Fanny 23 ans.
Charlotte de 20 ans
Little Mary 23 ans.
Rachel de 14 ans
Jeanne de 23 ans.
Phébé de 51 ans
Lucie de 40 ans.
Julienne de 45 ans.
Lisa de 40 ans.

Enfans.

Aimée de six ans
William de deux ans
Sam de huit ans
Miner de six ans.
Frank de deux ans
Elisa de quatre ans
Charles d'un an
Fenton de dix ans
Maria de six ans
Denis de cinq ans

Lesquelles propriétés resteront ainsi hypothéquées jusqu'au payement final et jusqu'au rachat de tous les susdits bons en capital et intérêts ou jusqu'à ce que les sieur et dame Marigny aient payé le montant de leurs actions, & qu'ils aient remboursé l'emprunt qu'ils pourront obtenir, à moins qu'ils n'aient auparavant transféré leurs actions et qu'ils n'aient été entièrement déchargés par la dite Banque.

Les dits sieur et dame Marigny consentent à ce que la présente obligation hypothécaire donnée par eux en garantie de mortgaged his sugar plantation in Assumption Parish with its fifty-two enslaved workers in exchange for 686 shares of Citizens' Bank stock, valued at $68,600. Under the terms of the contract, this property would remain under mortgage "until all the bonds issued by the Bank shall have been redeemed in Capital & interest." Alternatively, Tournillon could replace this mortgage with a cash payment for the shares (which few, if any, investors ever did), or transfer his shares to another planter with suitable property. In all cases, as long as he "shall have reimbursed the loan which he may have obtained as stockholder," he would be "entirely discharged by the said Bank."[46] The August 1834 mortgage for Charles Borromée Dufau similarly would exist "jusqu'au payement final et jusqu'au rachat de tous les dits bons en capital et intérêts" ["until the final payment and the final redemption of all the said bonds in capital and interest"]. Yet in one interesting departure, this contract for 813 shares worth $81,300 listed his property as a sugar plantation in the parish of Plaquemines and twenty-nine "têtes d'esclaves"—"head of slaves."[47] Whereas it was quite customary for people to refer to livestock as "head of" cattle, for example, this direct dehumanization was less common for enslaved individuals (at least in the banking records). The only other instances I have encountered of this term were in another francophone Citizens' Bank mortgage from 1837, and an 1838 anglophone auction advertisement.[48] But these instances were rare exceptions in the mortgage records.

Before accepting any stock subscriptions or mortgage loans, the bank sent a form to the local parish judge, requesting that he check the records for prior liens on any of the property. Since an earlier lienholder would have the priority of claim in the case of a foreclosure, the bank needed to know the terms and amount of these debts to assess how it should value the collateral being offered. When Jean Estévan applied in June 1837 for 150 shares of Citizens' Bank stock secured by his sugar plantation and twenty-nine enslaved individuals in Iberville Parish, the bank told the parish judge that it would accept his application unless "prior mortgages exist on the above described property and slaves, exceeding in amount $9750." If the liens against Estévan did prove excessive, he would have to get them "reduced to this sum, or the act cannot be passed."[49] Similarly, the judge in Lafayette Parish needed to confirm that the land and seven enslaved workers of another planter did not possess encumbrances exceeding $2,250 before the bank would approve his application for forty-five shares of stock.[50] In the case of St. Julien Tournillon, the

FIGURE 5.1. *Opposite*, "Hypothèque à la Banque des Citoyens par B. Marigny & son épouse," July 5, 1836, Notary Theodore Seghers, vol. 18, no. 131, p. 2, New Orleans Notarial Archives. Courtesy of the Hon. Chelsey Richard Napoleon, Clerk of Civil District Court, Parish of Orleans.

bank discovered that he had mortgaged the same property to secure a loan of $5,300 from the Bank of Louisiana in 1830. The latter bank agreed to give the priority of claim to the Citizens' Bank on the condition that Tournillon "shall exercise the privilege of borrowing on his stock as soon as the Citizens' Bank goes into operation" in order to pay off this prior debt. But "in case the Citizens' Bank do not go into operation within twelve months then this concession of priority shall be null & void."[51]

In a similar manner, Charles Dufau had a prior mortgage with the firm of Sieurs Lizardi frères (the Lizardi Brothers) to secure a debt of $29,857.13. Dufau promised to use a future loan from the Citizens' Bank "à éteindre leur créance sus dite" ("to extinguish the aforementioned loan") for which the Lizardi Brothers gave up their priority of claim to the bank ("à donner à la Banque des Citoyens priorité d'hypothèque.")[52] But in the case of Lucien Labranche, who in 1833 had mortgaged his sugar plantation and enslaved workers to the Union Bank in exchange for three hundred shares of bank stock, the Citizen's Bank required him to cancel ("radier") or write off that mortgage within three months, as a condition of subscribing with the new bank.[53] Finally, when Josiah Barker initially applied for seven hundred shares in May 1838, secured by his Long Wood sugar plantation and eighty enslaved lives in East Baton Rouge, the bank only approved him for 118 shares, due to a prior mortgage to the creditors William Kenner & Co. Yet "being desirous of Securing all the shares which he might be entitled to on his subscription," by January 1839 Barker convinced the bank to grant him all seven hundred by "renounc[ing] the right of Borrowing on his stock untill the aforementioned mortgage . . . should be paid." The only exception would be if "the said Loan be applied to the extinguishment in full of the said mortgage."[54]

Despite this widespread interest from planters in subscribing for Citizens' Bank stock, the institution initially failed to sell its mortgage-backed securities in the northeastern and foreign bond markets (much as the CAPL had similarly struggled to sell its original bonds). This failure delayed the bank from going into full operation as a lending institution. In January 1836, the bank board sent a letter to the legislature, petitioning for it to provide state backing for these bonds. Citing the "Happy precedents set by your honorable body" by backing the CAPL and Union Bank bonds, it assured the legislature that the support "subjects the State to little or no risk." It also touted plantation banks as the future of southern banking. "An experience of Several years has demonstrated the decided Superiority of Banks resting on the principles of the Citizens' Bank, over other monied institutions differently organized." Not only would the land and human property provide "inherent guarantees of ample security and stability," but the bonds would bring in "large amounts of foreign Capital so necessary to the full and rapid development of the great internal resources of our State." And the importance of the Citizens' Bank to the state's planters was even more pressing with the failure of Congress to renew the charter of the Second Bank of the United States. "The expediency of fostering the Citizens' Bank and bringing it into immediate operation under the existing contract, must press itself on the minds of your enlightened Body, when you reflect on the almost unavoidable embarrassment which will follow the winding of the Colossal institution about to expire" in 1836.[55]

The legislature responded favorably to this request later that month, authorizing the sale of up to $12 million in Louisiana state bonds, which would be secured with the mortgage collateral of the bank.[56] As had been the case with the Union Bank, the state would take one-sixth of the bank's profits in return for its backing (or a smaller percentage if it failed to sell the full $12 million bond issue). "The whole amount of these State profits shall be appropriated to the benefit of free schools, agreeably to the population of each parish."[57] Additionally, the bank would annually donate $5,000 to each of the scholarship funds of the College of Jefferson in St. James, the College of Franklin in Opelousas, and the College of Jackson in East Feliciana.[58]

With the proceeds of these bonds, the Citizens' Bank obtained the necessary funds to begin exercising "all the rights and privileges usually accorded to banks," including the ability to issue banknotes, "to discount bills, notes, and bills of exchange, . . . and to lend money upon mortgage or pledge of property, movable or immovable."[59] In the case of stockholders, they would be permitted to obtain loans "equal to one-half of the total amount of his stock," using the stock itself—which had already been secured with plantations and enslaved lives—as collateral.[60] This ability to borrow against one's bank stock was the main inducement to obtaining shares, although some subscribers (like the heirs of Victorin Roman) may also have invested in the hope of future dividends once the bonds had been repaid. St. Julien Tournillon, for example, immediately obtained a loan to repay his debt to the Bank of Louisiana, and the latter bank released him from his mortgage obligation on July 16, 1836.[61] Charles Dufau likewise paid $6,000 toward his debt with the Lizardi Brothers in June 1836.[62] Many other shareholders quickly began converting their stock to loans. One St. Bernard planter received a loan of $5,000 in the spring of 1837 "secured by a pledge of his stock and a mortgage on his plantation & slaves already mortgaged to secure said stock."[63] Another partnership similarly received a loan of $4,000, in addition to the $2,500 loan which "has already been granted,"[64] while a Pointe Coupée slaveholder received a loan of $15,700.[65] Non-shareholders also applied for mortgages, such as the $10,000 loan to one slaveholder in the summer of 1837, which was "secured by mortgage on his plantation on Sirily Island . . . valued at $22,400 & on sixteen slaves."[66]

The major advantage of Citizens' Bank mortgages over other bank loans was their length and size; debtors could renew these loans every twelve months, repaying annually the interest and one-fourteenth of the principal, for up to fourteen years.[67] The bank believed that these interest and principal payments would be sufficient to pay the annual interest on the bonds, as well as the principal which would come due in "equal portions, in fourteen, twenty-three, thirty-two, forty-one and fifty years."[68] Bernard Marigny used his 2,530 bank shares as collateral for borrowing against the bank, obtaining several loans from the bank totaling more than $100,000 (about $2.9 million in 2021). Marigny was required to pay the annual interest on his mortgage notes (ranging from 6.5 percent to 8 percent), plus one-twelfth of the principal when the notes fell due each May, making this a twelve-year mortgage. These proceeds would be used to pay the annual interest on the bonds. But if Marigny failed to pay this debt, the bank could foreclose on his mortgage, selling the land and human property to reimburse the bondholders.[69]

All profits from principal and interest payments on loans accrued to a sinking fund for the repayment of the bonds.[70] After each of these bond payments, the directors would "divide among the stockholders one-fifth of the profits made up to that time, if any there be," which they could then "appl[y] to loans on mortgages."[71] Stockholders could also transfer ownership of their stock shares, as long as the buyer of the shares could "furnish a mortgage to the satisfaction of a majority of all the directors."[72] Under the amended charter of 1836, individual stockholders could own no more than two thousand shares each, for a maximum potential loan amount of $100,000 (about $2.9 million in 2021).[73] During the summer of 1836, the bank reduced Marigny's mortgages to bring his subscription in line with this new limitation.[74]

Enslaved Lives as Long-Term Collateral

As these stock and loan applications began pouring in, the Citizens' Bank appointed parish-level commissioners "to examine and appraise the property of all persons who shall subscribe to the stock of said bank, or who shall desire to make loans on mortgages therefrom."[75] On preprinted forms (figure 5.2), the bank requested the dimensions of the property in arpents (a unit of measurement roughly equivalent to six-sevenths of an acre); the number of arpents in cultivation of sugarcane, cotton, and corn; the number of slaves, horses, mules, and cows; the dimensions of the sugarhouse and main dwelling house on the plantation; the power of any machinery or engines in use;

and the gross product of the crops. They were then to list the valuation of the land, dwelling house, slave houses, stables, barns, carts and farm implements, and livestock. Finally, they were directed to value enslaved men, women, and children separately, describing them by name and age on the back of the appraisal form ("Les noms et âge devront être décrits au dos de cette piece [*sic*]").[76]

These valuation lists, which almost always included a separate assessment of each enslaved individual, often also added descriptions to assist in identification and/or to justify the stated valuation. For Jean Estévan's twenty-nine enslaved workers, for example, the assessors included their function on the plantation (figure 5.3). The most highly valued, at $1,800 each, were thirty-three-year-old Maurice, who was a multi-talented "menusier [*sic*], charpentier, charon [*sic*], tonnelier & sucrier" ["joiner, carpenter, wheelwright, cooper & sugar maker"], and thirty-four-year-old "nègre de champ" ["field slave"] Clément. Those valued at $1,500 each included forty-six-year-old Honoré, who was "commandeur, sucrier, tonnelier & charpentier" ["commander"—presumably a driver or head of sugar production, "sugar maker, cooper, & carpenter"]; thirty-four-year-old Klem, who was a "nègre de champ & forgeron" ["field slave & blacksmith"]; and twenty-one-year-old Célestin, who split his time between fieldwork and serving in the main house ["domestique de maison"]. The other three men were all field slaves, valued at $1,800, $1,500, and $500 (the latter amount for forty-eight-year-old Cyprien, the eldest of the mortgaged enslaved men).[77]

The most highly valued women, at $1,000 each, were the teenagers: sixteen-year-old Séraphine, eighteen-year-old field slave Mélitte, and nineteen-year-old house slave Phélis. This valuation likely reflected their potential for producing more enslaved property; Mélitte already had a three-year-old son, and Phélis already had a four-year-old daughter and infant son. Séraphine's mother, Henriette, was also highly valued, at $800, reflecting both her flexible skills as a "field slave, cook, [and] laundress" ["négresse de champ, cuisinière, blanchisseuse"], but also her fertility. In addition to Séraphine, her children included six-year-old Eugène, three-year-old Cécile, and one-year-old Darius. The remaining five women included two field slaves in their thirties, each valued at $600; and three women between the ages of forty and fifty-five, each valued at $500, who multitasked as field slaves, cooks, and laundresses. The twelve children ranged in value from $900, for the eldest preteen boys capable of assisting in the fields, to $100 for the infants.[78]

The detailed descriptions of mortgaged lives by name and age, and sometimes by occupation, color, or other relevant descriptors, was necessary to ensure that the assessed value of the enslaved lives was accurate. If the bank

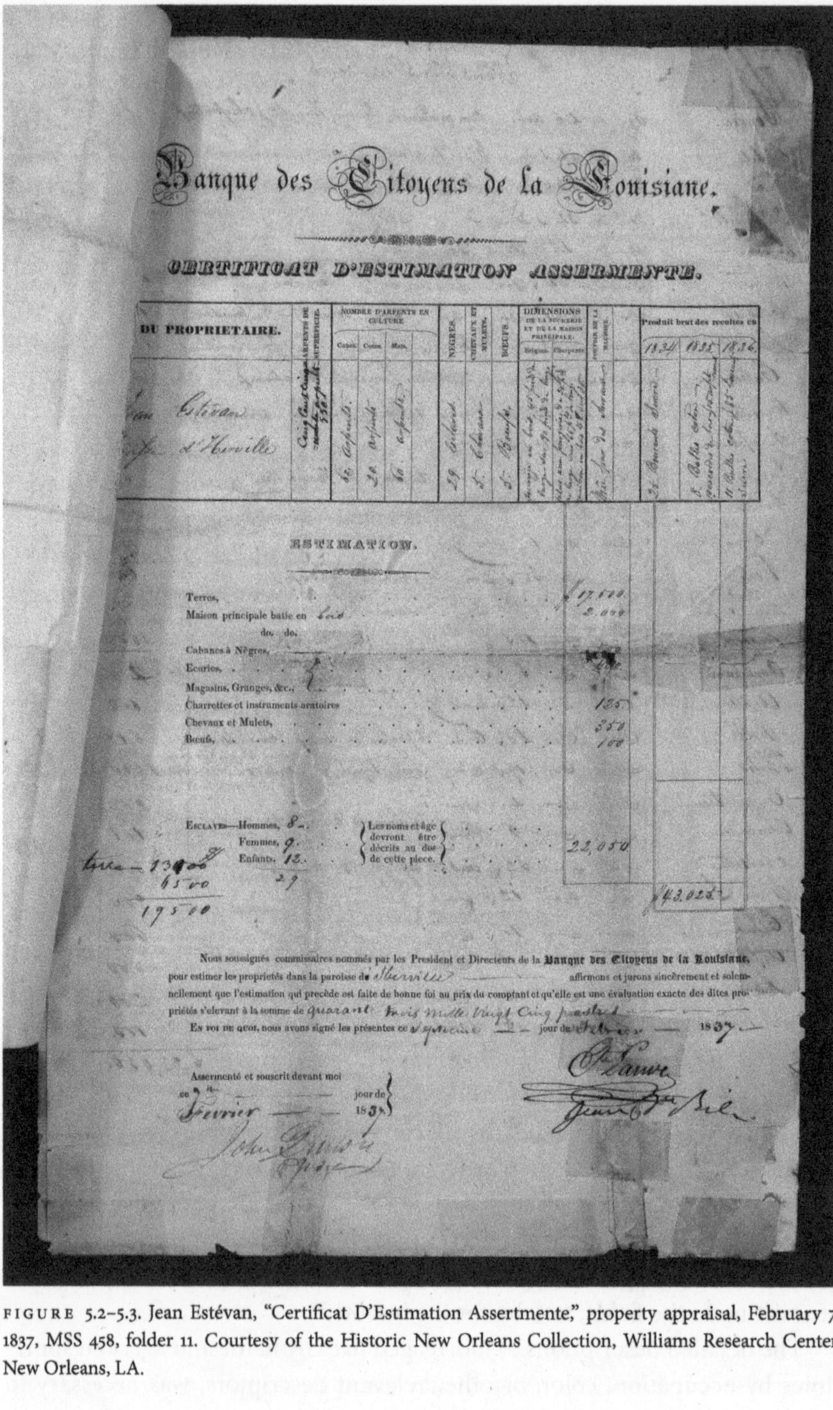

Banque des Citoyens de la Louisiane.

CERTIFICAT D'ESTIMATION ASSERMENTE.

DU PROPRIETAIRE.	ARPENTS DE SUPERFICIE.	NOMBRE D'ARPENTS EN CULTURE			NÈGRES.	CHEVAUX ET MULETS.	BŒUFS.	DIMENSIONS DE LA SUCRERIE ET DE LA MAISON PRINCIPALE.	POUVOIR DE LA MACHINE.		Produit brut des recoltes en		
		Cann.	Coton.	Maïs.							1834	1835	1836
Jean Estévan d'Iberville	530	60 arpents	20 arpents	60 arpents	29	5	5						

ESTIMATION.

Terres,	$17,500
Maison principale batie en bois	2,000
do. do.	
Cabanes à Nègres,	
Ecuries,	
Magasins, Granges, &c.,	
Charrettes et instruments aratoires	125
Chevaux et Mulets,	350
Bœufs,	100
Esclaves—Hommes, 8. Femmes, 9. Enfants, 12. (Les noms et âge devront être décrits au dos de cette piece.)	22,050
	$43,025

Nous soussignés commissaires nommés par les President et Directeurs de la Banque des Citoyens de la Louisiane, pour estimer les propriétés dans la paroisse de Iberville affirmons et jurons sincèrement et solemnellement que l'estimation qui precède est faite de bonne foi au prix du comptant et qu'elle est une évaluation exacte des dites propriétés s'elevant à la somme de quarante trois mille vingt cinq piastres

En foi de quoi, nous avons signé les présentes ce septième jour de février 1837.

Assermenté et souscrit devant moi ce 7 jour de Fevrier 1837.

FIGURE 5.2–5.3. Jean Estévan, "Certificat D'Estimation Assertmente," property appraisal, February 7, 1837, MSS 458, folder 11. Courtesy of the Historic New Orleans Collection, Williams Research Center, New Orleans, LA.

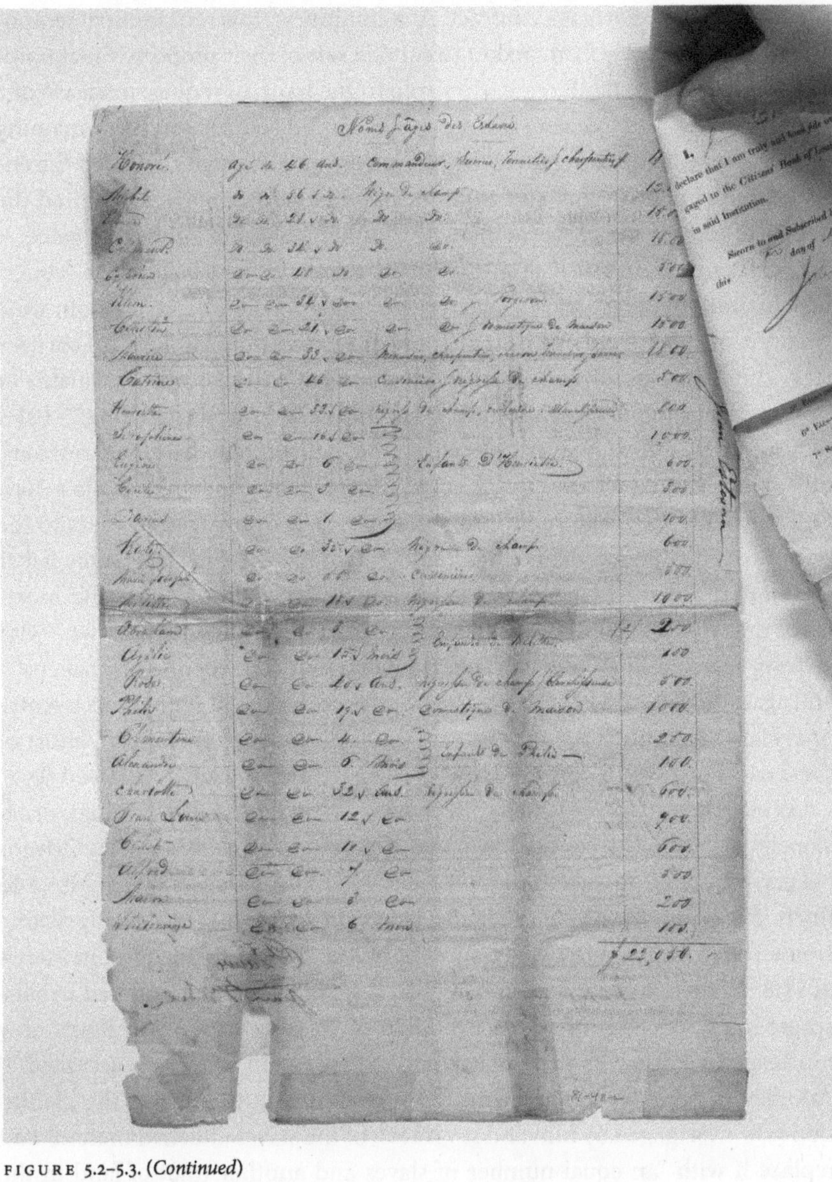

FIGURE 5.2–5.3. *(Continued)*

needed to seize and sell enslaved individuals in a foreclosure proceeding, this list would theoretically prevent the slaveholder from fraudulently substituting less valuable people for those in the original assessment. Yet by directly tying specific enslaved lives to the mortgage liens, debtors became unable to sell their human property without receiving a formal release of the enslaved person from the mortgage contract. At a minimum, this requirement temporarily delayed owners from making a sudden sale of their property. Stockholders of the Citizens' Bank regularly wrote to the bank to request a release of a particular enslaved life from the mortgage lien. In some cases, the remaining property was adequate to cover the obligation, and the board released the enslaved individual without substitution. In other cases, the bank required the debtor to replace the enslaved life with another person of equivalent value.

For example, in April 1836, the board granted one slaveholder's request to substitute "le negre [*sic*]" Isaac for the "mulatto" Bill, both of whom were twenty-three years old, on his stock mortgage with the bank.[79] In February 1838, the board permitted another slaveholder "to substitute a Mulatto of 22 years of age to the slave Marguerite whom she is desirous of selling."[80] Later that summer, a third planter "was allowed to substitute to his slave Davis another slave named Charles in his act of Mortgage to the Bank," while a New Orleans baker "was allowed to substitute the slave John aged 16 years to the slave Rose, now mortgaged to the Bank."[81] Two months later, this same baker substituted twenty-year-old Louise to release Jerry Ridon from the mortgage, then (two weeks later) replaced another Rose (age twenty-two) with sixteen-year-old Julia "attachée à la Boulangerie" ["attached to the bakery"], and again (three days later) replaced twenty-five-year-old Jenny with twenty-one-year-old Sanite.[82] As was the case with Marguerite, presumably most of these cases involved a slaveholder who wished to sell the newly released slave.

While these releases usually involved a single enslaved individual, occasionally a slaveholder wanted to make a larger swap. Another New Orleans bakery requested to substitute seven enslaved males—aged twenty-three to thirty-five—for the seven originally listed on the contract—mostly young women aged fourteen to twenty-six. The board granted this request in March of 1838.[83] The following September, "Mr. F. C. B. de St Aubin offered to substitute his slaves Sam of 31 years & Ellen of 50 years to the two slaves now mortgaged viz Isaac 27 years & Mariany 60 years—his offer was accepted."[84] Another slaveholder requested in the spring of 1839 to release "the plantation now mortgaged by him and seventeen of the slaves attached thereto" and replace it with "an equal number of slaves and another tract of land in the Parish of Ascension." The board also accepted this offer.[85] Bernard Marigny, who owned several large plantations in different parishes, similarly sought to release Celestin, Mariane, Grand Jeanne, and Anna from his mortgage, replacing them at his St. Tammany plantation with four others "who are on his plantation at Plaquemines"—twenty-six-year-old Marie Covington, twenty-five-year-old Marie Bell, ten-year-old Bigny, and thirty-five-year-old blacksmith John Magnan.[86] The following year, Marigny again requested to replace ten enslaved individuals with ten others (including Amélie, who was notable for having "yeux bleus" ["blue eyes"]), while simultaneously receiving a release on two children: seven-year-old Chemine and ten-year-old Pauline. The board agreed to both requests.[87] And in January 1845, a different planter sought to substitute twenty-four-year-old Ryley, fourteen-year-old Willis, and thirty-year-old Hannah with Big Henry, Lewis, and Ann—all of whom were in their early twenties. This slaveholder "produced the certificate" of two other bank stockholders "stating that the three slaves offered were superior to the ones above mentioned." The bank agreed to the release.[88]

In the summer and fall of 1838, John Fitz Miller purchased several pieces of land in St. Martin Parish to form a large cotton plantation, with the attached enslaved workers and over six hundred shares of Citizens' Bank stock.[89] Two years later, Miller sought to release twenty-five enslaved individuals from the mortgage, replacing them with twenty-seven different people. In doing so, Miller stipulated that these newly mortgaged people were distinct from any of the enslaved individuals under his other mortgage liens who shared similar names:

> The slave Denis mentioned in said certificate [of the recorder of mortgages] is a dark mulatto aged thirty five or thirty eight years whilst the slave Denis now mortgaged is a black boy aged fourteen years, that the slave Fanny mentioned in said certificate is a negrowoman fifty years old, whilst the Fanny now mortgaged is called Fanny Travis and is a dark mulatress aged thirty five years. That the slave Charlotte now mortgaged is called Charlotte Randolph and is a negro woman aged thirty two years whilst the other Charlotte mentioned in the said certificate was a griffonne bought by him from the Estate of Wm Cecil and resold by him several years ago to Mr. Leaumont. Whence it results that there are no mortgages on the above described slaves.

The bank agreed to this replacement, keeping the mortgage on the land as well as on thirty-seven-year-old Peter, twenty-year-old Manuel, and forty-seven-year-olds Sam and Dilly.[90]

If a slaveholder possessed adequate collateral to cover the debt—either because he or she had paid down part of the debt or because the remaining property was sufficient—the bank did not require a substitute. When one widow "applied for the release of her mortgage so far as it bears on the slave Jonas," the board concluded that she had "furnished an excess of Security for the stock" and thus "her request was granted."[91] Similarly, another slaveholder wished to release twenty-five-year-old Lucinda in April 1839. The board agreed, he having "furnished $500 more security than was required for the 200 shares he possesses."[92] After a different planter sold seventy shares of his stock in the Citizens' Bank in November 1840, he requested a release of three of the enslaved individuals. The directors assented, since "the property now mortgaged to secure his stock" was "of a much greater value than is required."[93] Upon paying off part of his loan in July 1841, another planter received a release on the mortgage of two of his bondspeople.[94] Similarly, after another debtor paid off $1,250 of his bank loan in November 1841, the directors released one of his enslaved people from the mortgage.[95]

In other cases, the release reflected the declining value of the enslaved individuals. Although one slaveholder had originally included forty-year-old Henrietta (also known as Harriet) as part of his collateral, the board granted her release in the summer of 1839 as she now "was considered of no value."[96] In January of 1840, the board agreed to another planter's proposal to replace "five worthless slaves which he is desirous of returning to his sellers" with five others, valuing them at "say $500 p[er]. slave."[97] Three years later, a different slaveholder offered to substitute another enslaved life for Hillard, who was a runaway. He also hoped to get a refund from the slave's vendor.[98]

These types of releases were common at other banks as well. When one husband and wife received a $3,500 loan from the Bank of Louisiana in April 1834, they mortgaged several enslaved individuals, including sixty-two-year-old David. Two years later, the bank agreed to allow the couple to substitute twenty-five-year-old Mary for David, whom they now valued at $400.[99] And in January of 1841, the same bank granted another planter a release of eighteen-year-old Louise, who was among the enslaved workers he had mortgaged to secure $2,500 in 1840, replacing her with sixteen-year-old Auguste.[100] In 1838, a slaveholding family mortgaged four enslaved individuals to the Bank of the State of Georgia to secure a note of $800 due in sixty-one days. A week before that note was due, the bank "agreed to cancel the said Mortgage, and to take a Mortgage upon other slaves for the same purpose," listing teenagers John, Joe, Rosa, and Julian on the new contract.[101]

In addition to the property appraisal and the judge's certificate listing any prior liens on the land and human property, applicants to the Citizens' Bank also needed to submit three more pieces of information to establish their rightful and continued ownership of the enslaved individuals being offered as collateral. The bank required "the bills of sale of the slaves," or other evidence of how the applicant had initially acquired the enslaved person, to demonstrate his or her ownership claim. And to ensure that the enslaved individual still remained his or her property, the applicant also needed to furnish "a certificate from the sheriff of his Parish that he pays taxes on these slaves," as well as "an affidavit that they are living and are now on the place mortgaged."[102] In July 1836, for example, John Reid "personally came and appeared" before the justice of the peace for East Baton Rouge, attesting that "he has personally known for ten years and upward the following named slaves as the property of Joshua Alexander." Reid swore that Alexander was "the bona fide owner in quiet possession of the same, who are offered as stock for the Citizens' Bank."[103]

Another slaveholder gave the bank title papers for ten of the enslaved individuals he mortgaged to secure two hundred shares of bank stock in April 1838; for the remaining twenty-four people, "whose names are designated by an asterisk," he stipulated that they "were born his property."[104] Several months later, when this same slaveholder purchased fifteen more shares, he submitted his sworn statement to the judge of St. Helena Parish in November 1838 that three additional enslaved lives, "Daniel, Maria, and Jesse included in an act of mortgage . . . to the Citizens Bank of Louisiana are now living on his plantation."[105] However, he also "declared that one of the slaves therein mentioned and named Aveline aged nine years, has died since said appraisement."[106]

Upon submitting all of these documents to the bank, the board of directors reserved "the sole and exclusive right to decide on the title to, and the value of, property offered as security for stock subscribed for, or money to be borrowed on mortgage."[107] They also stipulated that if, at any time, "the property now mortgaged is no longer of sufficient value to secure said stock . . . the bank shall have the right to exact additional security. . . . [or] will have the right to Cause said Stock to be sold in whole or in part, and to cause the property mortgaged to be sold."[108]

Applicants were not always happy with the decisions of the board, particularly when they believed that their property was undervalued or if the bank refused their application altogether. In 1834, one applicant sued the Union Bank for refusing his subscription for six hundred shares of stock, which he sought to secure a plantation and enslaved laborers in Jefferson Parish. The bank found that his title to the property, which he had purchased at the succession sale of the heirs of the previous owner, was "insufficient." The directors were not convinced that all the heirs had properly agreed to the sale, and they feared the potential future claims of the previous owner's minor children. The new owner believed that the rejection was "under pretexts entirely unfounded in law," and wanted the court to assess his title and force the bank's assent to his application. The supreme court of Louisiana, however, sided with the bank. Although the justices believed that the new owner likely had a valid claim on the property, that fact was not the issue at hand. According to the bank's charter, the directors "were made by law the judges of the validity of the titles, and of the sufficiency of the property offered to secure the stock of said bank, and that as long as they acted in good faith, they were not liable to be sued."[109] This failed stock subscriber may have suffered "*damnum absque injuria*," or a loss without injury, but the justices "see no ground to suspect capricious and improper views" on the part of the board. Even "if they [the bank directors] have erred" in their assessment of the title, that error was irrelevant. If the directors "are not perfectly satisfied their duty to the corporation, is to withold [*sic*] the expression of their satisfaction" and reject the application.[110]

Plantation Banking beyond Louisiana

The popularity and initial success of the Louisiana plantation banks had two major effects on the banking system. Within the state of Louisiana, traditional banks rapidly embraced long-term mortgages on enslaved lives in order to compete with the new plantation banks. For example, while the City Bank of New Orleans was not a plantation bank, its 1831 charter granted it "like privileges . . . in making loans on mortgage, taking security, and enforcing the payment thereof, as are now accorded by law to the Consolidated Association of the Planters of Louisiana."[111] Outside Louisiana, the plantation-bank model was soon duplicated in at least Arkansas, the Florida territory, and Mississippi. (Other states may have also attempted plantation banks, although these new banks quickly became victims of the Panic of 1837, leaving few surviving records.) In creating these banks, slaveholders were able to tap into their enslaved workers in a unique way, allowing for the expansion of the money supply to be linked explicitly to the market value of enslaved lives. This expansion of long-term lending, secured by enslaved people, also became intertwined with the efforts of Nicholas Biddle to salvage a national bank after the expiration of the Second Bank's charter in 1836.

In 1833, the territory of Florida incorporated the Union Bank of Florida with a capital stock of $3 million, "which capital shall be raised by means of a loan, on the faith of the Territory." To secure these territory-backed bonds, stock subscribers would give mortgages "on land and slaves." But the Florida institution embraced human collateral to an even greater degree than the Louisiana banks had. The Union Bank of Florida permitted enslaved individuals to comprise up to half of the mortgaged property (rather than just one-third), and it allowed shareholders to borrow up to two-thirds of the value of their stock (rather than just one-half) on mortgage. It also specified that "the increase of such slave or slaves," meaning any children born to enslaved women, "shall be subject to the same lien created by said mortgage." While mortgage documents often mentioned the "increase" of enslaved women, this was the first time a *charter* specifically mentioned unborn enslaved children.

Finally, recognizing the highly mobile nature of Florida's population, as well as the growing problem of indebted slaveholders fleeing with their property, the charter specifically empowered judges "to seize and take such slave or slaves" whenever the bank "verily believes that the said mortgagor intends removing or is about to remove, or has commenced to remove the said slave or slaves beyond the reach of the laws of this Territory."[112] Although some people questioned the constitutionality of a territorial legislature passing a law which would bind the faith and credit of a future state, Congress ultimately approved the legislation creating this bank.[113]

Despite the fact that Florida territorial governor William P. Duval had vetoed all previous bank charters for traditional commercial banks, he believed that "the time has arrived, when the great planting interest of Florida calls for such an institution" on the plantation-bank model. Contrasting them with traditional banks that "have, in many instances exploded, overwhelming their creditors with ruin, convulsing society, and destroying the happiness of thousands," the plantation model would avoid all these risks. "If the stockholders are true to their own interests,—nay,—unless they determine to ruin themselves, this institution will not only be secure, but must be as serviceable to the general interests of the country, as it will be profitable to the stockholders." Indeed, Duval perceived no risk to either the state or the holders of banknotes, since "if any loss should occur, it must fall on the stockholders; and as their lands and slaves will be pledged as ultimate security; nothing short of such a revolution, can destroy the value of their lands; or a sweeping pestilence, exterminate their slaves."[114] Once again, the imagination of bank promoters failed to encompass the possibility of another major economic panic.

Upon opening in 1835, the Union Bank of Florida "unleashed a flood of credit." In historian Edward Baptist's estimation, "attracted by the smell of standing money, interstate slave traders brought thousands of enslaved migrants to the region during the next few years" as part of this "Union Bank-funded burst of the slave trade."[115] That same year, the Territory of Florida also incorporated the Southern Life Insurance & Trust Company, which, despite its name, primarily operated as a plantation bank. Its $2 million capitalization was to be "secured by unencumbered real and personal estates, lying and being in the Territory of Florida, of double the value, in each case, of the sum so secured."[116] In practice, the Southern Life "concentrat[ed] specifically on cotton speculation" when issuing its loans.[117]

Despite the stated purpose of these Florida banks to support the planters of the territory, an 1840 congressional investigation into their operation found that they had failed to live up to their promise:

> The charter [of the Union Bank] intended that two thirds of the money borrowed by the sale of bonds, should be loaned on long mortgages to the subscribers, who had taken up the shares, and given their property as security. . . . and the remaining third . . . should remain in bank, to perform the commonly received legitimate business of banking—such as discounting promissory notes [that] have a short time to run, buying and selling bills of exchange, furnishing a paper medium of circulating currency, and affording such other facilities in money transactions.[118]

However, the stock quickly became concentrated in the hands of just a few wealthy planters, who dominated the bank's debtors while often offering insufficient credit.[119] Not only were loans "incautiously made in large amounts, on long time, to persons not previously considered rich," but the bank was also overly lax in assessing the property. For example, the enslaved individuals "which form so considerable a part of the security of the large stockholders" were often "simply enumerated, as 'Tom,' or 'Dick,' 'Sally,' or 'Mary,' with no further description, unless occasionally the age." This practice meant that the bank had to rely "upon the honor of their owners" as to the identity of the actual collateral. And since "slave property is *locomotive*," the investigators worried that "there would be little difficulty, were the parties so disposed, to remove the whole 2,682 slaves beyond the jurisdiction of the Territory in one night."[120] But beyond the specific missteps of this bank, the congressional committee condemned the very concept of plantation banks. "The idea of a bank founded on borrowed capital, had before been ill understood—now it was perfectly comprehensible. To become suddenly rich—to become off hand the proprietor of lands, negroes, houses, and equipages, simply by pledging property on a loan with thirty years' credit, which property could be bought with money thus obtained, was to enjoy in reality a vision of fiction."[121] (With only the removal of the word "negroes," this exact same statement could have been made in 2008.) The rapid rise and fall of the Real Estate Bank of Arkansas (1837–1842), which was also chartered as a plantation bank, was likewise tainted by mismanagement and political corruption.[122]

Throughout the frontier South, Nicholas Biddle and the Second Bank worked closely with these plantation banks to try and ensure their success. Writing in 1830 to a Pennsylvania congressman, Biddle explained that "With regard to the new Bank 'the Planters Association'"—meaning the CAPL in Louisiana—"its funds came principally through the Branch Bank & I believe the general intercourse is of the most friendly character."[123] The Second Bank was also actively involved with the sale of state-bond issues related to many of the other plantation banks.[124] In several instances, the Second Bank acted as the agent selling the bonds to investors in New York or Europe. For example, in 1834 Biddle discussed its negotiation of a million-dollar subscription by Baring Brothers to the banks in Louisiana.[125] In 1837, after Arkansas incorporated its Real Estate Bank, the United States Bank (now operating under a Pennsylvania charter) offered to help that state sell its bank bonds in Europe.[126] And in 1838, it was likewise at the center of negotiations with two New York financiers for the sale of 5 percent and 6 percent bonds of the State of Alabama for its state-owned bank (which was not a plantation bank).[127]

The bank's most intense involvement with the plantation banks came in Mississippi. In 1838, Biddle and the United States Bank of Pennsylvania obtained the contract to underwrite the $5 million bond issue (about $148 million) of the Union Bank of Mississippi, the newest of the plantation banks to receive a charter.[128] Biddle wrote to Samuel Jaudon, the US Bank's sales agent in Liverpool, regarding "the purchase of five millions of Mississippi State Bonds, 5 p.ct., payable in London, endorsed & guaranteed by the Union Bank of Mississippi."[129] As the underwriter, the US Bank actually purchased the bonds on credit for resale in smaller lots. As Biddle informed the bank's New Orleans agent in September 1838, "I have, as you are aware, large payments to make, on account of the Mississippi Loan taken by me, in the month of November next, & again another million of dollars in January."[130] Throughout that fall, as his agents unsuccessfully worked to sell the Union Bank bonds, Biddle wrote confidently that he believed that "Mississippi paper will be a profitable and safe investment" and that the "paper will rapidly appreciate."[131] He also purchased "some bonds of the Planter's Bank," another Mississippi bank that was partially owned by the state (although not a plantation bank), which he deemed "bonds that are very safe and bear a very good interest."[132] This heavy investment in southern bank bonds would contribute to the United States Bank of Pennsylvania's failure during the 1840s (chapter 8).

The Bank War and Proxy Banks

While banks of the old South were somewhat-reluctant participants in the financing of slavery's spread to the frontier, the Second Bank of the United States was increasingly willing. In addition to its branches in Savannah, Georgia (1817), and New Orleans, Louisiana (1817), the bank opened two additional frontier branches during the postwar boom in Mobile, Alabama (1826), and Natchez, Mississippi (1830). Yet the bank remained a controversial institution, and it had to balance between cultivating support among southern constituents and meeting the expectations and demands of its northern advocates. Although the Second Bank was chartered through 1836, President Andrew Jackson made his disdain for the financial institution known during his first

State of the Union address in 1829. Many people had blamed the bank for exacerbating the Panic of 1819, yet under the leadership of Nicholas Biddle during the 1820s, it had established itself as a stabilizing force in the economy and enjoyed relatively widespread popularity. Kentucky senator—and presidential hopeful—Henry Clay thus schemed that he could force the popular president into a bind by convincing Biddle to apply for a recharter of the bank four years early, during the presidential year of 1832. If Jackson vetoed the recharter, Clay was confident that Congress would override the veto, and Clay would be handed an issue on which to campaign against Jackson—especially in those states such as Pennsylvania where the bank was particularly popular. Biddle decided to go along with this plan, and applied for a recharter early in 1832.[133]

In March 1832, the House of Representatives convened a committee to examine the conduct of the Second Bank of the United States and to determine "whether the provisions of its charter have been violated" or "whether there have been any circumstances of mismanagement."[134] Initiated by several antibank congressmen, the purpose of these inquiries was to uncover some illegal actions or policies that they could use to sway public opinion against the institution. Short of that, they aimed to tarnish the reputation of both Biddle and the Second Bank while simultaneously delaying a vote on the recharter legislation until after the fall election. The highly partisan final committee report, which was filed on April 30, 1832, and supported by the four Jacksonians on the committee, found lots of questionable behavior and improprieties but no smoking gun.[135]

The three pro-bank members of the committee wrote a pointed dissent in which they attached the full documentation from the investigation, including a series of questions addressed to Biddle with his responses. Among the queries was: "Has the Bank any interest in slaves . . . ?" to which Biddle tellingly replied: "I am not aware that the Bank has any interest in slaves *except so far as they may be included in mortgages for debts in the Southern States*." Biddle then briefly mentioned that "the only direct interest in slaves" of the bank was in 1826, when it had seized a plantation and its enslaved workforce in Louisiana, holding all the property until it could be sold the following year.[136] Although in his concise description Biddle called this property a "cotton plantation," it is possible (based on the timing) that he was actually referring to the Magnolia Grove sugar plantation in Louisiana, which the bank possessed after foreclosing on Dennis A. Smith and Philemon C. Wederstrandt in the 1820s (chapter 2). Biddle's response to the committee was simultaneously honest and disingenuous. He freely admitted that enslaved lives were a common component of southern mortgage contracts, including those of the

Second Bank. Yet he downplayed this relationship, implying that it was both minor and indirect—likely in an attempt to avoid alienating northern supporters of the bank as well as the banking establishment, who still adhered to the belief in short-term discount notes as the core of a bank's loan portfolio.

Unfortunately for Biddle, Clay's predictions of how the affair would play out after Jackson vetoed the recharter legislation in July 1832 were wrong on all counts. Congress was not able to marshal enough votes for a veto override, and it was not a winning issue for Clay in the November election.[137] Although four years still remained on the charter, the prospects for obtaining a charter renewal with Jackson in the White House were slim, especially after Jackson successfully convinced the public that Biddle and the Second Bank were responsible for the recession of 1833–34 (rather than Jackson's removal of government deposits from the bank).[138]

With a federal charter out of reach, Biddle saved the bank from liquidation in 1836 by obtaining a state charter from Pennsylvania, yet he still sought to maintain the institution's extensive national reach, from which it drew most of its economic power. In order to continue providing financial services across the country, he needed to get around the various state laws which banned out-of-state banks from opening branches. One option was to establish close alliances with key banks in each state. Biddle's plan was to arrange for a newly chartered bank "to purchase the whole establishment of the [branch] Office near them, banking house, debts & all." Not only would this arrangement be "very advantageous" to the new bank, which would immediately obtain the "standing, capital, deposits & custom" of the branch office, but it would also eliminate the time, expense, and hassle of settling the business of each branch. Biddle also envisioned the former branch management taking over control of the new banks, tying them even more closely to the future United States Bank of Pennsylvania.[139]

The Lexington, Kentucky, branch was the perfect model of this process. As Biddle explained in an August 6, 1835, letter to John Huske, president of the Fayetteville, North Carolina, branch of the Second Bank: "The President & Cashier of the [Lexington] Office have been appointed the President & Cashier of the Northern Bank of Kentucky," which had been newly incorporated in 1835; the new bank agreed to assume all the assets and debts of the branch in the process. Biddle likewise encouraged Huske to accept the presidency of the new Fayetteville branch of the recently rechartered State Bank of North Carolina, or to "make a similar arrangement . . . with any other institution" that "would be satisfactory to us."[140] In October 1835, the bank urged its Natchez branch cashier Thomas Henderson to negotiate "for a sale to the Planters Bank of Miss[i] of the entire local debt of your office." Parent-bank cashier Samuel Jaudon explained the terms Henderson should offer, concluding, "Should the Planters Bank decline acceding to the terms proposed, you will see that your Board is authorized and instructed to offer the same terms to the Agricultural Bank, or such other Bank as they may think offers ample security, and to report the result to the parent Board for its final action."[141] Yet while this type of relationship would create a close alliance with the United States Bank, it would not provide the bank with any direct control of banking in these states.

Rather than state banks purchasing the assets of the former branches, another option was for the United States Bank to become the silent owner of out-of-state banks. Soon after formally incorporating with the state of Pennsylvania in February 1836, Biddle sought and received an addendum to its charter authorizing it "to purchase and hold any real estate belonging to the late Bank of the United States, and also to purchase and hold any bank stock."[142] This permission to purchase bank stock was critical to Biddle's plan for asserting even greater control over out-of-state banks. Biddle informed James Hunter, cashier of the Savannah, Georgia, branch, that "I did this under an impression that it might be well to buy the whole of the Stock of any new Bank incorporated in a good position, and convert it into an Agency." He then inquired if Hunter knew of "any such institution in Georgia, old or new" that would serve this purpose, yet warned him that "for obvious reasons, you will confine the knowledge of this letter to yourself alone."[143]

A few months later, Biddle put this plan into action with the newly chartered Merchants' Bank of New Orleans. Employing prominent slave trader James Erwin as his agent for this transaction, Biddle orchestrated a change to the bylaws of the Louisiana bank, which permitted the transfer of the bank's stock to "residents of Pennsylvania"—members of the bank's board who were designated by Biddle for this purpose. Once these transactions were completed and the United States Bank had operational control over the Merchants' Bank, the Pennsylvania institution would pay Erwin $100,000 (about $2.9 million in 2021) for his services.[144] The transfer occurred without a hitch and was completed by September 1836. Biddle next set his sights on Alabama, where he inquired of former Mobile branch cashier George Poe Jr. whether there was "any thing to be done in that way in Alabama? You mentioned the project of reviving an old broken down bank. Is any thing done, or will any thing be done in that matter?"[145] The bank ultimately failed to get a secure foothold in Alabama, where state laws made this type of transaction more difficult, although the bank did continue to conduct financial transactions through several agents in Mobile.[146] But later in 1836, it succeeded in getting control of the Insurance Bank of Columbus, Georgia.[147] One final attempt in

1839 to purchase controlling stock of the newly chartered Hamilton Bank of Baltimore fell through when that bank failed to open.[148]

Under the United States Bank's guidance, both the Merchants' Bank of New Orleans and the Fayetteville branch of the Bank of the State of North Carolina regularly engaged in the underwriting of enslaved people. Yet reflecting accepted local banking practices, the loans secured by human property in North Carolina tended to be relatively small, while the Louisiana mortgages reflected the extensive mortgages now common in that state. In purchasing the assets of the Fayetteville branch of the Second Bank, the North Carolina bank just continued the planter relations of its predecessor. For example, John M. Dobbin had obtained a loan of $4,515 from the Second Bank branch in 1829, offering his twelve enslaved people as collateral.[149] Ten months later, he used the same twelve named slaves plus fifteen additional enslaved individuals to secure the $3,000 remaining due on the original loan, as well as a new $500 loan from the bank.[150] Five years later, in 1835, Dobbin renewed these notes again—now owing $2,675 and $145—with twenty-four enslaved lives, most of whom had been listed on the 1830 deed. However, this third loan was with the Fayetteville branch of the Bank of the State of North Carolina, where John W. Huske—former president of the Second Bank branch in that city and Dobbin's son-in-law—was now president.[151] Similarly, Paris J. Tillinghast had obtained a $600 loan from the Second Bank branch in Fayetteville in November 1832, offering his slave Lucy Ann and her two daughters Julia Ann and Lucy Ann as collateral.[152] While Tillinghast owned eight enslaved males and nine females according to the 1830 census, these were the only three enslaved people he put in peril of sale.[153] Three years later, Tillinghast renewed his loan for $414, secured by the same three enslaved lives, but this time the lender was the Fayetteville branch of the State Bank of North Carolina.[154]

Whereas the North Carolina bank continued the lending practices of the Second Bank branch in that state, the Merchants' Bank of New Orleans specialized in loans to particularly large planters. Both the First and Second Banks occasionally underwrote a few large, long-term loans, such as the 1818 Smith mortgage granted by the Baltimore branch on the Magnolia Grove plantation in Louisiana, yet these loans were departures from both the banks' normal lending practices and their charter regulations. On the other hand, most of the debts of the Merchants' Bank involved it initiating or securing a large, long-term loan collateralized by human property. Alexander McNeill of Vicksburg, Mississippi, owed the United States Bank of Pennsylvania debts totaling over $38,000 (about $1.1 million in 2021), payable at the Merchants' Bank in two annual payments due in 1839 and 1840. To secure this debt, on January 15, 1838, McNeill mortgaged his plantation in the parish of Carroll,

Louisiana, along with forty named slaves—a fraction of the total enslaved community he owned between his Louisiana and Mississippi plantations.[155] Similarly, John P. Walworth and his wife Sarah Wren, both of Natchez, Mississippi, owed the United States Bank $70,000 (about $2.1 million in 2021) on four promissory notes due annually on May 1, from 1846 to 1849, and likewise payable at the Merchants' Bank. In 1841 they mortgaged their cotton plantation in Concordia, Louisiana, along with forty-two enslaved workers "and all the children of the said slaves belonging to the said appearers whether named in this act of mortgage or otherwise in all about sixty in number, also all their increase for and during the continuance of this act." As part of the agreement, Walworth and his wife promised "not to remove any of the said Slaves from the Plantation whereon they are now employed"—an important concession to protect the bank since the couple owned other plantations in Mississippi.[156]

Also in 1841, the heirs of Thomas Bibb—former governor of Alabama—obtained a mortgage of $125,046.38 (about $3.9 million in 2021) from the Merchants' Bank, guaranteeing the loan with a plantation and 245 enslaved individuals in Lafourche Parish, Louisiana. According to the terms of the mortgage, the heirs would pay back the loan in seventeen installments from 1842 through 1859.[157] That same day, they mortgaged the same property to the Bank of Louisiana to secure a separate debt of $54,000, and another plantation and enslaved workforce to the Commercial Bank of New Orleans for a $29,000 debt and to the Canal Bank for a $36,730 debt.[158] These immense loans rivaled even the largest mortgages underwritten by the plantation banks of the 1830s, and the Bibb heirs would spend the next decade struggling to meet these debt obligations (chapter 9).

❋

The plantation banks that developed in the 1830s were based on sophisticated financial concepts. While southerners might not have had the jargon to describe these ideas fully, they had found a way to monetize their human property. Enslaved labor was first an input in production, generating profitable crops for a global market. With the closing of the international slave trade, enslaved people became a store of value for their owners—particularly given their positive rate of natural increase in North America. Slaveholders could not only buy and sell people as needed like any other asset, but they could literally grow their wealth by breeding enslaved children. Yet this substantial investment in land and human property was not very liquid; it tied up capital and limited further investment in the region's economy.

Frontier banks, however, solved this problem by allowing slaveholders to leverage their stored wealth in enslaved people. Slaveholders could now borrow against the market value of enslaved bodies in anticipation of repaying the debt either from future profits or the appreciation in value of the enslaved life itself. Like a home equity loan, they could tap into the value of their human property while still enjoying the full advantage of their profitable labor, natural increase, and appreciating market value. Even more, enslaved people became abstract, fungible assets as part of bond instruments that could be bought and sold on the world's most modern financial exchanges. And unlike the slaveholders, traders of these instruments could remain willfully ignorant of the enslaved lives upon which their investments were based.

The success of both the plantation banks and those traditional banks engaged in large, long-term lending secured by property depended on the market stability of the underlying assets—land and enslaved people. Even with the memories of the Panic of 1819, no one was prepared for the possibility of the economy again collapsing. And just as leverage multiplies the wealth-producing effects of an asset in good economic times, it greatly exacerbates the losses in a downturn. Southerners quickly found that they had overleveraged their human property, and needed to figure out how to disentangle these enslaved lives from the collapsing banks without destroying the system of slavery itself.

PART III

The Collateral Damage of the Panics of 1837 and 1839

By the winter of 1836–1837—at the same time that the states of the frontier South were organizing both joint banking-improvement companies and new plantation banks focused on long-term loans secured by land and human property—London credit markets had already begun to tighten, and global cotton prices were in decline. From March to May 1837, the three major New Orleans merchant bankers principally responsible for the cotton trade with England closed their doors, sending shockwaves through the financial community. Banks throughout the nation began suspending specie payments, further contracting the money supply. Despite a brief recovery in 1838, a second panic hit in 1839 and the nation settled into a prolonged depression that lasted until around 1843.[1]

In many ways, the Panic of 1819 and the Panics of 1837 and 1839 were quite similar, at least in their macroeconomic effects on the US economy. As figure 2.1 from chapter 2 demonstrates, speculative bubbles in the prices of land and human property foreshadowed both periods, followed by a collapse in market values; commodity prices did not begin their gradual recovery until the mid-1820s and mid-1840s respectively. Although a comparison of the larger causes and effects of these panics is outside the purview of this book, the impact of the 1830s downturn was decidedly more widespread than that of the earlier panic. A much-larger proportion of the population had been directly integrated into the market economy by the 1830s, making them more vulnerable to wide swings in asset prices and to a collapse of financial institutions.[2] The involvement of commercial banks in fueling the speculative credit economy of the 1830s was also more explicit, especially on the western frontier. The ability and willingness of southwestern banks to finance large, long-term loans backed by the inflated valuations of land and enslaved individuals placed these financial institutions in a much more difficult position once the economy collapsed in the late 1830s.

As the economy faced another panic, debt defaults, *fieri facias* suits, and foreclosure proceedings predictably rose. And as during the Panic of 1819, banks had to choose between short-term leniency toward debtors (which might endanger the bank's solvency), and the hassle, expense, and risk of seizing and selling property in a depressed market. Having invested so heavily in plantations and enslaved lives during the 1830s, most banks chose to prop up the system of slavery, rather than oversee its systematic collapse. Yet despite this tendency toward leniency, banks often did find it necessary to foreclose on certain debtors (chapter 6). Even more so than during the early 1820s, southern banks of the 1840s faced extended foreclosure lawsuits, greater instances of fraud, and other challenges related to long-term mortgage contracts. Foreclosures were not only complicated by the claims of multiple creditors, and the confusing counterclaims of widows and heirs, but also newer difficulties such as the release of a debtor's obligations through federal bankruptcy proceedings, and the flight of debtors with enslaved people to the Republic of Texas (chapter 7). The willingness of banks to embrace long-term mortgages on land and human property, and their leniency toward many delinquent slaveholders during the depression itself, ultimately resulted in the failure of a large percentage of banks—particularly in the frontier South; these failures had wide repercussions for both the debtors and the enslaved men, women, and children who had been offered as collateral (chapter 8).

Despite—or perhaps because of—the collapse of the banking sector, banks substantially assisted slaveholders in weathering the depression and ultimately paved the way for the South to emerge as a global economic powerhouse by mid-century. Yet banks also received much of the blame for the hard times. As the frontier of the 1830s became more settled, legislatures aggressively pushed back against bank financing of slavery, forcing slaveholders to pursue other methods of financial support. Several Deep South states would eventually reconsider the wisdom of their anti-banking policies during the 1850s. Yet in doing so, they would return to the traditionally conservative banking principles of the North and the Eastern Seaboard, rejecting the innovative banking practices that had driven southern frontier development in the 1830s (chapter 9).

6

Foreclosing (or Not) on Delinquent Slaveholders

On January 24, 1837, "a cold, raw day" with "a drizzling rain from the northeast," Henry William Huntington of Natchez, Mississippi, wrote to his neighbor William Newton Mercer about the state of the local cotton crop. Mercer, who was on an extended tour of Europe, had left oversight of his four large cotton plantations with overseers, and relied on his neighbors and friends for periodic updates.[1] At his own Greenoak plantation, Huntington reported that "Our ploughing and manuring is going on very well, . . . and I am looking forward to 1200 bales for this years crop, and that without hard work." In political news, he related that "the Legislature of our State . . . has refused Banking privileges to the Natchez rail road company, and granted a charter to what they call a 'Union Bank' with 15000000 capital." Yet Huntington seemed a bit skeptical about this newest plantation bank, remarking sarcastically "Are we not in the high road to wealth?"[2]

By April, Huntington's letters to Mercer took a much-darker tone. Three enslaved individuals at Mercer's Ormond plantation—Joe, Edmund, and Sarah—had fallen ill with some kind of fever. Although "Joe particularly seemed very well, and I had no doubt that in a couple of days he would go out, . . . he suddenly became worse, and at 9 o'clock died." Edmund and Sarah, however, now seemed to be recovering and "there are no new cases." Later, when Huntington went into town, he "learned there that the small pox has made its appearance." He was going to talk to someone "about vaccinating" all of the enslaved workers across their five plantations. "It must be immediately attended to."[3]

But Huntington's greatest concern was for "the commercial distress at New Orleans and Natchez, and indeed all through the country" which was "unexampled." The finances of the commission merchants "have been so improvidently managed that they have suddenly failed, and thus the speculators have placed all[,] however slightly they were in debt, on an equality." As a result, "many, very many, have not an ounce of pork, and as they cannot get it without cash, they are not likely to have any, unless they sacrifice property." He proceeded to relate to Mercer a story he recently heard about a man in Vicksburg who had to sell an enslaved man for $400 to buy pork for his plantation. If he could have mortgaged or sold that same enslaved individual "on a credit of twelve months," he "would have brought him 1600 dollars." Yet the planter still needed the man's labor for "the cultivation of his crop." He thus immediately "gave his note to a trader for $1800, the price of a negro, inferior to the one he had sold."[4] Selling cheap and buying dear was a recipe for disaster.

Huntington was at a loss for how to halt the downturn, which he (correctly) predicted would only worsen. The legislature was debating various relief measures including stop laws to prevent debt foreclosures, but—in his opinion—"There wants but this to complete the ruin of the state, for though it is unconstitutional and of course void, it will give a shock to the credit of the state that will paralize [*sic*] all its projects of improvement and throw us back 20 years." But he saw no political alternatives either. "All they can do will not prevent a crash, which must as certainly come, as time will roll on. And when it does come I hope it will teach us better management."[5]

As for the banks, Huntington believed that they should treat the planter with leniency while being strict with delinquent merchants. "I think it would have been for the advantage of the country if instead of endeavouring [*sic*] to support the Commission houses, the Banks had let things go down; and if they granted loans let it be to the planters to pay the balances they owe." Huntington was likely self-interested in this assessment of how the banks should deal with planters, as he was facing foreclosure himself on Greenoak. "God knows what is to become of me and my poor family, but I will not despair. Whatever He wills is not only right, but best for me." In ending this long, depressing letter to Mercer, Huntington concluded: "I am glad that you are removed from all the turmoil which surrounds us. You will come home just when we are settling down in destruction and you will know nothing about it."[6]

In fact, as Huntington hoped, most frontier banks proved to be extremely lenient with delinquent slaveholders—especially with those who were politically powerful and well connected, but often also with smaller debtors (who were still wealthy enough to belong to the slaveholding minority). These financial institutions had become interwoven with the system of slavery, and it was in their long-term interest to ensure the success of the planter class, even as it placed their short-term survival in jeopardy. Especially in the case of the largest debtors, the banks often treated them as "too big to fail," repeatedly renegotiating loan contracts to avoid—at almost any cost—the seizure and sale of land and human property in the midst of the downturn. In this way, banks frequently (if inadvertently) prevented the large-scale breakup of enslaved communities that was often the hallmark of foreclosure proceedings. And in those cases where the bank did ultimately decide to foreclose, it still had to choose whether it was better to sell the property immediately (potentially at a great loss), or take ownership and managerial responsibility for a whole plantation with its enslaved workforce until market conditions improved. By serving as a financial safety net for slaveholders during the depression, frontier banks helped lay the foundations of the southern economic boom during the 1850s.

Relieving Delinquent Slaveholders through Slave Finance

Early in the depression, in 1838, the board of the Citizens' Bank blamed the problems with the banking system on the repeated renewals of short-term notes, known as accommodation paper, "the amount of which in our Banks is becoming alarmingly large." This "fictitious paper and kites"—meaning a loan taken out in one bank in order to pay a debt due to another bank—"has in a great measure destroyed all accountability; and that accountability is the only check to over-trading and its natural sequences." The board thus recommended that the bank pass a new rule, forbidding the renewal of short-term notes discounted for sixty days "unless forced by extraordinary circumstances, and in all such cases, the maker or endorser of such paper, shall be required to give a mortgage on Real Estate" which could not "exceed two-thirds of the cash value of said Estate."[7] In passing this short-term lending policy, the Citizens' Bank was especially concerned about the ability of the plantation banks to weather the downturn since "[u]nlike other monied Institutions property banks are essentially national. . . . [T]he preservation of that Capital, therefore, in its original integrity, is a national trust, and its loss would be a national calamity."[8] Yet the plantation banks were not alone in directly linking their survival to slave finance. As the depression dragged on and the market for land and human property remained severely undervalued, unpaid debts secured by enslaved lives piled up on the balance sheets of banks throughout the frontier South.

In Alabama, the Bank of Mobile (1818), the State Bank (1820), and the newly chartered Planters' and Merchants' Bank of Mobile (1836) all found themselves in dire financial straits very early in the Panic of 1837. In the words of one state historian: "As Alabama's banks suspended their specie payments, commerce and trade seriously declined and the price of land, cotton, and slaves were sent spiraling downward. The state's court dockets were filled with civil suits to recover debts owed creditors, and sheriffs were crying off property on the steps of courthouses."[9] Most of these bank debts originated as discount loans, since the Alabama banks were much more conservative than Mississippi or Louisiana banks regarding slave-backed mortgages during the 1830s. Historians of Alabama's banks also note that they were not particularly well run.[10]

In one of his last acts as governor, Clement Comer Clay called the legislature into special session in July and argued for "radical legislation" both to relieve debtors and to save the banks. He was especially concerned about the Bank of the State, since responsibility for the failure of this state-run entity would fall heavily on taxpayers, although the state also held a two-fifths interest in each of the other two banks.[11] The legislature quickly passed the Relief Act of 1837, which permitted all three banks to suspend specie payments temporarily without forfeiting their charters. More significantly, the act authorized the formal conversion of all short-term bank debts into three-year loans, payable 20 percent after one year, 30 percent after two years, and the remaining 50 percent after three years, secured by "deeds of trust on real or personal property."[12] (This debt conversion was very similar to the rule passed by the Citizens' Bank board of directors in Louisiana requiring property mortgages on short-term loan renewals.)

Finally, the state issued $5 million in new bonds, the proceeds of which were distributed equally between each of the five branches of the state bank. The act instructed these banks to lend the entirety of these new deposits "in sums not exceeding $2000" (about $57,000 in 2021) in an effort to stimulate the state's economy and counteract the monetary contraction.[13] In the annual governor's message that November, Clay's successor in office, Hugh McVay, praised the "beneficial effects" of the Relief Act and blamed the "evils of the times" on the "heedless creation of banks and the wild and prodigal issues of bank paper."[14] He did not mention the additional $5 million worth of "wild and prodigal" bank paper which the Relief Act provided. In trying to bail out slaveholders, the Relief Act formally authorized Alabama's banks to secure debts directly with mortgages upon land and human property for the first time.

Upon passage of the act, the various branches of the Bank of the State quickly drew up guidelines for compliance. At a July 12 meeting of the Montgomery branch, the directors resolved to require that "a deed of Trust or Mortgage on Double the am[oun]t of Property shall be taken before said Notes shall be discounted." In order to ensure that the security offered was sound, the board required debtors to "produce satisfactory Evidence to the Board that the Lands & Negroes proposed to be Mortgaged are worth double the am[oun]t called for" as well as "the certificate of the Clerk of the County Court of the proper County that the said Lands & Negroes are free from any Incumbrance of any description whatever." This requirement for double the value was repealed a week later, and then replaced on July 26 with a statement that the adequacy of all mortgage security should be "decided on their own merits." The directors appointed a three-person committee "to confer with the Bank Attorney to draw up a form of Note & Mortgage," since the bank had not previously dealt in mortgage security. Finally, they directed the cashier to "give notice in both the papers published in this town to all persons indebted to this institution by note Bills of Exchange or in judgment" of the proposed debt extension, as well as informing the public that they would offer new loans of up to $2,000 "upon the parties so applying giving Notes payable in one Two & Three Years with at least Two good & sufficient securities & a deed of Trust on Real Estate or Slaves."[15]

The board of the Huntsville branch met on July 27 to discuss similar resolutions, voting to "reserve to themselves the right to require a mortgage or deed of trust on real or personal property estimated to be worth double the amount of the debts intended to be secured, the value of such property to be ascertained by such person or persons as the Board may select." They gave debtors sixty days to apply to the bank for such an extension, warning that "On all debts extended, a failure to pay punctually the first or second instalment, or to give additional security when required by the Board, will authorise them to declare the whole debt due and they will proceed to collect it accordingly." Like the Montgomery branch, Huntsville also planned to offer new loans of up to $2,000 upon the same terms, "with the privilege reserved to the Board of requiring a mortgage or deed of trust on real or personal property."[16]

Applications for loan extensions quickly began flowing into the branch offices. One slaveholder offered to secure his $1,400 debt with a mortgage on his house and lot in the city of Mobile. When the directors deemed this property to "be not sufficient," he added "two negroes to be included in the mortgage," who were the entirety of the enslaved lives in his possession.[17] The directors accepted the loan extension with this additional human collateral, and the slaveholder paid off the debt with interest in three equal installments of $666. A Green County resident mortgaged his land and thirty-four enslaved individuals to secure his $14,462.64 debt, which he promptly paid on time.[18] A slaveholder in Mobile applied for an extension of his existing debt with the bank, offering to mortgage a city lot "for which I am now offered $6000 cash, & nine negroes." The bank accepted these terms as adequate to cover his debt of $5,644.44 (including interest), but this debt remained unpaid until 1851.[19] Another slaveholder initially proposed ten of his twenty-eight enslaved people as security for his $6,610 debt, but the bank rejected these assets as insufficient. He then added his brickyard on five acres of land in the city of Mobile, which was also rejected. Finally, he added the endorsement of Adam Cornelius Hollinger, who—as the owner of more than eighty individuals—was one of the largest slaveholders in the city. The bank finally accepted this offer as sufficient collateral for the debt.[20]

But the Bank of the State did not always scrutinize the collateral carefully enough. When one slaveholder requested an extension on his $2,317.68 debt secured by five enslaved lives (Dunmore, Jack, Dolly, Patty, and Juliett), the Mobile branch failed to record any relevant information about the enslaved individuals. "The mortgage merely gives the names of the negroes without any description by which they might be identified, the committee is therefore unable to form any estimate of their value." By December 1845, this debtor still owed $1,200.[21] In the case of another debt for $6,046.62, the bank insisted on the addition of a prominent endorser—William W. Fry—to supplement the seven slaves offered as collateral: Ben, William, and Charles (all in their forties), Semore, Louisa, and Joice (in their twenties), and fifteen-year-old Nevis. By the time this debtor settled with the bank in March of 1845, Fry was long dead, having passed in 1839 leaving an insolvent estate.[22] Likewise, the bank trusted that the property of another slaveholder—which consisted of his house, twenty-five acres of land, and five of his eleven bondspeople—was sufficient to secure his $3,151 debt. Yet when the bank sued him for nonpayment in August of 1840, the court could find "no property" to seize.[23]

William Fry was not only the endorser on several notes, but himself had discounted numerous bills of exchange with the bank. In 1837, he applied for the Relief Act's three-year extension on these debts, which by then totaled $37,450 (about $1.1 million in 2021). He offered to pay back this loan in eight installments over three years, totaling (with interest) $44,570.67, secured with a mortgage on thirty of his enslaved workers, valued at $30,000, and some other "country paper" valued at $10,217.62.[24] Despite the fact that this collateral barely covered the debt, the bank accepted these terms. Upon his death in October 1839, he still owed the bank $17,732.17. The bank seized twenty of the enslaved individuals and sold them at depression prices to fourteen separate buyers, scattering them throughout the community. One purchaser obtained twenty-four-year-old Dandy Jack, thirty-year-old Yellow Jack, thirty-five-year-old Sam Fox, and thirty-year-old Gabe for a total of $2,275. A second bought twenty-five-year-old Henry Strongfellow and twenty-six-year-old Benton Dick for a total of $1,165. A third acquired twenty-four-year-old Brown and thirty-five-year-old Jim Wragg for $1,115, while a fourth purchased twenty-three-year-old Barney (who was "a good Caulker") and twenty-year-old Paul for $1,700. The remaining ten men—Gilbert, Perry, Edward ("also a good Caulker"), Preston, James Lombort, Jim Bates, Jacob, Judge, Dan Ambercrombie, and Stratton—were all prime lives aged twenty-one to twenty-seven; each sold to separate buyers for $460 to $1050. The bank netted $13,785, not including lawyers' fees, court costs, advertising, and other costs associated with the transaction—for a significant loss on the original loan.[25]

The bank also suffered losses due to competing claims. The branch bank in Decatur sued Cornelius Allen of Morgan County in 1839 for nonpayment of his $1,500 debt, plus $75 in damages, $105 interest, $4 cost of protest, and $14.25 court costs ($1,698.25 total). The sheriff seized his property, which included sixteen enslaved individuals, a wagon, six mules, and some other plantation property, and proceeded to sell this property in three separate lots on October 7, November 2, and November 6, 1839. But before the sheriff finalized the sales, Benjamin D. Harris of Madison County claimed the property as his own, stopping the proceedings. The bank now had to sue Harris, averring that the enslaved individuals, wagon, and livestock were "not the property of the said Benjamin D. Harris but at the time of the said levy was the property of the said Cornelius Allen & subject to the said execution." Able to convince the court of its superior claim, the bank obtained a judgment requiring Harris to pay a "penal sum" of $3,024, unless he delivered the property to the courthouse at the next auction day. He was also required to pay "such cost & Damages as shall be recovered by putting in the Claim for delay."[26]

While many debtors were able to take advantage of the Relief Act, not everyone successfully satisfied the bank's collateral requirements. In February 1838, the branch bank in Montgomery adopted a resolution requiring bank officers "to use all dilligence [*sic*] in finding out the condition of the Principal & securities of the Notes, [and] the situation of all Real or Personal Estate Mortgaged for their payment." It planned to use this information "in order that the most efficient measures may be taken to secure such debts as are bad or doubtful either by requiring additional security or by declaring them instantly due."[27] Other branches proceeded in a similar fashion, with the Mobile branch quickly foreclosing on debts it classified as "bad" and seizing whatever property it could to satisfy the claim. In Marion County, it recouped $2,220 from the sale of one debtor's enslaved property in February 1839, and $1,510 from another in March 1840, although it failed to sell the property of a third; the bank suspected that the debtor in question had taken this property to Texas.[28] In Perry County, it recovered $81 in February 1839 from the sale of an unknown number of "negroes," while the sale of four others netted $248.55 (averaging just $62 each) in July of that year. The sale of several enslaved workers of a third slaveholder in February 1841 brought another $448.71. The bank sold the slaves of a fourth debtor in August 1842.[29] While the market value of individual slaves could vary widely based on age, health, and skill, these sale prices were all well below the average price of enslaved lives, which dropped just below $300 at their depression nadir.

The bank also deemed the debts "bad" of James Caulfield and E. T. Broughton of Monroe County, W. M. Story of Pickens County, Joel Shirley of Tuskaloosa County, Charles Davenport of Lowndes County, and G. W. Kinnard of Sumter County, and obtained court orders on the human property of each.[30] In Marengo County, it seized and sold the enslaved men, women, and children belonging to C. H. Taylor, K. K. Blouvet, G. W. Legroes, G. D. Connor, B. M. Banon, and P. W. Bearcon, all to satisfy "bad" debts between 1839 and 1843.[31] After receiving a favorable court judgment against the firm of King Upson & Co. for $6,745.56 in October 1840, the branch bank at Mobile claimed "Three Lots on Corner of State & Jackson Streets. . . . Also, 5 Negroes as follows viz: Nora aged 28 years & her two children Agga & Robert (ages not at hand), Justin 22 & Clarke 15 years of age," as well as some household furniture. Despite the hassle of seizing property, the bank was pleased with this outcome. "This property was taken . . . in payment of the debts . . . due this Bank, . . . the collection of which was extremely doubtful would be secured to the satisfaction of the Board."[32]

By 1840 and 1841, many of the debts that had initially qualified for debt extensions were falling due, and the bank was overwhelmed with collection lawsuits. During just the February 1841 court term, the branch bank in Mobile received judgments against two slaveholders in Lowndes County, two more (in three separate suits) in Conecuh County, another three in Clarke County, and one each in Dallas and Butler. In each case, the bank's claim was "levied on negroes" of either the principal debtor or one of their two endorsers; the failure of the debtor to fulfill his obligations directly resulted in the sale of these enslaved individuals. But successful judgments were not of much use if the bank could not take possession of the enslaved lives. In the Butler County case, for example, the bank successfully sued for $579.22 against Thomas B. Windham, yet "doubts arising as to the validity of the title" on the negro and "no person appearing on behalf of the Bank to indemnify the sheriff, the property was given up to the def[endan]t, and so it stands."[33]

Even with a favorable court judgment, these claims often took time to resolve, especially when the debtors challenged the ruling. In the case of Cyrus Gill of Conecuh County, this debtor claimed that the enslaved lives in question were actually the property of his daughter. He managed to keep the bank wrapped up in the courts until the fall of 1848, when it finally "succeeded in subjecting the negroes to the execution." Lucy, Dicey, Julia, and Jinney, valued at $950, were then seized and sold. The court additionally charged Gill $48.39 as "damages for delay."[34] Josiah W. Marshall owed the branch bank at Huntsville $2,100 from a bill of exchange he discounted in February 1836. In October, Marshall moved to Tennessee, selling his enslaved blacksmith for $2,100 before he left. When the bank received a court judgment against Marshall in April 1837 for $2,316 including interest and court costs, the sheriff returned the execution as "no property found." But the bank soon discovered the sale of the blacksmith, and alleged that Marshall had orchestrated the money to be paid to his brother-in-law "for the purpose of defrauding [the bank] and other creditors." Marshall's defense was that he owed his brother-in-law $2,100 separately on a prior debt, which he sold the enslaved man to pay. The bank fought this case to the Alabama Supreme Court. But despite its best efforts to demonstrate fraud, the court finally ruled in 1842 that the bank had not sufficiently demonstrated either fraud or its superior claim over other creditors to the blacksmith. It never recovered on the $2,100 loan.[35]

Oftentimes, the property offered as collateral was worth only a fraction of the debt due—especially as market prices for land and enslaved lives plunged. One slaveholder had mortgaged her property, including 25.6 acres of land as well as "some household and kitchen furniture and two negroes," as the endorser on a $6,733.18 debt. Unfortunately, there was a prior mortgage on this property of which the branch bank at Mobile had been unaware. In November 1841, the branch bank paid $5,110 to this superior claimant "to obtain title" to the property. Although it believed that the property was only worth about $10,000—much less than the debt and purchase price combined—this was its sole recourse since the endorser's property "was the only security the Bank had for the debt."[36]

Beyond the power to renew existing loans, each branch bank had been allotted an additional $1 million by the legislature to use in the issuance of new loans of up to $2,000 each. In practice, however, some of the branches went well beyond this limit. For example, in 1842, one woman who had "an Estate separate and apart from her said husband" obtained about two dozen enslaved individuals "for her separate use in addition to her former Estate." In order to pay for these people, "Mary became indebted to the Branch of the Bank of the State of Alabama at Mobile" for $7,500, which she agreed to pay over the next six years, plus $442.92 in interest. The enslaved individuals were both the object of the loan and the collateral for this mortgage. Although she remained current with the payment schedule through 1846, she soon fell behind and had to renegotiate with the bank. The debt was finally settled in January of 1852, when her husband paid the balance due of $2,596.43.[37] Another slaveholder similarly borrowed $9,065 from the same branch in December 1843, which he secured with several enslaved people.[38]

The overall effectiveness of the Relief Act of 1837 in Alabama was mixed. On the one hand, numerous delinquent debtors were saved from foreclosure by the extension of their loans for three years, enabling them to keep possession of their human property and preventing family breakups. In other cases, the state's forbearance merely delayed the foreclosure proceedings for a number of years. But whereas the intention of the act was also to save the Alabama banks themselves from failure, the lenient treatment of slaveholders hurt the banks' balance sheets. Delayed mortgage payments left the Bank of the State of Alabama, in particular, teetering on the edge of viability as the second wave of panic hit in 1839 (chapter 8).

Too Big to Fail in Louisiana

Placing a handful of enslaved individuals up for sale was much easier than trying to liquidate an entire plantation with a large enslaved workforce. Thus, in Louisiana, where the financial institutions had engaged in the most extensive underwriting of large mortgages secured by land and human property, the banks were reluctant to foreclose on delinquent debtors, preferring to find any possible alternative to placing property up for public auction. Further complicating many of these cases was the fact that the debtors were frequently prominent Louisiana politicians and businessmen who often simultaneously served as members of a bank's board of directors. Like the official Relief Act in Alabama, the results of this unofficial policy of forbearance were mixed. While in some cases the debtors eventually fulfilled their obligations with interest, in many other cases the practice just delayed the inevitable and the bank ultimately had to write off the debt as a partial or even total loss. As will be evident in subsequent chapters, Louisiana banks, in particular, continued to struggle with delinquent debts stemming from the Panic of 1837 throughout the 1840s and 1850s.

By its charter, the Bank of Louisiana was limited to $5,000 loans renewable for up to five years, yet it regularly lent much-larger amounts and renewed beyond five years rather than foreclosing. This policy was relatively unproblematic during the boom years when delinquencies and defaults were uncommon, but threatened the survival of the bank as defaults accelerated during and after the panic. For example, sometime after 1824, John C. Sullivan migrated from Virginia with his enslaved workforce and established a cotton plantation in Rapides Parish, Louisiana, known as the Bertrand plantation. In the 1830 census, he listed fifteen enslaved individuals.[39] John soon died, and his brother James Bailey Sullivan inherited the plantation. James was a surgeon who in 1829 had been "appointed by General Jackson as assistant surgeon in the United States Army." After serving in that post for several years, "he resigned his commission, and engaged in the cotton-planting business on Red River."[40] In August 1832, he mortgaged to the Bank of Louisiana his plantation along with twenty-six enslaved workers for $10,000; three months later, he added a second loan of $10,000 secured by the same property. All but eight of these enslaved individuals were under the age of twenty.[41] He later attested "all of which slaves are black . . . and all which came from the State of Virginia." While still repaying those two loans, he took out a third loan with the bank for $19,000 in October 1836.[42]

Although he made regular payments to pay off the first loan and a portion of the second, a decade later he still owed the bank $25,000 on these mortgages. Rather than foreclosing, the bank agreed to renew them in April 1843 but with additional property as collateral "in order the more fully to secure the final payment of the aforesaid sums of money." Sullivan added to the mortgage several tracts of land adjoining the originally mortgaged one, as well as forty-seven more enslaved individuals. In addition to the twenty-two people listed in the original mortgage (four children under the age of five were no longer listed, presumably having died), there were nineteen more children born since the first mortgage, and twenty-eight newly acquired adults—twenty-four of whom were between the ages of fifteen and twenty-five.[43] This roster likely represented his entire workforce, which he listed in the 1840 census as numbering sixty-five.[44] The bank's forbearance allowed him to continue growing his wealth. By the 1850 census, he listed one hundred enslaved individuals and $35,000 in real estate.[45] And by the start of the Civil War, he had 168 enslaved workers, and recorded his total real and personal wealth at $185,240 (about $6 million in 2021).[46] At some point, he successfully paid off all his debts to the Bank of Louisiana. In this instance, the bank's willingness and ability to wait for conditions to improve paid off.

At other times, forbearance failed to bear fruit and the Bank of Louisiana eventually decided to foreclose on long-delinquent mortgages, purchasing them at public sale and then reselling them in an attempt to recoup the value of the debt. For example, in May 1834, Manuel Garcia mortgaged his sugar plantation and fifty-six enslaved workers at Bonnet Carré in the parish of St. John the Baptist to secure a debt of $7,912.08 with the bank.[47] Although he promised to repay in twelve months, the debt still remained unpaid nine years later. Thus in September 1843, the bank purchased the sugar plantation with its then fifty-nine enslaved individuals, reselling it three months later to Thomas May. However, it included only forty-nine of the property's enslaved lives, since ten had managed to run away during the bank's brief management. May agreed to pay $45,000 for the property: $10,000 cash—covering the original principal and a portion of the accumulated interest on Garcia's loan—and an additional $35,000 on a mortgage renewable for five years. He secured the mortgage with the purchased plantation and enslaved workers, as well as six additional enslaved individuals whom he brought to work there.[48] Assuming May paid off this debt in a timely fashion—which is likely since he did continue to run this plantation successfully throughout the 1850s—the bank eventually made a substantial profit off Garcia's original loan.[49] And despite the loss of this plantation, Manuel Garcia remained a respected local citizen, serving as sheriff of Jefferson Parish in 1846 and later as a Whig elected to represent that parish in the Louisiana Senate beginning in 1847.[50]

In November 1843, the Bank of Louisiana similarly foreclosed on the sugar plantation of Edmond Fortier and his wife Matilde Labranche in St. Charles Parish, although it is unclear how many of the 105 enslaved people (listed in the 1840 census) the bank also seized.[51] In December, the bank resold ten enslaved individuals to Madame Fortier for $6,000 as her separate property. She gave two promissory notes for the purchase, both endorsed by her relative Lucien Labranche (who was a major stockholder of the Citizens' Bank), payable $2,000 in May 1844 and $4,000 in May 1845.[52] The land, however, the bank sold in January 1844 to Pierre Soniat for $28,000.[53] Soniat was a business partner of the Fortier family, with whom he owned a separate plantation in Jefferson Parish.[54] The bank secured the mortgage with the St. Charles plantation and the forty enslaved workers whom Soniat intended "to be placed on the said Plantation"—likely the thirty-eight individuals (plus their increase) whom he listed on the 1840 census in Jefferson Parish.[55] Again, the mortgage was renewable for five years, although the deed included a stipulation that "in case a crevasse or hurricane shall destroy the crop" at any point before the debt was paid, the bank would allow two extra years for payment.[56] The remainder of Fortier's enslaved property, apparently unneeded to satisfy the mortgage debt, the bank likely permitted him to keep. By the 1850 census, Soniat reported himself as a substantial planter in St. Charles Parish with $90,000 in real estate wealth (about $3.1 million in 2021) and ninety-five enslaved lives, despite the crevasse that flooded his plantation in 1849–50 and again in 1850–51. And both Madame Fortier (now widowed) and her son, Edmond Jr., had reestablished themselves on separate sugar plantations in St. Charles Parish.[57]

On the neighboring plantation from the Fortiers' in St. Charles Parish, Edmond's sister Adelaide Felicie Fortier and her husband Jean François Piseros also found themselves unable to pay their debts during the hard times. Piseros had mortgaged his plantation, with its seventy-six enslaved individuals, to the Citizens' Bank several years earlier.[58] Like the Bank of Louisiana, the Citizens' Bank was loath to foreclose too quickly on property or to take ownership of whole plantations unless as a last resort. Thus in the winter of 1842–43, the bank negotiated a deal with Piseros in which the bank seized his sugar crop in partial payment of the debt. In January 1843, Piseros "placed in the hands of the Bank 83 Hogsheads Sugar which stands pledged for his arrears to the Bank." The bank received "$2065.08 . . . for the net proceeds of 50 Hhds shipped to New York on which 3 cents advanced have been received."[59] In order to keep the plantation functioning, "the Bank has agreed to furnish the Corn that may be required which is estimated at 700 BUs [bushels] for the year, & clothing for the Negroes. Some molasses is retained for that purpose."[60] The bank effectively assumed financial control of the plantation, even as Piseros remained the titular owner.

In April 1843, several months after the Citizens' Bank had begun entering into crop garnishment agreements with a number of delinquent debtors like Piseros, the legislature endorsed this creditor tactic, permitting plantation banks "whether in liquidation or not" to negotiate with debtors "for a privilege and mortgage on the future crops, revenues and rents of the property mortgaged to secure their stock or stock loan." The banks likewise could receive direct transfers of property in payment of debts, as long as any such property was properly assessed by three appraisers: one "to be appointed by the Secretary of State, one by the debtor, and the other by the Managers."[61]

But crop garnishment was only one potential solution. An alternative pursued by several Louisiana banks was effectively to refinance the mortgage through the wife or another family member. In the fall of 1843, the Citizens' Bank seized the Piseros property. Then "Mrs. J. F. Piseros . . . acquired at Sheriffs Sale a plantation and slaves thereunto belonging together with the Stock thereon" for $62,500, which was slightly less than the $65,000 Piseros owed the bank. As part of the sale, Mrs. Piseros assumed "all the mortgages consented by her husband & herself in favor of the said Citizens Bank." In order to "enable her to extinguish the sum gradually," the bank allowed her to secure the payment "by mortgage on the Plantation & Slaves and pledge of Stock" as well as "all the Crops, Rents and revenues of said property for the payment of said debts." The bank would renew the remaining debt each year, provided that the entire "proceeds of the Crop of said plantation, after paying the

Expenses thereof" would be pledged to the bank. If Mrs. Piseros failed "to meet any of the payments herein stipulated, the whole of the debt assumed by her shall become due" and the bank would proceed with foreclosure.[62] By the 1850 census, the Piseroses had regained their financial footing, declaring $110,000 (about $3.8 million in 2021) in real estate wealth with ninety-three enslaved workers, although (like their neighbor) their plantation was flooded by the crevasse at Bonnet Carré in 1850. Although the mortgage with the bank remained in Adelaide's name, both the census and P. A. Champomier's *Statement of the Sugar Crop of Louisiana* listed Jean François as the head of household and owner of the enslaved individuals.[63]

In June 1853—almost a full decade after the original refinance and in the wake of the death of Jean François—Mrs. Piseros sold the 915 shares of Citizens' Bank stock and the plantation (but not the enslaved lives) to a neighboring planter. The bank agreed "that in lieu of the 74 slaves mortgaged by Mrs. Piseros to this bank, [the new owner] shall be allowed to substitute 70 slaves of his own, named & described in a list submitted to this board for reference."[64] Beginning in July, Mrs. Piseros separately listed "Fifty Five Acclimated Creole Slaves"—"lately belonging to Mr. Pisero [*sic*]"—for sale by auction.[65] While it is unknown how many buyers purchased the enslaved individuals, only a portion of them remained together after the auction. Eighteen months later, seventeen enslaved people "from the plantation of the late Mr. Pisero [*sic*]" reappeared for sale as part of "60 Very Choice Sugar Plantation Hands" being auctioned at Banks' Arcade in New Orleans. Included from Piseros's original gang were forty-seven-year-old Lewis, a "good carpenter and sugar maker a trusty and superior subject," and his forty-year-old-wife Sally, herself a "good field hand and hospital nurse, trusty"; twenty-seven-year-old Bob Jackson, who was an "extra No. 1 field hand and ploughman, understands machinery, can run centrifugal machines"; fifty-year-old Richard, who was a "gardener and field hand" despite his "sore legs"; and thirty-two-year-old Hans, an ox and mule driver who had been listed as a runaway during the original sale—he "has only one arm."[66] In 1857, the St. Charles plantation changed hands once again. The property and stock shares "with 47 slaves now surviving out of 79 originally mortgaged" was purchased by a third slaveholder, who partially financed the acquisition with a $26,535 Citizens' Bank mortgage on the property.[67]

This process of reorganizing debts among other family members recurred throughout the early 1840s in Louisiana. In 1837, Jean S. Armant mortgaged his St. James sugar plantation and twenty-seven enslaved workers to the Citizens' Bank in exchange for 110 shares of stock. He increased this portion to 450 shares in 1838, and then to 780 shares by 1839, adding more land and thirty-two additional enslaved lives to the mortgage, representing the entirety of his property. Based on these shares, he could obtain bank loans totaling $33,990.[68] He also served on the bank's board of directors from 1837 to 1839 and again from 1846 to 1847.[69] When he was unable to pay his debt by 1843, the board resolved that the bank's lawyer "be instructed to bid on the Plantation & Slaves mortgaged to this Bank to the sum of Forty Thousand Dollars," but that the bank should then make an offer for Madame Armant to buy the property back, which she did.[70] While still heavily indebted to the bank, in January 1846 Jean was appointed by the governor as one of the managers for the liquidation of this same institution.[71] Meanwhile, as of 1847, the bank still listed Madame Armant as the owner of the sugar plantation, fifty-one enslaved workers, and 728 shares of bank stock.[72] By 1850, Jean listed ninety-six enslaved workers on the census, even as Adelaide remained the legal owner by mortgage.[73] The Armants stayed current with their payments, and upon Madame Armant's death in 1853, the bank agreed to allow it to revert back to her husband for him to complete the remaining payments.[74] Jean retained possession of the plantation throughout the 1850s, even if the sugar harvest at the end of the decade was less than half of what it was during its height in 1853–54.[75]

These familial refinancings became one of several tools for the bank to avoid fully foreclosing on mortgaged property. On March 17, 1838, Martin Gordon Penn subscribed for 150 shares of Citizens' Bank stock, mortgaging his cotton plantation called Palestine and seventeen enslaved individuals in Washington Parish.[76] The same day, he received a $12,000 loan from the Union Bank, offering as collateral the same property as well as the 150 shares of Citizens' Bank stock.[77] By the following November, the Union Bank agreed to grant the Citizens' Bank priority of mortgage, on condition that Penn use a loan of up to $7,500 that he was permitted as a Citizens' Bank stockholder to repay his Union Bank loan. Then, in 1840, Penn obtained seventy-five more shares of Citizens' Bank stock (entitling him to an additional loan of up to $3,750), adding them to his existing mortgage contract.[78]

Within two years, Penn had fallen behind on his debts. In April 1842, he transferred his 225 shares back to the bank, and "the Bank caused to be seized and sold his plantation situate in the Parish of Washington and certain Slaves thereunto attached . . . the Bank became purchaser of all said property, resold a portion of the Slaves free of Mortgage"—meaning without the attached stock—". . . & made an arrangement with Mrs. Penn for the purchase by her from the Bank, of the Plantation and balance of Slaves." The bank acknowledged that this arrangement with Penn's wife was irregular—1842 was the first instance of a spousal refinance in the board of director minutes, predating both the Piseros and Armant sales—but the bank believed that by "the resale of 225 Shares of stock [it] could have realized on the market . . . an amount sufficient to cover said Penn's notes due." However, in this instance, the Penns failed to comply with the terms of the agreement, the proposed contract became null and void, and the bank ultimately took legal possession of the plantation and its enslaved workforce.[79] Yet the bank did not immediately try to sell the property, and it is likely that the bank actually left the Penns in a management role on the plantation as it resolved this debt dispute.

Five years later, the board "ordered that said Plantation and Slaves together with the Stock attached thereto, be advertised for sale," although it still planned to "giv[e] due notice . . . to Mr & Mrs Penn, that the Bank will give them a preferance [*sic*] for the purchase of said Plantation & Slaves," who numbered fifty-seven in 1847, if the couple could comply with the bank's terms.[80] By July 1847, the bank resold the Palestine plantation and bank shares back to Mrs. Penn, including nine enslaved individuals who were "now in the possession of said M. G. Penn." Thirty-five-year-old blacksmith Tom Hays, thirty-year-old Nelson, twenty-year-old Silvester, twenty-eight-year-old Sally, and Sally's eldest child Eliza had all been part of the original mortgage; Sally had since had four more children.[81] But Mrs. Penn still "failed to comply with the terms of the sale to her," and the board decided (again) to sell the property in April 1849. "The Cashier was directed to forward to her a copy of the advertisement and inform her that upon her complying with the conditions agreed upon . . . previous to the sale at auction, the property would be conveyed to her; otherwise it will be sold agreeably to advertisement."[82]

The Palestine plantation was indeed advertised for sale in April 1849, but Mrs. Penn begged the bank for forbearance once again—she needing more "time for the settlement of the cash portion accrued and accruing" on the debt.[83] The board initially agreed to give her until July 19 at noon, stating that "then the said Plantation & slaves with the 225 shares attached thereto, shall be sold at auction, on that day."[84] Yet just four days later, the board reversed its decision, granting her an additional "delay of one and two years from 1st March 1849." Mrs. Penn consented to add to the mortgage three additional enslaved individuals whom she owned in the parish of St. Tammany.[85] As the board minutes no longer mention the Penns after 1849, they presumably (finally) began making regular payments toward the extinguishment of this debt.

The bank also permitted other family members besides wives to assume responsibility for delinquent mortgages. When the bank foreclosed on the St. Bernard plantation of the widow Darcantel, it allowed the sheriff to sell the plantation, brickyard, stock shares, and enslaved workers to her relative Henry Darcantel (perhaps her brother or son) for $24,700. As part of the sale, he assumed "the existing mortgage in favor of the Citizens Bank."[86] Similarly, when the bank foreclosed on the land, human property, and 132 shares of stock of Constance Peyroux in St. Bernard Parish, her sister-in-law Aimi Carraby Peyroux (wife of her brother Pierre Oscar Peyroux) "proposed to pay and assume the whole amount of the debt due to this Bank."[87] Yet the 1849–50 report of the sugar crop reported neither the Darcantels nor the Peyrouxes as owners of these respective plantations.[88]

Like familial refinancings, the garnishment of crops was also a tactic repeated by the Citizens' Bank with other debtors who fell delinquent. Trasimond Landry was a Democrat politician representing the parish of Ascension in the Louisiana House from 1824 to 1831.[89] He was already a large slaveholder by this point, reporting eighty enslaved lives in the 1830 census.[90] During 1838 and 1839, he purchased 750 shares of Citizens' Bank stock from six different stockholders, for which he mortgaged his plantation "on the right bank of the Mississippi at about a mile below Donaldsonville. . . . valued at $50000 for Land & improvements, slaves $25000."[91] This purchase was in addition to the 1,100 shares for which he had separately subscribed in 1835 and 1836.[92] By the 1840 census, his human property had increased to 161 people.[93]

Yet as had been the case with Piseros, in the winter of 1842–43 the bank worked out an "arrangement" with Landry regarding his sugar crop. In January 1843, he "place[d] at the disposal of the Bank 510 Hogsheads Sugar to meet his arrears & Interest & Curtailments for 1843. Of the 510 Hogsheads 310 have been received and a regular pledge given for the same by Mr. Landry this day." Out of the proceeds of the remaining two hundred hogsheads (as well as an additional "30,000 Gallons of Molasses also placed at the disposal of the Bank"), Landry first needed to pay about $7,500 in other debts, including the salaries of two overseers, state and parish taxes, a $2,100 judgment owed to another creditor, a $600 interest payment to the Canal Bank of Donaldsonville, and a $400 interest payment to the Bank of Louisiana branch in Donaldsonville (both of which banks held prior mortgages on his land and human property). Landry would also retain "such a portion of the molasses as may be necessary to purchase provisions."[94] Unlike the case of Piseros, this arrangement was sufficient to get Landry's debt payments back on schedule; although the bank listed the property as "purchased by bank" on its 1847 books, Landry retained possession of the property and eventually reassumed full ownership.[95] Elected on the Democrat ticket as a Loco-Foco, the politically powerful Landry served a four-year term as the state's lieutenant governor, beginning in 1846.[96] By 1850 he was reporting 230 enslaved workers across three Ascension sugar plantations.[97] He had also begun actively purchasing additional shares of Citizens' Bank stock between 1850 and 1855.[98] In the 1860 census, his total wealth was $1,055,000 (about $35 million in 2021), including 316 enslaved lives.[99]

While the vast majority of Citizens' Bank stockholders were individual plantation owners or New Orleans merchants and traders, a few corporations—such as the Compagnie des Canaux de Barataria & de LaFourche (the Barataria & LaFourche Canal Company), the Levee Steam Cotton Press Company, and the Pontchartrain Rail Road Company—also subscribed for stock and borrowed money from the bank secured with mortgages on real estate and enslaved lives.[100] In February 1843, the board of directors of the Pontchartrain Rail Road "applied to this Bank for an extension of time to pay the amount due by them to this Institution." In order to further secure this loan, they offered twenty-eight additional enslaved individuals beyond their original collateral. The bank agreed to an extension on the debt, with the corporation paying the 8 percent interest up front (in eight monthly installments during 1843), and the loan principal in nine semiannual installments on February 1 and August 1, 1844 through 1848.[101] In August 1847, when the railroad should have been paying its penultimate installment, it still owed $55,000 plus $6,074.45 in "arrears interest." The bank granted them another twelve months to pay this interest (plus $364.47 additional interest), upon securing the payment with "a Mortgage upon Fourteen prime Slaves attached to said Road."[102]

While the Louisiana banks were often quite lenient in dealing with large debtors, sometimes these cases still devolved into extended court battles. Eliza Scott was the only daughter of Abram M. Scott, the sixth governor of the state of Mississippi. Just eight months after her March 1833 marriage to Preston Withers Farrar, a prominent lawyer in Woodville, Mississippi, her father died unexpectedly of cholera.[103] In 1837, the couple took possession of Eliza's half of her deceased father's plantation and enslaved workers in Rapides Parish, Louisiana. On May 26, 1838, she and her husband mortgaged the land and forty-three enslaved individuals to the Bank of Louisiana to secure a loan of $29,000.[104] Preston used the majority of the loan to repay his $24,443 debt to the New Orleans firm of Hermann, Briggs & Co. When the couple failed to repay more than "a small part of said loan," the bank sued to foreclose on the property.[105] Yet at the same time as he was struggling financially, the thirty-seven-year-old Preston was a rising star in Louisiana politics, serving as one of six representatives from Louisiana at the national nominating convention for the Whig Party in Baltimore in May.[106] But the couple's professional and political fortunes quickly faded with their economic woes. Preston lost the election for state legislature in July.[107] In September, their young son, Preston Withers Farrar Jr., died suddenly of cholera in Woodville, Mississippi.[108] Then "the Bank purchased and took possession of the said Slaves" along with the rest of the Rapides plantation on December 7—although it did not get the enslaved men Dred and O'Joe until February 1, 1845.[109]

At this point, Eliza tried to have the entire mortgage contract nullified. First, she claimed that when she signed the contract, she was "entirely ignorant and uninformed of its nature and effect upon her own rights." More importantly, her lawyers argued that "the contract is not a loan within the true intent and meaning of the charter." Although Louisiana law was clear that women could bind themselves in mortgage contracts, the lawyers tried to make a technical distinction that she could not "become the surety of her husband" for other types of loans. Her lawyers attempted to prove that Hermann, Briggs & Co., being on the verge of insolvency, had orchestrated the loan between Preston and the bank. "The transaction was made to assume the form of a loan, or discount on a bond secured by mortgage of Mrs. Farrar's property." Although "a pro forma check was drawn to the order of Farrar and wife," the lawyer alleged that "not one dollar was paid to Farrar or his wife." The lawyers were seeking to draw a distinction between a "loan or discount made by said bank to the defendant, or to her husband," which would "create such an hypothecary contract as a married woman is authorized to make," and a loan "to secure a debt due by the husband to third persons," which they alleged was a violation of her rights as a wife. Preston Farrar "made no defence" as to his purported misrepresentation of the loan; it was also in his best interest to have the contract nullified.[110]

The Louisiana Supreme Court, however, failed to see this distinction in either the law or the bank's charter, ruling that "if the contract made by Mr. Farrar is binding upon him, under the charter of the bank, it was one to which the defendant and appellant [Mrs. Farrar] could become a party, and bind her property for the performance of it."[111] This ruling was subsequently cited in numerous Louisiana cases in which justices argued that "objections taken to the validity of the plaintiff's obligation on account of her being a married woman, are without any foundation whatever."[112] By the time the Louisiana Supreme Court ruled in April 1846, Preston had just been elected to the state legislature as a representative for the fourth district of Orleans Parish.[113] Just one year later, he was elected as speaker of the Louisiana House of Representatives, serving in that position until he, also, died suddenly of cholera in 1850.[114]

It is unclear who was managing the Farrar property from the time of the bank's acquisition of it in December 1844, but with the lawsuit finally settled in April 1846, the Bank of Louisiana was free to advertise and sell the Rapides plantation with its enslaved lives. The buyer in November 1846 was Hugh McCausland Keary, who was already an extremely wealthy planter. By 1840, Keary and his younger brothers Will and Patrick were well-established on a plantation with ninety-five enslaved workers in Wilkinson County, Mississippi—the same county where Farrar lived and practiced law.[115] At some point during the 1840s, Hugh and William bought a sugar plantation in Avoyelles Parish, Louisiana, known as Catalpa Grove.[116] Hugh likely jumped at the opportunity to purchase a third plantation—the Farrar estate—in the neighboring parish of Rapides at such a bargain price. The bank sold him the property for $29,000, but Keary only needed to pay $4,000 in the near term. He promised to pay the remaining balance in six annual installments on January 1, from 1848 to 1853.[117]

Due to the plantation's unorthodox management while under the ownership of the bank, the bank was unwilling to provide Keary with any warranty on the state of the enslaved lives he had just purchased. The mortgage contract stipulated that:

> It is well understood and agreed to by and between the said parties to these presents that, the vendors do not guarantee, the number of the said Slaves to be correct, nor that, they are all on the said plantation at present, nor do they guarantee them or any of them to be of any particular age or Colour, nor do they guarantee them or any of them against any of the redhibitory vices, maladies and defects prescribed by law, the purchaser declaring that, he takes the said Slaves as they may be found under the foregoing description and conditions, without recourse against the Vendors for any defects in health or character, or any deficiency in number arising from death, desease [*sic*] or absence.

The bank could not even account for the number, age, or gender of any "Slaves born on said Plantation from those originally mortgaged to the said Bank." But Keary was likely willing to forgo these usual protections in exchange for the extremely favorable purchase terms.[118]

The Keary brothers successfully continued to develop these plantations, eventually selling the Mississippi property to focus on the two Louisiana sugar plantations. In 1850, they acquired 804 shares of Citizens' Bank stock, to be secured by Catalpa Grove, "the appraised value whereof . . . was fixed at $120,000."[119] They continued to purchase more stock shares throughout the summer, fall, and winter, until they had accumulated the full 1,200 shares that their $120,000 appraisal would permit; this would allow them to borrow up to $60,000 from the bank.[120] In the 1850 census, Patrick was still living with his wife Helen in Wilkinson, Mississippi, as a planter with $15,500 in real estate wealth and sixty-three enslaved individuals, while Hugh and Will lived in Avoyelles Parish, where Hugh listed real estate wealth of $200,925 (about $6.9 million in 2021), with 138 enslaved people in Avoyelles and another fifty in Rapides.[121] Ten years later, Patrick and Helen were now residing in Rapides with real estate wealth of $149,380 and personal wealth of $11,900 from the plantation and sixty-seven enslaved workers.[122] Like the former owner Preston Farrar, Patrick Keary was active in politics in both Mississippi and Louisiana—although as a Democrat—eventually being elected to represent Rapides in the state legislature.[123] Hugh and Will remained in Avoyelles, where Hugh declared real estate wealth of $450,000, plus another $25,000 in personal property (about $15.4 million total in 2021) from Catalpa Grove with its 140 enslaved individuals.[124] Unlike his younger brother, Hugh was an ardent Whig.[125] The brothers appear to have paid off their mortgages to both the Bank of Louisiana and the Citizens' Bank without incident.

Bank Ownership of Plantations and Enslaved Lives

As had been the case with the Farrar and Penn plantations, banks that chose to foreclose on delinquent debtors often ended up purchasing the property when it failed to sell at auction for a sufficient price to cover the original debt. Such a purchase forced the bank to manage the property for a period of months—sometimes years—until it could execute an appropriate sale. The limited evidence on these bank-owned properties indicates that the bank either hired an outside manager for the property, or contracted with the foreclosed owner to continue running the plantation until the completion of a final sale. For example, when the Mobile branch of the Bank of the State of Alabama took possession of the plantation and enslaved laborers of one Marengo County slaveholder, the bank's agent "was instructed to receive the property & contract for its hire till the 1 Jany 1844." In September 1843, the bank's liquidator directed the cashier to write to the agent "to report what has been done."[126]

In October 1845, the same branch bank at Mobile submitted for foreclosure the property of Augustus A. Winston, who owed the branch $33,571.13 on his 1843 mortgage. He had secured this debt with his plantation and thirty-four enslaved lives on a promise to pay $4,000 plus interest semiannually until fulfilled, but had quickly fallen into arrears.[127] A year later, the bank sent an agent with power of attorney to inventory the Winston property, which the bank had continued operating in the meantime (perhaps under Winston's management). The bank sold the property for an undisclosed amount to another slaveholder, conveying to him by December 1846 "all the property thereon consisting of Forty Seven Negroes, the Horses, Mules, Cattle, Hogs, Wagon, Plantation tools, Corn, fodder, Household & Kitchen furniture."[128] While it is unclear whether this sale covered the whole debt, the bank at least had successfully gotten the property off its books.

Banks that took possession of such property needed (at a minimum) to maintain the value of the land and enslaved lives, if not (more ideally) profitably run the plantation until it could be resold. Adam Cornelius Hollinger was not only a major debtor of the Bank of Alabama, but he likewise was the endorser for numerous others.[129] In December 1841, he still owed the bank on his own account $12,511.72, which he had secured with a mortgage on his land in Mobile County and thirty of his approximately eighty-two enslaved lives. Hollinger never paid off his debt, which by January 1846 had increased to $16,540.58 (with accrued interest). After five years of delinquency, Hollinger paid $1,500 in January 1846, another $550 in February, and $225 in March, in a last-ditch attempt to convince the bank not to liquidate his assets.[130] Perhaps he was trying to take advantage of the recently passed act of the Alabama legislature from 1846 permitting existing "good" debtors another extension on their debts until September 1847, provided they pay half the debt by June of 1846.[131]

By August, 1846, Hollinger was far short of the required 50 percent payback, and the bank placed his land and enslaved workers up for sale. Yet, unable to find a suitable buyer, the bank purchased most of the property on its own account for $9,738.11, leaving a balance still due by Hollinger on the debt (with accrued interest) of $5,151.74. Of the original thirty enslaved individuals listed on the mortgage, the bank acquired twenty-three, plus seven children born since 1841. Three of the enslaved lives from the original mortgage—twenty-year-old Lucy and seventeen-year-olds John and Mary—were claimed under a prior mortgage to another creditor and sold separately. Forty-year-old "Solomon was drowned," while twenty-three-year-old Mariah Harry was "delivered to the Register for sale" to another individual. Finally, Hollinger had failed to send twenty-year-old George Smith and forty-year-old Celeste; he forwarded them to the bank for sale by September.[132]

The bank now needed to find a use for this land and human property. Despite this foreclosure proceeding, Hollinger was "anxious to Rent the said land and hire the said Negroes, and ultimately to purchase the same from said Bank." The bank agreed to hire the enslaved people back to Hollinger, on the condition that he continue to repay the balance of the mortgage in four payments of $2,500 each between October 1846 and September 1847. If complied with, the bank would then "sell and Convey said land and Negroes to said Hollinger" with a new three-year mortgage for the remainder of their value. In effect, the bank was allowing him one more chance to take advantage of the extension law. If, on the other hand, he failed to meet any of these payments, he would have to "immediately on demand . . . redeliver the said slaves and give up the possession of said lands," which the bank would proceed to sell.[133]

The records do not indicate how much of this debt Hollinger paid. On the one hand, he did retain possession of the enslaved individuals until the early 1850s, and it is unclear whether he included these thirty or so hired laborers in the sixty-nine enslaved lives he listed in the 1850 census.[134] On the other hand, he listed no real estate wealth in 1850, and the bank did eventually foreclose on this property, dispersing the enslaved people across several buyers.[135] In May 1850, the bank sold twenty-five-year-old Matilda to one buyer for $650 at "Hollingers consent & request"; the bank had valued her at $710 in 1846. In May 1852, the bank sold forty-six-year-old Rachael, originally valued at $290, for $400 to a second purchaser. In January 1853, the bank sold twenty-three-year-old Jim, thirty-six-year-old Lucy, and the family of Richard, Maria (both around thirty-one years old), and their children, Richard Jr., Martha, and Israel, to a third slaveholder for an unreported amount. And then in June it sold the remaining sixteen slaves to a fourth buyer; Daniel and Delight had died in the interim.[136] With no further notations on his account, the bank appears to have considered this debt finally settled.

Louisiana foreclosures also sometimes ended in the bank taking possession of and running an active plantation. During the speculative land bubble of the 1830s, Nathaniel and James Dick obtained two pieces of land in the parish of Rapides. The first was a "cotton plantation" known as Bynum's Lower Plantation, along with its fifty-seven enslaved workers, all of which they purchased from Abner Robinson in 1834 for $75,000 (about $2.4 million in 2021). The brothers paid $43,979.27 "in ready current money," with the remainder to be paid by assuming two of Robinson's outstanding debts: $23,230.91, the "amount of principal and interest up to the sixth day of June last, due & owing by the said vendor to the United States Branch Bank," and the balance to another Rapides planter.[137] Their second purchase was an adjacent piece of land that they obtained directly from the United States government in 1835. In 1837, the Dicks used this property as collateral for a loan of $131,643 (about $3.8 million in 2021) from the Mechanics' and Traders' Bank of New Orleans, payable in four payments due in nine, ten, eleven, and twelve months, but with the possibility of renewal. They secured the loan by offering the two pieces of land, and seventy-one enslaved lives, as mortgage collateral.[138]

But the debtors soon succumbed to the hard times following the panic, and by November of 1840, the bank foreclosed on the property. The sheriff put the land and enslaved individuals up for public sale, but—not receiving an adequate offer at auction—the Mechanics' Bank took ownership of the property. The purchase price was then used to repay all debts owed by the Dicks, including the outstanding loan to the bank itself. Over the next fifteen months, the bank likely hired an agent to run the plantation for its own benefit while it sought a suitable buyer. In February of 1842, it finally sold the two tracts of land, including "all the buildings and improvements thereon, and all the farming utensils, and stock, consisting of horses, mules, oxen, cattle, &c. wagons, carts, ploughs, provisions, &c.," along with the 103 named slaves "attached to said Plantation," to Horatio Stephenson Sprigg and George Mason for $106,050. The new owners paid $10,000 in cash, financing the remainder with six promissory notes payable at 7 percent interest over the next six years. The bank required that the pair not only offer the purchased land and enslaved workers as collateral for these notes, but that they also obtain "an additional Mortgage on the Plantation and Slaves of H. S. Sprigg Situated in the Parish of Rapides called Evergreen" to secure the first three promissory notes.[139] Once again, the ultimate payment of this loan was significantly delayed by the repeated sales and refinancings.

Due to the problems of owning, operating, and reselling property, banks usually avoided taking possession of foreclosed property whenever possible. On May 3, 1834, Peter Petrovic requested a loan of $7,000 from the Natchitoches branch of the City Bank of New Orleans, offering to mortgage his cotton plantation and twelve enslaved workers—all prime hands between the ages of sixteen and twenty-four.[140] Two years later, he borrowed $14,000 from the New Orleans firm of Lambeth & Thompson, securing the loan with this same plantation and enslaved lives. Having repaid his first bank loan, in April 1837 he borrowed $25,000 from the City Bank, payable in five annual installments and still secured by his growing plantation and enslaved workforce.[141] He paid the first installment of this second bank loan, but by 1840 he was in arrears for both debts. In the summer of 1840, the bank received a writ of *fieri facias* to foreclose on Petrovic's property.[142] The cashier of the New Orleans branch advised the Natchitoches office that it needed to ensure that the collateral security was not lost. "I presume it will be unnecessary to say to you, that to protect the interest of the Bank, it will be necessary that you, or some one else should attend the sale on the part of the bank and bid up to the amount of the Bank debt," meaning that the property had to sell for at least $34,000 to cover both debts. The New Orleans cashier likewise cautioned that "I should think it advisable that a good look out should be kept, that the negroes are not transported to Texas." Mostly, the City Bank wished to avoid acquiring property on the bank's account except under extreme circumstances. "The Bank does not wish to become the purchaser of the property, unless it is to save the debt."[143] At the September 1840 auction, a local slaveholder stepped in to purchase the land and forty-seven enslaved lives for precisely $34,000, paying $14,000 to Lambeth & Thompson, assuming the mortgage of Petrovic to the City Bank for the remainder, and saving the bank from having to take ownership of the property.[144] Yet what seemed like an ideal solution would turn into an extended legal battle for the bank later in the 1840s (chapter 9).

As the New Orleans cashier's instructions to the Natchitoches branch indicate, the City Bank was wary of acquiring additional property that it would need to manage and then resell in the midst of the recession. Having recently foreclosed on the mortgage of William L. Cockerill, the City Bank was temporarily stuck with the ownership of his Natchitoches plantation. Fifteen of his enslaved workers, along with another tract of land, were separately mortgaged to R. B. Hyde to secure a note of $7,832.65. While Hyde considered the land to be "of little value," he wanted to make a deal with the bank regarding the human property. Hyde was "in want of money," and thus needed to foreclose on the loan. However, given the continued low valuations for enslaved people, he feared that "he will be obliged to buy them in, as it is not likely that any purchaser will be found able or willing to pay the full amount of the debt in cash." Early in 1842, a representative of Hyde's contacted the bank, offering to sell it the note and mortgage secured by Cockerill's enslaved workers, believing that it would be "to its interest to assume the present debt." Hyde's terms were $5,500 cash paid to him by the bank, and the balance of $2,332.65 plus interest in a year. The bank, however, had no interest in acquiring this additional property to consolidate the assets, and the offer was "not acceded to."[145]

At other times, the consolidation of debts worked to the advantage of both the debtor and the bank. Absalom Barney Gill and his wife Ann, both of Alexandria, Louisiana, had struggled to keep afloat even before the panic hit. The couple initially took out two loans from the Natchitoches branch of the City Bank of New Orleans in the early 1830s. The loans—one for $5,000 secured by promissory notes, and the other for $10,000 secured by a mortgage on their cotton plantation and enslaved workers—were repayable in five annual installments plus 10 percent interest. In November 1834 (well before the panic), the couple wrote the branch of their struggles with the cotton crop that year, which was impeding their ability to pay. "Owing to the unfortunate visitations which have cum [*sic*] upon the planters of this parish in the shape of worms and storms, we have many of us and my wife and myself among the rest now cut short with perhaps less than half a crop of cotton this year." They thus wrote with great "anxiety," hoping the bank would extend "your liberality to us" and "deal indulgently with us." The Gills believed that they would be able to pay "without great sacrafice [*sic*]" the required one-fifth curtailment of principal on the discounted note of $1,000, the interest on the remaining balance, as well as the interest (only) on the mortgage loan, but not the additional $2,000 in principal due on the mortgage.[146]

While they awaited the response of the branch bank, Mrs. Gill simultaneously subscribed for 610 shares in the new Citizens' Bank, offering their cotton plantation in Rapides Parish and forty-six enslaved individuals (who had only numbered ten people in the 1830 census) as collateral. Although the couple jointly agreed to mortgage the property, the deed clearly stated that the shares were "subscribed by the said Mrs. Gill."[147] This subscription entitled her to a loan of up to $30,500 from the Citizens' Bank. In considering this subscription, the Citizens' Bank required that the City Bank grant it "the priority of mortgage" over any City Bank claims. The cashier of the City Bank home office in New Orleans forwarded this request to the Natchitoches branch cashier, since "it is a matter which rests altogether with your direction." The New Orleans cashier instructed his counterpart that "in similar application made by persons indebted to the mother Bank on mortgage the request had been granted, on condition that the Citizens Bank, agree in the act of mortgage to apply the money, the applicant would be entitled to as stockholder, to the liquidation of the mortgage debt due the City Bank." Thus, as long as the Gills exercised their stockholder privilege with the Citizens' Bank to take out a loan and then used it to repay City Bank, the latter bank would renounce its lien priority on the property. If this loan repayment were not accomplished within "twelve months from the date of the act, they agree to rescind the mortgage."[148] The Gills effectively refinanced their five-year debt with City Bank, by replacing it with the ten-year loan of the Citizens' Bank.

Although the Gills listed forty-six enslaved individuals in the 1835 mortgage deed, their workforce had been reduced to thirty-five by the 1840 census; it is unknown if this reduction took place through death, sale, or escape. And the collapse in cotton prices during the panic again affected their ability to make prompt debt payments.[149] By the winter of 1842–1843, the Citizens' Bank foreclosed on the property, yet the sheriff was unable to find a buyer offering adequate money to cover the debt and the bank was forced to take ownership. In March 1843, the bank directors discussed what to do with "A. B. Gills Plantation & Negroes lately bought by the Bank at Sheriffs' Sale" in the parish of Rapides.[150] In the long term, it needed a plan for managing the property until it could resell it and recoup the outstanding debt. But the bank also had more pressing worries. Letters from both a prominent local stockholder, Evariste Archinard, and the bank's attorney raised concerns about the status of the property; many delinquent debtors were disappearing to Texas and perhaps they feared that Gill would likewise flee with his enslaved people. The board thus directed the attorney "to send the Slaves immediately to the City should he and Mr. Archinard be of opinion that the safety and interest of the Bank require such a course."[151] It is unclear how long the bank remained in possession of the property, but by 1847 it had sold the land on Bayou Marteau with its thirty-seven enslaved people and 464 (of the original 610) shares of bank stock to another slaveholder; the entire property was then appraised at $77,437 (about $2.6 million in 2021).[152]

When multiple creditors claimed the same property, the consolidation of debts was often preferable to disputes that arose when debtors scrambled to foreclose and assert their claims over a portion of the assets. In the summer of 1843, both the Bank of Louisiana and the firm of A. Rivarde & Co. received *fieri facias* judgments against Sylvester Bossier. The sheriff of Caddo Parish seized his cotton plantation and human property, and auctioned them off to the highest bidder. On September 3 and 6, the bank and A. Rivarde each purchased a portion of the plantation and enslaved workers, canceling Bossier's debts in the process.[153] Two years later, in 1845, A. Rivarde sold the firm's portion of the property to the bank for $12,000, giving the bank full ownership of the plantation and forty-one enslaved lives. The bank only paid $5,948.24 cash, with the remainder accounted for by canceling $6,051.76 in debts that Rivarde separately owed to the bank.[154] Another six years later, in 1851, the bank acquired ten more of Bossier's enslaved lives from a sheriff's sale initiated by the estate of another creditor.[155]

Based on the limited historical record, it is likely that Bossier never gave up possession and management of his land and human property, even as ownership legally passed to the Bank of Louisiana. As had been the case with Adam Hollinger and the Bank of the State of Alabama, the Bank of Louisiana must have reached an agreement with Bossier to enable him to buy back the property. In February 1853, almost a decade after the initial foreclosure, the bank resold the plantation and enslaved individuals to Bossier for $8,547.37 in cash, an amount that was presumably the remainder of the debt with interest that he owed to the bank. Although the mortgage listed fifty-one individuals by name and age, the bank could not say with any certainty which of them had since died nor how many enslaved children had been born in the interim. But this lack of knowledge was not a problem, since Bossier "declared that he acknowledges himself to be in possession of the property and slaves, and requires no guarantee from the vendors as to the number, names, and redhibitory vices, maladies and defects of the slaves, some of whom may have died since purchased by the Bank but he is entitled to all the increase thereof."[156] He had remained the active manager of the property and needed no further assurances of its status.

While the bank often auctioned land and enslaved lives together, a practice that helped to maintain the continuity of the enslaved communities on these large plantations, doing so was not always possible. Sometimes, new purchasers only desired the land and intended to bring their own enslaved workers from other plantations, as had been the case when a new owner purchased the Piseros plantation. At other times, the bank might only seize the enslaved individuals to satisfy the delinquent debt. In 1847, the Citizens' Bank board of directors were concerned that "this Bank has purchased at several Sheriffs Sales a number of Slaves attached at the time to Lands seized. . . . Their number being small, it has been found impracticable to sell them with Stock and the Lands to which they were attached." The board agreed that holding these enslaved people, especially separate from a plantation, was a liability. "Considering that the Bank is much exposed to loss from natural or other causes by holding said Slaves, It was resolved that the President be requested to have all the Slaves belonging to the Bank, brought to this City as soon as he may deem it prudent, in order that they may be disposed of as the Board may determine."[157] Presumably, these enslaved individuals were transported to New Orleans and sold at auction to the highest bidder.

The leniency of these frontier banks in treating with delinquent debtors after the Panics of 1837 and 1839 was critical to stabilizing the slave economy during the depression. The banks of the southern frontier actively operated to support and uphold plantation slavery, mitigating the worst effects of the downturn for slaveholders. Banks repeatedly refinanced mortgages that were significantly overdue and/or were figuratively underwater (meaning that the debt due surpassed the value of the property itself), and deliberately helped slaveholding families to maintain possession of their plantations. Rather than upholding their fiduciary responsibility to protect the interests of bank shareholders, bondholders, and noteholders, these banks instead jeopardized their balance sheets and placed their own survival at risk to protect the slaveholding aristocracy on the frontier. In doing so, they facilitated the triumph of the slave economy by mid-century, but at the expense of the southern banking system itself (chapter 8).

The Exemption of Human Property from Debts

Frontier banks were not the only institutions who treated delinquent debtors with leniency. Many state legislatures also quickly found ways to protect struggling citizens. During and after the panics, Pennsylvania (1836, 1842), Virginia (1837, 1842), Mississippi (1840), Ohio (1841), Illinois (1841), Indiana (1838, 1841), and Iowa (1843) all passed some combination of stay or stop laws that placed a temporary pause on foreclosure proceedings, and/or valuation laws that required foreclosed property to be sold for at least one-half to two-thirds of its appraised value—even if the courts later struck down many of these laws as violations of the US Constitution's contract clause.[158] Other states—including Georgia, Kentucky, Tennessee, Michigan, Missouri, and New York—expanded the type and value of property that was exempt from seizure under *fieri facias* proceedings. Exercising one of its few enumerated powers under the Constitution, Congress passed (and then quickly repealed) a federal bankruptcy act in 1841 to try and address these issues (chapter 7).[159]

The question of whether to exempt human property in particular from debt seizures was also debated periodically throughout the antebellum period. In 1825, in the wake of the Panic of 1819, "Phylanthropy" published an editorial in the *Centreville Gazette* of Maryland on "the justness of passing a law exempting slaves from execution for debt" given both "the embarrassed state of the country" and the evils of family separations due to sales.[160] This novel idea, while inspired by the many laws dating back to the colonial period that exempted items such as essential clothing, kitchen utensils, or certain household furnishings from seizure for debt, pushed the boundaries of what assets were essential for survival to include human property.[161] In countering this proposal, "Justicia" noted the unjustness of the law for creditors, even if only applied to future debts: "If a man borrows one thousand dollars, purchases slaves with this same money, and after purchasing, hires them out and lives upon the proceeds, according to Phylanthropy's plan, if he has no other property to execute, his creditor is robbed of his money!"[162] Justicia's argument prevailed, and this proposal gained little traction in the 1820s. Even in the wake of the nation's first major panic, southerners demonstrated no interest in protecting enslaved individuals from seizure for debts.

Two decades later, slavery had become more entrenched in the southern economy and human property was more essential as loan collateral. In the wake of the most recent panics of 1837 and 1839, southerners expressed increasing interest in protecting human assets from seizure for debts. As the constitutional convention in Louisiana was getting underway in the spring of 1845, an editorial in the *New Orleans Bulletin* written by "A Citizen" urged the delegates to consider "exempting slaves from seizure and sale, for debts created at future day." The writer promoted this idea as a means to counter the "unholy crusade against southern institutions" that was being waged by people in "Europe and the north." The South, "as a prudent people," would need "to adopt all means necessary and proper for our protection"; and this measure "would be beneficial alike to the master and the slave, to the debtor and the creditor, to the State and its citizens."[163]

After reviewing the many positive attributes of the system of slavery—"that the slave population of the south are the best fed and clad laboring community in the world" and "are generally warmly attached to their owners"—the author noted that "the only substantial drawback to their happiness is the liability, which at present exists, of a separation from their nearest and dearest relatives." While this same critique could easily have been leveled at the domestic slave trade, "A Citizen" instead focused on "the records of our mortgage officers" which revealed "the forced alienations monthly pervading every part of the State." It was the mortgage broker and not the slave trader—and certainly not the benevolent masters who "seldom voluntarily part with their slaves"—that was responsible for "the separation of husband and wife, parent and child, brother and sister." Not only would this revision in the law enable enslaved individuals to be born and die "from generation to generation in the same families and communities," but the master would likewise "feel no longer the remorse of rearing a large slave family, probably to witness its entire dismemberment."[164]

For those commercial-minded readers, the author argued that this policy would result in increased prices for enslaved lives, and as a result, "the present debtor will thereby be better enabled to discharge the obligations now in operation on his slaves"—presumably by *selling* this more valuable human property, but the author did not mention that contradiction. And as for the plantation banks, "for which the faith of the State is so deeply pledged," a change affecting the very equity upon which their capital stock was based would somehow be of "such decided advantages as to relieve the state from all apprehension of their inability to meet their debts." Since "A Citizen" only intended the law to apply to new debts, the (inevitable) rising prices of enslaved lives would positively affect the equity of all existing debts collateralized with slaves, including the outstanding bonds of the plantation banks. On the other hand, for those readers critical of the "made spirit of enterprise or aggrandizement which decennially overruns our country," this policy would provide "a wholesome check" by "plac[ing] slave property so far out of commerce, as to be beyond the reach of forced sales." Not only "would the claims of humanity and the best interests of Louisiana, public and private, profit by the change," but it would "be hailed in after time as one of the greatest achievements of an enlightened age."[165]

The editors of the *Democrat* in Huntsville, Alabama, the *Vicksburg Tri-Weekly Sentinel*, and the *Holly Springs Gazette* in Mississippi all republished the editorial in full. The Holly Springs and Huntsville papers both opined: "There are many distinguished individuals in our State who favor these views; and ere long we may expect to see the subject introduced to the attention of our law-makers."[166] The *Mississippi Free Trader and Natchez Gazette* agreed, comparing the proposal to a Virginia law that exempted land from execution for debts: "We think the dictates of humanity would be a strong plea in favor of extending it to slaves."[167] And a Kentucky editorial, republished in the *Natchez Gazette*, compared it to the "great revolutions in regard to the relation of debtor and creditor" such as the abolishment of debt prisons, which "the march of mind and the increased liberality consequent upon the increase of the educated classes, is destined" to produce. Pointing out the "advantages to the public interest" of such a law—both from increased slave prices and "the motives of humanity"—the author believed that even a law "exempting a certain amount in *value* of property" would be beneficial to society. He urged that this topic should "command the serious consideration of the next legislature of this State," alongside "'a law to protect the rights of married women by securing to them at least a portion of their own property."[168] Several months later, the Huntsville *Democrat* repeated its support for this proposal, which "would add, greatly, to their value, as a permanent species of property; and restore those familiar ties, which, in years past, existed in the older slave states of the Union."[169]

Despite the strong journalistic support, no mention of this proposal appeared in the proceedings of the Louisiana constitutional convention during the summer of 1845. In February 1846, Orleans Parish representative H. D. Ogden "gave notice that he would introduce a bill to exempt slaves from seizure to satisfy future debts," but his bill made no progress in the state legislature.[170] On the other hand, several states did begin passing homestead exemption laws, which set aside a certain amount and type of property from seizure. For example, Georgia's 1841 law allowed the head of household twenty acres of land "exempt from levy and sale," plus an additional five acres for each child under the age of fifteen, as well as "one horse or mule, not to exceed the value of fifty dollars, ten head of hogs and thirty dollars worth of provisions." An 1843 amendment extended this allotment to fifty acres, while another 1845 amendment allowed up to $200 of real estate in cities or towns.[171]

Four years later, in 1849, an editorial in the Augusta, Georgia, *Daily Constitutionalist* signed "Bibb" argued that the logical next step would be the addition of a new amendment "exempting from levy and sale under execution one slave of a debtor . . . to be selected by the debtor." While the "noble objective" of the existing homestead exemption was "to rescue the unfortunate debtor from hopeless penury," it was "defective—it does not go far enough. . . . [A]dd to this meagre inventory one slave, and you secure solid comfort to the unfortunate, you fence and till the fifty acres—you warm with cheerful fires the children of poverty, and rescue the fragile mother from wasting toil." The exemption would likewise further encourage the expansion of slaveholding in the state, as it would "hold out inducements to vest capital in this species of property." And like the Louisiana editorialist from 1845, Bibb believed that even the exemption of a single slave would help to "throw a gentle and salutary check" on "the wild, unlimited and unrestrained credit system [that] has convulsed as with the throes of a volcano." On the one hand, it would "cause capital to seek investment in slaves," while on the other it would "produce corresponding caution on the part of merchants and banks, in extending credit."[172]

The Georgia legislature debated this exemption during their December session. Whereas Mr. Shackelford of Cass County supported the bill because it gave "every individual in the State a direct and consequently a more active interest in the institution of slavery," Mr. McDougald of Muscogee "considered it an innovation of a dangerous character," and Mr. Robinson of Macon "thought that it would prejudice those who are unable to hold slaves, by exempting a species of property from execution which they could not possess and granting an immunity which they could never enjoy." Mr. Jones agreed, arguing that "it looked like buying support for the institution of slavery" which was "impolitic and unnecessary." The legislature went into recess and the bill never passed.[173]

That same year, in August 1849, the Virginia legislature passed an amendment that forbade the seizure of enslaved individuals "without the consent of the debtor" when there was sufficient other property available to satisfy the claim. In debating this amendment, one legislator remarked that "it would be very unjust to deprive a man of the last slave to wait on him," while another opined that it was "not only just and proper, but humane, in preventing the taking away a negro from the master's family and associates . . . which was, really, our strongest defence against the attacks of the enemies of our institutions."[174] Yet rather than exempting enslaved individuals, this law merely gave the debtor more flexibility in determining which assets would be sold first.

Four years later, in 1853, C. G. Baylor of Holly Springs, Mississippi, again took up this issue. Repeating many of the same points, he believed that the strongest argument in its favor was that it would encourage all southerners to become slaveholders. "As loudly as we may call on federal power to crush abolitionism *without*, we can no longer disguise the fact that we must also meet that abolitionism in its incipient form, AT HOME." Exempting human property from seizure "would make the South an unit on everything touching our slave property." It would also encourage farmers in the North and West to rethink their opinions on the slave system. "Let a man in Illinois know that he can own a negro to work for his family, *and that this property cannot be taken from him*, and he will most *ardently* desire to possess himself of one." On the other hand, Baylor asserted that the strongest opposition for the measure would come "from those northern banking influences now based purely on our slave population as property, and consequently a species of banking capital" who would argue that "to sweep from under the North such an amount of capital would endanger the stability of trade." Baylor, in contrast, believed that enslaved people were not "banking capital" but rather "an *agricultural* property alone."[175]

Ironically, some northern commentators entered this 1853 debate, supporting the measure as a step in the right direction toward abolition. A Connecticut editorialist stated that "any measure must be a proper one that will to any extent prevent the disruption of families now so common and so cruel at the South."[176] A St. Louis abolitionist argued that the idea, which was "gaining great favor at the South," would "be to a very great extent equivalent to declaring human beings no longer property." If southern legislatures followed up the exemption law with another "prohibiting in ordinary sales or in gifts the dispersion of slave families, and especially the separation of the mother from her young children," it would go a long way toward removing "the glaring barbarism . . . from our slave institution"—even if this "pretense of amelioration" fell short of the ultimate goal of full abolition.[177] Southerners who opposed the idea recognized this potential for abolitionists to "use the statute itself as an argument, to work its destruction." As one commenter in the *West Alabamian* opined, "Such a law . . . would . . . so derange and unsettle the whole civil polity of our people, that it should be rejected at the first move."[178]

In the fall of 1853, Huntsville, Alabama, representative Percy Walker introduced an act which would have permitted slaveholders to register up to five enslaved individuals as exempt from debts. Much like the recording requirements for mortgage deeds, slaveholders seeking this exemption would file an official notice with the county probate judge, listing the names, ages, and gender of the effected property, and paying a twenty-dollar filing fee for each enslaved individual. Upon moving to another county, the slaveholder would be required to re-register the enslaved individuals in order to retain the exemption. The funds raised through these registrations would be applied to a "Special Education Fund" for the promotion of public schools.[179] A Florida commentator deemed this law "a good one, and will doubtless interest other Southern States in its adoption."[180] Yet in his December message to the legislature, the newly elected Democrat governor John A. Winston expressed only mixed support for the bill. Its contractionary effect on credit was "not very objectionable" since "an excess of credit is certainly a great evil in this State, [and] often prejudicial to the interest of the debtor, occasionally so to the creditor—injurious to public morals and productive of much suffering in families." Yet he still questioned "what effect the measure referred to would have upon the institution of slavery at home [and] Whether public sentiment demands, or would approve it." Thus he concluded that "no enactment of such political importance should be passed without an assurance that popular opinion will sustain it, lest, by reaction, injurious consequences may result."[181] The act failed to pass, and by the winter of 1859–60 the Alabama legislature was still debating a new version of Walker's bill.[182]

Similar bills were also unsuccessfully proposed in Kansas in 1855, Mississippi and South Carolina in 1856, and Florida in 1858.[183] During the Kansas debates, which took place as part of the controversial proslavery legislative session after the disputed territorial elections, exemption proponents again argued for the humanity of the law in preventing family separations, as well as for the relief it would provide poor debtors. Dr. John H. Stringfellow, Speaker of the House, vehemently responded that he "did not think the principle of separating husband and wife or child and mother was wrong." The record quoted him as saying: "I don't call them evils; to sell slaves is a right—a right recognised by God himself—recognised by every Southern State." The measure was soundly defeated by a vote of seventeen to three.[184]

Despite this recurring interest throughout the 1840s and 1850s, as of 1859 no states had passed laws exempting enslaved individuals from execution for debt. Most southern states did allow debtors to retain a certain portion of their land, defined as a combination of acreage and value, free from seizure. This exemption ranged from just $150 of both real and personal property in Missouri, 40 acres of land up to $200 in Florida or 50 acres up to $200 in Georgia, 40 acres up to $400 in Alabama, up to 160 acres in Arkansas, and up to $500 in Tennessee. Kentucky, North Carolina, and Virginia permitted exemptions only for household goods and personal property up to $100, $50, and $25 respectively.[185] Even if enslaved people had been included under these laws, all these exemptions remained well below the average price of a single enslaved life, which was (on average) between $650 and $800 on the eve of the Civil War; these prices ballooned to above $1,500 for prime males in the New Orleans market (see figure 2.1).[186]

Mississippi and Texas, on the other hand, were much more generous, exempting 160 acres up to $1,500 and 200 acres up to $2,000 respectively, although these higher amounts were intended to account for more expensive residences in towns or cities and still did not include enslaved individuals. And Virginia remained the only state to exempt enslaved lives from seizure in cases "where there are other goods and chattels of such debtor sufficient for the purpose."[187] Whether it was because creditors did not want debtors to be able to hide their wealth in human property, because slaveholders wanted to be able to continue using their enslaved people as collateral, or because nonslaveholders did not think it was fair for indebted slaveholders to have more options for property exemption, these slave-exemption laws never gained much traction anywhere in the South.

❋

While enslaved lives were never explicitly exempted from debt collection, southerners did find another way to protect their human property from the claims of creditors through the passage of the Married Women's Property Acts, although this response—in the words of historian Woody Holton—had larger "unintended consequence."[188] The wave of foreclosures in the aftermath of the Panic of 1837 highlighted the risks of securing loans with enslaved lives. Beginning in 1835, the territory of Arkansas exempted a wife's property from seizure in the case of debts that the husband had incurred prior to the marriage, but this act did not address debts acquired during the marriage.[189] Then in 1839, Mississippi passed an act specifically targeted at protecting the human property of wives from foreclosure. "The Negroes which a woman owned at the time of her marriage or which she acquired afterwards were her separate property and exempt from her husband's debts. The husband, however, controlled and managed these slaves, and the receipts of their labor remained with him, just as they had under the common law."[190] The following year, Texas passed its own married women's property act, which established a separation of property between spouses along the model of Louisiana.[191]

The Mississippi law clarified the rights of creditors, debtors, and their wives, and applied these rights across all married couples without the need for separate trust deeds or marriage settlements, which were largely only accessible to the wealthy and well-informed.[192] By 1848, seven southern states (mostly in the frontier South) had adopted similar legislation.[193] By standardizing the property rights of women and explicitly placing this property outside the claims of creditors, married couples no longer needed to register trust deeds with local courthouses—a change which rendered slave-backed mortgages even riskier. Thus, whereas Holton's "unintended consequence" of the 1839 act was growing calls for women's equality by mid-century, another unintended consequence was making enslaved individuals potentially less desirable for creditors. Even so, while the Married Women's Property Acts, bankruptcy laws, and other debtor-protection measures made mortgage contracts more risky, fraudulent conveyances of property and the growing practice of "going to Texas" epitomized the problem of using human property as collateral.

7

Escaping Debt: Bankruptcy, Fraud, and Going to Texas

In December 1843, John D. Bracy obtained a $9,065 loan from the Mobile branch of the Bank of the State of Alabama, placing several enslaved individuals in trust to protect his endorsers should he fail to repay the obligation. When the bank sued him for nonpayment in November 1845, the trustee sold some of the enslaved individuals "to reduce the debt." Yet Bracy remained delinquent and quickly realized that the entirety of his property was in jeopardy. Within a few months, "Bracy privately left the State of Alabama," taking with him his remaining enslaved people and leaving no property behind for the bank to seize. First going to Mississippi, he moved to Louisiana by 1847, and then onto White County, Arkansas, in 1848, where he claimed a "tract of Government land" and began operating it as a cotton plantation. In 1849, he sold the enslaved individuals to his sister Margaret McRae for $3,500, which she promised to pay him in four installments from 1855 to 1858—several years in the future. McRae's son took possession of the enslaved lives and brought them to Louisiana.[1]

Also during 1849, McRae's husband died, leaving her a widow with eleven children and in possession of numerous enslaved people—her husband had reported owning forty-eight on their Alabama plantation in the 1840 census.[2] She soon joined her brother in Arkansas with her family and human property—which now included the enslaved lives purchased from that same brother. She took title to the cotton plantation, while Bracy managed it. Upon Bracy's death in 1852, he had accumulated over $14,000 in new debts, but only possessed property in his own name worth $345.90.[3] In contrast, McRae reported owning $4,000 in real estate wealth and fifty-five enslaved individuals in the 1850 census.[4] With average prices for enslaved lives at about $500, we can estimate her wealth in human property at approximately $27,500.[5]

When the bank learned of the location of Bracy's enslaved workers, it sued McRae as the fraudulent possessor of the individuals. McRae's defense was that "she purchased [the enslaved people] in good faith, and without any notice or knowledge whatever of a subsisting lien upon them." Yet the US Supreme Court justices unanimously rejected her assertion of innocence. "But we are all of opinion, that the sale to Mrs. McRae was in fraud of creditors, and especially of the bank." While Bracy's guilt in fleeing with the enslaved lives was undisputed, the legal consolidation of all his property so neatly into the hands of McRae was too convenient for them to believe her ignorance. "We think it enough to say, that the removal of the property from Alabama by Bracy, leaving the judgment of the bank unsatisfied, his insolvency, the relation between the parties, their subsequent residence together, the manner in which the property was held and managed, are causes of very grave suspicion." The court even questioned whether any sale had ever taken place, since no promissory notes from McRae were included in the inventory of Bracy's property, and McRae would not start paying her brother until six years afterward.[6] With this definitive ruling, McRae was forced to settle the full bank debt. The historical record does not indicate whether the bank took possession of the enslaved people—bringing them back to Alabama for sale—or if McRae repaid the debt in cash and kept the slaves on the Arkansas plantation. The physical mobility of enslaved lives made either solution a viable option.

While creditors had to weigh the pros and cons of foreclosure versus forbearance when dealing with debtors, debtors could also assert their own agency over the situation, through either legal or illegal means. Frauds committed to evade foreclosure were often distinct from frauds committed at the point of contract—such as mischaracterizing the value or ownership rights of property offered for collateral, or secretly mortgaging the same property to multiple creditors. Many foreclosure frauds instead involved the illegitimate or pretended sale of property, such as Bracy's sale to his sister. Questionable claims by wives of rights to property through dower or unrecorded trust deeds, fake conveyances of land or enslaved individuals to family or friends, and the nondisclosure of assets in bankruptcy filings could tie up foreclosure proceedings in court for years—sometimes decades (much like the Jarndyce estate in Charles Dickens's *Bleak House*). Even if the creditor ultimately prevailed, the delay usually left the property in the hands of the debtor until the final ruling, during which time they continued to benefit from the enslaved labor. But the most brazen means of evading foreclosure was to flee from creditors with the property in hand, as Bracy had done. Debtors who physically sought to escape their creditors had to leave behind their land, but they could remove their valuable human property. And when the independent

Republic of Texas existed along the southern border from 1836 to 1846, absconding debtors could literally hide in plain sight.

Beyond fraud, debtors also had a few legal options to stave off foreclosure. As we saw in the previous chapter, they could petition creditors for extensions of their loans, offer additional property as security, or refinance by soliciting a new loan to repay the old. Yet especially during periods of economic depression, debtors often lacked the assets and access to capital to pursue these options. Legally, their only other recourse for voiding a debt contract was to convince a court that it was somehow an invalid contract (as many women attempted to do), or to place themselves at the mercy of their creditors through bankruptcy proceedings. However, even as some states sporadically passed insolvency laws, these laws were of questionable constitutionality, tended to favor the interests of creditors, and were designed to make the process as cumbersome as possible to discourage applicants.[7]

In the US Constitution, establishing "uniform Laws on the subject of Bankruptcies throughout the United States" was one of the enumerated powers designated for Congress under Article I, Section 8, yet Congress had only exercised this power briefly, from 1800 to 1803.[8] In 1841, during the height of the depression, Congress passed a new federal bankruptcy law which went into effect on February 1, 1842. Under the terms of that act, an individual could voluntarily declare him or herself bankrupt and fully discharge his or her debts by surrendering all property to the courts. A court-appointed assignee would sell the property, paying off as much of the outstanding debt as possible. Critically, the debtor would then be absolved of whatever portion of the debts remained unpaid.[9] Designed as a uniform procedure to provide relief to a wide array of debtors, the highly controversial law satisfied few people. Unlike most state insolvency laws, which often required the agreement of a majority or supermajority of creditors to proceed, creditors had little say in the federal proceedings. The law also required assignees to sell property as quickly as possible, which—during the continued economic downturn—often meant that it sold at depressed prices. And legal and administrative fees frequently absorbed a large portion of the proceeds. On average, creditors received only ten cents on the dollar as a result of proceedings under the federal act. By March of 1843, Congress voted to repeal the unpopular legislation.[10] Yet while the act itself was short-lived, disputes stemming from the law often remained tied up in court for years.

Unlike individual creditors, large financial institutions had an advantage in navigating bankruptcy proceedings, challenging fraud, and retrieving enslaved lives. They had greater resources, legal knowledge, and experience which made successful pursuit more possible. They also possessed a wider portfolio of loans than most individual creditors, allowing them to spread the risk and expense of debt recovery across a broader array of contracts. Banks recognized that some fraction of loans would go bad, and tried to account for both the expense of recovery and the inevitable losses through their lending terms, interest rates, and requirements for endorsements and collateral. And yet, even banks faced an uphill, expensive battle in foreclosing on fraudulent and absconding debtors. The magnitude of these losses, alongside losses from extreme debtor forbearance, ultimately led to the failure of many of these frontier banks after the panics (chapter 8).

Escaping Debts through Bankruptcy

Thomas Barrett and Robert Bell typified the speculative frenzy of the frontier South during the 1830s. Barrett was the principal of the New Orleans commercial firm of Thomas Barrett & Co., while Bell—a Nashville, Tennessee, merchant—followed his brother to Iberville Parish, Louisiana, in 1813 to seek his fortune as a cotton or sugar planter (the brothers were not initially sure which to try). Bell brought with him two small sons and his young wife, Caroline Stanwick Butler, who had grown up in the household of Andrew Jackson; the future president had become her legal guardian after her father's death.[11] After a few failed attempts to establish himself as a planter, in 1826 Bell purchased for $30,000 "a beautiful plantation with forty negroes" in Iberville with his brother. The Bells set up house there by 1829, taking full ownership upon the brother's death that same year.[12] Around this time, Robert Bell met the merchant banker Barrett. Possibly, Bell used him as a factor to sell his sugar crop, or perhaps met him through his brother-in-law Edward George Washington Butler, who had discounted a promissory note with Barrett in 1829.[13] Within a few years, Bell and Barrett established a very active partnership in buying and running large plantations.

In March 1833, Barrett purchased Whitehall plantation in St. James Parish for $151,043 (about $4.9 million in 2021), paying most of the price by assuming the seller's mortgage agreement with the original owner—interest payments of $6,000 per year for twenty years, with a balloon payment of the principal at the end of the term.[14] Two days later, Barrett conveyed half ownership of the plantation and enslaved lives to Bell.[15] The Bells sold their Iberville plantation to Caroline's brother, who had recently purchased several adjacent tracts of land, and moved with their enslaved workers downriver to Whitehall.[16] It is unclear what terms of partnership Barrett and Robert Bell drew up for this plantation.

Soon after, Barrett and Bell again partnered to purchase the rights to land in Iberville Parish claimed by the Houma Native American tribe. In June 1834,

Congress had decided to give "preëmption rights to settlers on the public lands," and determined that settlers could claim these lands through the land office, and the partners took advantage of this opening.[17] By 1836, they had begun building a sugar plantation on the land, and in August and September of 1837, they separately mortgaged their respective halves of the plantation with its enslaved workers to the Citizens' Bank, in return for a combined loan of $50,000. In all likelihood, they used the loan to purchase additional enslaved individuals as well as all the expensive equipment needed for sugar production. The following year, they also obtained three hundred shares of Citizens' Bank stock, likewise secured by the same mortgage.[18]

As they rapidly expanded their plantation holdings, the partners quickly fell further and further into debt to several banks. Bell still owed $14,400 on an 1832 loan of $24,000 from the Bank of Louisiana. The Union Bank received several judgments against Barrett during 1837 and 1838 for unpaid debts, amounting to $55,513.19, upon which he still owed $23,164.59 by 1840. Both banks held a lien against the Iberville plantation for these judgments.[19] In February 1838, Barrett mortgaged nine other pieces of property and eighty enslaved lives in the parishes of Orleans and Jefferson to secure another five-year loan of $160,000 with the United States Bank of Pennsylvania, payable through its local proxy: the Merchants' Bank of New Orleans.[20] Either a shrewd businessman or a true speculator, Barrett was taking out long-term loans to invest in each of these properties (and possibly borrowing from one bank to repay debts due to another), believing that the skyrocketing prices of land and enslaved lives would enable him to repay the loans easily in the future. In this, he was not much different from the many Americans who borrowed extensively to purchase large homes in the decade before 2008; neither group recognized the bubble until it was too late.

Unfortunately for Barrett, prices plummeted before he could sell, particularly after the second wave of panic hit in 1839, and he quickly fell behind on his debts. In January 1838, March 1839, and April 1839, the original owner of Whitehall sued Barrett for nonpayment on two years of interest for the plantation, totaling $12,000.[21] By the summer of 1839, Bell and Barrett had not paid back any of their Citizens' Bank mortgage either, and the directors decided to foreclose on these unreliable, delinquent debtors. In the bank's estimation, "the plantation & slaves in question" were "of a value far superior to the amount due this bank." It believed that "the claim of the Bank" could be "perfectly secured by the Banks becoming purchaser of the property for cash & afterwards selling it on credit for good and approved paper secured by mortgage."[22] The bank thus sought to finance more-reliable slaveholders.

In August, 1839, the Citizens' Bank directed the local sheriff to seize the Iberville property. He advertised it for sale for the requisite thirty days, before the bank purchased it for its own account at the sheriff's sale of September 17, 1839, for $50,000. This was the exact amount of the principal on the 1837 debt, but did not take into account the opportunity cost of lost interest or the delay in receiving two principal payments. The bank did not put up any cash to take possession of this property; it merely "extinguished de facto" the two mortgages to the Citizens' Bank, although the claims from the Bank of Louisiana and Union Bank remained. Included in the sale were ninety-eight enslaved workers. While the sale document described most of these enslaved individuals merely by name and age, it included further descriptors for twenty. In addition to ten "field hands," forty-year-old Frank was a "driver and confidential negro"—meaning an enslaved man who could be trusted to do the bidding of the master with regard to his fellow slaves. Twenty-eight-year-old George McNayez was likewise a driver. There was also a carpenter, sawyer, layer, sugar maker, and handyman. Thirty-seven-year-old Ned was a "good blacksmith," while thirty-year-old Henry was a "good hand" and thirty-year-old Juliet a "good field hand." Twenty-five-year-old Eliza was "sickly." Somewhat ambiguously, the document designated thirty-year-old Eliza as having "very good character," although it mentioned no occupation for her; it is unclear if this description was meant to imply a reliable house servant or something more nefarious.[23]

Upon losing this valuable plantation, Barrett recognized the peril of his "embarrassed" financial situation. Facing total ruin, in May 1840 Barrett "applied for the benefit of the insolvent laws of Louisiana" under the terms outlined in that state's Civil Code of 1824.[24] For this process, he voluntarily needed to turn over all his assets to his creditors, who would then determine how best to sell the property and fairly disperse the proceeds among the various claimants. "In the schedule of property surrendered to his creditors is found an item of Whitehall plantation and one hundred and fifty slaves, valued at $210,000, subject to the bond for $100,000, and the interest due thereon." The heirs of the original owner argued that their mortgage claim on Whitehall—which amounted to $127,248.11 ½, including accrued interest—was superior to that of the other creditors despite the bankruptcy proceedings, and the courts agreed. Early in 1841, the property was "advertised and sold by the sheriff," with the heirs themselves purchasing it for the bargain price of $116,000, "paying" for it with their mortgage claims.[25] The heirs also separately sued Robert Bell for the residual amount due of $11,248.11 ½.[26] Forced to leave their residency at Whitehall with this sale, the Bells tried to salvage their plantation dreams by partnering with another slaveholder on a sugar plantation in St. James Parish, likely contributing the remaining enslaved laborers from their first Iberville plantation. Yet by the end of 1842, Robert Bell was dead, and Caroline decided to return permanently to Nashville, leaving her Louisiana economic interests in the hands of the St. James partner.[27]

Meanwhile, four months after acquiring Bell and Barrett's Iberville plantation at sheriff's sale, in January 1840 the Citizens' Bank resold the property, with its ninety-eight enslaved workers and 244 shares of capital stock, to George A. Botts and Abner Robinson—both of whom had a history of slave trading—for $75,000. This purchase price covered both the original loan and the outstanding debts still due to the Bank of Louisiana and the Union Bank.[28] The pair paid $5,950 immediately in cash, and promised another $10,000 on April 1, 1840. The bank divided the remaining debt plus interest into six annual installments payable between April 1841 and April 1846, ensuring that "all law charges, [and] fees for professional services in procuring the judicial sale of the property" would "be added to the claim of the Bank & included in the Notes & Mortgage."[29] Although this resale delayed payment on the principal of the original mortgage by a few years without adding any interest payments for that period, it preserved the bulk of the large debt for the overall benefit of the bank.

Unfortunately for the bank, Botts and Robinson were no more reliable as debtors than Bell and Barrett had been. Within two weeks of purchasing the property, Botts sold fifty-five of the enslaved people on the plantation back to Bell, who presumably added them to his new St. James plantation.[30] The enslaved individuals conveyed to Bell were a cross section of the entire workforce, including some of the skilled hands and men, women, and children of all ages.[31] Botts did this without the permission of the bank, who held the lien on these enslaved individuals through the mortgage contract. (The bank only appeared to learn of this sale in December 1842, and continued to claim the enslaved lives under mortgage until 1851.)[32] The sale also weakened the workforce on the plantation and signaled the liquidity problems of Botts.

In April, when the first $10,000 payment was due to the bank, Botts and Robinson already needed to renegotiate the mortgage. They paid the bank $5,000 in cash, yet they were "unable to pay in full." The bank gave them until January of 1841 to pay the remainder plus interest, but they had to add several other tracts of land to further secure the mortgage.[33] By September 1840, Robinson had sold his portion of the property back to Botts, in exchange for Botts assuming responsibility for paying all of the promissory notes; the bank did not grant approval for this transaction either, and it is even unclear when the bank first learned of the property transfer.[34] Several months later, on March 29,

1841, Botts mortgaged two enslaved women and an enslaved man (none of whom were part of the original mortgage) to Robinson, in exchange for $5,000.[35] By the timing of this loan, it is likely that Botts intended to make his scheduled payment of $5,954.88 to the Citizens' Bank, due April 1, 1841, using the proceeds.[36] In December 1842, Robinson died.[37]

Whether Botts was a poor sugar planter, a reckless speculator, or just another unfortunate victim of the "hard times," he was never able to repay any more of this debt. On October 25, 1842, in a desperate attempt to find a way out of his financial bind, he fraudulently conveyed the Iberville property and enslaved lives to a relative named Seth Botts.[38] It is also unclear when the Citizens' Bank first learned of this transfer. Then, on December 20, 1842, he transported eleven of his enslaved individuals to another slaveholder in Assumption Parish, advising the planter that if he liked them, he "was to take and pay him for [them] in March 1844 at the prices for which such negroes were selling in N. Orleans at that time." By pushing the final sale date off by fifteen months, Botts appeared to be trying to hide these assets in the possession of another planter, from whom he hoped to recoup their value once his debts had been cleared by the federal court proceedings (and slave prices had hopefully recovered).[39] Finally, on December 24, 1842, he filed for bankruptcy under the new federal law.[40] Perhaps recognizing that the conveyance of his Iberville plantation to Seth Botts in October had been fraudulent and thus in violation of the bankruptcy statute, he included this property and its remaining thirty-seven enslaved workers on his declaration of assets and made no mention of Seth.[41]

A week later, he informed the board of directors of the Citizens' Bank that he "had declared himself a Bankrupt before the U.S. District Court," and thus "desires the managers to take forthwith charge of the plantation & slaves mortgaged to the Citizens Bank by him, the said Botts having no money to carry it on."[42] This move by Botts caught the bank off guard and placed it in unchartered territory. If Botts succeeded in his bankruptcy petition, would the court cancel the bank's mortgage claim? This debt still amounted to $63,784 (with accrued interest) owed to the Citizens' Bank and $22,971.76 to the creditors of Bell and Barrett. What other debts did he owe to other creditors who might stake a claim to his property? Although the bank was not privy to the details of his bankruptcy petition, Botts additionally owed more than $60,000 to numerous other creditors, but his main possession was the Iberville plantation with its thirty-seven remaining bondspeople. His only other assets were three promissory notes totaling $3,462.90, and two runaway slaves.[43] If the bankruptcy court sold the property, how would it distribute the proceeds among the various creditors? The fact that the mortgage had been secured by the property did not guarantee that the bank would have priority over the proceeds; the rules of the bankruptcy court muddled these claims. This notification of the bankruptcy filing also appeared to be when the bank first learned "through Mr. Bell that a portion of the negroes mortgaged have been sold and taken away from the plantation," referring to the February 1840 sale of fifty-five enslaved individuals to Bell.[44]

With all these unknowns, the bank's board acted quickly "to take the necessary legal steps forthwith to protect the interest of the Bank." It immediately solicited its Iberville agent, E. G. W. Butler—Caroline Bell's brother—"to take possession of said plantation slaves &c. and to take an inventory of all the Negroes, Cattle, moveables, &c. belonging to said plantation, in presence of two witnesses of the neighborhood & to transmit a copy of the same as soon as possible to this Bank, and to supply the plantation with such provisions as may be absolutely necessary."[45] At some point during those first weeks of January, it must also have learned of the October 1842 alleged conveyance of the property to Seth Botts. Although the bank board always treated George as the sole owner of the plantation in its private correspondence, it decided that this confusion of ownership provided the bank with a potential way around the bankruptcy law. The bank obtained a writ of seizure and sale from the district court, by which the local sheriff "did seize said plantation and slaves as the property of one Seth Botts, and has advertized, and is about to proceed to the Sale thereof."[46] In justifying this move, the bank acknowledged that George had "put said aforesaid property on his [bankruptcy] schedule as if it still belonged to him, but the [bank] aver that the aforesaid acts [of sale to Seth] had all been recorded previous to said application in the proper offices according to the Registry laws of Louisiana and that said G. A. Botts had no longer any control over the said property." Although Seth tried to "rescind" the sale "a few days previous to the issuing" of the writ of seizure, the bank maintained that this move was "an act to the prejudice of the [bank], and that as to them it is null & void, it being intended to defraud them of their legal right."[47]

The assignee in charge of Botts's bankruptcy case, Francis B. Conrad, disputed the bank's interpretation of ownership. It was Conrad's duty to seize and sell as much of Botts's property as possible for the benefit of all his creditors, and the Iberville plantation and enslaved community were virtually his only asset. Seeking to stop the sheriff's sale, Conrad argued that George was "the Real owner of said property," and that "inasmuch as said property had been surrendered by him to his creditors [through the bankruptcy proceedings], [it] formed a part of the assets on his schedule, and could not be seized by a creditor pending said proceedings, but must be disposed of for the benefit of all his creditors in the due course of administration under his Bankruptcy."

If the court allowed the sheriff's sale to proceed, it would "expose said property to great sacrifice, & the interest of the mass of his creditors to material prejudice & injury." The court sided with Conrad, and issued a writ of injunction to halt the sheriff's sale.[48] Despite the bank's continued protestations, the court ruled on June 3, 1843, that "the aforesaid property was in reality the property of the Bankrupt George A. Botts, and that it should be treated as property of said Bankrupt Estate."[49]

Having lost this battle, the bank instead tried to impress upon the court the primacy of its claim to the Iberville plantation as both the former owner and mortgage holder. Not only had Botts failed to pay the majority of his debt to the bank (which had now increased through accrued interest), but he had actually reduced the overall value of the property. While the estate certainly "has been greatly diminished in value partly by the circumstances of the times and the great depreciation of real estate" after the panics, much of the blame lay with Botts's decision to sell off a large portion of the enslaved workers so "that instead of 99 slaves there are now on said property only between 35 and 40 slaves." As a direct result, "the absence of the greater part of the slaves embraced in the original mortgage" had reduced the value of the bank's collateral security. Based on this history, the bank concluded that it was "entitled to the whole proceeds which the sale of said property may be expected to yield," and that it should be "alone entitled to the choice of the terms of the sale." Considering the current state of both the plantation property and the real estate market, the bank proposed selling the land, slaves, and bank stock for $26,648.64, payable $8,784 in cash and the remainder in three annual payments of $5,954.88 plus interest (the three remaining promissory notes from the original mortgage). In October 1843, Judge Theodore H. McCaleb agreed to these terms.[50] At less than half the value of the principal and interest due, this proposal represented a considerable loss to the bank.

Yet when the bankruptcy assignee finally put the property up for sale, there were no buyers even at this price and on these conditions. Instead, the cashier of the Citizens' Bank purchased the property on January 23, 1844, for the fire-sale price of $10,000 cash, thus canceling Botts's mortgage with the bank.[51] Now finally free of the bankruptcy court, the bank proceeded on two separate fronts to recoup the substantial debt that remained from the original mortgage, which it estimated as "an amount of upwards of $40,000 still due," not including "Interest accrued & accruing thereon" at 8 percent.[52] First, the bank attempted to resell the property at its market value, which was still depressed due to the ongoing effects of the panic and the reduced enslaved community on the plantation. Second, it separately sued the estate of Botts's former partner, Abner Robinson.

First, the bank cashier planned to "resel [*sic*] said property under the direction of, and for the benefit of this Bank" (presumably taking back his $10,000 outlay as part of the deal).[53] Within two days, the bank had an offer on hand from the now-widowed (and absentee) Caroline Bell to pay the bank a total of $63,850.42 for the property: $4,000 in cash, $9,447.74 as "the stock debt of G. A. Botts with interest," and the remainder of $50,402.68 over four years. The whole sale was secured by a mortgage on the plantation as well as by additional enslaved individuals whom Bell offered as collateral.[54] Exactly three months later, Bell resold the same property to Samuel T. Harrison—a neighboring owner of the Annandale plantation in Iberville—and he assumed the same terms of mortgage.[55] These sales—once the mortgages were fully paid—would have satisfied the original debt as well as the outstanding loans to the Bank of Louisiana and the Union Bank, but again did not take into account the opportunity cost to the bank from the significant delay in payment and accrued interest. The widow Bell also retained the fifty-five enslaved individuals from the earlier sale, although the bank continued to assert its right to them as part of the original Botts and Robinson mortgage.[56]

However, by the late 1840s the bank's concern with this particular mortgage lay not only with its series of delinquent owners, but now with the validity of Bell and Barrett's original land claim. In September 1841, Congress granted Louisiana five hundred thousand acres of land "for purposes of internal improvement." By 1844, the state established "an office for the sale of the unlocated lands," which issued "warrants" to claim this land. Arthur Morgan Foley purchased two warrants, and in January 1847 used them to assert ownership of the land previously settled by Barrett and Bell under the Houma claim in the mid-1830s.[57] According to Foley, Bell and Barrett's rights were "cancelled . . . because the land on which the original settlements purported to have been made, were, at the time of said entries, not subject to the acts" under which they had made their claim. Not only was the land in question "not public land," but "the officers who undertook to adjudicate them were acting beyond the pale of their authority," thus nullifying all the stakes. Foley took Harrison—the new owner—to court to gain possession of the valuable sugar plantation.[58] As long as this case remained unresolved, Harrison was unwilling to pay his mortgage debt to the bank.

But the bank never intended to rely solely on the fulfillment of Harrison's mortgage contract. Simultaneously, it instructed its attorney "to prosecute the Banks claim against the Estate of Abner Robinson for the balance," with the executors of the estates of both Robert Bell and Thomas Barrett joining in this suit.[59] The crux of the case was that Robinson could not have legally removed himself from responsibility for the January 1840 mortgage without express permission of the bank, and thus the September 1840 "sale" of Robinson's half of the plantation and enslaved individuals to Botts was invalid. In court, the estate of Robinson—represented by his business partner and executor Joseph W. Tucker—tried to argue that Botts was always the true owner of the Iberville plantation, and that Robinson had "only lent his name to enable Botts to make the purchase on his own account." This was a critical admission (and mistake) on the part of Tucker. In the opinion of the Supreme Court of Louisiana, if the bank had only approved the mortgage with Robinson's endorsement, he could not later unilaterally remove himself from the mortgage contract without violating the agreement. The property sale to Botts "cannot have the effect of destroying or weakening the obligations contracted by Robinson towards the plaintiffs." The Louisiana Supreme Court thus ruled in the bank's favor in 1844. Robinson's promissory notes to the bank remained valid, and his estate was ultimately still responsible for his share of the original mortgage debts.[60]

The principal asset at Tucker's disposal was a large sugar plantation in the parish of Lafourche that he jointly owned with Robinson's heirs.[61] In September 1847, the bank authorized its attorney "to vote at any meeting of the Creditors of the Estate of Abner Robinson in the name of this Bank, for the sale of the Property of said Estate on such terms as he may think proper." In lieu of splitting and selling the property through a foreclosure proceeding, the bank wanted Tucker to purchase the other half, using the proceeds to pay the bank for Robinson's unredeemed debt.[62] Eighteen months later, after much haggling between Robinson's descendants, Tucker, and the bank, the parties reached a settlement in which Tucker bought the estate's half of the plantation for $86,000, paying "in cash as large a portion of the claim as practicable," with the remainder secured by mortgage.[63] Tucker issued sixteen promissory notes totaling $78,500.90, which "are the property of the Citizens' Bank of Louisiana & accrue to the same in payment of a debt due to said institution by the estate of Abner Robinson."[64] He mortgaged both Robinson's half of the plantation with sixty-two enslaved lives, as well as his own original half "and also the following [twenty-four] slaves who always were the exclusive property of the said Joseph W. Tucker."[65] Although the court reached this decision almost a decade after Robinson had signed the original mortgage contract, the debt was finally again on track for (eventual) repayment.

At the same time as this 1849 settlement with Robinson's estate, the Fifth District Court of New Orleans ruled on the property dispute between Foley and Harrison, nullifying the initial land claim of Bell and Barrett, and thus canceling the title of Harrison. The aggrieved debtor immediately appealed to the Louisiana Supreme Court in January 1850, with the Citizens' Bank cashier joining his defense. Unlike the lower court, the justices were "not prepared to concede that the entries were originally made in violation of law" despite the contradictory land statutes. Instead, such cases needed to be "determine[d] upon principles of equity and justice." In their judgment, Harrison—who "remained in possession and continued to urge his claim"—had "the better title."[66] Two years later, when the United States Supreme Court affirmed this decision, Justice John McLean chided Foley for "locat[ing] his warrants on a very valuable sugar plantation, of which the defendant had long been in possession." This maneuver did "not strongly recommend his equity."[67] Harrison's claim to the property was finally secure, and he also could begin paying his mortgage debt.

With all these disputes reaching resolution, in June of 1851 the bank "released . . . the 55 slaves belonging to Mrs C. S. Bell, said slaves being subject to a mortgage in favor of this bank granted by Botts & Robinson on 21st January 1840"; it is unclear how many of these enslaved individuals were still alive. The bank justified this decision by stating that the 1840 mortgage had been "superseded" by the sale of Botts's remaining property on mortgage from the bank cashier back to Bell in 1844, which she had subsequently sold to Harrison.[68] Tucker died in 1852, but with no further mention of him in either the legal record or the minutes of the bank, the heirs of Tucker presumably paid the remainder of their mortgage obligation.[69] His sons continued running the plantation, reporting combined assets of $300,000 in 1860 (about $9.7 million in 2021).[70]

Harrison, on the other hand, died in 1856 still indebted.[71] In May 1858, the sheriff of Iberville seized and advertised for sale Harrison's Annandale plantation, for the benefit of the Citizens' Bank. Included were all the land, buildings, and improvements on the sugar plantation; 228 shares of bank stock; and ninety-one enslaved individuals. The purchaser had to come up with $40,000 immediately, "payable in cash on the day of sale, that sum being the amount required to pay the debts due said bank and other debts due by said succession." For the balance of the sale price, the purchaser was permitted to pay in ten annual installments, with a mortgage on the property in the name of the Citizens' Bank.[72] Another neighbor purchased the Annandale plantation jointly with her son.[73] Approximately half of the ninety-one enslaved individuals had been born since the Citizens' Bank originally purchased the property in 1839. Another twenty remained from this original group, including six who were now in their fifties or sixties, five of whom were listed as "infirm."[74]

After more than twenty years of mortgages, foreclosures, negotiations, and court cases, by the late 1850s the Citizens' Bank finally seemed to have recouped a significant portion of the original debt, with pending payments by the heirs of Robinson and the newest owners likely compensating it for the remainder plus interest. For a creditor seeking to turn a profit, this loan contract was neither easy nor lucrative. Yet for a plantation bank, whose whole purpose was to fund the state's largest planters, this financially questionable business model largely worked. As long as the bank eventually received enough funds to repay its bond debt (which had been renegotiated after the state's initial repudiation in 1842), then the bank could argue that it was fulfilling its obligations to its shareholders, bondholders, and noteholders.

Outwitting Creditors through Fraudulent Conveyances

While debtor insolvency was a major problem for banks, especially after the panics, instances of fraud likewise increased substantially. For an insolvent debtor, successfully evading creditors through fraud was often preferable to starting over after declaring bankruptcy. Court dockets of the 1840s and even 1850s were thus filled with fraud cases stemming from the depression. For example, in the spring of 1837, Richard Abbey found himself deeply in debt to the Agricultural Bank of Mississippi.[75] The New York State native migrated to Natchez as a teen, where he became a clerk in the dry-goods store of P. F. Merrick & Co. After a few years, "by reason of his great diligence and excellent business capacity, he rose to the headship of the establishment."[76] He subsequently married and became a leader in the Natchez community. He was an active member of the local Methodist church and of the Anti-Gambling Society, and "he helped organize the first temperance society in the Southwest."[77] In May of 1833, he was elected a director of the newly formed Natchez Shipping Company, and appointed the company's secretary.[78]

Abbey bought out his partner just a month before Merrick's unexpected death in May 1833, at the age of thirty-six. Abbey immediately began operating a new partnership called R. Abbey & Co. out of the same address "on Main Street, directly opposite the United States Bank."[79] The firm became the local agency of the Aetna Insurance Company in September 1833, and then a few months later, took on the agency of the American Hydraulic Company of Windsor, Vermont, which made fire engines.[80] But the partners' main focus was dry goods, especially "Ladies Misses and childrens" clothing, boots, and shoes.[81] The firm also occasionally dabbled in other items that came its way, from small lots of printing paper and "fresh garden seed," to "Carpeting of excellent quality and the latest and most tasty patterns" and "A First Rate *Hartford-made Barouche*"—a large, horse-drawn "four-wheeled carriage with a driver's seat high in front, two double seats inside facing each other, and a folding top over the back seat."[82]

In December of 1833, R. Abbey & Co. also listed for sale a cotton plantation known as the Boston plantation, "situated on the Yazoo river 8 miles above Manchester," complete with "a good gin, convenient cabins, a good supply of plantation stock and utensils, and *Sixteen Negroes*, all first rate hands, between the ages of 11 and 40 years."[83] The Boston plantation had jointly belonged to his former partner Phineas Merrick and Hubbard Emerson, both natives of Massachusetts.[84] Perhaps Merrick had sold out the dry-goods firm to Abbey in 1833 to become a full-time cotton planter before his sudden death; Hubbard was an absentee owner, only returning to Mississippi each winter to check on his business interests.[85] After Merrick's death, his widow (her hands already full with several small children) desired to sell the plantation, with Hubbard's consent.[86] Abbey apparently purchased it for himself, "for between eighteen and nineteen thousand dollars."[87] By May 1835, Abbey sold out his stake in the dry-goods firm and settled full-time on the Boston plantation with his wife and surviving daughter; now it was his turn to live the life of the southern planter.[88]

Abbey may have been a talented businessman, but he initially struggled as a planter, accumulating large debts to both the Agricultural Bank of Natchez and the Commercial Bank of New Orleans. In March of 1837, Abbey attempted to sell the plantation, which he now listed as including "about *seventeen hundred acres of land*, 300 in cultivation; *fifty Negroes*, (43 hands, one of whom is a Blacksmith;) all kinds of Stock and Utensils necessary for a cotton plantation; Cotton gin; Railroad Mill; Blacksmith shop and tools; two large cement cisterns; and a reservoir for water, with houses and quarters all in good order." Always the salesman, he crowed that "This plantation is well known to be one of the best on the Yazoo; the land very high mostly 8 or 10 feet above the water of last year. I have never had a death, (except of cholera in 1834,) or a dangerous case of fever on the Boston Plantation." His asking price was $25,000 up front in cash, with "the balance in about 6 equal annual instalments."[89] Yet failing to find a buyer at these terms, three months later Abbey mortgaged the entire property to the Agricultural Bank "to secure a large debt due the bank."[90]

As the Panic of 1837 settled down on the region, Abbey was unable to repay either bank debt. In May 1839, the Commercial Bank successfully sued Abbey for payment of "a large sum of money" due, although this bank could not seize the plantation and Abbey's fifty-two enslaved lives as a result of the Agricultural Bank's prior lien.[91] The Agricultural Bank then foreclosed on the Boston plantation in the spring of 1840. Not finding an adequate buyer to satisfy Abbey's more-than-$40,000 debt, the bank itself took ownership of the property, and then repeatedly (and unsuccessfully) listed the plantation for sale in 1841 and 1842.[92] In the meantime, Abbey continued living on the plantation "as agent for the bank, and upon wages to be paid by the bank." At some point, the bank and Abbey came to a mutual agreement, in which the bank applied the profits from the annual crop sales toward Abbey's debt. If and when he was able to repay the debt in the future, the bank agreed to convey the property to Abbey's wife and daughter "as a compensation for his wife's dower in the property which she had conveyed by the mortgage."[93] By this arrangement, the property remained out of the reach of his other creditors, primarily the Commercial Bank.

Meanwhile, Abbey decided to apply for relief under the federal Bankruptcy Act. On February 20, 1843—just two weeks before Congress repealed the act on March 3—"the certificate of discharge of Abbey as a bankrupt [was] granted."[94] The following year, the "Assignee in Bankruptcy of Richard Abbey" sold his property and dispersed it to his creditors.[95] Critically, Abbey had not listed the Boston plantation on the required schedule of assets that he submitted to the bankruptcy court, and he remained the Agricultural Bank's "agent" on that property.[96] He even started to prosper as a planter. In December of 1844, the Jackson, Mississippi, *Southern Reformer* noted that Abbey had "raised the present season a very superior cotton plant. It is said to surpass the Mexican in the size of bolls, and to equal Sea Island in the softness and beauty of its staple."[97] By April 1848, Abbey and his "very superior cotton" had succeeded in repaying the debt, and the Agricultural Bank (through a third party to whom it had transferred the mortgage) conveyed legal title on the property to his wife and daughter.[98] By 1850, the Abbeys reported owning thirty-seven enslaved individuals and $16,000 in real estate.[99]

The Commercial Bank cried foul, accusing Abbey and the Agricultural Bank of making a "fraudulent arrangement, for the purpose of giving Abbey an opportunity to pay the debt by means of the crops upon long time, to secrete and secure it against other creditors, and to have it conveyed to his wife and daughter after the payment of the debt to the bank." In particular, it cited the Bankruptcy Act's requirement that debtors honestly list *all* their assets in order to be in compliance with the law, asserting that Abbey had "committed a *wilful concealment* of his property." Abbey, for his part, denied that he had misled the bankruptcy court. The Agricultural Bank was the legal owner of the property, and it was his wife (not Richard) who retained an interest in the property. In placing so much emphasis on the alleged violation of the Bankruptcy Act, the Commercial Bank actually hurt its own case. The main issue that the bank presented to the court was not whether the agreement between Abbey and the Agricultural Bank was fraudulent with regard to other creditors (and the court believed that it was possibly fraudulent), but whether he had specifically violated the terms of the federal statute.[100] The Mississippi appeals court ruled in 1857—*eighteen years* after the Commercial Bank's initial lawsuit—that since "the arrangement" with the Agricultural Bank "was made before the passage of the Bankrupt Act," it "could not be said to have been made in contemplation of bankruptcy."[101] The Abbeys got to retain the Boston plantation, and the Commercial Bank had to write off another bad debt.

Other debtors likewise took advantage of the leniency of bankers and the legal mechanism of the bankruptcy statutes to defraud legitimate claimants. The case of Peter Petrovic of Natchitoches Parish from chapter 6 is one example of such manipulation. When the City Bank foreclosed on Petrovic in 1840, Theophile E. Tauzin purchased the property for the precise amount of Petrovic's $34,000 debt, including the remaining mortgage of $20,000 to the bank.[102] A year later, Peter's wife Harriet sued him for a legal separation of property, claiming a portion of another plantation and thirteen enslaved lives as equivalent to the value of the property she had brought into the marriage. By the summer of 1842, Peter conveyed to her this property, and then declared bankruptcy under the 1841 federal act. Meanwhile, Harriet mortgaged the second property to the Union Bank of Louisiana for $12,268. One month later, she purchased the first Petrovic property and its enslaved workers back from Tauzin—presumably using the loan from the Union Bank—and assumed the $20,000 mortgage still due by Tauzin to the City Bank. It is unclear why Tauzin was willing to make the initial purchase (for the precise amount required), and then resell the same to Harriet, although he appears to have been intentionally trying to redeem the property for one or both of them; perhaps he was a relative. Either way, by 1847 it was clear to both banks that Harriet was not able to repay these debts, and each bank decided "to sell the lands and slaves respectively mortgaged to them" and then to "buy in the lands and slaves under her respective proceedings." The banks hoped to resell this property quickly to a third creditor, the firm of Messrs. A. Ledoux & Co. The City Bank would offer the firm a three-year mortgage, and the Union Bank would offer a five-year mortgage.[103]

Yet these contracts "were not intended to vest in [A. Ledoux & Co.] the absolute ownership of the property." Rather, the firm only "took the title to the property . . . as agents" on behalf of Peter Petrovic. This business model of a firm assuming financial control of a struggling plantation was becoming increasingly common in the late 1840s and 1850s (chapter 9). Ledoux contracted with Petrovic "to work the plantation and slaves, in the name of A. Ledoux & co., for the term of five years." If, during that time, he could repay the loans due to the City Bank, the Union Bank, and the firm, as well as the additional sum of $4,500 "for their name, trouble, risk and care on account of their assumption and attention aforesaid," then the firm would "reconvey" all the property to Petrovic, free of all encumbrances. Petrovic agreed to ship all cotton through the firm, paying "the usual commission of two and a half per cent. for selling and charges for their troubles," with "the net proceeds, after deducting expenses . . . to be by them applied in liquidation of the above debts." For his role as plantation manager, Petrovic would receive an annual salary of $500, with permission to employ one overseer at an additional salary of $400. Petrovic managed the plantation until his death in 1851, when his son Charles assumed the role and fulfilled the contract terms in 1853.[104]

As his father's sole heir, Charles now expected to inherit the entire property, but his step-siblings—his mother's children from a previous marriage—thought otherwise. The banks in 1847 had foreclosed on *Harriet's* debts, and it was Harriet who then conveyed the two plantations and their enslaved workers to Ledoux & Co. Under Louisiana law, "the husband is prohibited from purchasing the property of his wife in a direct sale." Although he might purchase the property at a public sale, in this case the banks had negotiated directly with Ledoux & Co., thereby preventing "a fair competition among the bidders." Since Harriet had been required by the banks to sell this property "to the agents of her husband," she had essentially been forced to sell "to the husband himself." The Louisiana Supreme Court concluded that, by extension, a husband could not "be permitted (for a price fixed beforehand) to acquire indirectly and by the machinery of legal proceedings, what he could not do directly." Finally, Peter was earning back the plantation "out of the revenues of the wife's property, her lands, the labor of her negroes and mules. . . . Indeed, the whole contract, were it to be considered as made on behalf of Peter Petrovic and valid, would have the effect of transferring to him the entire property of Mrs. Petrovic, without any equivalent, and without any trouble on his part, save that of passing the revenues through the hands of his agents, Messrs. Ledoux & Co." The court thus ruled that the land and human property had to be split between the three heirs of Harriet, rather than descend to the sole heir of Peter.[105]

Even when these frauds ultimately failed, the efforts to dispute seizures often left delinquent debtors in control of their land and human property for years after their debts were due—making these schemes at least a temporary success. Jeremiah Watson, for example, was an up-and-coming plantation owner in Concordia Parish, Louisiana. Having already reported thirty-seven enslaved lives in the 1830 census, he increased his holdings to one hundred and seventeen by 1840—putting him among the ten largest enslavers in the parish.[106] In the process, he also accumulated numerous debts, and by the late 1830s owed at least $400,000 (about $14.4 million in 2021) for both his own obligations and as the endorser for the debts of others. One note from 1835, for $20,000, had been discounted at the Planters' Bank of Mississippi, and two more from 1836, totaling $118,304.06, had been discounted with the Bank of the United States at Natchez. When the loans were not paid by the summer of 1836, the Planters' Bank sued Watson.[107] Meanwhile, on January 6, 1837, Watson mortgaged his plantation and ninety-seven enslaved workers in the parish of Concordia to the Bank of Louisiana to secure another loan of $25,000, due in one year—perhaps he intended to use this loan to repay some of his other outstanding debts.[108]

After numerous appeals on its 1836 lawsuit, the Planters' Bank finally received a favorable judgment in 1840, when the court ordered Watson to pay $28,533.33 on the first note, and $133,871.38 on the other two. However, while he was appealing the bank's suits, Watson conveyed the title to all his property, including his Grand View plantation in Concordia Parish, "a great number of slaves . . . [and] four hundred bales of cotton," to his son-in-law Samuel D. Walker. Walker, who owned another plantation with fifty-nine enslaved workers in Chicot County, Arkansas, was to pay Watson $280,000 for the property over the next eight years. Walker immediately appointed his father-in-law as his agent, "giving him the fullest and most extensive powers on the property," along with a salary of $1,500 and use of the dwelling house. Watson thus "continued to remain in possession of the plantation, slaves, and other property, and to administer them as if they still belonged to him."[109]

When the Planters' Bank received the foreclosure order from the court, the sheriff of Concordia Parish took the writs of seizure and sale but returned empty handed. He reported that "after diligent search and inquiry being made" there was "no property found in his parish, belonging to the defendant Watson, whereon to levy the writs." The bank sued Watson, accusing him of a "fraudulent and simulated . . . pretended sale." Watson denied this charge, avowing that the sale to Walker "was made in good faith and for a just price." Walker also came to his father-in-law's defense, asserting that he had already begun paying the installments on the property. He countersued the bank "for oppressing and harrassing [*sic*] him," claiming damages of $5,000 "for counsel's fees, personal expenses, loss of time, &c." At trial, the jury found for Watson and Walker and against the bank.[110] The jury was likely unaware that Watson had continued to claim the property as his own on the 1840 census returns.[111] In 1842, Walker mortgaged his father-in-law's plantation and enslaved workers to secure his own debts to the trustees of the Bank of the United States.[112] Again, the bank trustees appeared unaware of the ongoing lawsuit with the Planters' Bank over the property.

The Planters' Bank continued to appeal the ruling to the Louisiana Supreme Court, where the justices in October 1842 examined more closely the nature of Watson's indebtedness. Whereas his debts—for which lawsuits were pending in Concordia Parish as well as in the state of Mississippi—totaled more than $400,000, the entirety of his property he had sold to Walker for only $280,000. But even this value was a mirage, since that property had recently "been appraised, in 1836, at $170,000 or 180,000, cash." In assessing this evidence, the justices commented that Watson "must have considered himself, at the time of the sale, as he really was, in insolvent circumstances." Thus "it is not surprising" that "he attempted, by the sale in question, to screen his property from the pursuit of his creditors." Several witnesses even testified to hearing Watson state "that he would never pay the debt claimed" and that "he would dispose of his property in such a manner that they would not get a cent." Based on these facts, as well as the reality that Walker never even attempted to take physical ownership of the property, the justices concluded that "the verdict of the jury [is] manifestly erroneous" and "that the sale attacked in this suit, is fraudulent and simulated, and that it ought to be avoided and set aside." However, the justices did grant Watson a rehearing of the case, during which time he retained possession of the property.[113]

Meanwhile, early in 1843 the Bank of Louisiana applied to the district court for an order of seizure and sale of Watson's property, to satisfy his unpaid 1837 loan. Unlike his debts to the Planters' Bank and the Bank of the United States, which were unsecured, the Bank of Louisiana loan was specifically secured with a mortgage on his plantation and human property. Thus, Watson's defense of "selling" the property to his son-in-law would not work. In March, Isaac Franklin of Tennessee and John Armfield of Washington, DC, the principals in the famous slave-trading firm of Franklin & Armfield, "made a proposition . . . to pay the aforesaid debt." Watson renegotiated the debt with the bank, promising to pay one-fifth of the principal plus interest every year from 1844 to 1848, with this sum guaranteed by Franklin and Armfield.[114] Watson must have made a similar agreement to cover his Planters' Bank debts—either with Franklin and Armfield or with another endorser—since by the time the court was ready to rehear his case in 1844, the parties had "compromised their differences," and an "agreement was entered into between the parties, in pursuance of which the suit was dismissed."[115]

Within a year, Watson died and Walker advertised for sale his father-in-law's Grand View plantation, "on the Bank of the Mississippi river containing about two thousand acres of land upwards of one hundred slaves."[116] Presumably, he planned to use the proceeds to pay the various other debts. But with the property worth far less than the outstanding obligations, the priority of claims mattered. This dispute between the claimants remained tied up in court until 1848, with later creditors variously claiming ignorance of the initial lawsuit, the dispute over Watson's property sale to Walker, and/or the earlier liens of other creditors. Yet the judges were resolute that it was ultimately the creditor's responsibility to learn the history of a given property. The trustees of the Bank of the United States, for example, "took the mortgage [in 1842] with full actual notice that [Walker] was a fraudulent and simulated vendee, whose title was a mere shadow fraudulently cast upon the estate, and having no legal existence or efficacy." Likewise, the Bank of Louisiana was responsible for searching the mortgage records to check for judicial liens against the property or investigating the status of "an estate actually in litigation" before it granted the 1837 mortgage. "It is a rule of universal jurisprudence, and one which has been expressly recognized in our Civil Code, that every man is presumed to be attentive to what passes in the courts of justice of the State where he resides, or has transactions." Although "the rule may sometimes operate harshly, [it] is founded upon grave considerations of public policy, and must therefore be respected and enforced."[117]

It is unclear how much of these debts the Planters' Bank, the Bank of Louisiana, or the Bank of the United States eventually recovered from the Watson estate, but it seems likely that all three institutions suffered considerable losses. Regardless of the ultimate success of debtors who engaged in these shenanigans, these types of fraudulent conveyances continued to plague bank creditors, who had to expend considerable time and resources in legally pursuing large, delinquent debtors. It was arguably even more difficult when this pursuit became geographic.

Gone to Texas

While many frauds involved the illegitimate or pretended sale of property, enslaved individuals could also be physically moved and hidden from creditors. The relocation of mortgaged enslaved people was a problem throughout the antebellum period. Slaveholders moving to different jurisdictions not only made it difficult for new creditors to research the existence of prior mortgage liens, trust deeds, or bills of sale, but also enabled debtors to hide enslaved people bodily from creditors. The Planters' Bank of Vicksburg, Mississippi, thus specifically stipulated in its mortgages that if the debtor "shall at any time attempt to remove the said property or any part thereof from the said county" or if the creditor "shall have just cause to believe that the said property or any part thereof is about to be removed from the county," that would justify the immediate seizure and sale of the enslaved individuals to satisfy the mortgage.[118] Operating under the same principle, in November, 1841, the Montgomery branch of the Bank of Alabama "received information that Allen B. Knowles is about to run certain Negroes Mortgaged to this Institution." To prevent this removal, the branch president authorized "some person to take possession of said Negroes & convey it to this place."[119]

The emergence of the independent Republic of Texas greatly exacerbated this problem. Whereas Texas had served as a haven for debtors throughout the 1810s and 1820s, slavery was technically illegal there under Mexican law. Southerners wishing to migrate with their human property needed to exploit a legal loophole that permitted long-term indentured servitude contracts. Yet upon declaring independence in 1836, the new nation enshrined the system of slavery into its constitution. When the Panic of 1837 and ensuing depression set off a wave of foreclosures throughout the United States, debtors flocked to Texas, where land was cheap and extradition treaties were nonexistent. While absconding debtors had to leave behind their mortgaged land and homes, they could smuggle their valuable enslaved people out of the reach of their creditors.[120]

Although absconders came from all parts of the United States, it was certainly easiest for debtors from the neighboring state of Louisiana to slip over the border. During the late 1820s, Philip Minor Cuny helped his widowed mother to manage his family's cotton plantation, Clio, near Alexandria, Louisiana, with its forty-five enslaved workers. Cuny's grandfather had been one of the original settlers in what became the parish of Rapides in central Louisiana. In 1831, the twenty-four-year-old grandson purchased a nearby plantation on the right bank of the Bayou Rapides with its twenty-three enslaved workers.[121] Less than a decade later, Cuny abandoned this property and migrated to Texas, becoming a successful cotton planter and powerful state politician.[122] One historian of the family speculates that he made this move to pursue his political ambitions, seek new wealth opportunities, and mend a broken heart.[123] The more likely explanation was that he was running from his creditors.

Following the death of Cuny's first wife in 1834, after less than a year of marriage, the young man began piling up significant debts.[124] In 1834, he borrowed $3,000 from the New Orleans Canal & Banking Company, offering a tract of land (not his Bayou Rapides plantation) and some enslaved individuals as collateral. He then sold the same property to his sister-in-law (wife of his eldest brother), who soon resold the property. It is unclear if his sister-in-law knew that the property was under mortgage, and the debt remained unpaid in 1847.[125] In 1836, another brother purchased a tract of land for $6,350, payable to the seller in three equal installments. Cuny endorsed these promissory notes, which the seller then discounted at the Citizen's Bank where he was a stockholder; by 1845 neither brother had repaid these debts.[126]

In 1837, Cuny and his new wife, Eliza Ware, purchased two hundred shares of stock in the Citizens' Bank, mortgaging his Bayou Rapides plantation and enslaved workers.[127] Simultaneously, he jointly purchased another tract of land and enslaved lives for $60,000. Cuny and his partner promised to pay the full amount over six years, offering their promissory notes and securing the property with a mortgage.[128] However, when the Citizens' Bank learned of this additional $60,000 mortgage, it rescinded its stock sale.[129] Cuny tried to back out of the new deal and convey his portion of the property back to the seller, but the seller had already discounted some of the promissory notes, in the amount of $10,500. In return for canceling the remaining obligation, Cuny agreed to retain seven of the enslaved individuals and repay $10,500 to the seller. As of 1841, he was still in arrears.[130]

In 1838, the Cunys returned to the Citizens' Bank, successfully purchasing (now) 250 shares of stock in exchange for a mortgage on the Bayou Rapides plantation and enslaved workers.[131] The following year, Cuny purchased some more property from the estate of a local widow, offering three promissory notes of an undisclosed amount. The creditors sued the endorsers of these notes for nonpayment in 1844.[132] Cuny also jointly purchased a plantation with another sister-in-law, for which he owed $42,000 to the firm of Burke, Watt & Co. At least one brother and a sister-in-law were still disputing their obligations to pay Cuny's debts in 1845.[133]

By the middle of the depression in 1840, Cuny was deeply in debt—both as a primary debtor and as an endorser of several other obligations—and his creditors were pressing him for payment. It was under these circumstances that, in November, Cuny and his wife "absconded to Texas taking the slaves mortgaged to the [Citizens'] Bank with him." The Citizens' Bank resolved quickly "that his mortgage be forthwith foreclosed and his plantation & stock sold to liquidate his debt to the Bank."[134] In less than three months, the bank sold the Bayou Rapides plantation as well as the 244 shares of bank stock to an existing stockholder (one of Cuny's cousins). The new buyer secured the stock with a mortgage on the plantation and twenty additional enslaved people.[135]

While the claims of the Citizens' Bank were relatively straightforward, Cuny's other debts had been discounted and sold multiple times and his other creditors were now bogged down in court. In most cases, it was easier for them to sue intermediate owners of the notes rather than trying to track down Cuny himself in another country.[136] Cuny, for his part, literally got off scot-free. With his enslaved workers, he established a cotton plantation in southeastern Texas known as "Sunnyside." In 1843, he was elected to the Texas House of Representatives, beginning a long political career. By 1850, his brother Stephen had joined his Texas household, possibly also running from creditors. By the eve of the Civil War, Cuny was one of the richest men in the county, reporting real estate worth $293,900 and personal property of $31,100 (about $10.7 million total in 2021).[137] Before his death in 1866, he had fathered three children with Eliza, five children with his third wife, Adeline Spurlock, and (overlapping these marriages) another eight with his enslaved domestic servant Adeline Stuart.[138]

But whereas in this case the Citizens' Bank was able to recoup Philip Cuny's debt through the foreclosure of his land and bank stock without pursuing his human property, it was often necessary for banks to take even more drastic measures to recover lost enslaved lives taken to Texas. During the summer of 1841, the life of James Forbes of East Baton Rouge began to spiral out of control. Although he was listed in the 1840 census as owning eleven enslaved individuals, he was deeply in debt.[139] His wife successfully sued him for a separation of property in July 1841, to protect herself from "the embarrassed condition of her husband's affairs." She was granted the right to "retain and continue to administer her property as a feme sole," along with a judgment for $2,700.[140] When Forbes failed to pay this judgment by October, the court seized and sold his horses, cattle, hogs, and oxen on her behalf.[141] To settle a suit with another creditor, the court in November seized and sold "all the corn which is on the plantation where the defendant now resides and also three stacks of fodder."[142] Reflecting the complicated web of debt in early America, Forbes also received a favorable court judgment in July of 1841 as the aggrieved creditor, taking possession of an enslaved family in payment.[143] The Citizens' Bank, which possessed a mortgage on his plantation and enslaved workers, decided to foreclose on the land (but not the enslaved individuals) in February of 1842. When the land did not sell immediately for cash, the bank changed the terms to allow twelve months' credit to the buyer.[144] While it is unclear if the bank intended to foreclose on the human property as well, the Citizens' Bank learned in December of 1842 that James Forbes had fled with six of his mortgaged lives to Texas. Unlike in the case of Cuny, this time the bank board resolved "to take such measures as may tend to the recovery of said slaves, and to enter into such contract for reward . . . as may be necessary to secure the same."[145] Their agent was not successful. By 1845, the bank's directors were still pursuing Forbes in Texas, in addition to three other absconding debtors.[146]

During the winter of 1844, stockholder Joseph R. Thomas sold his plantation in West Feliciana Parish and nineteen enslaved lives—valued at $25,000—to George H. Patillo.[147] Patillo was already a stockholder with the Citizens'

Bank, having obtained two hundred shares in 1837 and another fifty in 1839, in exchange for a mortgage on his West Feliciana cotton plantation and eighteen enslaved individuals.[148] As was the norm with the sale of property mortgaged to the Citizens' Bank, Patillo agreed to assume the mortgage and bank loans in return for Thomas's 244 shares of bank stock. After the sale (but before the bank stock and loan obligations had been legally transferred) Patillo "had taken off the Slaves [from the plantation] and it was supposed had gone with them to Texas." The bank informed Thomas that he was still liable for the mortgage debt and "demanded of him other Security in the place of the Slaves." The board also directed the bank's attorney "to have [the enslaved people] pursued, and use every possible means to have them apprehended, authorising him to incur any necessary reasonable expense in the matter."[149]

As the person most knowledgeable about the missing enslaved individuals and with the most to gain if found, Thomas volunteered to pursue them himself "free of Charge," only asking for "an advance of Two Hundred Dollars" from the bank to "defray the Expense attending the journey." Thomas "offer[ed] also to undertake to claim for the Bank any other Slaves mortgaged to it and now in Texas, for a reasonable and just compensation in proportion to his success in Securing and bringing them back into the possession of the Bank." The bank president agreed to these terms, advancing Thomas $200 and allotting an additional $250 for Thomas to draw on "as may be required for conveyment [of the enslaved individuals] to this City." The bank granted him a power of attorney to act on its behalf to find "any Slave or slaves mortgaged to the Citizens Bank by G. H. Patillo, Robert Pool, George Dougherty and James Forbes, now in the Republic of Texas, or wherever they may be found."[150] The board made no further mention of this venture, and as of 1847, the bank still listed Thomas's human property as "run off to Texas."[151]

Another of the absconding debtors pursued by Thomas was Robert Pool, who owned a plantation on Richland Creek in the parish of East Feliciana. Between 1820 and 1840, his enslaved workforce grew from four adults and two children, to eighteen people; eleven were actively engaged on his plantation and the remaining seven were children under the age of ten. While the extent of his financial troubles is unclear, by the early 1840s Pool's wife was gone (she was no longer listed after the 1830 census), and this man in his midsixties decided to start anew with his enslaved workforce in Texas.[152] When Thomas failed to locate Pool in 1845, another resident of East Feliciana (presumably someone who knew Pool) volunteered to pursue him on behalf of the Citizens' Bank. This petitioner was already "engaged in a similar transaction for the Union Bank." He thus offered to seek out Pool as well, "upon condition that in case of success to secure said Slaves or any of them, or the recovery of the value thereof, he should receive one fourth of the amount thus recovered." The board agreed to these terms, granting him a power of attorney on behalf of the bank and up to $50 to defray his expenses.[153] By June of the following year, the bank had recovered at least one of Pool's slaves, "Jim aged about 45 years," whom it sold for $400.[154] More of Pool's enslaved people arrived by December 1848, with their recoverer—it is unclear which of the bank's representatives had succeeded—receiving "25% on the proceeds of Sale of the slaves . . . after delivery of said Slaves to the Bank in New Orleans."[155]

With many of these cases remaining unresolved well into the late 1840s and even 1850s, debtors had the extended benefit of their enslaved laborers even if the bank ultimately prevailed. Josiah Stafford migrated from Woodville, Mississippi, to Rapides, Louisiana, early in the 1830s. In 1832, the twenty-four-year-old married fourteen-year-old Jeannetta Kirkland, and the very young couple soon began accumulating property in Louisiana. In 1837 they obtained a $45,000 loan from the Union Bank, secured by their plantation and 102 enslaved individuals. The following year, they refused to pay, asserting that Jeannetta was still a minor and thus not legally able to contract with the bank. After several years of negotiation, the Staffords reached a new mortgage agreement with the bank in 1841, which they were to pay off in installments between 1844 and 1851.[156]

The couple had a separate mortgage on forty-eight of the same enslaved people to secure a $10,000 loan with the New Orleans Canal & Banking Company. When the Canal Bank foreclosed on these enslaved individuals in 1844, the sheriff could not find any buyers willing to bid for at least two-thirds of the appraised value, as required by law.[157] In such cases, "according to the usual course of proceeding," the property was "again offered for sale on a credit of one year . . . to the highest bidder." In this way, Josiah's younger brother purchased the people at the sheriff's sale for $12,853, due in one year.[158] Averaging $267 per enslaved person, this purchase reflected the depression nadir in the market value of human property.[159] Yet despite this alleged formal sale, the brother never took possession of the people. The court later noted that "Notwithstanding the complication of mortgages, sales, and transfers of the slaves now in question, it must be observed, that they have never been out of the possession of the respondents," Josiah and Jeannetta Stafford. And at the end of the year, the younger Stafford failed to pay the purchase price.[160]

With payments due to both banks in 1845, the couple had run out of delay tactics. In February, they took the mortgaged enslaved lives to Texas "for the purpose of evading the payment of this and other debts." Although Texas remained independent at this point, by December of 1845 Congress admitted it as a state. Josiah Stafford thus also "threatened to remove them out of that state to Mexico if such a step should be necessary to prevent them from being seized to satisfy his debts." The bank quickly sold the mortgaged land that remained behind in Louisiana, but "the amount for which the lands sold did not satisfy the first instalment of the principal of the mortgage."[161] Fearing that the Staffords intended "to scatter and secrete" the enslaved individuals "for the purpose of evading the just claims" of the banks, the Union Bank received a court order to seize the people.[162] "A receiver was appointed by the court, and . . . a part of the slaves have been taken into his possession with much difficulty and at great expense." While the parties disputed their claims in court, the receiver hired out the enslaved workers—apparently to the Staffords themselves.[163] In the 1850 census for Houston, Texas, Josiah listed himself as a planter with no real estate wealth and only nine enslaved people whom he owned outright.[164]

The Staffords tried to use every defense at their disposal to defeat the claims of the banks—from Jeannetta's youth to Texas's very pro-debtor statute of limitations—and they initially received a positive ruling in the Texas district court. The banks appealed, and the cases reached the US Supreme Court in 1851, where these arguments were less successful. Although Jeannetta had been a minor when she contracted for the first mortgage, she was "of full age" when she signed the revised mortgage. Nor could she successfully claim that the property fell under her dower rights, since the charter of the Union Bank—like most Louisiana banks—required wives to sign an affidavit relinquishing any claims on their separate property. In signing the mortgage contract, Jeannetta had agreed to these terms.[165]

The couple also tried to used Texas's "liberal construction of their statutes of limitations" which were "in favor of debtors, for the purpose of encouraging immigration" to circumvent the banks' claims. Yet the Supreme Court ruled that, in the case of mortgages, "whether the slaves in question be considered either as personalty or realty," the statute of limitations did not start running until the contract had fully expired; the Staffords had contracted to pay installments through 1851, and only then would the clock on the statute of limitations start. Additionally, the court ruled that "although a species of realty is movable, and may be carried away or fraudulently concealed from the pursuit of the mortgagee, such acts cannot" be used to "defeat the lien of a creditor" through the statute of limitations. The court could "not permit a party to plead his own fraud to defeat the equity of the complainant" by switching to a more debtor-friendly jurisdiction. The Supreme Court remanded the case back to the district court in 1851, where it ordered the lower court to rule in favor of the banks.[166]

Unfortunately for the banks, the district court was not scheduled to meet again until July 1853. In the meantime, the enslaved individuals remained in the hands of the receiver, who hired them out to work for the Staffords. The couple paid $25,379.39 in hiring fees, which they wished the bank to credit to their debt, and then again appealed for a one-year reprieve to pay the balance of the claim. The court finally settled the matter in the December 1854 term, ordering the sale of the people for the benefit of the banks. The only advertisement located for these individuals was the sale of thirty-four-year-old Mary Jake in November 1855.[167] By 1860, Josiah still listed himself in the census as a planter, and had accumulated a modest $5,000 in real property and $4,000 in personal property including enslaved lives; he died in 1862.[168] By 1870, Jeannetta was living with her adult children in Galveston; none of them listed any wealth, although the 1873 tax rolls valued her Houston property at $3,000 in 1873.[169]

Upon her death in September 1870, the *Galveston Daily News* described Jeannetta as "one of the early settlers at Houston, and a lady beloved and respected in this community for her many noble virtues and generous attributes of character."[170] Another paper noted that "an omnibus filled with colored people who had been her servants in time past, and who were still devoted to her as friends . . . followed her remains weeping to the grave, and wept over her as though she had been their mother instead of their mistress." The writer concluded, "with all the wrong and evil of slavery, happy is the master or mistress who can leave behind such a testimony as this to their gentleness and excellence."[171] No mention was made of her role in transporting human property to Texas to evade the claims of her creditors.

Although fleeing to Texas was particularly a problem for Louisiana banks, since the state shared a long border with the republic, banks in other southern states likewise encountered the problem of debtors going to Texas. Among the debtors to the Real Estate Bank of the State of Arkansas in 1840 were thirty-two-year-old Thomas J. Curl and his younger brother Henry Curl. Thomas was sheriff of St. Francis County, located just across the Mississippi River from Memphis, Tennessee, and a prominent member of the local Democrat Party.[172] The brothers had each discounted several notes with the bank in 1839 and 1840, with Thomas's debts totaling at least $5,786.50 and Henry's totaling at least $3,157.31.[173] Thomas was additionally listed as a security on at least six other discounted notes totaling $17,900. The bank renewed these notes every six to nine months, as long as the principal borrower continued to pay the accrued interest.[174] During the spring of 1840, the bank began protesting several of these notes for nonpayment, including an $1,800 note of Thomas and another for $4,320 which had been endorsed by both of the Curl brothers.[175]

By September 18, the bank had attained a court ruling in its favor, but the cashier of the Helena branch was sufficiently concerned about the status of the Curls' property that he dispatched an agent to "proceed to St. Francis County and take possession, as agent of the Real Estate Bank of the State of Arkansas, of the following named property, and guard and protect the same from loss or removal, by any means whatsoever." The property included Thomas's 320-acre farm "with all the improvements, buildings and hereditaments thereunto belonging" as well as eleven of his sixteen enslaved workers, all of his livestock, "all the houshold [*sic*] and kitchen furniture, farming utensils and personal property of all and every nature whatsoever," and the "standing crop of corn and other produce." The bank similarly instructed the agent to secure Henry's adjacent farm, with three enslaved children. The agent could, however, "suffer and permit the said Curl to remove such portion of the produce and stock as they may prepare to ship to New Orleans, advising me of the readiness of the same for shipment and awaiting further instructions from me."[176] The bank advanced the agent $20 to cover his expenses.[177]

The cashier was correct to be concerned, for another creditor had also attained a court order against Henry, whose land "is advertised for sale by the sheriff of St. Francis County"—presumably by Thomas Curl, who remained sheriff. The bank immediately wrote to the local circuit-court judge (who was also a bank stockholder), requesting that he "please examine the records and ascertain which [claim] has the priority of date." If the other creditor did indeed have the prior claim, the judge was to "examine the proceedings and ascertain if there is a positive defect therein, sufficient for the Bank to recover the Land." On the other hand, should the other creditor's claim prove valid and unassailable, the cashier wanted him to "buy the land in for the Bank, making arrangements with the sheriff to allow you sufficient time, for me to send up such funds as may be demanded," with the caveat "that the amount for which the land may be sold, shall not be so large, as to place the Bank in a worse position by the payment thereof, than it now stands or in which it would stand by permitting the land to be sold."[178]

Meanwhile, the agent reported back "that being accidently at Madison Court[house]," the county seat, "he there to his surprise found H[enry] H Curls three Negroes and all his land about to be sold for the sum of $300," presumably to satisfy the claim of the competing creditor. Luckily for the bank, "there being some defect in the execution it was thrown out of Court, but leaving the land still bound under it." The agent warned that "he thinks Curl is disposed to act otherwise than right." Upon arriving at the scene, the judge decided to become "responsible for the Amount of Execution ($300) and is in possession of the [enslaved] property." The bank president quickly issued a power of attorney to one of its bank directors, and the cashier instructed the director "to go immediately to St. Francis and act with your best judgment for the benefit of the Bank" to secure the land and human property of the Curls and a third debtor, in payment of Henry's note of $3,000 and Thomas's note of $6,000—payment on both of which had been overdue since July. Based on the agent's report, the cashier believed that "immediate action . . . is advisable."[179] The bank credited the agent with another $35.97 for his efforts.[180] At the end of November, the main branch in Little Rock reimbursed the judge for his $300 payment on behalf of the bank.[181]

Despite all these efforts, in just under a month, Thomas Curl managed "clandestinely" to leave the county, "taking with him some twelve or fifteen negroes" belonging to himself and his brother and "making his way either to Texas or Missouri."[182] With the branch president absent in Little Rock, and unable to consult "the whole of the Directory," the cashier took the initiative and granted a power of attorney to a bank agent "for the purpose of pursuing the said Curl and retaking the negroes and bringing them to this place to be disposed of." He hoped the president would "acknowledge the correctness of the act." The alternative was to allow Curl "to escape with the negroes," which was "all the available security that the Bank had for the debts."[183]

The cashier simultaneously drafted a letter to his counterpart at the Washington branch bank (which was located at the opposite corner of the state near the Texas border), informing him that the agent "is to retake the negroes and bring them back to this place to be sold . . . and he may posibly [*sic*] have to pursue them as far as Texas." He hoped that the Washington branch cashier would "extend to [the agent] any aid and assistance that he may require. And also pay the check . . . for such amount of money as he may need to defray his expenses."[184] For the next ten days, the agent and another bank representative pursued Curl, but with no luck. Unable to recover the enslaved individuals, the bank began proceedings to sell the land in St. Francis County.[185] The agent received an additional $239.03, which was the "bal[ance] of wages & traveling Expenses," while the second bank representative received $61 to defray his expenses.[186] The bank had spent more than $620 in the failed pursuit of this debtor. By December, the bank had moved both protested notes to its "suspended" account.[187] Four years later, the bank finally obtained court permission to sell Thomas Curl's land, advertising it for sale in March 1845 unless Curl "appear before this court" by that date.[188]

But Curl was long gone. With his wife, three children, four stepchildren (from his wife's first marriage), and enslaved community, he settled just over the border from Louisiana in Nacogdoches, Texas, near where his father-in-law and several brothers-in-law already resided in San Augustine. Like Philip

Minor Cuny, Thomas Curl was able to make a fresh start in Texas, finding both wealth and respect. In the 1850 census, he reported $2,000 in real estate and twenty-five enslaved workers.[189] In 1853, he was selected as one of the delegates to represent Nacogdoches County at a convention regarding the building of a railroad.[190] In 1854, he was appointed a commissioner for inspecting the construction of local bridges and roads.[191] Later that year, the local paper commented favorably on the cotton grown on his plantation.[192] By 1860, the fifty-two-year-old reported $11,000 in personal wealth (likely the value of his twenty-five enslaved people), and $20,850 in real estate.[193] His eldest son had branched off into "merchandizing" and reported $5,000 of his own personal wealth.[194] His brother, Henry, likewise settled in nearby San Augustine, but with less pecuniary success.[195]

The Bank of the State of Alabama also aggressively pursued absconding debtors as part of its efforts to liquidate the bank's affairs. Between 1836 and 1839, Joseph W. Tisdale had accumulated $18,439.46 in debt to the Mobile branch of the bank.[196] In response to the bank's demands for additional security on this substantial amount, on May 17, 1839, Tisdale and his wife Mary Amelia Wilson mortgaged several tracts of land, four horses, one mule, a carriage, one pair of harnesses, fifteen named enslaved adults, and two unnamed enslaved children.[197] He promised to repay the entire debt in four months' time, but failed to come up with the necessary funds.[198] As Tisdale grew worried by his inability to repay this debt, he sought the advice of his friend, Alfred Clinton Horton. Horton had been a prominent Alabama state legislator in the 1830s, until he joined the Texas revolution in 1835. Afterward, he settled in Texas, serving as a state senator from 1836 to 1838, representing several counties south of Galveston, and presiding over a plantation valued at mid-century at $100,000, plus over ninety enslaved individuals.[199] As Tisdale later reported their conversation, "I informed him of the whole transaction from begining [*sic*] to end, and of the mortgage of the negroes to the Bank." But Horton only increased Tisdale's anxiety about the debt by "several times . . . observ[ing] that the Bank could take the negroes when ever she found them in my possession." Horton thus "bargained" with Tisdale to place the enslaved individuals into his custody—it is unclear whether any money exchanged hands—and Horton then returned with them to Texas.[200] Tisdale himself might have considered absconding with his family and enslaved lives, as so many debtors did at the time. But having five children all under the age of ten, perhaps Tisdale (or his wife) did not see fleeing as a viable option.[201]

In 1840, the bank sold Tisdale's mortgaged real estate and the three enslaved lives who remained in his possession, but this sale only repaid about half his debt. Tisdale tried to negotiate a settlement of the remainder with the bank on several occasions in 1842 and 1843, but it "refused to treat with me."[202] Of course, by now the bank knew that he had fraudulently sent off the mortgaged human property to Texas, so he was hardly a sympathetic debtor. By 1843, the bank actively sought to go after the enslaved individuals in Horton's possession. The bank's attorney issued a lien of execution against the people, and believed that this claim should still apply outside the United States. The bank even conferred with Judge Abner Lipscomb on the matter, "enquiring how far it may be practicable to recover their debts."[203] Lipscomb had been Chief Justice of the Alabama circuit court until he resigned in 1835, entering private law practice in Mobile. In 1839, he also moved to Texas, where he served as Secretary of State during 1840.[204] As a lawyer familiar with both Alabama and Texas issues, he was the ideal counsel for the bank. Lipscomb concluded that the bank indeed had a valid claim and "that the property can be recovered with out any doubt," since Horton had knowingly—indeed fraudulently—removed mortgaged property from the state of Alabama.[205]

By 1844, Tisdale was ready to throw himself at the mercy of the bank in order to "bring my matters with the Branch Bank to a close, or as near to a settlement as the nature of circumstances will admit." Perhaps the bank was threatening to throw him into debtor's prison or deprive his family of a home. For whatever reason, he now decided to work on the institution's behalf to retrieve the enslaved individuals whom he had formerly "removed from the reach of the Bank." He admitted that "this request originates from no vain wish to reap the honor arising from the performance of an act of sheer justice, but in duty to myself to show the present Board and all succeeding ones that my intentions have been from the beginning of this transaction to act faithfully as it regarded the final payment of the debt." The bank agreed to pay Tisdale's up-front expenses to travel to Texas and retrieve the enslaved lives in question, although these expenses ultimately were tacked onto his debt and "embraced in the settlement." Once he delivered to the bank either the enslaved people "or their proceeds," he would "be released from all Liability on debts due by him to this b[an]k."[206]

As promised, Tisdale traveled with the bank's representative to Texas in 1844, where he identified for the representative the enslaved people in question as well as "a large waggon & a Horse" that presumably had also been part of the original mortgage lien. But Horton refused to hand over the enslaved lives, and then the bank representative died on the return trip to Alabama, leaving Tisdale with $50 in unpaid expenses and no recovered people.[207] At this point, the historical record goes cold. It is unclear whether or not the bank ever filed any court claims in Texas or sent any further representatives to recover these enslaved individuals. By 1845, Tisdale had relocated with his family to St. Tammany Parish, Louisiana, where he died by 1848. But the story doesn't quite end there.

In 1848, his widow, Mary Amelia Wilson, filed a writ of sequestration in the Fifth District Court of New Orleans to gain possession of an enslaved woman named Louisa, her seven-year-old daughter Lydia, and her unnamed mulatto mother. Mrs. Tisdale claimed all three as her separate property by dowry from her father. "Mrs. Tisdale charges that, about seven years ago, her late husband took Louisa from her and led her to believe that the slave had been removed to Texas and sold." Whereas Louisa's mother "is in fact still in Texas, held by one Albert C. Horton," the widow Tisdale had recently discovered that her husband had deceived her regarding the status of the daughter Louisa. Rather than being sent to Texas, the enslaved woman had been "living as Joseph Tisdale's concubine and passing for a white free person" in New Orleans. Giving the timing of this deception, it is highly likely that Joseph was also the father of seven-year-old Lydia. The widow Tisdale was petitioning "the court to declare them her property." Additionally, she sought "to gain ownership of Louisa's personal belongings, which include some furniture." The court "partially granted" this request, although it is unclear which part the widow received.[208]

The ability of the bank to navigate the complicated and expensive process of pursuing absconding debtors across state lines and retrieving enslaved individuals through various state court systems was even more apparent in another set of cases. Joseph McCarty and Robert Hazard (both postmasters in Washington County, Alabama) along with Ptolemy T. Harris (an Alabama circuit-court judge) jointly discounted four notes with the Mobile branch of the Bank of Alabama. The first three, dated January and March 1843, totaled $10,912; while the fourth, for $2,650, was discounted in April of the following year.[209] These men were three of the largest slaveholders in the county. In the 1840 census, McCarty listed fifty-six enslaved individuals and Hazard listed thirty-seven, making McCarty part of the top 1 percent of slaveholders in the county and Hazard part of the top 4 percent.[210] The bank partially secured these loans with a mortgage on eighteen of McCarty's enslaved workers. In the winter of 1845, when the three had defaulted on their payments, the bank foreclosed on the loan, obtaining a sheriff's order to seize and sell—as partial payment of the debts—the eighteen enslaved individuals of McCarty specifically listed in the mortgage. The sheriff sold these people, but before the sale could be finalized, they disappeared. McCarty had placed his forty-nine enslaved workers—including the eighteen from the mortgage—into the possession of John P. Hill, who was already on his way to Texas with them. Hazard had separately left the state with his twenty-two enslaved individuals.[211]

In January 1846, the bank hired an agent to pursue and retrieve the human property of both debtors. The agent "overtook and attached the property of Jos. McCarty in Claiborne Parish Louisiana." He first claimed the eighteen enslaved people listed in the mortgage agreement, who were now "held by title derived under a sale made by the Sheriff of Washington County Ala." The bank also instructed the agent to seize McCarty's other enslaved people to fulfill the remainder of the debts. Although McCarty had not explicitly secured his debts with these individuals, all of his property was liable to seizure once he had defaulted. As a compromise, McCarty offered the bank seventeen of the remaining thirty-one enslaved individuals, in return for a full release from all of his debts. In consultation with an attorney, the agent determined that this deal was in the best interests of the bank. On the one hand, the human property would likely become tied up in an extended court fight; "In as much as negroes in that State [Louisiana] were held as Real Estate and therefore could not be disposed of as perishable property, . . . [they] would have to remain in the Custody of the Sheriff during the periodicy of the suit." Even if the bank ultimately succeeded, the cost of a lengthy lawsuit would reduce the individuals' value to below "what I could now realize out of the Seventeen." The agent thus compromised with McCarty on behalf of the bank and took possession of the seventeen enslaved individuals. He offered either to bring the bondspeople back to the bank, or to sell them on the bank's behalf "to the best advantage." In addition to paying the agent's expenses, the bank would also pay him "25 per cent on the amount collected" for their sale, either "in a portion of the Negroes" or in cash.[212]

Once the agent had successfully completed this portion of his mission and had "shipped the Negroes which I got from McCarty on Board of a Steam Boat at Monroe on the Ouachitta River," he went in pursuit of Hazard, catching up to him and his enslaved lives in Franklin Parish. Without the legal backing of a mortgage, it was more difficult for the bank to assert its claim over these enslaved individuals. Hazard was determined to retain possession and refused to reach any compromise with the agent. The agent was thus "compelled to go down to New Orleans and take out an attachment from the Circuit Court of the United States." The marshal seized the property and brought the enslaved individuals down to New Orleans. Yet the agent's attorney was "of the opinion that it was extremely doubtful whether that Court would have jurisdiction of the Case or not and advised the dismissing of the case in that court and the taking out an attachment in the State Court which was done." The agent left the enslaved people in the hands of the court in New Orleans, where they remained until the resolution of the suit.[213]

The agent's expenses for this trip—including travel, per diem, professional services, and court costs—totaled $842.80. Additionally, for their services in the Hazard case, the agent's attorneys in New Orleans would be paid "a commission of 1½ per cent to furnish security on the attachment Bond, and 2½ per cent on the amount collected if by compromise before the case comes to trial, or 5 per cent on the amount collected at the end of the suit." In case the lawsuit ended unsuccessfully, the bank would merely owe them a flat $100 fee. Finally, the bank owed the agent 25 percent of the value of the seventeen enslaved people he recovered from McCarty.[214] Fourteen of these enslaved individuals were sold in April, and the remaining three in July to a second slaveholder, for a total of $4,600. The agent thus claimed $1,150 in commission in addition to his expenses.[215]

More than a year later, the court case between the bank and Hazard in New Orleans remained unresolved. In the bank attorney's report for November 1847, he noted that the claim on the twenty-one enslaved lives was on appeal to the Supreme Court of Louisiana, but that he believed the ultimate recovery of the individuals to be doubtful.[216] These enslaved people presumably remained in the possession of the court during this entire proceeding, their fate hanging in limbo as the legal process slowly unfolded.

⁂

As of 1859, the liquidator of the defunct Union Bank was still trying to recover on the debt of Thomas Barrett, the Louisiana merchant who in 1833 had first purchased the Whitehall plantation in St. James Parish. The bank's former president sued the Whitehall plantation creditors, claiming "one hundred and thirteen negroes, and their increase . . . and the revenues which had been derived from their labor" as due for "the payment of certain judgments which [the former president] says he owns, as the assignee of the Union Bank of Louisiana." But the court tossed out this frivolous claim. The bank's representatives had approved of the liquidation of Barrett's property in 1841 as part of Louisiana's insolvency law, and the bank's liquidators could not later challenge that settlement.[217] Yet the fact that this bank representative was still pursuing the financial assets of the institution on the eve of the Civil War is indicative of how problematic these contracts had become. Although all creditors faced similar challenges in terms of recouping debts secured by human property, banks were uniquely positioned to try and mitigate these issues. They employed experienced lawyers to challenge debtors in court, hired agents to pursue those who fled the state to Texas, and could spread the risk of default across a large portfolio of mortgages.

Despite these many institutional advantages, the lesson of the Panics of 1837 and 1839 was that the financialization of slavery was extremely risky. The benefits of long-term lending on enslaved lives during boom times were mirrored and magnified as disadvantages during the downturn, with the practice leaving in its wake a trail of failed banks (chapter 8). In the aftermath of the collapse of the banking system, frontier southerners found an easy scapegoat for their financial woes, and now rejected banking outright as a viable option for financing a slave economy. And yet, by the 1840s and 1850s, the innovative financialization of slavery by formal banking institutions was no longer necessary. By facilitating rapid expansion into the southern frontier during the 1820s and 1830s, and then providing stability for slaveholders during the depression, frontier banks had successfully entrenched plantation slavery in the Southwest, paving the way for the region's economic boom period by mid-century. When frontier legislatures reconsidered the role of banks by the 1850s, they were no longer seeking novel financial solutions for an emergent economy and could instead return to the more conservative structures of traditional banks (chapter 9).

8
When Banks Fail

When New Orleans readers opened their copies of the *Times-Picayune* on the morning of Sunday, May 14, 1837, they were met with an onslaught of bad news about banks. All week, the newspaper had been reporting about bank runs and business failures in New York, public meetings about bank suspensions in Mobile, Alabama, and closed-door sessions between bank presidents in their own city to discuss "the times."[1] Just two days earlier, on Friday evening, the presidents of the Bank of Louisiana, the City Bank, the Mechanics' & Traders' Bank, the New Orleans & Carrollton Railroad & Banking Company, the Atchafalaya Railroad & Banking Company, and the Bank of Orleans had decided to suspend specie payments—declining to redeem their banknotes on demand for gold and silver. Upon publishing this news in the Saturday papers, "the long anticipated climax of our calamities broke upon our city" and "a tremendous run was made upon all of them." Some people were "seen running to and from the Banks, and returning with their hands full of silver" while others "were obliged to return empty, finding no favor with the tellers."[2] Those "sober, steady men" who were denied specie ended up at the city's many bars. "Never was there so much liquor drank in Orleans in one day as yesterday, and all on account of the suspension of the banks . . . many a steady man found himself before night in a very unsteady situation."[3]

In the middle of the page, the *Times-Picayune* reprinted the justification of the presidents of the three banks in Mobile, Alabama, regarding their identical decisions to suspend payments, which were "Owing to the extraordinary exigency of the times, the unparalleled depreciation of the value of our agricultural products, the general prostration of confidence throughout the country, and the universal panic that is bringing home upon the monied institutions their entire circulation for redemption in specie." This determination had caused "great excitement" in that city, and resulted in calls for "a meeting of *all* the citizens of Mobile" to protest this decision and "rescue the *character* of the city of Mobile from the *odium* of the call upon the Banks."[4] And the news from the North was no better, where "the panic increases—not diminishes."[5] One headline screamed "IMPORTANT.—Buffalo Banks all Bursted," while another article cited 303 New York business failures in just one day."[6] The latter article remarked that "even the United States Bank begins to shake in the wind."[7]

Although figure 8.1 depicts a slightly later bank run, from the Panic of 1857, the crowd of desperate men and women jostling to get into a bank to redeem their banknotes or withdraw their deposits before the vault ran dry captures the general association of bank failure with a panicked bank run. In normal times, a bank's decision to suspend specie payments did often signal failure, as it placed the institution in direct violation of its charter. But as had been the case during the Panic of 1819, most states condoned the joint decision of a group of banks to suspend specie payments temporarily during the extreme "hard times" of 1837 and 1839. Of the six New Orleans banks suspending that weekend, the Bank of Louisiana, the Mechanics' & Traders', and the City Bank eventually resumed normal operations (although the City Bank would close when its charter expired in 1850); the Carrollton forfeited its banking privileges and continued solely as a railroad company; and the Atchafalaya and the Bank of Orleans—the latter being the eldest of the city's extant banks—went into liquidation.[8] Similarly, in Alabama, the Bank of Mobile survived the depression, while the Bank of the State of Alabama and the Planters' & Merchants' Bank of Mobile did not.[9] Whereas contemporaries focused on the sudden closing of bank vaults and decried the reduction of banknotes to useless "rags," the process of actually liquidating a bank was much more complicated and drawn out.[10] It could take years—sometimes decades—to recover the obligations of debtors, liquidate assets, and settle with creditors. And while bank suspensions usually signaled the start of a panic, bank failures frequently did not occur until much later in the depression.

Historians often mention the negative impact on enslaved people when individual slaveholders faced economic troubles, yet the more widespread impact of the failure of an entire bank is usually only discussed in broad, macroeconomic terms, especially when it occurred during periods of economic contraction such as after the Panics of 1819 or 1837 and 1839. Yet the unexpected closure of a bank or set of banks had important implications for the individuals involved. Debtors who had routinely and repeatedly renewed their loans—or who had relied on the leniency of banks to help them through the depression—suddenly had to meet their obligations, as the bank

FIGURE 8.1. "Run on the Seamen's Savings' Bank during the Panic," *Harper's Weekly*, October 31, 1857. Courtesy of the Library of Congress Prints and Photographs Division, Washington, DC.

called for the repayment of all outstanding loans. Whether or not their debts had been formally secured by enslaved individuals, any slaveholding debtors now faced the seizure and sale of their land and human property. Additionally, banks needed to liquidate any enslaved people they owned as a result of previous foreclosures. And all of these liquidations often occurred as market prices were collapsing. Even more disruptive than the failure of a large slaveholder, these mass seizures and sales could disrupt and displace a significant portion of the enslaved population in the affected regions. The embrace of large, long-term loans by many frontier banks in the years leading up to the panic only made this process more difficult and the effects more widespread.

Southern Failure

Approximately sixty-three southern banks (not including the failed United States Bank of Pennsylvania, which was still active in the South) closed between 1838 and 1843 as a result of the Panics of 1837 and 1839, contracting the overall number of southern banking institutions by one-third (table 8.1). These southern failures were overwhelmingly concentrated in the frontier states of Georgia, Florida, Alabama, Mississippi, Louisiana, and Arkansas

(94 percent), and only five of these closures (8 percent) were of older banks chartered before 1830. Thus, the vast majority of southern failures were newly chartered banks of the Southwest, reducing the number of banks in this region by two-thirds. As a result of these failures, Arkansas and Florida were left with no state-chartered banking institutions, while Mississippi and Alabama retained only one each. Finally, all the plantation banks went into active liquidation during this period, imperiling the state finances of Mississippi, Louisiana, and the Florida territory, each of which had sold state bonds based on the land and human property mortgaged by the stockholders of these banks. While similar large-scale bank failures occurred in some portions of the Midwest—the 1837 and 1839 panics wiped out all the banks in Wisconsin and Illinois, 98 percent of the banks in Michigan, and 74 percent of the banks in Ohio—these latter failures did not ripple out into the slave economy. In contrast, the well-established traditional commercial banks of the southern seaboard weathered the panic and post-panic depression with almost no casualties.[11]

A few of these closures were expected, with the bank closing when its charter expired as planned rather than receiving a charter renewal from the legislature. A few of these banks failed suddenly, shuttering their doors overnight. Most, however, went into either voluntary or involuntary liquidation, which was a much more controlled process that still involved a massive contraction of local credit.[12] Failure also looked very different depending on the nature of the bank's balance sheet, the liquidity of other local banks, and

TABLE 8.1 Southern bank charters, 1837–1843

Region	*Total banks end of 1837*	*New charters 1838–43*	*Closures 1838–43*	*Total banks end of 1843*	*Percentage of banks closed 1838–43*	*Growth rate of banking 1838–43*
Mid-Atlantic (MD, DE, DC)	36	2	(4)	34	11%	-6%
Old South (VA, NC, SC)	18	3	(0)	21	0%	17%
Upper frontier (KY, TN, MO, AR)	8	2	(2)	8	20%	0%
Lower frontier (GA, AL, MS, LA, FL)	58	19	(57)	20	74%	-66%
Totals	120	26	(63)	83	43%	-31%

Source: Weber, *Census of Early State Banks.*

the regulations established by the state legislature. A failed bank might immediately foreclose on all its loans, seize the property of delinquent debtors, sell all its assets as expeditiously as possible (even at a great loss), and then disperse the proceeds among its creditors (with many banks prioritizing the claims of stockholders over noteholders). Much less disruptive to debtors was if the bank sold its entire balance sheet to another solvent bank, transferring ownership of the loans. This kind of liquidation often occurred when a bank's charter expired, and the management was able to plan an orderly transition of its assets and liabilities.

For example, in anticipation of its charter expiration in 1850, the City Bank had stopped renewing notes and had received court orders against its remaining delinquent debtors. The bank sold all of the Baton Rouge branch real estate (including the banking house), movable effects, and assets to its branch cashier for $16,500 in October 1849. The mortgage assets amounted to $25,551 across thirty-three small claims, most of which were delinquent and for which the bank had already received court judgments that still required collection—a time-consuming process which likely would only partially succeed.[13] The remainder of the bank's real estate, assets, and liabilities at both the home office in New Orleans and its branch in Natchitoches—which the bank valued at about $2.2 million on each side of the balance sheet—it then transferred to the Louisiana State Bank in April 1850. In exchange, the State Bank promised to pay the City Bank's stockholders par value ($100 per share) for its stock on demand (amounting to $978,700), after first deducting any debts the stockholders individually owed the bank.[14] An August 1849 list of stockholders indicated that capital stock was spread widely across approximately 176 individuals, many of whom owned only a handful of shares. About 52 percent were residents of New Orleans, 43 percent from New York, and 5 percent from Philadelphia.[15]

A third option was for the bank to cease redeeming its notes, issuing new loans, or renewing loans, but to allow existing debtors to repay under the terms of their original contracts. For traditional commercial banks that mainly issued short-term loans, this process might look similar to immediate liquidation. But for those banks that engaged in long-term lending backed by land and human property, this option might extend the life of the bank significantly. A final option was for the bank to forfeit its charter, but to continue operating as a private, non-chartered bank—servicing and renewing existing loans as well as issuing new loans. Although the lack of charter usually meant relinquishing the right to issue bank notes, some banks were able to sustain limited operations as private institutions.

This chapter evaluates the impact of a handful of these failures on the system of slavery by examining a large state-run system (the Bank of the State of Alabama), a plantation bank (the Consolidated Association of the Planters of Louisiana), a smaller, traditional commercial bank (the Bank of Orleans), a joint banking-improvement company (the Exchange Banking Company of New Orleans), and the United States Bank of Pennsylvania. Both the Bank of Orleans (1812) and the Bank of the State of Alabama (1825) were chartered prior to the 1830s bubble. The continued operations of the Citizens' Bank of Louisiana—first as a private bank and then with a new charter—will mainly be discussed in chapter 9. These banks represent both the diversity of experiences of bank closure and, more pragmatically, the extant documentary sources. As a direct result of these closures and their wider impact on the region's economy, the legislatures of the frontier South would reject most banks altogether during the 1840s, putting in place severe restrictions on the chartering and function of financial institutions until the 1850s (chapter 9).

Good, Bad, and Doubtful Debts in Alabama

In Alabama, the Relief Act of 1837 had been designed as a combined rescue-stimulus package to save both the banks and the debtors. By converting bank debts into three-year loans, the legislature hoped to relieve the short-term pressure on debtors until the economy improved. And by injecting an additional $5 million of state funds—in the form of small loans up to $2,000—into the economy, it was attempting to counteract the monetary contraction of the specie suspension. But when the second downturn hit in 1839, the economy settled into a deep depression and these debts remained unpaid. Even more problematic was the decline in value of land and enslaved lives. Reflecting back on the condition of banking in 1830s Alabama a few years later, James Deas—the commissioner assigned to liquidate the Mobile branch of the bank—judged that "the money was loaned lavishly and the security if sufficient at the time was not so after the great sale of property in 1837."[16] In Deas's opinion, the legislature's choice of directors had been based "more to their popularity than their competentcy [*sic*] as bankers," a state of affairs that only compounded the banking crisis during the depression.[17]

With no recovery in sight, the legislature in 1843 decided that their attempts to stimulate the economy and ease the monetary contraction were not working. Instead, it adopted the opposite tactic and suddenly placed all five branches of the Bank of the State of Alabama into liquidation.[18] The legislature "classified the debts into good, bad, & doubtful, & placed the two latter into the hands of attorneys to collect."[19] For the debts classified as good, the legislature offered another three-year extension in payment, similar to the 1837 Relief Act.[20] In 1845, it passed still another extension law, although it required the immediate payment of one-third of the principal and interest in order for the debtor to receive an extension.[21] And in 1846, the legislature permitted existing "good" debtors an additional extension on their debts until September 1847, provided they pay half their debt by June of 1846.[22]

In settling accounts after 1843, the bank needed to foreclose on numerous debtors who had taken advantage of the 1837 extension, but who were now deemed "bad" or "doubtful." Yet even as it began foreclosure proceedings, these claims often took several years to resolve. One slaveholder in Mobile owed the bank $14,945.24, which he had secured with land and fifteen enslaved lives. Although the bank advertised the land and human property for sale in 1843, at least four of the people remained unsold until 1846.[23] Similarly, a slaveholder in Marengo County received an extension on his $51,354.61 debt to the bank in 1838, secured by his land and sixty-nine bondspeople. Although his brother had a "prior lien" on the enslaved lives of $23,000, "disinterested gentlemen" assessed the entire property at "say $87,800 being $10,800 over and above the amounts of the prior lease, and the debt due the Bank."[24] In October 1841, the bank claimed both the land and enslaved individuals, but it appears that it left the property in the hands of the debtor for the next two years. In November of 1843, citing the Alabama law closing the institution, the bank finally advertised the property for sale, but the sale was repeatedly postponed.[25] On February 3, 1844, Governor Ben Fitzpatrick advised the bank that it needed to postpone the sale once again, due to the excessive rains (although it is unclear why the governor and the legislature were taking such a personal role in this transaction):[26]

> The sale of 69 negroes late the property of F. B. Shepard which is advertised to take place on the 19th of this month, under a postponed sale, in Marengo County, I am satisfied from the unusual weather, the state of the Roads, &c, should be postponed to a more distant day, power was vested in me by certain joint Resolutions of the Last legislature to postpone the sale of that property until any period not beyond the first monday in April next. In conformity with the power vested in me by those Resolutions, I hereby notify you, that I have changed the Day of sale of said negroes, from the day now fixed, to the first monday in March next; you will please change the advertisement, so as to conform to the day above named.[27]

Another brother eventually purchased at least seven of these enslaved individuals, including a family of five, but the fate of the remaining sixty-two is unclear from the records.[28]

On numerous occasions, the Alabama bank's laxity in securing the debts came back to haunt it. For example, one pair of slaveholders owed the bank the considerable sum of $124,933.12 (about $3.5 million in 2021), which the bank allowed them to secure with land and nineteen enslaved lives. Yet when the pair failed to fulfill their contract (it is unclear how much they still owed) and the bank foreclosed in 1843, "it was found that nearly all the property had been sold under previous mortgages of older date." At this point, "the sale was postponed." In February 1846, the pair sent four enslaved individuals "to Texas by consent of Bank" where they were sold, presumably for the benefit of the bank. Finally, in June 1848, "the Register sold the entire interest in the mortgage, and the Branch Bank Mobile became the purchaser for 1000 dollars, and by this bid closed the whole property."[29] While the extant records do not reveal the bank's full loss on this particular loan, it appears to have been significant.

As commissioner James Deas later criticized, the bank often lost money by selling the property immediately at depressed prices. In June of 1840, Jonathan M. Bates and his wife Elizabeth mortgaged their property and twelve of their twenty-four bondspeople to secure a debt of $28,962.26. Payable in five installments from May 1841 to May 1845, the Bateses only partially fulfilled this contract.[30] In August of 1845, the branch bank at Mobile seized and sold all of this property. One buyer purchased the land, as well as thirty-five-year-old West, who was listed as "unsound." A second purchaser paid $1 for Annis, a ninety-year-old "Negro woman." A third slaveholder purchased the remaining ten enslaved individuals, a group that included three people in their forties and five children. Only two of those sold were prime male field hands, although the couple listed many prime hands in the 1840 census. The bank itself purchased the "store house & Lot in Greensboro" and the "Dwelling House & Lot" for $2,000, likely hoping to sell them for a profit in the future. Subtracting off this $2,000, the bank netted $5,050.20 for the sale.[31] The Bateses retained twelve of their enslaved workers, and quickly reestablished themselves in Greensboro, Alabama. By the 1850 census, they reported $3,500 in real estate wealth, plus thirty-nine enslaved lives.[32]

Despite the liquidation proceedings, the bank still occasionally offered leniency to delinquent debtors. In September 1844, one anxious debtor wrote the bank that "the sheriff will take my negroes soon." He owed $1,500 to the branch bank at Mobile, which had obtained a court judgment against him. Yet despite being in arrears, he sought to "ask your indulgence," as he was a reliable debtor and "my intention is to discharge my entire indebtedness to the Bank as early as possible," if it would just give him enough time. "As soon as the river rises," he would be able to sell his current cotton crop for $400.50

"for account of the Bank," and then pay the remaining debt with future crops. However, "if my [enslaved] hands are taken away I am undone." The bank appears to have allowed this proposition.[33] In February 1844, another Mobile debtor also hoped for an "indulgence . . . asking this Bank to relinquish its claim under the existing Judgment to a lot" in the city of Mobile, in exchange for "a levy on the following described negroes." The bank accepted a thirty-eight-year-old woman named Dido and her four children, aged seven to fifteen—who together comprised one-third of his human property—in substitution for the land.[34]

Not all desperate debtors were willing to rely on the indulgence of the bank board. When Eliza Kenan's indebted husband, Michael, died in 1843, he left her with many debts; the estate had "been subjected to great losses from securityships" [endorsements] that "reduced the property to its present state." Instead of petitioning the bank, she first went to the legislature to obtain "An Act To enable the Executrix of Michael J. Kenan to secure the payment of certain money to the Branch Bank at Mobile." With this act in hand, someone wrote the bank (on her behalf) requesting a refinancing of her husband's $11,598.89 debt ($13,532.05 with accrued interest) under terms that she could better afford. Based on Kenan's signature at the bottom of the appeal, she was likely barely literate and had someone else draw up the letter in her name. She proposed an annual payment schedule of "2000 dollars on the original and the interest due at the end of each year . . . until the debt is extinguished." She estimated the mortgaged land, twenty-seven enslaved individuals, mules, stock, and furniture worth "at the lowest calculation" $27,300. "I further pledge myself that if I can possibly pay more, than proposed, from the proceeds of my crops, after defraying the necessary expenses of my family, that I will do so; as I am very anxious to pay the debt and stop the accumulation of Interest." She hoped that "the Board will grant me the indulgence asked," enabling her "to pay the debt without sacrificing" property. The bank accepted this proposal.[35] Eliza steadily paid down the debt, as agreed. In 1846, she sold George and Solomon for $1,072.67, applying this amount "to the debt secured by the mortgage, the same being the proceeds of their sale." By February 1848, Eliza had reduced the debt to $3,322.89 (which was about $2,000 faster than she had promised), and the following month the bank "consented to extinguish the banks lien of the slaves Sandy & Amy," likely freeing her to sell them for her own profit. Her account with the bank was soon marked "Settled in full."[36]

Debtors often tried to use the depressed state of the economy as an argument for leniency. If the bank waited, the prices for land and enslaved individuals would (hopefully) rebound. And, in the meantime, the debtor might be able to make good on his or her overdue obligation. A bank director from Greensboro warned the branch bank at Mobile of the perils of selling during the current downturn, and encouraged it to continue offering credit terms. In February 1844, he advised it that the property of one debtor, including forty-five enslaved individuals, was scheduled for sale by the sheriff. While "it will not be possible to sell the land for cash at a fair price" given the current economic conditions, the director believed that "if sold on time [credit], I believe it will sell very well." He thus thought it "best for the Bank to authorise some person to act as its agent on the occasion," who could "agree to a credit sale of the land & some of the negroes."[37] The bank was caught in a bind. On the one hand, it was supposed to be liquidating debts and wrapping up the business of the bank rather than entering into new credit contracts. On the other hand, this director was probably correct that it would receive a better selling price if the buyer were permitted to purchase it on mortgage. However, while the various legislative acts related to the bank's liquidation permitted the extension of "good" debts, the legislature strictly forbade the bank from entering into new loan contracts.[38] The records do not definitively indicate how it proceeded in this case, but the lack of any further documentation implies that it most likely declined acting on this suggestion.

In the case of existing debtors, however, it had more flexibility to be lenient. In March 1844, Robert Huie wrote the Mobile branch on behalf of his brother, Josiah, whose property was being advertised for sale by the bank.[39] Another relative named James (possibly the father or another brother) had originally mortgaged this land in Autanga County with thirteen enslaved lives to secure a debt of $15,503 in 1837, but died before completing the repayment; the property and debts both then passed to Josiah. Robert warned the bank that "at this time [the property] cannot possibly bring enough to satisfy the debt for which it is mortgaged." He thus begged an indulgence for Josiah, so that the latter could "make an arrangement which will be entirely satisfactory to your institution," including "plac[ing] good notes as collateral security in your hands."[40]

The bank agreed to postpone the sale for two years, but finally seized the property and sold it at auction in February of 1846. One slaveholder purchased twenty-five-year-olds Daniel, Phil, and Peter for $1,875. A second buyer purchased thirty-four-year-old Bob and Lovey (a child) for $800. A third purchaser obtained thirty-one-year-old Bill and thirty-four-year-old Hannah for $975; and a fourth slaveholder bought twenty-seven-year-old Prince for $600. Thirty-two-year-old Charles and thirty-four-year-old Roda were "not accounted for," while twenty-two-year-old John had been "killed & p'd for by C. T. Pollans." The auctioneer tried to sell forty-four-year-old Jack (who was "lame"), thirty-six-year-old Lucy, and two children named Charlotte and Jack Jr. (ages four and one) separately in March, but failed. The bank instead bought this enslaved family itself and put it "in possession of H. A. Donaldson" until that fall, when it sold the family to another slaveholder for $650.[41] The failure of Josiah Huie thus caused the dispersal of his enslaved community across five separate buyers, although that sale was delayed for two years by the indulgence of the bank.

This shattering of enslaved communities was a common outcome of foreclosure proceedings. In April 1842, Louisa S. Owen—recent widow of George Owen—mortgaged her land and approximately thirty enslaved people to the branch bank at Mobile, to secure a debt of $28,172.05, which she promised to repay in five annual payments between March 1843 and March 1847. When she failed to pay these installments, the bank put the property into foreclosure in September 1845, and in April 1848 all but three of the enslaved individuals "were divided."[42] Most were hired out among ten local slaveholders, while all were simultaneously advertised for sale. The bank received $1,849.32 for the hiring but had to pay $488.77 in expenses for them, including $102.33 for life insurance premiums, $34 in city taxes, $38.44 in hiring fees, $6 for advertising, $71.50 in jail fees, $96 in doctor's bills, and $55.90 for clothing and shoes.[43]

The bank then gradually sold off the enslaved individuals. One slaveholder purchased nineteen-year-old Salena and her child for $700 in April 1848. In May, another buyer acquired eighteen-year-old Barbary for $550. In July, twenty-eight-year-old John sold for $725; another slaveholder obtained thirty-eight-year-old Hackey for $500; and a third acquired thirty-eight-year-old Sylvester for $450, forty-year-old Folih for $550, and forty-year-old Mack for $500. In October, twenty-four-year-old Bob Wiggins was purchased for $625, while the following month another slaveholder acquired twelve-year-old Romeo for $425. Also in November, a local minister deposited $500 for the purchase of the family of thirty-year-old Fanny and her four children Isabella, Thomas, Margaret, and Virginia, but changed his mind before finishing the sale. A local doctor paid the balance of $900 for the family in February, and received "a bill of sale." In January of 1849, the bank advertised for sale the family of forty-two-year-old Robert, his thirty-five-year-old wife Fanny, and their children sixteen-year-old Austin, twelve-year-old Sarah, and ten-year-old Washington, but ended up selling them together "at private sale" for $2,500. Similarly, thirty-five-year-old Ben was advertised for auction, but sold that same day "at private sale" to another slaveholder for $500.[44] Absent the liquidation proceedings, the bank might have extended Owen more time to pay her debts, keeping the enslaved community intact. But the bank's closure forced the sale and dispersal of these individuals across at least ten slaveholders.

Throughout its liquidation, the Bank of Alabama regularly used auctioneers to sell any enslaved individuals. In April 1843 the Mobile branch employed James Pickens and John T. Lomax to sell the forty-eight enslaved people who were "formerly the property of Prince & Garrett." The auctioneers scattered the enslaved people across at least nine different purchasers, each of whom bought (on average) four to five slaves. With a median price of $327 each, the sale prices ranged from $170 for Dick to $600 for Bob.[45] These amounts were consistent with the average prices for enslaved lives at this time in the depression.[46] The auctioneers took a 5 percent commission on the total sale of $15,701. This $785.05 payment likely included various state, city, and school-fund taxes assessed on slave auctions. The bank paid the auctioneers $50 in cash.[47]

But the branch bank at Mobile most commonly employed Edward B. Gayle as its auctioneer, a relative of bank cashier Billups Gayle.[48] When one slaveholder fell delinquent on paying his $17,672.75 debt, for which he had mortgaged twenty-four enslaved lives in 1842, the bank turned the enslaved individuals over to Edward Gayle for auction in February 1846. Gayle sold seventeen of the enslaved people to ten different purchasers for an average price of $275 each, netting the bank $4,675.50—less than one-quarter the original debt. Gayle charged the bank $25 for his services—a mere 0.5 percent, although this fee likely did not include taxes.[49] At other times, he charged the bank between 1 percent and 2.5 percent for his services, and separated out the tax assessments from his own fees. The bank also occasionally employed him to take care of odd lots of enslaved individuals, rather than the property of just one slaveholder. In December 1845, the bank hired Gayle to sell the human property of "Various Accounts," which included people from at least four different slaveholders.[50]

All these lawsuits and auctions were time-consuming and expensive for the bank, which often was only able to reclaim a fraction of the debt due. For example, the Huntsville branch received a court judgment against one slaveholder in September 1845 for $746.16. This amount included the original debt of $688.19, plus interest, damages, and $6.25 in court costs ($1.25 for clerk's fees, $2 in taxes, $2 for the attorney, and $2 for the sheriff). The sheriff then seized and sold four enslaved individuals in January 1846 for $1,074. However, another creditor "having a prior lien" claimed $409.11 of these proceeds, leaving only $664.89 for the bank ($81.27 less than the bank's original claim). The branch fared even worse in the case of another debtor. Although it received a court judgment against him in June 1844 of $1,500 plus $65.25 damages and $14.87 court costs, the sheriff did not seize his four enslaved lives until the fall of 1849. He was unable to sell them "for want of time" during the November auction, so they were to "remain in your hands" until the sheriff could "expose to sale the aforesaid property." Eight months later, on July 3, 1850, the sheriff finally sold the people for $271.95, paying the bank attorney a mere $259—less than one-sixth of the bank's full claim on this debtor.[51]

In his final analysis of the Bank of the State of Alabama's liquidation, commissioner James Deas believed that the legislature had made a grave mistake in rushing to foreclose on debtors. "This act I think lost to the State more than a million of dollars which under a different policy would have been collected." In particular, he noted that while attorneys of the bank went to court to seize and sell enslaved individuals, many debtors fraudulently sought to evade collection either through the "collusive transfers of property" to nondebtors or "by running off their negroes" to other states, including Texas, as was described in chapter 7.[52] For example, when the branch bank at Mobile sent the sheriff to claim the enslaved workers of two slaveholders in 1844, the sheriff returned the execution as "no property."[53] That same year, it accused administrators of a deceased slaveholder's estate of omitting "divers mules horses and cattle" as well as twenty-three enslaved individuals, which it claimed in payment of his $14,136.40 debt from 1841. In mounting their defense to the judge of the Clark County Court disputing the "validity and legality of the claim of the Bank against the estate," the administrators alleged that "Corporations . . . have no souls"—an obvious attempt to appeal to the sympathies of fellow slaveholders who might be similarly situated over the institutional rights of the bank.[54] And although the bank repeatedly tried to claim the forty-one enslaved individuals owned by still another slaveholder in payment of several notes from 1840 to 1842 totaling almost $6,000, the claim remained unresolved as of November 20, 1847, with "all concerned insolvent."[55] Even as Deas was only "guessing," he believed that "certainly [debtors] must have carried off three thousand negroes" by removing them from the state. Additionally, by adding so much property to an already weak market, "the winding up depressed much the value of the property and was a visible check to an onward progress" of the economy.[56]

Deas was writing this reflection in 1849, at the request of the president of the Bank of the State of South Carolina, Franklin Elmore. That state legislature was threatening to close its state bank, and Elmore was seeking to understand the implications of a rapid liquidation of the bank (and perhaps, looking for some ammunition to use against the bank's critics). In Deas's opinion, if the bank is "reasonably managed I should say continue them and let the closing up at some future day be by very gradual curtailments." The key was for the legislature to "give discretion" to the bank's management. "Discretion is liable to abuse certainly, but the derangements and evils of closing are certain to give the 'devil his due.'" Whereas Elmore likely appreciated his candor, Deas apologized for his impassioned critique. "I have wandered very much I fear from answering the questions propounded to me and may have mixed up with it too much of my opinions which I should certainly have more confidence in if they related to plantation cotton or corn."[57] Notwithstanding his passion, Deas was correct that the liquidation of the Bank of the State of Alabama had been messy, time-consuming, and expensive. What he omitted from his analysis was the impact on the enslaved lives at the center of many of these contracts, who were sold and dispersed in large numbers as the bank foreclosed on its extensive loan portfolio.

Dead Weight in Louisiana

The response in Louisiana was starkly different from that in Alabama, but it was partially a reflection of the very different banking terrain in that state. Whereas Alabama (and similarly Arkansas and Mississippi) contained only one or two major state-run banks with multiple branches, Louisiana had a much more robust and diverse banking industry, consisting of a mix of plantation banks, traditional commercial banks, and joint banking-improvement companies. Rather than rapidly liquidating troubled banks (or doing nothing), the state took a much more interventionist approach. In 1842, the Louisiana legislature put into place rules for banks either to resume specie payments and revive their charters, or go into formal liquidation. For a bank that voluntarily or involuntarily went into liquidation, the government would appoint a liquidation committee to take full inventory of its property.[58] Reviving banks—as part of the condition for continuing their charters—pledged that they would "receive at par" the banknotes of liquidating banks. These notes would be distributed equitably among the surviving banks, which would also receive an equitable proportion of the cash assets, bonds, or loan portfolio of the defunct banks. In effect, surviving banks would absorb the assets and debts of banks in liquidation, thereby allowing most long-term loans to remain intact.[59]

The Louisiana state legislators clearly believed that the biggest problem with banking during the 1830s had been the issuance of long-term mortgages on land and human property by the traditional commercial banks, a practice they sought to rein in. Reflecting these concerns, the first requirement of revival was for a bank to separate its short-term loans (defined as loans payable within ninety days) from "loans on capital to be composed of accommodations on personal security, or on mortgage, loans on stock by the property banks, and of all other investments of whatever nature not realizable in ninety days." These long-term loans "shall be denominated the 'dead weight,'" a somewhat damning designation. Chartered banks were banned from engaging in new "dead weight" investments until they accumulated specie equal to one-third of their cash liabilities, and "satisfactory paper, payable in full at maturity, and within ninety days" of at least two-thirds of their liabilities. For the commercial banks most engaged in long-term mortgage lending, following this requirement would entail a significant rebalancing of their loan portfolios. Additionally, short-term discount loans were no longer renewable; they "shall be considered *de facto* as payable in full at maturity."[60] Thus the legislature severely curtailed a bank's ability to issue long-term loans (including renewals of short-term loans) to one-third the value of its total liabilities. Existing dead-weight loans were renewable, as long as "ample and satisfactory security on real estate be furnished by" the debtor, and the debtor paid off at least 15 percent of the loan each year.[61] Finally, banks were permitted "in order to prevent a heavy loss, to purchase the property [previously] mortgaged," and hold on to it for later resale, "when it is advertised to be sold under seizure."[62]

But this sharp curtailment of long-term lending could not easily apply to those banks which, by charter design, primarily engaged in extended mortgages on land and enslaved lives. This group included both the state's plantation banks as well as the Bank of Louisiana, which by its charter was required to lend *at least* half its capital on mortgages renewable for five years, and could discount notes for up to four months.[63] Thus, the state's new liquidation policies would "not apply to those banks in which the state is a stockholder, or for which it has issued bonds, or for the debts or obligations of which the state is in any manner responsible"—a reference to the plantation banks and the Bank of Louisiana. If any of these latter banks were unable to continue full operations, it would forfeit its charter without dissolving and instead "retain its corporate powers and privileges" to manage its assets and loans, effectively operating as a private bank and employing any proceeds to the payment of the bonds or other obligations of the state.[64] If necessary, the government would appoint new directors to manage the affairs of these banks.[65]

In his 1844 message to the legislature, Governor Alexandre Mouton (who was allegedly an anti-bank Democrat) affirmed the success of Louisiana's 1842 banking legislation. "The Bank of Louisiana, the Louisiana State Bank, the Union Bank of Louisiana, the Mechanics' and Traders Bank, and the Canal Banking Company" were "all operating strictly within the requisitions of the law," and the legislation had proven to be "equally beneficial to the Stockholders and to the public." The weaker institutions, including the Merchants' Bank, the Bank of Orleans, the Exchange & Banking Company, and the Atchafalaya Railroad & Banking Company, were soon liquidated under the terms of the act. Finally, he judged "the liquidation of the Property Banks"—the Citizens' Bank, Union Bank, and the Consolidated Association—to be moving "in a satisfactory manner." He had "every reason to hope that the whole liabilities of those institutions will, under its operation be gradually extinguished." With regard to the plantation banks, in particular, the goal was "to put an end to these monuments of our thoughtless folly."[66]

The report of the board of currency, which oversaw both the revival and the liquidation of the banks, was even more pointed in its criticism of the entire banking landscape in Louisiana. Referring collectively to the seven active banks, the two plantation banks being operated by state commissioners, the four banks in involuntary liquidation, and the three banks liquidating voluntarily, the report warned that "the lessons of the past must not be lost upon us." In causing stockholders to lose approximately $16 million between 1837 and 1843, "the former administration of those institutions had brought more distress, sin and shame upon the land, than could have been inflicted by any other human agency." It was thus imperative for both the public and the legislature "to ascertain and to avoid hereafter the causes of that great evil."[67]

The report then proceeded to review how the global banking system led to the overspeculation of the 1830s. Whereas the committee placed considerable blame on the tariff of 1828, the transfer of funds from the Bank of the United States to the state banks, and the global bubble in cotton prices, the ultimate result of these factors was an expansion of bank lending for long-term loans secured by property. This "system of large accommodations has been the fundamental error in the past administration of the Banks," and current banking capital remained "to a great extent locked up in long loans." At present, all the banks could do was to "require nothing but the interest upon long loans well secured and to be contented with as much of the principal as the debtors can conveniently pay" in order to provide planters with "the delay [in payment] which they absolutely require." Although the committee believed that banks would eventually resume issuing new long-term loans, it advised bankers "to stop far short of the extent which they will soon have it in their power to go," advising that "all long loans must be secured by unincumbered real estate, the growing crop or a pledge of business paper."[68]

The liquidation committee in charge of the Union Bank described the creation of plantation banks as "done in a moment of infatuation which sometimes finds its way to the minds of men; but it is believed so severe has and may be the lesson, that it will not again occur. It certainly never should."[69] Similarly, the board of currency criticized the long-term nature of the mortgages in plantation banks: "[T]he permanency of such investments which constitutes their safety, unfits them at the same time for the purposes of banking. . . . [I]t is worse than madness to pretend that they could still have worked their task" even without the economic downturn. But the committee believed that "the Legislature was not again to be deceived" by these mechanisms of "unreal speculation and abstract finance." It must deal with "the consequences of past follies" by preventing their future repetition.[70] In scapegoating these institutions, these reports neglected to acknowledge the essential role of state banks in promoting and sustaining the expansion of the frontier South during the 1820s and 1830s. They may have failed as profitable financial institutions, but they succeeded in propping up and extending the system of slavery at an essential point in its historical development.

Liquidating Human Property

Even before passage of the 1842 banking acts, some of the most troubled Louisiana institutions had begun liquidating. Chartered in April 1835, the Exchange & Banking Company was tasked with "erecting a Hotel in the city of New-Orleans and its faubourgs, for the better accommodation of visitors and strangers," a task the accomplishment of which would "contribute to the advantage of the public and the prosperity of the city."[71] With the completion of the St. Charles Hotel & Exchange in 1838, the institution fulfilled this mission, but continued operating the hotel and exercising its banking privileges.[72] Among the bank's assets were four enslaved men (Reuben, Carey, Hannibal, and Washington) that it had acquired in June 1841 from the estate of a deceased debtor.[73] Yet by November 1841, the bank was struggling to stay solvent, and its president, Edward Yorke, decided to sell off as many of the non-hotel assets as he could—particularly those assets with disputed claims.

On November 4, 1841, the bank sold twenty-year-old Washington and twenty-five-year-old Cary for $1,500 to a Terrebonne Parish slaveholder.[74] Five days later, the bank subrogated to Thomas Fitzwilliam the mortgage of Alexander McNeill of Warren County, Mississippi. In 1837, McNeill had mortgaged forty-seven enslaved lives on his plantation in Carroll Parish to secure a loan of $18,750.[75] These people were unique from the forty enslaved individuals from the same plantation whom he later mortgaged to the United States Bank of Pennsylvania in 1838.[76] When McNeill died in 1839, the Exchange Bank debt remained unpaid. Fitzwilliam purchased under subrogation the mortgage claim from the bank for $22,891, which was slightly less than McNeill's estate now owed (with accumulated interest at 7 percent), giving his own promissory notes payable in twelve, eighteen, and twenty-four months. Acquiring all the privileges of the mortgage creditor, Fitzwilliam would have the legal right to foreclose on the enslaved individuals if McNeill's estate did not pay the debt.[77] McNeill's estate, however, quickly became mired in lawsuits brought by competing creditors and neither the bank nor Fitzwilliam was able to recover the debt until at least 1850.[78]

Four days later, on November 13, 1841, the Exchange & Banking Company reached an agreement with another creditor over a disputed property claim. The bank and this creditor each possessed several promissory notes of a Natchitoches slaveholder totaling $62,799.69, which were secured by his plantation and enslaved workers. The creditors had foreclosed on the property, but when they found it "impossible to find a purchaser willing to pay cash for said plantation and Slaves, at the Judicial Sale thereof," they eventually sold the property to another slaveholder for a mere $38,500, payable over four years. The bank's share of those proceeds was $887 a year, or $3,548 total.[79] And on November 19, 1841, the bank sold thirty-two-year-old Reuben Morgan ("a Mulatto, a carpenter") and twenty-three-year-old Hannibal to slave trader Isaac Franklin for $1,700, payable in three installments at four, eight, and twelve months.[80] Another creditor of the original owner soon sued for possession of all four enslaved men, and their ownership remained tied up in court until 1849.[81]

President Yorke, who himself was indebted to the bank for $200,000 (about $6.8 million in 2021), then absconded with $70,000 of bank funds in March 1842. While the governor offered a $500 reward for his apprehension, the legislature put the institution into formal liquidation, beginning with a full inventory of the bank's assets and liabilities.[82] The only remaining enslaved individuals in the possession of the bank were "Amy aged about [blank] and her live children," valued at $600.[83] The bank had acquired the family in 1840, as part of the settlement with the estate of another deceased debtor. In July 1842, the bank's liquidators sold the twenty-six-year-old Aimée (described as a "griffonne," or a woman of one-quarter white ancestry) with her six-year-old daughter Sarah and four-year-old son Cornelius to a merchant for $1,330 "payable in notes of the Exchange & Banking Company"; the sale price was likely inflated due to the merchant's desire to pay in the rapidly depreciating notes of the liquidating bank.[84] Two years later, in March 1844, the legislature incorporated the St. Charles Hotel Company to take over operation of that institution. According to the charter, "the Liquidating Commissioners of the Exchange and Banking Company [were] authorized and required to sell the portfolio, and other assets of the Bank, with the exception of the Hotel, at public auction, for the most they will fetch."[85] Yet by this point, all the enslaved individuals owned by the bank had already been sold.

As other Louisiana banks entered into liquidation under the 1842 acts, they likewise needed to sell any land and enslaved individuals that they had acquired from foreclosing on debtors. The Bank of Orleans, for example, had obtained several plantations and numerous enslaved individuals during the depression, which it still owned at the time of its liquidation. At some point it had become the joint owner with William H. Gay of a plantation and enslaved workers in Washington County, Mississippi, on Deer Creek, which the bank valued at $38,274; the bank had likely acquired this property as part of a mortgage foreclosure. Gay still owed the bank for his half of the purchase price, but he also managed the plantation on the bank's behalf, thereby alleviating the institution of the headache of having to hire competent managers or overseers for the property.[86] In the 1840 census, Gay listed himself as owner of its twenty-two enslaved workers.[87] On January 29, 1841, the Bank of Orleans purchased eighteen-year-old Julia, her twelve-month-old daughter Arianna, and seventeen-year-old Abby for $2,250 from the Virginia slave traders Walker & Hundley. That same day, it also purchased Armstead Warner for $1,000 from another slave trader named Thomas Boudar. Although it is unclear what happened to Abby (perhaps she died or ran away), the other three enslaved individuals went to work alongside Gay's twenty-two enslaved laborers on the Deer Creek plantation.[88]

The bank later acquired the plantation of William Armstrong in Rapides Parish, Louisiana. Armstrong had purchased the plantation on the Red River with its enslaved workforce in 1832. The following year, he mortgaged it to the Union Bank of Louisiana in exchange for eighty-four shares of bank stock. At some point, he also obtained a loan of $2,405.40 from the Union Bank secured by the same property, which he never repaid.[89] And in August 1834, he became separately indebted to Nathaniel Cox. After Cox's death in 1836, his widow, Ann B. Harrison, sued Armstrong, receiving a *fieri facias* court judgment against him for $4,307.02 in April 1838. Armstrong also failed to pay this judgment, although it appears that Ann Cox was able to seize one enslaved man named Sam in partial payment.[90] In November 1839, Armstrong used this same Rapides plantation with eight of his twenty enslaved workers, as well as his eighty-four shares of Union Bank stock, to obtain a loan of $13,573.68 from the Bank of Orleans; it is unclear if the bank knew about Cox's prior lien.[91]

Two years later, when the Bank of Orleans foreclosed on Armstrong for nonpayment, Mrs. Cox asserted her claim to the property. The bank purchased the plantation, twenty-two enslaved individuals, and the eighty-four

Union Bank shares at the Rapides Parish sheriff's sale in May 1841, for an undisclosed amount. The enslaved included Harry, Hetty, Lucy, and Anthony from the original 1833 sale, as well as eight children born in the interim.[92] Then in July, the bank settled with Cox, paying her $5,423.07 for her claim over the property.[93] The bank also separately purchased Sam from Cox. The bank held onto this property for the next two years, perhaps retaining Armstrong to manage it for an annual salary.[94]

The Bank of Orleans acquired even more enslaved property in January 1842, when it foreclosed on the debts of John A. Scott and C. F. Legrand of Mississippi. Scott owed the bank $8,333.33 on two promissory notes, and Legrand owed another $18,263.32 on three notes. Between them, the pair transferred to the bank 5,961 acres of "sundry lands" in the Mississippi counties of Bolivar, Carroll, Tallahatchie, and Washington. Scott additionally sold the bank the family of Humphrey and Molly (both about fifty years old), with their teenaged sons Wesley and Silas, as well as thirty-five-year-old Dick and seventeen-year-old Isaac. The bank valued this land and the enslaved individuals at exactly the sum due on the five notes.[95]

Finally, the Bank of Orleans acquired a sugar plantation in Jefferson Parish. The plantation had originally been the property of Michel Commagère, which he had mortgaged to the Union Bank in 1837. In March 1841, when he still owed $31,027 ($45,427 with accumulated 10 percent interest), the Union Bank foreclosed on the delinquent debtor. In May, it sold the entire plantation "in a lump" to Andrew Hodge (the bank's president) for $70,000 "cash," although Hodge did not actually pay this full amount in cash. He likely only paid $30,000 up front, which was the amount of the loan he had obtained from the Bank of Orleans the previous month. For this loan, he signed three promissory notes for $10,000 each, payable in twelve, eighteen, and twenty-four months, and endorsed by his brother. Hodge employed Commagère to continue managing the plantation, and the latter hired an overseer for $1,200 a year. Hodge sent seven of his own enslaved laborers to join the plantation workforce, and they hired nine more field-workers from the overseer. Yet Hodge failed to repay the three notes and remained indebted "for a very large amount" with the Bank of Orleans. In the fall of 1843, the bank liquidators obtained a writ of *fieri facias* against him and attempted to seize the property. The Union Bank, however, disputed this seizure, claiming that Hodge had not fully paid for the original purchase of the property, and thus that it still belonged to Commagère (upon whom the Union Bank retained a lien). But the court ruled that the Union Bank had been treating Hodge as the legal property owner, and thus no longer had a valid mortgage on the property.

The Bank of Orleans took possession of this plantation as well, releasing Hodge from $101,000 in mortgage debts, but not from his $30,000 loan from the Bank of Orleans.[96]

Yet even as the Bank of Orleans and the Union Bank were battling over the Hodge plantation, the Bank of Orleans failed to comply with the 1842 state-banking requirements, and the legislature placed it into liquidation. The governor appointed three liquidation commissioners who were charged with inventorying the bank's assets, selling off the property, and settling with the bank's creditors before dispersing any remaining assets to the stockholders. Per the liquidation acts, the bank's loan portfolio and bank notes were distributed proportionately among the surviving banks. The inventory, completed in July 1842, valued the bank's real estate assets at $146,739.51 (table 8.2). This valuation included the banking house ($30,228.26), another "granite building" ($24,885.38) and a plot of land ($3,864), all in New Orleans; some "wild lands" in Mississippi ($1,250.62); and the Mississippi property of Legrand and Scott, along with Scott's slaves ($26,596.65), Armstrong's plantation and enslaved property in Rapides Parish ($21,640.60), and Gay's Deer Creek plantation in Mississippi ($38,274).[97] With the inventory complete, the commissioners scheduled a meeting in December with the creditors "for the purpose of deliberating on the time, terms and conditions of the sale of the real property and Slaves belonging to the said Bank of Orleans." By this point, the Hodge plantation was also in the bank's possession, and the commissioners added it to the inventory. The eleven creditors ranged from Jacob Barker, who represented the firm of Horace Bean & Co. with its claim of $13,889, to John Turpin, who held just $5 in notes of the bank. A week later, Louisiana attorney general Christian Roselius added his approval to the plan on behalf of any "absent creditors." Not including these latter (presumably small) creditors, the total claims on the bank amounted to $32,512.08, a fraction of the assessed value of the bank's physical assets.[98] These creditors would need to be paid before any of the $500,000 in capital stock could be repaid to the bank's stockholders.

The commissioners turned all the property over to the auction firms of Hewlett & Cenas and Bach & Warfield to advertise and sell. On February 25, 1843, they "caused to be exposed for sale by Public Auction, at the St. Louis Exchange" in New Orleans, the first installment of the bank's assets. All the New Orleans land and buildings sold for $45,700, which was $13,277.64 less than their assessed valuation. The Mississippi lands of Legrand and Scott sold for $5,357.93, and Scott's enslaved property for $2,650; the overseer of the Hodge sugar plantation purchased Scott's enslaved family of four for $1,550,

TABLE 8.2 Bank of Orleans property sale, 1842–1843

Property	*Assessed value*	*Sale price*	*Gain/loss*
New Orleans banking house and lot;	$30,228.26		
granite building adjoining bank;	$24,855.38	$45,700 [all 3]	($13,277.64)
square of land in Faubourg Livandais	$3,864		
interest in Mississippi "wild lands"	$1,250.62	$180.00	($1,070.62)
sundry lands in Mississippi of C. F. Legrand and John A. Scott	$26,596.65 [land & slaves]	$5,357.93 [land]	($18,588.72)
plus Scott's six enslaved lives		$2,650 [slaves]	
William Armstrong's Rapides Plantation and seventeen enslaved lives	$21,640.60	$9,000	($12,640.60)
William H. Gay's Deer Creek Plantation and twenty-six enslaved lives	$38,274	$20,100	($18,174)
Totals	$146,739.51	$82,987.93	($63,751.58)

Source: "Inventory of the Property and Effects of the Bank of Orleans," July 28, 1842, vol. 45: 365–369, NONA; "Proces-Verbal of Sales of Real Estate & Slaves belonging to the Bank of Orleans," February 25, 1843, vol. 47, no. 314, NONA; "Sale of Plantation &c the Commissioners of the Bank of Orleans to Michael Welch," June 3, 1843, Notary William Christy, vol. 47: 616–620, NONA.

while Josiah Barker bought the other two Scott slaves for $1,100. This total came to $18,588.72 less than the combined valuation of these lands and enslaved individuals. The bank's half of the Gay plantation on Deer Creek in Mississippi, with its twenty-six enslaved laborers (including three of the four the bank had purchased from slave traders in 1841) sold for $20,100, which was $18,174 less than its valuation. The buyer agreed to "take the place and stead of the Bank of Orleans" with regard to Gay's debt for the other half of the plantation. All told, this first auction netted $73,987.93, or just about 60 percent of the property's assessed value. Additionally, the purchasers only paid one-sixth ($12,331.32) in cash, with one-sixth payable in four months, one-third in six, and the remaining one-third in twelve months.[99]

In May, the auctioneers advertised for sale the Armstrong plantation in Rapides, which included eighty-four shares of Union Bank stock and twenty-two enslaved workers. They also re-advertised the Deer Creek property and slaves; the earlier buyer must have failed to follow through on his purchase, as there is no record of the sale in the notarial archives. For the Armstrong plantation, Michael Welch was "the last and highest bidder" on the property, obtaining the full plantation, twenty-two enslaved individuals plus Sam, and eighty-four shares of Union Bank stock for the bargain price of $9,000, which was $12,640.60 less than its 1842 valuation. He agreed to pay the bank $1,500 immediately, $1,500 in four months, and $3,000 each in six and twelve months—with a mortgage on the property until paid. He also agreed to assume the $2,405.40 debt still owed to the Union Bank.[100] By the 1850 census, Welch valued the plantation at $25,000, in addition to the value of its sixty-four enslaved individuals.[101]

The commissioners faced considerable difficulty resolving Hodge's debt. By 1847, he still owed the bank $30,000 but apparently had no land or human property worth claiming. In June of 1847, the liquidation commissioners finally subrogated this mortgage to the firm of Fellowes Johnson & Co. The firm paid the bank $4,000, and in exchange assumed the full "rights, liens, and privileges" to Hodge's $30,000 debt "in the same manner, and to the same extent that they the said Commissioners might have done."[102] This firm was one of many that stepped in to take the place of banks in financing slavery after the depression (chapter 9).

Repudiation and the Death of the United States Bank of Pennsylvania

Beyond trying to orchestrate an efficient dismantling of their banking systems, several states also had to contend with the outstanding state bonds that had been sold in support of their banks. During the 1830s, states throughout the country had borrowed heavily to invest in internal improvements and banking institutions. Pennsylvania and Maryland were both intent on creating transportation infrastructures to compete with the success of New York's Erie Canal, issuing almost $50 million in state-backed bonds between them for this purpose (or about $19 and $32 per capita, respectively). A similar aggregate sum was borrowed by the growing states of the old Northwest Territory—Illinois, Michigan, Indiana, and Ohio—for elaborate canal and railroad projects to connect their lands to these market hubs (or about $28, $26, $19, and $7 per capita, respectively). In contrast, frontier southern states were mainly relying on their chartering powers to create corporations and joint banking-improvement companies to address their own internal-improvement needs, using their borrowing capacities instead to invest in new banking institutions—both state-owned banks and plantation banks—

to serve the needs of their large planters. By 1841, state debts for bank bonds amounted to $17.4 million in Louisiana (about $49 per capita, including the enslaved population) for its plantation banks and part ownership of the Bank of Louisiana, $15.4 million in Alabama (about $26 per capita) for state ownership of the Bank of the State of Alabama and part ownership of the Bank of Mobile and the Planters' & Merchants' Bank, $7 million in Mississippi (about $19 per capita) for the new Union Bank and part ownership of the Planters' Bank, $3.9 million in the sparsely populated Florida territory (about $72 per capita) across two plantation banks and the Bank of Pensacola, and $3.2 million in Arkansas (about $33 per capita) for its newly chartered Real Estate Bank and the state-owned State Bank.[103] If we were to calculate these figures based only on the free population, the per capita expenditures would be even more extensive.

Across these ten states, only Ohio and Alabama remained current with their bond obligations by 1841; the remaining eight went into default on their interest payments. Yet as the economy began recovering by the mid-1840s, Pennsylvania, Maryland, Illinois, and Indiana all resumed payments on their bonds and eventually repaid their entire debts with interest. The two prosperous mid-Atlantic states raised taxes to fund their obligations, while the midwestern states borrowed additional money to complete their transportation projects, which eventually allowed them to repay some of the bonds through infrastructure revenues.[104] But the four states of the frontier South (plus Michigan) repudiated some or all of these debts.[105]

As the bottom fell out of the market for land and enslaved lives, banks that were heavily invested in long-term property loans—or even more significantly, those whose very stock was based on rapidly depreciating plantations and enslaved people—found themselves on the brink of insolvency. Legislatures had placed the full faith and credit of their states behind the bond issues supporting these banks, which committed them to paying creditors by raising taxes, shifting revenues, or selling assets. Yet when approving these bond measures, bank proponents had repeatedly argued that state backing "subjects the State to little or no risk" (regarding the Citizens' Bank of Louisiana),[106] that "nothing short of such a revolution, can destroy the value of their lands; or a sweeping pestilence, exterminate their slaves" (regarding the Union Bank of Florida),[107] and that "it is further impossible that there ever can be a total failure of a Bank based on the planting interest of this State . . . it is hardly possible, even, with the most gross mismanagement, to sink the profits, much less the whole capital, of an institution so carefully guarded, and so firmly supported as the Planters' Bank [of Mississippi]."[108] State legislatures had contributed their names to the bonds, without fully committing themselves to the nature and extent of the risk they were undertaking. They quickly sought contract violations, technicalities, and other legal loopholes to evade payment on these bonds.

Both Louisiana and Mississippi differentiated between their obligations toward the creditors of the state-owned banks and their guarantees of the bonds of plantation banks. Louisiana, for example, resumed payment of the interest and principal on its Bank of Louisiana bonds by 1844, but denied any obligation to pay the bonds of the three plantation banks. As Governor André B. Roman (himself a stockholder in the Citizens' Bank) stated to the legislature in 1842, "in case of non-payment . . . of the capital or interest of the bonds issued" in favor of the plantation banks, "you will not be under the necessity of imposing additional taxes," since payment was the responsibility of "the stockholders of the institution for whose benefit they have been issued."[109] In the state's view, the plantation-bank stockholders remained liable for paying these obligations, and not the taxpayers. Unfortunately, the banks' main means of raising funds was to foreclose on delinquent debtors and sell the mortgaged plantations and human property of shareholders—all during a severe market downturn. Yet by renegotiating the debts with the bondholders, extending leniency to debtors, and assessing stockholders on their shares, the Louisiana plantation banks eventually repaid the debt obligations secured by the state.[110]

Mississippi also initially differentiated between its obligations to the bondholders of the partially state-owned Planters' Bank and the Union plantation bank. Additionally, the governor argued that the Union Bank bond sales had actually been conducted illegally through the United States Bank of Pennsylvania. Although contracted in Nicholas Biddle's name, the governor asserted that "by its charter" the United States Bank "could not legally purchase" the bonds. "Hence although Mississippi had received the money for the bonds, it was thus proposed to refuse to repay it on the ground that the purchaser had no right to buy them," which was a spurious argument at best.[111] On the other hand, although the state remained verbally committed to the Planters' Bank bonds, it made little effort to pay these debts, and by 1852 Mississippi repudiated payment on its remaining bond obligations.[112] In Arkansas, the governor argued that the bonds for the Real Estate Bank had been sold below par, in violation of the bank's charter, and refused to honor them. Although the state made some attempts at repayment in the 1850s (in an effort to reestablish its credit for internal-improvement projects), most of the debt remained unpaid.[113] Finally Florida claimed that, as a territory, responsibility for its obligations fell to the US Congress, since all the territorial officers involved in creating the banks had been agents of the federal government. During 1842 and 1843, the territorial legislature passed a series of resolutions repudiating the debts, and most were never paid.[114]

One of the biggest banking casualties of the panics and their aftermath was the former Second Bank of the United States, which was still one of the nation's most powerful financial institutions even with a Pennsylvania state charter. The bank's extensive investment in the frontier South, including its involvement in the bond issues of the plantation banks and its own underwriting of large, long-term mortgages secured by land and human property, took a toll on its liquidity. As market prices for land and enslaved lives plummeted, and as states began defaulting on their bond payments, the United States Bank found its investments severely squeezed. While few scholars have investigated the final demise of the United States Bank of Pennsylvania in terms of its relationship with southern slavery, it is highly likely that its heavy involvement with and investment in both plantation banks and long-term mortgages directly contributed to its closure in 1843.[115] As the *London Times* explained in 1849 (in reference to the state of Mississippi's 1842 decision to repudiate payment on its state bonds), the United States Bank owned most—if not all—of the $5,000,000 in bonds of the Union Bank of Mississippi, as well as another $2,000,000 of Planters' Bank bonds. Thus, up to one-fifth of the Bank's capital was wiped out by the Mississippi repudiation alone.[116]

When the United States Bank went into receivership in 1843, all the outstanding loans to the bank were called and, when the debtor was unable to pay, immediately foreclosed. In July 1843, the bank advertised for sale the property of one delinquent debtor, including fifty-two named enslaved individuals "together with about forty heads of horses and mules." Five years earlier, this debtor had received a loan from the Merchant's Bank for $8,100, but had failed to repay the notes. With the United States Bank now in liquidation, the shareholders sued him, forcing his property into receivership.[117] That same month, they likewise sued another slaveholder, seizing by court order his land and twenty-seven enslaved lives; an additional thirty-seven enslaved individuals were seized from this same debtor on behalf of the Union Bank of Mississippi. He owed the Second Bank $4,599.92 from a July 11, 1840 loan.[118] And in August, the receivers seized the land and sixty-two enslaved lives of a Washington, Mississippi, slaveholder. In 1840, this debtor had discounted seven notes totaling $16,512.29 with the Merchant's Bank. Payment on one of these notes was due every year from 1841 through 1847. Yet at the time of the bank's closure, it was already protesting the first two notes for nonpayment and decided to foreclose on his entire property.[119]

While a small percentage of the state bondholders were local investors, the vast majority of bonds had been sold in New York, Philadelphia, London, and Amsterdam; whether these northern and European investors knew that the bonds were supported by mortgaged plantations and enslaved lives has not yet been sufficiently examined by historians.[120] Nonetheless, these repudiations did significant and lasting damage to the credit reputations of these southern states, making it difficult for them to borrow for future internal-improvement projects and—more critically—during the Civil War. A full assessment of the impact of these repudiations on state finance also has yet to be made, and will have to be the purview of a future scholar. In the short term, however, these repudiations only added fuel to the anti-bank fire that had begun to rage across the South (chapter 9).

The Afterlife of a Plantation Bank

Due to the substantial state-backed debt that formed the basis of their capital, the liquidation of Louisiana's plantation banks was much more difficult than that of traditional commercial banks. While the state temporarily stopped payment on the annual bond interest for lack of funds coming from these banks, it expected the plantation banks to continue collecting on their mortgages—resuming payments of the bond interest and creating a sinking fund to pay off the bond principal as it came due. Although the banks lost the privilege of issuing new banknotes, they continued to oversee the long-term mortgages that formed the majority of their balance sheets. The Consolidated Association of Planters of Louisiana (CAPL) engaged in a slow liquidation of these mortgages that lasted until the 1880s. As long as debtors made a good-faith effort to pay a portion of the principal and accumulated interest on the loan, the bank allowed their debts to continue. But if the bank determined that the debtor was no longer willing or able to make an adequate payment of the debt due, it would foreclose on the debtor and sell the property. The CAPL applied the proceeds of all debt payments and foreclosure sales toward the payment of their bond obligations. In 1847, the legislature further amended the liquidation process, requiring the institution to "set apart a sufficient amount of assets . . . to pay the interest now due upon the bonds of the State."[121] With the approval of holders of 95 percent of the stock, the CAPL board passed a measure to assess their stockholders $6 per share annually from June 1849 to 1865 to meet this requirement.[122] As the bank placed delinquent properties into foreclosure, it now often resold the property separately from the stock, in order to free the purchasers from this assessment; the bank then retired those same stock shares.

In 1844, the CAPL sued the heirs of one slaveholder for nonpayment of his mortgage debt on a plantation in Lafayette Parish and thirty-four enslaved people. The slaveholder had first obtained the mortgage in 1830, and made regular payments from 1831 through 1838 before falling delinquent on the remaining $8,460 debt. Upon his death during the panic, his heirs refused to continue payments on the mortgage, claiming technical deficiencies in the original mortgage document. The Supreme Court of Louisiana ruled in the bank's favor in August 1848.[123] The bank immediately had the parish sheriff seize the property and advertise it for sale. By prior agreement with Judge E. Simon and Governor Alexandre Mouton (who presented himself as an anti-bank Democrat but willingly contracted with the CAPL), the bank purchased the property on December 2, 1848, and then resold the land to Governor Mouton for $3,200 and the enslaved individuals to Judge Simon for $16,880. Simon paid $3,000 in cash, and the men financed the remainder over four years, obtaining a "special mortgage" on the property rather than the normal stock mortgages of the plantation bank: "The property is sold free from all mortgages or incumbrances created on account of its original liability to the Bank, whether for stock or otherwise." This special agreement released the new purchasers from having to pay the $6-per-share assessment, but they also could not take advantage of the generous eighteen-year mortgages granted to existing stockholders. The board further stipulated "that the proceeds . . . shall be applied to the redemption of the outstanding Bonds of the State."[124]

Similarly, in February 1850, when a widow was no longer able to make the mortgage payments due to the CAPL for her St. Charles sugar plantation, she "gave and abandoned unto said institution" the estate and fifty-three enslaved individuals "in payment & settlement of her debt to said Institution."[125] The following November, the bank auctioned off the property "at 12 o'clock at the St. Louis Exchange." About 60 percent of the aging workforce was over the age of forty (one-third over fifty), and only 40 percent of the individuals were aged twenty or under. None of the enslaved were between the ages of twenty-one and forty, and only 11 percent were teenagers from fifteen to twenty. By the day of the sale, seventy-year-old field hand Azor had died, and forty-five-year-old Jean, a mulatto workman, was "now a run away." Another slaveholder purchased the entire plantation with this elderly workforce for $76,000, paying $16,000 cash and the remainder in ten annual installments from 1852 through 1861. Again, the CAPL sold the property "free of Bank Stock."[126]

Whereas the CAPL focused on gradually liquidating its existing mortgages in compliance with the spirit of the legislation, the Citizens' Bank continued its operations (with the exception of issuing new banknotes) as if it still possessed a valid state charter. The bank directors immediately committed the bank to meeting its bond obligations, declaring in June 1842: "[I]t is deemed of vital importance to this Institution that its obligations in Europe for which the stock is a guarantee should be punctually met and . . . it is considered a sacred duty on the part of the Board of Directors to provide for the same by every means in their power."[127] In particular, the board warned the legislature not to default on these bonds. "The protest of the State Bonds in Europe would not only discredit all the Banks resting on Capital borrowing in Europe on State Bonds but would be followed by results so disastrous to the State, to our own stockholders and to the whole community that the undersigned cannot but think that an event fraught with so much danger ought to be avoided as long as possible."[128] Yet when the state failed to step in and help the bank to make those payments, the district court ordered the bank into foreclosure in November, with the directors "called upon to deliver up the assetts [*sic*] of the institution to the commissioners of Liquidation appointed by the Executive."[129]

In his extended address to the board of directors on the question of liquidation, bank president Edmond Jean Forstall clearly stated "that the Interest of the State and the Stockholders is identical and that any injury or benefit done to the latter must be equally injurious or beneficial to the former." He then defiantly asserted his interpretation of the liquidation statutes. "So long as [the stockholders] punctually pay the interests & curtailments required upon the money loaned them on their stock, and so long as the moneys thus collected suffice to keep the faith of the state inviolate, they remain undisturbed in the possession of their property and ever guarded against seizure by other parties, the Mortgage in favor of the Bank, in the present prostrated condition of Real Estate, acting as a kind of protection." Indeed, Forstall considered it the bank's "duty to protect by every means in our power, the Real Estate whereupon the Bonds issued are based." Forstall intended the bank simultaneously to fulfill its obligations to the bondholders, while also continuing to serve the financial needs of the planters of Louisiana.[130]

Yet Forstall's statement was not merely an act of defiance against the state in protection of delinquent debtors. If the bank was to continue serving the slaveholders of the state, it would need to ensure the soundness of its balance sheet. Thus, three days after the president's speech, the board passed new rules and bylaws mandating that "every person, or subscriber applying for a transfer of Stock, or for a loan" provide complete documentation on the property including "a chain of titles for the last twenty five preceding years," "the certificate of appraisement," and a list of any current liens on the property.[131] Two months later, the board ordered a complete audit of the "true condition of the property mortgaged" in order "to ascertain the true condition of the Bank." It appointed three stockholders "from among those not in arrears" for each parish to form a standing committee "To ascertain the true condition of the property mortgaged to the Bank in said Parish & the income thereof.... To prevent, where Negroes are mortgaged with the Land, the removal of said Negroes . . . to suggest such measures as they may think necessary to the safety and welfare of the Bank.... To inform ... of any fraud that may come within their knowledge. . . . [and] to exercise a general supervision on all property mortgaged to the Bank."[132] With this information in hand, the Citizens' Bank essentially operated as a private (unchartered) plantation bank for the next decade. Unlike the CAPL, which behaved as a bank in active (if slow) liquidation, the Citizens' Bank interacted with its stockholders and debtors as a fully functioning bank—absent the banknotes (chapter 9).

*

Unlike the Panic of 1819, which led to an expansion of the relationship between banking and the system of slavery, the Panics of 1837 and 1839 precipitated an anti-banking backlash, particularly in those states that had suffered most from specie suspensions, bank failures, and foreclosures. These experiences left southerners seriously questioning the wisdom of banks in general, and long-term loans secured by land and human property in particular. Whereas the state of Louisiana had been at the forefront of southern banking during the 1830s, with bank expansion widely supported by both Whig and Democrat politicians, by the 1840s it became one of the most aggressive states on the anti-banking front. The combined failures of many plantation banks, improvement banks, and traditional commercial banks left the treasury empty and the state heavily in debt, particularly for millions of dollars in state-backed bonds. As early as 1841, there were calls for "a convention to remedy the glaring evils of the constitution of 1812." While a major goal of constitutional reformers was expanding the franchise to all white males and limiting the power of New Orleans over the rest of the state, a critical piece of that reform involved adding language to restrict the powers of the legislature to incorporate banks and other business institutions.[133] As one historian of Louisiana politics has summarized this debate, Democrats "believed that the best way to shield the people's liberty from these 'monsters' was for the state to outlaw banks and monopolies and to remove government support from all private commercial endeavors," as well as implementing "a more strict enforcement of the charters of existing corporations."[134]

Banks had helped to finance the movement of enslaved labor to the frontier and had facilitated slaveholders in weathering the depression, thereby paving the way for the South to emerge as a global economic powerhouse by mid-century. Yet as these frontier states became more established and entered a new, more mature stage of development, they actively rejected the further support of these same innovative banking establishments. Other financial institutions—including private banks, out-of-state banks, and cotton or sugar factors—quickly stepped in to fill the void. When southern states reconsidered the incorporation of banks during the 1850s, the more developed slave economy no longer required institutions specifically designed to support that system, and they instead largely embraced the conservative banking model of the Eastern Seaboard states.

9
From Commercial Banking to Private Finance

In his first state of the state address after narrowly winning election in 1844, the new Democrat governor of Louisiana, Alexandre Mouton, reflected the sentiments of many citizens when he laid the blame for the state's economic woes at the feet of the chartered corporations that benefited from the support of the state at the expense of the taxpayers. Describing the 1820s and 1830s as "the era of idleness, bank expansion and ruinous speculation," he simultaneously celebrated and lamented "that the capitalless [*sic*] banks have been shorn of their power to bring ruin on the country, while they ruin themselves." Among his recommendations for economic retrenchment were for "all attempts at internal improvement—which have signally failed—[to] be abandoned," and for the state to divest itself of its shares of bank stock in the semipublic Bank of Louisiana, as well as of the stock it had acquired in the Mechanics' & Traders' Bank. He ended with a call on the General Assembly to "afford the people every facility to exercise without restriction, their sovereign power" by holding a convention to amend the state constitution.[1] In two separate state referenda on the question, pro-convention forces prevailed, with 62 percent of the popular vote on the first and then 80 percent on the second referendum. Bending to this overwhelming popular will, the Whig legislature finally gave in, and the convention convened in August 1844.[2]

There was no shortage of anti-banking rhetoric at the constitutional convention.[3] One representative from New Orleans blamed the "present lamentable and deplorable condition of our State affairs" on the "wild and reckless spirit of extravagance which had been fostered by evil legislation" and spoke of "the creation of a vast banking capital—of an inflated currency, and of the thousand mad and ruinous schemes which had been projected by our State legislature, and which were the copious fountains from whence have flowed the evils that now impend upon us."[4] Another representative asserted that "so high did the banking mania rage here, that I heard a senator in his place say yesterday that the projects of charters flew about the city like falling leaves in autumn, and that they were piled up so high on the secretary's desk in the house of representatives, of which he was then a member, that he could not see the secretary's face for them." But, he asked, "for whose benefit were these banks chartered?"[5]

Answering his own question, he continued that it was "the merchant, broker, schemer and idler" rather than "the productive laborer," leading to "universal ruin" for all but "a few fortunate individuals." In the very chartering of banks, the legislature had taken the "sovereign power of the State" and "delegated and transferred" it "from the people to these soulless corporations" who were "out of the reach of any regulator." While he conceded "that the planters and others in the country"—besides New Orleans merchants—"have voluntarily borrowed large amounts from the banks, and have been as much benefited as the city merchant," their folly in having "borrowed large sums during the rage of the speculative mania" only hurt themselves. The merchant, on the other hand, never suffered for his gambles; he merely passed on his debts by "increas[ing] his profits upon the producer to a sufficient amount to enable him to pay his interest, and realize a profit besides, for himself." Thus "this enormous debt that has been fastened upon the banks, must all be paid by the product of useful labor," i.e., by the planters of the state. "They are the *real* paymasters, and the *real* sufferers, and when they become involved in the banks by mortgages or otherwise, it is fortunate if they escape without losing all they have."[6]

Despite these impassioned pleas, it remained to be seen if the anti-banking forces at the convention would be able to prevail on the majority, including many Democrats who were more moderate on the banking question. Indeed, the initial proposal that emerged from the committee on banking issues was only a mild revision of the banking laws. It suggested requiring six months' public notice for any proposed legislation regarding the creation, renewal, or extension of corporations "with banking or discounting privileges," limiting any future charters to a maximum length of twenty years, and including "a clause reserving to the legislature the power to alter, revoke, or annul the same whenever, in their opinion, it may be expedient to do so." Yet Mr. Brent of Rapides Parish, a mixed sugar-and-cotton area in central Louisiana, immediately moved to strike out the majority of this section, reducing it to "No corporate body shall be hereafter created, renewed or extended with banking privileges." Several committee members then spoke up with regards to the proposal. Mr. Lewis from St. Landry Parish (also a mixed agricultural region of central Louisiana)—who "was *in toto* an anti-bank man"—claimed that he had made a similar suggestion in committee "but was overruled."[7]

Yet his colleague, Mr. Conrad of Orleans Parish, was concerned about the long-term implications of such a drastic measure, and stood up to defend the initial, more moderate language by pointing out some flaws in the anti-banking logic. "What would it avail the State of Louisiana to prohibit the incorporation of banks within her limits, if the other States, particularly the adjoining States, should not imitate her example?" Anticipating the problems that would result "if we prohibit the establishment of banks," Conrad predicted that "our State will be flooded with the paper of the banks of other States, over which we can exercise no control, and thus we will be made to share their losses without being able to participate in their profits." As a result, he was in favor of "restricting the legislature in the power to incorporate banks, and to prevent the deplorable mischiefs which have resulted from the abuse of that power, but to deprive them of it entirely was farther than he was prepared to go."[8] Despite this defense, the bank supporters were vastly outnumbered, with the convention as a whole voting 38–19 *against* the original proposal and in favor of the more draconian, anti-banking clause.[9] In November of 1845, by a vote of 12,277 to 1,395, Louisiana voters overwhelmingly ratified this new constitution with its banking ban.[10]

Whereas innovative banking institutions had been essential to the expansion of the slave South during the 1820s and 1830s, southerners after the panics no longer viewed this relationship as necessary. The more mature plantation system of the late 1840s instead relied for its financing on the few remaining banks, private (unchartered) banks, and mercantile firms that were expanding into plantation finance. By the 1850s, several frontier states began to reconsider their strict anti-banking policies. Yet in returning to bank finance, they explicitly rejected the financialization of slavery by banking institutions, reverting instead to the much more conservative free-banking model that was then growing in popularity.

An Anti-Banking Backlash

In the aftermath of the panics, especially in those states of the Midwest and Southwest that experienced the worst banking failures, anti-banking legislators rose to power. Only four new banks received charters on the southern frontier between 1844 and 1850, and three of these were in the more settled states of Kentucky and Tennessee (table 9.1). The Tennessee legislature even hid the incorporation of the Lawrenceburg Bank (chartered in 1848 with a capital of $100,000–$300,000) within the charter of the Hartsville and Nashville

Glass and Soda Manufacturing Company; only the first two sections of the charter related to the manufactory, while the remaining four established the bank.[11] The Southern Bank of Kentucky—first chartered in 1839—and the Bank of East Tennessee only began operations in 1850.[12] A fourth institution in Florida never opened its doors. This anti-banking backlash was similar in the Midwest. In the wake of the depression, both Wisconsin and Illinois went without any state-chartered banks until 1847 and 1852 (respectively). Indiana had only its State Bank, with multiple branches throughout the state, until the 1850s. While two of the three new banks that Michigan chartered during the depression survived, it only added a third in 1845. The notable exception to this anti-banking trend in the Midwest was Ohio, where the legislature chartered a large, integrated banking system in 1845.[13]

In addition to Louisiana's constitutional ban on banking in 1845, Texas's first constitution, also in 1845, declared that "[n]o corporate body shall hereafter be created, renewed or extended with banking or discounting privileges," while Arkansas passed a constitutional amendment in 1846 stating that "[n]o Bank or Banking Institution, shall be hereafter incorporated, or established in this State."[14] The new constitutions of California (1849) and Oregon (1857) allowed only banks of deposit, but not note-issuing institutions.[15] Both Arkansas and Florida were left with no state-chartered banks until the eve of the Civil War. The Northern Bank of Mississippi—which had initially been chartered in 1837 as a joint railroad-banking company but then reorganized before opening its doors in 1838 as only a bank—was the sole institution to survive the depression and enjoyed a monopoly on banking in that state through 1858.[16] Similarly, the newly organized Bank of the State of Missouri

TABLE 9.1 Southern bank charters, 1843–1850

Region	*Total banks end of 1843*	*New charters 1844–50*	*Closures 1844–50*	*Total banks end of 1850*	*Percentage of banks closed 1844–50*	*Growth rate of banking 1844–50*
Mid-Atlantic (MD, DE, DC)	34	4	(5)	33	13%	-3%
Old South (VA, NC, SC)	21	2	(0)	23	0%	10%
Upper frontier (KY, TN, MO, AR)	8	3	(1)	10	9%	25%
Lower frontier (GA, AL, MS, LA, FL)	20	1	(4)	17	19%	-15%
Totals	83	10	(10)	83	10%	0%

Source: Weber, *Census of Early State Banks.*

(chartered in 1837) monopolized banking in that state until 1857, while the Bank of Mobile was the only institution in Alabama until 1851.

Without access to bank loans or the expanding money supply provided by fractional-reserve banking and banknotes, economic growth throughout the frontier South and Midwest was temporarily stifled. Yet as delegate Conrad had warned during the Louisiana constitutional convention, out-of-state banks stepped into this void. Between 1845 and 1853, historian Larry Schweikart estimates, banks from New York, Charleston, and Savannah opened ten to fourteen agencies in the state of Florida.[17] He also asserts that Louisiana banks stepped in to fill the gaps in Arkansas, Mississippi, Texas, and Missouri.[18] Yet given the severe contraction of banking capital in Louisiana—and, indeed, throughout most of the country—the ability of out-of-state banks to meet these banking needs was limited.

Even for those banks with monopolies in their respective states, their lending was constrained by the amount of their capitalization. The largest Louisiana bank to retain its charter was the Bank of Louisiana, with its $4 million in capital. Just as it had done before the panic, it continued offering large, long-term mortgages throughout the 1840s and 1850s—in violation of the $5,000 loan limit of its charter. In 1844, it lent $54,000 to one resident of Huntsville, Alabama, secured by the plantation and two hundred enslaved individuals she had recently inherited from her grandmother in the parish of Rapides.[19] That same year, another slaveholder secured a $30,000 loan with his sugar plantation and seventy-eight enslaved workers in Orleans Parish, while a third received $20,000 on three tracts of land and 107 enslaved lives in West Feliciana.[20] The bank's mortgages just for the month of January 1845 included $27,000 on a sugar plantation called "La Vacherie Dugué Livandais" and eighty-nine enslaved workers in Lafourche, and $20,000 each to planters in Madison, St. Mary, and (two in) West Feliciana—all secured by plantations and enslaved lives.[21] In 1846, another slaveholder received $47,000 on her St. James sugar plantation and eighty-six enslaved individuals.[22] The owners of the Bellechase sugar plantation and 103 lives (not including infants) received $50,000 in 1852.[23] Another planter received the same large sum in 1853 for his Orleans sugar plantation and 106 workers, while a third pair borrowed $60,000 for their Ardogne sugar plantation and eighty-five enslaved workers in Terrebonne.[24] The bank lent sums ranging from $6,000 to $60,000 to dozens of other planters throughout the state during this period, greatly benefiting some of the state's largest slaveholders. But the extent and overall impact of its lending was still curtailed by its capital limits.

A greater proportion of the demand that remained unmet by the surviving state-chartered banks was instead filled by "private bankers"—anyone who provided banking services without a valid state charter. This group included formerly chartered banks like the Citizens' Bank, which continued its operations after surrendering its charter; businessmen like Jacob Barker or James Robb, who operated unchartered firms that specialized in providing banking services; and commission merchants or factors, who increasingly offered banking services to their existing customers. Given the vagueness of the definition for private bankers, it is difficult to estimate their numbers with much precision. Private bankers seem to have targeted underbanked parts of the shifting southern frontier. Schweikart estimates that between twenty-six and fifty were located in Missouri by 1860, providing vital capital to farmers and slaveholders in the growing region.[25] Another historian estimates that 2,638 private firms offered $3 million in loans throughout Texas in 1858.[26] Although the operations of these private bankers is largely outside of the scope of this book, this chapter will examine a few examples of merchant bankers in action in Louisiana—particularly when they stepped in to replace a bank in an existing creditor-debtor relationship.

The Citizens' Bank as Private Banker

Even without a legal state charter, the Citizens' Bank continued all its banking functions except note issuance throughout the 1840s and 1850s. In December 1847, the bank's board resolved that it needed "an accurate record as to the nature and value" of the collateral securing its mortgages. The cashier was directed to write each stockholder, "inviting them to forward as soon as possible" a report on the status of their property, including "a statement of the Improvements" and "A List of all the Slaves now attached."[27] Perhaps realizing the folly of relying on the stockholders to self-report, several days later the board resolved to have the cashier "procure from the State Treasurer's office a list of the Slaves belonging to all the Stockholders of the Bank as have Mortgaged Slaves and Lands as security for their Stock."[28] The cashier was then "directed to prepare . . . the Record Book of Securities."[29] This report included the name of each stockholder and number of shares, parish, a concise description of the property including the number of enslaved lives, an appraisement of the property in 1847 (only provided in just over half the entries), the amount of delinquency or arrears as of February 1, 1847 (again only occasionally noted), and some purchase and sale comments. This unique compilation provides a rare snapshot of the bank's operations at mid-century (table 9.2).[30] Subsequent, undated notations to the text slightly complicate the document's interpretation. For example, most of the names are crossed out, likely indicating the completion of the contract (but with no indication of when it was

TABLE 9.2 Enslaved lives mortgaged to the Citizens' Bank of Louisiana, 1847

		Number of mortgages with slaves (number appraised)	*Average property appraisal*	*Number of enslaved people mortgaged*	*Average slaves per mortgage*	*Percentage of parish's enslaved people mortgaged*
Major sugar parishes 1840 & 1850	St. Bernard	16 (7)	$72,731.43	519	32	22.34%
	Plaquemines	16 (6)	$57,519.67	869	54	18.18%
	St. Charles	15 (9)	$49,766.67	562	37	13.60%
	St. James	19 (10)	$62,727.00	980	52	12.64%
	West Baton Rouge	13 (10)	$49,670.00	539	41	12.39%
	Iberville	39 (18)	$38,896.89	1,029	26	11.96%
	Assumption	30 (17)	$27,105.00	571	19	10.69%
	Remaining five	34 (19)	$49,711.76	938	28	3.09%
	Total	182 (96)	$47,941.43	6,007	33	8.88%
Minor sugar parishes 1840 & 1850	St. Tammany	10 (5)	$34,025.00	314	31	13.29%
	Jefferson	20 (11)	$58,670.91	684	34	11.04%
	Remaining thirteen	107 (63)	$35,320.70	3,154	29	3.41%
	Total	137 (79)	$36,814.08	4,152	30	4.12%
Twenty non-sugar parishes						
	Total	31 (16)	$42,376.25	1,121	36	1.47%

Source: Citizens' Bank 1847 Ledger, Canal Bank; Seventh Census, 1850, Louisiana, M-432, reels 242–247, Census (SS); *Compendium of the Enumeration of the Inhabitants and Statistics of the United States, Sixth Census* (Washington: Thomas Allen, 1841): 240; *Statistical View of the United States . . . being a Compendium of the Seventh Census* (Washington: A. O. P. Nicholson, 1854): 242–253.

completed). Several entries are marked "purchased by bank" without date, and other notations likewise appear to be additions.

In the twelve parishes with the highest concentration of sugar production per capita in 1840 and 1850, the Citizens' Bank held 182 mortgages on 6,007 enslaved lives, or almost 9 percent of the enslaved population in those parishes. Mortgages encompassed an even greater percentage of the enslaved in the individual parishes of St. Bernard (22 percent), Plaquemines (18 percent), St. Charles (14 percent), St. James (13 percent), West Baton Rouge (12 percent), Iberville (12 percent), and Assumption (11 percent). In the next fifteen parishes, which produced a lower percentage of sugar per capita, the Citizens' Bank held 137 mortgages on 4,152 enslaved lives, or just over 4 percent of the enslaved in those parishes. The slaveholders of St. Tammany (13 percent) and Jefferson (11 percent) held a significant number of mortgages, while the remaining minor sugar parishes possessed mortgages covering just 3 percent of their enslaved people. And in the twenty parishes that produced little or no sugar, the Citizens' Bank held only thirty-one mortgages on 1,121 enslaved lives, or about 1.5 percent of the enslaved population. Thus, even while technically in liquidation, the Citizens' Bank continued to finance a significant proportion of the sugar planters of the state.

Digging deeper into this data, the Citizens' Bank lent mainly to medium and large (but not the very largest) slaveholders in these parishes (table 9.3). According to the slave schedule of the 1850 manuscript census, 68 percent of slaveholders in St. Bernard Parish possessed ten or fewer people and only 3 percent possessed more than one hundred; the average slaveholder held eighteen individuals and the median slaveholder held just five. Yet the Citizens' Bank listed no small (ten or fewer) or extremely large (over one hundred) slaveholders as customers in this parish. Half their customers owned between twenty-six and fifty people; the average customer had thirty-two and the median had thirty-five enslaved individuals. The story in Plaquemines was similar. The vast majority of slaveholders (73 percent) possessed ten or fewer enslaved people, and only 6 percent owned over one hundred; the average slaveholder owned twenty and the median held five. The bank customers, by contrast, averaged fifty-four enslaved lives each, with a median of thirty-three. These customers were spread roughly evenly among the middle and large slaveholders: 31 percent held eleven to twenty-five; 19 percent held twenty-six to fifty; 25 percent held fifty-one to one hundred; and 19 percent held over one hundred. Although a larger percentage of bank loans financed small slaveholders with ten or fewer individuals in St. Charles (29 percent), St. Tammany (30 percent), West Baton Rouge (23 percent), and Iberville (21 percent), their lending still disproportionately went to large slaveholders owning twenty-six to one hundred enslaved lives.

As the board of directors' meeting minutes from the late 1840s and early 1850s make clear, the bank continued to grant mortgages to stockholders and collect loan payments, transfer mortgage liens and bank stock from one enslaver to another upon the sale of property, appraise the property being offered for mortgage, renegotiate contracts with some delinquent debtors, and foreclose on others. Indeed, the board of directors' minutes from this time period are remarkably similar to those from before the panic. Debtors, for example, routinely asked permission to substitute enslaved property on their mortgages. On March 27, 1849, "Mr. Bernard Marigny applied for a release of mortgage on the slave Celina and her two children and to mortgage in their stead the slave Anna aged 30 years and her two children François & Euladich which was granted after due appraisement shall have been made &

TABLE 9.3 Number of enslaved people in Citizens' Bank mortgages (1847) vs. number owned by average slaveholder in 1850 census

	St. Bernard Parish		*Plaquemines Parish*		*St. Charles Parish*		*St. Tammany Parish*		*West Baton Rouge Parish*		*Iberville Parish*	
Number of enslaved people	*Census*	*Bank*	*Census*	*Bank*	*Census*	*Bank*	*Census*	*Bank*	*Census*	*Bank*	*Census*	*Bank*
1–10	68%	0%	73%	6%	54%	29%	80%	30%	65%	23%	48%	21%
11–25	9%	37.5%	9%	31%	19%	29%	11%	20%	16%	31%	25%	41%
26–50	10%	50%	4%	19%	3%	7%	5%	30%	7%	8%	11%	21%
51–100	9%	12.5%	8%	25%	14%	36%	4%	20%	9%	31%	11%	15%
100+	3%	0%	6%	19%	10%	0%	0%	0%	3%	8%	4%	0%
Average	18	32	20	54	32	40	9	31	18	41	25	27
Median	5	35	5	33	9	22	4	25	6	22	11	21
Percentage under mortgage	22.34%		18.18%		13.6%		13.29%		12.39%		11.96%	

Source: Citizens' Bank 1847 Ledger, Canal Bank; *Seventh Census*, 1850, Louisiana, M-432, reels 244–247, Census (SS). Census data only includes whites who owned at least one enslaved person

accepted."[31] On June 7, 1849, "Mr Saml W. Logan of the parish of St Charles applied for a release of the mortgage . . . on the two slaves Eddy & his daughter Patsey," substituting two others.[32] On April 24, 1850, "Mrs. Mandeville Marigny [Bernard Marigny's wife] applied for a release of mortgage on the slave York whom she intends to sell, he being too weak for the work of her brick yard [in St. Tammany], offering to apply the proceeds of said sale to the purchase of another slave," who would then be encompassed in the original mortgage.[33]

Similarly, Albert Fabre requested "a release of mortgage of the mulatto slave Isidore aged 43 years[,] . . . the mulatto boy Theodore aged 17[,] . . . [and] Cécile aged 16 years, Milly aged 40, Augustine aged 17," because they were "not fit for the work of his plantation" and he wished to sell them. He offered "to transfer the mortgage" from Isidore to "the negro slave Jacques about 40," and from Theodore to "another slave to the satisfaction of the bank." For the remaining three, he requested "a delay of 60 days" so that he could obtain "other slaves to the satisfaction of the bank, to be purchased by him out of the proceeds of said sale & whom he binds himself to mortgage to the bank."[34] John F. Miller's January 28, 1851, application to release sixteen enslaved individuals from his mortgage included a mother and five children, a husband and wife, a set of young siblings, and a mother and son. He proposed to replace them with sixteen different enslaved people, including another husband-and-wife couple, a set of parents with their three children, and a mother and her four children.[35] The bank routinely granted these requests, but the extra delay and layer of bureaucracy involved continued to make enslaved lives less liquid as assets than non-mortgaged slaves.[36]

In May of 1849, the bank seized the plantation of a delinquent debtor named Charles Fagot. It planned to place the land, enslaved lives, and bank shares all up for sheriff's sale in July, but worried that it would not be able to attain an adequate purchase price to cover the entirety of the mortgage investment. If no bidder offered at least $18,010.50, the bank's representative was "authorized to employ an overseer or keeper, to be put in charge of [the] plantation . . . at a reasonable salary or compensation, or to take any other measure which he may deem necessary or expedient for the preservation of [the] property." As instructed, the bank's agent purchased the property at the sheriff's sale for $11,000 as the highest bidder. The agent immediately sold off the enslaved individuals separately, "with the exception of the slave Marie." The instructions for the sale made it clear that "After the property & slaves mortgaged shall have been sold, if the Bank is paid in full, the slave Marie shall not be sold. . . . If on the contrary the Bank is not paid in full, then the slave Marie shall be offered for sale . . . said slave together with her offspring remaining always subject to the mortgage securing the stock."[37] Clearly Fagot sought to protect Marie from sale; perhaps she possessed particularly valuable skills, or perhaps his interest in her was sexual—the record provides little guidance on this. And while the bank was not willing to release her entirely from the mortgage contract, it was willing to indulge this special request as long as it did not harm its financial claims. Despite the immediate sale of the enslaved lives, the bank retained the Fagot land until some future point when it could find a more profitable buyer.[38] In the fall of 1850 the bank would similarly purchase the plantation, enslaved workers, and stock shares of delinquent borrower S. Peyman at a sheriff's sale, successfully reselling the whole lot to Albert Fabre.[39]

Marie was not the only enslaved individual to receive special treatment from the bank. In 1852, the bank was willing to pay up to $500 to recover a young slave named Dick who worked on the plantation of Felix Garcia. For an unstated reason, the boy had "been arrested & sold at Liberty, Mississippi." While the bank was not disputing the reasons for the arrest and sale, they were willing to pay Fr. Dauncy $50 plus traveling expenses to find and repurchase Dick; he would receive only $25 if he failed to complete the task.[40] Dick must have been particularly valuable on the Garcia plantation to warrant such expensive efforts.

The persistence of the bank's operations is most evident in its extended interaction with one set of debtors from the 1830s through the 1850s. In the late 1830s, Felix Garcia was one of the most powerful politicians in Louisiana. He had been elected to the state senate around 1836 at the age of thirty-three, and by 1838 was selected as senate president—the position second in line to the governorship.[41] In September of 1838, he also served as the legal proxy ("fondé de pouvoir") for his mother-in-law with the Citizens' Bank. Marie Hortense Wiltz Arnauld, the widow of Jean Eleanor Arnauld, subscribed for 250 shares of stock in the bank and acquired 106 more from other stockholders. To secure these 356 shares, she mortgaged to the bank her sugar plantation in the parish of St. John the Baptist and its forty enslaved workers.[42] By the following month, she had acquired an additional 233 shares from the Compagnie des Canaux de Barataria & de LaFourche (the Barataria & LaFourche Canal Company). The bank agreed that the existing mortgage on her property was sufficient to cover these additional shares, making the assessed value of her property at least $58,900.[43]

As was her right as a stockholder, the widow Arnauld was permitted to borrow up to half the value of her stock from the bank as a formal loan—$29,450—renewable for up to ten years upon repayment of at least one-tenth of the principle plus interest every year.[44] In April 1839, Arnauld (with Garcia still acting as her proxy) borrowed an additional $5,000, "to be secured by Mortgage on her property & slaves already mortgaged to the bank for stock together with a pledge of said stock."[45] Although this loan was small relative to the appraised value of her property, her accumulated loans with the bank must already have surpassed the 50 percent limit. Thus she added fourteen more enslaved individuals to the mortgage, and promised to repay this amount in only five months, renouncing her right to annual renewals of up to ten years.[46] But the widow failed to fulfill this obligation, and in October requested an additional extension, secured by a note of Felix Garcia and his business partner, Achille Lorio.[47]

By the fall of 1839, Garcia was himself a member of the bank's board of directors, being elected by the legislature as one of the state's six bank representatives.[48] He simultaneously began acquiring Citizens' Bank stock in his own name. His first fifty-seven shares were secured by the sugar plantation he owned jointly with Lorio in the parish of St. Charles. The plantation "with the improvements other than the mill" was valued at $18,000, plus an additional $10,500 for its twenty-two enslaved individuals.[49] In March 1840, the partners purchased twenty-three more enslaved individuals at an auction in New Orleans; these individuals comprised about one-third of the workers from an estate-liquidation sale (at what is now the Whitney Plantation historic site).[50] Using this new human property as additional collateral, the partners added another 175 shares in April and July of 1840, for a total of 232 shares secured by their sugar plantation.[51] The following year, Garcia applied for a $30,000 loan from the bank, which far exceeded the $11,600 loan to which he was entitled. The bank demanded additional mortgages on his house, sawmill, and fifteen more enslaved individuals, as well as either additional third-party notes (if the bank's attorney deemed them adequately liquid) or an acceptable endorsement from another third party.[52]

One year later, in April 1842, Garcia and Adolphe Sorapuru—a judge in St. John the Baptist Parish and the father of a prominent Creole family of color—jointly mortgaged several different tracts of land in St. Charles Parish, a sugar mill, and seventy-two enslaved lives to the Consolidated Association of Planters of Louisiana (CAPL) in exchange for 240 shares of stock, valued at $120,000. The pair immediately obtained a $60,000 loan from the CAPL, secured by that stock.[53] The widow Arnauld likewise applied for and received an additional loan of $13,896 from the Citizens' Bank in May of 1843.[54]

Up to this point, the relationship of both the widow Arnauld and her son-in-law, Felix Garcia, with the Citizens' Bank and the CAPL was pretty typical. Both held stock in the banks, secured by their land and human property. Both continued to expand these holdings by acquiring additional shares from other stockholders. Garcia eventually owned 372 shares in the Citizens' Bank secured by the plantation, sawmill, and enslaved workers in St. Charles Parish; the assessed value of this property was $44,000. Arnauld's extensive sugar plantation on the left bank of the Mississippi River at Bonnet Carré in St. John the Baptist Parish contained sixty-nine to seventy-seven enslaved lives. It secured 831 shares of Citizens' Bank stock, representing a minimum value of $83,100. And both had acquired loans from the bank, collateralized with this property and stock.[55] It was also not unusual for large planters to obtain loans simultaneously from more than one bank, as Garcia had done.

But whereas many previous debtors had suffered as the result of economic downturns like the Panic of 1837 or the liquidation of the banks, the troubles for Garcia and Arnauld began with Mother Nature. At about ten o'clock in the morning on Thursday, August 1, 1844, the levee protecting the plantation of Madame Arnauld at Bonnet Carré broke, an event known locally as a crevasse. Within an hour, "the crevasse was fifteen feet wide and fifteen feet deep, and continued to increase with fearful rapidity."[56] By three o'clock in the afternoon, it "had extended sixty feet in width and eight feet in depth . . . the water was pouring through the place like a mill tail. The dwelling house was considered in much danger, as it was entirely surrounded by water." Workers traveled thirty-five miles to New Orleans to obtain a spile-driving machine (seen in figure 9.1 at the point of the breach of another crevasse), which could be used to drive small wooden pilings (known as spiles) into the ground to shore up the embankment and prevent further damage, but they were unsuccessful.[57] By Saturday, the crevasse was eighty-seven feet wide by twenty-two feet deep, "and the water was rushing through the opening with a velocity and in such a body that a current was drawn from the middle of the river." Several surrounding plantations were now also underwater. The local government had sent machines and laborers to assist with the breach, but locals feared "that the whole of the Trémé suburb will be flooded."[58]

A full week later, the flooding continued. "The water flows through it in a perfect torrent, and nothing but a fall of the river can put a stop to the destruction going on." Travelers on the river reported "that the roaring of the water through the breach can be heard at the distance of two miles."[59] Bonnet Carré and the surrounding plantations now resembled "a large lake."[60] The enterprising owners of several steamers began running sightseeing excursions to the disaster for the next few weeks. Charging between $1 and $1.50, passengers could take a round-trip tour from New Orleans, spending one to two hours at the crevasse; "[r]efreshments will be provided on board."[61] An image from another crevasse in 1858 shows sightseers similarly observing the disaster (figure 9.1).

FIGURE 9.1. *The Late Crevasse at Bell's Plantation, near New Orleans*, June 5, 1858. Wood engraving, 6½ × 10½ in. http://hnoc.minisisinc.com/thnoc/catalog/1/5303. Courtesy of the Historic New Orleans Collection, Williams Research Center, New Orleans, LA. Gift of Mr. Harold Schilke and Mr. Boyd Cruise.

On October 4, after the river had receded, the Citizens' Bank sent a member of the board of directors to assess the damage. He concluded that it would be impossible for the widow Arnauld to plant a crop "without great Expense for rebuilding the Levee anew," which he estimated would cost at least $4,200, in addition to the cost of "a supply of Cane for Planting and Supplies of provisions clothing &c for the Slaves &c before any revenue could be made thereon." The widow separately wrote the board, advising it that she was unable to make the repairs "for want of the necessary means." The bank, "as her largest creditor & holding the first mortgage on the Plantation," would have to invest in the levee itself. "Considering the very large amount due this Bank by Mrs. Arnauld secured by mortgage on said Plantation," the board resolved to rebuild the levee "with the Slaves of the Plantation, and to furnish the provisions & clothing necessary, until the plantation can be seized & sold."[62]

Despite being technically in a state of liquidation, the bank spent the next sixteen months trying to repair the levee and prepare the plantation for sale. It also needed to resolve any outside claims on the property. For example, the widow had purchased two new enslaved laborers—Brisson, aged thirty-seven, and Peter, aged twenty-five—from a local estate in April 1843 for $2,720. With accumulated interest, she still owed $1,200 to the estate. "The

Slaves being very valuable," the board decided that "it would be injurious to the interest of the Bank to permit them to be seized and sold separately to satisfy the claim." The bank negotiated with the estate, agreeing to pay $1,000 to settle the debt.[63] With this final claim resolved, the bank foreclosed on the Arnauld property, instructing the sheriff to seize and sell the plantation and enslaved individuals, and to advertise the property in several newspapers in both French and English.[64] Not receiving any attractive offers, the bank then proceeded to purchase the property on its own account.[65]

Meanwhile, Felix Garcia's finances were also teetering on the edge. In addition to the $30,000 loan from 1841, he had accumulated several additional debts with the bank through discounted notes, which were often endorsed by his partner, Achille Lorio, who died in 1845.[66] By 1846, these debts totaled $40,479.23, and were "mostly uncovered by proper securities." Garcia proposed a plan which would reorganize his debts with better security, while simultaneously taking the Arnauld plantation off the bank's hands. First, the bank would foreclose on seventeen of his mortgaged slaves, purchasing them at the sheriff's sale. It would also purchase an additional tract of land bordering the Arnauld plantation for $1,060. The bank would then sell to Garcia the seventeen enslaved individuals, the new tract of land, and the entirety of the widow Arnauld's plantation and enslaved people—including her 831 shares of bank stock—for $109,685. He would pay a mere $1,060 in cash as part of this refinance (essentially covering the purchase of the adjoining land). The remainder would be divided between a stock loan of $31,660.60 on the Lorio plantation and a mortgage of $76,964.80 on the Arnauld plantation, payable in ten annual installments at 7 percent interest. To further secure the mortgage, Garcia offered to mortgage two other tracts of land to which he held claims, as well as fifty shares of stock valued at $5,000 in a drainage company. Finally, the bank would hold a mortgage on the crops raised on the Arnauld plantation, and "the Overseer of said plantation shall be such as the Bank will approve." The board estimated that this arrangement "presents an additional Security to the Bank of upwards of Twenty Thousand Dollars towards securing the debt due by Felix Garcia."[67] It finalized this elaborate sale in September 1846, a full two years after the devastating crevasse.[68]

The entire refinancing was ill-conceived, and problems emerged immediately. Garcia quickly purchased $3,965 worth of horses and mules for the plantation from a bank board member, but by February 1847 was "unable to pay the amount out of the present crop," and the seller was threatening to seize and resell the animals as a "consequence of [Garcia's] embarrassed situation." Yet the board believed that this resale would "prove a serious injury to the interest of this Bank" since "it would put it out of [Garcia's] power to make a crop to meet his Instalments . . . and that a forced sale of said plantation would fall far short of the price stipulated with him." The bank resolved to give the creditor "priority of privilege over that of this Bank upon the next crop" until he was fully repaid.[69] Three months later, Garcia was again asking the bank for a three-year extension on repaying overdue notes, totaling $9,178.25, on the Lorio plantation.[70] And he missed his first annual payment on the Arnauld plantation.[71]

Garcia was not only indebted to the Citizens' Bank but also to the CAPL, to which his entire $60,000 debt with Sorapuru from 1842 remained unpaid. Additionally, he would have to start paying the new $6 per share annual assessment on his 240 shares of stock, or $1,440 per year, beginning in June 1848. (Ironically, as president pro tem of the senate, Garcia had signed the 1847 bill mandating that property banks provide additional assets to meet their bond obligations, which directly led to the stock assessments.)[72] In July 1847, he negotiated a "prolongation de délai" ["extension of time"] with the CAPL, arguing that "ces délais sont nécessaires pour . . . payer la dite dette" ["these delays are necessary in order . . . to pay the said debt."] The CAPL agreed to extend payments on the $60,000 debt with 7 percent interest over eighteen years. But Garcia also stated that he wanted to "déniger [*sic*] une contribution annuelle de six piastres par action de la part des actionnaires" ["denounce an annual contribution of six dollars per share from the shareholders"]. Perhaps reflecting Garcia's powerful position in state politics, the CAPL relented, stating that "the above contribution required of six dollars per share, should be considered as payment asserted on the mortgage obligation" ["la contribution ci-dessus exigé de six piastres par action, devra être considérée comme paiement fait à valoir sur l'obligation hypothécaire"]. In effect, the bank agreed to waive his stock assessment as long as he paid the annual principal and interest due on his substantial loan.[73]

Despite these repeated extensions and refinancings, Garcia was too far in debt to recover. One year later, he missed his second mortgage payment to the Citizens' Bank and the board reported that Garcia's plantations and enslaved individuals were "in a state of general abandonment requiring early measures for their preservation." The bank immediately moved to foreclose on the property and people.[74] In several letters between April and July 1848, Garcia begged the Citizens' Bank to reconsider, and—once again—it relented and refinanced the debt. Beginning in April 1849, he was permitted to pay his balance in fifteen equal annual installments, plus interest, which lowered his annual payments. The bank retained all the same rights "concerning the pledge of the crops, the choice by the Bank of a city factor for their consignment & sale & of the overseers on the plantations."[75] Yet once again Garcia failed to uphold his end of the contract. The Citizens' Bank finally decided to take a different approach with this severely delinquent debtor, by engaging the intermediary managerial help of a merchant establishment.

Dunlop, Moncure & Co. of Richmond, Virginia

Throughout the 1830s and 1840s, frontier banks balanced between the necessity of foreclosing on delinquent slaveholders—who might also be their friends, relatives, neighbors, or business partners—and finding ways to help them meet their overdue obligations. Leniency in enforcement, creative refinancing, crop liens, and other mechanisms allowed many slaveholders to keep possession of their property. During the 1840s, this oversight increasingly involved bringing in outside firms to manage the plantation with the hope of improving its profitability. The mercantile firm of Dunlop, Moncure & Co. of Richmond, Virginia, had become heavily involved with the sugar trade in New Orleans. As early as 1842, it was advertising itself in that city's newspapers as "Commission Merchants and Auctioneers" specializing in sugar and molasses.[76] By the mid-1840s, the firm had also begun administering troubled sugar plantations in the area as a means of turning a quick profit. Rather than purchasing a plantation outright (an expensive and risky proposition), the firm would assume responsibility for paying the debts of the plantation owner (known as *subrogation*) in return for a substantial portion of the short-term profits (known as *antichresis*). The intention was to help stabilize a troubled debtor's finances without forcing them to sell their plantation and enslaved workers. The firm, which was often already a creditor of the slaveholder in question, sought to secure the payment of its own existing investment, while hopefully also making a quick short-term profit if its intervention was successful. The merchants also profited from the commissions on selling the debtor's crops.

For example, in 1846, John W. Bowles of St. Mary Parish was indebted to several people, including Dunlop, Moncure & Co. and (separately) Henry Moncure, one of its partners. The firm took responsibility for administering and paying Bowles's debts (the subrogation). In return, for three years his crops would "be shipped to [Moncure's] house in Richmond. . . . One-third of said debt and interest was to be paid annually, from the proceeds of each crop" (the antichresis). Any remaining profit would then be used to retire Bowles's other debts. If Dunlop, Moncure & Co. were successful, it would recoup the value of its debts, and Bowles would be able either to resume full ownership and operation of his plantation in a stronger financial position, or to sell it more advantageously.[77] As historian J. Carlyle Sitterson notes, factors leveraged their capital in these types of relationships by making commissions on the sale of the crops and on the sale of the plantation supplies, as well as earning profits from the interest on the loan itself.[78]

Left unstated was how or why this firm was in a better position to run a sugar plantation than the owner. Perhaps the partners believed that the debtor in question was operating inefficiently or irresponsibly, and just needed the expertise of a successful businessman to get back on track. Whatever the rationale, Dunlop, Moncure & Co. repeated various versions of this model throughout the late 1840s and early 1850s, administering the finances and—sometimes—the final sale of several sugar plantations. In 1849, it became administrator of the estate of the late Alexander Gordon in Jefferson Parish. Dunlop, Moncure & Co. agreed to take shipment of the sugar crop in Richmond, Virginia, in return for paying off the estate's creditors, which included the Citizens' Bank.[79] The plantation and its eighty-six enslaved laborers were then sold, with the purchasers assuming the remaining mortgage of $21,333.28 due to the Consolidated Association of Louisiana Planters in sixteen equal installments.[80]

Also in 1849, Henry Moncure assumed responsibility for the sale of the Bel Air sugar plantation in Plaquemines Parish, including its 209 enslaved individuals and "1379 Shares of the Stock of the Citizens' Bank of Louisiana, secured by mortgage on said plantation and slaves." As part of the purchase price, the buyer would pay $25,000 in cash, and the remainder in four equal installments, in addition to assuming the $33,746.04 still due the Citizens' Bank for the mortgage loan.[81] Henry Doyal purchased the plantation, but by 1855 Charles Moncure (another partner) was jointly running the estate with Doyal on the firm's behalf.[82] And in the winter of 1854–55, Moncure administered the sale of the sugar plantation and thirty-two enslaved individuals of the late Mathew Rogers and Mary Bell on Bayou Teche in the parish of St. Mary.[83]

Through these many interactions, the Citizens' Bank was familiar with the firm of Dunlop, Moncure & Co., as it was trying to resolve the ongoing debt issues of Felix Garcia. In April 1849, when the first installment of Garcia's latest refinance was due, he claimed that he "had been prevented from complying with his recent contract with the Bank . . . in consequence of the loss by fire of a Sugar House and a portion of his crop." Despite continuing to throw good money after bad, the bank concluded that it was too heavily invested in the plantation to abandon it. "It is a fact beyond the possibility of doubt that, by seizure & sale of Mr Garcia's plantations at this time & under existing circumstances, a very heavy loss would be sustained by the Bank."[84] Yet it was also unwilling to negotiate another refinance with Garcia.[85]

Instead, Dunlop, Moncure & Co. offered temporarily to take over operations of the Lorio and Arnauld plantations in order to get them financially solvent again. Garcia would "pass an act of antichresis" transferring full possession of the property's assets and production to the firm (from April 1849 to April 1851), during which time the firm would exercise full operational control of both plantations. Dunlop, Moncure & Co. would "advance the necessary charges and supplies for the said plantations, and the means wherewith to erect a new Sugar House, steam Engine & Mill, machinery and appurtenances thereto, in place of the one lately destroyed by fire, sufficient to take off and secure a full crop on said Arnauld Plantation," all of which expenses would be capped at $8,000 per year. Additionally, the firm would "procure for the plantations . . . twenty five working slaves to be employed on the Arnauld & Lorio plantations, or either of them," with payment for these individuals to be added separately to Moncure's expenses (above the annual cap).[86]

In compensation for their efforts, Dunlop, Moncure & Co. "shall receive and sell the two first crops . . . of 1849–50 and 1850–51." If this sale did not cover the firm's advances, "they shall be compelled to leave the slaves on said plantations until the entire balance due them is paid by means of the appropriation . . . of the one sixth part of the nett proceeds of the succeeding crops, after deducting all the necessary charges, such as the yearly supplies, taxes, overseer's wages, &c." As soon as Dunlop, Moncure, & Co.'s advances were fully reimbursed, "the title to said slaves, or as many of them as may be living at the time, together with their offspring, shall be made to the Bank." If the firm failed to cover Garcia's debts, the bank reserved the right to foreclose on and sell the plantations, reimbursing the firm for its outstanding expenses from the proceeds.[87] The firm was betting that the two crops could earn them a profit above the expenses of running the plantation. And in contrast to buying a plantation outright, they had little downside risk, since the bank guaranteed to reimburse their advances. The bank and Garcia both hoped that this two-year intervention would return the plantations to financial solvency, allowing Garcia to resume management of the works and repayment of his debts.

While most of the bank's board members accepted this arrangement as a win-win solution for all involved, one member went on record as opposing the agreement for three reasons. First, he did not believe that the board had the "right to cause the Institution to assume the risks of twenty five slaves which, though bought by Mr Moncure in his own name, are in fact bought for the account of the Bank, as they are intended to be paid out of monies accruing to the Bank." Second, he feared that the numbers just didn't add up. Two years' worth of crops was unlikely to pay off Dunlop, Moncure & Co.'s expenses, and he didn't believe that "5/6th of the nett proceeds of the crop" in the ensuing years would be "sufficient to meet the yearly payment then due by Mr Garcia." Yet by guaranteeing the payment of the firm's expenses out of these crops, the contract would place the bank at a disadvantage. Finally, and most importantly, he believed that "the whole difficulty in the case of Mr Garcia rises from the fact that the Board are attempting to save a debt, which has been utterly lost since 1842." This director divided the debt into two parts: the current market "value of the mortgaged plantations" and "the excess of value of said plantations" which was "worth nothing . . . the only colour of its existence and availability being due to Mr Garcia's high sense of honor which has prompted him to speak and act, as if his energies were competent to meet it in the course of time." This director recognized that Garcia's stature in the community and relationship with the board had led them to make a series of poor decisions in an effort to prop up this major slaveholder. Yet despite these concerns, the board still voted in favor of the arrangement.[88]

It is impossible to determine whether Dunlop, Moncure & Co. would have been successful or if the critique was correct, because by January of 1850, the crevasse at Bonnet Carré had reopened, again flooding the Arnauld plantation.[89] Even worse than the 1844 flood, the crevasse expanded to 7,000 feet and persisted through July.[90] At the height of the flooding in May, newspapers reported that "the immense crevasse at Bonnet Carré still exists, defying the art and labor of man to stop it, and flowing in a destructive torrent over a dozen of the finest sugar plantations in the State." In particular, the author observed that "the planter not only loses his crop for this season but he is deprived of his plant-cane for the next year. His cattle are all destroyed, his shrubbery killed, his ditches filled up, his levee cut away, his sugar-house inundated, and his elegant villa ruined."[91] A wrecked steamer that found itself sucked into the crevasse "ran up 'slap-bang' against some obstacle. It proved to be a large sugar-house, lately erected, at an expense of $25,000, by Mr. Felix Garcia, and now nearly submerged."[92] Presumably this was the sugarhouse he needed to rebuild after the fire of the previous year. The Arnauld plantation would produce no sugar in either the 1850–51 or 1851–52 harvests.[93]

Henry Moncure immediately began requesting permission from the bank to advance additional funds to Garcia. In moving all the slaves from the Arnauld plantation, he needed $3,000 to put the Lorio plantation in "a better state of affairs & accommodation."[94] The following November, Moncure requested an additional $3,000 "for the construction of the levee ordered by the police jury of the parish of St. John Baptist to be made on the Arnauld plantation," and a further $1,500 for "negro clothing & other plantation supplies" which were "indispensably necessary for the maintenance of the slaves &

the gathering of the present crop." Moncure wanted these additional sums to be treated the same as the previous expenses, with the bank promising to "protect him from all loss & indemnify him within a reasonable time for said advance." The board approved this request, under the condition that a board member oversee the levee's construction, employing Garcia's enslaved laborers for the purpose "as he may deem proper . . . leaving [on the plantation] a sufficient form for the gathering of the present crop."[95] Despite the fact that Garcia's plantations were flooded—literally and figuratively—from both the crevasse and his many debts, he still listed himself in the 1850 census as a planter with $110,000 of real estate wealth and 132 slaves.[96] He also employed his brother Carlos as overseer of the Lorio plantation, presumably with the permission of the bank.[97]

By May 1852, Dunlop, Moncure & Co. had accumulated approximately $41,000 in expenses, which consisted of $16,000 to run the plantations over two years (the amount stipulated in the original contract), plus $7,500 for the flooding and levee repairs, and about $17,500 for the purchase of twenty-five additional enslaved laborers. The bank planned to sell off both plantations, as well as the purchased slaves, repaying the firm by the following year.[98] Meanwhile Carlos Garcia, as overseer, had seized the current sugar crop, claiming it for his wages. Although he had been paid $800 per annum, he believed that he was owed $1,800 "*quantum meruit*" [the amount he deserved as a reflection of his actual labor]. When the case reached the Louisiana Supreme Court, at issue was both the reasonableness of this amount in a case "where the overseer does not take the ordinary course of engaging for a fixed salary," as well as whether the antichresis agreement legally permitted Dunlop, Moncure & Co. to take the full crop with their own expenses paid first.[99]

In their decision, the justices chastised the firm for not taking full possession and responsibility for the plantations. "It is the essence of the contract of antichresis . . . that the creditor be put in actual possession of the property which it affects." Yet Dunlop, Moncure & Co. never took possession, but instead "suffered the plantations to remain in possession of their debtor, as owner, and made a contract with him in relation to the supplies they were to furnish." In consequence, the judges found that the firm could "set up no right under the antichresis, and . . . they stand in no better situation than their debtor towards the plaintiff."[100] The bank agreed to pay Carlos $2,875.43 to cover additional wages and expenses, while Moncure was responsible for the attorneys' fees.[101] By August 1852, the bank had foreclosed on both properties, purchased them at sheriff's sale, and advertised them separately for resale.[102] Throughout all of these proceedings, Felix Garcia somehow remained in the bank's good graces, being elected to the position of bank commissioner in

September of 1852.[103] The debts from Garcia's plantations would remain unpaid when the Civil War broke out a decade later (see the epilogue).

Brown Brothers of New York

Southern commission merchants were not the only firms who saw potential profit in plantation finance. During the 1820s and 1830s, the New York merchant-banking firm of Brown Brothers and Company had become an important intermediary in the cotton trade between Liverpool and southern merchants.[104] In the midst of the depression in 1838, George Brown wrote his brother James that "there is no use in having a house [i.e., agency] anywhere in this country . . . except in New Orleans . . . as that is the place to get some good business."[105] That same year, the firm opened its first agency in New Orleans. Headed by Samuel Nicholson until 1856, the office "was to be chiefly engaged in furthering the firm's foreign exchange and credit operations."[106] On behalf of the firm, Nicholson purchased the banking house of the defunct Bank of Orleans on the corner of Exchange Place and Canal Street in 1842 for the bargain price of $30,500.[107] Additionally, James Brown involved the firm in the financing of several large plantations in the area during the 1840s and 1850s, including the cotton and sugar plantations of P. M. Lapice.

Pierre Michel Lapice de Bergondy—more commonly known simply as P. M. Lapice, although he occasionally also referred to himself as Peter—was born in St. Domingo in 1797 in the midst of the Haitian Revolution. His brother Joseph François was also born on the island in 1800. Their family was one of many who fled the war-torn colony, settling in Louisiana sometime before its annexation to the United States in 1803.[108] In 1814, at age seventeen, Pierre joined the army to fight during the War of 1812. Following the war, he moved upriver and in 1817 became a partner in the dry-goods firm of James Berthe & Co. in Natchez, Mississippi.[109] The firm reorganized in 1821 as Berthe, Lapice & Co., and they began specializing in the cotton trade in addition to selling fancy goods, groceries, hardware, paints, and linens.[110]

At the end of 1822, they dissolved this partnership, although Lapice continued in business as a sole proprietor until 1828.[111] In October 1823, he advertised "Cash for Cotton," as well as selling "Scotch and Kentucky Bagging, Bale Rope and Twine, Sugar and Coffee, Whiskey, Fresh Flour, Molasses, Chewing Tobacco, Cotton Cards, Woollens, Liverpool fine Salt . . . Blankets . . . In short, he can furnish every article necessary for the Country use."[112] He also ventured into finance, offering "Drafts on New York for Sale."[113] Around this same time, Pierre acquired a cotton plantation across the Mississippi River in Concordia Parish, Louisiana. In March 1823, he advertised for rent "100 acres of the very best quality of land, under good fence, and ready for cultivation. There is a good Dwelling House, and extensive Negro-Quarters. Possession given immediately."[114] He advertised the property for sale in January, 1826, but had not yet sold it by December.[115] In all likelihood he kept it, the first of many plantations he would acquire in Concordia.

By the mid-1820s, Lapice was a fixture in the Natchez community. In January 1825, he was elected as both a city selectman and a director of the Bank of the State of Mississippi.[116] In May 1826, he was elected a warden of the fire company.[117] Later that summer, he added an agency of the Louisiana Insurance Company to his thriving business ventures.[118] He also regularly served as an intermediary for slaveholders looking to recover runaways, including "A Negro Boy, named Dick" who ran away from the Burthe plantation, Leon Gauthier's "mulatto boy named Jack," and George, who escaped from the plantation of Francis Troxler.[119] By 1827, he was secretary of the Natchez Steamboat Company.[120] And as a stockholder in the local theater, he was elected president of the managers in 1828, as well as a member of the committee of finance; he was still president of the theater in 1838.[121] He also wed Marie Louise Demée around this time. The couple quickly produced at least five children between 1827 and 1834, all of whom were born in Natchez, before Marie's death in 1834 at age thirty-one. Pierre did not remarry.[122] Although he continued to live with his young family in Natchez, by the end of 1828 he decided to "sell at Auction . . . HIS ENTIRE STOCK OF GOODS," in order to devote himself to his plantation interests.[123]

Lapice was always at the forefront of local innovations. During the summer of 1833, as a cholera outbreak raged in the region, Lapice allowed doctors to experiment with a treatment of red pepper and calomel on his plantations, with allegedly positive results despite the highly toxic nature of calomel.[124] "[A]t one of Mr. Lapice's plantations, out of 70 or 80 cases, it cured all but one; that at another plantation of the same gentleman, after losing more than a dozen negroes under the immediate management of 4 or more physicians, the pepper practice was finally adopted, and found to be the surest and the safest."[125] He was also on the cutting edge of new technology. By December 1833 his plantations were using "a new and useful improvement in the *Corn-sheller*," recently invented by William Hoyt.[126] Newspapers also raved—*"Beat this who can!"*—about his success with his "Connor Press," which produced seventy-one bales of cotton in only twelve hours on his White Hall plantation.[127] Several years later, he tested a "Repeating Cotton Thrasher, invented by Jb. Idler of Philadelphia, which clean the leaves and trash . . . out of the most dirty cotton in the seed; and cotton which has passed through this cleaner, will gin one-third faster and make a far cleaner cotton."[128]

But Lapice was even more devoted to finding a viable means of raising sugar on the land in and around Natchez, Mississippi, and Concordia, Louisiana, which was much farther north than the main sugar lands of Louisiana. As early as 1826, he was experimenting with sugar planting in Adams County, Mississippi.[129] This interest is likely what led to his partnership with James C. Wilkins, a prominent local banker who was involved in the 1830 chartering of the Planters' Bank.[130] Wilkins served as president of the board of the newly opened Bank of the United States branch in 1832, before assuming the presidency of the Planters' Bank by 1834.[131] In 1833, Lapice acted as Wilkins's agent in the purchase of some property in the sugar-growing parish of Iberville.[132] Yet despite Wilkins's significant banking connections, the pair needed much-greater financing than any local bank would be willing or able to provide if they wanted to transform a cotton plantation into a capital-intensive sugar plantation.

In 1835, Wilkins sent Lapice with several letters of introduction for use in securing large-scale financing for their schemes, suggesting that he either approach A. & J. Dennistoun & Co. of New Orleans (the same firm that was then financing the Louisiana plantation of the Corbin brothers and Edward Rawle [see chapter 5]) or seek out other options in the North.[133] In his letter to George Ralston, a director of the Girard Bank in Philadelphia, Wilkins explained that the partners were "embark[ing] on a large land speculation, which will be most productive of profit. . . . Mr Lapice will explain the affair to you confidentially and in detail." While a third partner, Mr. S. Davis (possibly Samuel Davis, father of future president of the Confederacy Jefferson Davis), could contribute his own substantial funds to the endeavor, both Lapice and Wilkins would "have to negotiate for the loan of money, either in Philadelphia or New York." To secure such funding, Lapice could offer as collateral his property that was "extensive, and most productive, yielding from 1000 to 1500 Bales of Cotton per annum." Wilkins's assets were tied up in "heavy investments in Lands in the Miss. and elsewhere, by which I expect to realize an immense profit. The passion for these new lands is increasing daily, and I have no idea the price will reach its maximum for five years to come." On the partners' behalf, Lapice was seeking a loan up of to $100,000, "giv[ing] security on real Estate and Negroes to four times the amount if it is asked." Wilkins suggested that Lapice should start by soliciting the firm of Brown Brothers in New York, of whom "I think it probable the loan may be obtained."[134] Although Brown Brothers was first mentioned in this 1835 letter, Lapice succeeded in securing funds in Philadelphia without the need to travel to New York; he reported to Wilkins in July that he had obtained the desired $100,000 loan from George Ralston and Thomas Flemming (another Philadelphia banker).[135]

Wilkins and Lapice may have used these substantial funds to convert one of Lapice's Concordia properties into an experimental sugar plantation. In 1841, the newspapers raved about the "Concordia Sugar Cane" grown on Lapice's plantation. "Look out for Concordia sugar at the Baton Rouge Agricultural fair!"[136] The following year, another article reported that the manager of Lapice's Arnandlia plantation near Vidalia had "for several years past . . . cultivated a small patch" of sugarcane "*invariably with success*. It is his belief that a crop would succeed here." Lapice estimated "that this cane would yield one and a half hogsheads sugar, sixty gallons molasses, which at the present rates would nett eighty-seven dollars per acre."[137] An 1843 article boasted that Lapice's experiments with acclimating sugarcane at his White Hall plantation would eventually allow "Louisiana to produce Sugar for the whole Union, at a low price." This author estimated that switching portions of cotton plantations to sugar "would yield three times the amount of the same land cultivated in cotton . . . the planter would realize better prices for his labor—a higher interest on his capital—and, while adding to his own wealth, materially increase the prosperity of the country, by supplying that deficiency in one article for which we are now indebted to the West Indies."[138] Indeed, whenever the newspapers wanted to cite the success of sugar growing north of "the mouth of the Red River, once considered the northern boundary of the cane-growing region," they always first cited the efforts of Lapice.[139]

Yet even as he was experimenting with sugar on his cotton lands, Lapice decided to start investing in the traditional sugar parishes of Louisiana. In April 1836, he purchased his first sugar plantation in St. James Parish. The following January, he and his brother Joseph entered into a formal partnership to share in the "expenses, costs, and charges" of running this and any future sugar plantations they might acquire. Between 1837 and 1840, the brothers expanded this plantation by purchasing several adjoining pieces of land, as well as at least 134 enslaved workers; 103 of these people they purchased from Archibald Dunbar of Adams County, Mississippi, in 1836 and 1837, transporting them south to St. James Parish. Pierre mortgaged all of this property to acquire 810 shares of Citizens' Bank stock, which entitled him to a loan of up to $40,500 from the bank, as well as three hundred shares of Union Bank stock. Then, in December 1840, the pair purchased an adjoining tract of land from the widow of Evariste Villavaso for $10,500, promising to pay her in three equal payments in March 1842, 1843, and 1844.[140]

Lapice was simultaneously using his Concordia plantations to secure loans. In May 1838, he mortgaged a plantation three miles from the town of Vidalia (next door to Arnandlia), and the 175 enslaved people who lived there, to the Merchants' Bank of New Orleans for a $20,000 loan. Having successfully repaid this loan after two years, he obtained a new loan from the same bank in April 1840, secured by the same property, of $100,000 payable over four years.[141] But the following month, Mother Nature dealt the plantation a severe setback when a tornado swept through Concordia.[142] "P. M. Lapice, Esq. suffered immensely in his Arno plantation, below Vidalia. His negro quarters were all blown down, four or five negroes killed outright, about twenty dangerously, some of them mortally wounded, and thirty or forty more slightly injured. His plantation has resounded with groans since the storm. He estimates his loss at thirty thousand dollars."[143]

Whether due to the ongoing effects of the depression, the (literal) blow dealt by the tornado in Concordia, or to the fact that his brother "has not paid any part of his share of the expenses, charges & costs" associated with the St. James property, Lapice's finances were in a dire condition by 1842. On April 23, 1842, he dissolved the partnership agreement with his brother, taking full control of all the land, enslaved lives, and bank stock associated with the St. James sugar plantation.[144] Five days later, in desperation, he turned to James Brown of Brown Brothers, New York, for help in paying off his creditors while "making [his plantations] productive." Lapice executed a mortgage in favor of Brown for $250,000 (about $8.5 million in 2021), secured by both his sugar and cotton plantations. Brown did not give the money directly to Lapice; rather, the loan was largely to be a combination of future debt payments to other creditors (a subrogation) and advances for use in the management and improvement of the plantations.[145] Brown immediately began consolidating and making annual payments on Lapice's other outstanding mortgages. On May 11, 1842, the City Bank of New Orleans (which, upon the liquidation of the Merchants' Bank in 1842, had acquired two of the promissory notes worth $40,333.33 owed by Lapice) subrogated the mortgage to Brown, who assumed future payment of these notes to the City Bank.[146] Perhaps not realizing the full extent of Lapice's indebtedness until then, Brown added another $150,000 to Lapice's mortgage debt the very next day.[147]

Lapice was also behind on his first two payments to the widow Villavaso, who demanded an immediate settlement in March 1843. James Brown stepped in and paid $7,000 cash directly to Villavaso, while Lapice issued a promissory note for the remaining $3,500, to be paid in March 1844 as previously agreed.[148] Two months later, Brown foreclosed on his two mortgages from 1842 in order to gain operational control of the Lapice plantations. On May 30, 1843, "Lapice executed in favor of Brown an act of pledge, by way of antichresis, of the same lands, to secure the above amount of $400,000, in which Brown acknowledged possession, and covenanted to appropriate the fruits and monies to the payment of his claims and interest." As part of the antichresis, Lapice agreed "to ship his crops to defendant's house 'so long as *Lapice* shall continue to be indebted to said *Brown*, and stipulated in his favor a lien upon them.'" Lapice, for his part, retained a "right of redemption," meaning that if he was able to repay his debt to Brown through the plantation profits, he could reclaim full ownership of the property.[149]

As of March 1844, the balance sheet of Brown Brothers listed Lapice's debt on his Concordia and St. James plantations at $573,377 (about $21.1 million in 2021).[150] That month, Brown Brothers paid the final installment of $3,500 to the widow Villavaso.[151] The firm also made regular payments on the mortgage debts due to the Citizens' Bank and the Union Bank,[152] and recorded additional expenses for such items as state and parish property taxes, "Negro clothing," a case of straw hats, medicine, 450 pairs of "Wax brogans" (shoes) in various sizes ("extra sizes," men's, youths, boys), as well as fifty pairs of "mens Water boots extra sizes," groceries, hardware, overseers' wages, and quinine.[153] In 1844 they paid for the patent application "for the improvement of the manufact[ure] of Sugar" taken out by Joseph Lapice.[154]

Brown permitted Pierre Lapice to live on the St. James plantation, although he placed his own agents in charge of running the sugar and cotton plantations. Yet "the long experience and capacity of *Peter M. Lapice*, were such as to induce me [James Brown], through my agent, to consult him on important matters connected with the management of said sugar plantations, its cultivation and the manufacture of sugar." Such was his respect for Lapice that "great weight was attached to his counsel and advice on these subject, the more especially, as he was to receive back the plantations after the payment of my claim, and consequently, was greatly interested in making them productive."[155] Despite the formal financial arrangement, Brown treated Lapice as a coequal partner in the plantations' management.

Viewing these plantations as long-term investments, Brown Brothers and Lapice plowed much of the profits into improvements rather than paying off the substantial debt. "Large sums of money have been expended in the erection of a new sugar house, and in the furnishing of a new apparatus for making sugar on said plantation," which Brown believed to be "necessary for making the plantation as productive as I could. These improvements were exclusively projected and devoted to augmenting the revenues of the said plantation, and not to embellishments of any kind."[156] While some of Lapice's other creditors contended that this practice of reinvesting the profits was purposely designed to defeat the claims of competing claimants, Brown defended their decisions. "The extreme desire always expressed by *Peter M. Lapice* to pay his creditors, had induced me, year after year, to continue without enforcing payment, so as to leave him the chance of paying me with the revenues, and thereby becoming able to satisfy all his other creditors. That his strong hope of success in the project, induced me to lend every indulgence in my power."[157]

Indeed, Lapice was one of the most innovative sugar planters of the region, experimenting with ways to make higher quality sugar while using fewer resources (time and fuel), as well as improving the production of the most highly valued white sugar. One 1847 newspaper article, which began as an overview of a new apparatus for producing white sugar without the intermediate step of brown sugar, noted that "the most remarkable and perfect of these apparatuses are those on the plantations of Messrs. V. Aime and P. M. Lapice, of the Parish of St. James, particularly on account of the economy in fuel resulting from the open condensers." The article then morphed into an advertisement for Lapice's branded product:

> The sugar made by Mr. Lapice is of a large grain, of marble whiteness, retains the aroma of the cane, and is in that respect superior to white refined sugar, although it is sold at a cent or a cent and a half lower. . . . Mr. Lapice's sugar house is well worth a visit. The industry and ability displayed by that enterprising gentleman deserves the highest credit. This clarified sugar, to which he has attached the name of *Paragon Sugar Works*, is very superior, and may be found at S. Nicholson's, Canal street.[158]

With the significant financial support of Brown, Lapice continued improving his sugar production process and promoting his Paragon brand. Two years later, yet another newspaper article sang the praises of "a *brick* of sugar made on the plantation of P. M. Lapice." In contrast to other producers, "this sugar is clarified by a process invented by Mr. Lapice—it is as white, and much purer than the loaf, and is sold at eight cents. The word *Paragon*, which is the name of the plantation, is beautifully stamped on one side of the brick." The article concluded, "We have no doubt that Mr. Lapice will find his new improvement in the art of clarifying sugar very profitable. The specimen before us, is a beautiful illustration of the perfection the art can be brought to."[159] Thus Brown had significant evidence that reinvesting the profits of the plantations was bearing long-term dividends.

In an attempt to further differentiate Lapice's brand from the bulk of sugar on the market, noted chemist Samuel Cartwright performed chemical analysis of the product in a New York lab and declared Lapice's output to be "purer and better than any of the double refined loaf sugar of commerce." In reporting these findings, the chemist declared that Lapice was not just an innovator in sugar, but that he also "for twenty-years or more was justly regarded as the Napoleon among the cotton planters, and whose improvements in that branch of industry, especially in ameliorating the condition of the slave population, have been generally adopted and have already entitled him to a place in the front rank of public benefactors."[160] While it is unclear of what these "ameliorating" innovations consisted in terms of his enslaved laborers, Lapice was revered by his peers at mid-century. During the 1849–1850 season, Lapice's St. James plantation reported producing 1050 hogsheads of sugar.[161] And despite his substantial indebtedness to Brown, Lapice listed his real estate wealth on the 1850 census as $150,000.[162]

Notwithstanding this success and the continued support of Brown Brothers, the plantations were still overextended. Lapice's debt to Brown had ballooned to $742,626.01 (about $26.2 million in 2021) by 1850, and production began to slow significantly.[163] Lapice and his Paragon Sugar Works only reported producing six hundred hogsheads in 1850–51, and 738 in 1851–52.[164] In the meantime, another creditor named W. C. Pickersgill—a commission merchant with offices in New York and Liverpool—won court judgments against Lapice worth over $100,000. Yet due to Brown's priority of claim on Lapice's properties, Pickersgill could not foreclose. Instead he acquired Lapice's "equity of redemption" for "all the plantations and slaves and that, as such purchaser, he stands in relation to that property in the place of Lapice."[165] Once the debts to Brown were paid, Pickersgill would take possession of the property. But whereas Brown was happy with the partnership arrangement he had with Lapice—which must have been quite profitable for his firm—he had no interest in this third-party deal. Brown immediately foreclosed on Lapice, rendering Pickersgill's right to an equity of redemption moot.[166]

In the legal battle that ensued, Pickersgill claimed a fraudulent relationship between Lapice and Brown. The purpose of the foreclosure, he alleged, was to "prostrate the creditors . . . for the sole benefit of *Lapice*, and to enable him to elude his creditors"; furthermore, Pickersgill charged that the relationship was "of a usurious character, to increase the amount of said loan beyond its true value in money." He concluded that "the granting of the mortgages, the confession of judgment, and the antichresis, were intended as means by which *Lapice* might frustrate his creditors."[167] The Louisiana Supreme Court, however, disagreed, and the sheriff placed all the properties up for auction.[168] Brown purchased Arnandlia with its ninety-one enslaved people for $120,000, White Hall and its enslaved population of 176 for $60,000, Lake and its seventy-three enslaved individuals for $50,000, and St. James with its 130–150 enslaved workers for $175,000.[169] The $405,000 total price tag was—conveniently—just about the principal on the original two mortgages from 1842. While creditors who, like the Citizens' Bank, possessed secured mortgages on Lapice's property would continue to be paid by Brown, the debts of unsecured creditors (like Pickersgill) were erased by this sale.

For the next three years, Brown continued to run the St. James plantation as the Paragon Sugar Works, taking advantage of the brand recognition that had come to be associated with the product.[170] Merchants, for example, regularly advertised that they stocked "paragon sugar" from "Lapice's St. James Sugar Refinery."[171] While the records do not indicate what happened to the Concordia plantations, sometime around 1855–56 Brown sold (under unknown terms) the St. James plantation back to Pierre's sons: Pierre Michel Bergondy (known simply as Bergondy), Joseph, Ambrose, and Emile, who formed the partnership of Bergondy Lapice & Brothers.[172] Bergondy and Joseph managed the plantation, while Ambrose and Emile ran "a general Mercantile and Commission business" in New Orleans.[173] Brown transferred all 756 shares of Citizens' Bank stock to the brothers (the original 810 shares having been reduced in 1853 due to an alteration in the bank charter), who operated the plantation now called Lauderdale through the outbreak of the Civil War.[174] Paragon sugar continued to be praised as a "fine article . . . a beautiful article, well worth the attention of families."[175] At the 1860 census, Pierre was still living with two of his sons and two daughters on the St. James plantation, declaring the family's wealth at $100,000 in real estate and $218,930 in personal (i.e., enslaved) property (about $10.6 million total in 2021).[176]

The involvement of Brown Brothers in the ownership and management of southern plantations was not limited to P. M. Lapice, although he was certainly the firm's most substantial acquisition, and the only one for whom it held the property in antichresis. While the firm ran numerous plantations during the 1840s and 1850s, it is unclear whether it acquired these holdings through debt foreclosure proceedings or—as in the case of Lapice—by rescuing troubled planters. Sometime around 1842, Brown Brothers came into possession of the Bellevue cotton plantation of James Girault—possibly the same person who had been indebted to the Bank of the State of Mississippi for various Natchez and Concordia plantations throughout the 1820s and 1830s (see chapters 2 and 4)—which it then valued at $115,477.06. It later sold the property in 1845 for about $38,000. Although this sale would appear to represent a significant loss for the firm, it is unclear from the books how much the firm originally paid (in cash), and how much profit it gleaned from this plantation in the intervening years. The plantation's seventy-one enslaved people, valued at $24,850, as well as seventeen mules worth $570, were transferred to its Lochleven property upon the sale of the land. Similarly, it acquired the Mississippi plantation of J. R. Crecy—valued at $41,327.67 in 1842—and declared significant losses through 1848 when it placed the property's value at only $6,018.60. The Mount Meigs plantation in Alabama was valued at $10,154.70 in 1842, but only worth $5,468.67 by 1844. The Lochleven & Artonish cotton plantations, valued at $178,604.45 in 1842, it sold in 1847 to D. Withers for $25,000 in cash plus an undisclosed amount on credit. Again, it is unclear whether Brown Brothers really took such substantial losses on these properties, or if these balance sheets are concealing a different story; a deeper examination of these holdings would be a potentially interesting project for a future researcher.[177]

Reassessing Banking (Again) in the Frontier South

Despite the efforts of the Citizens' Bank to operate as a fully functional private bank during the 1840s, its profitability was severely hobbled by its inability to issue banknotes. Selling the properties of delinquent debtors merely shifted an existing mortgage obligation to a new debtor, which often restarted the payment terms on the loan. This process further delayed mortgage payments and threatened the bank's ability to repay its bonds. In March 1850, the state-appointed Board of Bank Managers issued its annual report on the status of the bank to the Louisiana legislature. Not only was there "a very large deficit" on the bank's books, but "there appeared no prospect of [this deficit] being diminished by the lapse of time; on the contrary, there was every reason to believe . . . that it would continue to increase, until the period of the maturity of the series of bonds due in 1868." While the bank continued to serve the needs of the planters of the state, "little reliance could be placed on these stock-mortgages as a means of extricating the bank from her difficulties." The board concluded that the only means by which the bank might meet the future bond obligations would be for the legislature to restore its former charter with full banking privileges. Should this recommendation be adopted, they estimated that "in the course of five to seven years, the whole amount of the State bonds issued for said bank will be surrendered and the State relieved from responsibility; that no harm will come to any one, and much good be done to that portion of the stockholders of the bank, all of whom are citizens of this State, and who are involved in its fate."[178]

A major problem with this proposal was the constitutional ban on new banking institutions. The board of the bank hired "two distinguished lawyers" to look into this complication, paying them $500 apiece.[179] Focusing on the original bank charter, the attorneys concluded that the legislature in 1842 had no right to force the Citizens' Bank into liquidation. Whereas most bank incorporations contained a clause stipulating forfeiture of the charter as a punishment if the bank suspended payments, the Citizens' Bank charter instead merely imposed a 10 percent tax on the notes in question. Thus both noteholders and bondholders "anticipated a continuance of the banking privilege" for the entirety of its fifty-year charter, even in the event of a suspension of payments. "This was a leading inducement to our citizens to subscribe for stock in the Bank—this favourable feature of the charter which, having become to all intents and purposes, a vested right, under the guarantees of a contract, to which the State was a party, they never expected to see trampled under foot, and utterly disregarded by the Legislature, as it was by the act of 1842." In the same manner, "the foreign capitalists, on the faith of this charter—on the faith of the State—on the faith, common to all civilized nations, of the inviolability of contracts—advanced their money for the bonds of the State."[180] The long-term nature of the contracts underlying the bank's organizational structure necessitated the stability of its charter terms, and the legislature had blatantly violated the bank's charter privileges by forcing it into liquidation as if it were a traditional commercial bank.

Bank proponents used these arguments to continue pushing for a full reinstatement of the charter, arguing that the legislature in 1842 could never have intended to revoke the bank's privileges permanently, and thus a restoration would in no way violate the banking ban of the constitution: "The prohibition against issuing notes for circulation was a mere limitation of the powers confided to the agents of the State, which limitation the legislature might at any time relax or remove." Rather than seeking a new charter, the stockholders merely sought "the removal of this restriction . . . which only wants the Executive sanction to become a law."[181] Legislative resistance to the bank finally folded. As a condition of its reinstatement, the bank agreed to negotiate a $800,000 reduction of payments with bondholders, and to raise an additional $800,000 in cash, which it proposed to do by assessing stockholders $1 per share for seven years (from May 1851–1857).[182] An editorialist for the Baton Rouge *Democratic Advocate* concluded that the bank's restoration was in the best interests of the entire state of Louisiana:

> Unless the present mode of liquidation be abandoned, the institution will be lost, thousands of our citizens be ruined, and the State be compelled, ultimately to redeem the bulk of her bonds by taxation. Our people are now overtaxed; and be it remembered, likewise, that thousands and thousands have become citizens of the State, who never participated in the benefits of the Bank, and that they too, as things stand must bear the burden of this taxation, unless the plan sanctioned by the Legislature be carried into execution. . . . It will add to our capital, now that the community is deplorably in want of capital. It will stimulate our declining trade, until a system of freebanking can be matured. It will supply the vacuum to be created by the periodical extinction of the present Banks. It will disenthral[l] thousands of our citizens whose property is now neither available

> nor negotiable, and whose industry is therefore paralyzed. It will put an end to the bank monopoly which now exists in this city. It will release the State from a heavy liability which she is bound to redeem, and which she is without resources to redeem. It will relieve our citizens, who have brought their property into Louisiana since the fall of the banks, from a liability for those bonds, which it would be hard indeed to exact from them.[183]

Despite this impassioned plea that a reinstatement of the Citizens' Bank charter would conveniently solve most of the woes of the state, Governor Joseph Walker (a Democrat) vetoed the bill that reached his desk in March 1852, citing "constitutional objections."[184] Just a week later, both the Senate (evenly split between Democrats and Whigs) and the Whig-controlled House voted to overturn his veto, passing a bill that "restored to the stockholders [of the Citizens' Bank] in the same manner, with the same rights and privileges, to the same extent and with the same restrictions as if said decree of forfeiture [from 1842] had never been rendered."[185] By May 1853, the bank had successfully complied with the stipulations of the legislature, and its charter was restored.[186] The reversal represented not only a vote of confidence in the Citizens' Bank, but a changing attitude toward banking that was sweeping across many southern states at mid-century.

Free Banking and Human Property

As was the case in Louisiana, slaveholders across the southern frontier had limited access to bank loans during the 1840s, especially from state-chartered institutions. Debtors increasingly turned to out-of-state banks, private banks, and merchants to finance their operations. Thus, as some critics of the anti-banking fervor had predicted, minimizing or eliminating state-chartered banks just shifted demand to other institutions that fell outside the regulatory control of the state. While several southern states, such as Arkansas, Florida, Mississippi, and Missouri, remained staunchly anti-bank through most of the 1850s, the rest of the South began rethinking their banking systems. Yet unlike the 1820s and 1830s, when southern banks had adapted their banking policies and practices in response to the unique demands of southern planters and the system of slavery, during the late 1840s and 1850s, these banking conversations took place firmly within the national conversation over free banking. As a part of these debates, the main concern was the financial requirements of commercial interests like merchants and traders (with an indirect effect on planters), while they essentially ignored the large-scale, long-term financing needs of large slaveholders.

Free banking was a type of general incorporation statute that streamlined and democratized the process of creating banks. Free-banking laws all contained two features: first, ease of entry for anyone meeting the stipulated requirements, common to all general incorporation laws; and second, strict oversight of the issuance of banknotes. This latter provision was usually accomplished by requiring the bank to purchase bonds equal in value to their banknote issues. The bank would place these bonds on deposit with the state, although the institution would continue to earn any accrued interest from the investment. In the event the bank failed to redeem its notes for specie, the state could sell the bonds and reimburse the noteholders. Supporters of this system believed that this bond security would restrain banks from issuing too many notes while protecting the public in the event of a bank's failure. Although Michigan's 1837 experiment with free banking was a fiasco, New York's 1838 free-banking act—and especially its 1840 revision—became a model for the rest of the country.[187] In the South, the most widespread early discussions of free banking took place in the upper South states of Tennessee and Virginia, and the lower South states of Alabama and Louisiana. Yet whereas enslaved lives had been a prominent part of southern banking before the panics, and could have easily been incorporated into the asset requirements for free banks under the real estate provisions common in many free-banking statutes, southerners uniformly rejected this option.

In all of these state-banking debates, the two pressing needs voiced by banking advocates were for banknotes and short-term credit for trade; the need for long-term mortgages was never mentioned. In Knoxville, Tennessee, an 1849 editorial explained that "our banks now in existence do not accomplish the ends for which they were created—to furnish a currency readily convertible at all times into specie and supply the demand for exchange at reasonable rates."[188] At a public meeting of the citizens of Mobile, Alabama, in 1849, the attendees were most concerned with "the present condition of the circulating medium of the State." Even when "enumerat[ing] several very serious evils to the commercial interests of Mobile, and to the planting interests of the State, which they think result entirely from the want of adequate banking facilities," the committee boiled these evils down to "a too greatly restricted circulating medium."[189] The problems of planters, in their estimation, were not long-term but seasonal. "During this season the Bank [of Mobile] has been unable to purchase the exchange that was required to buy the planters' cotton. The bills that were offered were good, and they would readily have been purchased, but the circulation of the bank had nearly reached its limit, and it could afford no additional facilities for trade or negotiation." Planters were thus forced to "traffic . . . in notes furnished by the Banks of the neighboring States of Tennessee, Georgia and South Carolina, which notes are at a depreciation of two to five per cent for the notes of this bank or specie." Because the merchants lacked funds for buying the cotton, "the planter must then submit to the sacrifice of a sale under the most inauspicious circumstances, or to the operation of having his note shaved by the broker at a most ruinous discount." In this situation, the planter needs "the power (whether he chooses to exercise it or not,) of holding his cotton until business revives, or the market becomes settled. A bank judiciously managed, would be able and willing to discount his note for sixty or ninety days, and he could return home with the price of his cotton already realized, and with the hope of reaping the advantages of a rise in the market."[190] What was needed—even for the planting interests—were state-chartered banks whose operations focused on discounting short-term commercial paper.

Yet even if the operations of the free banks focused on short-term lending, southern legislatures could have designated real estate as an acceptable asset to underwrite the bonds required to support the issuance of banknotes. New York's free-banking law allowed banks to issue notes backed by bonds from New York State or the federal government, as well as "mortgages on real estate . . . in lieu of stocks, to the extent of one-half the bills transferred. . . . Said mortgages to be on good improved real estate to an amount not exceeding half the assessed value thereof." Under the 1840 revision to this law, the bonds and mortgages would be accepted only at their actual market value instead of their face value. Banks would need to supplement their bond or mortgage holdings whenever the market value of these assets declined.[191] Southern states, particularly those of the lower South, had considerable experience with state-issued bonds for both internal improvements and banks, as well as with the use of real estate (which they almost always understood to include enslaved lives) to secure the capital of plantation banks and as collateral for mortgage loans. Only a decade after the finances of several of these states had suffered considerably—as a result of the collapse of both bonds and real estate mortgages—many southerners were readily embracing a renewed engagement with the bond market through free banking. However, these southern promoters of free banking drew the line at bonds potentially backed by plantations and enslaved lives.

Among southern free-banking proponents, the main critique of New York's law was its use of real estate mortgages. Governor Collier of Alabama, for example, thought the entirety of the New York system "commends itself very favorably to our consideration" *except* in its use of real estate: "In this State, we certainly could not receive real estate as security to any extent; its value is so fluctuating and uncertain, that it is impossible to estimate what it would command in cash at the present moment, much less what it will sell for at any future indefinite period."[192] In Governor Walker's address to the Louisiana legislature in January 1852, he reluctantly expressed support for a more moderate system of free banking. "The first attempts at free banking were made upon a mixed basis of State stock and real estate, but this was abandoned, proof being adduced, that the valuation of such estate was sometimes too high, if not fraudulent, and the security to note-holders not ample." Ignoring the fact that New York actually still permitted mortgage-backed bonds, he contended that the success of New York's current system was because "United States stock and State stock, always at or near par value, form now the security for circulation in States where the free system seems most prosperous."[193] In Tennessee, the legislative committee that endorsed free banking declared: "The pledge of real estate is equally valu'less as the long and protracted proceedings incident upon the investigation of titles, and foreclosure of mortgages produced a delay which to the note holder, is little better than total insolvency."[194] In Mississippi, another free-bank supporter conceded that "all banks are dependent upon property of some kind or other for their solvency. In most all cases this solvency depends on both the real estate and personal property of the Bankers and their debtors." Yet this writer believed that a system of free banking could be set up based entirely on the state's developing railroads. "Good Railroads are therefore the very best property for a banking basis."[195]

Even as southern supporters of free banking were largely uninterested in accepting real estate as security for the notes, southern critics of free banking latched onto the real estate provision in the New York law as one of the main flaws in the whole system: "That Free Banking is but a revival, in part, of the old property bank system, with which Louisiana was once cursed, as it permits the use of bonds and mortgages on real estate as securities for the currency."[196] Based on past experience, an Alabama critic positively stated "that mortgages upon stocks or real estate can never be made the basis of a circulating medium."[197] Southerners on both sides of the free-banking debate were actively rejecting the use of their largest financial asset as the foundation for supporting and regulating the banking capital of their states.

The one state that seemed to embrace the possibility of basing a new free-banking system on real estate was Louisiana, which had been the originator and greatest developer of long-term property mortgages and plantation banks. An 1851 newspaper article published in the *New Orleans Delta* and reprinted in the *Concordia Intelligencer* opined, "Wealth we have in abundance, but it is dormant, idle, valueless, for trade or commerce. Your valuable real estate,—of what avail is that for the purposes of trade?" Rather than mortgaging property to release its equity, the author proposed "making it productive" through free banking. "By this, any number of individuals who can raise the capital may associate like other partners and issue paper and discount notes at fixed rates of interest." Although the main functions of the bank would be discounting and note issuance (rather than property mortgages), the valuable property would still be used to protect noteholders. "In case the State, or United States stocks cannot be procured, we know of no better security than bonds and mortgages on real estate, fairly assessed, and worth double or treble the amount for which it is mortgaged." This writer assured readers that this system did not have "the slightest similarity to the old Property Bank system" in which "the whole control was vested in a chartered company" that could not be trusted, rather than safely "in the hands of the State Comptroller."[198] Another Louisiana writer likewise asked: "Where have we the stocks to be deposited for the issue of notes, unless mortgages on real estate and negroes could be substituted?"[199]

But even in Louisiana there was significant dissent from this idea, especially as the November 1851 election approached with its crucial statewide referendum on calling another constitutional convention. One writer in the *New Orleans Crescent* thought that free banking was being pushed "to the great delight of landholders, who wished another 'land fever,' and to the certain creation of an immense and unhealthy speculation in lands, that a Banking system, based upon the vast complication of mortgaged real estate, should be established."[200] The *New Orleans Weekly Delta* endorsed the *Crescent*'s "examination of the absurdity of banking in real estate."[201] And an editorialist for the New Orleans *Times-Picayune* thought that the ongoing credit problems of the state would make the system unworkable for solving the "evils which are upon us" in the economy. "Dishonored bonds will scarcely furnish a basis for a circulating medium. Mortgages upon real estate, even if syndics [of creditors with prior claims] could not remove them, would as little answer the purposes of currency."[202] Free-banking legislation was under debate throughout the South—indeed throughout the country—but most southerners no longer viewed enslaved lives as an acceptable basis for banking institutions.

Between 1850 and 1853—when the various sections of the country could agree on little else—twelve state legislatures passed free-banking acts, including the New England states of Massachusetts (1851), Vermont (1851), and Connecticut (1852); the mid-Atlantic state of New Jersey (1850), which was joining New York (1838); the midwestern states of Illinois (1851), Ohio (1851), Indiana (1852), and Wisconsin (1852); and the southern states of Alabama (1850), Tennessee (1852), Florida (1853), and Louisiana (1853). Additionally, Kentucky (1850) and Virginia (1851) both passed hybrid laws that required bond security for note issuance but did not allow for general incorporation.

As in New York, the legislation of both New Jersey and Vermont included a provision for the use of real estate security. For example, the Vermont law stipulated that "one half of the circulation . . . may be secured by mortgages on improved farms at two fifths their value, exclusive of buildings."[203] The southern states, by contrast, all rejected this option. The Tennessee law, for example, allowed "any portion of the public stocks now created, or hereafter to be created, by this State, or bonds of incorporated companies indorsed by the State, or bonds of the United States," while additionally requiring that "at least three fourths of the securities so deposited shall be bonds of the State of Tennessee"; real estate was not included.[204]

With these new laws on the books, the number of southern banks doubled during the 1850s, with especially strong growth in the states of the upper frontier (table 9.4). But these absolute numbers overstate the importance of free banks in the South. Almost no banks were created under the law in Florida, and only a handful in Alabama.[205] Most of the new banks chartered in Tennessee had a small capitalization of only between $50,000 and $200,000; the Virginia banks were mostly capitalized between $100,000 and $300,000.[206] Due to their small capitalization, all these banks had to focus on discounting commercial paper, rather than on underwriting large property mortgages. Even the larger Bank of Mobile—which had been chartered in 1818 as a traditional commercial bank and now had a capital of $1.5 million—reported discounts of $771,345 in November 1847 and $1,467,158 in October 1851, but only $26,647 and $134,400 (respectively) in "mortgages and other loans."[207] While banks had been essential to the development of the slaveholding South during the 1820s and 1830s, this direct relationship had been severed by mid-century.

In Louisiana, the New Orleans *Times-Picayune* excitedly announced on May 5, 1853, that "a meeting of subscribers to the first bank under the free banking law, was held at the room of the Crescent Mutual Insurance Company last evening." The much-anticipated new bank, known as the Bank of New Orleans, was capitalized at $1,000,000. "More than half the stock has already been subscribed, and a charter was adopted last night."[208] Banking in Louisiana after the passage of the free-banking law grew at a moderate pace; the state definitely did not experience the rapid explosion of banks that anti-bankers feared and some free-bank supporters seemed to promote.[209] Six free banks, each capitalized between $600,000 and $2 million (including the Mechanics' & Traders' Bank, which reorganized as a free bank when its charter expired in 1853), operated alongside the Canal Bank of New Orleans, the Citizens' Bank, and the state's two semipublic banks (the Louisiana State Bank and the Bank of Louisiana). But whereas banking expansion was modest in Louisiana, the state quickly gained a reputation—alongside New York—for possessing the most stable,

TABLE 9.4 Southern bank charters, 1850–1861

Region	*Total banks end of 1850*	*New charters 1851–61*	*Closures 1851–61*	*Total banks end of 1861*	*Percentage of banks closed 1851–61*	*Growth rate of banking 1851–61*
Mid-Atlantic (MD, DR, DC)	33	21	(12)	42	22%	27%
Old South (VA, NC, SC)	23	39	(7)	55	11%	139%
Upper frontier (KY, TN, MO, AR)	10	47	(27)	30	47%	200%
Lower frontier (GA, AL, MS, LA, FL)	17	28	(7)	38	16%	124%
Totals	83	135	(53)	165	24%	99%

Source: Weber, *Census of Early State Banks.*

safe banking system in the nation. No Louisiana free banks failed before the Civil War. And from the limited extant evidence, these new banks seem to have reverted to the functions of traditional commercial banks—lending primarily on short-term discounted commercial paper. While these loans may still have been secured with mortgages on enslaved lives, they were not the large, long-term mortgages of the Citizens' Bank or the Bank of Louisiana.

❋

In all the anti-banking and free-banking debates from the 1840s and 1850s, the question of the relationship between banking and the system of slavery was only rarely mentioned. During the 1820s and 1830s, banks of the lower South consciously broke from traditional banking practices in response to the financing demands of slaveholders. But by the anti-banking debates in the 1840s, no one seemed to argue that the ability to obtain loans secured by land and human property had been a benefit to slaveholders, or that limiting the future financing options of planters might slow the extension of slavery into the western territories. Everyone instead fixated on the harm that resulted from debt, which had been encouraged and facilitated by greedy, opportunistic banks. During the free-banking debates at mid-century, few southerners endorsed the use of land or enslaved individuals to secure notes, although real estate was a part of the model New York legislation. In effect, southerners were declaring that the system of slavery no longer needed the support of banks.

EPILOGUE

Banks, Debt, Emancipation, Reparations, and Memory

Debt and Emancipation

In May of 1857, Jacob Denny of Arkansas and some associates purchased Sosthène Roman's Magnolia sugar plantation for $270,532.39 (about $8.5 million in 2021). The almost 4,000-acre property in St. James Parish, Louisiana, included 1,229 shares of Citizens' Bank stock and 120 enslaved people, who Roman guaranteed were "esclaves pour la vie" or "slaves for life."[1] Sosthène Roman was part of the plantation elite in St. James parish. His parents and siblings owned several neighboring plantations, and his younger brother André had served as governor of Louisiana during the 1830s and 1840s, as well as being a delegate to the state secession convention.[2] Roman's original mortgages with the Citizens' Bank from 1837 to 1839 had included 105 enslaved individuals, of whom forty-six survived in 1857; another forty-one were the offspring of the original community.[3] But Roman had fallen on hard times by the mid-1850s. Having reported $70,000 in real estate wealth as well as 141 enslaved workers in 1850, he now needed to liquidate his substantial property.[4] The only people not included in the 1857 sale were "Henry aged 42 years, Hutton 46, Antoinette 37, Grande Phillis 50, Fanchonette 27, Sophia 52, Manette alias Henriette 53, and George 42."[5] Denny paid Roman $50,000 in cash and assumed responsibility for Roman's remaining bank debt by issuing a series of promissory notes payable to Roman in six annual installments between 1858 and 1863. Denny obtained another mortgage for $34,174 from the Citizens' Bank, due in May 1858. He put up the Magnolia plantation and its enslaved community as the collateral security for each of these debts.[6]

When the Civil War broke out in April 1861, Denny and his associates still owed approximately $110,000 of the $270,000 purchase price, including $31,000 due in May 1831. At this point, Denny stopped making his payments and Roman filed a lawsuit to seize the property back, but the suspension of the Louisiana court system froze the claim.[7] Roman renewed his lawsuit at the conclusion of the war in 1865, and the "Very Superior and Highly Improved Estate" was seized; on April 25, 1866, Roman's heirs purchased the property at auction for the much-reduced price of $120,000.[8] In his countersuit filed that same day, Denny claimed that this sale price vastly overestimated the current value of the land as well as the value of his remaining debt. In particular, he argued that emancipation, by undermining Roman's warranty that the people were "slaves for life," canceled his obligation to pay this portion of the loan. He even accused Roman of having an active role in bringing about emancipation—and thus destroying the value of the property—by his actions in promoting the war. Denny estimated the value of the 120 enslaved individuals in the original purchase price as $1,000 each, or exactly $120,000—conveniently wiping out the remainder of the debt.[9] The Louisiana Supreme Court, however, dismissed this claim, ruling in 1874 that "a party can not be permitted to allow his property to be sold under a judicial process and then claim the proceeds, under the allegation that he did not owe the debt, which the property was sold to pay."[10] Denny could not just walk away from debts incurred in the purchase of enslaved lives.

This case was just one of many cases litigated in the aftermath of emancipation. As one legal historian of Louisiana notes, "After the war and abolition of slavery, the supreme court was flooded with cases in which people who owed debts for the purchase price or hire of slaves refused to pay and their creditors sued to collect."[11] While both the Emancipation Proclamation and the Thirteenth Amendment made clear that no slaveholder would be compensated for the loss of their human property, neither resolved the more complex question of who should suffer the financial loss when enslaved individuals were part of an ongoing debt contract. Did Denny still owe the residual of the $270,000 he originally agreed to pay for the Magnolia plantation and its 120 now-freed slaves? Or would Roman have to absorb the loss of the slaves? Like Denny, many "clever debtors who had paid some of the notes before and during the war claimed afterward that they had been paying the land portion of the debt and not the slave portion, and since debts for slaves could not now be enforced, they owed nothing."[12] And what about the Citizens' Bank, which also held a mortgage on the property? Could it still collect on a debt that had been secured with formerly enslaved people? Most southern banks failed during the war years, independent of and prior to the implementation of emancipation. Therefore, whereas there were many court cases involving debt-contract disputes due to emancipation, very few of these cases involved banks. The Citizens' Bank of Louisiana was one of the few southern banks to survive the war and to leave some record of disputes over formerly enslaved lives after emancipation.

In addition to the case between Denny and Roman, the Citizens' Bank was the defendant in an 1871 lawsuit brought by the widow of George Wailes. In 1852, the bank had foreclosed on Felix Garcia's Lorio and Arnaud plantations, purchasing them at sheriff's sale.[13] In December 1852, the bank advertised to "be sold at auction at the St. Louis Hotel Rotunda . . . a Sugar Plantation formerly known as the 'Arnauld Plantation,'" including 120 shares of Citizens' Bank stock.[14] One newspaper ad noted that the plantation offered "a fine opportunity for investment or speculation."[15] This auction successfully "disposed of" the Arnauld plantation, "together with the slaves [who] worked on said plantation."[16] At a similar auction in 1852, Charles and Theodore Roussel purchased the Lorio plantation, enslaved workforce, and 950 shares of bank stock for $80,000. About $17,000 was secured by various third-party promissory notes due in March of 1853, $31,000 was payable in four equal installments from 1854 to 1857, and the remaining $32,000 was mortgaged to the bank and payable in ten annual installments.[17]

When the Roussels failed to repay the loan by 1858, the bank reseized the plantation—now called Trinity—with its fifty-one enslaved workers, reselling it that same year for $80,000. Two years later, on the eve of the war, George Wailes purchased Trinity, including the enslaved individuals attached to the plantation and 830 shares of Citizens' Bank stock.[18] At this point, the outstanding amount due to the bank was $21,850. When Wailes failed to pay the balance of the mortgage, the bank foreclosed on the property. Yet by the time the courts reopened and the bank was able to act on the foreclosure in 1867, the enslaved workers had been emancipated and the bank could only claim the land. The bank paid $320 to a broker to find a suitable purchaser of the property, selling the land to Messrs. Mennier and Cherbonnier in December "together with the buildings, improvements and appertanances [*sic*] on the land, and 830 shares of Mortgage Stock reduced to 775, for the price of $32,971 10." The bank discharged the remaining debt of George Wailes, with Wailes agreeing to these proceedings.[19]

The following year, after Wailes had died, his wife filed a lawsuit against the bank, claiming that "at the time the order of seizure and sale was executed against said property, the said debt was not valid and obligatory in consequence of the emancipation of slaves." In her view, the value of the formerly enslaved individuals was much greater than the value of the land, and certainly more than the remaining debt owed to the bank. Since the people in question were no longer enslaved, the remaining debt was invalid, making the foreclosure also invalid. The widow demanded that the bank return to her the proceeds of the land sale.[20] The widow was actually on relatively solid legal footing in claiming that the debt was invalid. As these disputes over debt contracts involving formerly enslaved lives worked their way through the courts in each state, judges had to rule on how to treat these contracts; in most cases, justices based their decisions on contract law. In 1866, for example, the Florida Supreme Court ruled in favor of the debtor in a case in which the mortgage security was entirely made up of enslaved people. The creditor could no longer foreclose on a mortgage secured by enslaved individuals since the collateral security no longer existed, and thus the creditor had no further claim on the debt.[21]

But in many other cases, the debts involving enslaved lives included other property as part of the collateral. In these cases, contract law was on the side of the creditor. The Alabama Supreme Court ruled in 1867 that when a mortgage contract was signed, the debtor was required to fulfill the terms of the contract regardless of what happened to the property in the interim; it was the debtor who took on the risk of an enslaved person becoming ill or dying (or, in this case, being emancipated). Like Jacob Denny, this Alabama debtor tried to argue that emancipation meant that the creditor's warranty of the enslaved being "slaves for life" had been violated, canceling the contract. But the court disagreed. As long as the statement had been true when the mortgage was executed, the creditor could not be held liable for the change in status of the enslaved lives. It was no different from a purchased slave dying, or a piece of land getting damaged in a hurricane. The debtor still had to pay the balance of the debt.[22] The Georgia Supreme Court in 1867 agreed, stating that the creditor should not suffer the loss of emancipation; the mortgage debt must be paid regardless of the status of the property mortgaged.[23]

But the Louisiana Supreme Court took a decidedly different view of the question. Whereas the court cases in other states largely revolved around the question of whether the debtor or creditor should bear the pecuniary loss of emancipation—basic contract-law issues—Louisiana ruled instead based on natural law. It declared that emancipation immediately nullified all contracts involving enslaved lives, because—in their words—"Freedom . . . was a preexisting right; slavery, a violation of that right." If the court were to rule in favor of either the creditor or debtor, it would be validating the existence of slavery as an institution. Although this position was effectively a ruling in favor of the debtor—by canceling their remaining debt—the rationale reflected a natural-rights argument, rather than one upholding the rights of either creditors or debtors.[24]

The Reconstruction-era constitutions of Arkansas, Florida, Louisiana, South Carolina, and Georgia all endorsed this latter view, barring the enforcement of any debts involving formerly enslaved individuals. Although many critics argued that these articles violated the federal Constitution—no state being allowed to impair the obligation of a contract—these debt clauses initially passed and were approved by Congress.[25] Thus, the widow of George Wailes was on secure ground when she argued that the mortgage had been nullified by emancipation. Unfortunately for her, the foreclosure had already been finalized. Whereas Wailes could have chosen to challenge the foreclosure under Louisiana law, the courts would not allow his widow to undo a completed legal process. The Citizens' Bank prevailed in this case.[26]

By 1871, the United States Supreme Court finally weighed in on this question. In the case of *Osborn v. Nicholson*, the court ruled that emancipation had no effect on debt contracts; debtors were still obligated to fulfill these contracts. "Where an article is on sale in the market, and there is no fraud on the part of the seller, and the buyer gets what he intended to buy, he is liable for the purchase price, though the article turns out to be worthless." In reaching this conclusion, Justice Noah Swayne—a Lincoln appointee and the first Republican to serve on the court—rejected outright the natural-rights argument asserted by the Louisiana Supreme Court:

> Whatever we may think of the institution of slavery viewed in the light of religion, morals, humanity, or a sound political economy, -as the obligation here in question was valid when executed, sitting as a court of justice, we have no choice but to give it effect. We cannot regard it as differing in its legal efficacy from any other unexecuted contract to pay money made upon a sufficient consideration at the same time and place. . . . Neither the rights nor the interests of those of the colored race lately in bondage are affected by the conclusions we have reached.[27]

In opposition to this ruling stood the majority of Louisiana Supreme Court justices, freed blacks serving in southern legislatures, and US Supreme Court Chief Justice Salmon Chase, who wrote a prominent dissent. Chase, a fellow Republican and Lincoln appointee, stated "that contracts for the purchase and sale of slaves were and are against sound morals and natural justice, and without support except in positive law." Enforcing these contracts was tantamount to endorsing slavery as an institution, in violation of the Thirteenth Amendment, which "annulled" the state laws supporting slavery, and the Fourteenth Amendment, "which forbids compensation for slaves emancipated by the thirteenth."[28]

Despite this vocal opposition, most of the debate still revolved around the question of who should absorb the pecuniary loss of enslaved individuals. And unlike most debtor-creditor debates that pitted a wealthy creditor against a much-poorer debtor, this one was basically an argument among wealthy slaveholders and their slaveholding financiers. Many southerners who initially argued in favor of canceling all debts did so as a means of sharing the burden of emancipation. The debtor had already lost the enslaved individual he had purchased; he should not be penalized again by having to finish paying the purchase price. On the other hand, many of the southerners who advocated for enforcing the debts argued that the possibility of emancipation had been incorporated into the pricing for anyone who had purchased enslaved lives—especially during the war years. Those acquiring enslaved individuals were betting on the continued existence of the system of slavery. They knew the risks and those risks were factored into the sale price. These late purchasers should thus be forced to fulfill their debt obligations.[29]

The few banks to survive the war found themselves caught up in these debates. On the one hand, they could argue that they should not share the burden of emancipation, since they were technically not slaveholders (at least not usually)—just the financial intermediaries facilitating the economic life of the region. But, in fact, banks had been an integral part of the system of slavery, particularly during the critical decades of the 1820s through the 1840s, when large cotton and sugar plantations were developing in the frontier South. What consequences, if any, should those surviving banks suffer as a result of their historical involvement with slavery?

Banks and Reparations

Following several corporate reorganizations in the late nineteenth and early twentieth centuries, the descendant banks of both the Citizens' Bank and the New Orleans Canal & Banking Company eventually became part of J. P. Morgan Chase. In 2003, Chicago passed a Slavery Era Disclosure Ordinance that required businesses operating in the city to research and report whether they had ever profited from the slave system.[30] This law was modeled on California's 2002 and Illinois' 2004 Slavery Era Insurance Laws.[31] After combing their records, J. P. Morgan Chase determined that the two Louisiana banks it now owned had "accepted approximately 13,000 slaves as collateral for loans and ended up owning approximately 1,250 of them as a result of defaults." The company apologized, and set up a $5 million scholarship program for African American students in Louisiana. According to news reports of the fund, it was "believed to be the first time an American company has paid reparations for slavery." In response, one leader of the reparations movement stated that this was a "step in the right direction for a tainted corporation," although she didn't think this step went nearly far enough.[32]

How can modern Americans grapple with this past? What would be enough?

The reparations expert is correct that $5 million is merely a gesture. The Canal Bank had been incorporated in 1831 with $4 million in capital, and the Citizens' Bank in 1833 with $12 million.[33] Although it is difficult to inflate dollar amounts over such a long period, these amounts would be roughly equivalent to $130 million and $402 million, respectively, in 2021—vastly more than the proffered $5 million fund. Working backward instead, J. P. Morgan Chase's scholarship fund would have been approximately $155,000 in the 1830s, or about the value of a single, average-sized sugar plantation. In 2005, the bank reported net income of $8.5 *billion*.[34] This scholarship fund thus represented 0.06 percent—a fraction of a percent—of their net income for one year.

On the other hand, like the debate between creditors and debtors after emancipation, who *should* pay? Is J. P. Morgan Chase actually a guilty party—more guilty than other financial institutions? Are they really a "tainted corporation"—more tainted than other corporations? The nation's modern commercial-banking system is *not* a descendant of the innovations in southern frontier banking, but rather emerged largely from the free-banking system of New York State.[35] By the time these two banks were folded into J. P. Morgan Chase, it is extremely unlikely that anyone even had any recollection of the banks' past involvement with the system of slavery (which had ended more than a half century before). The parent bank certainly did not acquire these two institutions *because* of their slave connections. In many ways, it was unlucky to have inherited this past. Any one of the major world banks could have acquired these Louisiana institutions during the early twentieth century. For what, then, was J. P. Morgan Chase actually atoning? Bad luck? A negative public-relations story? And what if no southern banks had survived the Civil War—a perfectly credible proposition? What then? Would there be no one who could be held responsible? In some ways the bank's gesture, though incredibly small, was an important recognition—intentional or not—that it doesn't actually matter *how* its relationship to slavery came about. What matters is not establishing some direct link between an individual corporation and the descendants of enslaved individuals because—in reality—everyone who benefited from the rapid development of the nineteenth-century United States is tainted.

I first encountered these questions when researching my dissertation on life insurance, which roughly coincided with the passage of the various disclosure laws in California and Illinois. In retrospect, I think that an examination of the relationship between banking and slavery provides more clarity than the case of insurance ever could. Life insurers contributed only marginal support for slavery, and they were not critical to the system itself.[36] Banking, on the other hand, was. Frontier banks were central to the movement of vast numbers of people—both free and enslaved—to the fertile cotton and sugar lands of the South, which drove the rapid development of the United States by mid-century. In all likelihood, without this financial infrastructure, the settlement of the South would have been much slower, with smaller plantations and a much-reduced domestic slave trade. How much smaller? How much slower? That would be impossible to calculate. But the importance of the banking industry during the 1820s and 1830s is still undeniable. And as numerous recent scholars have documented, the effects of the southern cotton trade rippled throughout the US economy, regardless of one's direct involvement with slavery.[37] The United States as a nation benefited from this frontier expansion, and southern banks were at the core of its success.

This study has focused on the ways that banks directly, knowingly, and willingly participated in supporting and promoting the system of slavery. And yet, in the end, that attention to the conscious sin only further highlights the social sin that is slavery. It is not the numerous slaveholders—many of whom I deliberately tried to leave nameless—who primarily benefited from mortgages on enslaved lives. It is not the countless souls—whom I have tried to name whenever possible—who were the only victims of being assessed, collateralized, and foreclosed. As long as we continue to look for specific villains to target, we overlook the bigger picture. Everyone who is a beneficiary of this nation's economic past was a participant in slavery. Everyone who continues to suffer from its racial present is a victim.

I don't claim to know what reparations should look like or how much they should be. Slavery, at its core, was an economic system, so it makes sense to start with a monetary discussion. On the one hand, I believe that no matter what we do, it can never be enough to correct an immoral and inhumane history. At the same time, our limitations shouldn't stop us from trying to ameliorate what we can't undo. Yet slavery was not *just* an economic system, so I also believe that reparations can't *just* be in the form of money. Part of the process must include somehow remembering and acknowledging how and why this horrific past has shaped our present and continues to define our future.

Banks and Memory

So how can we remember and acknowledge the financialization of slavery? In 1978, the Mississippi Department of Archives and History registered the 1819 building housing the Woodville branch of the Bank of the State of Mississippi as a national historic site. Located "on the west side of the courthouse square" in the center of Woodville, the two-story brick building in the federal style had endured several renovations and even a fire circa 1912. In 1975, it was purchased by the Woodville Civic Club, who renovated the space and reopened it as an African American museum in 2004.[38] The stated purpose of the museum is to celebrate "four black individuals, and others," from the region "who left lasting impressions on music and the arts." The main exhibits center on blues musician Scott Dunbar (a lifetime resident of Woodville); civil rights activist and writer Anne Moody, whose 1968 autobiography *Coming of Age in Mississippi* recounts her childhood in Wilkinson County; renowned jazz saxophonist Lester Young, who was born in Woodville but grew up in New Orleans; and classical composer and conductor William Grant Still, who left Woodville as an infant. A local businessman who oversaw the completion of the project viewed the museum as a "depository for African-American history." Thomas Tolliver, chairman of the museum commission, hoped it would promote "ethnic tourism in Wilkinson County and southwest Mississippi." In his estimation, "we should always preserve history—good and bad."[39]

I wanted to know more about this museum and its founding. How does it achieve this balance of preserving both the good and the bad? Using a historic building once dedicated to the financing of plantation slavery to celebrate the challenges and the achievements of their descendants seemed like a good model. But were they conscious of the significance of the bank's history for the region's slave past? Unfortunately, I was unable to interview any of the African Americans involved in the museum's founding. Tolliver passed away in 2018.[40] Museum docent Gladys Conrad Hines likewise died in 2016.[41] I tried reaching out to local black pastors, the Mississippi branch of the NAACP, and other black community leaders, but I failed to find anyone to interview from the African American community with ties to the museum. I also contacted the Woodville Civic Club, owner of the building, who directed me to a gentleman who had been involved with the Civic Club from its founding in 1971, and he eagerly agreed to speak with me by phone in June 2021. This man, whom I will refer to as Mr. Jones, was fully aware that I was interviewing him for a book, and he never asked me to keep his name a secret, but I've chosen to keep his identity anonymous nonetheless.

Mr. Jones is a highly educated man, steeped in the history both of Woodville in general and the boyhood plantation home of Confederate President Jefferson Davis specifically. Indeed, he wanted me to understand that antebellum Woodville contained a much more highly educated population than other plantation areas, and—based on his research—he didn't think that the average slave owner beat their enslaved laborers. "I can't believe it," he insisted, noting as his supporting evidence that the slaveholders called them "servants" or "field hands" in their written documents. Not wanting to disrupt his willingness to talk by contradicting these gross historical errors, I instead redirected him to the decision to purchase the old building. Here, again, he became a bit sidetracked in explaining to me the context of race relations in Woodville when he arrived there in the late 1960s. Blacks and whites got along fine, he said. The problem was with outsiders like "that dreadful Coretta King"—notwithstanding the fact that Mr. Jones himself was also an "outsider" to the Deep South. Indeed, from his vantage point (as a non–African American man), lots of people at the time were "disgusted" with what was happening with the civil rights movement.[42] Again, not wanting to get sidetracked, I redirected him back to the foundation of the Civic Club.

As in many American cities in the late 1960s and early 1970s, the downtown area of Woodville was struggling. As the Civic Club's website relates, "there were lots of empty stores; business was bad, and the morale of our residents at an all-time low. It had a malaise that so many small towns across this country were suffering as the world seemed to shift and change so fast."[43] The Civic Club was thus organized in 1971 to keep the town from fading. Businesses were buying up historic buildings considered "eye sores" and replacing them with new, modern edifices. The Civic Club therefore focused on raising money to save these old buildings, starting with the old post office and (in 1973) the 1834 office and banking house of the West Feliciana Railroad; its landmark information lists it as "the third oldest extant railroad building in the United States." In 1991, the railroad building reopened as the Wilkinson County Museum.[44]

Bringing him back to the branch building of the Bank of the State of Mississippi, I again asked Mr. Jones how it became an African American museum. He never quite answered this question, but instead started describing the exhibits in the museum itself. In particular, he proudly explained the legacy of William Grant Still, a world-famous African American composer born in Woodville in 1895. Among his many accomplishments, Still was "the first African-American to conduct a major orchestra in 1936, when he conducted the Los Angeles Symphony."[45] He was also the first African American to have a symphony performed by a professional orchestra—initially by the Rochester Philharmonic and then by the New York Philharmonic at Carnegie Hall in 1935.[46] And in 1955, he made history again by conducting the New Orleans Philharmonic—the first black conductor of a major Deep South symphony orchestra. Although this "Dean of African-American Classical Composers" left Woodville when he was but a few months old, Mr. Jones still gushed over the talent and accomplishments of one of Woodville's favorite African American residents.[47]

On the other hand, Mr. Jones continued, "the word 'slavery' doesn't exist anywhere in the museum." Lulled by his eloquent description of Still, this comment left me momentarily speechless. How was that possible? How could a museum dedicated to the African American experience in Woodville,

Mississippi, *not* mention the word slavery? People "are tired of hearing about slavery," he replied.[48] Just as the reparations paid by J. P. Morgan Chase inadvertently exposed the complicity of all financial institutions in slavery, there is also some unintentional truth in Mr. Jones's shocking revelation. The African American experience is *more than* just an enslaved past. The histories we tell shouldn't be limited to the horrors of slavery. And yet, this focus on the success of Still and others felt less like a celebration of one man's triumph over the enslavement of his ancestors and his own struggles within the Jim Crow South, and more like a sweeping under the rug of all the challenges and racism that made Still, Young, Moody, Dunbar, and others so extraordinary.

As Clint Smith writes in his thought-provoking 2021 book *How the Word is Passed: A Reckoning with the History of Slavery Across America*, the intense celebration of people like Frederick Douglass during slavery or (in this case) William Grant Still during Jim Crow "is part of the insidiousness of white supremacy; it illuminates the exceptional in order to implicitly blame those who cannot, in the most brutal circumstances, attain superhuman heights. It does this instead of blaming the system, the people who built it, the people who maintained it."[49] Mr. Jones similarly seemed to be most interested in the cultural history of African American entertainers as a means of evading any local reckoning with slavery. Tolliver's stated goal to "preserve history—good and bad" had been truncated; only the good history had survived. I didn't bother to ask Mr. Jones for his opinions on monetary reparations.

Indeed, as I write this in early 2022, this same effort of partial remembrance is at the heart of recent debates over how we teach about race, race relations, and America's racial history in our schools. As of February 1, 2022, "35 states have introduced bills or taken steps . . . to limit how teachers can discuss racism and sexism." An example of these restrictions would allow teachers to talk about the success of Jackie Robinson in breaking Major League Baseball's color barrier, but not to discuss the reasons for the original ban on black players in sports. They could celebrate singer Marvin Gaye, but not dissect the political commentary on police brutality in his 1970 hit "What's Going On."[50] Representation matters, and students of all races and genders need to learn about and be inspired by the Barack Obamas, Oprah Winfreys, Thurgood Marshalls, and Mae Jemisons in our history. But when we do so without the larger racial context—when we make their stories "safe" for white consumption—the memory becomes distorted, and their histories again become erased. The greatness and accomplishments of LeBron James are for us to marvel at and enjoy. But should he speak about the racial strife of our nation's past and present, he is told by white pundits to "keep the political comments to yourselves. . . . Shut up and dribble."[51]

Banks, Debt, Emancipation, Reparations, and Memory

If I was seeking an example of how to remember and educate people about the financialization of slavery, the Woodville Branch Banking House of the Bank of the State of Mississippi and its African American museum was not it. Back in New Orleans, several of that city's original banking houses also remain. The Louisiana State Bank building is now a banquet facility known as Latrobes on Royal. In November 2019, the general manager was gracious enough to give me a full tour of the facility. Although they have carefully maintained the interior structure of the original bank, she seemed entirely unaware of the bank's past connections to slavery. The facility website highlights the architectural features of the building rather than its functions as a bank.[52] Across the street, a historical plaque dedicated to the Bank of Louisiana building also details its architecture and the many organizations that have inhabited it since the closure of the bank in 1867: the state capitol, an auctioneer, a combination concert hall and beer saloon, the superior criminal court, the juvenile court, an American Legion post, the Greater New Orleans Tourist and Convention Commission, and (currently) a precinct station for the New Orleans police department. Most interestingly, from 1879 to 1908 the building served as the Office of the Recorder of Mortgages and Conveyances; the notarial records detailing all the mortgage contracts using enslaved people as collateral would have been stored on this site—but that fact is not mentioned on the plaque.[53]

Just a few blocks away, the building housing the Citizens' Bank—the financial institution that easily had the greatest involvement with slavery—has now been renovated into a Walgreens pharmacy. A prominent plaque at the entrance credits the bank as being "The Birthplace of 'Dixie,'" due to the printing of *dix*, the French word for "ten," on its currency. "As this currency became widespread, people referred to its place of origin as 'the land of the Dix,' which was eventually shortened to 'Dixieland.'" Whether this myth is true or not, the Citizens' Bank itself promoted the idea when it reprinted in pamphlet form a 1913 London *Financial Times* article entitled "Remarkable Bank History: The Institution That Gave the Name 'Dixie' to the South."[54] While most enslaved people didn't physically pass through these bank doors, it was here in these buildings that they were turned into abstract, fungible assets. This history has again been erased.

A very different monument to the system of slavery is the Whitney Plantation, a historic sugar plantation about one hour outside of New Orleans, which has been dedicated to telling the stories of enslaved men, women, and children since 2014. The Whitney stands in vast contrast to the many dozens of plantation sites and museums that focus on the grandeur of plantation life with beautifully renovated mansion houses and meticulously landscaped grounds. Like the African American museum in Woodville and the New Orleans bank buildings, these "historic sites" often either erase or minimalize their slave past, leaving vacationing tourists unchallenged and making the grounds perfect sites for destination weddings.[55] The Whitney, on the other hand, inverts this relationship; the mansion house and its white residents are relegated to the background while the dank slave quarters, massive sugar kettles, and horrifying experiences of the enslaved individuals who lived and died there are brought to life.

While doing research for this book in New Orleans in 2017, I had the privilege of visiting this amazing and unique open-air museum. Near the entrance to the site is an immense granite "Wall of Honor" listing all the people known to have lived on the plantation.[56] The last panel of the wall documents the auction of sixty-two enslaved individuals by the owners in 1840 (figures E.1 and E.2). The auction was instigated by his creditors, and the people were sold under mortgage. The largest purchaser was Felix Garcia, who acquired twenty-three enslaved lives for his Lorio plantation in St. Charles Parish, and immediately placed them under mortgage with the Citizens' Bank.[57] Next to each individual name is the person's age, description, buyer—and the dollar amount for which they sold. They were identifiable people, now associated with their status as abstract financial assets. In his chapter dedicated to the Whitney Plantation, Clint Smith calls it "a laboratory for historical ambition, an experiment in rewriting what long ago was rewritten . . . a necessary, even if imperfect, corrective against a history that has been misrepresented or ignored for so long . . . a catalyst for discussion."[58] Paradoxically, perhaps people would be less "tired of hearing about slavery" if we had more sites like this to serve as "catalyst[s] for discussion." Yet as long as we are banning books and sanitizing school curricula in an effort to erase all memories of a complicated, painful past, this reckoning will never take place. Writing from the vantage point of 2022, I am as pessimistic as ever.

FIGURE E.1–E.2. Photos of Whitney Plantation "Wall of Honor" final panel. Photos taken by author, April 2017.

Auction of slaves attached to the estate of Jean Jacques Haydel, Jr. (April 30, 1840).

Sold at the Bath Saloon of the St. Louis Hotel, by Joseph Le Carpentier, Auctioneer, by virtue of an order from the Honorable the District Court for the First Judicial District of the State of Louisiana dated 24th March 1840, and at the request of the syndics of the creditors of Jean Jacques Haydel, after the advertisements required by law, to wit: In the Bee (State paper) in french and english, March 27th, April 13th, 20th & 30th, and in the Louisiana Courier in French and English, March 29th, April 13th, 20th & 29th, the following slaves.

Terms: One half payable in March 1841 and one half in March 1842 in notes satisfactorily endorsed and bearing mortgage until final payment. Said notes must be made payable in New Orleans and in case of non payment when due will bear from the day of expiration an interest of 10% per annum until final payment. Said clause not to be taken advantage of to defer the payment of any note. The slaves will be delivered to the purchasers when the conditions of the sale will be fulfilled. The acts of sale to be passed at the cost of the purchasers before Felix Grima, Esq., notary public.

Negroes

1. Little Guim, 50 years, African, sold to Mr. Etienne Villere, f.c.m., $170.
2. Paul, 48 years, Congo, sold to Cyprien Tremoulet, $300.
3. Achille 48 years, carter & ploughman, sold to Achille Lorio, $800.
4. George, 48 years, American, sold to Edmond Fazende, $650.
5. Big John, 45 years, American, carter & ploughman, sold to Phi Lambert, $675.
6. Borel, 30 years, American, carter & ploughman, sold to Felix Garcia, $1,325.
7. Lewis, 34 years, American, engineer, carter & ploughman, sold to Felix Garcia, $1,400.
8. Maille, 32 years, American, carter & ploughman, sold to Felix Garcia, $1,425.
9. Diastone, 32 years, American, carter & ploughman, sold to Sosthene Roman, $950.
10. Andre Jackson 36 years, American, carter & ploughman, sold to Felix Garcia, $1,225.

FIGURE E.1–E.2. (*Continued*)

Acknowledgments

This was not the book I intended to write. After the publication of my first book, on antebellum life insurance, I wanted—I needed—my next project to be on a topic that I could primarily accomplish using online databases. While I have always been an "archive rat," long trips away from home just aren't feasible when you have young children and a spouse with a full-time job (and travel obligations of his own). This book was thus supposed to be about the public perception of banking in and around the Panic of 1819, based on newspapers and other accessible print sources. As I tried to pull that project together, I published *Other People's Money: How Banking Worked in the Early American Republic* (2017). Based mainly on secondary sources, this "useful book" (as I like to think of it) explains the nuts and bolts of how money and banking worked from the Revolution to the Civil War. Yet my intended section on banking and slavery ended up being a mere two anemic paragraphs. Was that it? Was there really no larger story behind the financing of slavery? Indeed, in Joshua Rothman's assessment of this book in *Civil War Book Review* he lamented that "some greater attention to the significance of slavery in the development of the banking system would have been welcome." Thanks, Josh, but I'm already ahead of you. By 2015, before *Other People's Money* had even made it into page proofs, I had already pushed the topic of banking during the Panic of 1819 onto the back burner and had started digging into banking and slavery. Like people selecting wands in Mr. Ollivander's shop, I didn't choose the topic; the topic chose me.

Of course, I knew immediately that this could never be a "database" project. I also knew that this would not be a quick project but rather would likely take a decade or more to finish. I would need not only time and research money—always in short supply when teaching full-time at a liberal-arts college—but especially the flexibility to travel to archives while my children were still little. Every school break, every conference, every invited presentation, every vacation involved me doing a mad dash into some archive. I was greatly aided by changing technology and archival policies. Whereas virtually no one permitted the digital photographing of manuscripts when I was working on my dissertation, most archives now allowed researchers to capture images of documents on their phones. Rather than spending weeks combing through sources, typing notes, and flagging items for (often expensive) photocopies, I could now rapidly triage many collections. I took tens of thousands of photographs that I could worry about reading and sorting through back home. Although this quick method was not possible for most of the notarial records at the heart of this study, it still greatly expedited my time in other archives. Even more important was having a wonderful spouse, Ken, who held down the family fort while I was away on these many trips. He even doubled as my travel agent when I texted from inside archives, "need more time here; change my flight" or "done quicker than I thought; find me a rental car so I can drive to [x archive] in [y state]." In all, I traveled to dozens of archives—large and small—in at least fifteen different states. I couldn't have done it without him. In the process, I learned to love audiobooks as I traversed the South in a rental car.

I also could not have accomplished this project without the funding support I received from a large variety of sources. (Thank you to Ed Balleisen and Richard John for writing so many letters of recommendation for me!) These included a National Endowment for the Humanities summer stipend (2017) and a very generous travel grant from Providence College's Committee to Aid Faculty Research (2017–18). In the summer of 2018, I spent two weeks at the American Philosophical Society in Philadelphia supported by a Franklin Research Grant, where I read through the Stephen Girard papers. This collection was essential for providing information on early nineteenth-century banking, and especially the involvement of the First Bank of the United States with slave financing. I spent another two full weeks that summer at the Wilson Special Collections Library at the University of North Carolina at Chapel Hill, funded by a Hugh L. McColl Library Fund Research Fellowship. Initially, I expected much of my story to revolve around the more established banks of the old South. My deep dive into the Southern Historical Collection finally made me realize that I might be focusing in the wrong region. The many worthwhile gems I found during this trip almost always dealt with North Carolinians who were investing in or moving to the southern frontier. Even more importantly, the relative lack of interest in slave finance by old-South banks helped reshape my thesis around the expansion of slavery.

Sometimes, what you don't find is just as important as what you do. And since the Wilson Special Collections Library has (hands down) THE best finding aids I have ever seen, I departed relatively confident that I had left no major stone unturned.

I can't begin to thank all the wonderful archivists I encountered on these trips, but a few truly stand out. In addition to the stellar staff at UNC, I couldn't have done this project without the help of Siva Blake, Janine Smith, Sybil Thomas, and (at the end) Elizabeth Allen at the City of New Orleans Notarial Archives. The wonderful people at the Historic New Orleans Collection—especially Rebecca Smith—helped me with scans and permissions from their amazing digital collections. Back home, the interlibrary loan librarians at Providence College worked overtime to get me various collections that were available on microfilm (thank you especially to Carol Wiseman and Kevin Mattos). And in the very final weeks, Peter Rogers of the Providence College Library pulled together polished maps for the book. Several undergraduate students likewise contributed to my research at various points, especially Madison Palmieri, Christine Sullivan, Nick Moran, Kyle Burgess, and Kendall Hauerwas.

Amid all this traveling to archives, numerous people brightened my trips. I had meals with old high school and college friends Denise Harte Brandenburg, Stef Pratola Ferreri, Tracey Roach Koast, Amy Hayned Harned, and Debra Gaeta-Mineshima, and historian friends Wendy Woloson, Whitney Martinko, Jessica Roney, Shennette Garrett-Scott, Barbara Hahn, Aaron Sheehan-Dean, Jonathan Pritchett, and Rajesh Narayanan. Tim and Steph Murphy, Terry and Christie Murphy, Debra and Aiko Gaeta-Mineshima, and Whitney Martinko all let me stay in their guest rooms (often with little to no warning). I took in a Paul Simon concert in North Carolina with Tim and Steph, participated in a raucous mud-volleyball tournament with my extended Murphy family, got to see my talented godson Ryan Olowin compete in a regional gymnastics meet in Tennessee, and later attended his high school graduation party in Virginia.

While my husband and several fellowships were providing me with the flexibility and money I needed to travel, what I still lacked was *time*. Receiving a fellowship from the American Council of Learned Societies in 2018–19 was a game changer, allowing me to turn my one-semester sabbatical into a full year, and a decade-plus project into something doable on a potentially shorter timetable. By the end of that year, I had completed an article detailing the relationship between the First and Second Banks of the United States and the financing of slavery, which was published in September 2021 in the *Journal of Southern History*. (Thanks to Pat Breen and Steve Smith for helpful feedback on that article.)

As my sabbatical finished, I unexpectedly received an email from Nan Wolverton at the American Antiquarian Society in Worcester, MA, offering me an AAS-NEH fellowship for the fall of 2019; they had an unexpected, last-minute fellowship slot to fill. My provost Hugh Lena not only agreed to let me take this additional professional leave but also agreed to match the difference in my salary during the semester. My time at the AAS was amazing. Although I was commuting two hours every day (more audiobooks!), I still benefited from the "residential" aspects of this fellowship—daily lunches, regular dinners, numerous seminars, and countless other encounters with both the fellows and staff: Craig Friend, Karen Sanchez-Eppler, Rachel Miller, Christina Michelon, Megan Walsh, Don James McLaughlin, Matthew Suazo, Louise Walker, Corinne Field, Lauren Hewes, Ashley Cataldo, Elizabeth Watts Pope, Kevin Wisniewski, Stephen Bullock, Nan Wolverton—and others that I've missed. My lunchtime workshop on slave finance at the Nesbit Manufacturing Company turned into an article in *Enterprise & Society*. And again, the leave gave me much-needed time to finish organizing this unwieldy project. By the end of the semester, I had a working outline that would enable me to start drafting chapters. Then, in December 2019, I was awarded an NEH fellowship (third time's the charm!). Again, my provost agreed to allow me to take a professional leave—although I would delay it until the spring of 2021. Time and money.

Small workshops and seminars offer wonderful opportunities to share and discuss works in progress, and I benefited from participating in numerous such sessions. In the fall of 2015, I was invited to give a talk at the University of Virginia's MADCAP: Movements and Directions in Capitalism workshop. I decided that my alma mater was the perfect place to offer my initial, very inchoate thoughts on the topic. This talk was followed by seminars at the John F. Kennedy Institute for North American Studies at Freie Universität in Berlin (2016), the Economic History Workshop at Yale University (2017), the Columbia University Seminar in Economic History (2018), and the Brown University Early American Money Symposium (2020). In each of these settings, I benefited not only from fruitful discussions with a knowledgeable, interested audience but also from the collegiality (and good food and drink) that always accompanies such events. I likewise presented portions of this project in more-formal conference settings, including the Business History Conference (my intellectual home) in 2016 and 2020, the Histories of Capitalism v. 2.0 conference at Cornell University in 2016, the Society for Historians of the Early American Republic in 2018, the Organization of American Historians in 2021, and the American Society for Legal History in 2021. I can't even begin to list the people who made contributions to this book during those seminars and conferences, but I should at least try to thank Susie Pak, Ann Daly, Judge Glock, Sebastian Jobs, Jane Knodell, Naomi Lamoreaux, Sarah Milov, Kathryn Olivarius, and David Thomson. Ann, in particular, clued me into the Brown Brothers records at the New York Public Library.

I was extremely fortunate to have finished a significant amount of my research when the pandemic hit. In some ways, it forced me to stop looking for more scraps of primary sources and start writing. Thus, flanked by my children doing online school during May and June 2020, I dove in. The writing continued the following spring during my NEH leave. I had no more leaves coming and—even worse—I would become department chair in the fall. It was now or never. Yet my children were again doing online school from November through February. We sat in a row on our computers, and I wrote (while yelling at them to stop watching YouTube videos or playing games). As things opened up in the spring, I brought my computer everywhere. I wrote in the parking lot of swim practice. I wrote at the soccer field. I got up early to write and I stayed up late to write. By May, I had a working draft, ready to be workshopped. Provost Sean Reid, Dean Sheila Adamus Liotta, the Providence College Office of Academic Affairs, and my chair, Ted Andrews, all contributed money toward a manuscript workshop that June. The feedback I received from the careful reading and thoughtful comments of Caitlin Rosenthal, Peter Coclanis, Howard Bodenhorn, Seth Rockman, and Pat Breen absolutely transformed the draft for the better. Caitlin, it should be noted, had also been one of the blind reviewers on each of my two articles. She has more than "served her time" on this project.

These acknowledgments have been much too long, and yet I'm sure that I still forgot to thank people critical to this process. In addition to my amazing early Americanist colleagues Pat Breen, Ted Andrews, Adrian Weimer, and Steve Smith, other colleagues also provided much-needed support and comic relief—especially my history running crew of Jen Illuzzi, Alex Orquiza, Osama Siddiqui, Colin Jaundrill, and Alyssa Lopez. And in the end, I again must thank my husband and children, who give me not only much love and support, but also the flexibility to get this book done. This book is dedicated to my children, Amalia and Cono, who have literally lived and breathed this project. (Amalia even caught an error in one of my maps when reading over my shoulder one day.) As I was desperately trying to pull together this manuscript, I (quite seriously) commented that this might be my last book. I was exhausted and couldn't imagine starting another project. Amalia looked at me in horror. "Mama, you have to do another one." This is what their mom does. After all they have sacrificed for this book, they wouldn't have it any other way.

Portions of this book have been previously published in different forms:

Sharon Ann Murphy, "Collateral Damage: The Impact of Foreclosure on Enslaved People during the Panic," for a forum on the Panic of 1819 in the *Journal of the Early Republic* 40, no. 4 (Winter 2020): 691–96. ©Society for Historians of the Early American Republic. Reprinted with permission of the University of Pennsylvania Press.

Sharon Ann Murphy, "The Financialization of Slavery by the First and Second Banks of the United States," *Journal of Southern History* 87, no. 3 (August 2021): 385–426. Reprinted with permission of the Southern Historical Association.

Sharon Ann Murphy, "Gone to Texas: Deadbeat Debtors and their Human Property," *Journal of the Texas Supreme Court Historical Society* 11, no. 2 (Winter 2022): 27–43. Reprinted with permission of the Texas Supreme Court Historical Society.

Abbreviations

ALABAMA: Bank of the State of Alabama, Government Records Collections, Alabama Department of Archives and History, Montgomery, AL.

ARKANSAS: Real Estate Bank of Arkansas financial records, 1838–1855, Arkansas State Archives, Little Rock, AR.

BIDDLE: Letterbooks, 1823–1841, Nicholas Biddle papers, Manuscript Division, Library of Congress, Washington, DC, microfilm reels 42–46.

BROWN: Brown Brothers & Company records, Manuscripts and Archives Division, New York Public Library. http://archives.nypl.org/mss/410#c1101426.

BUS (BALTIMORE): Bank of the United States (Baltimore, MD) Records, Manuscript Division, Library of Congress, Washington, DC.

BUS (PA) Bank of the United States of Pennsylvania papers, 1390C, Historical Society of Pennsylvania, Philadelphia, PA.

BUS (PA-DISS.) Bank of the United States of Pennsylvania dissolution papers, 1390A, Historical Society of Pennsylvania, Philadelphia, PA.

CANAL BANK: Canal Bank records, collection #25, volume 58, Howard-Tilton Memorial Library, Tulane University, New Orleans, LA.

CENSUS (MCR): Manuscript Census Returns, National Archives Microfilm Series; all census documents accessed through http://www.familysearch.org.

CENSUS (SS): Slave Schedule, National Archives Microfilm Series; all census documents accessed through http://www.familysearch.org.

CITIZENS' BANK: "Citizens' Bank of Louisiana Minute Books and Records, 1833–1868," New Orleans, Louisiana collections #26 and #539 (Howard-Tilton Memorial Library, Tulane University, New Orleans, LA), Records of Ante-Bellum Southern Plantations from the Revolution through the Civil War, Series H, microfilm.

CITY BANK: City Bank records, #1785, Louisiana and Lower Mississippi Valley Collections, Louisiana State University Libraries, Baton Rouge, LA.

DAS: North American Slave Narratives, Documenting the American South. University Library, University of North Carolina at Chapel Hill. https://docsouth.unc.edu/neh.

ELMORE: Franklin H. Elmore papers, Library of Congress, Washington, DC.

GARR: Georgia Railroad Bank and Company records, 1834–40 Board of Directors Minutes, Reese Library Archives, Augusta University, Augusta, GA.

GEORGIA: Georgia State Archives, Morrow, GA.

GIRARD: Stephen Girard papers, 1793–1857, mss. film 1424 (American Philosophical Society, Philadelphia, PA), microfilm.

HSP: Historical Society of Pennsylvania, Philadelphia, PA.

KDLA BANK: Bank of Kentucky, Kentucky Department for Libraries and Archives, Frankfort, KY.

KDLA DEEDS: County court deeds, Kentucky Department for Libraries and Archives, Frankfort, KY, microfilm.

LLMVC: Louisiana and Lower Mississippi Valley Collections, Louisiana State University Libraries, Baton Rouge, LA.

LOC: Manuscript Division, Library of Congress, Washington, DC.

LOGAN: County Court Deeds, Logan County Archives and Genealogical Society, Russellville, KY.

MDAH: Mississippi Department of Archives and History, Jackson, MS.

MISSISSIPPI: Bank of the State of Mississippi records, Natchez Trace Collection, Briscoe Center for American History, University of Texas at Austin.

MSU: Bank of Mississippi records, mss. 19, Mississippi State University Libraries Special Collections, Starkville, MS, microfilm reel 3.

NARA: Bankruptcy Act of 1841 case files, US District Court for the Eastern District of Louisiana. New Orleans Term. National Archives Records Administration, Kansas City, MO.

NONA: New Orleans Notarial Archives, New Orleans, LA. Courtesy Hon. Chelsey Richard Napoleon, Clerk of Civil District Court, Parish of Orleans.

NYPL: Manuscripts and Archives Division, New York Public Library.

PETITIONS: Race & Slavery Petitions Project, University of North Carolina at Greensboro. https://library.uncg.edu/slavery/petitions/

PLANTATIONS: Records of Ante-Bellum Southern Plantations from the Revolution through the Civil War, microfilm, University Publications of America, Bethesda, MD.

PLANTERS BANK: The Planters Bank of Mississippi records, Mandeville (Henry D.) Family Papers, #491, 535, Correspondence, 1833–1873, Louisiana and Lower Mississippi Valley Collections, Louisiana State University Libraries, Baton Rouge, LA.

SANC: State Archives of North Carolina, Raleigh, NC.

SHC: Southern Historical Collection, Wilson Library, University of North Carolina at Chapel Hill.

THNOC: The Historic New Orleans Collection, Williams Research Center, New Orleans, LA.

TULANE: Citizens' Bank of Louisiana papers, New Orleans, Louisiana collection #539, Howard-Tilton Memorial Library, Tulane University, New Orleans, LA.

XAVIER: Charles F. Heartman Manuscripts of Slavery Collection, Archives and Special Collections, Xavier University of Louisiana, New Orleans, LA. https://cdm16948.contentdm.oclc.org/digital/collection/p16948coll6/.

Notes

Introduction

1. Fredrika Bremer, *The Homes of the New World; Impressions of America* vol. II (New York: Harper & Brothers, 1853), 193; George D. Green, *Finance and Economic Development in the Old South: Louisiana Banking 1804–1861* (Stanford, CA: Stanford University Press, 1972), 15.

2. Benjamin Moore Norman, *Norman's New Orleans and Environs* (New Orleans: B. M. Norman, 1845); L. Hirt, "Plan of New Orleans with Perspective and Geometrical Views of the Principal Buildings of the City," 1841, Historic New Orleans Collection, L. Kemper and Leila Moore Williams Founders Collection, http://hnoc.minisisinc.com/thnoc/catalog/1/2814. Among Norman's other publications were plantation account books, and an 1858 map of the lower Mississippi River, charting the owners of the cotton and sugar plantations from Natchez to New Orleans. Caitlin Rosenthal, *Accounting for Slavery: Masters and Management* (Cambridge, MA: Harvard University Press, 2018), 93; Marie Adrien Persac, Benjamin Moore Norman, and J. H. Colton & Co., "Norman's Chart of the Lower Mississippi River," map (New Orleans: B. M. Norman, 1858), https://www.loc.gov/item/78692178/.

3. Bremer, *Homes*, 194.

4. Norman, *Norman's New Orleans*, 143.

5. Richard Campanella, "The St. Louis and the St. Charles: New Orleans' Legacy of Showcase Exchange Hotels," *Preservation in Print* (April 2015): 16, https://cloud.3dissue.com/193333/193749/226507/April2015/index.html.

6. Norman, *Norman's New Orleans*, 143.

7. Norman, *Norman's New Orleans*, 143.

8. Sylvia Starns Mince, "The Power Struggle between Americans and Creoles in the First Half of the Nineteenth Century and Its Influence on the Architecture of New Orleans," (PhD diss., Louisiana State University, 2010), 148, https://digitalcommons.lsu.edu/gradschool_dissertations/136.

9. Campanella, "The St. Louis," 16.

10. Norman, *Norman's New Orleans*, 157; Rafael I. Pardo, "Bankrupted Slaves," *Vanderbilt Law Review* 71, no. 4 (May 2018), 1147; Maurie D. McInnis, "Mapping the Slave Trade in Richmond and New Orleans," *Buildings and Landscapes: Journal of the Vernacular Architecture Forum* 20, no. 2 (Fall 2013): 113.

11. Campanella, "The St. Louis," 16.

12. Bremer, *Homes*, 206.

13. McInnis, "Mapping," 112.

14. "Restaurant du Cardinal," New Orleans *Times-Picayune*, September 17, 1847, 3.

15. Green, *Finance*, 25.

16. Green, *Finance*, 22–23. In his history of Louisiana banking, Green makes the point that property banks like the Citizens' Bank are "incorrectly called 'plantation banks' by some historians." I disagree. While these banks were certainly still property banks, they were a specific subset that included and, indeed, depended on enslaved lives. The term "property bank" downplays this connection, while "plantation bank" emphasizes it. See p. 16.

17. Green, *Finance*, 5. Although Louisiana ranked third in banking capital behind New York and Massachusetts in 1840, the banks of Massachusetts were spread throughout that state, while Louisiana's banks were all concentrated in New Orleans with branches throughout the state.

18. Jean H. Baker, *Building America: The Life of Benjamin Henry Latrobe* (New York: Oxford University Press, 2020), 224–25; Adam Rothman, *Slave Country: American Expansion and the Origins of the Deep South* (Cambridge, MA: Harvard University Press, 2005), 184. The Louisiana State Bank building is now a banquet facility, but the interior structure of the original bank has largely been maintained. See http://www.latrobesonroyal.com/.

19. "Sale of Property by the President Directors & Company of the Bank of the United States to the New Orleans Gas-Light & Banking Company," January 22, 1836, Notary Jules Mossy, vol. 10, no. 39, *NONA*.

20. Norman, *Norman's New Orleans*, 155.

21. Green, *Finance*, 24–25.

22. Norman, *Norman's New Orleans*, 153–54.

23. Campanella, "The St. Louis," 16; Norman, *Norman's New Orleans*, 137–41.

24. Norman, *Norman's New Orleans*, 137–41.

25. Bremer, *Homes*, 194–5.

26. McInnis, "Mapping,"113; Norman, *Norman's New Orleans*, 139.

27. McInnis, "Mapping," 116.

28. Norman, *Norman's New Orleans*, 156.

29. McInnis, "Mapping," 120; Pardo, "Bankrupted Slaves," 1146–47; Bremer, *Homes*, 202–06.

30. Bremer, *Homes*, 195.

31. A. Rothman, *Slave Country*; Rosenthal, *Accounting*; Joshua D. Rothman, *The Ledger and the Chain: How Domestic Slave Traders Shaped America* (New York: Basic Books, 2021); Stephanie E. Jones-Rogers, *They Were Her Property: White Women as Slave Owners in the American South* (New Haven, CT: Yale University Press, 2019); Claudio Saunt, *Unworthy Republic: The Dispossession of Native Americans and the Road to Indian Territory* (New York: W. W. Norton, 2020); Robert Fogel and Stanley Engerman, *Time on the Cross: The Economics of American Negro Slavery* (New York: Little Brown and Company, 1974); Paul David and Peter Temin, "Explaining the Relative Efficiency of Slave Agriculture in the Antebellum South: A Comment," *American Economic Review* 69, no. 1 (1979): 213–18; Robert Fogel, *Without Consent or Contract: The Rise and Fall of American Slavery* (New York: W. W. Norton, 1989); Gavin Wright, *The Political Economy of the Cotton South* (New York: W. W. Norton, 1978); Gavin Wright, *Slavery and American Economic Development* (Baton Rouge: Louisiana State University, 2006); Alan Olmstead and Paul Rhode, "Biological Innovation and Productivity in the Antebellum Cotton Economy," *Journal of Economic History* 68 (December 2008): 1123–71; Sven Beckert, *Empire of Cotton: A Global History* (Cambridge, MA: Harvard University Press, 2015); L. Diane Barnes, Brian Schoen, and

Frank Towers, eds., *The Old South's Modern Worlds: Slavery, Region, and Nation in the Age of Progress* (Oxford: Oxford University Press, 2011); Edward Baptist, *The Half Has Never Been Told: Slavery and the Making of American Capitalism* (New York: Basic Books, 2014); Walter Johnson, *River of Dark Dreams: Slavery and Empire in the Cotton Kingdom* (Cambridge, MA: Harvard University Press, 2013); Christa Dierksheide, *Amelioration and Empire: Progress and Slavery in the Plantation Americas* (Charlottesville: University of Virginia Press, 2014).

32. Calvin Schermerhorn, *The Business of Slavery and the Rise of American Capitalism, 1815–1860* (New Haven, CT: Yale University Press, 2015); Edward E. Baptist, "Toxic Debt, Liar Loans, Collateralized and Securitized Human Beings, and the Panic of 1837," in Michael Zakim and Gary J. Kornblith, eds., *Capitalism Takes Command: The Social Transformation of Nineteenth-Century America* (University of Chicago Press, 2012): 69–92.

33. Joshua D. Rothman, "The Contours of Cotton Capitalism: Speculation, Slavery and Economic Panic in Mississippi, 1832–1841," in Sven Beckert and Seth Rockman, eds., *Slavery's Capitalism: A New History of American Economic Development* (Philadelphia: University of Pennsylvania Press, 2016): 122–45; J. Rothman, *Slave Traders*; Jeff Forret, "'How Deeply They *Weed* into the Pockets': Slave Traders, Bank Speculators, and the Anatomy of a Chesapeake Wildcat, 1840–1843," *Journal of the Early Republic* 39, no. 4 (Winter 2019): 709–736.

34. Richard Holcombe Kilbourne Jr., *Debt, Investment, Slaves: Credit Relations in East Feliciana Parish, Louisiana 1825–1885* (Tuscaloosa: University of Alabama Press, 1995); Bonnie Martin, "Slavery's Invisible Engine: Mortgaging Human Property," *Journal of Southern History* (November 2010): 817–66.

35. J. Carlyle Sitterson, *Sugar Country: The Cane Sugar Industry in the South, 1753–1950* (Westport, CT: Greenwood Press, 1973); Harold D. Woodman, *King Cotton & His Retainers: Financing & Marketing the Cotton Crop of the South, 1800–1925* (Lexington: University of Kentucky Press, 1968).

36. Larry Schweikart, *Banking in the American South from the Age of Jackson to Reconstruction* (Baton Rouge: Louisiana State University Press, 1987); Howard Bodenhorn, *State Banking in Early America: A New Economic History* (New York: Oxford University Press, 2003).

37. Richard Holcombe Kilbourne Jr., *Slave Agriculture and Financial Markets in Antebellum America: The Bank of the United States in Mississippi, 1831–1852* (London: Pickering & Chatto, 2006); Stephen W. Campbell, "'A Very Large Extent of Virgin Land': Nicholas Biddle, Cotton, and the Expansion of Slavery, 1823–1841," *Pennsylvania Magazine of History and Biography* 145 (January 2021): 33–65; Jane Ellen Knodell, *The Second Bank of the United States: "Central" Banker in an Era of Nation-Building, 1816–1836* (New York: Routledge, 2016); David Jack Cowen, *The Origins and Economic Impact of the First Bank of the United States, 1791–1797* (New York: Garland, 2000).

38. Stephen Mihm, "Follow the Money: The Return of Finance in the Early American Republic," *Journal of the Early Republic* 36, no. 4 (Winter 2016): 784–85.

39. Katharina Pistor, *The Code of Capital: How the Law Creates Wealth and Inequality* (Princeton, NJ: Princeton University Press, 2019), 3.

40. Peter J. Coleman, *Debtors and Creditors in America: Insolvency, Imprisonment for Debt, and Bankruptcy 1607–1900* (Madison: State Historical Society of Wisconsin, 1974); Winifred Rothenberg, *From Market-Places to a Market Economy: The Transformation of Rural Massachusetts, 1750–1850* (Chicago: University of Chicago Press, 1992); Bonnie Martin, "Neighbor-to-Neighbor Capitalism: Local Credit Networks and the Mortgaging of Slaves," in Beckert and Rockman, eds., *Slavery's Capitalism*: 107–21; Green, *Finance*, 8.

41. Sean Patrick Adams, "The Tao of John Quincy Adams. Or, The New Institutionalism and the Early American Republic," *Common-Place* 9 (October 2008), http://commonplace.online/article/tao-john-quincy-adams/.

42. For more on the idea of the erasure of enslaved voices, see Rosenthal, *Accounting*, 196–98; Marisa J. Fuentes, *Dispossessed Lives: Enslaved Women, Violence, and the Archive* (Philadelphia: University of Pennsylvania Press, 2016), 1–12; Stephanie E. Smallwood, *Saltwater Slavery: A Middle Passage from Africa to American Diaspora* (Cambridge, MA: Harvard University Press, 2008), 98.

Part I Introduction

1. US Department of Commerce, Bureau of the Census, *Historical Statistics of the United States: Colonial Times to 1970*, part 1 (Washington, DC: US GPO, 1975), 24–36, Series A 195–209.

2. Ira Berlin, *Generations of Captivity: A History of African-American Slaves* (Cambridge, MA: Belknap Press, 2003), 163.

3. Daniel S. Dupre, *Transforming the Cotton Frontier: Madison County, Alabama 1800–1840* (Baton Rouge: Louisiana State University Press, 1997), 1.

4. US Department of Commerce, *Historical Statistics*, 24–36, series A, 195–209.

5. James Oakes, *The Ruling Race: A History of American Slaveholders* (New York: Alfred A. Knopf, 1982), 76.

Chapter One

1. Bryan C. Rindfleisch, *George Galphin's Intimate Empire: The Creek Indians, Family, and Colonialism in Early America* (Tuscaloosa: University of Alabama Press, 2019), 3.

2. Bryan C. Rindfleisch, "The Last Will and Testament of George Galphin: Family, Empire, and Revolution in the Eighteenth-Century American South," *South Carolina Historical Magazine* 118 (July 2017): 192–98.

3. Rindfleisch, *Galphin's Intimate Empire*, 189.

4. Goodwyn v. State Bank, 4 Des. Eq. 389, 4 S.C. Eq. 389 (1813) at 390.

5. "An Act to Incorporate the State Bank," *Acts and Resolutions of the General Assembly of the State of South Carolina* (Columbia, SC: D. & J. J. Faust, 1802), 44.

6. *Goodwyn*, 4 Des.

7. *Goodwyn*, 4 Des. at 391 and 393.

8. "State Bank," *Acts and Resolutions*, 48.

9. For an interesting discussion of the early history of mortgaging and foreclosure, see K-Sue Park, "Money, Mortgages, and the Conquest of America," *Law and Social Inquiry* 41 (Fall 2016): 1006–35; and K-Sue Park, "Race Innovation, and Financial Growth: The Example of Foreclosure," in Destin Jenkins and Justin Leroy, eds., *Histories of Racial Capitalism* (New York: Columbia University Press, 2021), 27–51.

10. Peter J. Coleman, *Debtors and Creditors in America: Insolvency, Imprisonment for Debt, and Bankruptcy 1607–1900* (Madison: State Historical Society of Wisconsin, 1974); Winfred Rothenberg, *From Market-Places to a Market Economy: The Transformation of Rural Massachusetts, 1750–1850* (Chicago: University of Chicago Press, 1992); Bonnie Martin, "Neighbor-to-Neighbor Capitalism: Local Credit Networks and the Mortgaging of Slaves," in Sven Beckert and Seth Rockman, eds., *Slavery's Capitalism: A New History of American Economic Development*

(Philadelphia: University of Pennsylvania Press, 2016), 107–21; Peter A. Coclanis, *The Shadow of a Dream: Economic Life and Death in the South Carolina Low Country, 1670–1920* (New York: Oxford University Press, 1991), 104.

11. In 1774, 48.6 percent of southern wealth consisted of land, and 35.6 percent consisted of enslaved people, with various types of personal property accounting for the remaining sixth. See Claire Priest, "Creating an American Property Law: Alienability and Its Limits in American History," *Harvard Law Review* 120 (December 2006), 418.

12. On the coding of various assets as capital, see Katharina Pistor, *The Code of Capital: How the Law Creates Wealth and Inequality* (Princeton, NJ: Princeton University Press, 2019).

13. George M. Stroud, *Sketch of the Laws Relating to Slavery in Several States of the United States of America* (Philadelphia: Kimber and Sharpless, 1827), 22–23.

14. Sharon Ann Murphy, "Securing Human Property: Slavery, Life Insurance, and Industrialization in the Upper South," *Journal of the Early Republic* 25 (Winter 2005), 620–21.

15. Pistor, *Code of Capital*, 28.

16. For example, see Thomas D. Morris, *Southern Slavery and the Law, 1619–1860* (Chapel Hill: University of North Carolina Press, 1996), 61–62.

17. Morris, *Southern Slavery*, 64.

18. Priest, "American Property Law," 387–88.

19. Priest, "American Property Law," 419.

20. Morris, *Southern Slavery*, 66.

21. Priest, "American Property Law," 418–19.

22. Claire Priest, *Credit Nation: Property Laws and Institutions in Early America* (Princeton, NJ: Princeton University Press, 2021), 76.

23. Priest, "American Property Law," 389; Marylynn Salmon, *Women and the Law of Property in Early America* (Chapel Hill: University of North Carolina Press, 1986), 152–53; Pistor, *Code of Capital*, 39.

24. Priest, "American Property Law," 428–29.

25. Jones v. Langhorn, 1 Va. Colonial Dec. R109 (VA 1732) at R109; Jones v. Langhorn, 2 Va. Colonial Dec. 50, S.C. Jeff. 37 (General Court, VA 1736).

26. *Jones*, 1 Va. Colonial Dec.; *Jones*, S.C. Jeff. at 37 and 39.

27. Examples of southern mortgages secured by enslaved lives can be found in the Maryland cases of William Black v. William Digges's Executors, 1 H. & McH. 153 (Provincial Court, MD 1744); James Morgan's Lessee v. Richard Davis, 2 H. & McH. 9 (General Court, MD 1781); and William B. Lamar v. Jones and Clarke, 3 H. & McH. 328 (Appeals, MD 1793); the Virginia cases of Ross v. Norvell, 1 Va. 14 (Appeals, VA 1791); Joseph Woodson v. John Woodson, Wythe 129 (Chancery, VA 1791); and John Clayborn v. Hill, 1 Va. 177 (Appeals, VA 1793); the South Carolina cases of Hamilton and Lambright v. Greenwood, 1 Bay 173 (Common Pleas, SC 1791); Harrison v. Strother, 1 Bay 332 (Common Pleas, SC 1793); State v. Thackam and Mayson, 1 Bay 358 (Common Pleas, SC 1794); and Ann Garner v. Melcher Garner's Executors, 1 Des. 437 (Chancery, SC 1795); and the North Carolina case of Craik's Administrators v. Clark, 3 N.C. 22 (Law and Equity, NC 1797).

28. Neufville v. Mitchell, 1 Des. 480 (Chancery, SC 1796).

29. "The Mortgage," *Liberator* (Boston, MA), August 7, 1840, 128.

30. "A Loan Agreement between Poppaea Note and Dicidia Margaris, AD 61," *CIL* IV 3340.155, as reprinted in Alison E. Cooley and M. G. L. Cooley, *Pompeii and Herculaneum: A Sourcebook* (London: Routledge, 2014), 258–59.

31. Priest, "American Property Law," 448.

32. Morris, *Southern Slavery*, 71–74.

33. Morris, *Southern Slavery*, 74

34. Morris, *Southern Slavery*, 74; Judith Kelleher Schafer, *Slavery, the Civil Law, and the Supreme Court of Louisiana* (Baton Rouge: Louisiana State University Press, 1994), 8.

35. Edwin J. Perkins, *American Public Finance and Financial Services, 1700–1815* (Columbus, OH: Ohio State University Press, 1994), 113–14, 127–28.

36. Perkins, *Public Finance*, 235–38.

37. The remaining two branches were in Boston and New York. David Cowen, "The First Bank of the United States," in *Online Encyclopedia of Economic and Business History*, ed. Robert Whaples, EH.net, https://eh.net/encyclopedia/the-first-bank-of-the-united-states/.

38. "An Act to Incorporate the South-Carolina and State Banks," *Acts and Resolutions of the General Assembly of the State of South Carolina* (Columbia, SC: D. & J. J. Faust, 1802), 40–50; "An Act to Incorporate the State Bank," *Acts and Resolutions*, 44–63; J. Mauldin Lesesne, *The Bank of the State of South Carolina: A General and Political History* (Columbia, SC: University of South Carolina Press, 1970), 6–9; W. A. Clark, *The History of the Banking Institutions Organized in South Carolina Prior to 1860* (Columbia, SC: State Company, 1922), 45–54.

39. Warren E. Weber, *Census of Early State Banks in the United States* (2005), https://www.minneapolisfed.org/people/warren-e-weber; Lesesne, *Bank of the State*, 10–11.

40. The Planter's Bank first received a charter in 1807, but it was never organized. The state reissued the charter in 1810. Milton Sydney Heath, *Constructive Liberalism: The Role of the State in Economic Development in Georgia to 1860* (Cambridge, MA: Harvard University Press, 1954), 164.

41. "An Act, to Establish a Bank in the Mississippi Territory," *The Revised Code of the Laws of Mississippi* (Natchez, MS: Francis Baker, 1824), 465.

42. James Lyon, *Enquiry Relative to Banks* (New Orleans: Printed by Order of the Commissioners of the Louisiana Bank, 1804), 29.

43. Perkins, *Public Finance*, 113–36; Howard Bodenhorn, "Federal and State Commercial Banking Policy in the Federalist Era and Beyond," in *Founding Choices: American Economic Policy in the 1790s*, eds. Douglas A. Irwin and Richard Sylla (Chicago: University of Chicago Press, 2011), 153–58; and Sharon Ann Murphy, *Other People's Money: How Banking Worked in the Early American Republic* (Baltimore, MD: Johns Hopkins University Press, 2017), 42–49.

44. Robert E. Wright, "Origins of Commercial Banking in the United States, 1781–1830," in *Online Encyclopedia of Economic and Business History*, ed. Robert Whaples, EH.net, https://eh.net/encyclopedia/origins-of-commercial-banking-in-the-united-states-1781-1830/; Perkins, *Public Finance*, 124–26; and Murphy, *Other People's Money*, 47–49.

45. "The Citizen: On the Nature and Advantages of Banks," *Virginia Argus* (Richmond, VA), January 18, 1804, 1.

46. Howard Bodenhorn, *State Banking in Early America: A New Economic History* (New York: Oxford University Press, 2003), 54–57.

47. "Observations on the Act Entitled an Act to Establish a Bank," *Republican Star* (Easton, MD), May 7, 1805, 1.

48. For just a few examples: "Baltimore Office of Discount and Deposit," *Telegraphe and Daily Advertiser* (Baltimore, MD), July 213, 1800, 4; "The Office of Discount and Deposit," *Commercial Advertiser* (New York), October 30, 1801, 3; "Office of Discount and Deposit, Norfolk," *Commercial Register* (Norfolk, VA), August 16, 1802, 3; "Office of Discount and Deposit," *Columbian Museum* (Savannah, GA), March 18, 1803, 3; "Office of Discount and Deposit, New Orleans," *Salem* (MA) *Gazette*, February 27, 1810, 1; "Office of Discount and Deposit," *Democratic Press*

(Philadelphia), February 13, 1811, 2; "Office of Discount and Deposit," *Boston Daily Advertiser*, January 24, 1817, 2; "Office of Discount and Deposit," *National Advocate* (New York), June 17, 1817, 2; and "Office of Discount and Deposit," *City of Washington Gazette*, April 10, 1818, 3.

49. For example, the newly chartered Trenton Banking Company of New Jersey advertised in 1805 that it would discount "approved bills and notes," payable in sixty days. "The 'Trenton Banking Company,'" *Telegraphe and Daily Advertiser* (Baltimore, MD), May 10, 1805, 2.

50. *Senate Documents*, 61 Cong., 2 Sess., no. 571: John Thom Holdsworth and Davis R. Dewey, *The First and Second Banks of the United States* (Serial 5625; Washington, DC, 1910), 133.

51. Clark, *Banking Institutions*, 41; "Office of Discount & Deposit," *Columbian Museum and Savannah Advertiser*, September 14, 1802, 1.

52. "State Bank," *Acts and Resolutions*, 48.

53. Lyon, *Enquiry*, 31, 33.

54. "The Citizen: On the Nature and Advantages of Banks," 1.

55. "An Act to Incorporate the Union Bank of South Carolina," *Acts and Resolutions of the General Assembly of the State of South Carolina* (Columbia, SC: D. & J. J. Faust, 1811), 33.

56. Naomi Lamoreaux, "'No Arbitrary Discretion': Specialisation in Short-Term Commercial Lending by Banks in Late Nineteenth-Century New England," in Geoffrey Jones, ed., *Banks and Money: International and Comparative Finance in History* (London: Frank Cass, 1991), 93.

57. George D. Green, *Finance and Economic Development in the Old South: Louisiana Banking 1804–1861* (Stanford, CA: Stanford University Press, 1972), xi.

58. Priest, "American Property Law," 428.

59. "Sheriff's Sales," *City Gazette* (Charleston, SC), October 29, 1804, 1.

60. "Sheriff's Sales," *City Gazette* (Charleston, SC), December 3, 1804, 2.

61. "Sheriff's Sales," *City Gazette* (Charleston, SC), February 18 and March 4, 1805, 3.

62. M. St. Clair Clarke and D. A. Hall, eds., *Legislative and Documentary History of the Bank of the United States* (Washington, DC: Gales and Seaton, 1832), 31; Holdsworth and Dewey, *First and Second Banks*, 129.

63. "An Act to Incorporate the Stockholders of the Bank of New-York," *Laws of the State of New-York*, vol. II (Albany, NY: Charles R. and George Webster, 1802), 354–55; "An Act to Incorporate the Stockholders of the Bank of Albany," *Laws of the State of New-York*, vol. II, 362; "An Act to Incorporate the Stockholders of the Bank of Columbia," *Laws of the State of New-York*, vol. II, 369; "An Act to Incorporate the Stockholders of the Farmer's Bank," *Laws of the State of New-York*, vol. II, 378; "An Act to Incorporate the Stockholders of the New-York State Bank," *Laws of the State of New-York*, vol. III (Albany, NY: Charles R. and George Webster, 1804), 331; "An Act to Incorporate the Stockholders of the Merchants' Bank," *Laws of the State of New-York* (Albany, NY: Charles R. and George Webster, 1805), 63; "An Act to Incorporate the South-Carolina and State Banks," *Acts and Resolutions*, 43; "State Bank," *Acts and Resolutions*, 54–55; "An Act for Incorporating the Bank of Virginia," *The Revised Code of the Laws of Virginia*, vol. II (Richmond, VA: Thomas Ritchie, 1819), 72; "An Act Incorporating the Farmers Bank of Virginia," *Revised Code of the Laws of Virginia*, 88; John Haywood, "Bank of Cape Fear," *A Manual of the Laws of North-Carolina* (Raleigh, NC: J. Gales, 1819), 50; "Bank of Newbern," *Manual of the Laws*, 56; "State Bank," *Manual of the Laws*, 63; "Bank of Kentucky," *A Digest of the Statute Law of Kentucky*, vol. I (Frankfort, KY: Kendall and Russell, 1822), 142; Lucius Q. C. Lamar, "An Act to Incorporate a Bank, to Be Called the Bank of the State of Georgia," *A Compilation of the Laws of the State of Georgia* (Augusta, GA: T. S. Hannon, 1821), 89; Lucius Q. C. Lamar, "An Act to Incorporate the

Planter's Bank of the State of Georgia," *Compilation of the Laws*, 78; "An Act to Incorporate the Bank of Augusta," *A Compilation of the Laws of the State of Georgia* (Augusta, GA: Adams and Duyckinck, 1812), 592–93; Edward Scott, "An Act to Establish a Bank," *Laws of the State of Tennessee*, vol. II (Knoxville, TN: Heiskell & Brown, 1821), 49.

64. Lyon, *Enquiry*, 31.

65. Bank of the United States, Papers of Branch Offices, *Girard*, series II, reels 451–52.

66. Third Census, 1810, Georgetown County, SC, *Census (MCR)*, p. 217, M-252, reel 62. Dr. James Hamilton was a Revolutionary War veteran; he was a prisoner of war for a time on Long Island, and later commanded a battalion at the Battle of Yorktown. Elizabeth Lynch Hamilton was the daughter of a signer of the Declaration of Independence. Among their children was James, Jr., future governor of South Carolina and US Senator. Robert Tinkler, *James Hamilton of South Carolina* (Baton Rouge: Louisiana State University Press, 2004), 13–17.

67. "List of Bonds with Their Securities Held by the Office of Discount & Deposit Charleston," Bank of the United States, Papers of Branch Offices, Savannah, GA, *Girard*, series II, reel 451; Third Census, 1810, Charleston County, SC, *Census (MCR)*, p. 437, M-252, reel 60. While precise prices for enslaved lives varied widely by place and time, as well as by the age, gender, and condition of individual slaves, economic historians have compiled rough charts from the extant sources. In 1809, the average price of a South Carolina slave ranged from about $375 to $414. At these average prices, Laurens's workforce alone would have been valued between $93,750 and $103,500, about five times the $18,881.88 he still owed the bank. Peter C. Mancall, Joshua L. Rosenbloom, and Thomas Weiss, "Slave Prices and the South Carolina Economy," *Journal of Economic History* 61 (September 2001): 620. All monetary comparisons have been made using Samuel H. Williamson, "Purchasing Power Today of a US Dollar Transaction in the Past," MeasuringWorth, 2021, https://www.measuringworth.com/calculators/ppowerus/index2.php. There are many formulas for comparing dollar amounts across time, and I am in no way asserting that this one is the most accurate. It is intended purely as a rough yardstick to give the modern reader a better sense of how small or large were the dollar amounts referenced throughout the text.

68. "Sheriff's Sales," *Republican; and Savannah Evening Ledger*, July 25, 1809 (ad first ran July 1, 1809), 4. For a description of slave auction sales in Savannah, see Whittington B. Johnson, *Black Savannah, 1788–1864* (Fayetteville: University of Arkansas Press, 1996), 88–89.

69. "Return of Debts > $5000 Savannah Branch, February 28, 1811–October 31, 1812," Bank of the United States, Papers of Branch Offices, Savannah, GA, *Girard*, series II, reel 452.

70. Jeannette Holland Austin, *The Georgians: Genealogies of Pioneer Settlers* (Baltimore, MD: Genealogical Publishing Co., 1984), 140; Walter J. Fraser, Jr., *Savannah in the Old South* (Athens, GA: University of Georgia Press, 2005), 140, 146.

71. Rossiter Johnson, ed., "Habersham," in *The Twentieth Century Biographical Dictionary of Notable Americans*, vol. V: *Habb–Izard* (Boston, MA: Biographical Society, 1904); W. Calvin Smith, "Habersham Family," *New Georgia Encyclopedia*, last edited September 11, 2014, https://www.georgiaencyclopedia.org/articles/historyarchaeology/habersham-family/.

72. "Marshal's Sales Continued," *Republican; and Savannah Evening Ledger*, April 21, 1810 (ad first ran April 5, 1810), 4.

73. The Georgia population schedules of the federal census are missing for 1790, 1800, and 1810. "Census Records," *Georgia*, accessed March 2, 2022, https://www.georgiaarchives.org/research/census_records.

74. Austin, *Georgians*, 140.

75. "Return of Debts > $5000 Savannah Branch, February 28, 1811–October 31, 1812," and "List of the Real Estate of the Late Bank of the United States in and near Savannah," March 9, 1814, Bank of the United States, Papers of Branch Offices, Savannah, GA, *Girard*, series II, reel 452.

76. "Marshal's Sales," *Savannah Republican*, March 7, 1812, 3.

77. "Schedule of Notes, Bonds, Mortgages, etc. Belonging to Savannah Office, March 3, 1811," Bank of the United States, Papers of Branch Offices, Savannah, GA, *Girard*, series II, reel 452.

78. "Marshal's Sales Continued," *Republican; and Savannah Evening Ledger*, May 23, 1812 (ad first ran March 7, 1812), 4.

79. "Marshal's Sales Continued," *Republican; and Savannah Evening Ledger*, May 23, 1812 (ad first ran May 7, 1812), 4.

80. Untitled, *Telegraphe and Daily Advertiser* (Baltimore, MD), March 26, 1803, 3; Bank of the United States, List of Branch Offices 1810, *Girard*, series II, reel 453.

81. Samuel Howard court case, Bank of the United States, Papers of Branch Offices, Savannah, *Girard*, series II, reel 452.

82. "Marshal's Sales," *Savannah Republican*, June 2, 1810, 3.

83. "List of the Real Estate of the Late Bank of the United States in and near Savannah," March 9, 1814.

84. Samuel Howard, Savannah, to George Simpson, Cashier, Late Bank, March 22, 1815, Bank of the United States, Papers of Branch Offices, Savannah, GA, *Girard*, series II, reel 452.

85. "Marshal's Sales," *Savannah Republican*, July 23, 1811, 4.

86. "Public Sale," *Savannah Republican*, July 6, 1811, 3.

87. Samuel Howard, Savannah, to George Simpson, Cashier, Late Bank, March 22, 1815.

88. "Circuit Court Complaint of Daniel Howard v. David Lenox of the Bank of the United States," n.d., Bank of the United States, Papers of Branch Offices, Savannah, GA, *Girard*, series II, reel 452.

89. "Ranaway," *Georgia Gazette* (Savannah), June 25, 1789, 2; "Georgia," *Georgia Gazette* (Savannah), July 2, 1789, 3; "The Property," *Georgia Gazette* (Savannah), June 22, 1798, 4; "Runaway," *Georgia Gazette* (Savannah), July 6, 1798, 4.

90. *Minutes of the Union Society* (Savannah, GA: John M. Cooper & Company, 1860), 1–6, 12, 17, 30, 41, 58; Fraser, *Savannah*, 143.

91. "Return of Debts > $5000 Savannah Branch, February 28, 1811–October 31, 1812."

92. "Schedule of Notes, Bonds, Mortgages, etc. Belonging to Savannah Office, March 3, 1811."

93. "Tax Returns," *Savannah Republican*, October 3, 1809, 4.

94. "Schedule of Notes, Bonds, Mortgages, etc. Belonging to Savannah Office, March 3, 1811."

95. Donald R. Hickey, "American Trade Restrictions during the War of 1812," *Journal of American History* 68 (December 1981), 517–38; Fraser, *Savannah*, 179–81.

96. "List of the Real Estate of the Late Bank of the United States in and near Savannah," March 9. 1814; and "George Millen," Bank of the United States, Papers of Branch Offices, Savannah, GA, *Girard*, series II, reel 452.

97. "Marshal's Sales Continued," *Republican; and Savannah Evening Ledger*, May 17, 1810 (ad first ran March 31, 1810), 4.

98. "Marshal's Sales Continued," *Republican; and Savannah Evening Ledger*, March 14, 1811 (ad first ran March 2, 1811), 2.

99. "Marshal's Sales," *Republican; and Savannah Evening Ledger*, April 9, 1811 (ad first ran April 6, 1811), 4.

100. "Marshal's Sales Continued," *Republican; and Savannah Evening Ledger*, February 27, 1812 (ad first ran April 6, 1811), 4.

101. "Marshal's Sales," *Republican; and Savannah Evening Ledger*, May 19, 1812 (ad first ran March 7, 1812), 4.

102. "Marshal's Sales," *Republican; and Savannah Evening Ledger*, July 28, 1812 (ad first ran June 6, 1812), 4.

103. President, Directors & Co. of Bank of U.S. v. McLaughlin's Adm'r, 2 Cranch C.C. 20 (DC 1810) at 722.

104. "Return of Debts > $5000 Savannah Branch, February 28, 1811–October 31, 1812"; "Marshal's Sales," April 9, 1811, 4 (emphasis in original).

105. "Marshal's Sales," Savannah *Republican*, December 30, 1812 (ad first ran March 7, 1812), 3.

106. "Marshal's Sales," *Republican; and Savannah Evening Ledger*, July 28, 1812 (ad first ran May 2, 1812), 4.

107. Fourth Census, 1820, Chatham County, GA, *Census (MCR)*, p. 71, M-33, reel 8.

108. Pierce Butler to Roswell King, January 21, 1813, volume 1, Pierce Butler letterbooks, Am. 0368, *HSP*. According to one source, "in February 1815, the average price for 100 slaves sold by the marshal for the District of Georgia was $264.80 each," before rising to $312.60 the following year. Johnson, *Black Savannah*, 88.

109. Jacob Road to George Simpson, September 24, 1813, Bank of the United States, Correspondence 1802–1822, *Girard*, series II, reel 452.

110. William Stephens to David Lenox, January 28, 1815, Bank of the United States, Correspondence 1802–1822, *Girard*, series II, reel 452.

111. Samuel Howard, Savannah, to George Simpson, Cashier, Late Bank, March 22, 1815.

112. "List of the Real Estate of the Late Bank of the United States in and near Savannah, March 9, 1814," Ibid.

113. John H. Goff, "The Steamboat Period in Georgia," *Georgia Historical Quarterly* 12 (September, 1928): 238–39.

114. Samuel Howard, Savannah, to George Simpson, Cashier, Late Bank, March 22, 1815.

115. Goff, "Steamboat Period," 189–90.

116. "Sheriff's Sales," *City Gazette* (Charleston, SC), January 23, and February 14, 1815, 4.

117. "Marshal's Sale," *Savannah Republican*, August 29, 1815, 4.

118. "Marshal's Sale," *Alexandria Gazette*, October 4, 1815, 3.

119. "Schedule of Notes, Bonds, Mortgages, etc. Belonging to Savannah Office, March 3, 1811."

120. Bank of the United States, Papers of Branch Offices, New Orleans, LA, *Girard*, series II, reel 451.

121. "Return of debts > $5000 Savannah Branch, February 28, 1811–October 31, 1812," Bank of the United States, Papers of Branch Offices, Savannah, GA, *Girard*, series II, reel 452. As of 1844, the trustees of the First Bank were still "bringing to a final close the affairs of that institution." "First Bank of the United States," *Opelousas Gazette*, August 31, 1844, 1.

122. Bodenhorn, *State Banking*, 220.

123. Bodenhorn, *State Banking*, 221.

124. "An Act to Incorporate a Bank," *Republican Advocate* (Frederick, MD), June 14, 1805, 1–2.

125. "Observations on the Act Entitled an Act to Establish a Bank," *Republican Star* (Easton, MD), May 7, 1805, 1.

126. In 1807, Pennsylvania chartered the Farmers and Mechanics Bank of Philadelphia, yet the bank was only required to lend 10 percent of its $1.25 million capital for real estate mortgages to farmers. See Bodenhorn, *State Banking*, 139–40.

127. *Laws of the State of New-York* (1802), 351–79; *Laws of the State of New-York* (1804), 328–33; *Laws of the State of New-York* (1805), 62–66.

128. "From the Lansingburgh Gazette," *Balance* (Hudson, NY), December 17, 1801, 122.

129. Theodore Thayer, "The Land-Bank System in the American Colonies," *Journal of Economic History* 13 (Spring 1953), 146. Unlike a true bank, loan offices provided no financial-intermediation services (bringing together lenders and borrowers). They did not accept money on deposit or provide other financial services. They primarily served as a means of injecting much-needed liquidity into the economy. See also Perkins, *Public Finance*, 44–46; Katie A. Moore, "America's First Economic Stimulus Package: Paper Money and the Body Politic in Colonial Pennsylvania, 1715–1730," *Pennsylvania History: A Journal of Mid-Atlantic Studies* 83 (Autumn 2016), 529–57.

130. "Observations on the Act," May 7, 1805, 1. See also "The Farmer's Bank of Maryland," *Federal Gazette* (Baltimore, MD), August 28, 1804, 2; and "Letter from a Respectable Gentleman," *Republican Star* (Easton, MD), September 4, 1804, 2.

131. "Observations on the Act," May 7, 1805, 1. See also "Farmer's Bank," August 28, 1804, 2; and "Respectable Gentleman," September 4, 1804, 2.

132. "An Act to Establish a Bank," *Laws of the State of Delaware* (Wilmington, DE: M. Bradford and R. Porter, 1816), 102.

133. An Act to Establish a Bank," *Laws of the State of Delaware*, 560.

134. The Planters Bank of the State of Georgia was initially chartered in 1807, but never went into operation. The legislature repealed that charter and issued a new one in 1810. Thomas P. Govan, "Banking and the Credit System in Georgia, 1810–1860," *Journal of Southern History* 4 (May 1938), 166.

135. "An Act Incorporating the Planters' Bank in the City of New-Orleans," *Acts Passed at the Second Session of the Third Legislature of the Territory of Orleans* (New Orleans: Thierry, 1811), 86.

136. "An Act to Incorporate the Planters and Mechanics Bank of South-Carolina," *Acts and Resolutions of the General Assembly of the State of South-Carolina* (Columbia, SC: D. & J. J. Faust, State Printers, 1810), 69, 77.

137. "Bank of the State of South Carolina," *An Alphabetical Digest of the Public Statute Law of South Carolina*, vol. I (Charleston, SC: John Hoff, 1814), 56; Richard Sylla, John B. Legler, and John J. Wallis, "Banks and State Public Finance in the New Republic: The United States, 1790–1860," *Journal of Economic History* 47, no. 2 (June 1987), 398.

138. "Bank of the State," *An Alphabetical Digest*, 57.

139. "Bank of the State of So. Carolina," *Charleston Courier*, May 19, 1813, 1.

140. "No. 24 John Steele to Bank Cape Fear Weekly Return Jany 31, 1809 Salisbury Office of Discount," in the John Steele Papers #689, series 2, Financial and Legal, *SHC*.

Chapter Two

1. Bank of Kentucky v. Vance's Administrators, 4 Litt. 168 (Appeals KY 1823).

2. *Bank of Kentucky*, 4 Litt.; mortgage from Armistead Latham and Robert Latham to Bank of Kentucky, October 8, 1817, and December 30, 1818; mortgage from Armistead Latham and Robert Latham to Samuel Vance, July 20, 1819, *Logan*; William S. Waller, cashier Frankfort home

bank to Joseph D. Hamilton, cashier Russellville branch, November 11, 1817, and December 17, 1817, Home Bank Letter Book D 1816–1818, *KDLA Bank*.

3. *Bank of Kentucky*, 4 Litt.; mortgage from Armistead Latham and Robert Latham to Bank of Kentucky, October 8, 1817, and December 30, 1818; mortgage from Armistead Latham and Robert Latham to Samuel Vance, July 20, 1819, *Logan*.

4. Clyde A. Haulman, *Virginia and the Panic of 1819* (London: Pickering & Chatto, 2008), 10–15; Murray Rothbard, *The Panic of 1819: Reactions and Policies* (New York: Columbia University Press, 1962), 1–36; Harry L. Watson, *Liberty and Power: The Politics of Jacksonian America* (New York: Hill and Wang, 2006), 22–24; Dan Dupre, "Frontiers Knit Together and Unraveled: The Rhetoric of Land Relief in an Age of Boom and Bust," *Journal of the Early Republic* 40 (Winter 2020): 677–78.

5. Lucius Q. C. Lamar, "An Act to Incorporate a Bank, to Be Called the Bank of the State of Georgia," *A Compilation of the Laws of the State of Georgia* (Augusta, GA: T. S. Hannon, 1821), 91.

6. Lucius Q. C. Lamar, "An Act to Incorporate the Bank of Darien" *Laws of the State of Georgia*, 101; "An Act to Establish Two New Banks within This Commonwealth," *The Revised Code of the Laws of Virginia*, vol. II (Richmond, VA: Thomas Ritchie, 1819), 102; L. Moreau Lislet, "An Act to Establish a State Bank," *A General Digest of the Acts of the Legislature of Louisiana* vol. 1 (New Orleans: Benjamin Levy, 1828), 78.

7. George D. Green, *Finance and Economic Development in the Old South: Louisiana Banking 1804–1861* (Stanford, CA: Stanford University Press, 1972), 22; "General Assembly," *Louisiana State Gazette* (New Orleans), March 4, 1826, 2.

8. Notes on Wm Fleckner vs. Bank U.S., Langdon Cheves Papers, 1776–1864 (1166.00), Legal Papers, 1820–25, 12/54/14–20, South Carolina Historical Society, microfilm.

9. U.S. Bank v. Fleckner, 8 Mart (o.s.) 141 (SC LA 1820); Fleckner v. Bank of U.S., 21 U.S. 338 (1823).

10. Percy v. Millaudon, 3 La. 568 (SC LA 1832) at 573–74.

11. Percy v. Millaudon, 3 La. 568 at 578–79.

12. Max M. Edling, *A Hercules in the Cradle: War, Money, and the American State, 1783–1867* (Chicago: University of Chicago Press, 2014), 108–44.

13. John Thom Holdsworth and Davis R. Dewey, *The First and Second Banks of the United States* (Serial 5625; Washington, DC, 1910), 163–75.

14. The Augusta, Georgia branch was quickly closed in 1817, reducing the southern branches to ten. Jane Ellen Knodell, *The Second Bank of the United States: "Central" Banker in an Era of Nation-Building, 1816–1836* (New York: Routledge, 2016), 28–37.

15. "Acts to Charter the Bank of the United States, February 25; March 2, 1791" and "Act to Charter the Second Bank of the United States, April 10, 1816," in Herman E. Kroos, ed., *Documentary History of Banking and Currency in the United States*, vol. 1 (New York: McGraw-Hill, 1969), 310–11, 468–69.

16. Holdsworth and Dewey, *First and Second Banks*, 292.

17. Holdsworth and Dewey, *First and Second Banks*, 201.

18. Holdsworth and Dewey, *First and Second Banks*, 242.

19. J. Carlyle Sitterson, *Sugar Country: The Cane Sugar Industry in the South, 1753–1950* (Westport, CT: Greenwood Press, 1973), 28–29.

20. Loan indenture, October 5, 1818, box 1, *BUS (Baltimore)*; Charles Wederstrandt Document, May 15, 1827, Mss. 668, *LLMVC*.

21. Edward S. Kaplan, *The Bank of the United States and the American Economy* (Westport, CT: Greenwood Press, 1999), 62; "Board of Directors for the Bank of the United States, for 1818," *Baltimore Patriot*, January 7, 1818, 2; Dennis A. Smith to Alexander Brown, March 16, 1819, Jonathan D. Meredith Papers, box 9, *LOC*.

22. Dennis A. Smith to Alexander Brown, March 16, 1819.

23. Jessica M. Lepler, "Introduction: The Panic of 1819 by Any Other Name," *Journal of the Early Republic* 40 (Winter 2020): 665–70; Arthur H. Cole, *Wholesale Commodity Prices in the United States, 1700–1861*, Statistical Supplement (Cambridge, MA: Harvard University Press, 1938); Richard E. Ellis, *Aggressive Nationalism: McCulloch v. Maryland and the Foundation of Federal Authority in the Young Republic* (Oxford: Oxford University Press, 2007), 61; Rothbard, *Panic of 1819*, 1–36; Watson, *Liberty and Power*, 23–24; Andrew H. Browning, *The Panic of 1819: The First Great Depression* (Columbia: University of Missouri Press, 2019), 23, 84, 101–02, 112–20.

24. Ellis, *Aggressive Nationalism*, 62–64; Kaplan, *Bank of the United States*, 69; Walter Buckingham Smith, *Economic Aspects of the Second Bank of the United States* (New York: Greenwood Press, 1953), 108; Daniel Feller, *The Jacksonian Promise: America, 1815–1840* (Baltimore, MD: Johns Hopkins University Press, 1995), 41–48; John Lauritz Larson, *The Market Revolution in America: Liberty, Ambition, and the Eclipse of the Common Good* (Cambridge: Cambridge University Press, 2010), 40–43, 100; Watson, *Liberty and Power*, 38–39; Browning, *Panic of 1819*, 159–63.

25. Ellis, *Aggressive Nationalism*, 62–64; Kaplan, *Bank of the United States*, 69; Smith, *Second Bank*, 108; Feller, *Jacksonian Promise*, 41–48; Larson, *Market Revolution*, 40–43, 100; Watson, *Liberty and Power*, 38–39; Browning, *Panic of 1819*, 173–75.

26. *U.S. Bank*, 8 Mart (o.s.); *Fleckner*, 21 U.S.

27. *Percy*, 3 La. at 581.

28. *Percy*, 3 La. at 572.

29. "State of Louisiana, First Judicial District Court," *Louisiana State Gazette* (New Orleans), May 3, 1821, 1.

30. "Second Bank of the United States," *Documentary History*, volume 1: 468–69.

31. *U.S. Bank*, 8 Mart (o.s.); *Fleckner*, 21 U.S. at 344; Notes on Wm Fleckner vs. Bank U.S., Langdon Cheves Papers, 1776–1864 (1166.00), Legal Papers, 1820–25, 12/54/14–20, South Carolina Historical Society, microfilm.

32. *Fleckner*, 21 U.S. at 349–52.

33. *Fleckner*, 21 U.S. at 350–51.

34. Marigny v. Union Bank of Louisiana, 5 Rob. 354 (SC LA 1843) at 356.

35. Venable v. Bank of U.S., 27 U.S. 107 (1829). Although the court case spells his name "Norten," other documents indicate his name was Norton.

36. Fourth Census, 1820, Fayette County, KY, *Census (MCR)*, p. 59, M-33, reel 17; Price's Administrator v. Boswell, 3 B. Mon. 13 (Appeals KY 1842).

37. Fourth Census, 1820, Fayette County, KY, *Census (MCR)*, p. 101, M-33, reel 17.

38. Although the court case identifies the brother-in-law as George M'Donald, other documents including the federal census and a second court case identify him as George McDaniel. Fourth Census, 1820, Fayette County, KY, *Census (MCR)*, p. 108; "Notice," *Kentucky Gazette* (Lexington), November 3, 1826, 1.

39. *Venable*, 27 U.S. at 112.

40. *Venable*, 27 U.S. at 112 and 119.

41. *Price's Administrator*, 3 B. Mon.

42. *Bank of Kentucky*, 4 Litt.

43. Samuel Vance advertisement, *Weekly Chronicle* (Clarksville, TN), February 18, 1818, 4; mortgage from Armistead Latham and Robert Latham to Samuel Vance, July 20, 1819, *Logan*.

44. Samuel Vance advertisement, February 18, 1818; mortgage from Armistead Latham and Robert Latham to Samuel Vance, July 20, 1819.

45. Mortgage Jacob Holeman to Bank KY, July 22, 1822, Franklin County, KY, vol. K–L, *KDLA Deeds*, reel 266168.

46. Robert Alexander, president home bank to Thomas Prather, president Louisville branch bank, March 25, 1820, Home Bank Letter Book E 1818–1820, *KDLA Bank*.

47. *Bank of Kentucky*, 4 Litt.; *Weekly Messenger* (Russellville, KY), January 18, 1820 and September 23, 1820; "Louisiana, Orleans Parish Estate Files, 1804–1846," database with images, *FamilySearch*, Robert Latham, 1820, citing Robert Latham Estate, March 22, 1821, Orleans Parish, New Orleans Court of Probates, New Orleans City Archives; Robert Alexander, president home bank to Richard Bibb, Jr., president Russellville branch bank, December 17, 1819, Home Bank Letter Book E 1818–1820, *KDLA Bank*.

48. *Bank of Kentucky*, 4 Litt. at 171.

49. *Bank of Kentucky*, 4 Litt. at 176.

50. Fourth Census, 1820, Mount Sterling, Montgomery County, KY, p. 297, M-33, reel 25; Mosely v. Garrett, 1 J.J.Marsh. 212 (Appeals KY 1829) at 213.

51. *Mosely*, 1 J.J.Marsh. at 214 and 218.

52. "Sketch of Answer Bank vs. Green" and "The Answer of the President Directors & Company of the Bank of the State of Mississippi to the Bill of Complaint of Charles B Green," September 16, 1822, *Mississippi*, box 2E983c.

53. Sketch of Answer Bank vs. Green" and "The Answer of the President Directors & Company of the Bank of the State of Mississippi to the Bill of Complaint of Charles B Green," September 16, 1822.

54. "Two Valuable Farms for Sale," *Mississippi State Gazette* (Natchez), March 4, 1820, 4.

55. Charles B. Green to Samuel Postlethwaite, March 3, 1820, *Mississippi*, box 2E983c.

56. Samuel Postlethwaite to Charles B. Green, March 9, 1820, *Mississippi*, box 2E983c.

57. "Sketch of Answer Bank vs. Green" and "The Answer of the President Directors & Company of the Bank of the State of Mississippi to the Bill of Complaint of Charles B Green," September 16, 1822.

58. Charles B. Green to Samuel Postlethwaite, March 14, 1820, and Samuel Postlethwaite to Charles B. Green, March 15, 1820, *Mississippi*, box 2E983c.

59. Francis S. Girault to Samuel Postlethwaite, March 23, 1820, *Mississippi*, box 2E983c.

60. "The Answer of the President Directors & Company of the Bank of the State of Mississippi to the Bill of Complaint of Charles B Green," September 16, 1822.

61. Charles B. Green to Samuel Postlethwaite, March 24, 1820, *Mississippi*, box 2E983c.

62. Jane A. Girault to the bank, May 26, 1820, *Mississippi*, box 2E952.

63. "Whereas Francis S. Girault and Jane His Wife," undated, *Mississippi*, box 2E983c.

64. "Sketch of Answer Bank vs. Green" and "The Answer of the President Directors & Company of the Bank of the State of Mississippi to the Bill of Complaint of Charles B Green," September 16, 1822.

65. Samuel Postlethwaite to Charles B. Green, December 22, 1821, *Mississippi*, box 2E983c.

66. "Proposition" by Charles B. Green to bank, December 15, 1823, *Mississippi*, box 2E983c.

67. Charles B. Green to Samuel Postlethwaite, December 18, 1823, *Mississippi*, box 2E983c.

68. "Know All Men," release of obligation of Charles B. Greene, December 27, 1823, *Mississippi*, box 2E983c.

69. Charles B. Green to Gabriel Tichenor, April 27, 1826, and August 25, 1827, *Mississippi*, box 2E983c.

70. Edward Broughton to the Bank of the State of Mississippi, February 26, 1824, *Mississippi*, box 2E983c.

71. Edward Broughton to Samuel Postlethwaite, March 11, 1824, *Mississippi*, box 2E973; "Real Property for Sale," *Mississippi Republican* (Natchez, MS), June 7, 1824, 4.

72. James A. Girault to Gabriel Tichenor, November 5, 1824, *Mississippi*, box 2E973.

73. James A. Girault to the Bank of the State of Mississippi, November 16, 1831, *Mississippi*, box 2E967.

74. "Banque d'Orleans," *Louisiana State Gazette* (New Orleans), July 11, 1818, 4.

75. William McF. Saul to Gabriel Tichenor, January 27, 1819, *Mississippi*, box 2E951.

76. William McF. Saul to Gabriel Tichenor, November 8, 1819, *Mississippi*, box 2E951.

77. Katharina Pistor, *The Code of Capital: How the Law Creates Wealth and Inequality* (Princeton, NJ: Princeton University Press, 2019), 92; Peter A. Coclanis, *The Shadow of a Dream: Economic Life and Death in the South Carolina Low Country, 1670–1920* (New York: Oxford University Press, 1991), 102–03. This recording of mortgage contracts with the county court provides a paper trail of the transactions that used enslaved lives as collateral. In some jurisdictions, these notarial documents were indexed by the name of the creditor and/or debtor, enabling researchers to search for a bank as a party to the contract. In other jurisdictions, the name of the bank's president or cashier was instead used in the index, making the search more complicated. And in some locations, no index exists, forcing researchers to comb through the documents individually. Some states, including Georgia, Kentucky, and North Carolina, microfilmed all their county mortgage and deed records, and now have them centrally located in their respective state archives. The notarial records of the city of New Orleans, by contrast, are still in bound deed books at the city archives, organized by the names of the individual notaries who witnessed the agreements—although most of the volume indexes are microfilmed and available online.

78. Stephens' Administrator v. Barnett, 7 Dana 257 (Appeals KY, 1838) at 258.

79. Galt v. Dibrell, 18 Tenn. 146 (SC TN 1836).

80. *Galt*, 18 Tenn. at 159.

81. *Galt*, 18 Tenn.; Richard Sutch, "Appendix: The Value of the Slave Population, 1805–1860," in Roger Ransom and Richard Sutch, "Capitalists without Capital: The Burden of Slavery and the Impact of Emancipation," *Agricultural History* 62, no. 3 (Summer 1988), table A.1, 150–01.

82. *Galt*, 18 Tenn. at 151–52.

83. Claire Priest, "Creating an American Property Law: Alienability and Its Limits in American History," *Harvard Law Review* 120 (December 2006), 393.

84. *Galt*, 18 Tenn. at 150.

85. *Galt*, 18 Tenn.

86. "Alarming Times," *Frankfort Argus* (KY), April 16, 1819, 3.

87. Sommerville v. Horton, 12 Tenn. 541 (Appeals TN 1833) at 541–42.

88. "Maryland Legislature," *Easton Gazette*, February 8, 1819, 3.

89. Sterling Ruffin to Thomas Ruffin, September 3, 1819, in the Thomas Ruffin Papers #641, series 1.3, *SHC*.

90. Matthew G. Schoenbachler, *Murder and Madness: The Myth of the Kentucky Tragedy* (Lexington: University Press of Kentucky, 2009), 40; Browning, *Panic of 1819*, 133.

91. "Public Meeting," *Frankfort Argus*, May 14, 1819, 3 (emphasis in original).

92. "Public Sentiment in Kentucky," *Daily National Intelligencer* (Washington, DC), June 21, 1819, 3; "County Meetings," *Commentator* (Frankfort, KY), June 25, 1819, 3; "In Washington," *Daily National Intelligencer* (Washington, DC), June 25, 1819, 2.

93. Schoenbachler, *Murder and Madness*, 61; Howard Bodenhorn, *State Banking in Early America: A New Economic History* (New York: Oxford University Press, 2003), 240–41.

94. Mortgage C. Gill to Bank, July 1, 1819, Franklin County, KY, vol. H–I, *KDLA Deeds*, reel 266167.

95. Mortgage L. Castleman to Bank KY, September 1, 1819, vol. H–I, *KDLA Deeds*, reel 266167; Fourth Census, 1820, Franklin County, KY, *Census (MCR)*, p. 54, M-33, reel 22.

96. Mortgage Hickman to Bank KY, October 14, 1819, Franklin County, KY, vol. H–I, *KDLA Deeds*, reel 266167.

97. Mortgage Campbell to Bank KY, October 19, 1819, Franklin County, KY, vol. H–I, *KDLA Deeds*, reel 266167.

98. Mortgage W. Littell to Bank of KY, October 25, 1819, Franklin County, KY, vol. H–I, *KDLA Deeds*, reel 266167.

99. Fourth Census, 1820, Franklin County, KY, *Census (MCR)*, p. 62, M-33, reel 22.

100. August 11, 1821, Frankfort Minute Book D President & Directors 1821–1828, *KDLA Bank*; Pen Bogert, "Sold for My Account: The Early Slave Trade Between Kentucky and the Lower Mississippi Valley," *Ohio Valley History* 2 (Spring 2002): 11.

101. August 11, 1821, Frankfort Minute Book D President & Directors 1821–1828, *KDLA Bank*.

102. "Public Sale," *Argus of Western America* (Frankfort, KY), September 26, 1822, 3.

103. Mortgage Littell to Bank KY, June 10, 1823, Franklin County, KY, vol. K–L, *KDLA Deeds*, reel 266168.

104. Fourth Census, 1820, Franklin County, KY, *Census (MCR)*, p. 63, M-33, reel 22.

105. January 20, 1824, Frankfort Minute Book D President & Directors 1821–1828, *KDLA Bank*.

106. Bank of KY to J. Smith, February 29, 1828, Franklin County, KY, vol. M–N, *KDLA Deeds*, reel 266169.

107. Mortgage James B. and Thomas January to Bank US, May 3, 1821, Fayette County, KY, vol. S–U, 1818–1821, *KDLA Deeds*, reel c987743.

108. Fourth Census, 1820, Fayette County, KY, *Census (MCR)*, p. 63, 74, M-33, reel 17.

109. Mortgage Fletcher to Bank US, August 5, 1824, Fayette County, KY, vol. Y–2, 1824–1827, *KDLA Deeds*, reel c987745.

110. Fourth Census, 1820, Fayette County, KY, *Census (MCR)*, p. 176, M-33, reel 16.

111. Mortgage Fletcher to Bank US, August 5, 1824, Fayette County, KY, vol. Y–2, 1824–1827, *KDLA Deeds*, reel c987745.

112. Holdsworth and Dewey, *First and Second Banks*, 242; Ralph C. H. Catterall, *The Second Bank of the United States* (Chicago: University of Chicago Press, 1903), 400.

113. John Harvie, president home bank, to Samuel Murell, president, Glasgow branch bank, March 8, 1822, Home Bank Letter Book F 1820–1822, *KDLA Bank*.

114. May 13, 1823, Frankfort Minute Book D President & Directors 1821–1828, *KDLA Bank*.

115. Mortgage Taylor to Bank KY, November 12, 1819, Franklin County, KY, vol. H–I, *KDLA Deeds*, reel 266167.

116. Mortgage Morrison and Taylor to J. Harvie, March 20, 1826, Franklin County, KY, vol. M–N, *KDLA Deeds*, reel 266169.

117. "Mansion House," *Argus of Western America* (Frankfort, KY), December 10, 1823, 4.

118. Mortgage Morrison and Taylor to J. Harvie, March 20, 1826; Bank KY to Morrison &c, July 20, 1830, Franklin County, KY, vol. M–N, *KDLA Deeds*, reel 266169.

119. Bank KY to Morrison &c, July 20, 1830, Franklin County, KY, vol. M-N, *KDLA Deeds*, reel 266169.

120. Sitterson, *Sugar Country*, 170–71; "Wholesale Prices of Selected Commodities: 1800 to 1957," *Historical Statistics of the United States: Colonial Times to 1957* (Washington, DC: US Department of Commerce, Bureau of the Census, 1960), series E 101–12, pp. 122–24, esp. 124.

121. Dennis A. Smith to the Baltimore branch bank, March 17 and 24, 1820, Bank of the United States (Baltimore, MD) records, box 2, Manuscript Division, Library of Congress, Washington, DC.

122. Henry Thompson to the Baltimore branch bank, March 27, 1820; Philemon C. Wederstrandt to Henry Thompson, as quoted in Henry Thompson to the Baltimore branch, March 27, 1820, *BUS (Baltimore)*, box 2.

123. Mortgage agreement, March 30, 1820, *BUS (Baltimore)*, box 2.

124. Catterall, *Second Bank*, 40–50. Whereas the cashier spelled his name M'Culloh, the official Supreme Court transcripts used M'Culloch for the famous 1819 case of *M'Culloch v. Maryland*, and numerous contemporary and historical sources have adopted McCulloch. Mark R. Killenbeck, *M'Culloch v. Maryland: Securing a Nation* (Lawrence: University Press of Kansas, 2006), 90.

125. Dennis A. Smith to John White, New Orleans branch bank cashier, April 6, 1822; R. B. Magruder, Baltimore branch bank attorney, to John White, New Orleans branch bank cashier, September 9, 1822, *BUS (Baltimore)*, box 2; and Credit and Debit Account of the Baltimore branch with the New Orleans Branch, 1821–1825, *BUS (Baltimore)*, box 6.

126. Helen Wederstrandt to John White, New Orleans branch bank cashier, October 6, 1822, *BUS (Baltimore)*, box 2.

127. "Mortgage P. C. Wederstrandt to Bank U Office Disc & Dept," May 5, 1823, Notary Carlile Pollock, vol. 11, pp. 385–88, *NONA*; Charles Wederstrandt document, May 15, 1827, Mss. 668, *LLMVC*.

Part II Introduction

1. Adam Rothman, *Slave Country: American Expansion and the Origins of the Deep South* (Cambridge, MA: Harvard University Press, 2005), 168; Joshua D. Rothman, *The Ledger and the Chain: How Domestic Slave Traders Shaped America* (New York: Basic Books, 2021), 104–05.

2. John Craig Hammond, "Slavery, Settlement, and Empire: The Expansion and Growth of Slavery in the Interior of the North American Continent, 1770–1820," *Journal of the Early Republic* 32 (Summer 2012): 200.

3. A. Rothman, *Slave Country*, 170–71.

4. Gavin Wright, *The Political Economy of the Cotton South* (New York: W. W. Norton, 1978), 16, 20–21; *Historical Statistics of the United States: Colonial Times to 1957* (Washington, DC: US Department of Commerce, Bureau of the Census, 1960), 24–36, Series A 195–209.

5. Ira Berlin, *Generations of Captivity: A History of African-American Slaves* (Cambridge, MA: Belknap Press, 2003), 166, 179.

6. J. Carlyle Sitterson, *Sugar Country: The Cane Sugar Industry in the South, 1753–1950* (Westport, CT: Greenwood Press, 1973), 29.

7. Walter Johnson, *River of Dark Dreams: Slavery and Empire in the Cotton Kingdom* (Cambridge, MA: Harvard University Press, 2013), 32.

8. Joan E. Cashin, *A Family Venture: Men and Women on the Southern Frontier* (New York: Oxford University Press, 1991), 32–33.

9. Berlin, *Generations of Captivity*, 161.

10. Cashin, *Family Venture*, 38.

Chapter Three

1. "John Spear Smith," *Memorial Biographies of the New-England Historic Genealogical Society*, vol. VI: *1864–1871* (Boston, MA: Stanhope Press, 1905), 207–09; "Smith, Samuel, 1752–1839," *Biographical Directory of the United States Congress*, accessed March 8, 2022, https://bioguide.congress.gov/search/bio/S000609. Senator Samuel Smith of Maryland is not to be confused with Samuel Harrison Smith, the president of the Washington branch of the Second Bank.

2. "Samuel Smith," *Archives of Maryland Biographical Series*, MSA SC 3520–2827, accessed March 8, 2022, https://msa.maryland.gov/megafile/msa/speccol/sc3500/sc3520/002800/002827/html/2827sources.html.

3. "Mortgage Mrs. Hetty Carr & John Spear Smith to Bank U States," December 1, 1831, Notary William Christy, vol. 8, p. 289–91, *NONA*.

4. Nicholas Biddle to R. L. Colt, May 6, 1831, *Biddle*, reel 43.

5. Nicholas Biddle to R. L. Colt, May 10, 1831, *Biddle*, reel 43.

6. Nicholas Biddle to R. L. Colt, May 24, 1831, *Biddle*, reel 43.

7. "Mortgage Mrs. Hetty Carr & John Spear Smith to Bank U States," December 1, 1831.

8. "Mortgage Mrs. Hetty Carr & John Spear Smith to Harrison & Sterett," December 1, 1831, Notary Christy, vol. 8, pp. 291–95.

9. Nicholas Biddle to R. L. Colt, May 10, May 24, 1831, *Biddle*, reel 43.

10. Jessica M. Lepler, *The Many Panics of 1837: People, Politics, and the Creation of a Transatlantic Financial Crisis* (Cambridge: Cambridge University Press, 2013), 8–42; John Lauritz Larson, *The Market Revolution in America: Liberty, Ambition, and the Eclipse of the Common Good* (Cambridge: Cambridge University Press, 2010), 92; Harry L. Watson, *Liberty and Power: The Politics of Jacksonian America* (New York: Hill and Wang, 2006), 159–61; Peter Temin, *The Jacksonian Economy* (New York: W. W. Norton, 1969).

11. Stephen Mihm, "The Fog of War: Jackson, Biddle and the Destruction of the Bank of the United States," in *A Companion to the Era of Andrew Jackson*, ed. Sean Patrick Adams (Hoboken, NJ: Blackwell, 2013), 362–70; Watson, *Liberty and Power*, 150–56.

12. William Littell and Jacob Swigert, eds., "Bank of the Commonwealth," *A Digest of the Statute Law of Kentucky* vol. I (Frankfort: Kendall and Russell, 1822), 155–64.

13. "An Act passed December 26, 1820," in *A Digest of the Statute Law of Kentucky* vol. I, eds. Littell and Swigert, 149–54.

14. Edward Scott, ed., "An Act To Establish a Bank of the State of Tennessee," *Laws of the State of Tennessee* vol. II (Knoxville, TN: Heiskell & Brown, 1821), 619–25.

15. Matthew G. Schoenbachler, *Murder and Madness: The Myth of the Kentucky Tragedy* (Lexington: University Press of Kentucky, 2009), 62.

16. Scott, "Bank of the State of Tennessee," 619–25.

17. Littell and Swigert, eds., "Bank of the Commonwealth," 155–64; Scott, "Bank of the State of Tennessee," 619–25.

18. Littell and Swigert, eds., "Bank of the Commonwealth," 162.

19. John Harvie, president home bank to Mark Hardin, president Shelbyville branch bank, April 9, 1822, Home Bank Letter Book F 1820–1822, *KDLA Bank*.

20. Bank of Kentucky v. Vance's Administrators, 4 Litt. 168 (Appeals KY 1823).

21. Mortgage Daniel Weisiger to Bank of KY, January 5, 1821, Franklin County, KY, vol. H–I, *KDLA Deeds*, reel 266167.

22. For example, see also Mortgage Catesby Gill to Bank of KY, July 1, 1819; Mortgage Eliza P. Hickman to Bank of KY, October 14, 1819; Mortgage John R. Campbell to Bank of KY, October 19, 1819, vol. H–I, *KDLA Deeds*, reel 266167; Mortgage William Littell to Bank of KY, October 25, 1819; Mortgage Richard Taylor to Bank of KY, November 12, 1819; Mortgage Henry Wingate to Bank of KY, October 20, 1820; Mortgage Benjamin Hickman to Bank of KY, June 2, 1821; Mortgage Jacob Creath to Bank of KY, March 20, 1822; Mortgage Samuel Ralph to Bank of KY, June 11, 1822; Mortgage Jacob H. Holeman, July 22, 1822; Mortgage Henry and John Perkins to Bank of KY, July 26, 1822, vol. K–L, *KDLA Deeds*, reel 266168.

23. "Public Sale," *Kentucky Gazette*, March 25, 1824, 3.

24. Mortgage Perkins to Bank of KY, January 5, 1821, Franklin County, KY, vol. K–L, *KDLA Deeds*, reel 266168.

25. "Public Sale," *Kentucky Reporter* (Lexington), June 27, 1825, 4.

26. Mortgage Fletcher to Bank US, September 2, 1822, Fayette County, KY, vol. V–X, 1821–1824, *KDLA Deeds*, reel c987744.

27. Mortgage Fletcher to Bank US, August 5, 1824, Fayette County, KY, vol. Y–2, 1824–1827, *KDLA Deeds*, reel c987745.

28. Nicholas Biddle to J. M. Salazar, January 27, 1825, *Biddle*, reel 42.

29. Nicholas Biddle to P. Bacot, cashier Charleston branch, and J. Hunter, cashier Savannah branch, August 29, 1833, *Biddle*, reel 43.

30. John Thom Holdsworth and Davis R. Dewey, *The First and Second Banks of the United States* (Serial 5625; Washington, DC, 1910), 243; Ralph C. H. Catterall, *The Second Bank of the United States* (Chicago: University of Chicago Press, 1903), 100.

31. Holdsworth and Dewey, *First and Second Banks*, 244; Catterall, *Second Bank*, 152.

32. Holdsworth and Dewey, *First and Second Banks*, 244.

33. Fourth Census, 1820, Fayette County, KY, *Census (MCR)*, p. 112, M-33, reel 17.

34. Mortgage Lowry to Bank US, February 2, 1822, Fayette County, KY, vol. V–X, 1821–1824, *KDLA Deeds*, reel c987744.

35. Mortgage Pindell to Bank U. States, January 24, 1824, Fayette County, KY, vol. V–X, 1821–1824, *KDLA Deeds*, reel c987744.

36. Mortgage Blanton to Bank US, March 17, 1824, Franklin County, KY, vol. K–L, *KDLA Deeds*, reel 266168.

37. Mortgage John Smith to Bank US, June 12, 1825, Franklin County, KY, vol. K–L, *KDLA Deeds*, reel 266168.

38. Mortgage John Smith to Bank of Kentucky, February 29, 1828, Franklin County, KY, vol. K–L, *KDLA Deeds*, reel 266168.

39. Mortgage Smith to Bank US, May 12, 1827, Franklin County, KY, vol. M–N, *KDLA Deeds*, reel 266169.

40. "Sheriff's Sales," *Daily Georgian* (Savannah), February 8, 1825, 4.

41. "Cuyler, Jeremiah La Touche," Federal Judicial Center, accessed March 9, 2022, https://www.fjc.gov/history/judges/cuyler-jeremiah-la-touche; Gail Moyer, *The Life and Tines of William*

Henry Cuyler, August 1, 1984, Special Collections, Lane Library, Armstrong Atlantic State University, courtesy Georgia State University Digital Commons, https://digitalcommons.georgiasouthern.edu/cgi/viewcontent.cgi?article=1043&context=sav-bios-lane.

42. Indenture, March 4, 1828, in the Planters Bank of Savannah Records, no. 1256, *SHC*.

43. "Sheriff's Sales," *Georgian* (Savannah), November 11, 1825, 4; "Sheriff's Sales," *Georgian* (Savannah), January 9, 1826, 2; "Marshal's Sale," *Georgian* (Savannah), March 29, 1826, 2.

44. "Marshal's Sales," *Georgian* (Savannah), February 13, 1826, 3; "Marshal's Sales—continued," *Georgian* (Savannah), June 6, 1826 (ad first run March 9, 1826), 3.

45. "Marshal's Sale," *Daily Georgian*, January 26, 1828, 4.

46. "Sheriff's Sales," *Georgian*, September 7, October 19, 1824, 3.

47. *House Documents*, 24 Cong., 2 Sess., no. 28, *Memorial of Eleazar Early* (Serial 302; Washington, DC, December 20, 1836).

48. "Sheriff's Sales, Continued" *Georgian* (Savannah), November 15, 1824, 2.

49. "Sheriff's Sales, Continued" *Georgian* (Savannah), December 15, 1824, January 3, 1825, 4.

50. "An Act to Establish a Bank at Milledgeville," *Compilation of the Laws of the State of Georgia* (Milledgeville: Grantland and Orme, 1831), 86–87.

51. "Central Bank," *Daily Georgian* (Savannah), December 15, 1828, 2.

52. "An Act, to Alter and Amend the Twenty-First Section of an Act, to Establish a Bank at Milledgeville," *A Digest of the Laws of the State of Georgia* (Athens, OH: Oliver H. Prince, 1837), 118.

53. "Banks," *Daily Georgian* (Savannah), December 31, 1828, 2.

54. "Banks a Curse to Farmers," *Hampshire Gazette* (Northampton, MA), February 4, 1829, 2; *New-Bedford Mercury*, February 20, 1829, 1; *Augusta Chronicle*, March 14, 1829, 185 (emphasis in original).

55. "Central Bank Agency," *Augusta Chronicle*, April 18, 1829, 225.

56. "Better Times," *Daily Georgian* (Savannah), June 11, 1829, 2.

57. Arthur Foster, ed., "An Act to Provide for the Improvement of the Roads and Rivers in This State," *A Digest of the Laws of the State of Georgia* (Philadelphia: C. Sherman & Co., 1831), 297–98.

58. Ralph Betts Flanders, *Plantation Slavery in Georgia* (Chapel Hill: University of North Carolina Press, 1933), 218.

59. Flanders, *Plantation Slavery in Georgia*, 218–20.

60. "Sale of Public Hands, &c.," and "118 Negroes &c for Sale," *Macon Weekly Telegraph*, January 23, 1834, 3.

61. "118 Negroes &c for Sale," *Macon Weekly Telegraph*, March 28 and April 4, 1834, 4.

62. "Sale of Public Hands," *Macon Weekly Telegraph*, June 5, 1834, 1.

63. Wilson Lumpkin, "Message," *Georgia Telegraph*, November 6, 1834, 2.

64. Wilson Lumpkin, "Governor's Message," *Macon Weekly Telegraph*, November 12, 1835, 2.

65. Mortgage of Ann Box to Bank of the State of Georgia, June 9, 1837, Chatham Co., Georgia Deeds, vols. 2V–2W, RH 1059, microfilm 66–66, *Georgia*.

66. Mortgage of Robert Pooler to Gaudry & Branch, July 5, 1837, Chatham Co., Georgia Deeds, vols. 2V–2W, RH 1059, microfilm 66–66, *Georgia*.

67. Mortgage of Gurdon Miller to Henrietta Miller, July 8, 1837, Chatham Co., Georgia Deeds, vols. 2V–2W, RH 1059, microfilm 66–66, *Georgia*.

68. Mortgage of George Glen to Bayard & Hunter, December 19, 1837, Chatham Co., Georgia Deeds, vols. 2V–2W, RH 1059, microfilm 66–66, *Georgia*.

69. Mortgage of John Gardner to Planters' Bank of the State of Georgia, October 16, 1837, Chatham Co., Georgia Deeds, vols. 2V–2W, RH 1059, microfilm 66–66, *Georgia.*

70. Mortgage of Alexander Drysdale to Planters' Bank of the State of Georgia, February 2, 1838, Chatham Co., Georgia Deeds, vols. 2V–2W, RH 1059, microfilm 66–66, *Georgia.*

71. Mortgage of John F. G. Davis to Bank of the State of Georgia, May 19, 1838, Chatham Co., Georgia Deeds, vols. 2V–2W, RH 1059, microfilm 66–66, *Georgia.*

72. Mortgage of Jane E. Postell to Bank of the State of Georgia, June 28, 1838, Chatham Co., Georgia Deeds, vols. 2V–2W, RH 1059, microfilm 66–66, *Georgia.*

73. Allen Gunn to Joseph Totten, January 14, 1835, series 17, Joseph Silas Totten papers, in the Caswell County Historical Association Collection no. 5401, *SHC.*

74. J. Rothman, *Slave Traders*, 167–68, 178–79.

75. Isaac Franklin to Rice Ballard, January 9, 1832, in the Rice C. Ballard papers no. 4850, reel 1, folder 4, *SHC*; J. Rothman, *Slave Traders*, 179.

76. Isaac Franklin to Rice Ballard, June 8, 1832, in the Rice C. Ballard papers no. 4850, reel 1, folder 7, *SHC.*

77. Sharon Ann Murphy, *Other People's Money: How Banking Worked in the Early American Republic* (Baltimore, MD: Johns Hopkins University Press, 2017), 58–59.

78. R. P. N. Windfor to Rice Ballard, October 6, 1834, in the Rice C. Ballard papers no. 4850, reel 1, folder 7, *SHC.*

79. "Stephen Girard's Bank. Rough Minutes of the Board," June 26, 1834 and June 4, 1835, *Girard*, series II, reel 449.

80. "Stephen Girard's Bank. Rough Minutes of the Board," March 6 and July 21, 1834 and May 25 and 28, 1835, *Girard*, series II, reel 449.

81. "Stephen Girard's Bank. Rough Minutes of the Board," December 8, 1834; February 19, April 30, June 4, July 6, August 3, and September 3, 1835; and May 4 and 30, 1836. *Girard*, series II, reel 449.

82. Bills of Exchange, in the Rice C. Ballard papers no. 4850, reel 1, folders 5–12, *SHC.*

83. Bills of Exchange, in the Rice C. Ballard papers no. 4850, reel 1, folders 5–6, *SHC.*

84. Stephen Duncan, August 26, 1826, *Mississippi*, box 2E973.

85. Isaac Franklin to Rice Ballard, June 8, 1832, in the Rice C. Ballard papers no. 4850, reel 1, folder 7, *SHC.*

86. M. C. Stephens to William Gaston, July 3, 1833, in the William Gaston papers no. 272, *SHC.*

87. M. C. Stephens to William Gaston, July 3, 1833.

88. Larry Schweikart, *Banking in the American South from the Age of Jackson to Reconstruction* (Baton Rouge: Louisiana State University Press, 1987), 51.

89. M. C. Stephens to William Gaston, March 27, 1834, in the William Gaston papers, no. 272, *SHC.*

90. Thomas Green to Dr. G. Brockenbrough, May 2, 1837, R. A. Brock, *Virginia Banks Collection, 1841–1879*, Library of Virginia, microfilm.

91. Katharina Pistor, *The Code of Capital: How the Law Creates Wealth and Inequality* (Princeton, NJ: Princeton University Press, 2019), 92; Peter A. Coclanis, *The Shadow of a Dream: Economic Life and Death in the South Carolina Low Country, 1670–1920* (New York: Oxford University Press, 1991), 102–03.

92. Marylynn Salmon, *Women and the Law of Property in Early America* (Chapel Hill: University of North Carolina Press, 1986), 15–16.

93. Elizabeth Bowles Warbasse, *The Changing Legal Rights of Married Women, 1800–1861* (New York: Garland Publishing, 1987), 10–13; Salmon, *Women and the Law of Property*, 141–43. Husbands could override these minimums through the provisions of a will, but a widow could always claim her dower rights if she felt that the will treated her less favorably. Warbasse, *Changing Legal Rights*, 11.

94. Salmon, *Women and the Law of Property*, 153.

95. Salmon, *Women and the Law of Property*, 147–49; Carole Shammas, "Re-Assessing the Married Women's Property Acts," *Journal of Women's History* 6 (Spring 1994): 10.

96. Salmon, *Women and the Law of Property*, 156.

97. Salmon, *Women and the Law of Property*, 4, 149–53.

98. Sara Brooks Sundberg, "Women and Property in Early Louisiana: Legal Systems at Odds," *Journal of the Early Republic* 32 (Winter 2012): 646–48.

99. Venable v. Bank of U.S., 27 U.S. 107 (1829)

100. John E. Palmer v. Ann Cross, 1 Smedes & M. 48 (Appeals MS 1843). For an excellent, detailed description of trusts, see Pistor, *Code of Capital*, 42–44.

101. *Palmer*, 1 Smedes & M.

102. *Palmer*, 1 Smedes & M. at 62. In making this argument, the defense cited the recently decided case of the Bank of the United States v. Lee, 38 U.S. 107 (1839). See Sharon Ann Murphy, "The Financialization of Slavery by the First and Second Banks of the United States," *Journal of Southern History* 87, no. 3 (August 2021): 406–09.

103. *Palmer*, 1 Smedes & M. at 68.

104. Milly v. Smith, 2 Mo. 36 (SC M) 1828); Milly v. Smith, 2 Mo. 171 (SC MO 1829).

105. *Milly*, 2 Mo. (1828); Lea VanderVelde, *Redemption Songs: Suing for Freedom before Dred Scott* (Oxford: Oxford University Press, 2014), 90.

106. VanderVelde, *Redemption Songs*, 91.

107. Records of the Circuit Court (State Supreme Court Cases, box 542, no. 37, Milly vs. Stephen Smith, 31 August 1829; Missouri State Archives, Jefferson City, Missouri), *Petitions* 211 82708.

108. *Milly*, 2 Mo. (1828) at 37–38.

109. Records of the Circuit Court (State Supreme Court Cases, box 542, no. 37, Milly vs. Stephen Smith, 31 August 1829; Missouri State Archives, Jefferson City, Missouri), *Petitions* 21182708.

110. *Milly*, 2 Mo. (1828) at 39.

111. *Milly*, 2 Mo. (1829) at 173 and 175.

112. Fenwick v. Macey's Ex'rs, 1 Dana 276 (Appeals KY 1833) at 279–80.

113. *Milly*, 2 Mo. (1829) at 175–76.

114. Macey v. Fenwick's Adm'r, 9 Dana 198 (Appeals KY 1839) at 200.

115. Moses Grandy, *Narrative of the Life of Moses Grandy* (London: C. Gilpin, 1843), 65, *DAS* 1996.

116. Grandy, *Narrative of the Life*, 14.

117. Grandy, *Narrative of the Life*, 51 and 55.

118. Grandy, *Narrative of the Life*, 22–23.

119. Lunsford Lane, *The Narrative of Lunsford Lane* (Boston, MA: J. G. Torrey, 1842), 14–15, *DAS* 1999.

120. Erin Bartels, summary of *The Narrative of Lunsford Lane*, *DAS* 1999.

121. Josephine Brown, *Biography of an American Bondman, by His Daughter* (Boston: R. F. Wallcut, 1856), 17, *DAS* 2000; Jenn Williamson, summary of *Biography of an American Bondman, by His Daughter*, *DAS*.

122. William Wells Brown, *Clotel; or, The President's Daughter, a Narrative of Slave Life in the United States* (London: Partridge and Oakley, 1853), 57 and 60, *DAS* 2004; Mary Alice Kirkpatrick, summary of *Clotel; or, The President's Daughter*, *DAS*.

123. Brown, *Clotel*, 59, 62, and 163.

124. Brown, *Clotel*, 62 and 85.

125. Brown, *Clotel*, 204–05.

126. J. W. Loguen, *The Rev. J. W. Loguen, as a Slave and as a Freeman* (Syracuse, NY: J. G. K. Truair, 1859), 64–65, *DAS* 1999.

127. Loguen, *Rev. J. W. Loguen*, 109–10.

128. Loguen, *Rev. J. W. Loguen*, 213.

129. Jenn Williamson, summary of *The Rev. J. W. Loguen, as a Slave and as a Freeman*, *DAS* 1999.

130. Lewis Garrard Clarke, *Narrative of the Sufferings of Lewis Clarke* (Boston, MA: David H. Ela, 1845), 23–24, *DAS* 1999.

131. Clarke, *Narrative of the Sufferings*, 30.

132. Clarke, *Narrative of the Sufferings*, 72–73.

133. Solomon Northup, *Twelve Years a Slave: Narrative of Solomon Northup, a Citizen of New-York, Kidnapped in Washington City in 1841, and Rescued in 1853* (Auburn, NY: Derby and Miller, 1853), 106, *DAS* 1997.

134. Northup, *Twelve Years a Slave*, 116.

135. William Craft, *Running a Thousand Miles for Freedom; or, The Escape of William and Ellen Craft from Slavery* (London: William Tweedie, 1860), 10–12, *DAS* 2001.

136. Benjamin Drew, *A North-Side View of Slavery: The Refugee: or the Narratives of Fugitive Slaves in Canada Related by Themselves* (Boston, MA: John P. Jewett and Company, 1856), 177, *DAS* 2000.

137. Drew, *A North-Side View of Slavery*, 370.

138. William Walker, *Buried Alive (Behind Prison Walls) for a Quarter of a Century: Life of William Walker* (Saginaw, MI: Friedman & Hynan, 1892), 48–49, *DAS* 2003.

139. Annie L. Burton, *Memories of Childhood's Slavery Days* (Boston, MA: Ross Publishing Company, 1909), 5, *DAS* 1996.

140. Charles Willson to Thomas Ruffin, February 15, 1825, in the Thomas Ruffin papers no. 641, series 1.3, *SHC*.

Chapter Four

1. "Auction by T. Mossy," *Orleans Gazette*, February 11, 1820, 2.

2. March 20, 1820, Louisiana State Bank Records, 1817–1825, no. 1785, folders 1–25 (1), *LLMVC*.

3. March 20, 1820, Louisiana State Bank Records, 1817–1825. Translation by author.

4. "An Act to Grant Certain Privileges to the Louisiana State Bank, and for Other Purposes," *A General Digest of the Acts of the Legislature of Louisiana* vol. I (New Orleans, LA: Benjamin Levy, 1828), 76.

5. Sharon Ann Murphy, *Other People's Money: How Banking Worked in the Early American Republic* (Baltimore, MD: Johns Hopkins University Press, 2017), 43–47.

6. Larry Schweikart, *Banking in the American South from the Age of Jackson to Reconstruction* (Baton Rouge: Louisiana State University Press, 1987), 50–60; Howard Bodenhorn, *State Banking in Early America: A New Economic History* (New York: Oxford University Press, 2003), 6, 234.

7. *An Act to Incorporate the Subscribers to the Bank of Louisiana* (New Orleans, LA: Benjamin Levy, 1838), 3, 6–8.

8. *An Act to Incorporate the Subscribers to the Bank of Louisiana*, 19, 25–26.

9. "Letter from the Secretary of the Treasury Transmitting Statements Showing the Condition of Certain State Banks, January 4, 1837," *Executive Documents, Twenty-Fourth Congress*, 2nd session, House of Representatives, doc. no. 65, 150; "An Act to Establish a State Bank," *General Digest*, 70.

10. *An Act to Incorporate the Subscribers to the Bank of Louisiana*, 25–26.

11. "Rules and Regulations for Conducting the Business of the Bank of Louisiana," *An Act to Incorporate the Subscribers to the Bank of Louisiana*, 47.

12. "An Act to Amend the Act Entitled 'An Act to Establish a State Bank,'" *General Digest*, 79.

13. Sara Brooks Sundberg, "Women and Property in Early Louisiana: Legal Systems at Odds," *Journal of the Early Republic* 32 (Winter 2012): 646–48, at 648.

14. Sundberg, "Women and Property"; Elizabeth Bowles Warbasse, *The Changing Legal Rights of Married Women, 1800–1861* (New York: Garland Publishing, 1987), 53.

15. *An Act to Incorporate the Subscribers to the Bank of Louisiana*, 10, 19, 25–27.

16. "Rules," *An Act to Incorporate the Subscribers to the Bank of Louisiana*, 48–49.

17. "Mortgage Manuel Garcia to Bank of Louisiana," May 29, 1834, Notary Christy, vol. 18, no. 522, *NONA*.

18. Bank of Louisiana v. Farrar, 1 La.Ann. 49 (SC LA 1846) at 55.

19. *An Act to Incorporate the Subscribers to the Bank of Louisiana*, 25–26.

20. "Release of Mortgage Bank of Louisiana to Jacques Charbonnet Senr," March 31, 1838, Notary Christy, vol. 31, pp. 407–08, *NONA*.

21. "Release of Mortgage Bank of Louisiana to Richd G. Ellis and Thos Butler," June 1, 1839, Notary Christy, vol. 36, pp. 472–73, *NONA*.

22. "Release of Mortgage Bank of Louisa to Macarty and Lanusse," February 5, 1836, Notary Christy, vol. 23, pp. 199–200, *NONA*.

23. "Release of Mortgage Bank of Louisiana to Josias Gray," August 3, 1838, Notary Christy, vol. 33, pp. 17–18, *NONA*.

24. "Release of Mortgage Bank of Louisiana to James Freret," April 23, 1838, Notary Christy, vol. 31, pp. 600–01, *NONA*.

25. "Mortgage James P. Freret to the Bank of Louisiana," April 24, 1838, Notary Christy, vol. 31, pp. 604–07, *NONA*.

26. "Release of Mortgage Bk of Louisiana to B. Barrow and assumption by M. Courtney," March 31, 1836, Notary Christy, vol. 24, pp. 579–80, *NONA*; "Release of Mortgage Bank of Louisa to Philip Hicky," June 15, 1836, Notary Christy, vol. 25, pp. 355–56, *NONA*.

27. "Acceptation de l'Hypothèque de Philip Hicky et son épouse," July 6, 1838, Notary Theodore Seghers, vol. 29, no. 261, *NONA*.

28. "Acceptance of Mort. Bennet H. Barrow to Bank of Louis[ian]a," January 22, 1845, Notary Christy, vol. 52, pp. 52–53, *NONA*.

29. V. M. Garesche to Hon. R. B. Taney, Secretary of the Treasury, *Documents of the Congress of the United States, in Relation to the Public Lands* (Washington, DC: Gales & Seaton, 1860), 224.

30. George D. Green, *Finance and Economic Development in the Old South: Louisiana Banking 1804–1861* (Stanford, CA: Stanford University Press, 1972), 22–23; "Letter from the Secretary of the Treasury Transmitting Statements Showing the Condition of Certain State Banks, January 4, 1837," *Executive Documents, Twenty-Fourth Congress*, 150.

31. "An Act to Incorporate the Subscribers to the Merchants' Bank of New-Orleans," *Acts Passed at the Second Session of the Twelfth Legislature of the State of Louisiana* (New Orleans, LA: Jerome Bayon, 1836), 59.

32. "An Act to Incorporate the City Bank of New-Orleans," *Acts Passed at the First Session of the Tenth Legislature of the State of Louisiana* (New Orleans, LA: John Gibson, 1831), 38.

33. "City Bank," *Tenth Legislature*, 32.

34. Percy v. Millaudon, 3 La. 568 (SC LA 1832) at 575.

35. "John B. Kleinpeter, Louis Kleinpeter, and John Grager Office of the City Bank of New Orleans at Baton Rouge," May 1, 1832, folders 1–15, *City Bank*.

36. "Statement of Loans on Mortgage Security Made by This Office up to the 31st May 1832," folders 1–15, *City Bank*.

37. Office of the City Bank of New Orleans at Baton Rouge, May 8, 1832, folders 1–15, *City Bank*.

38. William Winfree, Office of the City Bank of New Orleans at Baton Rouge, May 1, 1832, folders 1–15, *City Bank*.

39. Office of the City Bank of New Orleans at Baton Rouge, May 8, 1832, folders 1–15, *City Bank*.

40. "Statement of Loans on Mortgage Security Made by This Office up to the 30th June 1832," folders 1–15, *City Bank*.

41. Office of the City Bank of New Orleans at Baton Rouge, May 15, 1832, folders 1–15, *City Bank*.

42. Office of the City Bank of New Orleans at Baton Rouge, May 8, 1832.

43. Office of the City Bank of New Orleans at Baton Rouge, May 15, 1832.

44. Office of the City Bank of New Orleans at Baton Rouge, May 22, 1832, folders 1–15, *City Bank*.

45. Office of the City Bank of New Orleans at Baton Rouge, May 8, 1832.

46. Robert Flecker, Office of the City Bank of New Orleans at Baton Rouge, May 15, 1832, folders 1–15, *City Bank*.

47. "Statement of Loans on Mortgage Security Made by his Office up to the 30th June 1832," folders 1–15, *City Bank*.

48. Office of the City Bank of New Orleans at Baton Rouge, May 15, 1832, folders 1–15, *City Bank*.

49. "Statement of Loans on Mortgage Security Made by his Office up to the 30th June 1832," folders 1–15, *City Bank*.

50. "General Statement of the Office of the City Bank of New Orleans, at Baton Rouge," July 31, 1832, folders 1–15, *City Bank*.

51. Samuel Watts, Office of the City Bank of New Orleans at Baton Rouge, May 15, 1832, folders 1–15, *City Bank*.

52. A. B. and Ann Gill to the board of Directors of the City Bank of New Orleans at Natchitoches, November 20, 1834, and Robert J. Palfrey, City Bank cashier New Orleans, to Jean Vignaud, City Bank cashier, Natchitoches, December 3, 1834, folders 1–15, *City Bank*.

53. Cesaire Fonteneau, City Bank notary form, April 13, 1838, with Frederick Williams, notary Natchitoches, folders 16–41, *City Bank*.

54. Richard William Hertzog mortgage, Natchitoches, May 7, 1839, folders 16–41, *City Bank*.

55. Harry Toulmin, ed., "An Act to Establish the Tombeckbe Bank" and "An Act to Establish a Bank in the Town of Mobile," in *A Digest of the Laws of the State of Alabama* (Cahawba, AL: Ginn & Curtis, 1823), 40–52.

56. Toulmin, ed., "An Act to Incorporate the Subscribers to the Bank of the State of Alabama," in *State of Alabama*, 53–61; John G. Aiken, ed., "Bank of the State of Alabama," in *A Digest of the Laws of the State of Alabama* (Philadelphia: Alexander Towar, 1833), 55–56.

57. Aiken, ed., "Bank of the State of Alabama," in *Digest of the Laws* (1833), 57–58, 64; John G. Aiken, ed., "Bank of the State and Branches," in *A Digest of the Laws of the State of Alabama* (Tuscaloosa, AL: D. Woodruff, 1836), 578–91.

58. John G. Aiken, ed., "Banks in Mobile," in *Digest of the Laws* (1836), 592–96.

59. Francis Newton Thorpe, "Constitution of Mississippi—1817," *The Federal and State Constitutions*, vol. IV (Washington, DC: Government Printing Office, 1909), 2044.

60. "An Act, Supplemental to an Act Entitled 'An Act, to Establish a Bank in the Mississippi Territory," *The Revised Code of the Laws of Mississippi* (Natchez, MS: Francis Baker, 1824), 468–72; William C. Davis, *A Way Through the Wilderness: The Natchez Trace and the Civilization of the Southern Frontier* (New York: Harper Collins, 1995), 213–14; Robert C. Weems, Jr., "Mississippi's First Banking System," *Journal of Mississippi History* 29 (December 1967), 386.

61. "An Act, to Amend the Charter of the Bank of the State of Mississippi," *Revised Code of the Laws of Mississippi*, 472.

62. Augustus Griswold to Gabriel Tichenor, April 5, 1821, *Mississippi*, box 2E953.

63. Martha Jane Brazy, *American Planter: Stephen Duncan of Antebellum Natchez and New York* (Baton Rouge: Louisiana State University Press, 2006), 69–70; Marvin Bentley, "The State Bank of Mississippi: Monopoly Bank on the Frontier (1809–1830)," *Journal of Mississippi History* 40 (1978), 312; Davis, *Through the Wilderness*, 214.

64. "Notice," *Ariel* (Natchez, MS), January 9, 1826, 6.

65. John Richards to Gabriel Tichenor, March 7, 1826, *Mississippi*, box 2E957.

66. "Obituary," *Mississippi State Gazette* (Natchez), January 8, 1820, 3.

67. "State of Louisiana, Probate Office," *Ariel* (Natchez, MS), April 21, 1826, 11; "State of Louisiana, Probate Office," *Mississippi Statesman*, February 14, 1827, 1.

68. Kempe's Heirs v. Hunt, 4 La. 477 (SC LA 1832).

69. *Kempe's Heirs*, 4 La.; indenture between Thomas Hunt, Francis Girault, and the Kempe siblings, July 2, 1832, *Mississippi*, box 2E983c.

70. "Rifle Point Plantation for Sale," *Mississippi Statesman* (Natchez), November 15, 1827, 1.

71. "Rifle Point Plantation for Sale," (emphasis in original).

72. Rifle Point Plantation receipts, *Mississippi*, box 2E983c.

73. *Kempe's Heirs*, 4 La.

74. "Sheriff's Sale," *Mississippi Statesman* (Natchez), May 1, 1828, 4.

75. *Kempe's Heirs*, 4 La.

76. Reynolds v Rowley, 2 La.Ann. 890 (SC LA 1847) at 893.

77. Indenture between Thomas Hunt, Francis Girault, and the Kempe siblings, July 2, 1832.

78. F. S. Girault to A. N. Ogden, August 9, 1832; and A. N. Ogden to Dr. Stephen Duncan, President Bank of the State of Mississippi, August 30, 1832, *Mississippi*, box 2E983c.

79. *Kempe's Heirs*, 4 La. at 484–85.

80. Interrogatories for Doctor Thomas Hunt, January 30, 1834, *Mississippi*, box 2E983c.

81. "An Act Granting Certain Powers, in the State of Louisiana, to the Bank of the State of Mississippi," *Acts Passed at the Second Session of the Eleventh Legislature of the State of Louisiana* (New Orleans: Jerome Bayon, 1834), 84–85.

82. Samuel Gustine to the Bank of the State of Mississippi, January 4, 1834, *Mississippi*, box 2E983c.

83. Thomas Hunt to Stephen Duncan, January 30, 1834, *Mississippi*, box 2E983c .

84. Thomas Hunt to the president and directors of the Bank of the State of Mississippi, January 30, 1834, *Mississippi*, box 2E983c.

85. Thomas Hunt to the president and directors of the Bank of the State of Mississippi, January 31, 1834, *Mississippi*, box 2E983c.

86. Brazy, *American Planter*, 71; "Executor's Sale," *Concordia Intelligencer*, January 2, 1847, 4.

87. "Executor's Sale," 4.

88. "An Act, to Establish a Planters' Bank in the State of Mississippi," in *Laws of the State of Mississippi* (Jackson, MS: Printed for the State, 1838), 237.

89. Brazy, *American Planter*, 71.

90. "Planters' Bank," in *Laws of the State of Mississippi* (1838), 241; Schweikart, *Banking*, 179.

91. Stephen W. Campbell, "'A Very Large Extent of Virgin Land': Nicholas Biddle, Cotton, and the Expansion of Slavery, 1823–1841," *Pennsylvania Magazine of History and Biography* 145 (January 2021): 33–65, at 51–52; Bodenhorn, *State Banking*, 255, 258; Calvin Schermerhorn, *The Business of Slavery and the Rise of American Capitalism, 1815–1860* (New Haven, CT: Yale University Press, 2015), 133.

92. H. G. Runnells, "Governor's Message," *Weekly Mississippian* (Jackson), January 23, 1835, 2.

93. Bentley, "State Bank of Mississippi," 317.

94. "An Act to Incorporate the Subscribers to the Mississippi Union Bank," *Natchez Weekly Courier*, September 22, 1837, 4.

95. "Planters' Bank," in *Laws of the State of Mississippi* (1838), 245–46.

96. "An Act, to Amend an Act Supplemental to an Act Entitled 'An Act to Amend the Charter of the Bank of the State of Mississippi," in *Laws of the State of Mississippi* (1838), 218–19.

97. Brazy, *American Planter*, 70.

98. "Communications," *Southern Clarion* (Natchez), August 26, 1831, 3.

99. "Planters' Bank of Mississippi," Natchez *Southern Clarion* (Natchez), May 20, 1831, 3.

100. David Gordon to Stephen Duncan, November 30, 1831, *Mississippi*, box 2E967.

101. C. M. Harris to Gabriel Tichenor on behalf of D. R. Ransom, December 26, 1831, *Mississippi*, box 2E968.

102. S. A. Edmondson to Stephen Duncan, December 28, 1831, *Mississippi*, box 2E968.

103. Gabriel Tichenor to John Fleming, June 24, 1831, letter book, March 26, 1821—September 13, 1833, *MSU*.

104. Stephen Duncan to Horace Binney, July 7, 1831, letter book, March 26, 1821—September 13, 1833, *MSU*.

105. Stephen Duncan to Horace Binney, July 9, 1831, letter book, March 26, 1821—September 13, 1833, *MSU*.

106. Stephen Duncan to Horace Binney, July 7, 1831, letter book, March 26, 1821—September 13, 1833, *MSU*.

107. Stephen Duncan to Horace Binney, July 9, 1831, letter book, March 26, 1821—September 13, 1833, *MSU*. One of the leading legal minds of the nation, Kent had just finished publishing his four-volume *Commentaries on American Law*.

108. Stephen Duncan to Daniel Webster, September 22, 1831, letter book, March 26 1821—September 13, 1833, *MSU*.

109. "For the Natchez Gazette," *Natchez Gazette*, November 2, 1831, 1; Brazy, *American Planter*, 71.

110. "The General Assembly of the State of Mississippi," *Natchez Gazette*, November 30, 1831, 2; Brazy, *American Planter*, 71.

111. Stephen Duncan to Samuel Gustine, November 17, 1831, letter book, March 26 1821–September 13, 1833, *MSU*; Brazy, *American Planter*, 71.

112. George Tichenor to James Duncan, November 17, 1831, letter book, March 26 1821–September 13, 1833, *MSU*.

113. "The Opinion of Daniel Webster, Esq.," *Natchez Gazette*, December 14, 1831, 1.

114. "The Bank.—Mr. Webster's Opinion," *Natchez Gazette*, December 14, 1831, 2.

115. "Agricultural Bank," *Natchez Weekly Courier*, March 8, 1833, 3; Brazy, *American Planter*, 72.

116. Charles W. T. Ward to bank, February 4, 1832, *Mississippi*, box 2E968.

117. F. W. Baird to Gabriel Tichenor, March 19, 1832, *Mississippi*, box 2E969.

118. "Planters' Bank," in *Laws of the State of Mississippi* (1838), 247.

119. Indenture of John Tucker, February 2, 1835, indentures 1835–1839, folder 72, box 7, *Planters Bank*.

120. Indenture of Peter C. Goosey June 5, 1835, indentures 1835–1839, folder 72, box 7, *Planters Bank*.

121. Indenture of Thomas and Mary Nash, October 7, 1840, indentures 1835–1839, folder 72, box 7, *Planters Bank*.

122. Richard Sylla, John B. Legler, and John J. Wallis, "Banks and State Public Finance in the New Republic: The United States, 1790–1860," *Journal of Economic History* 47, no. 2 (June 1987), 391–403.

123. "Manhattan Bank," *Laws of the State of New-York*, vol. II (Albany, NY: Charles R. and George Webster, 1802), 374.

124. Bodenhorn, *State Banking*, 134–135. In Pennsylvania, the vaguely-named Lancaster Trading Company (1814) and Marietta & Susquehanna Trading Company (1814) were also institutions that had likely adopted the "ploy of assuming banking practices while hiding behind a nonbank title." The same could be said for the Miami Exporting Company (1805) and the Zanesville Canal & Manufacturing Company (1816) in neighboring Ohio. Of these Pennsylvania and Ohio firms, all but the Lancaster Trading Company would fold as a direct result of the Panic of 1819. Bodenhorn, *State Banking*, 142–143; Warren E. Weber, *Census of Early State Banks in the United States* (2005), https://www.minneapolisfed.org/people/warren-e-weber.

125. Bodenhorn, *State Banking*, 134.

126. John Joseph Wallis, "Constitutions, Corporations, and Corruption: American States and Constitutional Change, 1842 to 1852," *Journal of Economic History* 65, no. 1 (March 2005), 213.

127. "An Act Incorporating the Farmers' Bank of Virginia," *The Revised Code of the Laws of Virginia* (Richmond, VA: Thomas Ritchie, 1819), 82; "An Act for Extending the Charter of the Bank of Virginia," *Revised Code of the Laws of Virginia*, 77.

128. "Legislature of Virginia," *Niles' Weekly Register*, February 24, 1816, 149; Wallis, "Constitutions," 241.

129. "An Act to Establish Two New Banks within This Commonwealth," *Revised Code of the Laws of Virginia*, 97.

130. "Kentucky. Governor's Message to the Legislature," *National Register, a Weekly Paper*, January 4, 1817, 5.

131. Untitled, *Rhode-Island American* (Newport), January 20, 1818, 3.

132. Bodenhorn, *State Banking*, 229.

133. "An Act, to Establish a Planters' Bank in the State of Mississippi," in *Laws of the State of Mississippi* (Jackson, MS: Printed for the State, 1838), 237.

134. Green, *Finance*, 22–23, 32–34.

135. "An Act to Incorporate the Subscribers to the New-Orleans Canal and Banking Company," *Acts Passed at the First Session of the Tenth Legislature* (New Orleans, LA: John Gibson, 1831); "An Act to Amend the Act Entitled 'An Act to Incorporate the Clinton and Port Hudson Rail-Road Company," *Second Session of the Eleventh Legislature*; "An Act to Incorporate the New-Orleans Gas Light and Banking Company," *Acts Passed at the First Session of the Twelfth Legislature of the State of Louisiana* (New Orleans: Jerome Bayon, 1835); *An Act to Incorporate the Commercial Bank of New-Orleans* (New Orleans: E. Johns & Co., 1833); "An Act to Incorporate the Exchange and Banking Company of New-Orleans," *First Session of the Twelfth Legislature*; "An Act to Amend the Act to Incorporate the New Orleans and Carrollton Rail Road Company," *Second Session of the Twelfth Legislature;* "An Act Granting Banking Privileges to the New-Orleans Improvement Company," *Second Session of the Twelfth Legislature*; "An Act Supplementary to an Act Entitled 'An Act to Incorporate the Pontchartrain Rail Road Company," *Second Session of the Twelfth Legislature.*

136. "Gas Light and Banking Company," *First Session of the Twelfth Legislature*, 103; *Commercial Bank of New-Orleans*, 13; "Exchange and Banking Company," *First Session of the Twelfth Legislature*, 200; "New-Orleans Improvement Company," *Second Session of the Twelfth Legislature*, 47.

137. "Clinton and Port Hudson Rail-Road Company," *Second Session of the Eleventh Legislature*, 116.

138. "Clinton and Port Hudson Rail-Road Company," *Second Session of the Eleventh Legislature*, 120; "Pontchartrain Rail Road Company," *Second Session of the Twelfth Legislature*, 41.

139. "The New Orleans Gas Light and Banking Co.," *Niles' Weekly Register*, November 14, 1835, 181.

140. "Mortgage Wm H. Sparks to the New Orleans Gas-Light & Banking Company," March 8, 1836, Notary Christy, vol. 24, 385–89, *NONA*.

141. "Sale of Slave [by] Jacob L. Florance to the N. O. Gas-light and Bank[in]g Company," June 4, 1836, 275–78; "Sale of Slave [b] Thomas Toby to the New Orleans Gaslight and Banking Comp[an]y," June 15, 1836, 361–64; "Sale of Slave [by] Thos C. Cash to the New Orleans Gaslight and Banking Comp[an]y," June 15, 1836, 365–68; "Sale of Slaves [by] John Minturn to the New Orleans Gaslight and Banking Co.," June 23, 1836, 413–16; and "Sale of Slaves John Minturn to the N. O. Gaslight & Bank[in]g Co.," June 23, 1836, 417–20, Notary Christy, vol. 25, *NONA*.

142. "Sale of Slave Jacob L. Florance to the N. O. Gas-light and Bankg Company," June 4, 1836, Notary Christy, vol. 25, 275–78, *NONA*.

143. "Sale of Slave Patrick Summers to the N. O. Gaslight & Banking Compy," March 7, 1838, Notary Christy, vol. 31, 279–80, *NONA*.

144. "Mortgage Mrs. Catharine Wilkinson and Robert A. Wilkinson to the New Orleans Gaslight and Banking Compy," November 12, 1838, Notary Christy, vol. 33, 339–45, *NONA*.

145. "Sale of Slave Lemuel Bullock to the New Orleans Gaslight and Banking Company," November 14, 1838, 367–68; "Sale of Slave Lepage Brothers to the New Orleans Gaslight and Banking Compy," November 14, 1838, 369–70; "Sale of Slaves New Orleans Gaslight and Banking Company to Edwards Ogden," November 30, 1838, 449–50, Notary Christy, vol. 33, *NONA*.

146. For example, see "Sale of Slave Thomas McCargo to the Gas Bank," January 25, 1841, 139–40; "Sale of Slave Mark Davis to the Gas Bank," January 25, 1841, 141–42; "Sale of Slave Edward Lockett to the Gas Bank," January 25, 1841, 145–46; "Sale of Slave Thomas Boudar to the Gas Bank," January 25, 1841, 147–48; "Sale of Slave Thos McCargo to the Gas Bank," February 11, 1841, 267–68; "Sale of Slave J. A. Barelli to Gas Bank," February 23, 1841, 315–16, Notary Christy, vol. 41, *NONA*.

147. "Sale of Slave Beverley Sydnor to the N. O. Gas Light & Banking Co.," February 28, 1838, Notary Christy, vol. 31, 277–83, *NONA*.

148. "Sale of Slaves by J. M. Bach to Commercial Bank of N. O.," February 25, 1836, Notary Hilary Breton Cenas, vol. 6, 497–500, *NONA*; Steven Deyle, *Carry Me Back: The Domestic Slave Trade in American Life* (Oxford: Oxford University Press, 2005), 99.

149. "Sale of Slave by J. M. Bach to The Commercial Bank of N Orleans," February 26, 1836, Notary Cenas, vol. 6, 597–600, *NONA*.

150. "Extract from the Minutes of the Commercial Bank of New Orleans, June 9, 1848," attached to "Sale of Slave by George A. Botts to Commercial Bank of New Orleans," July 7, 1848, Notary Cenas, vol. 40, 637–39, *NONA*.

151. "Pledge by F. P. Corbin, R. B. Corbin & E. Rawle to A. & J. Dennistoun & Co.," May 16, 1837, Notary Felix Grima, vol. 16, no. 436, *NONA*.

152. "Sale of Slaves F. P. & R. B. Corbin & Edward Rawle to N. O. Canal & Banking Company," May 18, 1837, Notary Grima, vol. 16, no. 453, *NONA*.

153. "Sale of Slave Martial Dupierris to the New Orleans Canal and Banking Compy," November 9, 1838, Notary Christy, vol. 33, 335–38, *NONA*.

154. "Mortgage Glendy Burke to the New Orleans Canal and Banking Co.," November 24, 1838, Notary Christy, vol. 33, 409–12, *NONA*.

155. Untitled, *Boston Post*, January 20, 1843, 2.

156. "An Act to Incorporate the Insurance Bank of Columbus," *A Digest of the Laws of the State of Georgia* (Athens, GA: Oliver H. Prince, 1837), 102.

157. Sharon Ann Murphy, "Securing Human Property: Slavery, Life Insurance, and Industrialization in the Upper South," *Journal of the Early Republic* 25 (Winter 2005), 634–35.

158. Mortgage of Patrick Houstoun Jr. to the Marine & Fire Insurance Bank, February 3, 1838, Chatham Co., Georgia Deeds, vols. 2V–2W, RH 1059, microfilm 66–66, *Georgia*.

159. Mortgage of George W. Ross to Merchants' Bank of New York, June 19, 1838, Muscogee Co., Georgia Deeds, book H1, RHS 4224, microfilm 147–62, *Georgia*.

160. "From Our Correspondent," *Macon Weekly Telegraph*, November 26, 1835, 2.

161. "From Our Correspondent," *Georgia Constitutionalist* (Augusta), November 27, 1835, 1.

162. For example, see "Georgia," *Macon Weekly Telegraph*, January 14, 1836, 2.

163. March 26 and 29, 1836, *GARR*.

164. October 25, 1836, and February 28, 1837, *GARR*.

165. "$25 Reward," *Georgia Constitutionalist* (Augusta), April 21, 1837, 3.

166. November 28, 1837, *GARR*.

167. September 18, 1838, *GARR*.

168. Sale of slaves of John B. Gaudry to Central Railroad and Banking Company, February 11, 1839, Chatham Co., Georgia Deeds, vols. 2V–2W, RH 1059, microfilm 66–66, *Georgia*.

169. "Third Semi-Annual Report, of the Engineer of the Central Rail Road and Banking Company," *Macon Weekly Telegraph*, June 25, 1839, 2.

170. May 5 and June 14, 1836, *GARR*.

171. "An Act to be Entitled an Act to Incorporate the Commercial and Rail Road Bank of Vicksburg," "An Act to Incorporate the Grand Gulf Rail Road and Banking Company," and "An Act further to Extend the Powers and Privileges of the West Feliciana Rail Road Company within the State of Mississippi," in *Laws of the State of Mississippi* (Jackson, MS: George R. Fall, 1834), 125–34, 140–47, 151–55; "An Act to Incorporate the Commercial Bank of Rodney," "An Act to Establish the Commercial Bank of Manchester," "An Act to Incorporate the Commercial Bank of Columbus, Mississippi," "An Act to Incorporate the Lake Washington and Deer Creek Rail-Road and Banking Company," "An Act to Incorporate the Tombigbee Rail-Road Company," "An Act to be Entitled an Act to Incorporate the Aberdeen and Pontotoc Rail-Road and Banking Company," "An Act to Incorporate the Commercial Bank of Natchez," in *Laws of the State of Mississippi* (Jackson, MS: G. R. & J. S. Fall, 1836), 132–51, 203–43, 247–55; "An Act to Incorporate the Northern Bank of Mississippi," "An Act Supplementary to an Act, Entitled an Act, to Incorporate the Mississippi Rail Road Company," "An Act to Incorporate the Benton and Manchester Rail Road and Banking Company," "An Act to Incorporate the Vicksburg Water Works and Banking Company," "An Act to Incorporate the Hernando Rail Road and Banking Company," "An Act to Amend the Charter of the Mississippi and Alabama Rail Road Company," in *Laws of the State of Mississippi* (1838), 582–90, 702–17, 721–35, 814–15.

172. "An Act to Incorporate the Citizens' Bank of Madison County," "An Act to Incorporate the Bank of Vicksburg," "An Act to Incorporate the Bank of Grenada, Mississippi," "An Act to Incorporate the Bank of Port Gibson," "An Act to Establish the Bank of Lexington," *Laws of the State of Mississippi* (1838), 590–603, 649–56, 659–66, 671–76.

173. "Benton and Manchester Rail Road and Banking Company," *Laws of the State of Mississippi* (1838), 707–10.

174. "Mississippi and Alabama Rail Road Company," *Laws of the State of Mississippi* (1838), 814.

175. The final southern improvement bank was the South Western Rail Road Bank, which was jointly incorporated in 1836 by separate acts of South Carolina, North Carolina, Tennessee, and Kentucky. Organized as a conservative commercial bank, the South Western Rail Road Bank was technically only permitted to discount notes for sixty days. "An Act to Confer Banking Privileges on the Stockholders of the Louisville, Cincinnati and Charleston Rail Road Company," in *Acts and Resolutions of the General Assembly of the State of South Carolina* (Columbia, SC: Weir, 1837), 7–16. Yet during the ensuing panic and depression, it became directly involved in the financialization of industrial slavery in South Carolina, when it agreed to guarantee a $150,000 bond issue secured by the ironworks and enslaved laborers of the Nesbitt Manufacturing Company in 1839. Although this deal with London investors ultimately fell through, the South Western Bank was willing to risk a substantial portion of its capital for this venture. See *Elmore*, minutes of stockholders' meeting, May 24, 1839, Business Correspondence, box 3; resolutions of the board of directors, May 24, 1839, Business Correspondence, box 3; and draft of indenture between South Western Rail Road Bank and the Nesbitt Manufacturing Company, n.d., Business Correspondence, box 6. See also Sharon Ann Murphy, "Enslaved Financing of Southern Industry: The Nesbitt Manufacturing Company of South Carolina, 1836–1850," *Enterprise & Society: The International Journal of Business History* (2021), 1–44, https://doi.org/10.1017/eso.2020.78.

Chapter Five

1. "Inventaire de titres et autres objets [Inventory of securities and other objects]," July 25, 1833, reel 13, *Citizens' Bank*.

2. "Main levée par la Banque des Citoyens à Rawle & Corbin," May 10, 1836, Notary Seghers, vol. 18, no. 60, *NONA*.

3. "The Corbin Family," *Virginia Magazine* 31 (January 1823), 80; Finding Aid, Francis Porteus Corbin papers, *NYPL*.

4. Robert Corbin to Francis Corbin, October 2, 1834, Francis Porteus Corbin papers, box 1, *NYPL*.

5. "Mortgage R. B. Corbin Edw. Rawle F. P. Corbin & A. S. C. Rawle to Bank of Louisiana," April 16, 1831, Notary Adolphe Mazureau, vol. 2, no. 140, *NONA*.

6. "Bank of Louisiana in Favour of R. B. & F. P. Corbin and Edward Rawle," April 29, 1837, Notary Christy, vol. 29, no. 501–02, *NONA*.

7. "Release of Morte A. & P. Denistoun & Co to Corbin & Rawle," May 16, 1837, Notary Grima, vol. 16, no. 434, *NONA*.

8. Stephen Mihm, "The Fog of War: Jackson, Biddle and the Destruction of the Bank of the United States," in *A Companion to the Era of Andrew Jackson*, ed. Sean Patrick Adams (Hoboken, NJ: Blackwell, 2013), 362–70, at 364.

9. Robert Corbin to Francis Corbin, November 12, 1834, Francis Porteus Corbin papers, box 1, *NYPL*.

10. Robert Corbin to Francis Corbin, October 2, 1834, Francis Porteus Corbin papers, box 1, *NYPL*.

11. Robert Corbin to Francis Corbin, November 12, 1834, Francis Porteus Corbin papers, box 1, *NYPL*.

12. "Main levée par la Banque des Citoyens à Rawle & Corbin," May 10, 1836, Notary Seghers, vol. 18, no. 60, *NONA*.

13. "Charter of the Citizens' Bank of Louisiana," *Charter of the Citizens' Bank of Louisiana and Acts Amendatory Thereto* (New Orleans, LA: Catholic Propagator Job Office, 1873), 9–10, Citizens' Bank of Louisiana papers, folders 1–2, *LLMVC*.

14. Robert Corbin to Francis Corbin, January 19, 1836, Francis Porteus Corbin papers, box 1, *NYPL*.

15. "Main levée par la Banque des Citoyens à Rawle & Corbin," May 10, 1836, Notary Seghers, vol. 18, no. 60, *NONA*.

16. "Bank of Louisiana in Favour of R. B. & F. P. Corbin and Edward Rawle," April 29, 1837, Notary Christy, vol. 29, no. 501–02, *NONA*; "Release of Morte A. & P. Denistoun & Co to Corbin & Rawle," "Release of Mortgage F. P. Corbin to R. B. Corbin & E. Rawle," "Pledge by F. P. Corbin, R. B. Corbin & E. Rawle to A. & J. Dennistoun & Co.," and "Pledge E. Rawle & R. B. Corbin to F. P. Corbin," May 16, 1837, Notary Grima, vol. 16, no. 434, 435, 436, and 438, *NONA*.

17. "Pledge by F. P. Corbin, R. B. Corbin & E. Rawle to A. & J. Dennistoun & Co.," May 16, 1837, Notary Grima, vol. 16, no. 436, *NONA*.

18. "Sale of Slaves F. P. & R. B. Corbin & Edward Rawle to N. O. Canal & Banking Company," May 18, 1837, Notary Grima, vol. 16, no. 453, *NONA*.

19. Statement of sale, June 12, 1837, Francis Porteus Corbin papers, box 6, *NYPL*.

20. "Pledge by F. P. Corbin, R. B. Corbin & E. Rawle to A. & J. Dennistoun & Co.," May 16, 1837, Notary Grima, vol. 16, no. 436, *NONA*. I have found no record of a separate sale of the land.

21. J. Carlyle Sitterson, *Sugar Country: The Cane Sugar Industry in the South, 1753–1950* (Westport, CT: Greenwood Press, 1973), 170–71.

22. Gavin Wright, *The Political Economy of the Cotton South* (New York: W. W. Norton, 1978), 14, 29, 83.

23. Sitterson, *Sugar Country*, 158–62.

24. George D. Green, *Finance and Economic Development in the Old South: Louisiana Banking 1804–1861* (Stanford, CA: Stanford University Press, 1972), 112–13; Reginald C. McGrane, *Foreign Bondholders and American State Debts* (New York: MacMillan Company, 1935), 168.

25. L. Moreau Lislet, "An Act to Incorporate the Subscribers to the Consolidated Association of the Planters of Louisiana," *A General Digest of the Acts of the Legislature of Louisiana* vol. II (New Orleans, LA: Benjamin Levy, 1828), 394–406.

26. For an overview of the founding of plantation banks, see Calvin Schermerhorn, *The Business of Slavery and the Rise of American Capitalism, 1815–1860* (New Haven, CT: Yale University Press, 2015), 95–109.

27. "State Legislature," *New Orleans Argus*, February 15, 1828, 2; *Membership in the Louisiana House of Representatives: 1812–2020*, report, David R. Poynter Legislative Research Library, August 17, 2018.

28. *Act to Incorporate the Subscribers of the Union Bank of Louisiana* (New York: Clayton & Van Norden, 1832), 5.

29. *Union Bank of Louisiana*, 6–7; and "Letter from the Secretary of the Treasury . . . January 4, 1837," 150.

30. *Union Bank of Louisiana*, 16–17.

31. *Union Bank of Louisiana*, 15–16.

32. Schermerhorn, *Business of Slavery*, 117.

33. *Union Bank of Louisiana*, 3–4.

34. "Letter from the Secretary of the Treasury . . . January 4, 1837," 150.

35. "Mortgage by J. H. Shepherd & J. F. Miller to the Union Bk of Louis," November 15, 1832, Notary Mazureau, vol. 5, no. 108, *NONA*.

36. "Mortgage by Mr. Ed Jn Forstall & Wife & Mr. Ala Gordon to the Union Bank of Louisiana," November 28, 1832, Notary Mazureau, vol. 5, no. 134, *NONA*; Irene D. Neu, "Edmond Jean Forstall and Louisiana Banking," *Explorations in Economic History* (Summer 1970): 387.

37. "Mortgage by Mr. Pl Pandely & Wife to the Union Bk of Louisiana," November 29, 1832, no. 143; "Mortgage by Chs Coffin & Wife to the Union Bk of Louisa," November 29, 1832, no. 153; "Mortgage by Mr. Joachim Bermudez & Wife to the Union Bank of Louisiana," November 30, 1832, no. 150; "Mortgage by Mr. A. Ch. Doriocourt & Wife to the Union Bank of Louisiana," November 30, 1832, no. 157, Notary Mazureau, vol. 5, *NONA*.

38. "Mortgage on Land and Slaves Given by Mr. & Mrs. John L. Lobdell," CFH03.04.1.007, *Xavier*.

39. "An Act to Incorporate the Citizens' Bank of Louisiana," *First Session of the Eleventh Legislature* (New Orleans: Jerome Bayon, 1833), 172–77, 193–94.

40. List of subscriptions by parish, May 12, 1834, Minute Book, vol. 1, reel 13, *Citizens' Bank*; *Compendium of the Enumeration of the Inhabitants and Statistics of the United States, Sixth Census* (Washington, DC: Thomas Allen, 1841), 240; *Union Bank of Louisiana*, 15; "New-Orleans Canal and Banking Company," *Acts Passed at the First Session of the Tenth Legislature* (New Orleans, LA: John Gibson, 1831), 58.

41. "Hypothèque à la Banque des Citoyens par B. Marigny & son épouse," July 5, 1836, Notary Seghers, vol. 18, no. 131, *NONA*. All translations by the author.

42. "Hypothèque par B. Marigny & son ép[ou]se à la Banque des Cit[oy]ens," May 9, 1836, no. 57; "Mainlevée partielle d'hyp[othè]que par la B[an]que des Citoyens en faveur de Bernard Marigny," August 11, 1836, no. 250, Notary Seghers, vol. 18, *NONA*.

43. "Probate Court Proceedings Allowing Mortgage of Property to the Citizens Bank of Louisiana," CFH03.05.1.014, *Xavier*.

44. October 10, 1836, Minute Book, vol. 1, reel 14, *Citizens' Bank*.

45. "Mortgage on Plantation Taken by Mr. & Mrs. Lucien Labranche," CFH03.05.1.019, *Xavier*.

46. "Mortgage on Land and Slaves Taken by St. Julien Tournillon," CFH03.06.1.001, *Xavier*.

47. "Mortgage on Plantation Taken by C. B. Dufau," CFH03.05.1.018, *Xavier*.

48. "Deposition Stating Financial Condition of Mr. and Mrs. Sosthene Roman," CFH03.08.1.014, *Xavier*; Hewlett and Raspiller auction notice for the sale of twenty-four slaves from the Iberville Parish estate of Johnathan Erwin, 1838, *THNOC* 73-701-L. Ed Baptist also references an 1824 mortgage for "from 90 to a 100 head of first rate slaves." See Edward Baptist, *The Half Has Never Been Told: Slavery and the Making of American Capitalism* (New York: Basic Books, 2014), 230.

49. Jean Estévan, prior mortgage form, June 7, 1837, MSS 458, folder 11, *THNOC*.

50. John B. Theall, prior mortgage form, September 28, 1837, folder 13-B, box 1, *Tulane*.

51. "Mortgage on Land and Slaves Taken by St. Julien Tournillon," CFH03.06.1.001, *Xavier*.

52. "Mortgage on Plantation Taken by C. B. Dufau," CFH03.05.1.018, *Xavier*.

53. "Mortgage on Plantation Taken by Mr. & Mrs. Lucien Labranche," CFH03.05.1.019, *Xavier*.

54. "Acceptation by the Citizens' Bank of Josiah Barker's Mortgage," January 22, 1839, Notary Seghers, vol. 34, no. 6, *NONA*.

55. January 2, 1836, Minute Book, vol. 1, reel 14, *Citizens' Bank*.

56. "An Act Amendatory and Supplementary to the Several Acts Relative to the 'Act to Incorporate the Citizens' Bank of Louisiana,'" *Charter of the Citizens' Bank*, 22, *LLMVC*.

57. "An Act Amendatory," *Charter of the Citizens' Bank*, 23.

58. "An Act Amendatory," *Charter of the Citizens' Bank*, 27.

59. "Charter of the Citizens' Bank," 8.

60. "Charter of the Citizens' Bank," 9–10.

61. "Mortgage on Land and Slaves Taken by St. Julien Tournillon," CFH03.06.1.001, *Xavier*.

62. "Main levée par Lizardi frère Co à C. B. Dufau," June 28, 1836, Notary Seghers, vol. 18, no. 124, *NONA*.

63. March 25, 1837, Minute Book, vol. 1, reel 14, *Citizens' Bank*.

64. March 22, 1837, Minute Book, vol. 1, reel 14, *Citizens' Bank*.

65. May 17, 1837, Minute Book, vol. 2, reel 14, *Citizens' Bank*.

66. July 15 1837, Minute Book, vol. 2, reel 14, *Citizens' Bank*.

67. "Charter of the Citizens' Bank," 9–10, *LLMVC*. The original charter allowed renewals for up to ten years, but this policy was revised in 1836. "An Act Amendatory," *Charter of the Citizens' Bank*, 28.

68. "Charter of the Citizens' Bank," 5.

69. "Hypothèque par B. Marigny & son ép[ou]se à la Banque des Cit[oy]ens," May 9, 1836, no. 57; "Hypothèque à la Banque des Citoyens par B. Marigny & son épouse," July 5, 1836, no. 131; "Mainlevée partielle d'hyp[othè]que par la B[an]que des Citoyens en faveur de Bernard Marigny," August 11, 1836, no. 250, Notary Seghers, vol. 18, *NONA*.

70. McGrane, *Foreign Bondholders*, 169–72.

71. "Charter of the Citizens' Bank," 19.

72. "Charter of the Citizens' Bank," 18.

73. "An Act Amendatory," *Charter of the Citizens' Bank*, 26.

74. "Mainlevée partielle d'hypque par la Bque des Citoyens en faveur de Bernard Marigny," August 11, 1836, Notary Seghers, vol. 18, no. 250, *NONA*.

75. "Charter of the Citizens' Bank," 16–17.

76. Gabriel Lebreton Deschapelle, Certificat D'Estimation Assertmente, July 25, 1836, folder 13-A, box 1, *Tulane*.

77. Jean Estévan, Certificat D'Estimation Assertmente, February 7, 1837, MSS 458, folder 11, *THNOC*.

78. Jean Estévan, Certificat D'Estimation Assertmente, February 7, 1837.

79. April 7, 1836, Minute Book, vol. 1, reel 14, *Citizens' Bank*.

80. February 12, 1838, Minute Book, vol. 2, reel 14, *Citizens' Bank*.

81. August 10 and September 6, 1838, Minute Book, vol. 2, reel 14, *Citizens' Bank*.

82. November 8, 1838, Minute Book, vol. 2, reel 14, *Citizens' Bank*; "Hypothèque par Michel Nicaud et son épouse & main levée par la Banque," November 21, 1838, no. 396, and "Hypothèque par M. Nicaud et son épouse et mainlevée par la Banque," November 24, 1838, no. 397, Notary Seghers, vol. 29, *NONA*.

83. March 3, 1838, Minute Book, vol. 2, reel 14, *Citizens' Bank*; "Hypothèque par C. Desanes Poincy, Charles E. Forstall et leurs épouses & main levée par la Banque," November 10, 1838, Notary Seghers, vol. 29, no. 390, *NONA*.

84. September 3, 1838, Minute Book, vol. 2, reel 14, *Citizens' Bank*.

85. May 23, 1839, Minute Book, vol. 3, reel 14, *Citizens' Bank*.

86. March 21, 1839, Minute Book, vol. 2, reel 14, *Citizens' Bank*; "Hypothèque par B. Marigny à la Banque des Citens et mainlevée par elle," March 23, 1839, Notary Seghers, vol. 34, no. 44, *NONA*.

87. February 1, 1840, Minute Book, vol. 3, reel 14, *Citizens' Bank*; "Changement d'hypothèque par B. Marigny sur certain esclaves et mainlevée par la banque sur dix esclaves," March 7, 1840, Notary Seghers, vol. 34, no. 242, *NONA*.

88. January 30, 1845, Minute Book, vol. 5, reel 15, *Citizens' Bank*.

89. "Deposition Statement for Mortgage on Land and Slaves taken by John Fitz Miller," CFH04.01.1.041, *Xavier*; "Hypothèque par John F. Miller," September 18, 1838, no. 350, and "Reversion d'hypothèque de Jonas Marsh, prise par John F. Miller," September 25, 1838, no. 359, Notary Seghers, vol. 29, *NONA*.

90. "Substitution of Sundry Slaves by John F. Miller in the Place of Others and Release on the Latter by the Citizens' Bank," March 18, 1840, Notary Seghers, vol. 34, no. 248, *NONA*.

91. September 3, 1838, Minute Book, vol. 2, reel 14, *Citizens' Bank*.

92. April 4, 1839, Minute Book, vol. 2, reel 14, *Citizens' Bank*.

93. November 12, 1840, Minute Book, vol. 3, reel 14, *Citizens' Bank*.

94. July 1, 1841, Minute Book, vol. 4, reel 15, *Citizens' Bank*.

95. November 15, 1841, Minute Book, vol. 4, reel 15, *Citizens' Bank*.

96. July 1, 1839, Minute Book, vol. 3, reel 14, *Citizens' Bank*.

97. January, 23, 1840, Minute Book, vol. 3, reel 14, *Citizens' Bank*.

98. January 28, 1843, Minute Book, vol. 5, reel 15, *Citizens' Bank*.

99. "Release of Mortgage Bank of Louisa to Jas. C. Wilson," March 3, 1836, p. 355, and "Mortgage James C. Wilson to the Bank of Louisiana," March 4, 1836, p. 363–36, Notary Christy, vol. 24, *NONA*.

100. "Partial Release Bank of Louisiana to Philippe Guesnon," January 22, 1841, p. 99–100, and "Mortgage Philippe Guesnon to the Bank of Louisiana," January 22, 1841, p. 101–02, Notary Christy, vol. 41, *NONA*.

101. Mortgage of the Rossignol family to the Bank of the State of Georgia, February 21, 1838, Chatham Co., Georgia Deeds, vols. 2V–2W, RH 1059, microfilm 66–66, *Georgia*.

102. Jean Estévan, prior mortgage form, June 7, 1837, MSS 458, folder 11, *THNOC*; John B. Theall, prior mortgage form, September 28, 1837, folder 13-B, box 1, *Tulane*.

103. John Reid affidavit, July 16, 1836, Citizens' Bank of Louisiana papers, mss 254, etc., folder 1:1a, *LLMVC*.

104. April 14, 1838 mortgage, papers, reel 17, *Citizens' Bank*; "Acceptation de l'Hypothèque de Demcy Kemp et son épouse," May 3, 1838, Notary Seghers, vol. 28, no. 175, *NONA*.

105. Demcy Kemp affidavit, November 21, 1838, Citizens' Bank of Louisiana papers, mss 254, etc., folder 1:1a, *LLMVC*.

106. "Acceptation de l'Hypothèque de Demcy Kemp & son épouse," September 8, 1838, Notary Seghers, vol. 29, no. 340, *NONA*.

107. "Charter of the Citizens' Bank," 17.

108. "Demcy Kempe and Wife Mortgage to Citizens Bank of Louisiana," April 1, 1838, papers, reel 17, *Citizens' Bank*.

109. Walden v. Union Bank, 6 La. 248 (SC LA 1834) at 249.

110. *Walden*, 6 La. at 254.

111. "An Act to Incorporate the City Bank of New-Orleans," *Acts Passed at the First Session of the Tenth Legislature of the State of Louisiana* (New Orleans, LA: John Gibson, 1831), 34.

112. "An Act to Incorporate the Subscribers of the 'Union Bank of Florida,'" in *Public Documents Printed by Order of the Senate of the United States* vol. VII (Washington: Blair and Rives, 1840); "An Act to Incorporate the Subscribers to the Mississippi Union Bank," *Natchez Weekly Courier*, September 22, 1837, 4; Howard Bodenhorn, *State Banking in Early America: A New Economic History* (New York: Oxford University Press, 2003), 251; Edward E. Baptist, *Creating an Old South: Middle Florida's Plantation Frontier before the Civil War* (Chapel Hill: University of North Carolina Press, 2002), 112–13.

113. McGrane, *Foreign Bondholders*, 224–25.

114. "Legislative Acts," *Floridian and Advocate* (Tallahassee), February 16, 1833, 2; Larry Schweikart, *Banking in the American South from the Age of Jackson to Reconstruction* (Baton Rouge: Louisiana State University Press, 1987), 170.

115. Baptist, *Creating an Old South*, 73.

116. "An Act to Incorporate the Southern Life Insurance and Trust Company," in *Public Documents Printed by Order of the Senate of the United States* vol. VII, 136; Schweikart, *Banking*, 52.

117. Schweikart, *Banking*, 52.

118. "Report of the Committee on Banks," in *Public Documents Printed by Order of the Senate of the United States* vol. VII, 34.

119. Schweikart, *Banking*, 197–98.

120. "Report of the Committee on Banks," 40–41 (emphasis in original).

121. "Report of the Committee on Banks," 35.

122. Schweikart, *Banking*, 69, 82.

123. Nicholas Biddle to Joseph Hemphill, February 8, 1830, reel 43, *Biddle*.

124. Nicholas Biddle to Walter Gregory, December 14, 1834; Biddle to J. S. Skinner, January 10, 1837; Biddle to [illegible] Carson, October 3, 1837; Biddle to W. R. King and Frederick S. Lyon, June 7, 1838; Biddle to Samuel Jaudon, August 31, 1838, reels 45–46, *Biddle*.

125. Nicholas Biddle to Horace Binney, January 1, 1834, reel 45, *Biddle*.

126. Nicholas Biddle to [illeg.] Carson, October 3, 1837, reel 46, *Biddle*.

127. Nicholas Biddle to W. R. King and F. S. Lyon, June 7, 1838, reel 46, *Biddle*.

128. Richard Holcombe Kilbourne Jr., *Slave Agriculture and Financial Markets in Antebellum America: The Bank of the United States in Mississippi, 1831–1852* (London: Pickering & Chatto, 2006), 68.

129. Nicholas Biddle to Samuel Jaudon, August 31, 1838; Biddle to James Hagaty, November 25, 1838, reel 46, *Biddle*.

130. Nicholas Biddle to W. W. Frazier, September 18, 1838, reel 46, *Biddle*.

131. Nicholas Biddle to W. W. Frazier, September 18, September 29, 1838, reel 46, *Biddle*.

132. Nicholas Biddle to C. A. Davis, September 29, 1838, reel 46, *Biddle*.

133. Mihm, "Fog of War," 355–59.

134. *Reports of Committees of the House of Representatives at the First Session of the Twenty-Second Congress*, report no. 460, vol. IV, December 7, 1831 (Washington, DC: Duff Green, 1831), 1.

135. *Reports of Committees of the House of Representatives*, report no. 460, 1–29; Mihm, "Fog of War," 358.

136. *Reports of Committees of the House of Representatives*, report no. 460, 531–32 (emphasis added).

137. Mihm, "Fog of War," 359–62.

138. Mihm, "Fog of War," 362–64.

139. Nicholas Biddle to John Huske, August 6, 1835, reel 45, *Biddle*.

140. Nicholas Biddle to John Huske, August 6, 1835.

141. Samuel Jaudon to Thomas Henderson, October 6, 1835, Bank of the United States, Natchez Office Records, Mss. 708, Cashier's Letter Book #1, *LLMVC*.

142. *An Act to Incorporate the Stockholders of the Bank of the United States, by the State of Pennsylvania* (Philadelphia: W. F. Geddes, 1838), 20.

143. Nicholas Biddle to J. Hunter, April 25, 1836, reel 46, *Biddle*.

144. Nicholas Biddle to James Erwin, June 25, 1836, reel 46, *Biddle*; Kilbourne, *Slave Agriculture*, 58.

145. Nicholas Biddle to George Poe Jr., September 28, 1836, reel 46, *Biddle*.

146. Mobile Agency, Correspondence 1841–49, box 10, *BUS (PA)*.

147. Nicholas Biddle to Joseph L. Roberts, January 13, 1837, reel 46, *Biddle*.

148. "Report of the Committee of Investigation Appointed at a Meeting of the Stockholders of the Bank of the United States," *Richmond Whig*, April 20, 1841, 4.

149. "Mortgage John M. Dobbin to Duncan Murchison and John W. Sandford, Cash[ie]r," October 24, 1829, Cumberland County, NC, vol. 36–38, reel 40013, *SANC*.

150. "Mortgage John M. Dobbin to John W. Sanford, Cash[ie]r," August 12, 1830, Cumberland County, NC, vol. 39–41, reel 40014, *SANC*.

151. "Mortgage John M. Dobbin to Ichabod Wetmore, Cash[ie]r," October 20, 1835, Cumberland County, NC, vol. 39–41, reel 40014, *SANC*.

152. "Mortgage Paris J. Tillinghast to John W. Sandford, Cash[ie]r," November 10, 1832, Cumberland County, NC, vol. 39–41, reel 40014, *SANC*.

153. Fifth Census, 1830, Carteret County, Fayetteville, NC, *Census (MCR)*, p. 88, M-19, reel 120.

154. "Mortgage Paris J. Tillinghast to Ichabod Wetmore, Cash[ie]r," November 16, 1835, Cumberland County, NC, vol. 39–41, reel 40014, *SANC*.

155. Mortgage Alexander McNeill, January 15, 1838, New Orleans papers, box 3, *BUS (PA-Diss.)*. McNeill is the "cruel" slaveholder described by Henry Watson in his autobiography.

Henry Watson, *Narrative of Henry Watson, a Fugitive Slave* (Boston, MA: Bela Marsh, 1848), 12, *DAS* 2000.

156. Bank of the United States of Pennsylvania, Liquidation 1841–43, New Orleans papers, box 3, *BUS (PA-Diss.).*

157. Bank of the United States of Pennsylvania, Liquidation 1841–43.

158. "Mortgage by The Heirs of Thomas Bibb Dec[ease]d to Bk of Louisiana," June 24, 1841, Notary Cenas, vol. 24, p. 661, *NONA.*

Part III Introduction

1. Jessica M. Lepler, *The Many Panics of 1837: People, Politics, and the Creation of a Transatlantic Financial Crisis* (Cambridge: Cambridge University Press, 2013), 19–20, 43–66, 123–56; Stephen Mihm, "The Fog of War: Jackson, Biddle and the Destruction of the Bank of the United States," in *A Companion to the Era of Andrew Jackson*, ed. Sean Patrick Adams (Hoboken, NJ: Blackwell, 2013), 370–73; Harry L. Watson, *Liberty and Power: The Politics of Jacksonian America* (New York: Hill and Wang, 2006), 156–59; John Lauritz Larson, *The Market Revolution in America: Liberty, Ambition, and the Eclipse of the Common Good* (Cambridge: Cambridge University Press, 2010), 92–96; Scott Reynolds Nelson, *A Nation of Deadbeats: An Uncommon History of America's Financial Disasters* (New York: Knopf, 2012), 117–21.

2. The only recent examination of the Panic of 1819 is Andrew H. Browning, *The Panic of 1819: The First Great Depression* (Columbia: University of Missouri Press, 2019). For an extensive discussion of the causes of the Panics of 1837 and 1839, see Lepler, *Many Panics of 1837*; and for the effects of this panic, see Alasdair Roberts, *America's First Great Depression: Economic Crisis and Political Disorder after the Panic of 1837* (Ithaca, NY: Cornell University Press, 2013). For comparisons of the two periods, see Watson, *Liberty and Power*; Larson, *Market Revolution*; Daniel Feller, *The Jacksonian Promise: America, 1815–1840* (Baltimore, MD: Johns Hopkins University Press, 1995); Peter Temin, *The Jacksonian Economy* (New York: W. W. Norton, 1969); Daniel Walker Howe, *What Hath God Wrought: The Transformation of America, 1815–1848* (Oxford: Oxford University Press, 2007); Sharon Ann Murphy, *Other People's Money: How Banking Worked in the Early American Republic* (Baltimore, MD: Johns Hopkins University Press, 2017).

Chapter Six

1. Stephen Duncan to William Newton Mercer, August 7, 1837, William N. Mercer papers, 1829–1854, *Plantations*, series H; Finding Aid, William Newton Mercer Papers, Mss. 292, 1051, 1233, etc., *LLMVC*; Martha Jane Brazy, *American Planter: Stephen Duncan of Antebellum Natchez and New York* (Baton Rouge: Louisiana State University Press, 2006), 10.

2. Henry William Huntington to William Newton Mercer, January 24, 1837, William N. Mercer papers, 1829–1854, *Plantations*, series H.

3. Henry William Huntington to William Newton Mercer, April 4, 1837, William N. Mercer papers, 1829–1854, *Plantations*, series H.

4. Henry William Huntington to William Newton Mercer, April 4, 1837.

5. Henry William Huntington to William Newton Mercer, April 4, 1837.

6. Henry William Huntington to William Newton Mercer, April 4, 1837. Huntington lost possession of Greenoak later that year, and relocated with his family to Catahoula, Louisiana.

See National Register of Historic Places nomination form for Green Oak plantation, September 29, 1976, Mississippi Department of Archives and History, https://www.apps.mdah.ms.gov/nom/prop/2140.pdf. This document states that Huntington had to sell Greenoak in 1836 to John Hutchins due to "financial reverses," but the deed-book record cited in the document is actually from 1837 (Deed Book Z:159). Quickly regaining his financial footing, he reported owning fifty-three enslaved individuals in the 1840 census, an increase over the thirty-three he listed a decade earlier in Mississippi (see Fifth Census, 1830, Adams County, Mississippi, *Census (MCR)*, p. 20, M-19, reel 70; and Sixth Census, 1840, Catahoula Parish, Louisiana, *Census (MCR)*, p. 49, M-704, reel 127–28). And in 1850, he reported real estate wealth of $35,000, in addition to fifty-two enslaved workers (see Seventh Census, 1850, Catahoula Parish, Louisiana, *Census (SS)*, p. 183–85, M-432, reel 243; and Seventh Census, 1850, Catahoula Parish, Louisiana, *Census (MCR)*, p. 52, M-432, reel 230).

7. *Report of the Committee of Investigation (Selected from the Stockholders.) Appointed by the Direction of the Citizens' Bank of Louisiana, in Conformity with the Resolution of the Board of 18th October, 1838* (New Orleans: E. Johns & Co., 1839), 5–6.

8. *Report of the Committee of Investigation.*

9. Herbert James Lewis, *Alabama Founders: Fourteen Political and Military Leaders Who Shaped the State* (Tuscaloosa: University of Alabama Press, 2018), 98.

10. Howard Bodenhorn, *State Banking in Early America: A New Economic History* (New York: Oxford University Press, 2003), 245; Larry Schweikart, *Banking in the American South from the Age of Jackson to Reconstruction* (Baton Rouge: Louisiana State University Press, 1987), 153.

11. The popular governor stepped down from his post later that month, upon being appointed by the legislature to the US Senate. Lewis, *Alabama Founders*, 98; "Banks in Mobile," in *A Digest of the Laws of the State of Alabama* (Tuscaloosa: D. Woodruff, 1836), 592–96; "An Act to Establish a Bank in the City of Mobile," in *Digest of the Laws of the State of Alabama*, 596–603.

12. "Alabama," *Albany Evening Journal*, July 14, 1837, 2.

13. Alabama," *Albany Evening Journal*, July 14, 1837, 2.

14. "Governor's Message," *Selma Free Press*, November 11, 1837, 2.

15. July 12, 14, and 26, 1837, Branch Bank at Montgomery Minute Book, 1835–1838, SG4066, *Alabama.*

16. July 27, 1837, Branch Bank at Huntsville Minute Book, 1835–1841, SG3745, *Alabama.*

17. Sixth Census, 1840, Mobile, Alabama, *Census (MCR)*, p. 72, M-704, reel 9.

18. "W. J. Hendon Mortgage," mortgage deeds Mobile, p. 42, SG3792, *Alabama.*

19. "Wm Taylor," Branch Bank at Mobile applications for loans and extensions of notes, 1837–1839, p. 222, SG3791, *Alabama.*

20. "S. Thrower," branch bank at Mobile applications for loans and extensions of notes, 1837–1839, p. 53, SG3791, *Alabama.*

21. "Thomas R. Bolling in Acct with Br Bk St of Ala at Mobile," Mobile Correspondence 1840–1847, SG2769, *Alabama*; "Mortgage of Thomas R. Bolling," mortgage deeds Mobile, p. 2, SG3792, *Alabama*; Sixth Census, 1840, Mobile, Alabama, *Census (MCR)*, p. 76, M-704, reel 9.

22. "George Wragg Mortgage," mortgage deeds Mobile, p. 44, SG3792, *Alabama*; Sixth Census, 1840, Mobile, Alabama, *Census (MCR)*, p. 81, M-704, reel 9; "Fry vs. the Branch Bank at Mobile," in *Reports of Cases Argued and Determined in the Supreme Court of Alabama* (Montgomery, AL: J. H. & T. F. Martin, 1849): 282–85.

23. John F. Everett, Branch Bank at Mobile applications for loans and extensions of notes, 1837–1839, SG3791, *Alabama*; "Marion Bad Debts," Branch Bank at Mobile execution docket, 1841–1853, SG4158, *Alabama*; Sixth Census, 1840, Mobile, Alabama, *Census (MCR)*, p. 72, M-704, reel 9.

24. "W. W. Fry," branch bank at Mobile applications for loans and extensions of notes, 1837–1839, SG3791, *Alabama*.

25. "Sale of W. W. Fry property," Mobile account sales register, SG3682, *Alabama*; "Mortgage of W. W. Fry," mortgage deeds Mobile, SG3792, *Alabama*.

26. "The State of Alabama Marshall County," Bank of State of Alabama Decatur records, SG4153, *Alabama*.

27. February 10, 1838, Branch Bank at Montgomery Minute Book, 1835–1838, SG4066, *Alabama*.

28. "Marion Bad Debts," Branch Bank at Mobile execution docket, 1841–1853, SG4158, *Alabama*.

29. "Perry Bad Debts," Branch Bank at Mobile execution docket, 1841–1853, SG4158, *Alabama*.

30. "Monroe County Bad Debts," "Pickens Bad Debts," "Tuskaloosa Bad Debts," Lowndes County Bad Debts," "Sumter Bad Debts," Branch Bank at Mobile execution docket, 1841–1853, SG4158, *Alabama*.

31. "Marengo Bad Debts," Branch Bank at Mobile execution docket, 1841–1853, SG4158, *Alabama*.

32. "King Upson & Co," Register of real estate claimed by Branch Bank at Mobile, 1842, SG3921, p. 24, *Alabama*.

33. "Feby Term 1841," Branch Bank at Mobile register of writs of execution, 1840–1841, SG3967, *Alabama*.

34. "The President & Directors v. Cyrus Gill Claimant in Trustee for His Daughter," Branch Bank at Mobile correspondence & related materials, 1840–1847, SG2769, *Alabama*.

35. Branch Bank at Huntsville v. Marshall, 4 Ala. 60 (AC AL 1842) at 61–62.

36. "S. T. Douglass," register of real estate claimed by Branch Bank at Mobile, 1842, SG3921, p. 25, *Alabama*.

37. "Mary S. Reavis & Turner Reavis to Branch Bank," mortgage deeds Mobile, SG3792, p. 174, *Alabama*.

38. McRea v. Branch Bank of Alabama, 60 U.S. 376 (1856).

39. Fifth Census, 1830, Rapides Parish, Louisiana, *Census (MCR)*, p. 104, M-19, reel 44.

40. House of Representatives, 43rd Congress, 1st Session, report no. 750, Committee on War Claims, June 22, 1874 (Washington, DC: Government Printing Office, 1874), 1.

41. "Affidavit Certifying the Existence of a Mortgage on Property and Slaves of James Sullivan," CFH09.02.2.008, *Xavier*.

42. "Mortgage J. B. Sullivan to Bank of Louis[ian]a" and "Mortgage Jas B. Sullivan to the Bank of Louisiana," April 29, 1843, Notary Christy, vol. 47, p. 468 and 472, *NONA*.

43. "Mortgage J. B. Sullivan to Bank of Louis[ian]a" and "Mortgage Jas B. Sullivan to the Bank of Louisiana," April 29, 1843.

44. Sixth Census, 1840, Rapides Parish, Louisiana, *Census (MCR)*, p. 220, M-704, reel 127–28.

45. Seventh Census, 1850, Rapides Parish, Louisiana, *Census (MCR)*, p. 45, M-432, reel 239; Seventh Census, 1850, Rapides Parish, Louisiana, *Census (SS)*, p. 995, M-432, reel 245.

46. Eighth Census, 1860, Rapides Parish, Louisiana, *Census (MCR)*, p. 222, M-653, reel 423; Committee on War Claims, 1.

47. "Mortgage Manuel Garcia to Bank of Louisiana," May 29, 1834, Notary Christy, vol. 18, p. 522–26, *NONA*.

48. "Sale of Plantation &c Bank of Louisiana to Thomas May," December 9, 1843, Notary Christy, vol. 48, p. 371–72, *NONA*.

49. P. A. Champomier, *Statement of the Sugar Crop of Louisiana of 1849–50* (New Orleans: Cook, Young & Co., 1850), 22; P. A. Champomier, *Statement of the Sugar Crop of Louisiana of 1858–59* (New Orleans: Cook, Young & Co., 1859), 16.

50. "State of Louisiana," *Times-Picayune* (New Orleans), January 3, 1846, 3; "Louisiana Legislature," *Concordia Intelligencer*, November 20, 1847, 3.

51. "Sale of Slaves Bank of Louisiana to Madame E. Fortier," December 14, 1843, Notary Christy, vol. 48, p. 411–12, *NONA*; Sixth Census, 1840, St. Charles Parish, Louisiana, *Census (MCR)*, p. 235, M-704, reel 135.

52. "Sale of Slaves Bank of Louisiana to Madame E. Fortier," December 14, 1843, Notary Christy, vol. 48, p. 411–12, *NONA*.

53. "Sale of Plantation the Bank of Louisiana to Pierre Soniat," January 18, 1844, Notary Christy, vol. 49, p. 73–74, *NONA*.

54. "Strayed or Stolen," *Times-Picayune* (New Orleans), November 5, 1847, 3.

55. "Sale of Plantation the Bank of Louisiana to Pierre Soniat," January 18, 1844; Sixth Census, 1840, Jefferson Parish, Louisiana, *Census (MCR)*, p. 232, M-704, reel 129–30.

56. "Sale of Plantation the Bank of Louisiana to Pierre Soniat," January 18, 1844.

57. Sixth Census, 1850, St. Charles Parish, Louisiana, *Census (MCR)*, p. 174, M-432, reel 239; Sixth Census, 1850, St. Charles Parish, *Census (SS)*, p. 155, M-432, reel 246; Champomier, *Sugar Crop . . . 1849–50*, 24–25; P. A. Champomier, *Statement of the Sugar Crop of Louisiana of 1850–51* (New Orleans: Cook, Young & Co., 1851), 19.

58. Sixth Census, 1840, St. Charles Parish, Louisiana, *Census (MCR)*, p. 235, M-704, reel 135; January 21, 1837, Minute Book, vol. 1, reel 14, *Citizens' Bank*.

59. January 7 and 28, 1843, Minute Book, vol. 5, reel 15, *Citizens' Bank*.

60. January 28, 1843, Minute Book, vol. 5, reel 15, *Citizens' Bank*.

61. "An Act to Facilitate the Liquidation of the Property Banks Chartered by this State," in *Acts Passed at the First Session of the Sixteenth Legislature of the State of Louisiana* (New Orleans: Alexander C. Bullitt—State Printer, 1843), 57–58.

62. November 2, 1843, Minute Book, vol. 5, reel 15, *Citizens' Bank*.

63. Seventh Census, 1850, St. Charles Parish, Louisiana, *Census (MCR)*, p. 173, M-432, reel 239; Seventh Census, 1850, St. Charles Parish, Louisiana, *Census (SS)*, p. 87–88, M-432, reel 246; Champomier, *Sugar Crop . . . 1849–50*, 25; *Sugar Crop . . . 1850–51*, 19.

64. June 23, 1853, Minute Book, vol. 7, reel 16, *Citizens' Bank*; P. A. Champomier, *Statement of the Sugar Crop of Louisiana of 1852–53* (New Orleans: Cook, Young & Co., 1853), 20; P. A. Champomier, *Statement of the Sugar Crop of Louisiana of 1853–54* (New Orleans: Cook, Young & Co., 1854), 19.

65. "Long Credit Sale at Auction," *Times-Picayune* (New Orleans), July 21, 1853, 3.

66. "Long Credit Sale at Auction,"; "60 Very Choice Sugar Plantation Hands," *Times-Picayune* (New Orleans), February 27, 1855, 3.

67. April 23, 1857, Minute Book, vol. 8, reel 16, *Citizens' Bank*; P. A. Champomier, *Statement of the Sugar Crop of Louisiana of 1857–58* (New Orleans: Cook, Young & Co., 1858), 19.

68. November 4, 1853, Minute Book, vol. 7, *Citizens' Bank*, reel 16. Armant reported owning sixty-six enslaved individuals in the 1840 census. Sixth Census, 1840, St. James Parish, Louisiana, *Census (MCR)*, p. 268, M-704, reel 135.

69. April 8, 1837, Minute Book, vol. 1, reel 14, *Citizens' Bank*; May 21, 1838, Minute Book, vol. 2, reel 14, *Citizens' Bank*; February 25, 1839, Minute Book, vol. 2, reel 14, *Citizens' Bank*; April 9, 1846, Minute Book, vol. 5, reel 15, *Citizens' Bank*; April 22, 1847, Minute Book, vol. 6, reel 15–16, *Citizens' Bank*.

70. June 6, 1843, Minute Book, vol. 5, reel 15, *Citizens' Bank*.

71. "Appointments," *Baton-Rouge Gazette*, January 17, 1846, 2.

72. Citizens' Bank 1847 ledger, *Canal Bank*.

73. Seventh Census, 1850, St. James Parish, Louisiana, *Census (MCR)*, p. 301, M-432, reel 246.

74. November 4, 1853, Minute Book, vol. 7, reel 16, *Citizens' Bank*.

75. Champomier, *Sugar Crop . . . 1853–54*, 15; *Sugar Crop . . . 1858–59*, 14.

76. "Hypothèque par Martin Gordon Penn," March 17, 1838, Notary Seghers, vol. 28, no. 90, *NONA*.

77. "M. G. Penn to Union Bank Mortgage," March 17, 1838, Notary Mazureau, nol. 18, p. 211–13, *NONA*.

78. "Acceptation by the Citizens' Bk of M. G. Penn's Mortgage," March 7, 1840, Notary Seghers, vol. 34, no. 245, *NONA*.

79. June 15, 1847, Minute Book, vol. 6, reel 15–16, *Citizens' Bank*.

80. June 15, 1847, Minute Book, vol. 6, reel 15–16, *Citizens' Bank*; Citizens' Bank 1847 ledger, *Canal Bank*.

81. "Acceptation by the Citizens' Bk of M. G. Penn's Mortgage," March 7, 1840; July 16, 1847, Minute Book, vol. 6, reel 15–16, *Citizens' Bank*.

82. March 23, 1849, Minute Book, vol. 6, reel 15–16, *Citizens' Bank*.

83. "Extensive Sale of Very Valuable Real Estate," *Times-Picayune* (New Orleans), April 10, 1849, 1; April 13, 1849, Minute Book, vol. 6, reel 15–16, *Citizens' Bank*.

84. April 13, 1849, Minute Book, vol. 6, reel 15–16, *Citizens' Bank*.

85. April 17, 1849, Minute Book, vol. 6, reel 15–16, *Citizens' Bank*.

86. November 20, 1843, Minute Book, vol. 5, reel 15, *Citizens' Bank*.

87. July 8, 1844, Minute Book, vol. 5, reel 15, *Citizens' Bank*.

88. Champomier, *Sugar Crop . . . 1849–50*.

89. *Membership in the Louisiana House of Representatives 1812–1820*, revised February 1, 2022 (David R. Poynter Legislative Research Library, Louisiana House of Representatives), https://house.louisiana.gov/H_PDFdocs/HouseMembership_History_CURRENT.pdf.

90. Fifth Census, 1830, Ascension Parish, Louisiana, *Census (MCR)*, p. 31, M-19, reel 43.

91. November 8 and 19, 1838, Minute Book, vol. 2, reel 14, *Citizens' Bank*; "Main levée par la Banque à Joseph Landry" and "Main levée par la Banque à Raphaël Mollère," November 30, 1838, Notary Seghers, vol. 29, nos. 403 and 405, *NONA*; "Main levée par la Banque à L. Seely," December 7, 1838, Notary Seghers, vol. 29, no. 410, *NONA*; "Mainlevée par la B[an]que des Cit[oy]ens à Achille Hébert," June 1, 1839, Notary Seghers, vol. 34, no. 101, *NONA*.

92. "Deposition Statement for Mortgage on Land and Slaves Taken by Mr. & Mrs. Trasimon Landry," CFH04.01.1.019, *Xavier*.

93. Sixth Census, 1840, Ascension Parish, Louisiana, *Census (MCR)*, p. 275, M-704, reel 135.

94. January 28, 1843, Minute Book, vol. 5, reel 15, *Citizens' Bank*.

95. Citizens' Bank 1847 ledger, *Canal Bank*.

96. John M. Sacher, *A Perfect War of Politics: Parties, Politicians, and Democracy in Louisiana, 1824–1861* (Baton Rouge: Louisiana State University Press, 2003), 125, 128–29; "Editors' Correspondence," *Daily National Intelligencer* (Washington, DC), August 5, 1845, 3; "By Authority," *Jeffersonian Republican* (New Orleans), July 4, 1846, 1.

97. Seventh Census, 1850, Ascension Parish, Louisiana, *Census (MCR)*, p. 69, 71, 99, 151, 153, M-432, reel 242; Champomier, *Sugar Crop . . . 1849–50*, 17–18.

98. April 24, 1850, May 1, 1850, Minute Book, vol. 6, reel 15–16; and November 22, 1853; December 16, 1853; May 15, 1855; June 5, 1855, Minute Book, vol. 7, reel 16, *Citizens' Bank*.

99. Eighth Census, 1860, Ascension Parish, ward 3, Louisiana, *Census (MCR)*, p. 107, M-653, reel 407; Eighth Census, 1860, Ascension Parish, ward 2, Louisiana, *Census (SS)*, p. 66, M-653, reel 427.

100. "Hypothèque par la Companie des Canaux de Barataria & de la Fourche," September 28, 1838, Notary Seghers, vol. 29, no. 362, *NONA*; November 7, 1843, Minute Book, vol. 5, reel 15. *Citizens' Bank*.

101. February 1 and 4, 1843, Minute Book, vol. 5, reel 15, *Citizens' Bank*.

102. August 17, 1847, Minute Book, vol. 6, reel 15–16, *Citizens' Bank*.

103. Robert Lowry and William H. McCardle, *A History of Mississippi, from the Discovery of the Great River by Hernando DeSoto, Including the Earliest Settlement Made by the French under Iberville, to the Death of Jefferson Davis [1541–1889]* (Jackson, MS: R. H. Henry & Co., 1891), 269–76.

104. "Sale of Plantation & Slaves Bank of Louisiana to Hugh M. Keary," November 3, 1846, Notary Christy, vol. 55, p. 281–84, *NONA*.

105. Bank of Louisiana v. Farrar, 1 La.Ann. 49 (SC LA 1846) at 49.

106. Untitled, *Times-Picayune* (New Orleans), May 5, 1844, 2.

107. "State Elections," *New-Orleans Commercial Bulletin*, July 1, 1844, 2; *Membership in the Louisiana House of Representatives 1812–1820*.

108. "The Sickness at Woodville, Miss.," *Times-Picayune* (New Orleans), September 14, 1844, 2.

109. "Sale of Plantation & Slaves Bank of Louisiana to Hugh M. Keary," November 3, 1846, Notary Christy, vol. 55, p. 281–84, *NONA*.

110. *Bank of Louisiana*, 1 La.Ann. at 49–52 and 56.

111. *Bank of Louisiana*, 1 La.Ann. at 57.

112. Posey v. Bank of Louisiana, 5 La.Ann. 187 (SC LA 1850) at 188. See also Farrar v. New Orleans Gaslight & Banking Co., 2 La.Ann. 873 (SC LA 1847); Mechanics' & Traders' Bank v. Rowly, 2 La.Ann. 372 (SC LA 1847); Eyssallenne v. Citizens' Bank, 3 La.Ann. 663 (SC LA 1848); Ledoux v. Rucker, 5 La.Ann. 500 (SC LA 1850); Mechanics' & Traders' Bank v. Jones, 6 La.Ann. 123 (SC LA 1851).

113. "Louisiana Legislature," *Jeffersonian Republican* (New Orleans), February 5, 1846, 2.

114. "Louisiana Legislature," *Concordia Intelligencer*, January 16, 1847, 2; "Obituary," *New Orleans Crescent*, March 9, 1850, 2.

115. Sixth Census, 1840, Wilkinson, Mississippi, *Census (MCR)*, p. 301, M-704, reel 217.

116. Louisiana Mutual Insurance Company v. New Orleans Insurance Company, 13 La.Ann 246 (SC LA 1858); Champomier, *Sugar Crop . . . 1850–51*, 2.

117. "Sale of Plantation & Slaves Bank of Louisiana to Hugh M. Keary," November 3, 1846, Notary Christy, vol. 55, p. 281–84, *NONA*.

118. "Sale of Plantation & Slaves Bank of Louisiana to Hugh M. Keary," November 3, 1846.

119. July 2, 1850, Minute Book, vol. 6, reel 15–16, *Citizens' Bank*.

120. July 9, August 6, and October 22, 1850; February 4, 1851, Minute Book, vol. 6, reel 15–16, *Citizens' Bank*.

121. Seventh Census, 1850, Wilkinson, Mississippi, *Census (MCR)*, p. 300, M-432, reel 382; Seventh Census, 1850, Wilkinson, Mississippi, *Census (SS)*, p. 765, M-432, reel 389; Seventh Census, 1850, Avoyelles, Louisiana, *Census (MCR)*, p. 138, M-432, reel 229; Seventh Census, 1850, Avoyelles, Louisiana, *Census (SS)*, p. 37, M-432, reel 242; Seventh Census, 1850, Rapides, Louisiana, *Census (SS)*, p. 807, M-432, reel 245.

122. Eighth Census, 1860, Rapides, Louisiana, *Census (MCR)*, p. 223, M-653, reel 423; Eighth Census, 1860, Rapides, Louisiana, *Census (SS)*, p. 449, M-653, reel 430.

123. "Democratic Meeting," *Woodville Republican*, April 19, 1853, 2; "State Election," *New Orleans Times-Picayune*, November 21, 1857, 1.

124. Eighth Census, 1860, Assumption, Avoyelles Parish, Louisiana, *Census (MCR)*, p. 74, M-653, reel 407; Eighth Census, 1860, Assumption, Avoyelles Parish, Louisiana, *Census (SS)*, p. 44, M-653, reel 427.

125. "Whig State Convention," *New Orleans Times-Picayune*, March 22, 1852, 4.

126. "The Committee on the Real Estate in Their Investigations into the Titles therefor Held by the Bank," Branch Bank at Mobile correspondence, real estate settlements, etc., 1842–1851, SG2788, *Alabama*.

127. "Augustus A. Winston Mortgage," mortgage deeds Mobile, SG3792, *Alabama*.

128. John B. Willy to H. B. Holcombe, December 26, 1846, Branch Bank at Mobile attorney's report, SG3724, *Alabama* (emphasis in original).

129. "S. Thrower," Branch Bank at Mobile applications for loans and extensions of notes, 1837–1839, p. 53, SG3791; "Hollinger" and "Robert B. Owen," Bank of State of Alabama mortgage deeds Mobile, SG3792, *Alabama*.

130. "A. C. Hollinger," mortgage deeds Mobile, SG3792, *Alabama*, p. 182–85; Sixth Census, 1840, Mobile Country, Alabama, *Census (MCR)*, p. 99, M-704, reel 9–10, p. 99.

131. "An Act to Regulate the Affairs of the Banks," *Democrat* (Huntsville, AL), February 11, 1846, 3.

132. "A. C. Hollinger," mortgage deeds Mobile, SG3792, *Alabama*, p. 182–85.

133. "A. C. Hollinger," mortgage deeds Mobile, 186–88.

134. Seventh Census, 1850, Mobile County, Alabama, *Census (SS)*, p. 195–97, M-432, reel 22.

135. Seventh Census, 1850, Mobile County, Alabama, *Census (MCR)*, p. 927, M-432, reel 11.

136. "A. C. Hollinger," mortgage deeds Mobile, 182–85.

137. "Purchase of Plantation Abner Robinson to Nathl and James Dick," July 7, 1834, Notary Cenas, vol. 1, no. 103; "Sale of Plantation & Slaves by the Mechanics & Traders Bank of New-Orleans to Horatio S. Sprigg and Geo M. Graham," February 7, 1842, Notary Cenas, vol. 26, no. 193, *NONA*.

138. "Mortgage of Landed Property and Slaves by Nathaniel & James Dick to the Mechanics' and Traders' Bank of New Orleans," August 30, 1837, Notary Cenas, vol. 15, p. 363–68, *NONA*.

139. "Sale of Plantation & Slaves by the Mechanics & Traders Bank of New-Orleans to Horatio S. Sprigg and Geo M. Graham," February 7, 1842, Notary Cenas, vol. 26, p. 193, *NONA*.

140. "P. Petrovic au President, Directeurs & Co de l'office du Bureau d'Escompte & de Depot de la Banque de cité de la Nlle Orleans à Natchitoches," May 3, 1834, folders 16–41, *City Bank*.

141. R. J. Palfrey, cashier at New Orleans, to Thomas R. Colquhoun, cashier at Natchitoches, August 11, 1840, folders 16–41, *City Bank*; Parnell v. Petrovic, 14 La.Ann. 601 (SC LA 1859).

142. State of Louisiana parish of Natchitoches, September 16, 1840, folders 16–41, *City Bank*.

143. R. J. Palfrey, cashier at New Orleans, to Thomas R. Colquhoun, cashier at Natchitoches, August 11, 1840.

144. State of Louisiana parish of Natchitoches, September 16, 1840.

145. J. P. Cass to the City Bank at Natchitoches president and directors, January or February 1842, folders 42–67, *City Bank*.

146. A. B. and Ann Gill to the board of directors of the City Bank of New Orleans at Natchitoches, November 20, 1834, folders 1–15, *City Bank*.

147. "Acceptation par la B[an]que des Citoyens d'Hyp[ote]que de dame Gill," May 15, 1835, Notary Seghers, vol. 10, no. 221, *NONA*; Fifth Census, 1830, Rapides, Louisiana, *Census (MCR)*, p. 92, M-19, reel 44.

148. Robert J. Palfrey to Jean Vignaud, December 3, 1834, folders 1–15, *City Bank*.

149. Fifth Census, 1830, Rapides, Louisiana, *Census (MCR)*, p. 92, M-19, reel 44; Sixth Census, 1840, Rapides, Louisiana, *Census (MCR)*, p. 216, M-704, reel 127–28.

150. March 23, 1843, Minute Book, vol. 5, reel 15, *Citizens' Bank*.

151. March 23, 1843, Minute Book, vol. 5, reel 15, *Citizens' Bank*.

152. Citizens' Bank 1847 ledger, *Canal Bank*.

153. "Sale of Plantation & Slaves A. Rivarde & Co to Bank of Louisiana," July 7, 1845, Notary Christy, vol. 52, p. 508–09, *NONA*; "Sale of Plantation & Slaves A. Rivarde & Co to Bank of Louisiana," September 11, 1845, Notary Christy, vol. 53, p. 33–35, *NONA*; "Acceptance of Sale A. Rivarde & Co to Bank of Louis[ian]a," October 24, 1845, Notary Christy, vol. 53, p. 89, *NONA*; "Sale of Property & Slaves by Bank of Louisiana to Sylvester Bossier," February 2, 1853, Notary Cenas, vol. 55, p. 393–97, *NONA*.

154. "Sale of Plantation & Slaves A. Rivarde & Co to Bank of Louisiana," July 7, 1845; "Sale of Plantation & Slaves A. Rivarde & Co to Bank of Louisiana," September 11, 1845; "Acceptance of Sale A. Rivarde & Co to Bank of Louis[ian]a," October 24, 1845.

155. "Sale of Property & Slaves by Bank of Louisiana to Sylvester Bossier," February 2, 1853.

156. "Sale of Property & Slaves by Bank of Louisiana to Sylvester Bossier," February 2, 1853.

157. August 17, 1847, Minute Book, vol. 6, reel 15–16, *Citizens' Bank*.

158. Charles Warren, *Bankruptcy in United States History* (Cambridge, MA: Harvard University Press, 1935), 87–88; Katharina Pistor, *The Code of Capital: How the Law Creates Wealth and Inequality* (Princeton, NJ: Princeton University Press, 2019), 40–41. For example, the 1843 case of *Bronson v. Kinzie* deemed valuation laws unconstitutional. See Woody Holton, "Equality as Unintended Consequence: The Contracts Clause and the Married Women's Property Acts," *Journal of Southern History* 81 (May 2015), 335; Charles W. McCurdy, *The Anti-Rent Era in New York Law and Politics: 1839–1865* (Chapel Hill: University of North Carolina Press, 2001), 107–10

159. Warren, *Bankruptcy*, 79–85.

160. "For the Star," = *Republican Star* (Easton, MD), May 3, 1825, 2.

161. Peter J. Coleman, *Debtors and Creditors in America: Insolvency, Imprisonment for Debt, and Bankruptcy 1607–1900* (Madison: State Historical Society of Wisconsin, 1974), 9.

162. "For the Star," 2.

163. "Exemption of Slaves from Execution," *Democrat* (Huntsville, AL), April 9, 1845, 3.

164. "Exemption of Slaves from Execution," *Democrat*, 3.

165. "Exemption of Slaves from Execution," *Democrat*, 3.

166. "To the Editor of the Bulletin," *Vicksburg Tri-Weekly Sentinel*, March 7, 1845, 2; "Exemption of Slaves from Execution," *Holly Springs Gazette* (MS), April 5, 1845, 2; "Exemption of Slaves from Execution," *Democrat*, 3.

167. Untitled, *Mississippi Free Trader* (Natchez), March 26, 1845, 1.

168. Untitled, *Mississippi Free Trader and Natchez Gazette*, April 12, 1845, 1.

169. "Report on Slave Introduction," *Democrat* (Huntsville, AL), January 28, 1846, 3.

170. "Louisiana Legislature," *Times-Picayune* (New Orleans), February 27, 1846, 2.

171. "The Exemption of One Slave of a Debtor from Levy and Sale," *Daily Constitutionalist* (Augusta, GA), August 16, 1849, 2.

172. "The Exemption of One Slave of a Debtor from Levy and Sale," 2.

173. "Things in Milledgeville," *Augusta Chronicle*, December 17, 1849, 2.

174. "Virginia Legislature," *Richmond Enquirer*, August 7, 1849, 2.

175. C. G. Baylor, "Messrs. Editors," *Mississippi Free Trader* (Natchez), July 5, 1853, 1.

176. "Exemption of Slaves from Attachment," *Hartford Courant*, September 19, 1853, 2.

177. "Slaves Exempt from Sale under Execution," *Alton Daily Morning Courier* [IL], September 20, 1853, 2.

178. "Exemption of Slaves," *Weekly Advertiser* (Montgomery, AL), September 21, 1853, 1.

179. "Exemption of Slaves," *Weekly Advertiser* (Montgomery, AL), October 19, 1853, 1.

180. "Exemption of Slaves from Sale," *Daily Constitutionalist and Republic* (Augusta, GA), November 12, 1853, 2.

181. "Governor's Message (Concluded)," *Democrat* (Huntsville, AL), December 8, 1853, 2.

182. "Alabama," *Greensboro Times* [NC], December 10, 1857, 2; *Journal of the Seventh Biennial Session of the Senate of the State of Alabama, Session of 1859-'60* (Montgomery, AL: Shorter and Reid, 1860), 69, 220, 226, 254.

183. "Kansas," *National Era* (Washington, DC), September 20, 1855, 4; "Legislative Proceedings," *Charleston Daily Courier*, December 1, 1856, 1; "Editor of Dallas Gazette," *Cahaba Gazette* (AL), November 28, 1856, 2; "Exemption of Slaves from Sale for Debt," *Richmond Dispatch*, October 2, 1856, 2; *A Journal of Proceedings of the House of Representatives of the General Assembly of the State of Florida* (Tallahassee, FL: Dyke and Carlisle, 1858), 29–30.

184. "Kansas," *National Era*, September 20, 1855, 4.

185. *The New World in 1859*, part IV (London: H. Baillere, 1859), 83–85.

186. Richard Sutch, "Appendix: The Value of the Slave Population, 1805–1860," in Roger Ransom and Richard Sutch, "Capitalists without Capital: The Burden of Slavery and the Impact of Emancipation," *Agricultural History* 62, no. 3 (Summer 1988), table A.1, 150–51.

187. *New World in 1859*, 83–85.

188. Holton, "Equality," 315.

189. Elizabeth Bowles Warbasse, *The Changing Legal Rights of Married Women, 1800–1861* (New York: Garland Publishing, 1987), 159.

190. Warbasse, *Changing Legal Rights*, 142.

191. Warbasse, *Changing Legal Rights*, 160.

192. Richard H. Chused, "Married Women's Property Law: 1800–1850," *Georgetown Law Journal* (1983): 1359–1425; Holton, "Equality," 324–25.

193. Warbasse, *Changing Legal Rights*, 245.

Chapter Seven

1. McRea v. Branch Bank of Alabama, 60 U.S. 376 (1856) at 376–377. McRea appears to be a misspelling in the court transcript of McRae.

2. Sixth Census, 1840, Clarke County, Alabama, *Census (MCR)*, p. 243, M-704, reel 2; Faye O. Strother, "Dandridge McRae—An Arkansas General," *Arkansas Democrat*, December 20, 1962, http://www.argenweb.net/white/wchs/Dandridge_McRae_Files/Dandridge_McRae.html.

3. *McRea*, 60 U.S.

4. Seventh Census, 1850, Harrison Township, White County, Arkansas, *Census (MCR)*, p. 931, M-432, reel 31; Seventh Census, 1850, Harrison Township, White County, Arkansas, *Census (SS)*, p. 618, M-432, reel 32.

5. Richard Sutch, "Appendix: The Value of the Slave Population, 1805–1860," in Roger Ransom and Richard Sutch, "Capitalists without Capital: The Burden of Slavery and the Impact of Emancipation," *Agricultural History* 62, no. 3 (Summer 1988)," table A-1, 150–51; Stanley L. Engerman, Richard Sutch, and Gavin Wright, "Slavery," chapter Bb in Susan B, Carter et al., *Historical Statistics of the United States*, vol. 2 (New York: Cambridge University Press, 2006), 369–86.

6. *McRea*, 60 U.S. at 377–78.

7. Peter J. Coleman, *Debtors and Creditors in America: Insolvency, Imprisonment for Debt, and Bankruptcy 1607–1900* (Madison: State Historical Society of Wisconsin, 1974), 31–36; Scott A. Sandage, *Born Losers: A History of Failure in America* (Cambridge, MA: Harvard University Press, 2005), 195–96; Edward J. Balleisen, *Navigating Failure: Bankruptcy and Commercial Society in Antebellum America* (Chapel Hill: University of North Carolina Press, 2001), 69, 126; Charles Warren, *Bankruptcy in United States History* (Cambridge, MA: Harvard University Press, 1935), 91.

8. Coleman, *Debtors*, 17–18; Sandage, *Born Losers*, 30–31.

9. Edward Balleisen, "Vulture Capitalism in Antebellum America: The 1841 Federal Bankruptcy Act and the Exploitation of Financial Distress," *Business History Review* 70 (Winter 1996), 479–80; Rafael I. Pardo, "Bankrupted Slaves," *Vanderbilt Law Review* 71, no. 4 (May 2018), 1074, 1086, 1090.

10. Coleman, *Debtors*, 23; Balleisen, "Vulture Capitalism," 479–80.

11. David D. Plater, *The Butlers of Iberville Parish, Louisiana: Dunboyne Plantation in the 1800s* (Baton Rouge: Louisiana State University Press, 2015), 4; 33–34. Upon the death of Edward Butler in 1803, Andrew Jackson became the legal guardian of Caroline and her siblings, Eliza Eleanor, Edward George Washington, and Anthony. Caroline married Bell around 1805 at the age of sixteen.

12. Plater, *Butlers*, 36–38, 42–43.

13. Plater, *Butlers*, 43.

14. Adams v. Preston, 63 U.S. 473 (1859) at 481.

15. *Adams*, 63 U.S.

16. Plater, *Butlers*, 55–56.

17. Foley v. Harrison, 5 La.Ann. 75 (SC LA 1850) at 76.

18. "Sale of Land & Slaves & Stock by the Citizens Bk to Botts & Robinson," January 31, 1840, Notary Seghers, vol. 34, no. 232, *NONA*.

19. "Sale of Land & Slaves & Stock by the Citizens Bk to Botts & Robinson," January 31, 1840.

20. "Mortgage by Thomas Barrett and His Wife to the Bank of the United States," February 26, 1838, Notary Mossy, vol. 16, no. 28, *NONA*; Thomas Barrett title papers 1831–38, New Orleans papers, box 4, *BUS (PA-Diss.)*.

21. Hampton's Heirs v. Barrett, 9 La. 336 (SC LA 1836); *Adams*, 63 U.S.

22. July 29, 1839, Minute Book, vol. 3, reel 14, *Citizens' Bank*.

23. July 29, 1839, Minute Book, vol. 3, reel 14, *Citizens' Bank*.

24. Wheelock S. Upton and Needler R. Jennings, "Art. 1980," in *Civil Code of the State of Louisiana* (New Orleans: E. Johns & Co, 1838), 308.

25. *Adams*, 63 U.S. at 482–85.

26. *Adams*, 63 U.S. at 482–85.

27. Plater, *Butlers*, 85–86.

28. Walter Johnson, *Soul by Soul: Life Inside the Antebellum Slave Market* (Cambridge, MA: Harvard University Press, 1999), 47, 53, 114; Michael Tadman, *Speculators and Slaves: Masters, Traders, and Slaves in the Old South* (Madison: University of Wisconsin Press, 1989), 21.

29. "Sale of Land & Slaves & Stock by the Citizens Bk to Botts & Robinson," January 31, 1840; July 29, 1839, Minute Book, vol. 3, reel 14, *Citizens' Bank*.

30. Citizens Bank of Louisiana v. Tucker, 6 Rob. 443 (SC LA 1844).

31. Comparison of list of slaves sold to Botts & Robinson in 1840, with list of slaves sold to Lesassier in 1844. "Sale of Land & Slaves & Stock by the Citizens Bk to Botts & Robinson," January 31, 1840; "Sale of Plantation, Slaves & Stocks Francis B. Conrad, Assignee of George A. Botts, Bankrupt to Louis Lesassier," February 3, 1844, Notary Lucien Hermann, vol. 8, no. 33, *NONA*.

32. December 30, 1842, Minute Book, vol. 5, reel 15, *Citizens' Bank*; and June 24, 1851, Minute Book, vol. 6, reel 15–16, *Citizens' Bank*.

33. "Change of Notes and Additional Mortgage by Botts & Robinson to the Citizens' Bank," April 7, 1840, Notary Seghers, vol. 34, no. 258, *NONA*.

34. "Mainlevée sur billets à George A. Botts & Abner Robinson," July 23, 1840, Notary Seghers, vol. 38, no. 840, *NONA*; *Citizens' Bank*, 6 Rob.; March 16, 1847, Minute Book, vol. 6, reel 15–16, *Citizens' Bank*.

35. Bankruptcy petition 545, Certificate of Mortgages, July 20, 1843, *NARA*.

36. "Sale of Land & Slaves & Stock by the Citizens Bk to Botts & Robinson," January 31, 1840.

37. March 16, 1847, Minute Book, vol. 6, reel 15–16, *Citizens' Bank*; Hill v. Tucker, 54 U.S. 458.

38. Bankruptcy petition 545, Citizens' Bank answer to assignee petition, May 11, 1843, *NARA*.

39. Bankruptcy petition 545, letter of Augustin Pugh to F. B. Conrad, February 10, 1843, attached to Petition of F. B. Conrad, February 25, 1843, *NARA*.

40. Bankruptcy petition 545, Bankruptcy petition schedule, December 24, 1842. For an extensive discussion of this bankruptcy case from the perspective of the government, see Rafael I. Pardo, "Racialized Bankruptcy Federalism," *Michigan State Law Review*, forthcoming 2022. Many thanks to Pardo for sharing the bankruptcy documents in this case, since I was unable to obtain them from the National Archives due to the pandemic.

41. Bankruptcy petition 545, *NARA*.

42. December 30, 1842, Minute Book, vol. 5, reel 15, *Citizens' Bank*.

43. Bankruptcy petition 545, bankruptcy petition schedule, December 24, 1842; and supplemental petition, January 24, 1843, *NARA*.

44. December 30, 1842, Minute Book, vol. 5, reel 15, *Citizens' Bank*.

45. December 30, 1842, Minute Book, vol. 5, reel 15, *Citizens' Bank*.

46. Bankruptcy petition 545, Marshall's return, February 28, 1843, *NARA*.

47. Bankruptcy petition 545, Citizens' Bank answer to assignee petition, May 11, 1843, *NARA*.

48. Bankruptcy petition 545, Petition of F. B. Conrad and Order to Federal Marshall, February 24, 1843, *NARA*.

49. Bankruptcy petition 545, Petition of Citizens' Bank for sale of certain property, October 19, 1843, *NARA*.

50. Bankruptcy petition 545, Petition of Citizens' Bank for sale of certain property, October 19, 1843, *NARA*.

51. Bankruptcy petition 545, rule, January 23, 1844, *NARA*.

52. March 16, 1847, Minute Book, vol. 6, reel 15–16, *Citizens' Bank*.

53. February 7, 1844, Minute Book, vol. 5, reel 15, *Citizens' Bank*.

54. February 9, 1844, Minute Book, vol. 5, reel 15, *Citizens' Bank*.

55. *Foley*, 5 La.Ann.; Plater, *Butlers*, 104.

56. June 24, 1851, Minute Book, vol. 6, reel 15–16, *Citizens' Bank*.

57. Foley v. Harrison, 56 U.S. 433 (1853) at 446–47.

58. *Foley*, 56 U.S. at 76.

59. March 16, 1847, Minute Book, vol. 6, reel 15–16, *Citizens' Bank*; Hullen v. Tucker, 6 Rob. 448 (SC LA 1844); Executrix and Universal Legatee of Bell v. Tucker, 6 Rob. 443 (SC LA 1844).

60. *Citizens Bank*, 6 Rob. at 447.

61. "Mortgage J. W. Tucker to Estate of A Robinson," April 7, 1849, Notary Mossy, vol. 33, no. 41, *NONA*.

62. September 14, 1847, Minute Book, vol. 6, reel 15–16, *Citizens' Bank*; "Mortgage J. W. Tucker to Estate of A Robinson," April 7, 1849, Notary Mossy, vol. 33, no. 41, *NONA*.

63. March 16, 1849, Minute Book, vol. 6, reel 15–16, *Citizens' Bank*.

64. "Additional Mortgage Joseph W. Tucker to Estate of Abner Robinson," April 7, 1849, Notary Mossy, vol. 33, no. 43, *NONA*.

65. "Exchange of Notes & Mortgage by J. W. Tucker to Estate of A. Robinson," April 10, 1849, Notary Mossy, vol. 33, act 46, *NONA*.

66. *Foley*, 5 La.Ann. at 79, and 90–91.

67. *Foley*, 5 La.Ann. at 450.

68. July 11, 1849, Minute Book, vol. 6, reel 15–16, *Citizens' Bank*.

69. "Joseph William 'J. W.' Tucker," *Find a Grave*, added June 16, 2012, https://www.findagrave.com/memorial/92011887/joseph-william-tucker.

70. Eighth Census, 1860, Lafourche Parish, Louisiana, *Census (MCR)*, p. 89, M-653, reel 413; P. A. Champomier, *Statement of the Sugar Crop of Louisiana of 1858–59* (New Orleans: Cook, Young & Co., 1859), 27.

71. "Died," *Times-Picayune* (New Orleans), November 13, 1856, 2.

72. "Citizens' Bank of Louisiana vs. Samuel T. Harrison," *Times-Picayune* (New Orleans), May 11, 1858, 6.

73. P. A. Champomier, *Statement of the Sugar Crop of Louisiana of. 1857–58* (New Orleans: Cook, Young & Co., 1858), 10; *Sugar Crop . . . 1858–59*, 10.

74. "Sale of Land & Slaves & Stock by the Citizens Bk to Botts & Robinson," January 31, 1840; "Citizens' Bank of Louisiana vs. Samuel T. Harrison," 6.

75. Abbey v. Commercial Bank of New Orleans, 5 George 571 (Appeals MS 1857).

76. "Richard Abbey," in *Minutes of the Annual Conferences of the Methodist Episcopal Church* (Nashville, TN: Barbee & Smith, 1891), 138; "Notice," *Natchez Weekly Democrat*, June 19, 1830, 7.

77. "Richard Abbey," *Minutes*, 138; "Married," *Natchez Weekly Courier*, May 6, 1831, 6; "Anti-Gambling Society," *Mississippi Free Trader*, November 3, 1835, 3.

78. "Natchez Shipping Company," *Natchez Weekly Courier*, May 10, 1833, 3.

79. "Notice," *Natchez Weekly Courier*, April 26, 1833, 3.

80. "Aetna," *Natchez Weekly Courier*, August 2, 1833, 3; "Fire Engines," *Weekly Mississippian* (Jackson), May 16, 1833, 1.

81. "R. Abbey & Co.," *Natchez Weekly Courier*, May 3, 1833, 2.

82. "A Small Lot," *Natchez Weekly Courier*, June 14, 1833, 3; "Fresh Garden Seed," *Natchez Weekly Courier*, December 6, 1833, 3; "Carpeting," *Natchez Weekly Courier*, November 1, 1833, 4; "Barouche," *Natchez Weekly Courier*, July 5, 1833, 3 (emphasis in original); *Merriam-Webster*, s.v. "barouche *(n.)*," accessed April 13, 2021, https://www.merriam-webster.com/dictionary/barouche.

83. "Plantation and Negroes for Sale," December 6, 1833, *Natchez Weekly Courier*, 3 (emphasis in original).

84. "The State of Mississippi," *Natchez Weekly Courier*, March 3, 1837, 4; American Life Insurance & Trust Co. v. Emerson, 4 Smedes & M. 177 (Appeals MS 1845).

85. *American Life Insurance*, 4 Smedes & M.

86. "The State of Mississippi," *Natchez Weekly Courier*, March 3, 1837; Abbey v. Merrick, 5 Cushm. 320 (Appeals MS 1854).

87. "The State of Mississippi," *Natchez Weekly Courier*, March 3, 1837.

88. Untitled, *Natchez Weekly Courier*, July 8, 1835, 4.

89. "Boston Plantation for Sale," *Mississippi Free Trader* (Natchez), March 4, 1837, 2 (emphasis in original).

90. *Abbey*, 5 George at 572.

91. *Abbey*, 5 George at 572; Sixth Census, 1840, Yazoo County, Mississippi, *Census (MCR)*, p. 314, M-704, reel 217.

92. "Sheriff's Sale," *Yazoo City Whig and Political Register*, April 3, 1840, 3; "Chancery Sale," *Yazoo City Whig and Political Register*, February 12, 1841, 2; "Marshal's Sale," *Yazoo City Whig and Political Register*, June 17, 1842, 3.

93. *Abbey*, 5 George at 573.

94. *Abbey*, 5 George at 573.

95. "Bankrupt Sale," *Western Statesman* (Carrollton, MS), June 20, 1844, 3.

96. *Abbey*, 5 George at 573.

97. "Richard Abbey," *Southern Reformer* (Jackson, MS), December 13, 1844, 3.

98. "Richard Abbey," *Southern Reformer*, 3; *Abbey*, 5 George.

99. Seventh Census, 1850, Yazoo County, Mississippi, *Census (MCR)*, p. 520, M-432, reel 382; Seventh Census, 1850, Yazoo County, Mississippi, *Census (SS)*, p. 427, M-432, reel 390.

100. *Abbey*, 5 George at 573–74 (emphasis in original).

101. *Abbey*, 5 George at 575.

102. State of Louisiana parish of Natchitoches, September 16, 1840, folders 16–41, *City Bank*; Parnell v. Petrovic, 14 La.Ann. 601 (SC LA 1859).

103. *Parnell*, 14 La.Ann. at 602.

104. *Parnell*, 14 La.Ann. at 602–04.

105. *Parnell*, 14 La.Ann. at 604–05.

106. Fifth Census, 1830, Concordia Parish, Louisiana, *Census (MCR)*, p. 156, M-19, reel 43; Sixth Census, 1840, Concordia Parish, Louisiana, *Census (MCR)*, p. 165, M-704, reel 129–30.

107. Planters' Bank of Mississippi v. Watson, 9 Rob. 267 (SC LA 1844); Sixth Census, 1840, Oden Township, Chicot County, Arkansas, *Census (MCR)*, p. 25, M-704, reel 17–20.

108. "Mortgage Jeremiah Watson to the Bank of Louisiana," January 6, 1837, Notary Christy, vol. 28, p. 29–35, *NONA*; "Guarantee by Franklin & Armfield to Bank of Louisiana," March 20, 1843, Notary Christy, vol. 47, p. 272–73, *NONA*.

109. *Planters' Bank*, 9 Rob.; Sixth Census, 1840, Oden Township, Chicot County, Arkansas, *Census (MCR)*, p. 25, M-704, reel 17.

110. *Planters' Bank*, 9 Rob.

111. Sixth Census, 1840, Concordia Parish, Louisiana, *Census (MCR)*, p. 165, M-704, reel 130.

112. Gillespie v. Cammack, 3 La.Ann. 248 (SC La. 1848).

113. *Planters' Bank*, 9 Rob.

114. "Guarantee by Franklin & Armfield to Bank of Louisiana," March 20, 1843, Notary Christy, vol. 47, p. 272–73, *NONA*.

115. *Planters' Bank*, 9 Rob. at 267; *Gillespie*, 3 La.Ann.

116. "Grand View for Sale," *Concordia Intelligencer*, January 11, 1845, 3.

117. *Gillespie*, 3 La.Ann. at 252.

118. February 2, 1835, mortgage, Mandeville (Henry D.) family papers, #491, 535, correspondence, 1833–1873, Planters Bank of Mississippi records, indentures 1835–1839, folder 72, box 7, *LLMVC*.

119. November 3, 1841, Branch Bank at Montgomery Minute Book, 1838–1843, SG4069, *Alabama*.

120. Mark E. Nackman, "Anglo-American Migrants to the West: Men of Broken Fortunes? The Case of Texas, 1821–46," *Western Historical Quarterly* 5, no. 4 (October 1974): 448–50.

121. Douglas Hales, *A Southern Family in Black and White: The Cuneys of Texas* (College Station: Texas A&M University Press, 2003), 4; Fifth Census, 1830, Rapides Parish, Louisiana, *Census (MCR)*, p. 102, M-19, reel 44; "Acceptation de l'Hypothèque de Philip M. Cuny et son épouse," October 22, 1838, Notary Seghers, vol. 29, no. 381, *NONA*; "Land Claims in Louisiana," June 22, 1813, in *Documents Legislative and Executive of the Congress of the United States, from the Second Session of the Eleventh to the Third Session of the Thirteenth Congress* (Washington: Gales and Seaton, 1834), no. 217, 1st session, 13th Congress, p. 775. In the records, the last name is spelled both Cuny and Cuney.

122. Thomas W. Cutrer, "Cuney, Philip Minor," *Handbook of Texas Online*, accessed January 6, 2021, https://www.tshaonline.org/handbook/entries/cuney-philip-minor.

123. Hales, *A Southern Family*, 5–6.

124. Hales, *A Southern Family*, 6.

125. Lynch v. Kitchen, 2 La.Ann. 843 (SC LA 1847) at 844–45.

126. Citizens' Bank v. Cuny, 12 Rob. 279 (SC LA 1845) at 280; "Hypothèque par Littleton Bayley," July 11, 1838, Notary Seghers, vol. 29, no. 268, *NONA*.

127. "Acceptation de l'Hypothèque de Philip M. Cuny et son épouse," October 22, 1838. Both Hales and Cutrer state that Cuny married Eliza Wales in 1842 after his arrival in Texas. However, she appears in the notarial records of 1837 and 1838 as Cuny's wife. Hales, *A Southern Family*, 6; Cutrer, "Cuney."

128. Duncan v. Elam, 1 Rob. 135 (SC LA 1841) at 137–38.

129. "Acceptation de l'Hypothèque de Philip M. Cuny et son épouse," October 22, 1838.

130. *Duncan*, 1 Rob. at 137–38.

131. "Acceptation de l'Hypothèque de Philip M. Cuny et son épouse," October 22, 1838.

132. Flint v. Franklin, 9 Rob. 207 (SC LA 1844) at 208.

133. Cuny v. Brown, 12 Rob. 82 (SC LA 1845) at 82–83.

134. November 12, 1840, Minute Book, vol. 3, reel 14, *Citizens' Bank*.

135. February 24, 1841, vol. 3, reel 14, *Citizens' Bank*; Citizens' Bank 1847 ledger, *Canal Bank*.

136. *Duncan*, 1 Rob.; *Flint*, 9 Rob.; *Cuny*, 12 Rob.; *Citizens' Bank*, 12 Rob.; *Lynch*, 2 La.Ann.

137. Eighth Census, 1860, Hempstead Precinct, Austin County, Texas, *Census (MCR)*, p. 22, M-653, reel 1287.

138. Cutrer, "Cuney."

139. Sixth Census, 1840, East Baton Rouge Parish, Louisiana, *Census (MCR)*, p. 86, M-704, reel 129.

140. Nancy Collins, "State of Louisiana," *Baton Rouge Gazette*, July 17, 1841, 2.

141. "State of Louisiana," *Baton Rouge Gazette*, October 23, 1841, 1.

142. "State of Louisiana," *Baton Rouge Gazette*, November 20, 1841, 2.

143. "State of Louisiana," *Baton Rouge Gazette*, July 24, 1841, 2.

144. "State of Louisiana," *Baton Rouge Gazette*, February 12, March 19, and June 18, 1842, 2.

145. December 20, 1842, Minute Book, vol. 5, reel 15, *Citizens' Bank*.

146. March 27, 1845, Minute Book, vol. 5, reel 15, *Citizens' Bank*.

147. January 16, 1845, Minute Book, vol. 5, reel 15, *Citizens' Bank*; Citizens' Bank 1847 ledger, *Canal Bank*.

148. "Acceptation par la Banque des Citoyens de l'hypotheque de George H. Patillo & son épouse," August 30, 1837, Notary Seghers, vol. 24, no. 387; and "Acceptance by the Citizens' Bank of Geo. H. Patillo's mortgage," February 2, 1839, Notary Seghers, vol. 34, no. 12; *NONA*.

149. January 16, 1845, Minute Book, vol. 5, reel 15, *Citizens' Bank*.

150. March 27, 1845, Minute Book, vol. 5, reel 15, *Citizens' Bank*.

151. Citizens' Bank 1847 ledger, *Canal Bank*.

152. Fourth Census, 1820, Rich Land Creek, East Feliciana Parish, Louisiana, *Census (MCR)*, p. 58, M-33, reel 31; Fifth Census, 1830, East Feliciana Parish, Louisiana, *Census (MCR)*, p. 204, M-19, reel 43; Sixth Census, 1840, East Feliciana Parish, Louisiana, *Census (MCR)*, p. 272, M-704, reel 130, page 272.

153. February 4, 1847, Minute Book, vol. 6, reel 15–16, *Citizens' Bank*.

154. May 23 and December 18, 1848, vol. 6, reel 15–16, *Citizens' Bank*.

155. December 18, 1848, vol. 6, reel 15–16, *Citizens' Bank*.

156. Union Bank of Louisiana v. Stafford, 53 U.S. 327 (1851).

157. *Union Bank*, 53 U.S.; New Orleans Canal & Banking Co. v. Stafford, 53 U.S. 343 (1851).

158. *Union Bank*, 53 U.S. at 339.

159. Sutch, "Appendix," table A-1, 150–51.

160. *Union Bank*, 53 U.S. at 342.

161. *Union Bank*, 53 U.S. at 337 and 339.

162. *New Orleans Canal & Banking Co.*, 53 U.S. at 344.

163. *Union Bank*, 53 U.S. at 337.

164. Seventh Census, 1850, Houston, Harris County, Texas, *Census (MCR)*, p. 20, M-492, reel 911; Seventh Census, 1850, Houston, Harris County, Texas, *Census (SS)*, p. 583, M-492, reel 917.

165. *Union Bank*, 53 U.S. at 338.

166. *Union Bank*, 53 U.S. at 340–341.

167. "Marshal's Sale," *Weekly Confederate* (Galveston, TX), October 20, 1855, 2.

168. Eighth Census, 1860, Houston Ward 4, Harris County, Texas, *Census (MCR)*, p. 155, M-653, reel 1296.

169. Ninth Census, 1870, Galveston Ward 4, Galveston, Texas, *Census (MCR)*, p. 10, M-593, reel 1586.

170. "Died," *Galveston Daily News*, September 25, 1870, 2.

171. "Death of Mrs. J. K. Stafford," as posted on "Jeannetta Kirkland Stafford," Find a Grave, accessed March 28, 2022, https://www.findagrave.com/memorial/65208085/jeannetta-stafford.

172. "$30 Reward," *Arkansas Gazette* (Little Rock), December 25, 1833, 4; "Negro in Jail," *Weekly Arkansas Gazette* (Little Rock), February 7, 1838, 4; "Democratic Meeting in St. Francis," *Weekly Arkansas Gazette*, April 22, 1840, 2.

173. General ledger 1839–1846, box 8, item 11, p. 36, *Arkansas.*

174. Discount and credit book 1838–1852, box 19, item 29, *Arkansas.*

175. Instruments of protest 1838–1841, box 23, item 38, *Arkansas.*

176. Charles W. Adams, cashier, to Henry F. Mooney, Helena, AR, September 18, 1840, letterbook 1839–1842, box 8, item 10, *Arkansas*; Sixth Census, 1840, St. Francis County, Arkansas, *Census (MCR)*, p. 194, M-704, reel 20.

177. Invoice book, 1839–1841, box 10, item 16, *Arkansas.*

178. Charles W. Adams, cashier, to Hon. W. K. Sebastian, Helena, AR, September 23, 1840, letterbook 1839–1842, box 8, item 10, *Arkansas*; "Sale of Lands for Taxes," *Arkansas State Democrat* (Helena), October 23, 1840, 3; Ted R. Worley, "The Control of the Real Estate Bank of the State of Arkansas, 1836–1855," *Mississippi Valley Historical Review* 37, no. 3 (December 1950), 417.

179. John H. Draper, clerk, to W. F. Moore, and Henry F. Mooney, Helena, AR, September 30, 1840, letterbook 1839–1842, box 8, item 10, *Arkansas*; *Report of the Accountants* (Little Rock, AR: True Democrat Office, 1856), 28; "St. Francis County," *Encyclopedia of Arkansas*, last updated February 4, 2022, https://encyclopediaofarkansas.net/entries/st-francis-county-810/.

180. Invoice book 1839–1841, box 10, item 16, *Arkansas.*

181. Invoice book 1839–1841, box 10, item 16, *Arkansas.*

182. Charles W. Adams, cashier, to E. Brittin, cashier, Helena, AR, November 3, 1840, and to Colonel H. L. Briscoe, president, Helena branch, November 4, 1840, letterbook 1839–1842, box 8, item 10, *Arkansas.*

183. Charles W. Adams, cashier, to Colonel H. L. Briscoe, president, Helena branch, November 4, 1840, , letterbook 1839–1842, box 8, item 10, *Arkansas.*

184. Charles W. Adams, cashier, to E. Brittin, cashier, Helena, AR, November 3, 1840; *Report of the Accountants*, 28. This letter was never sent.

185. Charles W. Adams, cashier, to Colonel W. F. Moore, Helena, AR, November 14, 1840, letterbook 1839–1842, box 8, item 10, *Arkansas.*

186. Invoice book 1839–1841, box 10, item 16, *Arkansas.*

187. Journal 1839–1844, box 7, item 8, *Arkansas.*

188. "State of Arkansas, County of St. Francis," *Arkansas Weekly Gazette* (Little Rock), October 2, 1844, 3.

189. Seventh Census, 1850, Nacogdoches County, Texas, *Census (MCR)*, p. 58, M432, reel 913; Seventh Census, 1850, Nacogdoches County, Texas, *Census (SS)*, p. 176, M432, reel 918.

190. "Proceedings of a Railroad Meeting," *Nacogdoches Chronicle*, October 4, 1853, 2.

191. "Notice," *Nacogdoches Chronicle*, January 24, 1854, 3.

192. Untitled, *Nacogdoches Chronicle*, June 20, 1854, 2.

193. Eighth Census, 1860, Nacogdoches County, Texas, *Census (MCR)*, p. 74, M653, reel 1301; Seventh Census, 1850, Nacogdoches County, Texas, *Census (SS)*, p. 19, M653, reel 1311.

194. Eighth Census, 1860, Nacogdoches County, Texas, *Census (MCR)*, p. 82, M653, reel 1301.

195. Seventh Census, 1850, San Augustine County, Texas, *Census (MCR)*, p. 74, M432, reel 914; slave schedule, Seventh Census, 1850, San Augustine County, Texas, *Census (SS)*, p. 6, M432, reel 918; Eighth Census, 1860, Smith County, Texas, *Census (MCR)*, p. 97, M653, reel 1305.

196. "State Branch Bank Report," *Wetumpka Argus*, August 21, 1839, 2.

197. "Mortgage J. W. Tisdale & Wife," mortgage deeds Mobile, SG3792, *Alabama*.

198. Joseph W. Tisdale to the bank, March 6, 1844, branch bank at Mobile correspondence, SG2769, *Alabama*.

199. Matthew Ellenberger, "Horton, Albert Clinton (1798–1865)," *Handbook of Texas Online*, Texas State Historical Association, accessed February 12, 2020, https://tshaonline.org/handbook/online/articles/fho62.

200. Joseph W. Tisdale to the bank, September 4, 1844, branch bank at Mobile correspondence, SG3770, *Alabama*.

201. Sixth Census, 1840, Franklin County, Alabama, *Census (MCR)*, p. 83, M-704, reel 2.

202. Joseph W. Tisdale to the bank, March 6, 1844, branch bank at Mobile correspondence, SG3769, *Alabama*.

203. Report of James F. Deas, chair of the Real Estate Committee, September 8, 1843, branch bank at Mobile real estate settlements, SG2788, *Alabama*.

204. Abner S. Lipscomb, *Alabama's Supreme Court Justices*, Alabama Department of Archives and History, accessed February 12, 2020, https://archives.alabama.gov/judicial/lips.html.

205. Joseph W. Tisdale to the bank, September 4, 1844, branch bank at Mobile correspondence, SG3769, *Alabama*.

206. Joseph W. Tisdale to the bank, March 6, 1844, branch bank at Mobile correspondence, SG3769, *Alabama*.

207. Joseph W. Tisdale to the bank, September 4, 1844.

208. Records of the Fifth Judicial District Court, November 9, 1848 (document no. 1,634, reel 6, Louisiana collection, New Orleans Public Library, New Orleans, Louisiana), *Petitions* 20884846.

209. Report of Crawford and Magee, no. 287, November 20, 1847, branch bank at Mobile attorney's report, SG3724, *Alabama*.

210. Sixth Census, 1840, Washington County, Alabama, *Census (MCR)*, p. 271, M-704, reel 16. Harris was not listed in the 1840 census, but owned thirty-four slaves in the 1830 census. See Fifth Census, 1830, Washington County, Alabama, *Census (MCR)*, p. 248, M19, reel 3.

211. "Report of William Magee, Agent to Pursue Negroes Run off by R. F. Hazard & J McCarty," March 4, 1846, branch bank at Mobile attorney's report, SG3724, *Alabama*. Although McCarty listed fifty-seven slaves in the 1840 census, these forty-nine slaves appear to have been the total of his enslaved property in 1845. Similarly, Hazard's total slave property appears to have been reduced from thirty-seven to twenty-two enslaved individuals between 1840 and 1845. Given the ongoing depression in the country and their status as debtors, it is likely that Hazard and McCarty either sold off these missing slaves or sent them out of state prior to 1845.

212. "Report of William Magee, Agent to Pursue Negroes Run off by R. F. Hazard & J McCarty," March 4, 1846.

213. "Report of William Magee, Agent to Pursue Negroes Run off by R. F. Hazard & J McCarty," March 4, 1846.

214. "Report of William Magee, Agent to Pursue Negroes Run off by R. F. Hazard & J McCarty," March 4, 1846.

215. "Statement of the Disposition Made of Seventeen Negroes Captured by Magee & Crawford," July 18, 1846, Bank of State of Alabama Mobile account sales register, SG3682, *Alabama*.

216. Report of Crawford and Magee, no. 287, November 20, 1847.

217. *Adams*, 63 U.S. at 481.

Chapter Eight

1. For example, see page 2 of the New Orleans *Times-Picayune* from May 12 and 13, 1837.

2. "Suspension of Specie Payments," *Times-Picayune* (New Orleans), May 14, 1837, 2.

3. Untitled, *Times-Picayune* (New Orleans), May 14, 1837, 2.

4. "To the Public," *Times-Picayune* (New Orleans), May 14, 1837, 2; untitled, *Times-Picayune* (New Orleans), May 14, 1837, 2.

5. "Times at the North," *Times-Picayune* (New Orleans), May 14, 1837, 2.

6. "IMPORTANT.—Buffalo Banks all Bursted," and "Times at the North," *Times-Picayune* (New Orleans), May 14, 1837, 2.

7. "Times at the North," *Times-Picayune* (New Orleans), May 14, 1837, 2.

8. George D. Green, *Finance and Economic Development in the Old South: Louisiana Banking 1804–1861* (Stanford, CA: Stanford University Press, 1972), 22–23.

9. Warren E. Weber, *Census of Early State Banks in the United States* (2005), https://www.minneapolisfed.org/people/warren-e-weber.

10. Untitled, *Times-Picayune* (New Orleans), May 14, 1837, 2.

11. This accounting of closure rates is based on Weber, *Census of Early State Banks*. Other states experienced lower (yet still significant) rates of bank closure between 1838 and 1843: Maine (36 percent), New Hampshire (29 percent), New York (18 percent), Vermont (16 percent), Massachusetts (15 percent), Maryland (12 percent), New Jersey (11 percent), Pennsylvania (10 percent), Washington, DC (7 percent), and Rhode Island (2 percent). No banks closed in Connecticut, Delaware, Iowa, Indiana, Kentucky, Missouri, North Carolina, South Carolina, Tennessee, or Virginia from 1838 to 1843.

12. While there are clear differences between these various types of closures—voluntary and involuntary, planned and sudden—I am treating all closures in this time period as "failures" so as to simplify the language. Many bank closures blurred the lines between these categories (for example, closing at a charter expiration when it was also insolvent, or claiming to be voluntarily liquidating when the legislature would have otherwise forced it into involuntary liquidation). These distinctions do not have a material effect on the experiences of slaveholders or the enslaved, and thus do not affect the argument.

13. "Sale of Real Estate & Assets by City Bank of N. O. to Louis Sheppers," October 24, 1849, Notary Cenas, vol. 43, p. 381–89, *NONA*.

14. "Sale of Property by City Bank of New Orleans to Louisiana State Bank," April 27, 1850, Notary Cenas, vol. 46, p. 213–18 and attachments, *NONA*.

15. "List of Stock Holders City Bank of New Orleans Stock 10th August 1849," folders 68–92, *City Bank*.

16. James Deas to Franklin Elmore, November 18, 1849, *Elmore*, business correspondence, box 6.

17. James Deas to Franklin Elmore, November 18, 1849.

18. *Acts Passed at the Annual Session of the General Assembly of the State of Alabama* (Tuscaloosa, AL: Phelan & Harris, Printers, 1843), 11, 37, 47, 53, 74.

19. *A Digest of the Laws of the State of Alabama* (Tuskaloosa [*sic*], AL: Marmaduke J. Slade, 1843), 119; James Deas to Franklin Elmore, November 18, 1849.

20. James Deas to Franklin Elmore, November 18, 1849.

21. "Abstract of the Provisions of the Extension Law of 1845," *Sumter County Whig* (Livingston, AL), March 4, 1845, 4.

22. "An Act to Regulate the Affairs of the Banks," *Democrat* (Huntsville, AL), February 11, 1846, 3.

23. "Mortgage of James G. Lyon," mortgage deeds Mobile, SG3792, *Alabama.*

24. S. T. Douglass, register of real estate claimed by branch bank at Mobile, 1842, p. 25, SG3921, *Alabama*; "Mortgage F. B. Shepard," mortgage deeds Mobile, SG3792, *Alabama.*

25. "Mortgage F. B. Shepard."

26. "The Cotton Crop," *Jacksonville Republican*, January 3, 1844, 1; "The Coon Party," *Democrat* (Huntsville, AL), January 11, 1844, 2; untitled, *Wetumpka Argus*, February 14, 1844, 2.

27. "Branch of the Bank of the State of Ala.," newspaper clipping, branch bank at Mobile correspondence and related materials, 1840–1847, SG2769, *Alabama.*

28. "Sales at Auction of Negroes," Mobile account sales register, p. 24, SG3682, *Alabama.*

29. "George Dobson and N. F. Williams Mortgage," mortgage deeds Mobile, SG3792, *Alabama.*

30. "Mortgage Jno M. Bates & Elizabeth Bates," mortgage deeds Mobile, SG3792, *Alabama*; Sixth Census, 1840, Greene County, Alabama, *Census (MCR)*, p. 108, M704, reel 5.

31. "Account of Sale of Property Mortgaged by Jno M. Bates," Mobile account sales register, p. 31, SG3682, *Alabama*; Sixth Census, 1840, Greene County, Alabama, *Census (MCR)*, p. 108, M704, reel 5.

32. Seventh Census, 1850, Greene County, Alabama, *Census (MCR)*, p. 266, M432, reel 6; Seventh Census, 1850, Greene County, Alabama, *Census (SS)*, p. 399, M432, reel 19.

33. Colonel R. S. Jones to General T. L. Toulmin, president, September 9, 1844, branch bank at Mobile correspondence and related materials 1840–1847, SG2769, *Alabama.*

34. Extract of letter of James Innerarity for minutes of the board, February 29, 1844, branch bank at Mobile correspondence and related materials 1840–1847, SG2769, *Alabama*; Sixth Census, 1840, Mobile, Alabama, *Census (MCR)*, p. 76, M704, roll 9–10.

35. Eliza Kenan to the branch bank, March 11, 1844, branch bank at Mobile correspondence and related materials, SG2770, *Alabama*; "An Act to Enable the Executrix of Michael J. Kenan to Secure the Payment of Certain Money to the Branch Bank at Mobile," in *Acts Passed at the Annual Session of the General Assembly of the State of Alabama* (Tuscaloosa, AL: John McCormick, State Printer, 1844), 123–24.

36. "Eliza Kenan's Mortgage," mortgage deeds Mobile, SG3792, p. 91, *Alabama.*

37. William Armistead to W. P. Gould, February 19, 1844, branch bank at Mobile correspondence and related materials 1840–1847, SG2769, *Alabama*; "Sale of Land and Negroes," *Alabama Beacon* (Greensboro, AL), February 24, 1844, 3.

38. *Acts Passed at the Annual Session of the General Assembly of the State of Alabama* (Tuscaloosa, AL: Phelan & Harris, Printers, 1843), 11.

39. "Branch of the Bank of the State of Alabama at Mobile," *Wetumpka Argus*, April 10, 1844, 3.

40. Robert Huie to the branch bank, March 29, 1844, branch bank at Mobile correspondence and related materials, SG2770, *Alabama.*

41. "James Huie Mortgage," mortgage deeds Mobile, SG3792, *Alabama*; "Account Sales of Twenty Slaves Belonging to the Branch Bank," Mobile account sales Register, SG3682, p. 42, *Alabama.*

42. "Mortgage of Louisa S. Owen," mortgage deeds Mobile, SG3792, p. 86, *Alabama.*

43. "No. 331 Peter Hamilton Admr G. W. Owen Estate Report of Hire of Negroes," branch bank at Mobile attorney's report, SG3724, p. 529, *Alabama.*

44. "Sales," Mobile account sales register, p. 46–55, SG3682, *Alabama.*

45. "List of Negroes of the Branch Bank," Mobile account sales register, p. 27–28, SG3682, *Alabama.*

46. Richard Sutch, "Appendix: The Value of the Slave Population, 1805–1860," in Roger Ransom and Richard Sutch, "Capitalists without Capital: The Burden of Slavery and the Impact of Emancipation," *Agricultural History* 62, no. 3 (Summer 1988)," table A-1, 150–51.

47. "Sale of Negroes by James Pickens and John T. Lomax," Mobile account sales register, p. 29–30, SG3682, *Alabama.*

48. "Sales at Auction," p. 22, 23, 33, 34, 69; "Sales of 5 Negroes," p. 37–39, and "Sales of 6 Negroes," p. 68, Mobile account sales register, SG3682, *Alabama.*

49. "Alfred Fowler's Mortgage," mortgage deeds Mobile, SG3792; "Sales at Auction," Mobile account sales register, p. 23, SG3682, *Alabama.*

50. "Act Sales at Auction," Mobile account sales register, p. 24, SG3682, *Alabama.*

51. Court summons for Farly D. Thompson, September 30, 1845, and court summons for Edward A. Oneal, September 30, 1850, Bank of State of Alabama Decatur records, SG4153, *Alabama.*

52. James Deas to Franklin Elmore, November 18, 1849, *Elmore*, business correspondence, box 6.

53. William F. Pierce to Henry B. Holcombe, March 24, 1844, Branch Bank at Mobile correspondence and related materials, SG2770, *Alabama.*

54. F. S. Blount to branch bank, April 16, 1844, Branch Bank at Mobile correspondence and related materials, 1840–1847, SG2769, *Alabama.*

55. "Report Crawford & Magee," November 20, 1847, branch bank at Mobile attorney's report, SG3724, p. 405, *Alabama.*

56. James Deas to Franklin Elmore, November 18, 1849, *Elmore*, business correspondence, box 6.

57. James Deas to Franklin Elmore, November 18, 1849.

58. "An Act to Provide for the Liquidation of Banks," in *Acts Passed at the Second Session of the Fifteenth Legislature of the State of Louisiana* (New Orleans: J. C. De St. Romes, State Printer, 1842), 238–40.

59. "An Act to Revive the Charters of the Several Banks Located in the City of New Orleans, and for Other Purposes," in *Second Session of the Fifteenth Legislature*, 48–50; "An Act to Amend an Act Entitled, 'An Act to Revive the Charters of the Several Banks Located in the City of New Orleans, and for Other Purposes,' Approved February 5, 1842," in *Second Session of the Fifteenth Legislature*, 216; Green, *Finance*, 22–23.

60. "An Act to Revive the Charters," in *Second Session of the Fifteenth Legislature*, 34–36.

61. "An Act to Revive the Charters," in *Second Session of the Fifteenth Legislature*, 38.

62. "An Act to Amend," in *Second Session of the Fifteenth Legislature*, 224.

63. *An Act to Incorporate the Subscribers to the Bank of Louisiana* (New Orleans: Benjamin Levy, 1838), 19, 25–26. Although the City Bank of New Orleans was chartered under the same principles as the Bank of Louisiana, its impending expiration in 1850 made it less of an issue.

64. "An Act to Provide for the Liquidation of Banks," in *Acts Passed at the Second Session of the Fifteenth Legislature of the State of Louisiana*, 250.

65. "An Act to Provide for the Liquidation of Banks," in *Second Session of the Fifteenth Legislature*, 252; "An Act Amendatory of the Charter of the Citizens' Bank of Louisiana," in *Second Session of the Fifteenth Legislature*, 396.

66. *Journal of the Senate: Second Session of the Sixteenth Legislature of Louisiana* (New Orleans: Alexander C. Bullitt—State Printer, 1844), 4–5.

67. *Journal of the Senate*, 14, statement E.

68. *Journal of the Senate*, 15–16.

69. *Journal of the Senate*, 40.

70. "Response of the Board of Currency to the Governor," in *Journal of the Senate*, appendix M, XXI.

71. "Exchange and Banking Company," in *Acts Passed at the First Session of the Twelfth Legislature of the State of Louisiana* (New Orleans: Jerome Bayon, 1835), 197.

72. Richard Campanella, "The St. Louis and the St. Charles: New Orleans' Legacy of Showcase Exchange Hotels," *Preservation in Print* (April 2015): 16, https://cloud.3dissue.com/193333/193749/226507/April2015/index.html; Benjamin Moore Norman, *Norman's New Orleans and Environs* (New Orleans: B. M. Norman, 1845), 137–41.

73. McAuley v. His Creditors, 4 La.Ann. 52 (SC LA 1849).

74. "Sale of Slaves by Exchange and Banking Company to Jesse Beaty of Parish of Terrebonne," November 4, 1841, Notary Hilary Breton Cenas, vol. 25, p. 417, City Archives of New Orleans.

75. "Subrogation of Mortgage by Exchange & Banking Co to Thomas Fitzwilliam of New Orleans," November 9, 1841, Notary Cenas, vol. 25, no. 473, *NONA*.

76. Mortgage Alexander McNeill, January 15, 1838, New Orleans papers, box 3, *BUS (PA-Diss.)*.

77. "Subrogation of Mortgage by Exchange & Banking Co to Thomas Fitzwilliam of New Orleans," November 9, 1841.

78. Lowry v. Erwin, 6 Rob. 192 (SC LA 1843); Erwin v. Lowry, 2 La.Ann. 314 (SC LA 1847); Erwin v. Lowry, 48 U.S. 172 (1849); Lowry v. Erwin, 5 La.Ann. 205 (SC LA 1850).

79. "Transaction between Exchange Bank and Ambrose Lanfear of New Orleans," November 13, 1841, Notary Cenas, vol. 25, no. 497, *NONA*.

80. "Sale of Slaves by Exchange Bank to Isaac Franklin of Sumner County, TN," November 19, 1841, Notary Cenas, vol. 25, no. 513, *NONA*.

81. *McAuley*, 4 La.Ann.

82. "Governor Roman," *Times-Picayune* (New Orleans), April 7, 1842, 2; Beaumon v. Thomas, 1 La.Ann. 284 (SC LA 1846).

83. "Inventory of the Exchange and Banking Company of New Orleans," March 23, 1842, Notary Cenas, vol. 26, no. 457, *NONA*.

84. "Sale of Slaves by Commissioners of the Exchange Bank to Thos H. Barker," July 13, 1842, Notary Cenas, vol. 26A, no. 609, *NONA*.

85. "An Act to Incorporate the St. Charles Hotel Company," *Acts Passed at the First Session of the Sixteenth Legislature of the State of Louisiana* (New Orleans: Alexander C. Bullitt—State Printer, 1843), 57–58.

86. "Inventory of the Property and Effects of the Bank of Orleans," July 28, 1842, Notary Christy, vol. 45, p. 365–69, *NONA*.

87. Sixth Census, 1840, Washington County, Mississippi, *Census (MCR)*, p. 245, M-704, reel 217.

88. "Sale of Slaves Walker & Hundley to the Bank of Orleans," January 29, 1841, vol. 41, no. 203; "Sale of Slave Thomas Boudar to the Bank of Orleans," January 29, 1841, vol. 41, no. 205; "Inventory of the Property and Effects of the Bank of Orleans," July 28, 1842, Notary Christy, vol. 45, p. 365–69, *NONA*.

89. "Sale of Plantation &c the Commissioners of the Bank of Orleans to Michael Welch," June 3, 1843, Notary Christy, vol. 47, no. 616, *NONA*.

90. "Subrogation Succ[essio]n of Nathl Cox to Bank of Orleans," July 6, 1841, Notary Christy, vol. 43, no. 43, *NONA*; "Nathaniel Cox," *Find a Grave*, July 17, 2011, https://www.findagrave.com/memorial/73499267/nathaniel-cox.

91. "Sale of Plantation &c the Commissioners of the Bank of Orleans to Michael Welch," June 3, 1843; Sixth Census, 1840, Rapides Parish, Louisiana, *Census (MCR)*, p. 201, M-704, reel 128.

92. "Sale of Plantation &c the Commissioners of the Bank of Orleans to Michael Welch," June 3, 1843*A*.

93. "Subrogation Succ[essio]n of Nathl Cox to Bank of Orleans," July 6, 1841.

94. "Sale of Plantation &c the Commissioners of the Bank of Orleans to Michael Welch," June 3, 1843; "Sale of Slaves John A. Scott to Bank of Orleans," January 3, 1842, Notary Christy, vol. 44, no. 5, *NONA*.

95. "Inventory of the Property and Effects of the Bank of Orleans," July 28, 1842.

96. Commissioners of Bank of Orleans v. Hodge, 8 Rob. 450 (SC LA 1844) at 450–56; "Release of Mortgage by Bank of Orleans to And Hodge Jr.," July 3, 1844, Notary Cenas, vol. 32, p. 269–70; "Transfer of Claims &c Commrs of Bank of Orleans to Fellowes Johnson & Co.," June 9, 1847, Notary Christy, vol. 57, no. 682, *NONA*.

97. "Inventory of the Property and Effects of the Bank of Orleans," July 28, 1842.

98. "Meeting of Creditors of the Bank of Orleans," December 15, 1842, Notary Christy, vol. 46, p. 837, *NONA*.

99. "Proces-Verbal of Sales of Real Estate & Slaves Belonging to the Bank of Orleans," February 25, 1843, vol. 47, no. 314; "Sale of Slaves the Commissioners of the Bank of Orleans to Andrew S. Barker," March 31, 1843, vol. 47 p. 330–32; "Sale of Slaves the Commissioners of the Bank of Orleans to Thomas H. Saul," March 31, 1843, vol. 47 p. 334–35; "Sale of Slaves John A. Scott to Bank of Orleans," January 3, 1842, *NONA*.

100. "Sale of Plantation &c the Commissioners of the Bank of Orleans to Michael Welch," June 3, 1843.

101. Seventh Census, 1850, Rapides Parish, Louisiana, *Census (MCR)*, p. 49, M-432, reel 239; Seventh Census, 1850, Rapides Parish, Louisiana, *Census (SS)*, p. 23, M-432, reel 245.

102. "Transfer of Claims &c Commrs of Bank of Orleans to Fellowes Johnson & Co.," June 9, 1847.

103. William B. English, "Understanding the Costs of Sovereign Default: American State Debts in the 1840's," *American Economic Review* 86, no. 1 (March 1996), 261–67; John Joseph Wallis, "Constitutions, Corporations, and Corruption: American States and Constitutional Change, 1842 to 1852," *Journal of Economic History* 65, no. 1 (March 2005), 217.

104. English, "Sovereign Default," 263–66; Reginald C. McGrane, *Foreign Bondholders and American State Debts* (New York: MacMillan Company, 1935), 80–81, 98–101, 121–25, 140–42.

105. Wallis, "Constitutions" 217.

106. January 2, 1836, Minute Book, vol. 1, reel 14, *Citizens' Bank*.

107. "Legislative Acts," *Floridian and Advocate* (Tallahassee), February 16, 1833, 2.

108. "Planters' Bank of Mississippi," *Southern Clarion* (Natchez), May 20, 1831, 3.

109. McGrane, *Foreign Bondholders*, 181.

110. McGrane, *Foreign Bondholders*, 181–82; English, "Sovereign Default," 265–66.

111. "Mississippi Repudiation," *Charleston Mercury*, August 29, 1849, 2.

112. McGrane, *Foreign Bondholders*, 199–201; English, "Sovereign Default," 265–67.

113. McGrane, *Foreign Bondholders*, 255–62; English, "Sovereign Default," 265–66.

114. McGrane, *Foreign Bondholders*, 240–43; English, "Sovereign Default," 265–67; Howard Bodenhorn, *State Banking in Early America: A New Economic History* (New York: Oxford University Press, 2003), 252.

115. Walter Buckingham Smith, *Economic Aspects of the Second Bank of the United States* (New York: Greenwood Press, 1953), 218; Namsuk Kim and John Joseph Wallis, "The Market for American State Government Bonds in Britain and the United States, 1830–43," *Economic History Review* 58, no. 4 (November 2005), 746.

116. "Mississippi Repudiation," *Charleston Mercury*, August 29, 1849, 2.

117. "Sheriff's Office to C Adams Jr Esq. Agt & Received for Debts," regarding W. Tigner, July 15, 1843, New Orleans papers, box 3, *BUS (PA-Diss.)*.

118. "Sheriff's Office to C Adams Jr Esq. Agt & Received for Debts," regarding C. R. Bass, July 15, 1843, New Orleans papers, box 3, *BUS (PA-Diss.)*.

119. "Sheriff's Officials to W. W. Frazier & C Adams Jr Receivers &c," regarding F. G. Turnbull, August 9, 1843, New Orleans papers, box 3, *BUS (PA-Diss.)*.

120. English, "Sovereign Default," 261.

121. "An Act to Protect the State against Loss on Account of Its Liabilities for Bonds Issued for the Use of the Property Banks," in *Acts Passed at the Second Session of the First Legislature of the State of Louisiana* (New Orleans: W. Van Benthuysen, 1847), 77.

122. Consolidated Association of Planters v. Claiborne, 7 La.Ann. 318 (SC LA 1852); The President and Directors of the Consolidated Association of the Planters of Louisiana, v. Lord, 35 La.Ann. 425 (SC LA 1883) at 435.

123. Consolidated Associated v. Comeau, 3 La.Ann. 552 (SC LA 1848).

124. Extract from CAPL sitting of Tuesday, February 13, 1849, attached to "Vente de terre et d'esclaves par L'Association Consolidée à Messrs Edouard Simon et Alexandre Mouton," February 28, 1849, Notary Amédée Ducatel, vol. 38, no. 82, *NONA*.

125. "Sale of Plantation by Consolidated Association of the Planters of Louisiana to Ambrose Lanfear," November 14, 1850, Notary Ducatel, vol. 46a, no. 603, *NONA*.

126. "Sold by Joseph LeCarpentier, Auctioneer," attached to "Sale of Plantation by Consolidated Association of the Planters of Louisiana to Ambrose Lanfear," November 14, 1850, Notary Ducatel, vol. 46a, no. 603, *NONA*.

127. June 4, 1842, Minute Book, vol. 4, reel 15, *Citizens' Bank*.

128. June 6, 1842, Minute Book, vol. 4, reel 15, *Citizens' Bank*.

129. November 5, 1842, Minute Book, vol. 4, reel 15, *Citizens' Bank*.

130. November 12, 1842, Minute Book, vol. 4, reel 15, *Citizens' Bank*.

131. November 15, 1842, Minute Book, vol. 4, reel 15, *Citizens' Bank*.

132. January 14, 1843, Minute Book, vol. 5, reel 15, *Citizens' Bank*.

133. John M. Sacher, *A Perfect War of Politics: Parties, Politicians, and Democracy in Louisiana, 1824–1861* (Baton Rouge: Louisiana State University Press, 2003), 82.

134. Sacher, *Perfect War*, 85. For a more in-depth discussion of state constitutional reform during this period, see Wallis, "Constitutions, Corporations, and Corruption."

Chapter Nine

1. "The Governor's Message," *Times-Picayune*, January 3, 1844, 2.

2. "State Legislature," *Times-Picayune*, January 11, 1844, 2; Samuel C. Hyde Jr., *Pistols and Politics: The Dilemma of Democracy in Louisiana's Florida Parishes, 1810–1899* (Baton Rouge: Louisiana

State University Press, 1998), 58; John M. Sacher, *A Perfect War of Politics: Parties, Politicians, and Democracy in Louisiana, 1824–1861* (Baton Rouge: Louisiana State University Press, 2003), 102–04.

3. Some historians present this constitutional debate as largely a political showdown between Whigs and Democrats. For example, see James Roger Sharp, *The Jacksonians versus the Banks: Politics in the States after the Panic of 1837* (New York: Columbia University Press, 1970), 114–15; and Sacher, *Perfect War*, 104. But as economic historian John Joseph Wallis rightly points out, "the major split over the convention was within the Democratic party, not between the Democrats and the Whigs." See John Joseph Wallis, "Constitutions, Corporations, and Corruption: American States and Constitutional Change, 1842 to 1852," *Journal of Economic History* 65, no. 1 (March 2005), 243.

4. *Proceedings and Debates of the Convention of Louisiana* (New Orleans: Besancon, Ferguson & Co, 1845), 110.

5. *Proceedings and Debates of the Convention of Louisiana*, 343.

6. *Proceedings and Debates of the Convention of Louisiana*, 343.

7. *Proceedings and Debates of the Convention of Louisiana*, 848.

8. *Proceedings and Debates of the Convention of Louisiana*, 848.

9. *Proceedings and Debates of the Convention of Louisiana*, 848–49.

10. Sacher, *Perfect War*, 107.

11. "An Act for the Charter of the Hartsville and Nashville Glass and Soda Manufacturing Company," in *Acts of the State of Tennessee* (Jackson, TN: Gates & Parker, 1848), 359–60; Warren E. Weber, *Census of Early State Banks in the United States* (2005), https://www.minneapolisfed.org/people/warren-e-weber.

12. "The Southern Bank of Kentucky," *Courier-Journal* (Louisville, KY), March 25, 1850, 2.

13. Sharon Ann Murphy, *Other People's Money: How Banking Worked in the Early American Republic* (Baltimore, MD: Johns Hopkins University Press, 2017), 115–16.

14. *Constitution of the State of Texas* (Houston, 1845), 20; "Notice," *Weekly Arkansas Gazette* (Little Rock), May 5, 1845, 3; Larry Schweikart, *Banking in the American South from the Age of Jackson to Reconstruction* (Baton Rouge: Louisiana State University Press, 1987), 167.

15. Sharp, *Jacksonians*; and Howard Bodenhorn, *State Banking in Early America: A New Economic History* (New York: Oxford University Press, 2003).

16. "An Act to Incorporate the Northern Bank of Mississippi," in *Laws of the State of Mississippi* (Jackson: Printed for the State of Mississippi, 1838), 582–90; "An Act to Alter and Amend an Act, Passed April 28, 1837, Incorporating the Northern Bank of the State of Mississippi," in *Laws of the State of Mississippi* (1838), 832–34.

17. Schweikart, *Banking*, 41, 72, 174.

18. Schweikart, *Banking*, 256.

19. "Mortgage Mrs. Mary S. Colhoun to the Bank of Louisiana," May 4, 1844, vol. 50, no. 615; and "Acceptance of Mortgage Mrs. Mary S. Colhoun to Bank of Louisiana," January 3, 1845, Notary Christy, vol. 52, no. 1, *NONA*.

20. "Mortgage John B. Leprêtre to Bank of Louisiana," May 2, 1844, vol. 50, no. 591; and "Mortgage Ruffin G. Stirling to Bank of Louisiana," December 17, 1844, Notary Christy, vol. 51, no. 459, *NONA*.

21. "Mortgage George H. Wyatt to Bank of Louisiana," January 7, 1845, vol. 52, no. 6; "Mortgage Wm J. Fort to Bank of Louisiana," January 7, 1845, vol. 52, no. 11; "Mortgage John Perkins to Bank of Louisiana," January 10, 1845, vol. 52, no. 25; "Mortgage F. A. Frère to Bk of Louis[ian]a," January 20, 1845, vol. 52, no. 49; and "Acceptance of Mort. Bennet H. Barrow," January 22, 1845, Notary Christy, vol. 52, no. 53, *NONA*.

22. "Mortgage Mad[a]me E. Robin Delogny to the Bank of Louisiana," April 4, 1846, Notary Christy, vol. 54, no. 513, *NONA*.

23. "Mortgage J P Benjamin & Theo J Packwood to Bank of Louisiana," May 12, 1852, Notary Cenas, vol. 54, no. 105, *NONA*.

24. "Mortgage &c by Caliste Villeré & Wife to Bank of Louisiana," February 7, 1853, vol. 55, no. 433; and "Mortgage by James J. Hanna & Mrs. Sarah Yorke to Bank of Louisiana," June 14, 1853, Notary Cenas, vol. 57, no. 1065, *NONA*.

25. Schweikart, *Banking*, 41, 71–72, 169, 174, 256–57, 271.

26. Joe Ericson, *Banks and Bankers in Early Texas* (New Orleans: Polyanthos, 1976), 30–79.

27. December 2, 1847, Minute Book, vol. 6, reel 15–16, *Citizens' Bank*.

28. December 7, 1847, Minute Book, vol. 6, reel 15–16, *Citizens' Bank*.

29. December 2, 1847, Minute Book, vol. 6, reel 15–16, *Citizens' Bank*.

30. Citizens' Bank 1847 ledger, *Canal Bank*.

31. March 27, 1849, Minute Book, vol. 6, reel 15–16, *Citizens' Bank*.

32. June 7, 1849, Minute Book, vol. 6, reel 15–16, *Citizens' Bank*.

33. April 24, 1850, Minute Book, vol. 6, reel 15–16, *Citizens' Bank*.

34. October 15, 1850, Minute Book, vol. 6, reel 15–16, *Citizens' Bank*.

35. January 28, 1851, Minute Book, vol. 6, reel 15–16, *Citizens' Bank*.

36. For example, see also, March 27, June 7, and November 7, 1849; January 7, January 15, April 9, and November 18, 1850; and January 28, 1851, all in the Minute Book, vol. 6, reel 15–16, *Citizens' Bank*.

37. May 15, 1849, Minute Book, vol. 6, reel 15–16, *Citizens' Bank*.

38. May 15, May 18, June 20, July 14, and August 22, 1849, Minute Book, vol. 6, reel 15–16, *Citizens' Bank*.

39. September 10, 1850, Minute Book, vol. 6, reel 15–16, *Citizens' Bank*.

40. May 20, 1852, Minute Book, vol. 7, reel 16, *Citizens' Bank*.

41. "Legislature of Louisiana," *True American* (New Orleans), January 8, 1839, 2; "Brief Biographical Sketches," *Times-Picayune* (New Orleans), September 5, 1844, 2. The 1845 state constitution created the position of lieutenant governor for the first time. See Edwin W. Edwards, "The Role of the Governor in Louisiana Politics: An Historical Analysis," *Louisiana History* 15, no. 2 (Spring 1974), 108.

42. Seventh Census, 1850, St. Charles Parish, Louisiana, *Census (MCR)*, p. 172, M-432, reel 239; Stanley Clisby Arthur, ed., *Old Families of Louisiana* (Baltimore, MD: Clearfield, 1997), 232; "Hypothèque par Dame Vve Arnauld, et concession de priorité à la Banque par Théodore Segond," September 12, 1838, Notary Seghers, vol. 29, no. 344, *NONA*; *Commissioners of Patents' Journal* 388, September 22, 1857, 1224.

43. "Hypothèque par Veuve Jean Eléonor Arnauld & concession de priorité par Théodore Segond," October 2, 1838, Notary Seghers, vol. 29, no. 365, *NONA*; September 6, 1838, Minute Book, vol. 2, reel 14, *Citizens' Bank*.

44. *Charter of the Citizens' Bank of Louisiana and Acts Amendatory Thereto* (New Orleans, LA: Catholic Propagator Job Office, 1873), 9.

45. April 18, 1839, Minute Book, vol. 2, reel 14, *Citizens' Bank*.

46. "Hypothèque par Veuve Arnauld à la B[an]que des Cit[oy]ens et nantissement," April 20, 1839, Notary Seghers, vol. 34, no. 71, *NONA*.

47. October 3, 1839, vol. 3, reel 14, *Citizens' Bank*.

48. "Election by the Legislature," *Times-Picayune* (New Orleans), March 3, 1840, 2.

49. November 7, 1839, Minute Book, vol. 3, reel 14, *Citizens' Bank.*

50. "Louisiana Slave Auction," *Whitney Plantation*, accessed April 1, 2022, https://www.whitneyplantation.org/history/slavery-in-louisiana/auction-of-the-slaves/.

51. April 23 and July 20, 1840, Minute Book, vol. 3, reel 14, *Citizens' Bank.*

52. April 22, 1841, Minute Book, vol. 3, reel 14, *Citizens' Bank.*

53. Adolphe Sorapuru may also have been a cousin of the Widow Arnauld. See Mary Gehman, "The Role of Slaves and Free People of Color in the History of St. Charles Parish," *St. Charles Parish Virtual Museum*, 2017, https://scphistory.org/role-slaves-free-people-color-scp/; "Hypothêque par Messrs Garcia & Sorapuru et Dame Jn Garcia fav[ou]r L'Association Consolidée des Cultivateurs de la Lne," April 20, 1842, vol. 22, no. 66; and "Prolongation de délai [extension of time] par L'Association Consolidée fav[ou]r Mr & Mme Félix Garcia et Mr A[dol]phe Sorapuru," July 24 1847, Notary Ducatel, vol. 32, no. 245, *NONA*.

54. May 24, 1843, Minute Book, vol. 5, reel 15, *Citizens' Bank.*

55. Citizens' Bank 1847 ledger, *Canal Bank*; Sixth Census, 1840, St. John the Baptist Parish, Louisiana, *Census (MCR)*, p. 239, M-704, reel 135.

56. "The Crevasse!" *Times-Picayune* (New Orleans), August 2, 1844, 2.

57. "The Crevasse!" *Times-Picayune* (New Orleans), August 3, 1844.

58. "More of the Crevasse," *Times-Picayune* (New Orleans), August 4, 1844, 2.

59. "The Crevasse," *Times-Picayune* (New Orleans), August 8, 1844, 2.

60. "Crevasse," *Times-Picayune* (New Orleans), August 10, 1844, 2.

61. "For the Crevasse," *Times-Picayune* (New Orleans), August, 6, 1844, 2; August 9, 1844, 3; and August 18, 1844, 2.

62. October 4, 1844, Minute Book, vol. 5, reel 15, *Citizens' Bank.*

63. February 19, 1846, Minute Book, vol. 5, reel 15, *Citizens' Bank.*

64. February 26 and March 12, 1846, Minute Book, vol. 5, reel 15, *Citizens' Bank.*

65. April 9, 1846, Minute Book, vol. 5, reel 15, *Citizens' Bank.* Under Louisiana law, creditors could not directly seize foreclosed property. The property had to be advertised and sold at a public auction, at which point the creditor could purchase the property.

66. "Achille Lorio," *Biographical and Historical Memoirs of Louisiana*, vol. I (Chicago: Goodspeed Publishing Company, 1892), 549.

67. April 16, 1846, Minute Book, vol. 6, reel 15–16, *Citizens' Bank.*

68. September 24, 1846, Minute Book, vol. 6, reel 15–16, *Citizens' Bank.*

69. February 4, 1847, Minute Book, vol. 6, reel 15–16, *Citizens' Bank.*

70. May 20, 1847, Minute Book, vol. 6, reel 15–16, *Citizens' Bank.*

71. February 6, 1849, Minute Book, vol. 6, reel 15–16, *Citizens' Bank.*

72. "An Act to Protect the State against Loss on Account of Its Liabilities for Bonds Issued for the Use of the Property Banks," in *Acts Passed at the Second Session of the First Legislature of the State of Louisiana* (New Orleans: W. Van Benthuysen, 1847), 78.

73. "Prolongation de délai," [extension of time] par L'Association Consolidée fav[ou]r Mr & Mme Félix Garcia et Mr A[dol]phe Sorapuru," July 24, 1847, Notary Ducatel, vol. 32, no. 245, *NONA*.

74. June 30, 1848, and February 6, 1849, Minute Book, vol. 6, reel 15–16, *Citizens' Bank.*

75. February 6, April 10, and May 1, 1849, Minute Book, vol. 6, reel 15–16, *Citizens' Bank.*

76. "Dunlop, Moncure & Co," *New-Orleans Commercial Bulletin*, January 14, 1842, 4.

77. Bowles v. His Creditors, 6 La.Ann. 679 (SC LA 1851) at 680–81.

78. J. Carlyle Sitterson, *Sugar Country: The Cane Sugar Industry in the South, 1753–1950* (Greenwood Press, 1973), 198.

79. Dunlop v. Gordon, 10 La.Ann. 243 (SC LA 1855) at 243–45.

80. "Unreserved Sale at Auction of a Sugar Plantation," *New Orleans Crescent*, January 3, 1850, 3.

81. "Valuable Sugar Plantation and 209 Slaves for Sale," *Times-Picayune* (New Orleans), April 9, 1850, 3.

82. P. A. Champomier, *Statement of the Sugar Crop of Louisiana of 1850–51* (New Orleans: Cook, Young & Co., 1851), 22; and *Statement of the Sugar Crop of Louisiana of 1855–56* (New Orleans: Cook, Young & Co., 1856), 21.

83. "Valuable Sugar Estate," *Times-Picayune* (New Orleans), December 15, 1854, and January 20, 1855, 3.

84. May 1, 1849, Minute Book, vol. 6, reel 15–16, *Citizens' Bank*.

85. *Dunlop*, 10 La.Ann. at 243–45.

86. May 1, 1849, Minute Book, vol. 6, reel 15–16, *Citizens' Bank*.

87. May 1, 1849, Minute Book, vol. 6, reel 15–16, *Citizens' Bank*.

88. May 1, 1849, Minute Book, vol. 6, reel 15–16, *Citizens' Bank*.

89. "The River and Levees," *Times-Picayune*, January 23, 1850, 2; "Look Out for Another Inundation," *Planters' Banner* (Franklin, LA), January 24, 1850, 1.

90. Captain A. A. Humphreys and Lieutenant H. L. Abbot, eds., *Report upon the Physics and Hydraulics of the Mississippi River* (Washington, DC: Government Printing Office, 1867), 143; *Flood Control in the Mississippi Valley*, House of Representatives report no. 1072, 70th Congress, 1st session, March 29, 1928, p. 8.

91. "Crevasses," *New Orleans Weekly Delta*, May 6, 1850, 1.

92. "A Night (Almost) in the Crevasse," *New Orleans Weekly Delta*, May 13, 1850, 4.

93. Champomier, *Sugar Crop . . . 1850–51*, 18; P. A. Champomier, *Statement of the Sugar Crop of Louisiana of. 1851–52* (New Orleans: Cook, Young & Co., 1852), 18.

94. March 5, 1850, Minute Book, vol. 6, reel 15–16, *Citizens' Bank*.

95. November 22, 1850, Minute Book, vol. 6, reel 15–16, *Citizens' Bank*.

96. Seventh Census, 1850, St. Charles Parish, Louisiana, *Census (MCR)*, p. 172, M-432, reel 239; Seventh Census, 1850, St. Charles Parish, Louisiana, *Census (SS)*, p. 139, M-432, reel 246.

97. Garcia v. Garcia, 7 La.Ann. 525 (SC LA 1852) at 526.

98. May 20, 1852, Minute Book, vol. 7, reel 16, *Citizens' Bank*.

99. *Garcia*, 7 La.Ann. at 527.

100. *Garcia*, 7 La.Ann. at 527.

101. May 20 and November 18, 1852, Minute Book, vol. 7, reel 16, *Citizens' Bank*.

102. August 5, 1852, Minute Book, vol. 7, reel 16, *Citizens' Bank*.

103. September 9, 1852, Minute Book, vol. 7, reel 16, *Citizens' Bank*.

104. John Crosby Brown, *A Hundred Years of Merchant Banking: A History of Brown Brothers and Company Brown, Shipley & Company and the Allied Firms* (New York: privately printed, 1909), 255–62.

105. Brown, *Merchant Banking*, 267

106. John A. Kouwenhoven, *Partners in Banking: An Historical Portrait of a Great Private Bank Brown Brothers Harriman & Co. 1818–1968* (New York: Doubleday, 1968), 40, 48.

107. "Proces-Verbal of Sales of Real Estate & Slaves Belonging to the Bank of Orleans," February 25, 1843, Notary Christy, vol. 47, no. 314, *NONA*.

108. United States passport applications, 1795–1925, no. 9,867, July 19, 1855, vol. 115, series M1372, roll 52, *NARA*; Seventh Census, 1850, Concordia, Louisiana, *Census (MCR)*, p. 158, M-432, reel 230.

109. "James Berthe," *Mississippi Free Trader* (Natchez), December 13, 1817, 1.

110. "Notice," *Mississippi Free Trader* (Natchez), October 16, 1821, 3; "Fresh Goods," *Natchez Gazette*, April 6, 1822, 1.

111. "Disolution [*sic*] of Partnership," *Mississippi Free Trader* (Natchez), December 26, 1822, 3.

112. "Cash for Cotton," *Natchez Gazette*, October 4, 1823, 3.

113. "Exchange," *Mississippi Free Trader* (Natchez), November 26, 1823, 3.

114. "Concordia Land," *Natchez Gazette*, March 5, 1823, 3.

115. "First Rate Concordia Land for Sale," *Ariel* (Natchez), January 9, 1826, 6; "Return of the Commissioners of the Lower Levee District," *Natchez Gazette*, December 23, 1826, 3.

116. "City Election," *Natchez Gazette*, January 8, 1825, 3; "Bank of the State of Mississippi," *Natchez Gazette*, January 8, 1825, 3; "Bank Directors," *Weekly Natchez Courier*, January 26, 1827, 6.

117. "Fire Company," *Natchez Newspaper and Public Advertiser*, May 9, 1826, 3.

118. "Louisiana Insurance Company," *Natchez Gazette*, August 16, 1826, 3.

119. "20 Dollars Reward," *Natchez Gazette*, March 26, 1825, 3; "$20 Reward," *Natchez Gazette*, May 28, 1825, 4; "Stop Him!" *Natchez Gazette*, November 25, 1826, 4.

120. Smith v. Natchez Steamboat Co., 1 Howard 479 (Appeals MS 1837) at 480.

121. "Dramatic," *Natchez Weekly Democrat*, May 17, 1828, 2; "Natchez Theatre," *Natchez Daily Courier*, February 21, 1838, 3.

122. "Marie Louise Demie Lapice," *Find a Grave*, added September 7, 2012, https://www.findagrave.com/memorial/96667206/marie-louise-lapice.

123. "Selling Off at Auction," *Natchez Weekly Courier*, December 13, 1828, 7.

124. "An Enquirer," *Natchez Weekly Courier*, July 19, 1833, 3. Calomel is mercury chloride, a highly toxic cathartic that was commonly used in medical treatments from the sixteenth through the nineteenth century. See *Encyclopedia Britannica Online*, Academic ed., s.v. "calomel (Hg_2Cl_2)," July 31, 2012, academic-eb-com/levels/collegiate/article/calomel/18721.

125. "Cholera," *Mississippi Free Trader* (Natchez), July 19, 1833, 2.

126. "New Invention," *Natchez Weekly Courier*, December 13, 1833, 1.

127. "*Beat This Who Can!*," *Weekly Mississippian* (Jackson), October 7, 1836, 3. Lapice's White Hall plantation was a distinct property from the Whitehall plantation in St. James Parish, discussed in chapter 7.

128. "Cotton Thrasher," *Mississippi Free Trader* (Natchez), February 26, 1839, 2.

129. "Adams Sugar Cane," *Natchez Newspaper and Public Advertiser*, November 1, 1826, 2.

130. "Charter of the Planters' Bank," *Vicksburg Whig*, September 23, 1831, 1.

131. "Office Bank United States," *Natchez Weekly Courier*, March 2, 1832, 6; "Planter's Bank," *Mississippi Free Trader* (Natchez), March 29, 1833, 2; "Planter's Bank," *Weekly Mississippian* (Jackson), March 20, 1835, 3.

132. [Illegible] to James C. Wilkins, March 27, 1833, Wilkins papers, *Plantations*, series G, part 5, reel 40.

133. James Wilkins to A. & J. Dennistoun & Co., New Orleans, and James Wilkins to George Ralston, Philadelphia, PA, April 18, 1835, Wilkins papers, *Plantations*, series G, part 5, reel 41.

134. James Wilkins to George Ralston, Philadelphia, April 18, 1835, Wilkins papers, *Plantations*, series G, part 5, reel 41.

135. P. M. Lapice to James Wilkins, July 2, 1835, Wilkins papers, *Plantations*, series G, part 5, reel 41.

136. "Concordia Sugar Cane," *Times-Picayune* (New Orleans), October 26, 1841, 2.

137. "Concordia Sugar Cane," *Vicksburg Daily Whig*, November 3, 1842, 2 (emphasis in original).

138. "Capacity of Louisiana to Produce Sugar for the Whole Union, at a Low Price," *Baton-Rouge Gazette*, November 4, 1843, 2.

139. "Cane Culture in Concordia," *Baton-Rouge Gazette*, April 4, 1846, 2; "Cotton Manufacturing in Natchez," *Natchez Daily Courier*, April 27, 1849, 2; "The Sugar Culture," *Concordia Intelligencer*, April 23, 1853, 1.

140. "Hypothèque à la Banque des Cit[oy]ens par P. M. Lapice," March 10, 1837, vol. 23, no. 96; "Hypothèque à la Banque des Citoyens par P[ier]re Michel Lapice," August 5, 1837, vol. 24, no. 359; "Hypothèque par P. M. Lapice," February 13, 1838, vol. 28, no. 49; "Hypothèque par Pierre M. Lapice & Joseph F. Lapice," September 11, 1838, vol. 29, no. 343; "Hypothèque par P. M. Lapice & Jh F. Lapice à la Banque des Cit[oy]ens," March 23, 1839, Notary Seghers, vol. 34, no. 43; "Dissolution of Partnership between P. M. Lapice & J. F. Lapice and Sale of und. ½ of Property &c by the Latter to the Former," April 23, 1842, Notary Mossy, vol. 22, no. 56, *NONA*.

141. "Mortgage by Pierre Michel Lapice in Favor of the Merchants Bank of New Orleans," April 4, 1840, Notary Mossy, vol. 19, no. 61, *NONA*.

142. "Dreadful Visitation of Providence," *Rodney Telegraph*, May 16, 1840, 2.

143. "Remarkable Preservation of Life," *Mississippi Free Trader* (Natchez), May 23, 1840, 2.

144. "Dissolution of Partnership between P. M. Lapice & J. F. Lapice and Sale of und. ½ of Property &c by the Latter to the Former," April 23, 1842.

145. Pickersgill v. Brown, 7 La.Ann. 297 (SC LA 1852) at 303.

146. "Subrogation &c by City Bank of New Orleans to James Brown," May 11, 1842, Notary Cenas, vol. 26A, no. 81, *NONA*.

147. *Pickersgill*, 7 La.Ann.

148. "Sale of Property by Widow E[variste]. Villavaso to P. M. Lapice and mortgage by Him to James Brown," March 25, 1843, Notary Mossy, vol. 24, no. 37, *NONA*.

149. *Pickersgill*, 7 La.Ann. at 298 and 306.

150. "Balance Sheet—Real Estate Valuations," vol. 123, 1842–1852, p. 58, *Brown*.

151. "Balance Sheet—Real Estate Valuations," vol. 123, 1842–1852, p. 50.

152. "Balance Sheet—Real Estate Valuations," vol. 123, 1842–1852, p. 8, 274; vol. 125, p. 260; vol. 126, 20, 310, 586; vol. 127, p. 122, 133, 274, 310.

153. "Balance Sheet—Real Estate Valuations," vol. 123, 1842–1852, p. 7, 9, 63, 85, 122, 136, 340, 211.

154. "Balance Sheet—Real Estate Valuations," vol. 123, 1842–1852, p. 150; *List of Patents and Designs Issued by the United States* (Washington, DC: J. & G. S. Gideon, 1847), 117; J. Leander Bishop, *A History of American Manufacturers from 1608 to 1860*, vol. II (Philadelphia: Edward Young & Co., 1868), 442.

155. *Pickersgill*, 7 La.Ann. at 303.

156. *Pickersgill*, 7 La.Ann. at 303.

157. *Pickersgill*, 7 La.Ann. at 304.

158. "Improvements in Sugar-Making," *Concordia Intelligencer*, December 11, 1847, 4.

159. "Mrs. Prewitt," *Mississippi Free Trader* (Natchez), December 19, 1849, 2.

160. "From the New Orleans Bee," *Opelousas Courier*, January 29, 1853, 2; "Fabrication du Sucre," *Opelousas Courier*, January 29, 1853, 1.

161. P. A. Champomier, *Statement of the Sugar Crop of Louisiana of 1849–50* (New Orleans: Cook, Young & Co., 1850), 19.

162. Seventh Census, 1850, St. James Parish, Louisiana, *Census (MCR)*, p. 213, M-432, reel 239.

163. *Pickersgill*, 7 La.Ann.

164. Champomier, *Sugar Crop . . . 1850–51*, 14; *Sugar Crop . . . 1851–52*, 15.

165. *Pickersgill*, 7 La.Ann. at 298.

166. "U. S. Marshall's Sale," *New Orleans Crescent*, February 23, 1850, 1.

167. *Pickersgill*, 7 La.Ann. at 298–99.

168. "Sheriff's Sale," *Concordia Intelligencer*, July 3, 1852, 2.

169. "Balance Sheet—Real Estate Valuations," vol. 127, 1842–1852, p. 173, 274, *Brown*; "Monition," *Concordia Intelligencer*, December 4, 1852, 3.

170. Champomier, *Statement of the Sugar Crop of Louisiana of 1852–53* (New Orleans: Cook, Young & Co., 1853), 15; *Statement of the Sugar Crop of Louisiana of 1853–54* (New Orleans: Cook, Young & Co., 1854), 15; *Statement of the Sugar Crop of Louisiana of 1854–55* (New Orleans: Cook, Young & Co., 1855), 14.

171. "Paragon Sugar," *Natchez Daily Courier*, November 27, 1852, and June 28, 1854, 3.

172. "Notice of Copartnership," *Times-Picayune* (New Orleans), February 1, 1856, 4; Champomier, *Sugar Crop . . . 1855–56*, 14.

173. "Notice of Copartnership," *Times-Picayune* (New Orleans), February 1, 1856, 4; "Notice of Copartnership," *Times-Picayune* (New Orleans), February 2, 1856, 2.

174. April 10, 1855 and February 15, 1856, Minute Book, vol. 7, reel 16, *Citizens' Bank*; P. A. Champomier, *Statement of the Sugar Crop of Louisiana of 1857–58* (New Orleans: Cook, Young & Co., 1858), 13; *Statement of the Sugar Crop of Louisiana of 1858–59* (New Orleans: Cook, Young & Co., 1859), 13.

175. "The 'Paragon Sugar,'" *Times-Picayune* (New Orleans), March 23, 1856, 4; "Paragon Sugar Works Sugars," *Times Picayune* (New Orleans), November 20, 1861, 3.

176. Eighth Census, 1860, St. James Parish, Sixth District, Louisiana, *Census (MCR)*, p. 70, M-653, reel 423.

177. "Balance Sheet—Real Estate Valuations," vol. 123, 1842–1852, p. 54–57, *Brown*.

178. John M. Bell, "To the Voters of New Orleans," *Daily Delta* (New Orleans), March 16, 1850, 2.

179. December 24, 1849, Minute Book, vol. 6, reel 15–16, *Citizens' Bank*.

180. "The Citizen's Bank," *Democratic Advocate* (Baton Rouge), July 31, 1851, 2–3.

181. "The Citizen's Bank," *Democratic Advocate* (Baton Rouge), July 31, 1851, 2–3.

182. May 18, 1850, Minute Book, vol. 6, reel 15–16, *Citizens' Bank*.

183. "The Citizen's Bank," *Democratic Advocate* (Baton Rouge), July 31, 1851, 2–3.

184. "The Veto on the Citizens' Bank Bill," *Times-Picayune* (New Orleans), March 3, 1852, 2.

185. "An Act for the Relief of the Citizens' Bank of Louisiana," in *Charter of the Citizens' Bank*, 34–37.

186. May 24, 1853, Minute Book, vol. 7, reel 16, *Citizens' Bank*.

187. Hugh Rockoff, "The Free Banking Era: A Reexamination," *Journal of Money, Credit and Banking* (May 1974), 141–67; Arthur J. Rolnick and Warren E. Weber, "New Evidence on the Free Banking Era," *American Economic Review* 73 (December 1983): 1080–91; Hugh Rockoff, "New Evidence on Free Banking in the United States," *American Economic Review* 75 (September 1985): 886–89; and Howard Bodenhorn, "Entry, Rivalry and Free Banking in Antebellum America," *Review of Economics and Statistics* 72, no. 4 (November 1990), 682–86.

188. "Our Legislature," *Knoxville Register*, December 5, 1849, 2.

189. "More Banking Facilities," *Alabama Beacon* (Greensboro), April 28, 1849, 2.

190. "To the People of the State of Alabama," *Alabama Beacon* (Greensboro), April 28, 1849, 1.

191. "Banking in the State of New-York," *Bankers' Magazine, and Statistical Register* V, no. XI (May 1856), 863; "Free Banking," *Daily Delta* (New Orleans), March 18, 1851, 2.

192. "Banking in Alabama," *Bankers' Magazine, and Statistical Register* IV, no. VII (January 1850), 639.

193. "Banking in Louisiana," *Bankers' Magazine, and Statistical Register* I, no. IX (March 1852), 753.

194. "Free-Banking—Majority Report," *Memphis Daily Eagle*, December 8, 1849, 2.

195. "New Banking System," *Monroe Democrat*, October 20, 1852, 4.

196. Logan McKnight, "Free Banking. Part IV," *De Bow's Review* XIV, no. I (January 1853), 157.

197. A Democrat, "Free Banking—No. 2," *Democrat* (Huntsville, AL), June 13, 1849, 2.

198. "Free Banking," *Concordia Intelligencer*, April 19, 1851, 2.

199. Planter, "Banking System for New Orleans," *New Orleans Weekly Delta*, March 24, 1851, 1.

200. "Free Banking," *New Orleans Crescent*, October 31, 1851, 2.

201. "Spirit of the Press," *New Orleans Weekly Delta*, November 3, 1851, 5.

202. "The Election and Its Promises," New Orleans *Times-Picayune* (New Orleans), November 12, 1851, 2.

203. "General Banking Law of Vermont," *Bankers' Magazine, and Statistical Register* I, no. X (April 1852), 64.

204. "The Free Bank Law of Tennessee," *Bankers' Magazine, and Statistical Register* I, no. X (April 1852), 763.

205. "The Banks of the United States," *Bankers' Magazine, and Statistical Register* IX, no. 1 (July 1859), 6; "Banks of the United States," *Bankers' Magazine, and Statistical Register* XI, no. 12 (June 1860), 992.

206. "Banks of the United States," *Bankers' Magazine*, 989–90, 998.

207. "Bank Statistics," *Bankers' Magazine, and Statistical Register* I, no. VIII (February 1852), 663.

208. "New Bank," *Times-Picayune* (New Orleans), May 5, 1853, 2.

209. On the limited growth of free banks, see Kenneth Ng, "Free Banking Laws and Barriers to Entry in Banking, 1838–1860," *Journal of Economic History* 48, no. 4 (December 1988), 877–89.

Epilogue

1. "The Courts," *Daily Picayune* (New Orleans), April 27, 1866; "M. Jacob Denny," *L'Avant-Coureur* (Lucy, LA), May 5, 1866, 1.

2. Stanley Clisby Arthur, ed., *Old Families of Louisiana* (Baltimore, MD: Clearfield, 1997), 270–71.

3. April 8, 1837, vol. 1, reel 14; July 15, 1837, vol. 2, reel 14; May 18, 1857, vol. 8, reel 16, Minute Book, *Citizens' Bank*.

4. Seventh Census, 1850, St. James Parish, Louisiana, *Census (MCR)*, p. 430, M-432, reel 239; Seventh Census, 1850, St. James Parish, Louisiana, *Census (SS)*, p. 313–17, M-432, reel 246.

5. April 8, 1837, vol. 1, reel 14; July 15, 1837, vol. 2, reel 14; May 18, 1857, vol. 8, reel 16, Minute Book, *Citizens' Bank*.

6. "The Courts," *Daily Picayune* (New Orleans), April 27, 1866; "M. Jacob Denny," *L'Avant-Coureur* (Lucy, LA), May 5, 1866, 1; Sosthene Roman v. J. Denny, 19 La.Ann. 521 (SC LA 1867).

7. "The Courts," *Daily Picayune* (New Orleans), April 27, 1866; "M. Jacob Denny," *L'Avant-Coureur* (Lucy, LA), May 5, 1866, 1; The State v. The Judge of the Second District of New Orleans, 16 La.Ann. 390 (SC LA 1861); *Sosthene Roman*, 19 La.Ann.; Horatio Weedon v. Arthemise Landreaux, 26 La.Ann. 729 (SC LA 1874).

8. "Very Superior and Highly Improved Estate," *Times-Picayune* (New Orleans), April 15, 1866, 8.

9. "The Courts," *Daily Picayune* (New Orleans), April 27, 1866; "M. Jacob Denny," *L'Avant-Coureur* (Lucy, LA), May 5, 1866, 1.

10. *Weedon*, 26 La.Ann. at 729.

11. Judith Kelleher Schafer, *Slavery, the Civil Law, and the Supreme Court of Louisiana* (Baton Rouge: Louisiana State University Press, 1994), 294.

12. Schafer, *Supreme Court of Louisiana*, 295.

13. August 5, 1852, Minute Book, vol. 7, reel 16, *Citizens' Bank*.

14. "Valuable Sugar Plantation," *Times-Picayune* (New Orleans), December 23, 1852, 1.

15. "A Fine Opportunity," *Times-Picayune* (New Orleans), December 28, 1852, 2.

16. January 13, 1853, Minute Book, vol. 7, reel 16, *Citizens' Bank*.

17. August 26, 1852, Minute Book, vol. 7, reel 16, *Citizens' Bank*.

18. April 4, 1860, Minute Book, vol. 8, reel 16–17, *Citizens' Bank*.

19. December 12 and 19, 1867, Minute Book, vol. 8, reel 16–17, *Citizens' Bank*; Mrs. George Wailes v. The Citizens' Bank of Louisiana, 23 La.Ann. 524 (SC LA 1871).

20. *Mrs. George Wailes*, 23 La.Ann. at 525.

21. William Judge v. Forsyth's Executors, 11 Fla. 257 (SC FL 1866).

22. Haskill v. Sevier, 25 Ark. 152 (SC AR 1867) at 154.

23. John F. Tucker v. Henry L. Toomer, 36 Ga. 138 (SC GA 1867).

24. Thomas Wainwright v. Mrs. Alice F. Bridges, 19 La.Ann. 234 (SC LA 1867) at 238; Schafer, *Supreme Court of Louisiana*, 297–98.

25. Andrew Kull, "Freedom: Personal Liberty and Private Law," *Chicago-Kent Law Review* 70 (1994), 496–97; Schafer, *Supreme Court of Louisiana*, 300.

26. *Mrs. George Wailes*, 23 La.Ann.

27. Osborn v. Nicholson, 80 U.S. 654 at 658–59 and 663.

28. *Osborn*, 80 U.S. at 663–64.

29. Kull, "Freedom," 507–10.

30. Sabrina L. Miller and Gary Washburn, "New Chicago Law Requires Firms to Tell Slavery Links," *Chicago Tribune*, October 3, 2002.

31. California Department of Insurance, "Slavery Era Insurance Registry Report to the California Legislature" (May 2002), http://www.insurance.ca.gov/01-consumers/150-other-prog/10-seir/upload/Slavery-Report.pdf; Illinois General Assembly, Public Act 093-0333, accessed February 1, 2022, https://www.ilga.gov/legislation/publicacts/fulltext.asp?name=093-0333; Sharon Ann Murphy, *Investing in Life: Insurance in Antebellum America* (Baltimore, MD: Johns Hopkins University Press, 2010), 196.

32. Ken Magill, "From J. P. Morgan Chase, an Apology and $5 Million in Slavery Reparations," *New York Sun*, February 1, 2005.

33. George D. Green, *Finance and Economic Development in the Old South: Louisiana Banking 1804–1861* (Stanford, CA: Stanford University Press, 1972), 23.

34. "JPMorgan Chase Net Income 2010–2021," Macrotrends.net, accessed April 5, 2022, https://www.macrotrends.net/stocks/charts/JPM/jpmorgan-chase/net-income.

35. Sharon Ann Murphy, *Other People's Money: How Banking Worked in the Early American Republic* (Baltimore, MD: Johns Hopkins University Press, 2017), 158–59.

36. Sharon Ann Murphy, "Securing Human Property: Slavery, Life Insurance, and Industrialization in the Upper South," *Journal of the Early Republic* 25 (Winter 2005)," 635–36.

37. For just a few examples, see Claudio Saunt, *Unworthy Republic: The Dispossession of Native Americans and the Road to Indian Territory* (New York: W. W. Norton, 2020); Gavin Wright, *Slavery and American Economic Development* (Baton Rouge: Louisiana State University, 2006); Sven Beckert, *Empire of Cotton: A Global History* (Cambridge, MA: Harvard University Press, 2015); Edward Baptist, *The Half Has Never Been Told: Slavery and the Making of American Capitalism* (New York: Basic Books, 2014); Walter Johnson, *River of Dark Dreams: Slavery and Empire in the Cotton Kingdom* (Cambridge, MA: Harvard University Press, 2013); Christa Dierksheide, *Amelioration and Empire: Progress and Slavery in the Plantation Americas* (Charlottesville: University of Virginia Press, 2014); and Sven Beckert and Seth Rockman, eds., *Slavery's Capitalism: A New History of American Economic Development* (Philadelphia: University of Pennsylvania Press, 2016).

38. "Branch Banking House Bank of Mississippi," *Historic Resources Inventory Fact Sheet, MDAH*, accessed June 1, 2021, https://www.apps.mdah.ms.gov/Public/prop.aspx?id=30370&view=facts&y=728; "Branch Banking House," *National Register of Historic Places Inventory*, United States Department of the Interior, March 30, 1978, https://www.apps.mdah.ms.gov/nom/prop/30370.pdf; Woodville Civic Club, Inc., accessed December 1, 2021, https://www.historicwoodville.org/.

39. Dave Parker, "Showcasing Woodville's Black History," *Enterprise-Journal* (McComb, MS), February 18, 2004, 13; Beth Wild, "Community Effort," *Enterprise-Journal* (McComb, MS), October 3, 2004, 21; "William Grant Still (1895–1978) Biographical Notes," *William Grant Still Music*, accessed December 1, 2021, http://www.williamgrantstillmusic.com/BiographicalNotes.htm.

40. Carlee Reed, "Thomas C. Tolliver Jr.," *Natchez Democrat*, August 23, 2018, https://m.natchezdemocrat.com/2018/08/23/thomas-c-tolliver-jr/.

41. "Gladys Hines," *Advocate* (Baton Rouge), October 5, 2016, https://obits.theadvocate.com/us/obituaries/theadvocate/name/gladys-hines-obituary?id=17384012.

42. Author interview with "Mr. Jones," conducted by phone, June 11, 2021.

43. Woodville Civic Club, Inc.]

44. "Office and Banking House of the West Feliciana Railroad," *Historic Resources Inventory Fact Sheet, MDAH*, accessed December 1, 2021, https://www.apps.mdah.ms.gov/Public/prop.aspx?id=30297&view=facts&y=728.

45. Woodville Civic Club, Inc.

46. "William Grant Still, 1895–1978," *Library of Congress*, accessed December 1, 2021, https://www.loc.gov/item/ihas.200186213.

47. Author interview with "Mr. Jones," June 11, 2021; "William Grant Still (1895–1978) Biographical Notes."

48. Author interview with "Mr. Jones," June 11, 2021.

49. Clint Smith, *How the Word is Passed: A Reckoning with the History of Slavery across America* (New York: Little, Brown and Co., 2021), 64.

50. Russell Contreras, "New Rules are Limiting How Teachers Can Teach Black History Month," *Axios*, updated February 6, 2022, https://www.axios.com/black-history-month-critical-race-theory-2e021dfb-8604-4d23-8a11-36069c93dde9.html.

51. Emily Sullivan, "Laura Ingraham Told LeBron James to Shut Up and Dribble; He Went to the Hoop," *NPR*, February 19, 2018, https://www.npr.org/sections/thetwo-way/2018/02/19/587097707/laura-ingraham-told-lebron-james-to-shutup-and-dribble-he-went-to-the-hoop.

52. Latrobe's on Royal, accessed December 1, 2021, http://www.latrobesonroyal.com/.

53. "Bank of Louisiana Erected 1826," Historical Marker Database, last updated May 27, 2018, https://www.hmdb.org/m.asp?m=117860.

54. "Remarkable Bank History: The Institution that Gave the Name 'Dixie' to the South," *Financial Times* (London), September 27, 1913, 10; *The Story of "Dixie" and the Citizens Bank of Louisiana*, Citizens' Bank and Trust Co., reel 17, *Citizens' Bank*.

55. Andrea Gallo, "Louisiana's Plantations are Reckoning with Their Racist Past; Here's How Some Are Evolving," *NOLA.com*, September 4, 2020, https://www.nola.com/news/article_937000dc-d5d0-11ea-b150-237b10ac5da1.html.

56. "The Wall of Honor," *Whitney Plantation*, accessed April 4, 2022, https://www.whitneyplantation.org/history/the-big-house-and-the-outbuildings/the-wall-of-honor/.

57. April 23 and July 20, 1840, April 22, 1841, Minute Book, vol. 3, reel 14, *Citizens' Bank*; "Louisiana Slave Auction," *Whitney Plantation*, accessed April 4, 2022, https://www.whitneyplantation.org/history/slavery-in-louisiana/auction-of-the-slaves/.

58. Smith, *How the Word is Passed*, 83–84.

Index

Page numbers in italics refer to figures.

Banks with no closure dates in parentheses survived past 1861.